COMPUTER ORGANIZATION

McGraw-Hill Computer Science Series

McGraw-Hill Series in Computer Organization and Architecture

COMPUTER ORGANIZATION

Third Edition

V. Carl Hamacher

University of Toronto

Zvonko G. Vranesic

University of Toronto

Safwat G. Zaky

University of Toronto

McGraw-Hill, Inc.

New York St. Louis San Francisco Auckland Bogotá
Caracas Lisbon London Madrid Mexico Milan
Montreal New Delhi Paris San Juan Singapore
Sydney Tokyo Toronto

COMPUTER ORGANIZATION

3 4 5 6 7 8 9 0 DOC DOC 9 5 4 3 2

ISBN 0-07-025685-3

This book was set in Times Roman by Publication Services.
The editor was David M. Shapiro;
the production supervisor was Friederich W. Schulte.
The cover was designed by John Hite
New drawings were done by Dan and Paul Vranesic.
Project supervision was done by Publication Services.
R. R. Donnelley & Sons Company was printer and binder.

Library of Congress Catalog Card Number:

90-60431.

ABOUT THE AUTHORS

V. CARL HAMACHER is a Professor in the Departments of Electrical Engineering and Computer Science, and the Chairman of the Division of Engineering Science at the University of Toronto. He received the B.A.Sc. degree in Engineering Physics from the University of Waterloo, Canada; the M.Sc. degree from Queen's University, Kingston, Canada; and the Ph.D. degree from Syracuse University, the latter two in electrical engineering. During 1978–1979, Dr. Hamacher was a Visiting Scientist at the IBM Research Laboratory in San Jose, California, and he was a Research Visitor at the Polytechnic Institute of Grenoble, France, in 1986. From 1984 to 1988 he was Director of the Computer Systems Research Institute at the University of Toronto. A Senior Member of the IEEE and a member of ACM, Sigma Xi, and the Association of Professional Engineers of Ontario, Dr. Hamacher is involved in research on local area networks and multiprocessor systems.

ZVONKO G. VRANESIC is a Professor of Electrical Engineering and Computer Science at the University of Toronto, where he received his B.A.Sc., M.A.Sc., and Ph.D. degrees in electrical engineering. Before working at the University of Toronto, he was a design engineer with the Northern Electric Company, Ltd. in Bramalea, Ontario. He was a Senior Visitor in the Computer Laboratory of the University of Cambridge, England, during 1977–1978, and in the Institut de Programmation of the University of Paris 6, France, during 1984–1985. Dr. Vranesic's current research interests include computer architecture, fault-tolerant computing, local area networks, and multiple-valued logic systems. He is a Senior Member of the IEEE and a member of the Association of Professional Engineers of Ontario.

SAFWAT G. ZAKY is a Professor of Electrical Engineering and Computer Science at the University of Toronto. Prior to joining the University of Toronto in 1973, he was with Bell Northern Research for three years, where he worked on applications of electro- and magneto-optics in telephone switching. During 1980–1981 he was a Senior Visitor in the Computer Laboratory of the University of Cambridge, England.

Dr. Zaky holds a B.Sc. in Electrical Engineering and a B.Sc. in Mathematics, both from Cairo University. He completed his M.A.Sc. and Ph.D. degrees in electrical engineering at the University of Toronto. His current research interests are in the areas of computer architecture, computer hardware, and computer communications. Dr. Zaky is a member of the IEEE and the Association of Professional Engineers of Ontario.

To Liz, Anne, and Shirley

CONTENTS

PREFACE

This book is intended for use in a first-level course on computer organization in computer science and electrical engineering curricula. It is self-contained, assuming only that the reader has a basic knowledge of computer programming in a high-level language. Many students who study computer organization will have had an introductory course on digital logic circuits, so we chose not to cover that subject in the main body of the book. We have provided an extensive appendix on logic circuits, however, for those students who need it.

Our resolve to write the original version of the book stemmed from our experience in teaching computer organization to three distinct types of undergraduates: computer science specialists, electrical engineering undergraduates, and engineering science undergraduates. We have always approached teaching courses in this area from as practical a point of view as possible. Thus, a major choice in shaping the contents of the three editions of this book was to illustrate the principles of computer organization with a number of extensive examples drawn from commercially available computers.

We believe that it is important to recognize that digital system design is not a straightforward process of applying "optimal design" algorithms. Many design decisions are based largely on heuristic judgment and tend to be a compromise between alternatives: it is our goal to convey these notions to the reader.

We have also endeavored to provide sufficient details to force the student to dig beyond the surface when dealing with ideas that seem intuitively obvious. We believe that this is best accomplished by giving real, adequately documented examples. Block diagrams are a powerful means of describing organizational features of a computer, but they can easily lead to an oversimplified view of the problems involved. Hence, they must be accompanied by the details of implementation alternatives.

We use a number of real machines for illustrative purposes. Our main examples are drawn from the following computers: PDP-11; Motorola 680X0 family, 6809, and 88000; VAX-11; IBM 370; HP3000; and Intel 80X86 family. The PDP-11 and

68000 are used as detailed examples early in the book. Their manageable size and complexity make them suitable for teaching purposes.

The book is designed for a one-semester course in computer science or engineering programs. It is suitable for both hardware- and software-oriented students, although we put greater emphasis on hardware because we believe that this is the way computer organization should be taught. It is a mistake to describe computer structures solely through the eyes of a programmer, particularly for people who work with systems that involve a variety of equipment, interfacing, and communication facilities. However, although the emphasis is on computer hardware, we have addressed a number of software issues and discussed representative instances of software-hardware trade-offs in the implementation of various components of a computing system.

Let us review the topics covered in sequence, chapter by chapter. The first eight chapters cover the basic principles of computer organization and the remaining five chapters deal with peripheral devices, microprocessor systems, RISC architecture, multiprocessors, and computer communications.

Chapter 1 provides an overview of computer hardware and software and informally introduces terms that are dealt with in more depth in the remainder of the book. It includes a discussion of the role of system software and of the basic ways standard functional units are interconnected to form a complete computing system.

Chapter 2 gives a methodical treatment of addressing techniques and instruction sequencing. We use the PDP-11 and Motorola 68000 to illustrate basic concepts. Numerous program examples at the machine instruction level discuss loops, subroutines, and simple input-output programming.

Chapter 3 continues the discussion of instruction sets that was begun in Chapter 2. It focuses on the CISC approach to computer architecture. Instruction sets in the VAX-11, the IBM 370, and the HP3000 are introduced. The influence of high-level language programming on the design of these machines is discussed.

Chapter 4 begins with a register-transfer-level treatment of instruction fetching and execution in a processor. The constraints imposed by various busing arrangements are explained, followed by a discussion of both hardwired and microprogrammed control.

Chapter 5 extends the discussion of microprogrammed control. The alternatives of fully decoded command words and partially encoded command words are treated, along with a detailed analysis of the "next-address" generation problem in microprogram sequencing. The use of bit slices in designing microprogrammed machines is also discussed.

Input-output organization is developed in Chapter 6. The basics of I/O data transfer synchronization are presented, and a series of increasingly complex I/O structures is explained. Direct memory access methods and interrupts are introduced, and the role of software interrupts in operating systems is discussed. Bus protocols and standards are also presented.

Chapter 7 treats the arithmetic unit of a computer. It begins with a discussion of fixed-point add, subtract, multiply, and divide hardware that operates on 2's-complement numbers. Lookahead adders and high-speed array multipliers are included. Floating-point number representations, operations, and the IEEE standard are presented.

Semiconductor memories are the subject of Chapter 8. Multiple-module memory systems and caches are explained as ways of increasing main memory bandwidth. Virtual-memory systems and memory management are also discussed in detail.

Peripheral devices are dealt with in Chapter 9. Video terminals and graphic displays are described as well as magnetic disks, drums, and tapes. Workstation and file-server systems are briefly presented.

Microprocessor chip families are considered in Chapter 10, with detailed examples from the Motorola 6809 and 680X0 chips and the Intel 80X86 family. Input-output aspects of microcomputer systems are emphasized, including a thorough discussion of a typical peripheral interface chip.

Chapter 11 deals with the subject of Reduced Instruction Set Computers (RISCs). Pipelining and other RISC features are carefully examined. The Motorola 88000 is used to illustrate the RISC approach.

An introductory presentation of multiprocessor systems is given in Chapter 12. This chapter covers issues such as interconnection schemes, caches, and techniques necessary for correct handling of shared variables in SIMD and MIMD machines.

Chapter 13 briefly presents a number of topics in computer communications. A presentation of synchronous and asynchronous protocols for data transmission is followed by a discussion of local area and wide area networks.

Our book is suited for the usual undergraduate class teaching environment, but we believe that it is also appropriate for self-study by graduates who have taken introductory computer courses or have work experience in the area. The use of commercially available computers in our examples makes the book attractive to the latter readership.

Major changes in the third edition. There are three major additions in the third edition:

- Chapter 2 has been expanded to include a thorough discussion of the instruction set of the Motorola 68000 microprocessor. The treatment parallels the material on the PDP-11, which has been retained for its simplicity and pedagogical value. The chapter is organized to allow concentration on only one of the two processors. The other processor may be ignored without loss of continuity.
- Chapter 11 on RISC processors is new.
- Chapter 12 on multiprocessors is new.

Chapter 10 of the second edition, which dealt with system software issues, has been deleted. Instead, system software topics are discussed where relevant in other chapters to illustrate the interaction between hardware and software.

Many smaller changes have been made throughout the book to update the material and improve the clarity of presentation.

We wish to express our thanks to the people who have helped during the preparation of this third edition. Professors Paul Chow, Moshe Krieger, and Richard Reid provided helpful suggestions for improvements to the presentation, and Susan McClure, Gail Dragan and Inge Weber cheerfully helped with the technical preparation of the manuscript. Reviews acquired by McGraw-Hill came from Paul Chow, University of Toronto; G. Taiho Decker, Rockwell International; James R. Goodman, University of Wisconson–Madison; Thomas J. Jantos, Rockwell International; Moshe Krieger, University of Ottawa; Richard Reid, Michigan State University; Jerome Rothstein, Ohio State University; and Charles T. Wright, Iowa State University. Our editor, David Shapiro, enthusiastically encouraged us and provided prompt support when needed.

V. Carl Hamacher
Zvonko G. Vranesic
Safwat G. Zaky

COMPUTER ORGANIZATION

CHAPTER

1

BASIC STRUCTURE OF COMPUTER HARDWARE AND SOFTWARE

This book is about computer organization. It studies the function and design of the various units of digital computers that are responsible for storing and processing information. It also deals with other units used to bring information into a computer and to send computed results to the outside world. Most of the material is devoted to what has been termed *computer hardware* and *computer architecture*. Computer architecture is defined here to mean the functional operation of the individual hardware units in a computer system and the flow of information and control among them.

Many aspects of programming and software components in computer systems are also discussed in the book. It is important to consider both hardware and software aspects of the design of various computer components in order to achieve a good understanding of computer systems.

This chapter will introduce a number of hardware and software concepts, present some commonly used terminology, and give a broad overview of the fundamental aspects of the subject. A more detailed discussion will follow in subsequent chapters.

1.1 FUNCTIONAL UNITS

Let us first define the term *digital computer,* or simply *computer*, because it is often misunderstood despite the fact that most people take it for granted. In its simplest form, a contemporary computer is a fast electronic calculating machine that accepts digitized input information, processes it according to a list of internally stored instructions, and produces the resultant output information. The list of instructions is called a computer *program*, and internal storage is called computer *memory*.

There are many types of computers that differ widely in size, speed, and cost. It is fashionable to use more specific words to represent some subclasses of computers. The smallest machines are called *microcomputers*. Their most common version is the personal computer that has found wide use in homes, schools, and business offices. The next higher level of machine is called the *minicomputer*. This may be time-shared by a number of users and has reasonable magnetic disk storage capacity for program and data files. Minicomputers are used extensively in payroll, accounting, and scientific computing applications. High-performance *workstations* with graphics input/output capability have a computational power in the minicomputer class. They are often used in engineering applications, especially for interactive design work.

Beyond minicomputers and workstations, a range of large and very powerful computer systems exist that are called *mainframes* at the low end of the range and *supercomputers* at the high end. Mainframes are typically used for business data processing in medium to large corporations whose computing and storage capacity requirements are larger than minicomputers can handle. Supercomputers are used for large-scale numerical calculations such as weather forecasting and aircraft design and simulation.

In its simplest form, a computer consists of five functionally independent main parts: input, memory, arithmetic and logic, output, and control units. These are illustrated in Figure 1.1. The input unit accepts coded information from human operators, from electromechanical devices such as the keyboard of a video terminal, or from

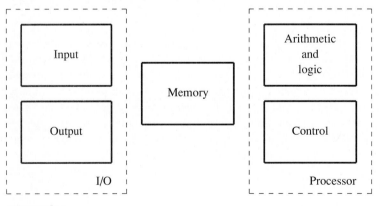

FIGURE 1.1
Basic functional units of a computer.

other computers over digital communication lines. The information received is either stored in the memory for later reference or immediately used by the arithmetic and logic circuitry to perform the desired operations. The processing steps are determined by a program stored in the memory. Finally, the results are sent back to the outside world through the output unit. All of these actions are coordinated by the control unit. The diagram in Figure 1.1 does not show the connections between the functional units, though these connections of course exist. There are a number of ways in which the connections can be made and they will be discussed in many places throughout the book.

It has been traditional to refer to the arithmetic and logic circuits in conjunction with the main control circuits as a *central processing unit* (CPU), or simply a *processor*. The word central was originally used because most of the control functions in early computers were centralized in a single processing unit. Modern systems often contain many processors, as we will see later, but the term CPU is still widely used.

Input and output equipment is usually combined under the term *input-output unit* (I/O). This is reasonable because some standard equipment provides both input and output functions. The simplest example of this is the often-encountered video terminal, consisting of a keyboard for input and a cathode-ray tube display for output. We must emphasize that input and output functions are separated within the terminal. Thus, the computer sees two distinct devices, even though the human operator associates them as being parts of the same unit.

In large mainframe computers, the main functional units may comprise a number of separate and often sizeable physical parts. Figure 1.2 is a photograph of such a

FIGURE 1.2
A large mainframe computer. (IBM Corp. Ltd.)

computer. Minicomputers and microcomputers are much smaller in size, often of desktop dimensions. A cabinet containing the processor and main memory of a minicomputer system is shown in Figure 1.3.

At this point we should take a closer look at the information fed into a computer. It is convenient to categorize this information as either instructions or data. *Instructions* are explicit commands that:

- govern the transfer of information within a computer as well as between the computer and its I/O devices
- specify the arithmetic and logic operations to be performed

A set of instructions that perform a task is called a *program*. The usual mode of operation is to store a program in the memory. The processor then fetches the instructions comprising the program from the memory one at a time and performs the desired operations. The computer is under complete control of the *stored program*, except for the possibility of external interruption by the operator or by I/O devices connected to the machine.

Data are numbers and encoded characters that are used as operands by the instructions. This is not a hard definition, because the term is often used to symbolize any digital information. Even within our definition of data, it is quite feasible that an entire program (that is, a set of instructions) may be considered as data if it is to be processed by another program. An example of this is the task of *compiling* a

FIGURE 1.3
A minicomputer processor and main memory cabinet. (Digital Equipment Corp.)

high-level language source program into machine instructions and data. The source program is the input data for the compiler program. The *compiler* translates the source program into a machine language program.

Information handled by a computer must be encoded in a suitable format. Most present-day hardware (electronic and electromechanical equipment) employs digital circuits that have only two stable states, ON and OFF (see Appendix A). Each number, character, or instruction is encoded as a string of binary digits called *bits*, each having one of two possible values. Numbers are usually represented in the positional binary notation, as Chapter 7 will discuss in detail. Occasionally, the *binary-coded decimal* (BCD) format is employed, in which each decimal digit is encoded by 4 bits.

Alphanumeric characters are also expressed in terms of binary codes. Several appropriate coding schemes have been developed. Two of the most widely encountered schemes are ASCII (American Standard Code for Information Interchange), in which each character is represented as a 7-bit code, and EBCDIC (Extended Binary-Coded Decimal Interchange Code), in which 8 bits are used to denote a character. A more detailed description of binary notation and coding schemes is given in Appendix D.

INPUT UNIT. Computers accept coded information through input units, devices capable of reading such data. The simplest of these is the keyboard of a video terminal, which is electronically connected to the processing part of a computer. The keyboard is wired so that whenever a key is depressed, the corresponding letter or digit is automatically translated into its corresponding code and is sent directly to either the memory or the processor. Figure 1.4 shows a keyboard that is a part of a workstation.

Many other kinds of input devices are available, including joysticks, trackballs, and mice. They are often used as graphic input devices in conjunction with video

FIGURE 1.4
A workstation. (Sun Microsystems)

displays. Detailed discussion of input devices and their operation can be found in Chapter 9.

MEMORY UNIT. The function of the memory unit is to store programs and data. There are two classes of memory devices called primary and secondary storage.

Primary storage, or *main memory*, is a fast memory capable of operating at electronic speeds. Programs are stored in the main memory during their execution. The main memory contains a large number of semiconductor storage cells, each capable of storing one bit of information. These cells are rarely read or written as individual cells, but are instead processed in groups of fixed size called *words*. The main memory is organized so that the contents of one word, containing n bits, can be stored or retrieved in one basic operation.

To provide easy access to any word in the main memory, a distinct address is associated with each word location. Addresses are numbers that identify successive locations. A given word is accessed by specifying its address and issuing a control command that starts the storage or retrieval process.

The number of bits in each word is often referred to as the *word length* of the computer. Large computers usually have 32 or more bits in a word, and microcomputer word lengths range from 8 to 32 bits. The capacity of the main memory is one factor that characterizes the size of a computer. Small machines may have only a few hundred thousand words, whereas medium and large machines normally have millions of words. Data are usually manipulated within a machine in units of words, multiples of words, or parts of words. A typical access to the main memory results in one word of data being read from the memory or written into it.

As mentioned above, programs must reside in the main memory during execution. Instructions and data can be written into the memory or read out under control of a processor. It is essential to be able to access any word location within the main memory as quickly as possible. Memories in which any location can be reached in a short, fixed amount of time after specifying its address are called *random-access memories* (RAM). The time required to access one word is called the *memory access time*. This is a fixed time, in the range of about 50 to 500 nanoseconds (ns) for most modern computers.

Although primary storage is essential, it tends to be expensive. Thus additional, cheaper *secondary storage* is used when large amounts of data have to be stored, particularly if some of the data need not be accessed very frequently. A wide selection of suitable devices is available, including *magnetic disks*, *drums*, and *tapes*. Figures 1.5 and 1.6 show disk and tape units.

Chapter 8 provides a detailed description of main memory components and their usage, and secondary storage devices are discussed in Chapter 9.

ARITHMETIC AND LOGIC UNIT. Execution of most operations within a computer takes place in the arithmetic and logic unit (ALU) of a processor. Consider a typical example. Suppose two numbers located in the main memory are to be added. They are brought into the arithmetic unit where the actual addition is carried out, and the sum may then be stored in the memory.

FIGURE 1.5
A magnetic disk unit. (IBM Corp. Ltd.)

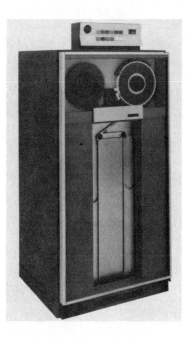

FIGURE 1.6
A magnetic tape unit. (IBM Corp. Ltd.)

Any other arithmetic or logic operation (for example, multiplication, division, or comparison of numbers) is initiated by bringing the required operands into the ALU, where the necessary operation is performed. We should point out that not all operands used in a computation reside in the main memory. Processors normally contain a number of high-speed storage elements called *registers*, which may be used for temporary storage of often-used operands. Each register can store one word of data. Access times to registers are typically 5 to 10 times faster than memory access times.

The control and arithmetic units are usually many times faster than other devices connected to a computer system. This enables a single processor to control a number of external devices such as video terminals, magnetic tape and disk memories, sensors, displays, and mechanical controllers. This is possible only because of the vast difference in speed, which enables the fast processor to organize and control the activity of many slower devices.

OUTPUT UNIT. The output unit is the counterpart of the input unit. Its function is to send processed results to the outside world.

A number of units provide both an output function and an input function. This is the case with video terminals and graphic displays. This dual role of some units is the reason for using the single name of I/O unit.

Of course, devices exist that are used for output only. The most familiar example of such a device is a high-speed *printer*. It is possible to produce printers capable of printing as many as 10,000 lines per minute. These are tremendous speeds in the mechanical sense, but are still very slow compared to the electronic speeds of a processor unit. Printers employ either mechanical impact heads, ink jet streams, or photocopying techniques to perform the printing function. A high-speed line printer is shown in Figure 1.7.

CONTROL UNIT. The previously described units provide the necessary tools for storing and processing information and providing input or output operations. Their operation must be coordinated in some organized way, which is the task of a control unit. This unit is effectively the nerve center, used to send control signals to other units and to sense their state.

A line printer will print a line only if it is specifically instructed to do so. This is typically effected by a Write instruction executed by a processor. To process this instruction, the control unit sends *timing signals* to and from the printer.

In general, we can say that I/O transfers are controlled by software instructions that identify both the devices involved and the type of transfer. However, the actual timing signals that govern the transfers during execution are generated by the control circuits. Data transfers between a processor and memory are also controlled by the control unit in a similar fashion.

In concept it is reasonable to think of a control unit as a well-defined, physically separate unit that interacts with other parts of the machine, but in practice this is seldom the case. Much of the control circuitry is physically distributed throughout

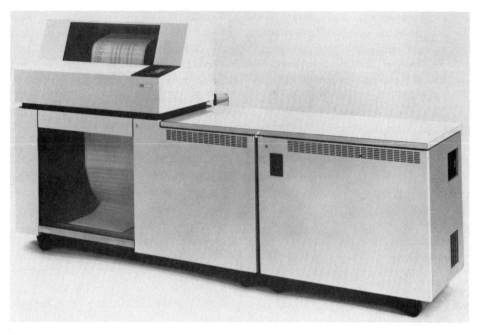

FIGURE 1.7
A line printer. (IBM Corp. Ltd.)

the machine. A large set of control lines (wires) carries the signals used for timing and synchronization of events in all units.

The operation of a computer can be summarized as follows

- The computer accepts information (programs and data) through an input unit and transfers it to the memory.
- Information stored in the memory is fetched, under program control, into an arithmetic and logic unit to be processed.
- Processed information leaves the computer through an output unit.
- All activities inside the machine are directed by the control unit.

1.2 BASIC OPERATIONAL CONCEPTS

In the previous section we stated that the activity within a computer is governed by instructions. To perform a given task, an appropriate program consisting of a set of instructions is stored in the main memory. Individual instructions are brought from the memory into the processor, which executes the specified operations. Data used as operands are also stored in the memory. A typical instruction may be

Add   LOCA,R0

This instruction adds the operand at memory location LOCA to the operand in a register in the processor, R0, and places the sum into register R0. This instruction requires performance of several steps. First, the instruction must be transferred from the main memory into the processor. Then the operand at LOCA must be fetched and added to the contents of R0. Finally, the resultant sum is stored in register R0.

Transfers between the main memory and the processor are started by sending the address of the memory location to be accessed to the memory unit and issuing the appropriate control signals. The data are then transferred to or from the memory.

Figure 1.8 shows how the connection between the main memory and the processor can be made. It also shows a few details of the processor that have not been discussed yet but are operationally essential. The interconnection pattern for these components is not shown explicitly, since at this point we will discuss their functional characteristics only. Chapter 4 will deal with the interconnection details as part of processor design.

The processor contains arithmetic and logic circuitry as the main processing elements. It also contains a number of registers used for temporary storage of data. Two registers are of particular interest. The *instruction register* (IR) contains the instruction that is being executed. Its output is available to the control circuits, which generate the timing signals for controlling the processing circuits needed to execute the instruction. The *program counter* (PC) register keeps track of the execution of a program. It contains the memory address of the instruction currently being executed. During the execution of the current instruction, the contents of the PC are updated to

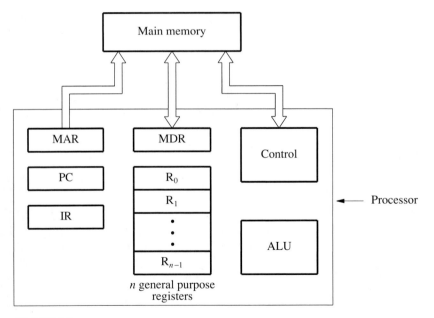

FIGURE 1.8
Connections between the processor and the main memory.

correspond to the address of the next instruction to be executed. It is customary to say that the PC *points* to the instruction that is to be fetched from the memory.

Besides the IR and PC there are usually several *general-purpose registers*. Their roles will be explained in Chapter 2.

Finally, two registers facilitate communication with the main memory. These are the *memory address register* (MAR) and the *memory data register* (MDR). As the name implies, the MAR is used to hold the address of the location to or from which data are to be transferred and the MDR contains the data to be written into or read out of the addressed location.

Let us now consider some typical operating steps. Programs reside in the main memory and usually get there through the input unit. Execution of the program starts when the PC is set to point to the first instruction of the program. The contents of the PC are transferred to the MAR and a Read control signal is sent to the memory. After a certain elapsed time corresponding to the memory access time, the addressed word (in this case the first instruction of the program) is read out of the memory and loaded into the MDR. Next, the contents of the MDR are transferred to the IR, at which point the instruction is ready to be decoded and executed.

If the instruction involves an operation to be performed by the ALU, it will be necessary to obtain the required operands. If an operand resides in the memory (it could also be in a general-purpose register in the processor), it will have to be fetched by sending its address to the MAR and initiating a Read cycle. When the operand has been read from the memory into the MDR, it may be transferred from the MDR to the ALU. Having fetched one or more operands in this way, the ALU can perform the desired operation. If the result of this operation is to be stored in the memory, then the result is sent to the MDR. The address of the location where the result is to be stored is sent to the MAR, and a Write cycle is initiated. During instruction execution, the contents of the PC are incremented to point to the next instruction to be executed. This way, as soon as the execution of the current instruction is completed, a new instruction fetch may be started.

In addition to transferring data between the main memory and the processor, the computer must have the ability to accept data from input devices and to send data to output devices. Thus, some machine instructions with the capability of handling I/O transfers must be provided.

Normal execution of programs may sometimes be preempted if some device requires urgent servicing. For example, a monitoring device in a computer-controlled industrial process may detect a dangerous condition and to deal with the situation quickly, the normal flow of the running program must be interrupted. To achieve this, the device can raise an *interrupt signal*. An interrupt is a request from the I/O device for service by the processor. The processor provides the requested service by executing an appropriate *interrupt-service routine*. Because such diversions may alter the internal state of the processor, its state must be saved in memory locations before servicing the interrupt. This normally involves storing the contents of the PC, the general registers, and some control information. Upon termination of the interrupt-service routine, the state of the processor is restored so that execution of the interrupted program may continue.

The processor unit shown in Figure 1.8 can be implemented in a variety of ways. In most small and medium sized machines, all elements are realized as a single VLSI chip, but in larger machines, several VLSI chips may be needed.

1.3   BUS STRUCTURES

So far we have discussed the functional characteristics of individual parts of a computer. To form an operational system, these parts must be connected together in some organized way. There are many ways of doing this. We will consider three popular structures.

If a computer is to achieve a reasonable speed of operation, it must be organized so that all units can handle one full word of data at a given time. When a word of data is transferred between units, all its bits are transferred in parallel. This requires a considerable number of wires (lines) to establish the necessary connections. A collection of wires that connects several devices is called a *bus*. In addition to the wires that carry the data, the computer must have some lines for addressing and control purposes.

Figure 1.9 shows the simplest form of a *two-bus* computer. The processor interacts with the memory through a *memory bus* and handles input and output functions over an *I/O bus*. Data passes through the processor on its way to the memory. In such configurations the I/O transfers are usually under direct control of the processor, which initiates transfers and monitors their progress until completion.

A different version of a two-bus structure is given in Figure 1.10. Here the positions of the processor and memory are reversed. Again, a memory bus exists for communication between them, but I/O transfers are made directly to or from the memory. Since the memory lacks adequate circuitry to control such transfers, it is necessary to establish a different control mechanism. A standard technique is to provide the necessary control circuitry as part of the I/O equipment, in circuits called *I/O channels*. An I/O channel is actually a special-purpose processor, also called a *peripheral processor*. The main processor initiates a transfer by passing the required information to the I/O channel. The channel then takes over and controls the actual transfer of data.

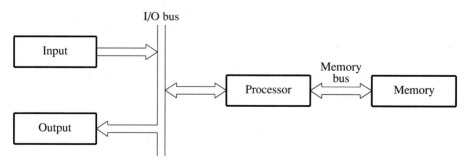

FIGURE 1.9
A two-bus structure.

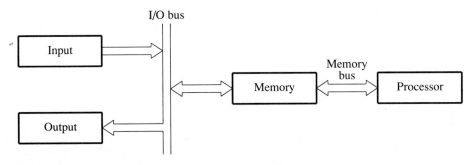

FIGURE 1.10
An alternative two-bus structure.

We have already mentioned that a bus consists of a collection of distinct lines that serve different purposes. There are three main groupings of lines: *data*, *address*, and *control*. The data lines are used for transmission of data, and the number of them corresponds to the number of bits in a word. Address lines specify the location of data in the main memory, and control lines indicate the direction of data transfer and coordinate the timing of events during the transfer.

Some machines have several distinct buses, but their operation is adequately represented by the two-bus examples. The main reason for including additional buses is to improve the operating speed through more parallelism.

A significantly different structure, which has a *single bus*, is shown in Figure 1.11. All units are connected to this bus, so it provides the sole means of interconnection. Because the bus can be used for only one transfer at a time, only two units can actively use the bus at any given instant. Bus control lines are used to arbitrate multiple requests for use of the bus. The main virtue of the single-bus structure is its low cost and flexibility for attaching peripheral devices, but the trade-off is lower operating speed. It is not surprising that a single-bus structure is primarily found in small machines, namely minicomputers and microcomputers.

Differences in bus structure have a pronounced effect on the performance of computers. From the conceptual point of view (at least at this introductory level of detail), however, they are not crucial in any functional description. The fundamental principles of computer operation are essentially independent of bus structure.

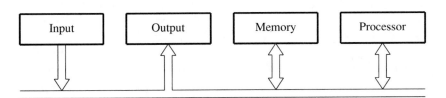

FIGURE 1.11
Single-bus structure.

In general, transfer of information over a bus cannot be done at a speed comparable to the operating speed of all devices connected to the bus. Some electromechanical devices are relatively slow, such as keyboards and printers, but others, like disks and tapes, are considerably faster. Main memory and processors operate at electronic speeds, making them the fastest parts of a computer. Because all these devices must communicate with each other over a bus, an efficient transfer mechanism that is not constrained by the slow devices and that can be used to smooth out the differences in timing among processors, memories, and external devices is necessary.

A common approach is to include *buffer registers* with the devices to hold the information during transfers. To illustrate this technique, consider the transfer of an encoded character from a processor to a character printer where it is to be printed. The processor sends the character over the bus to the printer output buffer. Since the buffer is an electronic register, this transfer requires relatively little time. Once the buffer is loaded, the printer can start printing without further intervention by the processor. At this time the bus and the processor are no longer needed and can be released for other activity. The printer continues printing the character in its buffer and is not available for further transfers until this process is completed. Thus, buffer registers smooth out timing differences among processors, memories, and I/O devices. These registers prevent a high-speed processor from being locked to a slow I/O device during a sequence of data transfers. This allows the processor to switch rapidly from one device to another, interweaving its processing activity with data transfers involving several I/O devices.

1.4 SOFTWARE

In order for a user to enter and run an application program, the computer must already have some system software. *System software* is a collection of programs that is executed as needed to perform functions such as

- receiving and interpreting user commands
- entering and editing application programs and storing them as files in secondary storage
- managing the storage and retrieval of files in secondary storage
- running standard application programs such as spreadsheets or games with data supplied by the user
- controlling I/O units to receive input information and produce output results
- translating programs from source form entered by the user into object form consisting of machine instructions
- linking and running user-written application programs with standard routines (e.g., a numerical computation package) that exist on the system

System software is thus responsible for the coordination of all activities in a computing system. The purpose of this section is to introduce briefly some basic aspects of system software.

Application programs are usually written in a high-level programming language such as Pascal or Fortran in which the programmer expresses mathematical or text-processing operations in a format independent of the particular computer to be used to execute the program. Thus, it is not necessary for the high-level programmer to be aware of the details of machine program instructions such as "Add LOCA,R0" that was discussed in Section 1.2. A system software program called a *compiler* is used to translate a high-level language program into a suitable machine language program containing instructions such as the Add instruction.

Another important system program that is familiar to all programmers is the text entry and editing program. The user of such a program interactively executes commands that allow statements of a source program entered at a video terminal keyboard to be accumulated in a *file*. A file is simply a sequence of alphanumeric characters or binary data that can be stored in memory or in secondary storage and can be referred to by a name chosen by the user.

We will not pursue the details of compilers, editors, or file systems in this book, but we will take a closer look at a key system software component called the *operating system* (OS). This is a large program, or more properly a collection of routines, that is used to control the sharing of and interaction among various computer units as they execute application programs. The OS routines perform the tasks required to assign computer resources to individual application programs. These tasks include assignment of main memory and magnetic disk space to program and data files, moving data between memory and disk units, and handling I/O operations.

In order to understand the basics of operating systems, let us consider a system with one processor, one disk, and one printer. We will discuss first the steps involved in running one application program. Once we have explained these steps, describing how the operating system manages the execution of more than one application program at the same time will be easy. Assume that the application program has been compiled from high-level language form into machine language form and stored on the disk. The first step is to transfer this file into the main memory. When the transfer is complete, execution of the program is started. Assume that part of the program's task involves reading a data file from the disk into the main memory, performing some computation on the data, and printing the results. When execution of the program reaches the point where the data file is needed, the program requests the operating system to transfer the data file from the disk to the memory. The OS performs this task and passes execution control back to the application program, which then proceeds to perform the required computation. When the computation is completed and the results are ready to be printed, the application program again transfers control back to the operating system. An OS routine is then executed to cause the printer to print the results.

In the discussion above, we have seen how execution control passes back and forth between the application program and OS routines. A convenient way to illustrate this sharing of the processor execution time is a time line diagram (see Figure 1.12). During the time period t_0 to t_1, an OS routine initiates loading the application program from disk to memory, waits until the transfer is completed, and then passes execution control to the application program. A similar pattern of activity occurs during periods

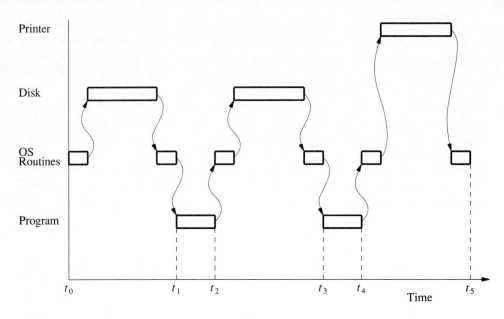

FIGURE 1.12
User program and OS routine sharing of the processor.

t_2 to t_3 and t_4 to t_5, when the operating system transfers the data file from the disk and prints the results. At t_5, the operating system may load and execute another application program.

Let us now briefly point out the way that computer resources can be used more efficiently if several application programs are to be processed. Notice that the disk and the processor are idle during most of the time period t_4 to t_5. It is possible for the operating system to load the next program to be executed into the memory while the printer is operating. Similarly, during t_0 to t_1, the operating system can arrange to print the previous program results while the current program is being loaded from the disk. Thus, the operating system is responsible for utilizing the computer resources as efficiently as possible when a number of application programs are to be executed.

1.5   DISTRIBUTED COMPUTING

Computer systems have evolved from machines based on a single processing unit into configurations that contain a number of processors. The processors can serve different roles. An instruction-set processor, for example, may execute the computation steps of a program, whereas an I/O processor performs the I/O tasks. It is also possible to use a number of identical processors to perform certain tasks in parallel. There are many ways in which processors can be interconnected via buses and communication lines with memory units and I/O devices to form complete computing systems.

Computer systems with multiple processors are attractive because large computations can often be partitioned into a set of tasks and some can be executed in parallel. For example, a computer-aided design (CAD) system may consist of one large computer and a number of workstations. Each workstation is a computer in its own right with graphics input and output capability. A designer working at one of these stations generates a digitized description of a desired object using these graphics capabilities. The large computer provides facilities for simulation and test generation, which may require a large amount of computing power. Since the large computer is not involved in the time-consuming interactive graphics tasks, it can support a number of workstations. The workstations might be distributed throughout a building, and connected to the large computer by communication lines consisting of optical fibers or coaxial cables. When the computer-aided design functions are spread over a collection of units in this manner, we say that the total system provides *distributed computing*.

1.6 CONCLUDING REMARKS

This chapter has considered many aspects of computer structures and operation. Much of the terminology needed to deal with the subject was introduced quickly, and many important design concepts were sketched superficially. The subsequent chapters will provide complete definitions of the terms used. We hope that this chapter has provided readers with an overall impression of what constitutes a computer system and how it works, though we fully realize that readers will not be able to place the various parts of this chapter into proper perspective until they have read the remainder of the book.

1.7 PROBLEMS

1.1. Give a point-form list of the steps needed to execute the machine instruction

Add   LOCA,R0

in terms of transfers between the components of Figure 1.8 and some simple control commands. Assume that the instruction itself is stored in the main memory at location INSTR, and that this address is initially in register PC. The first two steps might be expressed as

- Transfer the contents of register PC to register MAR.
- Issue a Read command to the main memory, and then wait until it has transferred the requested word into register MDR.

Do not forget to include the steps needed to update the contents of PC from INSTR to INSTR +1 so that the next instruction can be fetched.

1.2. (*a*) Give a short sequence of machine instructions for the task "Add the contents of memory location A to those of location B, and place the answer in location C." Instructions such as

Move   LOC,R*i*

and

Move   Ri,LOC

can be used to transfer data between the main memory and general purpose register R_i. Do not destroy the contents of either location A or B. The second operand in any Add instruction must be in a general purpose register.

(b) If both operands of the Add and Move instructions can be in the main memory, is it possible to use fewer instructions to accomplish this task? If yes, give the sequence.

1.3. Consider Figures 1.9 and 1.10. Discuss which of these two busing arrangements allows the most parallelism in activity, leading to faster execution of operations that involve both processing and I/O transfers.

1.4. (a) The discussion involving Figure 1.12 indicated how certain steps of a collection of programs like the one shown could be overlapped to reduce the total time needed to execute them. Let each of the six OS routine execution intervals be 1 unit of time. Estimate the ratio of best overlapped time to non-overlapped time for a long sequence of programs. Ignore startup and ending transients.

(b) Are there any more opportunities for overlap than those discussed in Section 1.4 for programs that have about equal balance among input, compute, and output parts? If yes, give the resulting ratio of best overlapped time to non-overlapped time.

CHAPTER

2

ADDRESSING METHODS AND MACHINE PROGRAM SEQUENCING

This chapter will consider the way in which programs are executed in a computer. The discussion is presented from the programmer's viewpoint. Chapter 1 introduced the general concept that both program instructions and data are stored in the main memory. We will study the ways in which sequences of instructions are brought from the main memory into the central processing unit (CPU) and executed to perform a given task. Most instructions specify operations to be performed on data located either in the main memory or in general-purpose registers in the CPU. We refer to such data, whether numeric or character data, as operands for these instructions.

The techniques that are in common use for addressing main memory locations and CPU registers will be discussed, followed by specific examples of the way that addressing is implemented in two commercially successful products: the PDP-11 computers manufactured by Digital Equipment Corporation and the 68000 microprocessors manufactured by Motorola Company. These machines will also be used in examples illustrating instruction formats, program branching, subroutine entry and exit, and stack manipulation. A simple example of program-controlled I/O (input-output) for a video terminal will be discussed. A number of programs at the assembly language level will be used to illustrate all of the principles introduced.

We chose the PDP-11 and 68000 computers as illustrative examples for several reasons. Both of these processors have attained wide acceptance in practical applications and have been used in teaching laboratories in many schools. Design principles learned from studying them are directly applicable to a variety of machines. Although the PDP-11 reached the height of its popularity in the late 1970s, some of its features, most notably its addressing modes, have been incorporated into the presently popular series of VAX computers. The lower complexity of the PDP-11, in comparison with the VAX machines, makes this processor almost ideal for teaching purposes. This was a strong consideration in our choice. The 68000 microprocessor is somewhat more complex than the PDP-11. However, its architecture is the basis for a series of widely used microprocessor chips that includes the 68020 and 68030 chips, which are the central parts of popular workstations and personal computers made by companies such as SUN Microsystems Inc., Apple Computer Inc., Atari Corp., and Apollo Computer Ltd.

This chapter is written in a way that allows the reader to focus on only one of the two processors that serve as examples. Each concept is first discussed in general terms. Then, separate identical examples are given for both the PDP-11 and the 68000 in clearly labeled subsections. The reader choosing to follow the 68000 only should simply ignore all subsections pertaining to the PDP-11, and vice versa. Of course, if time permits, it is beneficial to become acquainted with the characteristics of both processors.

2.1 MEMORY LOCATIONS, ADDRESSES, AND ENCODING OF INFORMATION

The main memory consists of a large number, usually many millions, of storage *cells*, each of which can store a binary digit, or *bit*, having the value 0 or 1. Since a single bit represents only a very small amount of information, bits are seldom handled individually. The usual approach is to deal with them in groups of fixed size. For this purpose, the main memory is organized so that a group of n bits can be stored or retrieved in a single basic operation. Each group of n bits is referred to as a word of information, and n is called the *word length*. As mentioned in Chapter 1, word lengths in microcomputers and minicomputers range from 8 to 32 bits, and large computers usually have 32 or more bits in a word.

Accessing the main memory to store or retrieve a single word of information requires distinct names or *addresses* for each word location. It is customary to use the numbers from 0 to $M-1$ as the addresses of successive locations in a memory consisting of M words (see Figure 2.1). The M addresses constitute the *address space* of a given computer. Using binary encoding of addresses, m bits are needed to represent all addresses, where $2^m = M$.

The contents of memory locations can represent either instructions or operands; the latter may be either numbers or characters. Figure 2.2 illustrates three possible ways in which a 32-bit word can be used to represent information. Figure 2.2a shows the most straightforward way that a 32-bit pattern can be used to represent a signed integer. The leftmost bit, b_{31}, is called the *sign bit*. It is 0 for positive numbers and 1 for negative numbers. The magnitude of the number is determined from bits b_{30} through b_0 by the formula

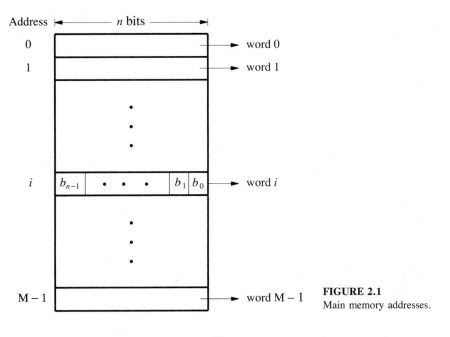

FIGURE 2.1
Main memory addresses.

$$\text{Magnitude} = b_{30} \times 2^{30} + \cdots + b_1 \times 2^1 + b_0 \times 2^0$$

The range of magnitudes that can be represented in this way is from 0 to $2^{31} - 1$, and the numbers are said to be in the binary positional notation.

The encoding format in Figure 2.2a is called the sign and magnitude representation. Two other binary number representations are frequently used: 1's complement and 2's complement. In both these schemes, the representation of positive numbers is the same as in the sign and magnitude method. The differences among the three methods are in the way in which negative numbers are represented. However, in all three schemes, the leftmost bit—b_{31} in our example—is 0 for positive numbers and 1 for negative numbers.

The choice of number representation scheme has a direct influence on how easily arithmetic operations are performed by logic circuits in the CPU. In fact, the 2's-complement representation is the most suitable one to use. Details of number representations and their influence on the design of logic circuits for performing arithmetic operations will be discussed in Chapter 7.

In this chapter, we will use the decimal sign and magnitude representation when we wish to give numerical examples. Of course, these values are represented in the computer by binary patterns based on one of the previously mentioned schemes. The only technical detail about the binary representations that we will need in this chapter is that the sign bit is always the leftmost bit. This is true for 8-bit numbers, which we will have occasion to use, as well as for 32-bit numbers or numbers of any other length.

In addition to numbers, computers must be able to handle characters. Characters can be letters of the alphabet, decimal digits, punctuation marks, and so on. They

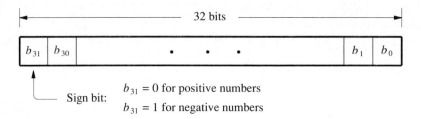

$b_{31} = 0$ for positive numbers

Sign bit:

$b_{31} = 1$ for negative numbers

Magnitude $= b_{30} \times 2^{30} + \cdots + b_1 \times 2^1 + b_0 \times 2^0$

(a) A signed integer

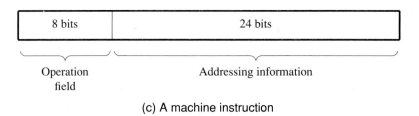

(b) Four characters

8 bits	24 bits

Operation field   Addressing information

(c) A machine instruction

FIGURE 2.2
Examples of encoded information in a 32-bit word.

are represented by codes that are usually six to eight bits long. Figure 2.2b indicates how four characters in either the ASCII or EBCDIC codes can be stored in a 32-bit word. These codes are described in Appendix D.

A main memory word can also be used to encode an instruction. In this case, one part of the word specifies the operation to be performed. Other parts may be used to specify operand addresses. It is customary to use the name *field* for each of these parts. An example of a possible format for a 32-bit machine instruction is given in Figure 2.2c. The 8-bit operation field can encode $2^8 (= 256)$ distinct instructions, and the 24-bit address field can encode an address in the range 0 through $2^{24} - 1 (= 16777215)$.

In general, it is not possible to determine whether a main memory location contains an instruction or an operand merely by inspecting its contents, because a given binary pattern may be interpreted according to any of the formats given in Figure

2.2. The additional information required is available inside the CPU. It was pointed out in Chapter 1 that one of the important elements inside the CPU is the program counter, or PC (see Figure 1.8). All memory words that the PC points at are interpreted as instructions. Memory words whose addresses are specified by the instructions are interpreted as operands. Whether an operand is a character or a numeric data item is determined by the operation field of the instruction.

2.2 MAIN MEMORY OPERATIONS

To execute an instruction, it is necessary for the CPU control circuits to cause the transfer of the instruction from the main memory to the CPU. It is also necessary to move operands and results between the main memory and the CPU. Thus there is an obvious need for two basic operations involving the main memory, namely, *Fetch* (or *Read*) and *Store* (or *Write*).

The Fetch operation transfers the contents of a specific main memory location to the CPU. The word in the main memory remains unchanged. To start a Fetch operation, the CPU sends the address of the desired location to the main memory and requests that its contents be read. The main memory reads the data stored at that address and sends it to the CPU.

The Store operation transfers a word of information from the CPU to a specific main memory location, destroying the former contents of that location. The CPU sends the address of the desired location to the main memory, together with the data to be written into that location.

The details of the hardware implementation of the above operations will be treated in Chapters 4, 5, and 8. In this chapter, we are taking the programmer's viewpoint. Thus we will concentrate on the logical handling of instructions and operands. Specific hardware components, such as CPU registers, will be discussed only to the extent necessary to aid the reader in understanding the execution of machine instructions and programs.

2.3 INSTRUCTIONS AND INSTRUCTION SEQUENCING

A typical program involves a number of functionally different steps to be performed. It is reasonable to assume that different classes of instructions should be available. We might roughly describe the classes as corresponding to:

- data transfers between the main memory and the CPU registers
- arithmetic and logic operations on data
- program sequencing and control
- I/O transfers

We will begin by discussing possible instructions in the first two classes. However, prior to this discussion, we should introduce some simple notation to help us describe the transfer of information from one location in a computer to another. Possible locations involved in such transfers are memory locations and registers in either the CPU or the I/O subsystem. In general, we will identify a location by a name. For example, names for main memory locations may be LOC, PLACE, A, VAR2, and so on; typical register names may be R_0, R_5, IOREAD, and so on. The contents of a location or a register will be denoted by placing the corresponding name in square brackets. Thus, the expression

$$R_1 \leftarrow [LOC]$$

will indicate that the contents of memory location LOC are transferred into register R_1.

The operation of adding two numbers is a fundamental capability in any computer. We will use an Add instruction to illustrate some possibilities for instruction formats. From the programmer's viewpoint, the simplest form of addition is $C \leftarrow [A] + [B]$, where A, B, and C are the names of three variables. Let the values of these variables be stored in distinct memory locations. We will associate the variable names A, B, and C with the addresses of these locations. The above expression then has the following meaning: The operands in memory locations A and B are to be fetched from the memory and transferred into the CPU, where they will be added in the ALU (arithmetic and logic unit). Then, the resulting sum is to be stored into memory location C.

To specify the complete process by a single machine instruction, a field specifying three operands, A, B, and C, is needed, together with the operation field that specifies the addition operation. This *three-address* instruction can be represented symbolically as

Add   A,B,C

Operands A and B are called the *source* operands and C is called the *destination* operand. A problem with this approach is that the inclusion of three addresses in an instruction may require a large number of bits. If *m* bits are needed to specify each address, the instruction must contain $3m$ bits for addressing purposes, in addition to the bits needed to denote the operation to be performed.

An alternative approach is to perform the desired calculation by using a sequence of instructions, each requiring fewer than three memory addresses. If two addresses are used in an Add instruction to specify the two operands A and B, an implicit assumption will need to be made about where the sum is to be sent. A number of computers have *two-address* Add instructions that send the sum back into memory to one of the operand locations, thus destroying the original operand. The instruction

Add   A,B

performs the operation $B \leftarrow [A] + [B]$. A single two-address Add instruction cannot be used to solve our original problem, which is to add the contents of locations A and B, destroying neither of them, and place the sum in location C. The problem can be solved through the use of another two-address instruction that copies the contents of one memory location into another. Such an instruction is

$$\text{Move} \qquad \text{B,C}$$

which performs the operation C ← [B]. Thus, the operation C ← [A] + [B] can be performed by executing the two instructions

$$\text{Move} \qquad \text{B,C}$$
$$\text{Add} \qquad \text{A,C}$$

Although the order of specifying the source and destination operands is arbitrary, a commonly used convention is to write two-operand instructions in the form

$$\text{Operation} \qquad \text{source,destination}$$

In the Move instruction, a copy of the source operand is placed in the destination location. In instructions requiring two source operands, such as the Add instruction, the second source operand comes from the destination location. The result is placed in the destination location.

The next possibility is to consider using only *one-address* instructions. Of course, since addition is a two-operand operation, an implicit assumption must be made regarding the location of one of the operands as well as the result. A general-purpose CPU register, usually called an *accumulator*, may be used for this purpose. The machine instruction

$$\text{Add} \qquad \text{A}$$

then means add the contents of memory location A to the contents of the accumulator and place the sum into the accumulator. Let us also introduce the one-address instructions

$$\text{Load} \qquad \text{A}$$

and

$$\text{Store} \qquad \text{A}$$

Execution of the Load instruction moves the contents of memory location A into the accumulator, and execution of the Store instruction moves the contents of the accumulator into memory location A. The operation C ← [A] + [B] can then be performed by executing the sequence of instructions

$$\text{Load} \qquad \text{A}$$
$$\text{Add} \qquad \text{B}$$
$$\text{Store} \qquad \text{C}$$

Note that the operand specified in the operand field may be either a source or a destination. In the Load instruction address A specifies the source operand, and the destination location (the accumulator) is implicit. On the other hand, C denotes the destination location in the Store instruction, and the source (the accumulator) is implicit.

Many computers have a number of general-purpose CPU registers, each of which can be used as an accumulator. If there are 8 (or 16) registers, then 3 (or 4) bits will be needed in a field of an instruction to address the register that is to take part in the operation. This is considerably less than the number of bits needed to address a location in the main memory. Let R_i represent a CPU general-purpose register. Then, the instructions

$$\text{Load} \qquad \text{A,}R_i$$
$$\text{Store} \qquad R_i\text{,A}$$

and

$$\text{Add} \qquad \text{A,}R_i$$

are generalizations of the earlier Load, Store, and Add instructions of the single-accumulator case. The Load instruction copies the contents of memory location A into register R_i, and Store copies the contents of register R_i into memory location A.

The Add instruction adds the contents of memory location A to the contents of register R_i and then places the result in register R_i. This type of instruction, in which one address always refers to a location in the main memory and the other, shorter address always refers to a CPU register, is intermediate to the one- and two-address formats discussed earlier. Because of this property, it is called a $1\frac{1}{2}$-address format. Machines with multiple CPU registers also include instructions that permit operations among the registers themselves. Thus,

$$\text{Add} \qquad R_i\text{,}R_j$$

adds the contents of register R_i to those of register R_j and places the answer in register R_j.

A number of general-purpose registers are often used in computers with two-address instruction formats. In general, the registers improve processing efficiency by reducing the number of main memory accesses required when a particular data item is used repeatedly in a computation. In machines that have the two-address format, it is usually possible to specify a register instead of a main memory location in either of the address fields. Thus, the instructions

$$\text{Move} \qquad \text{A,}R_i$$

and

$$\text{Move} \qquad R_i\text{,A}$$

achieve the same results as the instructions

Load   A,R_i

and

Store R_i,A

in the more restrictive $1\frac{1}{2}$-address format discussed earlier. In fact, in the two-address format it makes little sense to use unidirectional instructions such as Load and Store. The more general Move instruction is much more appropriate in this case.

We have discussed three-, two-, and one-address instructions. It is also possible to use instructions where the locations of all operands are defined implicitly. These depend on the use of a method for storing operands in what is called a *pushdown stack*, which will be discussed in Section 2.9. Such instructions are sometimes referred to as *zero-address* instructions.

2.3.1 Instruction Execution and Straight-Line Sequencing

In the above discussion of instruction formats, we used the task C ← [A] + [B] for illustration. A possible program segment for this task as it appears in the main memory of a computer with a two-address instruction format and a number of general-purpose CPU registers is shown in Figure 2.3. The three instructions of the program are placed in successive memory locations whose addresses increase in the order in which the instructions are to be performed, starting at location i.

Let us consider how this program is executed. The CPU contains a register called the *program counter* (PC), which holds the address of the instruction to be executed next. To begin the execution of a program, the address of its first instruction (i in our example) must be placed into the PC. The CPU control circuits automatically proceed to fetch and execute instructions, one at a time, in the order of increasing addresses. This is called *straight-line sequencing*. As each instruction is executed, the PC is advanced to point to the next instruction. Note that location $i + 3$ contains the first instruction of the next program segment.

Execution of a given instruction is a two-phase procedure. In the first phase, called *instruction fetch*, the instruction is fetched from the main memory location whose address is in the PC. This instruction is placed in the instruction register (IR) in the CPU. At the start of the second phase, called *instruction execute*, the instruction in the IR is examined to determine which operation is to be performed. The specified operation is then performed by the CPU. This may involve fetching operands from the main memory to the CPU, performing an arithmetic or logic operation, and storing the result into the main memory. Sometime during this two-phase procedure, the contents of the PC are advanced to point at the next instruction. Therefore, when the execute phase of an instruction is completed, the PC contains the address of the next instruction, and a new instruction fetch phase can begin.

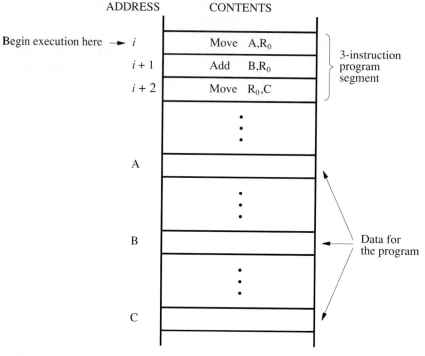

ADDRESS   CONTENTS

Begin execution here → i | Move A,R_0
$i + 1$ | Add B,R_0
$i + 2$ | Move R_0,C

3-instruction program segment

A

B   Data for the program

C

FIGURE 2.3
A program for C ← [A] + [B].

2.3.2 Branching

Consider the task of adding a list of n numbers. A generalization of the program in Figure 2.3 leads to the program outlined in Figure 2.4a. The addresses of the memory locations containing the n numbers are symbolically given as NUM_1, NUM_2, . . . , NUM_n, and the resulting sum is placed in memory location SUM. Instead of using a long list of Add instructions, it is possible to place a single Add instruction in a program loop and arrange to have it executed the required number of times. This is illustrated in Figure 2.4b.

The fundamental idea in program loops is to cause a straight-line sequence of instructions to be executed repeatedly. The number of repetitions, which obviously depends on the problem, must be controlled by means of additional instructions. In the above example, register R_1 is used as a counter. It is initially loaded with the value n from memory location N. The instruction

$$\text{Decrement} \quad R_1$$

decrements the contents of R_1 by 1 each time through the loop.

We now introduce the concept of a branch instruction. To cause a return to the first instruction of the loop, the conditional branch instruction

$$\text{Branch} > 0 \quad\quad \text{LOOPSTART}$$

is used. This causes branching to the instruction at the location indicated if the specified condition is fulfilled; otherwise, straight-line sequencing of instructions continues. The mechanics of causing a branch during the execution of a conditional branch instruction are simple. If it is determined that branching is to take place, the PC is loaded with the address named in the instruction; otherwise, the PC is incremented in the usual way.

Branch conditions are usually related to the result of a preceding arithmetic or logic operation. Since the Decrement instruction in Figure 2.4b immediately precedes the conditional branch instruction, this means that a branch to LOOPSTART occurs as long as the contents of R_1 remain greater than 0. After the loop has been executed n times, R_1 will have been decremented to 0, and the branch will not occur. Instead, the next instruction moves the final result from R_0 into the memory location SUM.

The capability for testing conditions and subsequently choosing one of a set of alternative ways to continue computation has many more applications than just loop

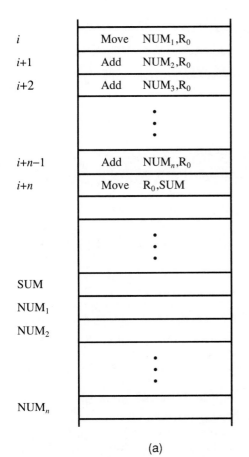

FIGURE 2.4

(a)

Two programs for adding n numbers.

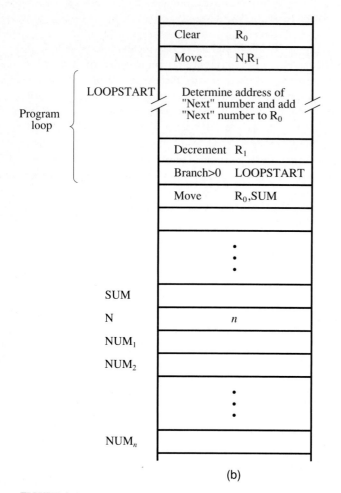

(b)

FIGURE 2.4
(*continued*)

control. This capability is embedded in the instruction sets of all computers and is fundamental to the programming of most nontrivial tasks.

Until now, we have considered only instructions where operand addresses are explicitly given within the instruction. This simple addressing mechanism means that the address field of the Add instruction in the unspecified block of instructions in Figure 2.4b must be modified in successive passes through the loop. It is possible to do this by adding 1 to the operand address of the Add instruction each time it is executed. However, the approach of directly modifying instructions is bad programming practice. It leads to difficulties in debugging and reusing the program. The problem is resolved through the introduction of different schemes for specifying addresses of operands. These schemes are called *addressing modes*. They are intended to provide more flexibility in specifying operand addresses. With some of these schemes, it is possible for a given instruction to refer to different operands when it is executed a number of times; the instruction itself is not changed, however. The next section will examine some of the important possibilities in detail.

2.4 ADDRESSING MODES

In Section 2.3, we used only one mode for addressing operands in memory, the absolute mode. Let us define this mode as

- *Absolute mode:* The address of the location of the operand is given explicitly as a part of the instruction.

We have actually used two versions of this mode in our examples. These are memory absolute mode, where the operand is in a main memory location, and register mode, where the operand is in one of the CPU registers.

Next, we will consider other important addressing modes and indicate how they can be used in the loop program of Figure 2.4*b*.

- *Immediate mode:* The operand is given explicitly in the instruction.

This mode is used in specifying address and data constants in programs. For example, the instruction

$$\text{Move} \qquad 200_{\text{immediate}}, R_0$$

places the value 200 in register R_0. The immediate mode is used to specify the value of a source operand. It makes no sense as a destination because it does not specify a location for an operand. Using a subscript to denote the immediate mode, as above, is rather awkward. Instead, it is common to use the "#" symbol in front of the immediate value. Thus, the above instruction is written as

$$\text{Move} \qquad \#200, R_0$$

In the definition of the next two modes and in subsequent discussions, we will refer to the address of the location of the operand as its *effective address*.

- *Indirect mode:* The effective address of the operand is in the register or main memory location whose address appears in the instruction.

We will denote this mode by placing the address in the instruction in parentheses. This location is said to be a *pointer* to the location of the operand. Figure 2.5 gives examples of indirect addressing. The execution of the Add instruction in Figure 2.5*a* starts by fetching the contents of pointer location A from the main memory. This value, B, is the effective address, which is then used to fetch the desired operand from

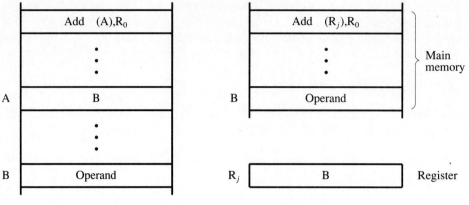

(a) Through a memory location   (b) Through a general-purpose register

Address	Contents		
	Clear	R_0	⎫
	Move	N,R_1	⎬ Initialization
	Move	$\#NUM_1,R_2$	⎭
LOOPSTART	Add	$(R_2),R_0$	
	Increment	R_2	
	Decrement	R_1	
	Branch>0	LOOPSTART	
	Move	R_0,SUM	

(c) The use of indirect addressing in the program of Figure 2.4b

FIGURE 2.5
Indirect addressing.

the memory. Finally, the operand is added to the contents of register R_0. Similarly, in Figure 2.5b the operand is accessed indirectly through register R_j.

Let us now return to the loop program in Figure 2.4b. The indirect addressing mode can be used in accessing successive numbers in the list, which are used as operands in the addition operation, resulting in the program shown in Figure 2.5c. Register R_2 is used as a pointer to numbers in the list; that is, the operands are accessed indirectly through R_2. The first two instructions in the loop implement the unspecified instruction block starting at LOOPSTART in Figure 2.4b. The initialization section of the program clears R_0 to 0, moves the counter value n into R_1, and places the address value NUM_1 into R_2 using the immediate addressing mode. The first time through the loop, the Add instruction fetches the operand at location NUM_1 into the CPU and adds it to R_0. The Increment instruction then adds 1 to the contents of the pointer R_2 so that it will contain the address value NUM_2 when the Add instruction is executed in the second pass through the loop.

The next addressing mode can also provide the addressing flexibility required in the addition loop example.

- *Index mode:* The effective address of the operand is generated by adding a constant value to the contents of a register.

The register used may be either a special register dedicated to this purpose, called the *index register*, or, more commonly, it may be any one of a set of general-purpose registers in the CPU. We will indicate the index mode symbolically as

Value(R)

where Value denotes a constant and R is the name of the register involved. We should note that Value may be given either as an explicit number or as a name representing a numerical value.

In the process of generating the effective address, the contents of the register are not changed. Figure 2.6 illustrates generation of an effective address by the index mode. There are two possibilities for using the index mode, as shown in the figure. In 2.6a the contents of the index register, R_1, are used to define an address in the memory, and the constant given in the instruction defines an *offset* (also called a *displacement*) between the address given and the actual location of the desired operand. An alternative use is illustrated in 2.6b. Here, the constant corresponds to a memory address, and the contents of the register define the offset to the operand.

To see the usefulness of indexed addressing, consider a simple example involving a list of marks for tests in a given course. The list is structured as shown in Figure 2.7. There is a four-word item for each student, consisting of the student's identification number (ID), followed by the marks obtained in three tests. There are n students in the class. The value of n is given at the start of the list. We are interested in computing the sums of the marks obtained in test 2 and 3, respectively. A possible program for this task is given in Figure 2.8.

The program makes use of the index addressing mode presented in Figure 2.6a to access the marks of each student. Register R_0 is used as the index register and is initially set to point to the ID location of the first student record. The main part of the program consists of a loop that accesses successive student records by adding 4 to R_0 at the end of each pass through the loop. Register R_1 serves as the loop counter. It is initialized with the number of students in the class. Registers R_2 and R_3 are used to accumulate the sums of the marks obtained in test 2 and test 3, respectively. The index mode provides a simple means for accessing the third and fourth words in each student record. We should emphasize again that the contents of the index register, R_0, are not changed while the third and fourth words are accessed. In this program the contents of R_0 are changed only by the last Add instruction in the loop. After the last pass through the loop, the resulting sums are stored in memory locations SUM2 and SUM3.

In general, the index mode facilitates access to an operand whose location is defined relative to the beginning of the data structure in which it appears. Each of the four-entry student records in Figure 2.7 is an example of such a data structure.

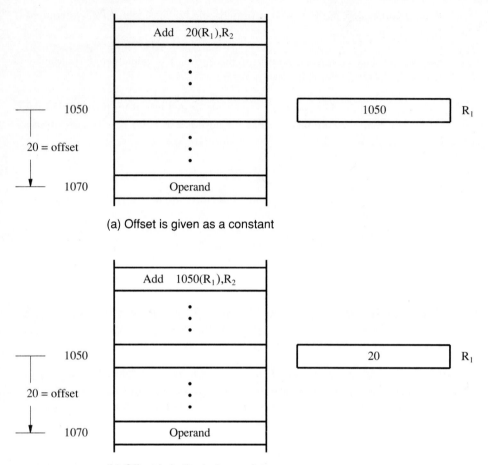

(a) Offset is given as a constant

(b) Offset is in the index register

FIGURE 2.6
Indexed addressing.

We have introduced the most basic form of indexed addressing. Many computers provide a more complex version of the index mode that uses two registers instead of one. Such a mode may be written in the form

$$\text{Value}(R_i, R_j)$$

where the effective address is the sum of the constant Value and the contents of registers R_i and R_j. We will discuss the use of this mode later.

So far we have discussed the four basic addressing modes that are found in most computers. While these modes suffice for general computation, it is often useful to provide some additional modes. Let us consider two other modes that are useful for accessing data items in successive locations in the memory.

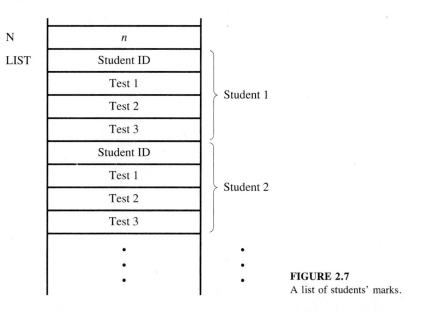

FIGURE 2.7
A list of students' marks.

- *Autoincrement mode:* The effective address of the operand is the contents of a register specified in the instruction. After accessing the operand, the contents of this register are incremented to point to the next item in a list.

We will denote the autoincrement mode by putting the specified register in parentheses to show that the contents of the register are used as the effective address, followed by a " + " sign to indicate that these contents are to be incremented. Thus, using register R_4, the autoincrement mode is written as

	Move	#LIST,R_0	
	Move	N,R_1	Initialization
	Clear	R_2	
	Clear	R_3	
LOOPSTART	Add	2(R_0),R_2	
	Add	3(R_0),R_3	
	Add	#4,R_0	
	Decrement	R_1	
	Branch>0	LOOPSTART	
	Move	R_2,SUM2	
	Move	R_3,SUM3	

FIGURE 2.8
Use of indexed addressing.

	Clear	R_0	⎫
	Move	N,R_1	⎬ Initialization
	Move	$\#NUM_1,R_2$	⎭
→ LOOPSTART	Add	$(R_2)+,R_0$	
	Decrement	R_1	
	Branch>0	LOOPSTART	
	Move	R_0,SUM	

FIGURE 2.9
Use of autoincrement addressing.

$$(R_4)+$$

Using the autoincrement mode, it is possible to eliminate the Increment instruction in Figure 2.5c. The desired operation can be combined with the preceding Add task, as shown in Figure 2.9.

A companion mode for the autoincrement mode, where operands are accessed in the reverse order is defined as follows:

- *Autodecrement mode:* The contents of a register specified in the instruction are decremented. Then, these contents are used as the effective address of the operand.

We will denote the autodecrement mode by putting the specified register in parentheses, preceded by a "−" sign to indicate that the contents of the register are to be decremented prior to being used as the effective address. Thus, we will write

$$-(R_4)$$

This mode allows accessing of operands in the direction of descending addresses. Note that the register contents are decremented before being used as an address. This is in contrast with the autoincrement mode, where the register contents are incremented after being used as an address. A reason for this will be given in Section 2.9, where it will be shown how the autoincrement and autodecrement modes can be used to implement a stack data structure.

The addressing modes defined in this section have been illustrated by simple examples. This has allowed us to introduce the basic concepts without a need to discuss the details of their implementation in a particular computer. The various possible instruction formats, as well as straight-line and loop sequencing, have also been discussed in earlier sections without reference to any specific computer.

2.5 ASSEMBLY LANGUAGE

Machine instructions are represented by patterns of 0s and 1s. Such patterns are awkward to deal with when discussing or preparing programs. Therefore, we use symbols to represent the patterns. For example, in the case of the Move and Add instructions, we use the symbolic names MOVE and ADD to represent the corresponding operation code patterns. Similarly, we use the notation R3 to refer to register 3. A complete set of such symbolic names and some rules for their use constitute a programming language, generally referred to as an *assembly language*. The symbolic names are called *mnemonics*; the set of rules for using the mnemonics in the specification of complete instructions and programs is called the *syntax* of the language.

Programs written in an assembly language can be automatically translated into a sequence of machine instructions by a special program called an *assembler*. The assembler, like any other program, is stored as a sequence of machine instructions in the main memory of the computer. A user program is usually entered via a terminal and stored either in the main memory or on a magnetic disk. At this point, the user program is simply a set of lines of alphanumeric characters in ASCII or EBCDIC coding. When the assembler program is executed, it reads the user program, analyzes it, and then generates the desired machine language program. The user program is called a *source program*, and the assembled machine language program is called an *object program*. We will discuss further how the assembler program works in Section 2.5.2. Now, we will present a few more aspects of the assembly language itself.

The assembly language syntax is likely to require us to write the previously used instruction

$$\text{Move} \qquad R_0, \text{SUM}$$

as

$$\text{MOVE} \qquad R0, \text{SUM}$$

The mnemonic MOVE represents the operation performed by the instruction. It will be translated into a binary code that is understood by the computer when it executes the instruction. The actual binary code is usually referred to as the *OP code*, because it specifies the operation denoted by the mnemonic.

The OP-code mnemonic is followed by at least one blank space. Then, the information that specifies the operands is given. In our example, the source operand is register 0. It is followed by the specification of the destination operand, separated from the source operand by a comma. The destination operand is in the memory location whose address is represented by the name SUM.

Since operands can be given in terms of various addressing modes, the assembler syntax must define how each mode should be specified. For example, a name (such as SUM) may be used to denote the absolute mode. This name must be associated with a numerical value somewhere in the program. Alternatively, the absolute mode may be specified by writing the address explicitly as a numerical value.

It is customary to use the sharp sign, #, to denote an immediate operand, as suggested in Section 2.4. Thus, the instruction

$$\text{ADD} \qquad \#5, \text{SUM}$$

adds the number 5 to the contents of location SUM and puts the result back into SUM.

If SUM represented the address 1000, then the instruction could also be written as

ADD   #5,1000

Indirect addressing is usually specified by placing brackets around the name or symbol denoting the pointer to the operand. For example, if the number 5 is to be placed in a memory location whose address is held in pointer register R2, the desired action can be specified as

MOVE   #5,(R2)

2.5.1   Assembler Commands

In addition to providing a mechanism for representing instructions in a program, the assembly language allows the programmer to specify other information needed to assemble the program. For example, if the programmer uses names to represent numerical values, it is necessary to declare the association between them. Suppose that the name SUM is used to represent a memory location whose address is 200. This fact may be conveyed to the assembler program through a statement such as

SUM   EQU   200

This is not an instruction that will be executed when the object program is being run; in fact, it will not even appear in the object program. It merely supplies information to the assembler that the name SUM should be replaced by the number 200 wherever it appears in the program. Such statements are called *assembler commands*. They are used by the assembler while translating a source program into an object program.

To illustrate further the nature of an assembly language, let us reconsider the program in Figure 2.5c. In order to run this program on a computer, it will be necessary to write its source code in the required assembly language, specifying all information needed to generate the corresponding object program. Suppose that each instruction and each data item occupies one word of memory. This is an oversimplification, but it will help keep the example straightforward. Suppose also that the object program is to be loaded in the main memory as shown in Figure 2.10. The figure shows the memory addresses where the machine instructions and the required data items are to be found.

We have given the instructions in a descriptive format, rather than as patterns of 0s and 1s, to make the figure easier to understand. If the assembler is to produce an object program that will reflect this arrangement, it will have to know the following:

- how to interpret the names
- where to place the object program in the memory
- how many memory locations will be needed to hold the data

To meet these requirements, the source program may be written as shown in Figure 2.11. The program begins with the assembler commands. We have already discussed

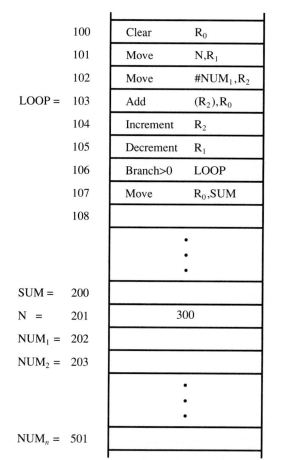

100	Clear	R_0
101	Move	N,R_1
102	Move	$\#NUM_1,R_2$
LOOP = 103	Add	$(R_2),R_0$
104	Increment	R_2
105	Decrement	R_1
106	Branch>0	LOOP
107	Move	R_0,SUM
108		

SUM = 200

N = 201   300

NUM_1 = 202

NUM_2 = 203

NUM_n = 501

FIGURE 2.10

Main memory arrangement for the program in Figure 2.5c.

the Equate command, EQU. The second assembler command, ORIGIN, tells the assembler program where in the main memory to place the instructions and data that follow. In this case, the location specified is at address 201. Since this location is to be loaded with the value 300 (which is the number of entries in the list), a DATA command is used to inform the assembler of this requirement. It states that the data value 300 is to be placed in the memory at address 201 and that this address may be referred to in the rest of the program by the name N. The next assembler command says that the next address (202) is to be known as NUM1 and that 300 consecutive words starting at this address are to be reserved for storing data. The command does not cause the actual data to be loaded in these locations. Such data may be loaded in the memory using an input procedure, as will be discussed later in this chapter.

The instructions of the object program are to be loaded in the memory starting at address 100, which is specified in the second ORIGIN command. The source program instructions are written in the assembly language format, using the symbols and rules discussed earlier in this section. The last statement in the source program is the assembler command END, which indicates to the assembler that this is the end

	Memory address label	Operation	Addressing or data information
Assembler commands	SUM	EQU	200
		ORIGIN	201
	N	DATA	300
	NUM1	RESERVE	300
		ORIGIN	100
Statements that	START	CLR	R0
generate		MOVE	N,R1
machine		MOVE	#NUM1,R2
instructions	LOOP	ADD	(R2),R0
		INC	R2
		DEC	R1
		BGTZ	LOOP
		MOVE	R0,SUM
		RETURN	
Assembler command		END	START

FIGURE 2.11
Assembly language representation for the program in Figure 2.5*b*.

of the source program. The END command includes the label START, which is the address of the location at which the execution of the program is to begin.

We have explained all statements in Figure 2.11, except the RETURN instruction. This instruction terminates the execution of the program, as will be explained in Section 2.10.

Most assembly languages require that statements in a source program be written in the form

Label   Operation   Operand(s)   Comment

The four fields are separated by an appropriate delimiter, typically one or more blank characters. The label is a name associated with the memory address where the machine language instruction produced from the statement will be loaded. Labels may also be associated with addresses of data items. In Figure 2.11 there are four labels: N, NUM1, START, and LOOP.

The operation field contains the operation mnemonic of the desired instruction or assembler command. The operand field contains one or more operands, depending on the type of instruction. The comment field is ignored by the assembler program. It is used for documentation purposes, to make the program easy to understand.

We have introduced some basic characteristics of assembly languages. These languages differ in detail from one computer to another. In Sections 2.6 and 2.7 we will discuss specific examples of assembly languages for the PDP-11 and 68000 computers.

2.5.2 Assembly and Execution of Programs

A source program written in an assembly language must be assembled into a machine-code object program before it can be executed. This is done using an assembler program. The assembler replaces all names and symbols with the numerical values that they represent. Symbols denoting operations and addressing modes are replaced by the binary codes used in machine instructions, and names and labels are replaced by their actual values.

The assembler assigns the addresses to instructions and data blocks. The starting address is specified by an ORIGIN assembler command. The assembler also inserts constants that may be given in DATA commands and reserves memory space as requested by RESERVE commands.

A key part of the assembly process is the determination of the values that replace the names. In some cases, where the value of a name is specified by an EQU command, this is a straightforward task. In other cases, where a name is defined in the label field of a given instruction, the value represented by the name is determined by the location of this instruction in the assembled object program. For example, in Figure 2.10 the names N and NUM1 represent the values 201 and 202, respectively, which are the memory addresses that hold the number of items and the first item in a data list. The value 201 for N is determined by the ORIGIN command statement in Figure 2.11. Since the assembler assigns consecutive addresses as required by the successive statements in a source program, the address associated with NUM1 is 202.

There are cases where the assembler does not directly replace a name representing an address with the actual value of this address. For example, in a branch instruction, the name that specifies the location to which a branch is to be made (the *branch target*) is not replaced by the actual address. As we will see later in this chapter, a branch instruction is implemented in machine code by specifying the distance between this instruction and the instruction at the branch target. The assembler computes this distance, called the *branch offset*, and puts it into the machine instruction.

The branch offset can be in either the forward or the backward direction. As the assembler scans through the source program, it keeps track of all names and the numerical values that correspond to them in a *symbol table*. Thus, it can resolve a backward branch without any difficulty. However, if a forward branch is required, the assembler will not be able to determine the offset, because the address of the branch target has not yet been recorded in the symbol table. A simple, commonly used solution to this problem is to have the assembler scan through the source program twice. During the first pass it creates the complete symbol table. Having done this, the assembler goes through the source program again. During the second pass, it substitutes the values from the symbol table for all names and computes the offsets for the branch instructions. Such an assembler is called a *two-pass assembler*.

Let us next consider the execution of assembled programs. The assembler, like most utility programs that are a part of system software, will store the object program on a magnetic disk. To execute this program, it must be loaded into the main memory of the computer. In order to load a program into the main memory, we must assume that another program, called a *loader*, is already in the main memory. The execution of the loader performs the proper sequence of input operations needed to transfer a machine language program from a magnetic disk into a specified location in the main memory. Having loaded the object code, the loader starts execution of the object program by branching to its first instruction. In order to transfer an object program from the disk to the main memory, the loader must know the length of the program and its starting address in the main memory. This information is usually placed by the assembler in a header preceding the object code.

When execution of the object program begins, it will proceed to completion if not prevented by logical errors in the program. To help the user find such errors, which are not of the syntax type that would have been detected by the assembler, the system software usually includes a *debugger* program. This program provides capabilities such as the ability to stop execution of the object program at some points of interest and to examine the contents of various processor registers and memory locations. We will consider program debugging in more detail in Chapter 6.

2.6   THE PDP-11 ADDRESSING MODES AND INSTRUCTIONS

The PDP-11 is a computer with a 16-bit word length and eight CPU registers. The names $R_0, R_1, \ldots, R_7$ will be used for these registers. Each of them contains 16 bits. Only registers R_0 through R_5 are used as truly general-purpose registers; R_7 is the program counter, and the use of register R_6 will be explained in Section 2.9.

The main memory is organized in 16-bit words, where each word can be interpreted as two separate 8-bit *bytes*. To facilitate referencing of individual bytes, each byte location is assigned a distinct address, as shown in Figure 2.12. Successive

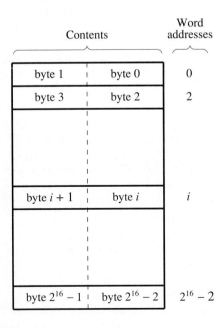

FIGURE 2.12
Map of addressable locations in the PDP-11.

words are given the even address values, 0, 2, 4, and so on. The word at an even-numbered address i consists of the bytes at addresses i and $i + 1$. The low-order byte of a word occupies the location with the even address i, and the high-order byte occupies location $i + 1$. Addresses are 16 bits long, so that up to 65,536 ($= 2^{16}$) bytes or 32,768 ($= 2^{15}$) words can be addressed. Instructions in the PDP-11 can deal with operands that consist of either one byte or one word. It is interesting to note the way in which addresses are assigned to the two bytes of a word in Figure 2.12. The low-order byte has an even address, which is the same as that of the word. The high-order byte has the next higher odd address. This is one way of assigning addresses. In some computers, for example the 68000, which will be discussed in Section 2.7, the high-order byte of a 16-bit word is assigned the even address, and the low-order byte the odd address.

2.6.1 Addressing

The PDP-11 has a number of addressing modes, including those described in Section 2.4. There are both one- and two-operand instruction formats. We will begin our discussion of addressing in the context of the one-operand format, shown in Figure 2.13a. The instruction is divided into two fields. Bits b_6 to b_{15} specify the operation to be performed and hence are called the OP-code field. Bits b_0 to b_5 constitute the address field. This short 6-bit field obviously cannot contain a full 16-bit address. The way that this field is interpreted to generate a 16-bit address will be discussed in the remainder of this section.

The detailed interpretation of the 6-bit address field is shown in Figure 2.13b. The rightmost 3-bit field names one of the eight registers R_0 through R_7. We will refer to this register as R_n. The other 3-bit field specifies the addressing mode. Thus there are eight possible modes, summarized in Table 2.1. The table is organized into five columns, indicating the 3-bit code, its decimal equivalent as a convenient abbreviation, the name of the mode, the PDP-11 assembler syntax, and the operational

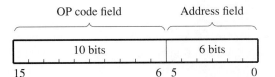

(a) One-operand instruction format

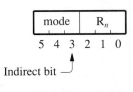

(b) Address field

FIGURE 2.13
The 6-bit address field in PDP-11 instructions.

TABLE 2.1 PDP-ll Addressing Modes

$b_5b_4b_3$	Decimal equivalent	Name	Assembler syntax	Meaning
0 0 0	0	Register	Rn	$A_{effective} = R_n$ (that is, Operand $= [R_n]$)
0 1 0	2	Autoincrement	(Rn)+	$A_{effective} = [R_n]$; Increment R_n
1 0 0	4	Autodecrement	−(Rn)	Decrement R_n; $A_{effective} = [R_n]$
1 1 0	6	Index	X(Rn)	Fetch X; Increment PC; $A_{effective} = X + [R_n]$
0 0 1	1	Register indirect	@Rn	$A_{effective} = [R_n]$
0 1 1	3	Autoincrement indirect	@(Rn)+	$A_{effective} = [[R_n]]$; Increment R_n
1 0 1	5	Autodecrement indirect	@−(Rn)	Decrement R_n; $A_{effective} = [[R_n]]$
1 1 1	7	Index indirect	@X(Rn)	Fetch X; Increment PC; $A_{effective} = [X + [R_n]]$

meaning for each mode. The assembler syntax column indicates the way in which the addressing mode is represented by a sequence of alphanumeric characters in the assembly language of the PDP-11. We will discuss the assembly language later when we introduce example programs. In the last column, the square-brackets notation, [L], means the contents of the location whose address is L, as used earlier in this chapter. The address L can be that of a main memory location or a register.

The organization of Table 2.1 indicates that bits b_5 and b_4 specify four basic addressing modes. Determination of the effective address of an operand can be viewed as follows. The bit pattern in b_5 and b_4 specifies how to obtain an address value. If bit $b_3 = 0$, this value is the effective address of the operand, denoted $A_{effective}$ in the table; but if $b_3 = 1$, the value obtained is the address of a location that contains the effective address. Thus bit b_3 is used to designate indirect addressing. Let us now consider the four basic addressing modes in detail.

- *Register mode.* When $b_3 = 0$, the operand is the contents of register R_n. In the indirect version of this mode, that is, when $b_3 = 1$, the register R_n contains the effective address of the operand.
- *Autoincrement mode.* The effective address is in R_n. After the contents of R_n have been used to fetch the operand, the register is automatically incremented. If the operand is a byte, as specified in the OP-code field of the instruction, register R_n is incremented by 1. If the operand is a word, R_n is incremented by 2. In the indirect case, the effective address is contained in the memory location pointed at by R_n before incrementing is performed, and R_n is always incremented by 2.
- *Autodecrement mode.* The contents of R_n are decremented and then used as the effective address. For byte operands, R_n is decremented by 1; for word operands, R_n is decremented by 2. In the indirect version, the effective address is contained in the memory location pointed at by R_n after it has been decremented, and R_n is always decremented by 2.
- *Index mode.* The effective address is generated by adding the contents of R_n to the constant X, which is contained in the word immediately following the OP-code word. If indirection is specified, it is performed after indexing.

As we have already mentioned, the autoincrement and autodecrement addressing modes provide a simple mechanism for referencing a list of data items in successive word or byte locations in the memory on successive passes through a program loop. The autoincrement indirect mode can be used to reference a list of addresses of data items instead of the data items themselves; an example of this will be given in Section 2.10, where a list of addresses is passed to a subroutine as parameters from a main program. The autodecrement indirect mode does not seem to have any obvious, important uses. Indeed, an extensive study[1] has found that it is seldom, if ever, used in practice. As we shall see in Chapter 3, this addressing mode is not included in the VAX-11 addressing modes, which were designed based on the experience gained from the use of the PDP-11.

An example of a one-operand instruction using the index mode is shown in Figure 2.14. Note that the instruction occupies two consecutive memory word locations.

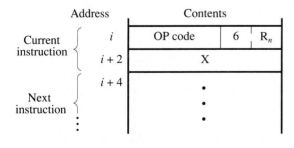

$$A_{effective} = X + [R_n]$$

FIGURE 2.14
Indexed addressing in the PDP-11.

Before the instruction is fetched into the CPU, the PC points at the first word of the instruction. After this word is fetched into the instruction register, IR, the PC is incremented by 2 to point at the second word, which contains the value X. Similarly, after fetching X, the PC is incremented again to point at the first word of the next instruction. Upon completion of this step, the contents of register R_n and the value X are added to generate the effective address of the operand. If R_n contains the starting address of a list of data items, then the index mode can be used to access an individual item by using X as its displacement from the starting address. Another important use for the index mode is where the program counter is used as the index register. This will be described in the next section.

2.6.2 The Role of the Program Counter in Addressing

The PC is actually register R_7 in the PDP-11 computer. When it is specified as the register R_n in the address field, some interesting and useful addressing actions result. Because we have already discussed all eight possible addressing modes, this section does not introduce anything that cannot be deduced from Table 2.2. We are merely highlighting the features that result when R_n = PC. Of course, these features are not accidental; they represent a central idea in the implementation of the addressing modes in the PDP-11.

- *Immediate mode* results from the autoincrement mode with R_n = PC. After the first word of an instruction has been fetched, the PC points at the following word. Since in the autoincrement mode the contents of the specified register (in this case, the PC) are used as the address of the operand, the second word of the instruction is the immediate operand. The PC is again incremented by 2, so that it points at the next word after the immediate operand. The PC is incremented by 2 whether the immediate operand is a word or a byte.
- *Absolute mode* results from the autoincrement indirect mode with R_n = PC. By adding a further level of indirection to the immediate mode, the second word of the instruction is interpreted as the effective address of the operand. This implements absolute addressing as defined earlier.
- *Relative mode* results from the index mode with R_n = PC. The effective address of the operand is the sum of the value X and the contents of the PC. This means that X represents the displacement in bytes from the word immediately following X to the location of the operand. In other words, the memory address of the operand is given relative to the instruction. Figure 2.15 shows a specific example of this addressing mode. Note that X can be negative as well as positive. Therefore, operands with addresses lower than that of the instruction, as well as those with higher addresses, can be specified.
- *Relative indirect mode* results from the index indirect mode with R_n = PC. The memory location containing the address of the operand is specified relative to the instruction.

TABLE 2.2 PDP-ll Addressing Modes with R_n = PC

$b_5b_4b_3$	Decimal equivalent	Name	Assembler syntax	Meaning
0 1 0	2	Immediate (autoincrement)	#n	$A_{effective}$ = [PC]; Increment PC (that is, operand n follows instruction)
0 1 1	3	Absolute (autoincrement indirect)	@#A	$A_{effective}$ = [[PC]]; Increment PC (that is, $A_{effective}$, which is A, follows instruction)
1 1 0	6	Relative (index)	A	Fetch X; Increment PC; $A_{effective}$ = X + [PC] (that is, $A_{effective}$ is A. It is specified relative to [PC] by displacement X in word following instruction)
1 1 1	7	Relative indirect (index indirect)	@A	Fetch X; Increment PC; $A_{effective}$ = [X + [PC]] (that is, the address A of location containing $A_{effective}$ is specified relative to [PC] by displacement X in word following instruction)

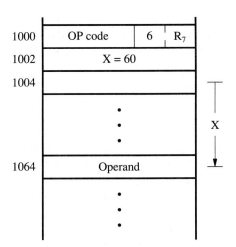

FIGURE 2.15
An example of relative addressing in the PDP-11.

Table 2.2 summarizes these four addressing modes. Note that special assembly language syntax is used for them. The use of the PC as R_n in the register and register indirect modes is of limited usefulness. Neither version of the autodecrement mode should ever be used with R_n = PC.

2.6.3   Some PDP-11 Instructions and a Simple Program

This section and several sections that follow will discuss some basic aspects of the PDP-11 instruction set. We will introduce instructions and their formats through simple examples. Some aspects of the PDP-11 assembly language will also be described. A complete listing of the PDP-11 instruction set is given in Appendix B.

Let us start by introducing the two-operand instructions that have the format shown in Figure 2.16a. The abbreviation src is used to denote the effective address of the first operand, called the *source* operand. Correspondingly, dst is used to denote the effective address of the second operand, called the *destination* operand. The values of src and dst are generated by using the information in the corresponding 6-bit fields of the instruction, as indicated in Figure 2.13b and Tables 2.1 and 2.2.

Figure 2.16b shows an example of the Add instruction. It is represented in the assembly language as

$$\text{ADD} \qquad \#17,\text{R3}$$

and performs the action

$$\text{dst} \leftarrow [\text{src}] + [\text{dst}]$$

The source operand, 17, is contained in the word immediately after the OP-code word and is accessed by the immediate addressing mode; that is, by the autoincrement mode, with R_n = PC. The destination operand is contained in register R_3.

The same format is used to provide a Subtract instruction, which has the OP code SUB and performs the action

$$\text{dst} \leftarrow [\text{dst}] - [\text{src}]$$

Another useful instruction in the two-operand format is the Move instruction that performs the action

$$\text{dst} \leftarrow [\text{src}]$$

The OP code for this instruction is MOV.

We can now write a PDP-11 program for the task $C \leftarrow [A] + [B]$ that was discussed in Section 2.3.1. Figure 2.3 showed that the three-instruction sequence

Move	A,R_0
Add	B,R_0
Move	R_0,C

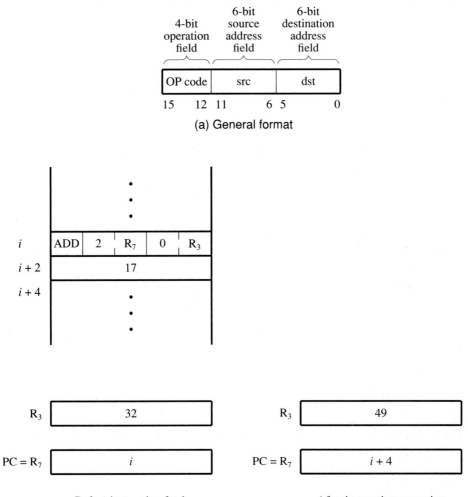

(a) General format

(b) Example of the Add instruction

FIGURE 2.16
The two-operand instruction format in the PDP-11.

can be used to perform the task in a machine with a two-address instruction format.

A PDP-11 program for this task is given in Figure 2.17. In this program, operands A, B, and C are addressed using the relative mode. The first Move instruction occupies two words, because the generation of the source address requires a relative displacement value. At the time that the source address is calculated, the PC contains 1204. Therefore, the displacement value must be −54, so that the operand address value will be 1204 − 54 = 1150.

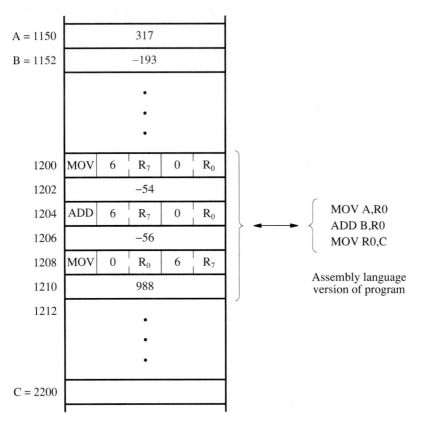

After program execution, [2200] = 124

FIGURE 2.17
A PDP-11 program for C ← [A] + [B].

The Add instruction and the second Move instruction both use the same addressing modes as the first Move instruction. The reader is encouraged to check that the displacement values −56 and 988 are correct.

2.6.4 The PDP-11 Assembly Language

We have introduced the general concepts of assembly languages in Section 2.5. In this section we will consider specific aspects of the PDP-11 assembly language. The discussion of general concepts in Section 2.5 applies to this particular assembly language, but different notation is used in some cases.

Consider again the program in Figure 2.17, loaded in the memory locations shown. A corresponding assembly language source program is given in Figure 2.18. The assembler commands perform the same functions as the corresponding commands in Figure 2.11, but the notation is different. The Equate command uses the " = " sign. The ORIGIN command is indicated with the ". = " symbol. A 16-bit data item is

	Memory address label	Operation	Addressing or data information
Assembler commands		C =	2200.
		. =	1150.
	A:	.WORD	317.
	B:	.WORD	−193.
		. =	1200.
Statements that generate machine instructions		MOV	A,R0
		ADD	B,R0
		MOV	R0,C
Assembler command		.END	

FIGURE 2.18
A complete assembly language program for the program of Figure 2.17.

placed in a given location with the .WORD command. Note that the labels A and B associated with these commands are followed by a colon. All labels in a PDP-11 assembly language program must be terminated by a colon. The end of the source program is indicated with the .END command.

Until now in this chapter, we have used the decimal number representation for convenience when referring to numerical quantities. However, several other number representations are used in programming. In addition to binary, two other frequently used representations are octal and hexadecimal, which will be described later. It is necessary for the programmer to specify the representation used. In the example of Figure 2.18, and in the PDP-11 assembly language in general, decimal numbers are indicated by a "." following the number.

We should emphasize that when using the relative addressing mode, the value of the displacement (-54 in the first instruction of our example) need not be explicitly specified in the assembly language program. Such displacements are computed by the assembler program based on its knowledge of the location of the instruction and the address of the operand involved.

In the assembly language program examples that are used in the remainder of this book, we will not always include the assembler command statements unless they are essential for an understanding of the points being illustrated. The reader should be aware that they are required if the programs are to be assembled and executed.

2.6.5   Branch Instructions and Condition Codes

We introduced the program loop idea in Section 2.3.2. The conditional branch instruction was found to be an essential part of loop control. In general, conditional branches are used in any programming situation in which one of two possible paths for continuing the computation must be chosen. This choice is usually based on an arithmetic or logical property or condition of the result of a recently performed operation.

The format of PDP-11 branch instructions is shown in Figure 2.19a. The 8-bit OP-code field specifies the branch condition to be tested. If the condition is true, or satisfied, a branch takes place. The branch address, that is, the address to be loaded into the PC, is computed by adding two times the value in the offset field to the current contents of the PC. When this addition is performed, the PC has already been advanced to point at the word following the branch instruction. Therefore the offset is the distance in words between that word and the branch address. The 8-bit offset value is interpreted as a signed number in 2's-complement representation. This number representation will be discussed in detail in Chapter 7. The offset can have any value in the range -128 through 127.

As an example of the use of a branch instruction, consider the program segment shown in Figure 2.19b. The three instructions correspond to the addition loop in Figure 2.9. The Decrement instruction, with the OP code DEC, has the one-operand format shown in Figure 2.13a. The branch instruction BGT specifies that a branch is to take place if the result of the most recent operation was greater than 0. Because the immediately preceding operation was performed by the DEC instruction, the branch will take place if the decremented value is greater than 0. Observe that the operations that influence the branch conditions are performed before the branch instruction is

OP code	Offset

15   8 7   0

Branch address = [updated PC] + 2 × offset

(a) General format and branch address determination

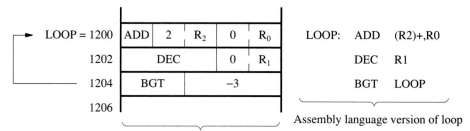

LOOP = 1200	ADD	2	R_2	0	R_0
1202	DEC			0	R_1
1204	BGT		−3		
1206					

LOOP:	ADD	(R2)+,R0
	DEC	R1
	BGT	LOOP

Assembly language version of loop

Appearance of loop in memory

PC = 1206 when a branch address is computed
Branch address = 1206 + 2 × (−3) = 1200 = LOOP

(b) Example of using a branch instruction in the loop program of Figure 2.5c

FIGURE 2.19
PDP-11 branch instructions.

fetched into the CPU; hence, it is necessary to temporarily store the status of such test conditions. A number of bit-storage elements, referred to as the *condition code* bits or flags, are used for this purpose.

In the PDP-11 there are four condition code flags:

N (negative)   Set to 1 if the result is negative; otherwise, cleared to 0.
Z (zero)   Set to 1 if the result is 0; otherwise, cleared to 0.
V (overflow)   Set to 1 if arithmetic overflow occurs; otherwise, cleared to 0.
C (carry)   Set to 1 if a carry-out results from the operation; otherwise, cleared to 0.

The usefulness of the V and C flags will become apparent in the discussion of arithmetic in Chapter 7. Most of the one- and two-operand instructions affect the setting of the condition codes. The detailed effects for all instructions are given in Appendix B. The branch instructions themselves do not affect the condition codes. They only inspect them to determine whether branching should take place.

A PDP-11 program for the full program of Figure 2.9 is given in Figure 2.20. The first instruction is a one-operand instruction that clears register R_0. The second instruction uses the relative addressing mode to load counter R_1 with the value n in memory location N. The next instruction loads the address value NUM into the pointer register R_2 by using the immediate addressing mode. We have already discussed the loop portion of the program in the explanation of the PDP-11 branch instructions. The last Move instruction places the sum into memory location SUM. Note that comments have been added to each instruction to make the program self-explanatory. Comments are ignored by the assembler program.

	CLR	R0	R_0 is used to accumulate the sum.
	MOV	N,R1	N contains n, the number of numbers to be added, and R_1 acts as a counter register in determining how many times to execute the loop.
	MOV	#NUM,R2	R_2 is a pointer register, and it is initialized to contain the address, NUM, of the location containing the first number of the list of numbers.
LOOPSTART:	ADD	(R2)+,R0	Successive numbers are added in R_0.
	DEC	R1	The counter register R_1 is decremented.
	BGT	LOOPSTART	If [R_1] have not reached 0, that is, if the loop has not been executed n times, branch back and execute the loop again.
	MOV	R0,SUM	Store the sum in SUM.

FIGURE 2.20
A PDP-11 assembly language program for the addition program in Figure 2.9.

2.6.6 Byte Operands

The operands of the PDP-11 ADD, SUB, MOV, CLR, and DEC instructions that we have introduced are 16-bit words. With the major exception of the Add and Subtract instructions, most one- and two-operand instructions can also be applied to byte operands. The leftmost bit of the OP code is set to 0 to specify word operands and to 1 to specify byte operands. The assembler mnemonics for the OP codes, as we have used them until now, have been the word operand versions. The letter B is appended to the OP codes to signify byte operands. As an example

$$\text{MOVB} \qquad \text{LOC1,LOC2}$$

moves the byte from memory byte location LOC1 into memory byte location LOC2. If a CPU register R_i is the source or destination location for a byte operand, the low-order 8 bits of the register are used.

In many computer applications, it is convenient to use byte-sized operands. A common example is manipulation of text performed by a word-processing program. In such tasks, the data are in the form of characters, which are usually represented by 8-bit codes.

To introduce further features of the PDP-11 instruction set and to discuss character manipulation in general, we will use an example program that sorts a list of bytes. Each byte encodes a character from the set of letters A through Z. It is desired to sort them into alphabetical order. Assume that either the ASCII or EBCDIC code is used for encoding individual characters. Appendix D gives the details of these codes. Observe that the letter sequence A, B, C, . . . , Z is represented by a sequence of binary code patterns that have increasing values when interpreted as positive integers. We can therefore regard the list as a set of positive integers that are to be sorted into increasing numerical order. The list has n bytes, not necessarily distinct, and is stored at consecutive byte locations LIST through LIST$+n-1$. The sorted list is to occupy the same memory locations as the original list. If necessary, it is permissible to use a few additional temporary storage locations in performing the required operations. This is called an *in-place* sort.

The specific algorithm that we will use is called the *straight selection sort*. The main idea is as follows: Find the smallest number first and place it in the first position of the list (location LIST), leaving the remaining numbers in the sublist consisting of the last $n - 1$ positions. Then, find the next smallest number and place it in location LIST$+ 1$, leaving the remaining numbers in the sublist consisting of the last $n - 2$ positions. This procedure is repeated until the list is sorted.

A Pascal-like program for the sorting algorithm is given in Figure 2.21a. In this program, the list elements are referenced as the one-dimensional array LIST(0), LIST(1), . . . , LIST($n-1$). For each sublist LIST(j) to LIST($n-1$), the current value of element LIST(j) is compared to successive elements of the sublist. The subscripts of these elements are specified by the loop variable k in the inner for-loop. Whenever a smaller element is encountered, it is interchanged with element LIST(j). The search is then repeated for all values of j from 0 to $n - 2$.

for j: 0 **to** n−2 **do**
 begin
 for k: j+1 **to** n−1 **do**
  begin
  if LIST(j) > LIST(k) **then**
   begin
   TEMP : LIST(j);
   LIST(j) : LIST(k);
   LIST(k): TEMP
   end
  end
 end

(a) Pascal-like program for sorting

	CLR	R1	Initialize outer loop control
			variable j to 0 in R_1.
OUTER:	MOV	R1,R2	Initialize inner loop control
	INC	R2	variable k to j +1 in R_2.
INNER:	CMPB	LIST(R1),LIST(R2)	Compare LIST(j) to
	BLOS	ENDINNER	LIST(k) and interchange
	MOVB	LIST(R1),R3	if LIST(j)>LIST(k).
	MOVB	LIST(R2),LIST(R1)	
	MOVB	R3,LIST(R2)	
ENDINNER:	INC	R2	Increment R_2 to contain
	CMP	R2,#n−1	next k value and
	BLOS	INNER	check for end of inner loop.
	INC	R1	Increment R_1 to contain
	CMP	R1,#n−2	next j value and
	BLOS	OUTER	check for end of sort.
	next instruction		

(b) PDP-11 program implementation

FIGURE 2.21
A byte-sorting program.

A PDP-11 assembly language program for the sorting algorithm is shown in Figure 2.21b. This program is written in a straightforward manner to correspond directly to the program in Figure 2.21a. Registers R_1 and R_2 are used to hold the loop variables j and k. Register R_3 is used as a temporary storage location during the interchange operation. The index addressing mode in the form LIST(R1) and LIST(R2) is used to access individual bytes in the list. Note that this use of the index mode corresponds to the option illustrated in Figure 2.6b.

The assembler commands needed to define the values of n and LIST should be added to the program. This can be done in a style similar to that shown in Figure 2.18.

The use of the expressions $n - 1$ and $n - 2$ in the immediate addressing modes toward the end of the program illustrates a common assembler feature. The values of these expressions are computed at assembly time and then used in place of the expressions.

The above program has a subtle flaw. The check for loop termination is done at the end of each loop. This means that there will be at least one pass through the loop, irrespective of the value n. Therefore, the program is unsuitable for lists shorter than two elements.

The reader should also note that this program is not very general, because the values LIST and n are constants that are fixed at assembly time. In a more general sorting routine, these parameters would be programmed as variables whose values are determined at execution time. (See Problem 2.12.)

In the sort program given in Figure 2.21b, the Compare instruction is used on both word operands and byte operands, represented by the OP codes CMP and CMPB, respectively. It performs the operation

$$[\text{src}] - [\text{dst}]$$

and manipulates the condition code bits based on the result of the subtraction operation. This instruction does not affect either of the operands; it affects only the condition code bits. It is normally followed by a branch instruction, as it is in the sort program. The Compare, Branch sequence is used to make a branching decision based on the relative order of the values of the two operands of the Compare instruction. For example, the instructions

```
CMP     R2,#n-1
BLOS    INNER           (Branch if Lower Or Same)
```

in lines 10 and 11 of the program cause a branch to the instruction in memory location INNER if $[\text{R2}] \le n - 1$.

The only other new instruction introduced in this program is the Increment instruction, INC. It is a one-operand instruction that adds 1 to the operand.

In the above examples, we have used two conditional branch instructions, BGT and BLOS. The way in which these and other conditional branch instructions use the four condition code flags is specified in detail in Appendix B. The use of these flags is obvious for some conditional branch instructions. For example, in executing the instruction BMI (Branch if MInus), the branch is taken if the result of the previous operation was negative, that is, if the N flag is equal to 1. For other branch instructions, the tests performed on the condition code flags are more complicated. These tests depend on the details of how arithmetic is performed on signed numbers. We will return to this topic in Chapter 7.

2.6.7   Logic Instructions

Until now, we have performed only arithmetic operations or comparisons on word and byte data. In many applications, it is necessary to manipulate some of the individual bit positions of byte or word data. Most computers have a few instructions, called logic instructions, that perform standard logic operations on the operands.

Let us consider some specific examples. The PDP-11 has three logic instructions in the two-operand instruction format. They are

$$
\begin{array}{ll}
\text{Bit-clear (BIC, BICB):} & \text{dst} \leftarrow \overline{\text{[src]}} \wedge \text{[dst]} \\
\text{Bit-set (BIS, BISB):} & \text{dst} \leftarrow \text{[src]} \vee \text{[dst]} \\
\text{Bit-test (BIT, BITB):} & \text{[src]} \wedge \text{[dst]}
\end{array}
$$

Each of these instructions manipulates the condition code bits as follows:

N   Set to 1 if the most significant bit of the result is 1.
Z   Set to 1 if the result is 0.
V   Set to 0.
C   Not affected.

The AND ($\wedge$) and OR ($\vee$) logic operations in these instructions are applied to corresponding bit positions in the source and destination operands. For example, let

$$[\text{src}] = A = a_{15} \ldots a_1 a_0$$

and

$$[\text{dst}] = B = b_{15} \ldots b_1 b_0$$

Then, the Bit-clear operation

$$\text{dst} \leftarrow \overline{[src]} \wedge [\text{dst}]$$

means

$$\text{dst}_{15} \leftarrow \overline{a}_{15} \wedge b_{15}$$
$$\ldots\ldots\ldots\ldots\ldots$$
$$\text{dst}_1 \leftarrow \overline{a}_1 \wedge b_1$$

and

$$\text{dst}_0 \leftarrow \overline{a}_0 \wedge b_0$$

The Bit-clear instruction clears the bits in the destination at each bit position where there is a 1 in the corresponding bit of the source operand. The destination bits that correspond to 0 bits in the source operand remain unchanged. The Bit-set instruction sets destination bits to 1 wherever there are 1s in the source operand. The Bit-test instruction does not change either operand; it manipulates the condition code bits as specified above, based on the result of performing an AND operation on the two operands.

Consider a data-processing problem that uses decimal digits, encoded in the binary-coded decimal (BCD) code, described in Appendix D. Assume that four digits are packed into the 16-bit word at location DIGITS in the main memory. It is required to set the digit in bit positions $b_7 b_6 b_5 b_4$ to the value $9_{10} = 1001_2$, where the subscripts on these two numbers denote decimal (base 10) and binary (base 2) representations, respectively. A simple way of doing this is to first clear the desired bits with a Bit-clear instruction and then insert the required pattern using a Bit-set instruction. Both instructions can include the required binary source operand patterns as immediate operands. These patterns, often called *masks* in this context, are shown in Figure 2.22. The masks are also given in octal (base 8) notation, which can be used to specify bit patterns concisely. The octal version of a binary number is derived by grouping the bits in threes from the least significant end of the binary number. The octal digit corresponding to each group of 3 bits is simply the value represented by that group.

The two instructions required to perform the above task are

$$\begin{array}{ll} \text{BIC} & \text{\#000360,DIGITS} \\ \text{BIS} & \text{\#000220,DIGITS} \end{array}$$

where the immediate operands are expressed in octal notation. In the PDP-11 assembly language, numerical quantities are considered to be in octal notation unless they are followed by a decimal point, in which case they are taken to be decimal numbers.

	Decimal digits			
[DIGITS] initially	$b_{15}\ b_{14}\ b_{13}\ b_{12}$	$b_{11}\ b_{10}\ b_9\ b_8$	$b_7\ b_6\ b_5\ b_4$	$b_3\ b_2\ b_1\ b_0$
Binary mask for BIC instruction	0 0 0 0	0 0 0 0	1 1 1 1	0 0 0 0
Octal notation	0 0	0	3	6 0
[DIGITS] after execution of BIC instruction	$b_{15}\ b_{14}\ b_{13}\ b_{12}$	$b_{11}\ b_{10}\ b_9\ b_8$	0 0 0 0	$b_3\ b_2\ b_1\ b_0$
Binary mask for BIS instruction	0 0 0 0	0 0 0 0	1 0 0 1	0 0 0 0
Octal notation	0 0	0	2	2 0
[DIGITS] after execution of BIS instruction	$b_{15}\ b_{14}\ b_{13}\ b_{12}$	$b_{11}\ b_{10}\ b_9\ b_8$	1 0 0 1	$b_3\ b_2\ b_1\ b_0$

Inserted digit 9_{10}

FIGURE 2.22
An example of digit insertion using logic operations.

Leading zeros need not be shown explicitly. In our example, they are included only to emphasize the correspondence with Figure 2.22. The figure shows the effect of executing the two instructions on the location DIGITS.

The third logic instruction mentioned above, Bit-test, serves a purpose similar to the Compare instruction. It is useful in testing the status of one or more bits in a byte or a word, in order to set the condition code flags for use by a subsequent conditional branch instruction. For example, if a branch is to take place to PROCEED when bit b_2 of memory location STATUS is equal to 1, the following two instructions can be used:

<pre>
        BIT   #4,STATUS
        BNE   PROCEED
</pre>

The OP-code mnemonic BNE denotes the Branch if Not Equal to 0 conditional branch instruction. If two or more bits of the test pattern are set to 1, branching will take place if any one of the corresponding bits of the destination operand is equal to 1.

2.7 THE 68000 MICROPROCESSOR
ADDRESSING MODES AND INSTRUCTIONS

The 68000 microprocessor is the original member of a family of microprocessors that have essentially the same architecture. It is characterized by a 16-bit external word length, because it has 16 data pins on the chip. However, data are manipulated internally in registers that contain 32 bits. The more advanced models of this family, the 68020, 68030, and 68040 microprocessors, come in larger packages and have 32 data pins. Thus, they can deal with data both internally and externally in 32-bit quantities. We will use the 68000 as our main example, because it is somewhat simpler to describe, yet it portrays the salient features of the entire family.

2.7.1 The 68000 Register Structure

The 68000 register structure is shown in Figure 2.23. There are eight data registers and eight address registers, each 32 bits long. The data registers serve as general-purpose accumulators and as counters.

The 68000 instructions deal with operands of three different lengths: A 32-bit operand is said to occupy a *long word*, a 16-bit operand constitutes a word, and an 8-bit operand is known as a byte operand. When an instruction uses a byte or a word operand of a register, the operand is in the low-order bit positions of the register. In most cases, such instructions do not affect the remaining high-order bits of the register, but some instructions extend the sign of a shorter operand into the high-order bits. For example, the sign of a byte operand is extended by replicating the bit in position b_7 into the bits in positions b_8 through b_{31}. Sign extension does not change the value of the operand, as will be explained in Chapter 7.

The address registers hold information used in determining the addresses of memory operands. This information may be given in either long word or word quantities. When the address of a given memory location is in an address register, the

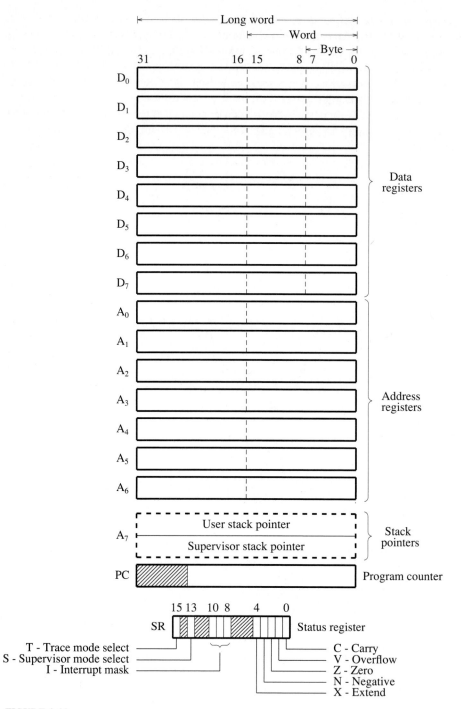

FIGURE 2.23
The M68000 register structure.

register serves as a pointer to that location. Both address and data registers can also be used as index registers. One address register, A_7, has a special function of being a stack pointer. The stack structure and the role of this register will be discussed in Section 2.9.

The address registers and address calculations involve 32 bits. However, due to pin limitations of the 68000 package, only the least-significant 24 bits of an address are used. The 68000 chip has a total of 64 pins, of which 16 connect to the data bus and 24 to the address bus. The remaining 24 pins are used for control and power supply purposes. As noted above, the 68020, 68030, and 68040 microprocessors come in larger packages, which allow them to have 32 address pins and 32 data pins.

The last register shown in Figure 2.23 is the processor *status* register, SR. It contains five condition code bits, which will be described in Section 2.7.5; three interrupt bits, which will be discussed in Chapter 6; and two mode-select bits, which will be explained in Section 2.9.

2.7.2 Addressing

The main memory of a 68000 microcomputer is organized in 16-bit words. Each word consists of two bytes that have distinct addresses. Two consecutive words can be interpreted as a single 32-bit long word. The memory addresses are assigned as shown in Figure 2.24. A word must be aligned on an even boundary, that is, its address is an even number. The byte in the high-order position of a word has the same address as the word, while the byte in the low-order position has the next higher address. (This is opposite to the scheme used in the PDP-11 computers.)

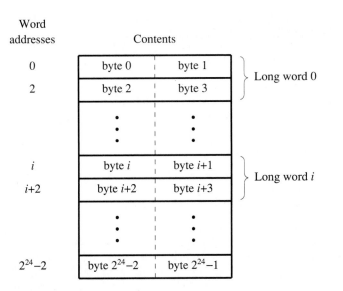

FIGURE 2.24
Map of addressable locations in the 68000.

As explained in the previous section, the 68000 generates 24-bit addresses. Therefore, the addressable space is $2^{24}(=16777216)$ bytes or 2^{23} words. The number 16777216 is usually referred to as 16M, hence one speaks of the addressable space as being 16 megabytes. The 68000 has a number of addressing modes, including the ones discussed in Section 2.4. It has many instructions that fit into a 16-bit word, but also some where additional words are required for extra addressing information. The first word of an instruction specifies the operation that is to be performed and possibly some addressing information. This word is called the OP-code word. The rest of the addressing information, if any, is given in the subsequent words. The available addressing modes are defined as follows:

- *Immediate mode*. The operand is contained in the instruction. There are four sizes of operands that can be specified. The byte, word, and long-word operands are given in the bytes that follow the OP-code word. The fourth type of immediate operand, consisting of very small numbers, can be included directly in the OP-code word in some instructions.

- *Absolute Mode*. The absolute address of an operand is given in the instruction, following the OP-code. There are two versions of this mode, long and short. In the long mode a 24-bit address is specified explicitly. In the short mode a 16-bit value is given in the instruction to be used as the low-order 16 bits of an address. The sign bit of this value is extended to provide the high-order 8 bits of the address. Since the sign bit is either 0 or 1, it follows that in the short mode only two *pages* of the addressable space can be accessed. These are the 0 page and the $FF8_{16}$ page, each consisting of 32K bytes.

- *Register mode*. The operand is in a CPU register specified in the instruction.

- *Register indirect mode*. The effective address of the operand is the contents of an address register specified in the instruction.

- *Autoincrement mode*. The effective address of the operand is the contents of an address register A_n specified in the instruction. After the operand is accessed, the contents of A_n are incremented by 1, 2, or 4, depending on whether a byte, a word, or a long-word operand is involved, respectively.

- *Autodecrement mode*. An address register A_n specified in the instruction is decremented by 1, 2, or 4, depending on whether a byte, a word, or a long-word operand is involved, respectively. Then, the effective address of the operand is the contents of A_n.

- *Basic index mode*. A 16-bit signed offset and an address register A_n are specified in the instruction. The sum of this offset and the contents of A_n is the effective address of the operand.

- *Full index mode*. An 8-bit signed offset, an address register A_n, and an index register R_k (either an address or a data register) are given in the instruction. The effective address of the operand is the sum of the offset and the contents of registers A_n and R_k. Either all 32 bits or the sign-extended low-order 16 bits of R_k are used in the derivation of the address. In the former case the specification of R_k in the assembler syntax must be stated as Rk.L, while the latter is the default case, which can also be indicated as Rk.W.

- *Basic relative mode*. This is the same mode as the basic index mode except that the program counter is used instead of an address register, A_n.
- *Full relative mode*. This is the same mode as the full index mode except that the program counter is used instead of an address register A_n.

The addressing modes and their assembler syntax are summarized in Table 2.3.

The reader should note that there are two versions of the index mode. The basic index mode corresponds to the mode depicted in Figure 2.6. The full index mode

TABLE 2.3   68000 Addressing Modes

Name	Assembler syntax	Addressing function
Immediate	#Value	Operand = Value
Absolute Short	Value	EA = Sign Extended WValue
Absolute Long	Value	EA = Value
Register	Rn	EA = R_n that is, Operand = $[R_n]$
Register Indirect	(An)	EA = $[A_n]$
Autoincrement	(An)+	EA = $[A_n]$; Increment A_n
Autodecrement	−(An)	Decrement A_n; EA = $[A_n]$
Indexed basic	WValue(An)	EA = WValue + $[A_n]$
Indexed full	BValue(An,Rk.S)	EA = BValue + $[A_n]$ + $[R_k]$
Relative basic	WValue(PC) or Label	EA = WValue + [PC]
Relative full	BValue(PC,Rk.S) or Label (Rk)	EA = BValue + [PC] + $[R_k]$

Notes:

EA	=	effective address
Value	=	a number given either explicitly or represented by a label
BValue	=	an 8-bit Value
WValue	=	a 16-bit Value
A_n	=	an address register
R_n	=	an address or a data register
S	=	a size indicator: W for sign-extended 16-bit word and L for 32-bit long word

involves the contents of two registers and an offset constant given in the instruction. The size of the offset constant is different for the two modes, being 16 bits long in the basic mode and 8 bits long in the full mode.

The second register, R_k, in the full index mode can be used in two ways: Either all 32 bits or only the low-order 16 bits are used. The two possibilities are indicated to the assembler by appending a size indicator, S, which is L for a long-word and W for a word. If the size indicator is omitted, the assembler assumes by default that $S = W$. When a 16-bit word is used in the computation of a 32-bit effective address, this word is sign extended.

The index modes may be used with the program counter in place of the address register. These special cases are called the relative modes, because the effective address is computed relative to the instruction where it is used. Figure 2.25 shows an example of the full relative mode, used in the instruction

$$\text{ADD} \qquad 100(\text{PC},\text{A1}),\text{D0}$$

The instruction consists of two words. The OP-code word specifies the Add operation, the destination register, D_0, and the fact that the full relative addressing mode is used for the source operand. The second word, often called the extension word, specifies that register A_1 is used as the index register and it also contains the 8-bit offset. Assume that A_1 contains the value 6. When the OP-code word of this instruction is being decoded by the processor, the program counter is pointing at the next word, which means that its contents are 1002.

Therefore, the effective address of the source operand is

$$\text{EA} = [\text{PC}] + [\text{A1}] + 100$$

$$= 1002 + 6 + 100$$

$$= 1108$$

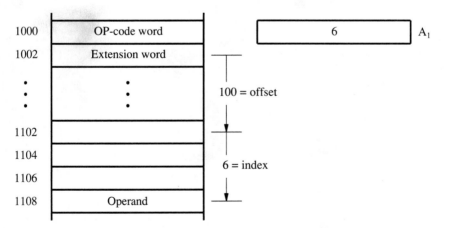

FIGURE 2.25
An example of full relative mode, for the instruction ADD 100(PC,A1),D0.

The figure suggests how this addressing mode can be used to access an entry in an array whose position is defined relative to the location of the instruction that needs to access the entry. If the array starts at address 1102, then the desired operand is the fourth word in the array.

We have written the full relative index mode in a very explicit format. Most assemblers allow this mode to be specified in a simpler way. Let the name ARRAY = 1102. Then, the instruction in Figure 2.25 can be written as

$$\text{ADD} \qquad \text{ARRAY(A1),D0}$$

The assembler would interpret this specification of the source operand as being in the full relative mode, and it would compute the offset as indicated in the figure. At assembly time it is not necessary to know what the contents of register A1 will be when the instruction is executed.

The limitation of the full relative mode is the fact that the offset is an 8-bit number, thus restricting its values to the range -128 to $+127$ bytes.

Finally, we should observe that the 68000 does not have indirect versions of all of its addressing modes. The only indirect mode is the register indirect mode.

2.7.3 Some 68000 Instructions and a Simple Program

The 68000 instruction set has been designed to conveniently support high-level programming languages. It provides an extensive set of instructions, most of which can operate on any of the three possible sizes of operands. The instruction set is summarized in Appendix C. All addressing modes can be used in a uniform way with most instructions. Instruction sets that exhibit this feature are often said to be *orthogonal*.

The 68000 has both one-operand and two-operand instructions. A two-operand instruction is written as

$$\text{OP} \qquad \text{src,dst}$$

where the operation OP is performed using the source and destination operands. The result is placed in the destination location. An example is given in Figure 2.26, which shows the instruction

$$\text{ADD} \qquad \text{\#9,D3}$$

Figure 2.26a depicts the general format of the ADD instruction, where the source operand can be specified in any addressing mode, but the destination operand must be in a data register (see Table C.4 in Appendix C). The OP code consists of five bits as shown. Note that these bits are not in a contiguous field, but this presents no difficulty in interpreting the meaning of the instructions as long as a unique bit pattern is assigned to each distinct OP code. Since the destination operand location must be one of the eight data registers, a 3-bit field suffices to identify it. Register D_3 is represented by the binary pattern 011. The source operand is identified as explained in Ta-

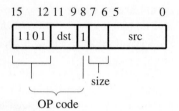

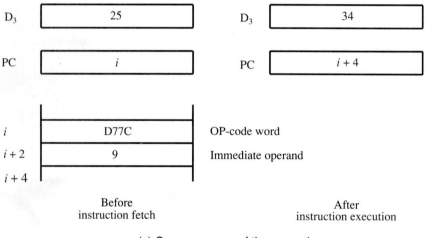

(a) Format of the OP-code word for an ADD instruction

(b) Encoding of the OP-code word

(c) Consequences of the execution

FIGURE 2.26
The 68000 instruction ADD #9,D3.

ble C.4 of Appendix C. An immediate source operand is identified with the pattern 111100 in the src field. As we have already mentioned in the previous subsection, the 68000 instructions may use operands of three different sizes. The desired size is indicated in the two-bit size field. In our example, the size of the operands is not stated explicitly in the assembly language statement, in which case it is assumed to be 16 bits. As seen from Table C.3, word-size operands are denoted by the pattern 01.

From the discussion above, it follows that the OP-code word for our ADD instruction is 1101011101111100. Such long binary patterns are awkward to write and read. A common practice is to represent the pattern in a higher-radix notation. Since in the 68000, and indeed in most computers, information tends to be represented in multiples of bytes, it is convenient to use the *hexadecimal* (hex) notation. In this notation, four bits are represented as a single hex digit. The notation is a direct extension of the BCD code given in Appendix D. The six 4-bit patterns 1010, 1011, . . . , 1111 are represented by the capital letters A, B, . . . , F. The first ten patterns 0000, 0001, . . . , 1001 are represented by the digits 0, 1, . . . , 9 as in BCD. Therefore, our OP-code word may be represented by the hexadecimal number D77C, as indicated in Figure 2.26b.

The Add instruction performs the action

$$dst \leftarrow [src] + [dst]$$

The immediate source operand, 9, is in the word following the OP-code word, as shown in Figure 2.26c. Before fetching the instruction, the program counter points at the OP-code word at address i. As each word is fetched from the memory, the contents of the PC are incremented by 2. Thus, upon completing execution of the instruction, the PC points at the OP-code word of the next instruction at address $i + 4$. As a result of the Add instruction, the number in register D_3 is increased by 9.

A similar instruction using the same format is the Subtract instruction, SUB, which performs the operation

$$dst \leftarrow [dst] - [src]$$

As can be seen from Table C.4, the ADD and SUB instructions allow the full range of 68000 addressing modes in accessing the source operand. However, in this case, the destination operand must be the contents of a data register. Most other two-operand instructions have the same type of restriction. The only instruction where both the source and the destination operands may be specified in terms of most of the addressing modes is the Move instruction, MOVE, which performs the action

$$dst \leftarrow [src]$$

Let us now consider a simple routine for the task $C \leftarrow [A] + [B]$, corresponding to Figure 2.3. In that figure it was shown that the required task can be performed as follows

Move	A, R_0
Add	B, R_0
Move	R_0, C

These instructions map directly into the 68000 instruction set. Figure 2.27 gives a possible routine, using a particular set of values for the operands. The operands are assumed to be 16 bits long, and their addresses are specified in the absolute mode. Note that the long version of the absolute mode is needed because the desired addresses

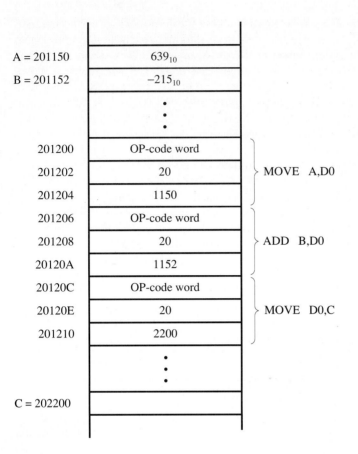

After execution, $[202200] = 424_{10}$

FIGURE 2.27
A 68000 routine for $C \leftarrow [A] + [B]$.

cannot be represented in 16 bits. When all 32 bits of an address are stored, the high-order 16 bits are placed in the lower address word and the low-order 16 bits in the higher address word, as shown in the figure.

2.7.4   The 68000 Assembly Language

The discussion of assembly languages in Section 2.5 applies generally to the 68000 assembly language. Some minor differences and additions will be explained in this section.

Because 68000 instructions can deal with three different sizes of operands, it is necessary to indicate the desired size in an assembler instruction. This is done by appending the size indicator to the operation mnemonic. The size indicator is L for longword, W for word, and B for byte. Thus, if an Add instruction is to operate on long-word operands, its operation mnemonic is written as ADD.L. When no size indication is given, the operand size is taken to be one word. That is, the instructions ADD.W #20,D1 and ADD #20,D1 are identical.

Numbers in a source program are assumed to be in decimal representation unless marked with the prefix $ for hexadecimal or % for binary. Alphanumeric characters placed between single quotes are replaced by the assembler with their ASCII codes. Several characters may be specified in a string between quotes. For example, a valid character string is 'STRING3'.

All of the assembler commands discussed in Section 2.5 can be used with only slight differences in notation. The starting address of a block of instructions or data is specified with the ORG command. The EQU command equates names with numerical values. Data constants are inserted into an object program using the DC (Define Constant) command. The size indicator is appended to specify the size of the data items, and several items may be defined in one command. For example, the commands

$$\text{ORG} \qquad 100$$
$$\text{PLACE} \qquad \text{DC.B} \qquad 23,\$4F,\%10110101$$

result in hex values 17 ($=23_{10}$), 4F, and B5 being loaded into memory locations 100, 101, and 102, respectively.

A block of main memory can be reserved for data by means of the DS (Define Storage) command. For instance, the command

$$\text{ARRAY} \qquad \text{DS.L} \qquad 200$$

reserves 200 long words and associates the name ARRAY with the address of the first long word.

A simple example of a 68000 assembly language program that corresponds to Figure 2.27 is given in Figure 2.28.

	Memory address label	Operation	Addressing or data information
Assembler commands	C	EQU	$202200
		ORG	$201150
	A	DC.W	639
	B	DC.W	−215
		ORG	$201200
Statements that		MOVE	A,D0
generate machine		ADD	B,D0
instructions		MOVE	D0,C
Assembler command		END	

FIGURE 2.28
Assembly language representation for the program in Figure 2.27.

2.7.5 Branch Instructions and Condition Codes

In order to implement program loops, it is necessary to have branch instructions, as was explained in Section 2.3.2. In general, a branch instruction tests a branch condition and then causes execution to proceed along one of two possible paths in the program, depending on the state of this condition. Several different conditions may be tested. Their state is determined by a recently performed operation.

Condition code flags. Certain properties of the result of an operation are stored in condition code flags, which are represented by a bit in the status register, shown in Figure 2.23. There are five flags, with the following meaning:

N (negative)	Set to 1 if the result is negative; otherwise, cleared to 0.
Z (zero)	Set to 1 if the result is 0; otherwise, cleared to 0.
V (overflow)	Set to 1 if arithmetic overflow occurs; otherwise, cleared to 0.
C (carry)	Set to 1 if a carry-out results from the operation; otherwise, cleared to 0.
X (extend)	Set in the same way as the C flag, but it is not affected by as many instructions.

The state of a flag reflects the result of the most recent operation that affects that flag. Table C.4 in Appendix C shows which flags are affected by each instruction. Consider the Add instruction, which affects all five flags. The N and Z flags are set to indicate whether the sum is negative or zero. The V flag is set to 1 if the sum does not fit within the operand length specified. The C flag is set to 1 if a carry occurs from the most-significant bit position. Note that because the operand can be specified in any of the three possible lengths, the C bit depends on the carry-out from bit positions 7, 15, or 31, for byte, word, or long-word operands, respectively. We will consider arithmetic operations in detail in Chapter 7, illustrating the various situations that result in carry-out and overflow conditions. In that chapter we will also consider the question of multiple-precision addition and subtraction, where the operand length exceeds 32 bits. Such operations require the use of carry-out information, which is available in the C flag. The 68000 saves the same information in the X flag. As we will see in Chapter 7, this apparent duplication is convenient, because the state of the X flag is not altered by a number of instructions that affect the C flag.

Table C.4 shows that even MOVE affects the flags. This provides useful information about the operand moved, namely whether it is positive, negative, or zero. Note that the C and V flags are cleared by the MOVE instruction, but the X flag is not affected unless the destination specified is the status register itself.

Branch instructions. A conditional branch instruction causes program execution to continue with the instruction at the branch target address if the branch condition is met. This address is determined from the branch offset in the operand field. Otherwise, if the branch condition is not met, the instruction that immediately follows the branch instruction is executed. The 68000 provides branch instructions with two types of offset. In the first type, a short offset of eight bits is included in the OP-code word. These instructions can be used when the branch target is within $+127$ or -128 bytes of the value in the program counter at the time the branch address is computed. Recall that the PC contents are incremented as each word is fetched from the memory, which means that the offset defines the distance from the word that follows the branch instruction OP-code word. In the second type, a 16-bit offset is specified in the extension word that follows the OP-code word. This provides for a much greater range within which the branch target can be located. In this case, the offset is the distance from the extension word to the branch target.

Figure 2.29 illustrates the use of a short-offset branch instruction. It shows how the program loop in Figure 2.9 may be implemented on a 68000 microprocessor. The reader may observe that the program in Figure 2.9 used a Decrement instruction. Since the 68000 does not have such an instruction, we have used the Subtract Quick instruction, SUBQ, which subtracts the immediate operand 1 from the contents of register R_1. As shown in Table C.4, a 3-bit immediate operand is included within the OP-code word of the SUBQ instruction, thus only one word is needed to represent the entire instruction.

```
15           8 7           0
┌──────────┬──────────┐
│ OP code  │  Offset  │
└──────────┴──────────┘
```

Branch address = [updated PC] + offset

(a) Short-offset branch instruction format

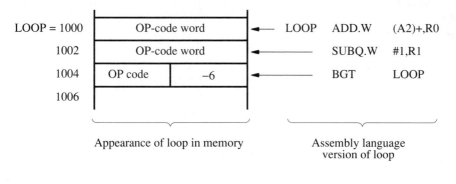

[PC] = 1006 when a branch address is completed
      Branch address = 1006 − 6 = 1000

(b) Example of using a branch instruction in the loop of Figure 2.9

FIGURE 2.29
Short-offset branch instructions.

The 68000 has 16 conditional branch instructions, each with 8- and 16-bit offsets. It also has an unconditional branch instruction, BRA, where the branch is always taken. Tables C.5 and C.6 give the details of these instructions.

A complete 68000 program for the program in Figure 2.9 is given in Figure 2.30. It uses data registers D_0 and D_1 to accumulate the sum and to act as a counter, respectively. It uses address register A_2 to point to the operands as they are fetched from the memory. Note that an address register is used, because in the autoincrement addressing mode only address registers are allowed.

Decrement and branch instructions. In addition to the normal branch instructions, the 68000 has a set of more complex branch instructions that incorporate a counting mechanism. Such a facility is useful for implementing loop control. These instructions are written in the format

$$\text{DBcc} \quad \text{Dn,LABEL}$$

where the suffix cc denotes a branch condition. For example, if GT is used in place of cc, the resultant instruction, DBGT, is the Decrement and Branch unless Greater Than instruction. The full set of possible branch conditions is given in Table C.6. The way in which the branch condition is used in these instructions is opposite to that in normal branch instructions. The action is as follows:

- If the condition specified by cc is satisfied, then the instruction that immediately follows the DBcc instruction is executed next.
- If the condition is not satisfied, then the least-significant 16-bits of register D_n are decremented by 1. If the result is equal to -1, the instruction that follows

	CLR.L	D0	D_0 is used to accumulate the sum.
	MOVE.L	N,D1	N contains n, the number of numbers to be added, and D_1 acts as a counter register in determining how many times to execute the loop.
	MOVEA.L	#NUM,A2	A_2 is a pointer register, and it is initialized to contain the address, NUM, of the location containing the first number of the list of numbers.
LOOP	ADD.W	(A2)+,D0	Successive numbers are added in D_0.
	SUBQ.L	#1,D1	Decrement the counter.
	BGT	LOOP	If $[D_1]$ have not reached 0, that is, if the loop has not been executed n times, branch back and execute the loop again.
	MOVE.L	D0,SUM	Store the sum in SUM.

FIGURE 2.30
A 68000 program for the addition program in Figure 2.9.

the DBcc instruction is executed next. If the result is not equal to -1, a branch is made to the instruction at location LABEL.

The DBcc instructions are more powerful than the normal branch instructions, because the decision on whether the branch is to be taken depends on two conditions rather than one. If the same action were specified using normal branch instructions, it would be necessary to use a sequence of three instructions: First, a branch instruction that tests the cc condition; then, an instruction that decrements the contents of the counter register; and finally, another branch instruction that causes a branch based on the result of the decrement operation. For example, the instruction

DBcc   D0,LOOP

is equivalent to the sequence

	Bcc	NEXT
	SUBQ	#1,D0
	BGE	LOOP
NEXT	next instruction	

A useful way of thinking about the DBcc instructions is to view them as providing convenient means for loop control where early exit from the loop occurs when a given condition is met. The number of times that the loop can be executed is limited by the contents of the counter register.

One DBcc instruction, DBF (Decrement and Branch if False), uses a test condition that is always false. Thus, the decision on whether a branch is to be made is based solely on the result of decrementing the counter register. This instruction is very useful in cases where a loop is always executed a predetermined number of times. It is even given a second name, DBRA.

To demonstrate the usefulness of decrement and branch instructions, the program of Figure 2.30 may be rewritten as shown in Figure 2.31. We can eliminate the Subtract instruction in the loop by using the DBRA instruction. Because the DBRA instruction causes a branch when the counter register contains a value equal to or

	CLR.L	D0	
	MOVE.L	N,D1	Put $n - 1$ into the
	SUBQ.W	#1,D1	counter register D_1.
	MOVEA.L	#NUM,A2	
LOOP	ADD.W	(A2)+,D0	
	DBRA	D1,LOOP	Loop back until $[D_1] = -1$.
	MOVE.L	D0,SUM	

FIGURE 2.31
An alternative program for the program in Figure 2.9.

greater than zero, register D_1 is initialized to the value $n-1$, rather than n as was done in Figure 2.30. The total number of instructions in the two programs is the same, but the program in Figure 2.31 takes less time to execute because of the shorter loop.

2.7.6 A Sorting Program Example

So far we have considered some basic aspects of the 68000 instruction set using very simple examples as illustrations. Now, let us consider a somewhat more complex example, which involves the task of sorting a list of bytes. Assume that the list consists of n bytes, not necessarily distinct, where each byte contains the ASCII code for a character from the set of letters A through Z. In the ASCII code, presented in Appendix D, the letters A, B, . . . , Z are represented by 7-bit patterns that have increasing values when interpreted as positive integers. When an ASCII character is stored in a byte location, it is customary to set the most-significant bit position to 0. Using this code, we can sort a list of characters alphabetically by sorting their ASCII patterns in increasing numerical order.

Let the list be stored in memory locations LIST through LIST$+n-1$ and the value n be a 16-bit value stored at address N. The sorting is to be done in place, that is, the sorted list is to occupy the same memory locations as the original list.

We will sort the list using a *straight selection sort* algorithm. First, the largest number (byte value) is found and placed at the bottom of the list, in location LIST$+n-1$. Then, the largest number in the remaining sublist of $n-1$ numbers is placed at the bottom of that sublist, in location LIST$+n-2$. The procedure is repeated until the list is sorted. A Pascal-like program for this sorting algorithm is shown in Figure 2.32a, where the list is treated as a one-dimensional array LIST(0) through LIST($n-1$). For each sublist LIST(j) to LIST(0), the number in LIST(j) is compared with other numbers in the sublist. Whenever a larger number is found in the sublist, it is interchanged with the number in LIST(j).

Note that this program traverses the list backward. This is not a natural way to write a high-level language program; however, this order of traversal simplifies loop termination in an assembly language program, because exit from the loop takes place when an index is decremented to zero.

A 68000 program that implements the sorting algorithm is given in Figure 2.32b. The comments given in the program explain the use of various registers. The current maximum value found while scanning a sublist during a pass is kept in register D_3. This enables a comparison with the numbers that follow. A direct comparison of two operands in the main memory cannot be done, because the 68000 CMP instruction requires one of the operands to be in a data register.

The inner loop in the program is terminated by the DBRA instruction. However, a DBRA instruction cannot be used to terminate the outer loop, because the final value for j is 1 rather than 0.

Finally, we should note that the program works correctly only if the list has at least two elements. This is because of the fact that the check for loop termination is done at the end of each loop. Hence, there will be at least one pass through the loop, irrespective of the value of n.

```
for  j: = n − 1 downto 1 do
     begin
     for k: = j − 1 downto 0 do
          begin
          if     LIST (j) < LIST(k) then
                 begin
                 TEMP  := LIST(j);
                 LIST(j) := LIST(k);
                 LIST(k) := TEMP
                 end
          end
     end
```

(a) Pascal-like program for sorting

```
           MOVEA.L   #LIST,A1           Pointer to the start of the list.
           MOVE      N,D1               Initialize outer loop
           SUBQ      #1,D1                 index j in D₁.
OUTER      MOVE      D1,D2              Initialize inner loop
           SUBQ      #1,D2                 index k in D₂.
INNER      MOVE.B    (A1,D1),D3         Current maximum value in D₃.
           CMP.B     (A1,D2),D3         Compare LIST(k) and LIST(j).
           BCC       NEXT               If LIST(j) is higher or same go
                                           to next entry.
           MOVE.B    (A1,D2),(A1,D1)    Interchange LIST(k)
           MOVE.B    D3,(A1,D2)            and LIST(j).
NEXT       DBRA      D2,INNER           Decrement counters
           SUBQ      #1,D1                 and branch back
           BGT       OUTER                 if not finished.
           next instruction
```

(b) 68000 program implementation

FIGURE 2.32
A byte-sorting program.

2.7.7   Logic Instructions

In previous sections, we have considered instructions that move operands and perform arithmetic operations such as addition or subtraction. The operands involved in these instructions have a fixed length of 32, 16, or 8 bits. In some applications it is desired to manipulate other sizes of data, perhaps only individual bits, performing logic operations on these data. The 68000 has several instructions for such purposes. In particular, there are instructions that perform logical AND, OR, and EXCLUSIVE-

OR operations. There are also instructions that shift and rotate operands in several different ways.

To illustrate the use of logic instructions, let us consider two simple examples. Suppose that register D_1 contains some 32-bit binary pattern and we want to determine if the pattern in bit positions b_{18} to b_{14} is 11001. This can be done using the instructions

$$
\begin{array}{ll}
\text{AND.L} & \#\$7C000,D1 \\
\text{CMPI.L} & \#\$64000,D1 \\
\text{BEQ} & \text{YES}
\end{array}
$$

The first instruction performs the logical AND of individual bits of the source and destination operands, leaving the result in register D_1. The hex number 7C000 has 1s in bit positions b_{18} to b_{14} and 0s elsewhere. Thus, as a result of the AND operation, the five bits in positions b_{18} to b_{14} in register D_1 retain their original values, while the remaining bits are cleared to 0. The subsequent Compare instruction tests whether these five bits correspond to the desired pattern.

As a second example, assume that two decimal digits represented in ASCII code are stored in memory locations LOC and LOC + 1. Suppose that we wish to represent these digits in a packed BCD format and store them in a single byte in location PACKED. The required task is to extract the low-order four bits in LOC and LOC + 1 and concatenate them into a single byte. This can be done by the program in Figure 2.33. Because it is easier to manipulate the data in registers, the two ASCII bytes are brought into registers D_0 and D_1. The LSL instruction shifts the byte in D_0 four bit positions to the left, filling the low-order four bits with zeros. The first entry in the operand field of this instruction is a count that indicates the number of bit positions by which the operand is to be shifted. Table C.4 shows that the count may also be specified in another data register. Hence, the same effect can be achieved with

$$
\text{LSL.B} \qquad \text{D2,D0}
$$

if the contents of D_2 have been set to 4 earlier. The ANDI instruction sets the high-

MOVEA.L	#LOC,A0	A_0 points to data.
MOVE.B	(A0)+,D0	Load first byte into D_0
LSL.B	#4,D0	Shift left by 4 positions.
MOVE.B	(A0),D1	Load second byte into D_1.
ANDI.B	#$F,D1	Eliminate 4 high-order bits.
OR.B	D0,D1	Concatenate the digits.
MOVE.B	D1,PACKED	Store the result.

FIGURE 2.33
Use of logic instructions in packing BCD digits.

order four bits of the second byte to 0. Finally, the 4-bit patterns that are the desired BCD codes are ORed together in D_1 and stored in memory location PACKED.

The AND and OR instructions operate simultaneously on all corresponding bit pairs of their operands. The 68000 instruction set also has instructions that manipulate single bits only. We will introduce these instructions in the next section and show how they may be used in programs that deal with I/O devices.

2.8 SIMPLE INPUT-OUTPUT PROGRAMMING

In this section, the instructions needed to transfer data between the CPU and peripheral devices will be discussed. Consider the general situation of programming a task that requires character input from the keyboard of a video terminal and produces character output that is to be displayed on the screen of the same unit. We will discuss only the part of the program that directly controls the I/O activity, using the method known as *program-controlled I/O*. The video terminal, consisting of a keyboard unit and a display unit, is a simple I/O device. The operation of such a device is easily understood and can be conveniently used to illustrate the basic principles of program-controlled I/O.

The rate of data transfer from the keyboard of a video terminal to a computer depends essentially only on the typing speed of the operator, which is unlikely to exceed a few characters per second. The rate of output transfers from the computer to the terminal display is much higher. It is limited by the rate at which characters can be transmitted over the link between the computer and the terminal and is typically about 1,000 characters per second. This is still much slower than a CPU that can execute upward of 1 million instructions per second. The different speeds of the CPU and the video terminal pose the problem of synchronizing their operation.

A solution to this problem is as follows. The CPU sends the first character, then waits for a signal from the terminal that the character has been displayed. It then sends the second character, and so on. An analogous situation exists with input from the keyboard. The CPU must wait for a signal indicating that a character key has been struck and that its code is available to be read by the CPU.

We have described the keyboard and display as separate devices inside the video terminal. This means that when the terminal is operating under computer control, the action of striking a key on the keyboard does not automatically cause the corresponding character to be displayed on the screen. In most applications, when a key is struck to send a character code to the computer, it is natural that this character should also be displayed on the screen. The way in which this actually happens is that one block of instructions in the I/O program transfers the character into the CPU and another associated block of instructions causes the character to be displayed. This process of sending the received character to the display is called *echoback*. It allows a form of error checking in that if the operator does not see the correct character printed, it is immediately apparent that something has gone wrong in the process of transmitting the character to or from the computer.

Let us now consider the problem of moving a character code from the keyboard to the CPU. Striking a key stores the corresponding character code in an 8-bit buffer register associated with the keyboard. We will call this register DATAIN. To inform the CPU that a valid character is in DATAIN, a synchronization control flag, CIN, is set to 1. The CPU can monitor CIN, so that when CIN = 1, the CPU will read the contents of DATAIN. When the character is transferred to the CPU, CIN is cleared to 0. If a second character is entered at the keyboard, CIN is again set to 1 and the process repeats.

An analogous synchronization process takes place when transferring characters from the CPU to the display. For this purpose, an 8-bit buffer register, DATAOUT, and a synchronization control flag, COUT, are provided. When COUT = 1, the terminal is ready to display a character. The CPU can thus monitor COUT, and when COUT is set to 1, the CPU can transfer a character code to DATAOUT. The transfer of a character to DATAOUT clears COUT to 0, and when the character has been displayed, COUT is set to 1 and the process can be repeated.

Peripheral devices such as video terminals are usually connected to the CPU via a bus as indicated in Figure 2.34. The computer must have instructions that can be used to check the status of the control flags and transfer data between the CPU and specific devices on the bus. These instructions are similar in general format to those we have already discussed for moving data between the CPU and the main memory. For example, the CPU can monitor the keyboard control flag CIN and transfer a character from DATAIN to register R_1 by the following sequence of operations:

> READWAIT Branch to READWAIT if CIN = 0
>   Input from DATAIN to R_1

The Branch operation is usually implemented by two machine instructions. The first

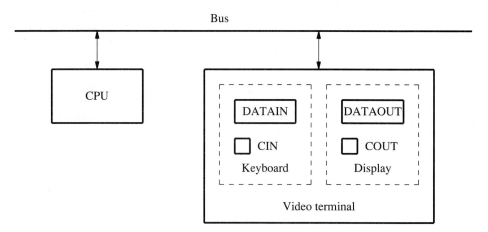

FIGURE 2.34
Connection of a video terminal to a CPU.

tests the control flag and the second performs the branch. While the details vary from computer to computer, the main idea is that the CPU monitors the control flag by executing a short *wait loop* and proceeds to the actual input data transfer operation when CIN is set to 1. In addition to transferring the character from DATAIN to R_1, the above Input operation resets CIN to 0.

An analogous sequence of operations is used for output to the display, for example,

WRITEWAIT   Branch to WRITEWAIT if COUT = 0
              Output from R_1 to DATAOUT

Again, the Branch operation is normally implemented by two machine instructions. The control flag COUT is set to 1 by the terminal when it is free to display a character. The Output operation clears COUT to 0 when it transfers a character from R_1 to DATAOUT to be displayed.

The above discussion assumes that the initial state of CIN is 0 and the initial state of COUT is 1. This initialization is normally performed by the device control circuits when the devices are placed under computer control before program execution begins.

Until now, we have assumed that the addresses issued by the CPU to access instructions and operands always refer to main memory locations. However, in many computers some of the address values are used to refer to peripheral device buffer registers such as DATAIN and DATAOUT. This means that the computer does not need to have specific I/O instructions. Data and status information can be transferred to and from peripheral devices by the two-operand Move instruction that we have already discussed. In particular, the contents of the keyboard character buffer DATAIN can be transferred to the CPU register R_1 by the instruction

Move   DATAIN,R_1

Similarly, the contents of register R_1 can be transferred to DATAOUT by the instruction

Move R_1,DATAOUT

The control flags CIN and COUT are automatically cleared when the buffer registers DATAIN and DATAOUT are referenced. These two instructions directly implement the general Input and Output operations discussed above.

So far, we have established that the two data buffers in Figure 2.34 may be addressed as if they were two memory locations. It is possible to deal with the status flags CIN and COUT in the same way, by assigning them distinct addresses. However, for a device such as a video terminal it is more usual to include both CIN and COUT in a single status register. Let us assume that bits b_3 and b_4 in register STATUS correspond to CIN and COUT, respectively. Then, the read operation described above may be implemented as

READWAIT	Testbit	#3,STATUS
	Branch = 0	READWAIT
	Move	DATAIN,R_1

The write operation may be implemented as

WRITEWAIT	Testbit	#4,STATUS
	Branch = 0	WRITEWAIT
	Move	R_1,DATAOUT

The Testbit instruction tests the state of one bit in the STATUS location. The bit position to be tested is indicated by the first entry in the operand field. If the bit is equal to 0, then the branch instruction interprets the branch condition as being true, and a branch is made to the beginning of the wait loop. Otherwise, the status of the I/O device is determined as being ready, hence data is read from the input buffer or written into the output buffer.

We will now consider the implementation of such I/O transfers in PDP-11 and 68000 computers.

2.8.1 Program-Controlled I/O (PDP-11)

In PDP-11 computers, the status and data buffers in I/O device interfaces are addressed as if they were memory locations. Therefore, the general I/O scheme described above is applicable to these computers.

The read operation can be programmed as

READWAIT:	BITB	#10,STATUS
	BEQ	READWAIT
	MOVB	DATAIN,R1

The Bit-test instruction, BITB, was discussed in Section 2.6.7. It performs a logical AND of the octal number 10 and the contents of location STATUS. Because 10_8 has a 1 in bit position b_3 and 0s elsewhere, the instruction causes the condition code flag Z to be set to 1 if b_3 of the STATUS location is equal to 0. The BITB instruction does not alter the contents of the destination location. This is important, because we must not destroy any other status flags in STATUS, for example, the COUT flag in b_4.

The write operation is performed similarly as

WRITEWAIT:	BITB	#20,STATUS
	BEQ	WRITEWAIT
	MOVB	R1,DATAOUT

In this case, the octal value 20 has a 1 in bit position b_4.

	MOV	#LOC,R1	Initialize pointer register R_1 to contain the address of the first location in main memory where the characters are to be stored.
READ:	BITB	#10,STATUS	Wait for a character to be entered
	BEQ	READ	into the keyboard buffer DATAIN.
	MOVB	DATAIN,@R1	Transfer the character from DATAIN to main memory (this clears CIN to 0).
ECHOBACK:	BITB	#20,STATUS	Wait for the display to
	BEQ	ECHOBACK	become ready.
	MOVB	@R1,DATAOUT	Move the character just read to the output buffer register DATAOUT for display (this clears COUT to 0).
	CMPB	(R1)+,#CR	Check to see if the character just read
	BNE	READ	is "carriage return" (CR). If it is not CR, branch back and read another character. The pointer register R_1 is incremented, anticipating that another character will be read.
	next instruction		

FIGURE 2.35
A PDP-11 program that reads a line of characters from a video terminal.

The scheme in which I/O devices are accessed as memory locations is called *memory-mapped I/O*.

Let us now consider a program for reading a line of characters entered at a terminal keyboard and terminated by a "carriage return." The program must check each character as it is read to see whether it is the carriage return code. Each character is to be echoed back to the display. The characters are to be placed in successive memory byte locations beginning with location LOC. A program for this task is shown in Figure 2.35.

2.8.2   Program-Controlled I/O (68000)

The 68000 microprocessor requires that all status and data buffers in interfaces of I/O devices be addressable as if they were memory locations. This means that program-controlled I/O in a 68000 computer can be achieved as described in the general discussion above.

The read operation is accomplished with

```
READWAIT    BTST.B    #3,STATUS
            BEQ       READWAIT
            MOVE.B    DATAIN,D1
```

The Test-a-bit instruction, BTST, tests the state of one bit of the destination operand and sets condition code flag Z to be the complement of the bit tested. The position of the bit to be tested is indicated as the first entry in the operand field. This is b_3 in our example.

Similarly, the write operation is performed with

```
WRITEWAIT    BTST.B    #4,STATUS
             BEQ       WRITEWAIT
             MOVE.B    D1,DATAOUT
```

In this case, the status bit tested is b_4.

When using a video terminal, it is useful to echo back and display any characters read from the keyboard. A program that reads one line of characters, stores them in the main memory, and echoes them back to the terminal is given in Figure 2.36. It assumes that each line is terminated when the carriage return key is pressed. The characters are stored in memory byte locations starting with location LOC.

Program-controlled I/O requires continuous involvement of the CPU in I/O activities. Let us assume that the keyboard and the display handle characters at the rates of 10 and 1000 per second, respectively. The CPU may execute more than a million instructions per second. This means that for every character read and displayed by the terminal, enough time has elapsed for about 100,000 instructions to be executed.

	MOVEA.L	#LOC,A1	Initialize pointer register A_1 to contain the address of the first location in main memory where the characters are to be stored.
READ	BTST.B	#3, STATUS	Wait for a character to be entered
	BEQ	READ	in the keyboard buffer DATAIN.
	MOVE.B	DATAIN,(A1)	Transfer the character form DATAIN to main memory (this clears CIN to 0).
ECHOBACK	BTST.B	#4,STATUS	Wait for the display
	BEQ	ECHOBACK	to become ready.
	MOVE.B	(A1),DATAOUT	Move the character just read to the output buffer register for display (this clears COUT to 0).
	CMP.B	#CR,(A1)+	Check if the character just read is CR
	BNE	READ	(carriage return). If it is not CR, then branch back and read another character. Also, increment the pointer to store the next character.
	next instruction		

FIGURE 2.36
A 68000 program that reads a line of characters from a video terminal.

Almost all the 100,000 executions are accounted for in the two wait loops, while the CPU is waiting for a character to be struck or for the display to become available.

In many situations it is desirable to avoid "wasting" the CPU time in this way. Other I/O techniques, based on the use of interrupts, may be employed to improve the utilization of the CPU. Such techniques will be discussed in Chapter 6.

2.9 STACKS

We will now introduce the topic of *stacks*. They constitute an important data structure that is used in a variety of programming situations.

A stack is a list of data elements, usually words or bytes, with the accessing restriction that elements can be added or removed at one end of the list only. This end is usually called the top of the stack, with the other end being called the bottom, and the structure is sometimes referred to as a *pushdown* stack. The term pushdown is motivated by the analogy with a pile of trays in a cafeteria. Customers pick up new trays from the top of the pile, and clean trays are added to the pile by pushing them onto the top of the pile. Another descriptive phrase, *last-in first-out* (LIFO) stack, is also used to describe this type of storage mechanism; the last data item placed on the stack is the first one removed when retrieval begins. The terms *push* and *pop* are often used to describe placing a new item on a stack and removing the top item from the stack, respectively.

A stack can be stored in the main memory of a computer, with successive elements in the stack occupying successive memory locations. Assume that the first element placed in the stack occupies memory location BOTTOM and that successive items are placed in lower-address locations. There is no reason why we could not have assumed that the stack grows in the direction of increasing memory addresses (which in fact will be the case in Section 3.6). However, because the addressing modes in the PDP-11 and 68000 computers make the former assumption more convenient, this is our choice in this chapter.

Figure 2.37 shows a stack as it might be implemented in the main memory of a computer. For convenience, we will assume that the stack contains numerical values, with 43 on the bottom and −28 on the top in the example. Register SP is used as the *stack pointer*; that is, it contains the address of the current top element of the stack. The two basic operations of push and pop can be implemented easily using the instructions

$$\text{Move} \quad \text{NEWITEM}, -(\text{SP}) \quad \text{(push)}$$

and

$$\text{Move} \quad (\text{SP})+, \text{TOPITEM} \quad \text{(pop)}$$

The first instruction moves (pushes) the word from the memory location NEWITEM onto the top of the stack, decrementing the pointer register before the move. The second instruction moves (pops) the top value from the stack into memory location

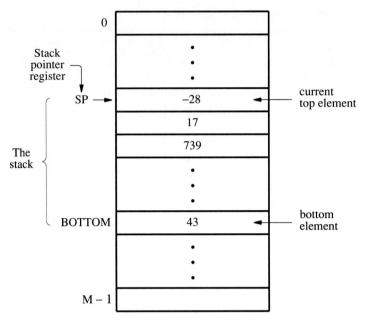

FIGURE 2.37
A stack in the main memory.

TOPITEM and increments the pointer register so that it points to the new top element. Figure 2.38 shows the effect of these two operations on the stack of Figure 2.37.

One of the uses of the stack data structure is in holding operands and intermediate computations in a sequence of arithmetic operations. A standard arithmetic operation on stacks is one that pops the two top values from the stack, adds (subtracts, multiplies, etc.) them, and then pushes the result onto the stack. An Add operation of this type can be performed by the single instruction

$$\text{Add} \qquad (SP)+,(SP)$$

Its effect is shown in Figure 2.38*d*. The reader should carefully work through the execution of this instruction to see that it indeed achieves the desired action. This example assumes that address calculations and operand fetches proceed strictly left to right in two-operand instructions. All steps required in the source address determination and operand fetch, including the autodecrementing and autoincrementing operations, are completed before destination operand addressing or fetching is begun.

In many cases where stacks are used in programming, it is necessary to carefully avoid popping an item from an empty stack or pushing an item onto a full stack. In this discussion we assume that the stack is allocated some fixed amount of main memory. Suppose that a stack runs from location 2000 (BOTTOM) down no farther than location 1500. If the stack is initially empty, then SP is loaded initially with the address value 2001. To prevent making either of the errors mentioned above,

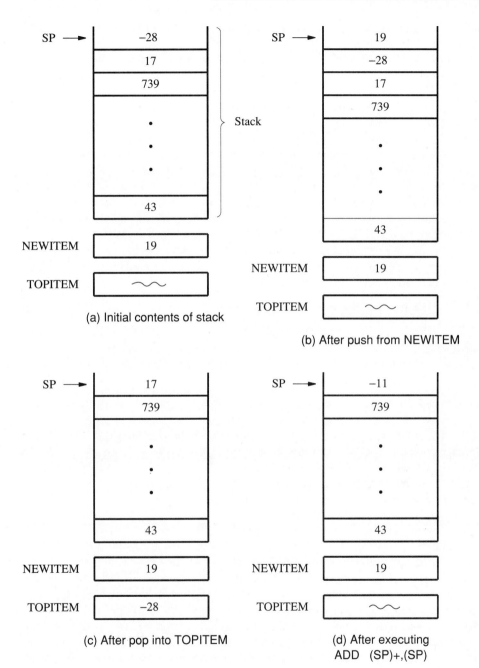

(a) Initial contents of stack

(b) After push from NEWITEM

(c) After pop into TOPITEM

(d) After executing
ADD   (SP)+,(SP)

FIGURE 2.38
Examples of stack operations.

we replace the simple one-instruction push and pop operations by the instruction sequences shown in Figure 2.39.

In PDP-11 computers a stack structure can be implemented using any register as a stack pointer, other than R_7, which is the program counter. As we will see in the next section and in Chapter 6, a particular stack, called the *processor stack*, is used automatically by most computers when dealing with subroutines and interrupts. For these functions a designated stack pointer must exist. In PDP-11 computers the processor stack pointer is always register R_6.

The 68000 microprocessor uses address register A_7 as the processor stack pointer, as indicated in Figure 2.23. Note that the figure shows that two different 32-bit registers serve as this stack pointer. The 68000 provides for two different modes of operation, called the user and supervisor modes. Each mode has its own stack pointer, referred to as A_7. In the supervisor mode, the 68000 can execute all machine instructions. In the user mode, some privileged instructions cannot be executed. Application programs are normally run in the user mode, while the system software uses the supervisor mode. One bit, S, in the status register of the 68000 is used to determine which of the two modes is active.

SAFEPOP	Compare	#2000,SP	Check to see if the stack pointer contains an address value greater than 2000. If it does, the stack is empty. Branch to the routine EMPTYERROR for appropriate action.
	Branch>0	EMPTYERROR	
	MOVE	(SP)+,TOPITEM	Otherwise, pop the top of the stack into memory location TOPITEM.

(a) Routine for a safe pop operation

SAFEPUSH	Compare	#1500,SP	Check to see if the stack pointer contains an address value equal to or less than 1500. If it does, the stack is full. Branch to the routine FULLERROR for appropriate action.
	Branch≤0	FULLERROR	
	MOVE	NEWITEM,−(SP)	Otherwise, push the element in memory location NEWITEM onto the stack.

(b) Routine for safe push operation

FIGURE 2.39
Checking for empty and full errors in pop and push operations on a stack.

This completes our brief introduction to stacks. A further and more important example of their use will be given in the next section, and a discussion of how they may affect computer design itself will be presented in Chapter 3.

2.10 · SUBROUTINES

The last topic to be discussed in this chapter is the special form of instruction sequencing needed to implement the *subroutine* concept. In a given program, it is often necessary to perform a particular task a number of times on different data values. Such a task is normally implemented as a subroutine. Examples of this include a subroutine to evaluate the *sine* function or a subroutine to sort a list of values into increasing or decreasing order.

It is possible to include the block of instructions that constitute a subroutine at every place where it is needed in any program. However, this is wasteful of memory space. It is better to place only one copy of this block of machine instructions in the main memory and have any program that requires the use of the subroutine branch to its starting location. This is usually termed *calling* the subroutine. After the subroutine has been executed, it is necessary to return to the program that called it. Since the subroutine is intended to be called from different locations in a calling program, provision must be made for branching back, or *returning*, to the appropriate location. In each case, this location contains the instruction immediately following the one that called the subroutine. The way in which any particular computer makes it possible to call and return from subroutines is referred to as its *subroutine linkage* method.

2.10.1 Subroutine Linkage
and Parameter-Passing Methods

It is obvious that the contents of the program counter at the time a subroutine is called must be preserved to enable the return to the appropriate place. This is necessary since there is only one PC in the CPU, and it must be used to control sequencing through the subroutine. The simplest linkage method is to preserve the contents of the PC in a specific location, for example, memory location LINK. The return to the calling program can be achieved by branching indirectly through memory location LINK, as illustrated in Figure 2.40*a*. This simple method has the problem that a subroutine cannot call another subroutine. If it did, the return address for the first call, which is stored in location LINK, would be destroyed when the second call places a new return address in LINK. Because it is a very reasonable and practical programming technique to allow one subroutine to call another, we will discard this possibility for subroutine linkage.

The situation where one subroutine calls a second subroutine can clearly be extended to the case where the second subroutine calls a third subroutine and so on. This process, called *subroutine nesting*, can be carried out to any depth. Eventually, the last subroutine called completes its computations and returns to the subroutine that called it. Note that the return address involved in this first return operation is the

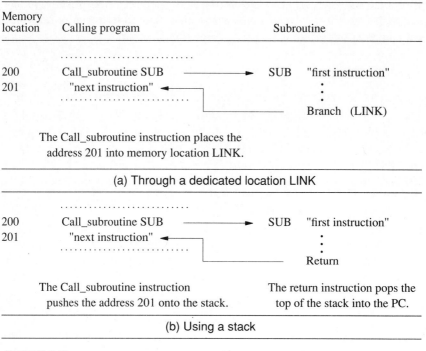

FIGURE 2.40
Subroutine linkage possibilities.

last one that was generated in the nested call sequence. In other words, the return addresses are stored and recalled in a last-in first-out order. We are thus naturally led to suggest that the return addresses associated with subroutine calls should be pushed onto a stack. This mechanism is indicated in Figure 2.40b. Execution of the Call-subroutine instruction consists of two steps. First, the return address, which is 201 in the example in the figure, is pushed onto the return address stack. Second, the address of the first instruction of the subroutine, symbolically given as SUB in the example, is loaded into the PC. This enables a branch to the subroutine. Now, suppose that this subroutine runs to completion without calling any other subroutines. Execution of the Return instruction pops the top of the stack into the PC. Therefore, the return address 201 will be placed into the PC, effecting the branch back to the proper location in the calling program. On the other hand, if the first subroutine calls another subroutine, and so on, the return addresses associated with the nested call sequence will be pushed onto the stack. The ordering of these addresses is correct, because they should be accessed in a last-in first-out order by the Return instructions. The returns, then, proceed in reverse order to the calls, with the final return being to the original calling program.

As well as preserving the PC value, that is, the return address, it is usually necessary to provide a means for sending operands or their addresses to the subroutine and for returning results from the subroutine to the calling program. This is referred to as *parameter passing*. In a multiregister machine it is possible to pass the parameters via some of the registers. Alternatively, the parameters can be passed through memory locations.

There are two commonly used schemes for passing parameters via the memory: by placing them after the Call instruction or by placing them on the stack. In the first scheme, the parameters are placed in the memory locations that immediately follow the Call instruction. When execution of the subroutine begins, the parameters can be read from the memory by using the return address on the stack as a pointer to them. Recall that at the time a subroutine is called, the return address stored on the stack is the address of the location following the Call instruction, which is normally the location of the next instruction to be executed in the calling program.

Figure 2.41 shows how this scheme can be used to write the program of Figure 2.9 as a subroutine. The program adds a list of n numbers and stores the result in a memory location SUM. The address of the first number in the list is assumed to be given as the contents of another memory location, NUMADR, whose address is passed to the subroutine. The value n is also not passed to the subroutine directly. It is given as the contents of location N, whose address is passed to the subroutine. Passing addresses, rather than actual values of parameters, allows the subroutine to be used in a general way, to operate on different lists with varying lengths. Note that the parameter addresses are placed in the calling program using the assembler Data command.

Calling program

	Call_sub	ADDNUM	Call subroutine ADDNUM.
	Data	N	Address of parameter n.
	Data	NUMADR	Address of location that contains the address of the list.
	Move	R_0,SUM	After return from subroutine store the sum in SUM.
	next instruction		
	$\vdots$		
Subroutine			
ADDNUM	Move	(SP),R_3	Register R_3 points to parameter addresses.
	Move	$((R_3)+),R_1$	Load n into register R_1.
	Move	$((R_3)+),R_2$	Register R_2 points to the list.
	Move	R_3,(SP)	Correct the return address.
	Clear	R_0	
LOOP	Add	$(R_2)+,R_0$	Accumulate sum in R_0.
	Decrement	R_1	
	Branch>0	LOOP	
	Return		Return from subroutine with sum in R_0.

FIGURE 2.41
Program of Figure 2.9 written as a subroutine.

When the subroutine is entered, the return address on the stack is loaded into register R_3. It points to the address of the parameter n. The second instruction reads n from the memory using the autoincrement indirect addressing mode. The autoincrement feature is used to automatically increment the pointer in R_3 to point to the address of the second parameter. Indirection is needed because addresses are being passed, rather than actual parameter values. After the second parameter has been accessed, the contents of R_3 will be the address of the Move instruction in the calling program. This is the instruction that must be executed on return from the subroutine; therefore, the corrected return address, which is in R_3, must replace the existing return address on the stack. This is accomplished by the Move instruction that follows the loading of parameters in the subroutine.

The subroutine in Figure 2.41 uses registers R_1, R_2, and R_3 for its computation. We have assumed that the calling program is not using any of these registers for holding valid data of its own at the time it calls the addition subroutine. Should this not be the case, the subroutine must be written such that it first saves the contents of these registers. It then restores them to the original values just before returning to the calling program. A convenient way of doing this is to save the register contents on the stack.

Parameters can also be passed to a subroutine via the processor stack. The calling program places the parameters on the stack. When the subroutine is executed, the parameters are read from the stack and used as needed. Upon return from the subroutine, the calling program must remove the parameters from the stack. Note that it is inconvenient to have the subroutine remove the parameters from the stack, because the return address is on top of the parameters and is needed to return to the calling program.

2.10.2 Subroutine Linkage (PDP-11)

Let us now consider the subroutine linkage and parameter-passing protocols that are used in the PDP-11. As pointed out in Section 2.9, stacks can be easily implemented in the PDP-11 through the use of the autoincrement and autodecrement address modes. Although any CPU register can be used by the programmer as a stack pointer, register R_6 is used by the processor as a pointer to the processor stack. This stack is used as part of the subroutine linkage mechanism. It is also used in connection with interrupt-controlled I/O, as will be discussed in Chapter 6.

The instruction

$$JSR \qquad R_L,dst$$

implements the call operation by branching to the location specified by the dst field. This location is the starting point of the subroutine program. The value in the PC, which has been incremented to point at the instruction after the JSR instruction, is preserved in the CPU register R_L, which is called the *linkage register*. The previous contents of R_L are pushed onto the processor stack. This instruction may seem overly complicated, given that all we require, based on our previous discussion, is that the contents of the PC be pushed onto a stack. The reason for introducing R_L is to facilitate the passing of parameters, as will be explained shortly.

The return from a subroutine to the calling program is achieved by the instruction

$$\text{RTS} \qquad R_L$$

This instruction moves the saved PC value from R_L into the PC and pops the top of the processor stack into register R_L. The computation then continues at the instruction following the JSR instruction, with the original contents of R_L restored.

Passing parameters from the calling program to a subroutine can be implemented conveniently in two ways in the PDP-11. If there are only a few operands or results to be exchanged between the calling program and the subroutine, it may be convenient to pass them via the CPU registers R_0 through R_5. As an alternative, the parameters can be passed by placing their addresses in memory locations immediately following the JSR instruction. The PC value that is saved in register R_L when the JSR instruction is executed is the address of the first of these locations. The subroutine can then access the parameters by using the autoincrement indirect addressing mode, $@(R_L)+$. After the last parameter has been accessed, the contents of R_L point to the next instruction to be executed in the calling program. This is exactly what is required to implement the return via the RTS instruction.

Figure 2.42 shows the addition routine presented earlier in Figure 2.20 written as a subroutine. The parameter addresses N and NUMADR are placed immediately

Calling program	JSR	R5,ADDNUM	Call the subroutine ADDNUM
	.WORD	N	using R_5 as the
	.WORD	NUMADR	linkage register.
	MOV	R0,SUM	After return from the subroutine store the sum in SUM.
Subroutine ADDNUM:	CLR	R0	
	MOV	@(R5)+,R1	Initialize register R_1 to contain n $(=[N])$.
	MOV	@(R5)+,R2	Initialize register R_2 to contain the address NUM.
LOOPSTART:	ADD	(R2)+,R0	Accumulate sum in R_0.
	DEC	R1	
	BGT	LOOPSTART	
	RTS	R5	Return from subroutine with sum in R_n.

FIGURE 2.42
Program of Figure 2.18 written as a subroutine.

after the JSR instruction. The sum of the n numbers, beginning at NUM, will be passed back to the calling program through register R_0.

The provision for a linkage register in the JSR instruction makes accessing parameters simpler than in the general case discussed in the previous section. In Figure 2.41, it was necessary to use the return address on the stack as a pointer to the parameters by loading it into one of the CPU registers. The PDP-11 uses the linkage register automatically to achieve the same effect.

After the subroutine in Figure 2.42 has been called by the JSR instruction, the linkage register R_5 points to the memory location containing the address N. The contents of location N are moved into register R_1 by the second instruction of the subroutine. The third instruction moves the address NUM into register R_2. At this time, R_5 has been incremented to point to the MOV instruction in the calling program. This permits a return to the correct location by the RTS instruction when the subroutine has finished its computation. Upon return to the calling program, the MOV instruction places the sum of the n numbers into main memory location SUM, the sum having been passed from the subroutine to the calling program through register R_0.

We have seen that the use of any one of the registers R_0 through R_5 as the linkage register in a subroutine call facilitates passing parameters to the subroutine through main memory locations. However, if parameters are passed through CPU registers, it is more appropriate to use R_7, the PC, as the linkage register. This eliminates the need for using one of the registers R_0 through R_5 as the linkage register. The net effect of the instruction

$$\text{JSR} \qquad \text{R7,dst}$$

is to push the updated contents of the PC onto the processor stack and load the subroutine address (specified by the dst field) into the PC. The return instruction

$$\text{RTS} \qquad \text{R7}$$

pops the top of the processor stack into the PC, thus implementing a proper return to the calling program.

We should note that register R_6 must always contain an even number. This is necessary because R_6 is used as the processor stack pointer. It must always be available for pushing and popping addresses associated with subroutine call and return operations. The CPU hardware is organized such that when register R_6 is used in either the autoincrement or autodecrement mode, it is always incremented or decremented by 2, even for byte instructions. For obvious reasons, register R_7 is treated in the same manner.

NESTED SUBROUTINES. Figure 2.42 shows the basic way that subroutine entry and exit are achieved by the JSR and RTS instructions in the PDP-11. The use of the linkage register in passing parameter addresses through memory is also illustrated. Let us now consider an example where one subroutine calls another subroutine.

Figure 2.43 shows a part of a main program that calls subroutine SUB1, which in turn calls subroutine SUB2. Subroutine SUB2 returns to SUB1, which eventually returns to the main program. The contents of the processor stack are shown in Figure 2.44 at a number of different points during the execution of the two subroutines.

A few comments are in order about this nested call sequence. It is assumed that subroutine SUB1 uses registers R_0 and R_1 in its calculations. Because these registers

Memory location	Instructions		Comments
Main program	$\vdots$		
2000	JSR	R5,SUB1	Call SUB1, passing addresses
2004	.WORD	PARAM	PARAM and ANSWER
2006	.WORD	ANSWER	through memory locations.
2008	next instruction		
	$\vdots$		
Subroutine			
2200 SUB1:	MOV	R0,−(R6)	Save $[R_0]_{main}$ and $[R_1]_{main}$
	MOV	R1,−(R6)	on the processor stack.
	MOV	@(R5)+,R0	Load parameter into R_0.
	$\vdots$		
	MOV	LOC,R1	Place a parameter into R_1
2250	JSR	R7,SUB2	and call SUB2.
2254	next instruction		
	$\vdots$		
	MOV	RESULT,@(R5)+	Send [RESULT] as a "result" into location ANSWER in the main program.
	MOV	(R6)+,R1	Restore original contents
	MOV	(R6)+,R0	of registers R_0 and R_1
	RTS	R5	
Subroutine			
3000 SUB2:	MOV	R0,−(R6)	Save $[R_0]_{sub1}$ on the processor stack.
	$\vdots$		
	ADD	R0,R1	Send a result to SUB1 through R_1.
	MOV	(R6)+,R0	Restore R_0.
	RTS	R7	

FIGURE 2.43
Nested subroutine calls.

may contain meaningful data for the main program, it is necessary to save these values when SUB1 is entered and restore them just before returning to the main program. This is accomplished through the use of the processor stack. The first two MOV instructions of SUB1 push the contents of R_0 and R_1 onto the processor stack, and the last two MOV instructions restore them.

Parameter addresses PARAM and ANSWER are accessed through the linkage register R_5. Subroutine SUB1 performs the first part of its calculations and calls subroutine SUB2. Parameter passing between subroutines SUB1 and SUB2 takes place through register R_1. Furthermore, it is assumed that subroutine SUB2 uses R_0 in its internal calculations. Hence, the contents of R_0 are saved on the processor stack. Note that the program counter, R_7, is used as the linkage register in calling SUB2, since parameter passing is done via a register.

After control is passed back to SUB1 from SUB2, subroutine SUB1 completes its calculations and stores the result into location ANSWER. The MOV instruction that stores this result also autoincrements the linkage register R_5 for the second time in SUB1. As a result, R_5 contains the correct return address, 2008, when control is passed back to the main program by the RTS instruction. The return is executed after the contents of registers R_0 and R_1 have been restored from the processor stack. The reader is encouraged to study the contents of the processor stack, as shown in Figure 2.44, as the execution of these programs proceeds.

2.10.3   Subroutine Linkage (68000)

In this section, we will describe the subroutine linkage and parameter-passing schemes used in the 68000 microprocessor. The 68000 provides for implementation of stacks as explained in Section 2.9, that is, through the use of the autoincrement and autodecrement addressing modes. Address register A_7 serves as a pointer to the processor stack, which is used in subroutine linkage.

A Branch-to-Subroutine instruction, BSR, is used to call a subroutine. It is implemented in the same way as any other branch instruction, but its action also causes the contents of the program counter to be stored on the stack prior to branching. In this case, the branch target is the first instruction in the subroutine. Upon completion of the subroutine, a Return-from-Subroutine instruction, RTS, is used to return to the calling program. It moves the return address at the top of the stack into the program counter. The BSR and RTS instructions allow implementation of the subroutine linkage mechanism as described in general terms in Section 2.10.1.

Figure 2.45 shows how the program in Figure 2.30 can be written as a subroutine. It follows almost exactly the scheme presented in Figure 2.41. The only significant difference is that two Move instructions are needed to load each parameter into a register, because the 68000 does not have an indirect autoincrement addressing mode.

NESTED SUBROUTINES. We have considered the simple case of a program calling a subroutine. Next, we will discuss the case of nested subroutines, where one subroutine calls another.

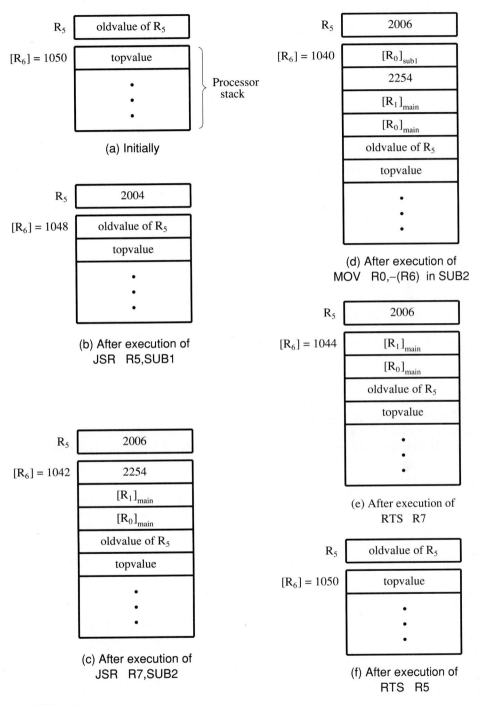

FIGURE 2.44
The contents of register R_5 and the processor stack as execution proceeds in the programs of Figure 2.43.

Calling program

	BSR	ADDNUM	Call subroutine ADDNUM.
	DC.L	N	Address of parameter n.
	DC.L	NUMADR	Address of location that contains address of the list.
	MOVE.L	D0,SUM	After return from subroutine, store the sum in SUM.
	next instruction		

$\vdots$

Subroutine

ADDNUM	MOVEA.L	(A7),A0	Use register A0 to point to parameter addresses.
	MOVEA.L	(A0)+,A1	
	MOVE.W	(A1),D1	Load n into register D_1.
	MOVEA.L	(A0)+,A1	Load the address, NUM,
	MOVEA.L	(A1),A2	of the list into A_2.
	MOVEA.L	A0,(A7)	Set the correct return address.
	CLR.L	D0	
LOOP	ADD.L	(A2)+,D0	Accumulate sum in D_0.
	SUBQ.W	#1,D1	
	BGT	LOOP	
	RTS		

FIGURE 2.45
Program of Figure 2.30 written as a subroutine.

Figure 2.46 gives an example of a main program that calls subroutine SUB1, which in turn calls subroutine SUB2. Upon completion of SUB2, a return to SUB1 is made. SUB1 is then completed and a return to the main program is made.

Two methods of passing parameters are illustrated in the example. The main program passes the addresses of the parameters to SUB1 as was done in Figure 2.41. The most direct way of passing parameters is used with the second subroutine, where SUB1 simply places the desired parameter into register D_0 prior to calling SUB2.

It is often the case that a program has information stored in some CPU registers at the time of calling a subroutine that it does not want destroyed by the subroutine. This information will be used by the calling program after the return from the subroutine. If the subroutine needs to use these registers for its own purposes, it must first save their contents when it is entered and later restore them before returning to the calling program. Figure 2.46 shows how this may be achieved using the processor stack as temporary storage. The first instruction in SUB1 saves the contents of registers D_0, D_1, D_2, A_0, and A_1 by pushing them onto the processor stack. The 68000 has a special instruction that facilitates this operation. The Move-Multiple-Registers instruction, MOVEM, moves the contents of the registers specified in the operand field to or from the main memory. In our example, the main memory location is given in the autodecrement mode using A7 as the pointer register, in order to save the registers on the processor stack. Note that any number of registers can be specified

Memory location	Instructions		Comments
Main program	:		
2000	BSR	SUB1	Call SUB1, passing addresses
2004	DC.L	PARAM	PARAM and ANSWER
2008	DC.L	ANSWER	through memory locations.
2012	next instruction		
	:		
Subroutine			
2200 SUB1	MOVEM.L	D0−D2/A0−A1,−(A7)	Save registers.
2204	MOVEA.L	20(A7),A0	Get pointer to parameter address.
	MOVEA.L	(A0)+,A1	Get address of first parameter.
	MOVE.L	(A1),D0	Load a parameter into D_0.
	:		
	MOVE.L	LOC,D1	Place a parameter into D_1
2250	BSR	SUB2	and call SUB2.
2254	next instruction		
	:		
	MOVEA.L	(A0)+,A1	Get address of second parameter.
	MOVE.L	RESULT,(A1)	Store the result in ANSWER.
	MOVE.L	A0,20(A7)	Set the correct return address.
	MOVEM.L	(A7)+,D0−D2/A0−A1	Restore registers
	RTS		and return.
Subroutine			
3000 SUB2	MOVE.L	D0,−(A7)	Save register D_0.
	:		
	ADD.L	D0,D1	Send a result to SUB1 through D_1.
	MOVE.L	(A7)+,D0	Restore D_0.
	RTS		

FIGURE 2.46
Nested subroutines.

in the MOVEM instruction. The assembler syntax uses slashes to delineate registers in the operand field and dashes to indicate a sequence of successive registers. Prior to leaving SUB1, another MOVEM instruction restores the original contents of the registers.

Figure 2.47 shows the contents of the stack after the first instruction of subroutine SUB2 has been executed, assuming that the object program is loaded in the memory locations indicated in Figure 2.46. We assume that the top of the stack is at location 1050 prior to executing the BSR instruction that calls SUB1. The execution of the BSR instruction pushes the return address, 2004, on the stack. The first instruction

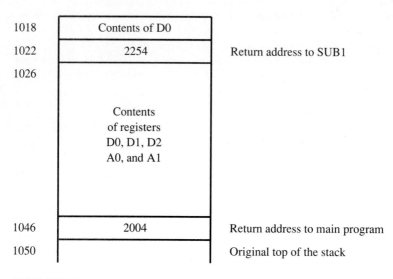

1018	Contents of D0	
1022	2254	Return address to SUB1
1026		
	Contents of registers D0, D1, D2 A0, and A1	
1046	2004	Return address to main program
1050		Original top of the stack

FIGURE 2.47
The processor stack for the program in Figure 2.46.

in SUB1 saves the contents of five CPU registers on the stack. The top of the stack at this point is at location 1026. When the BSR instruction that calls SUB2 is executed, the return address 2254 is pushed on the stack. Finally, the first instruction of SUB2 saves the contents of register D_0, resulting in the stack contents shown in the figure.

At the end of each subroutine, the saved contents of registers are popped and loaded back into the registers. The return addresses are removed when RTS instructions in the subroutines are executed. Note, however, that subroutine SUB1 will modify the return address to the main program after it accesses the address of the parameter ANSWER. The new return address, 2012, will be placed in location 1046, enabling the return to the correct instruction in the main program.

2.11 CONCLUDING REMARKS

This chapter introduced the representation and execution of instructions and programs at the machine level as seen by the programmer. The emphasis was on the basic principles of addressing techniques and instruction sequencing. To illustrate these fundamental notions, we used the PDP-11 and 68000 instructions in our examples.

The ease and flexibility of programming at the machine instruction level is strongly influenced by the addressing modes in a given computer. A significant part of the chapter was devoted to a discussion of addressing methods in general, followed by a complete and detailed description of those used in the PDP-11 and 68000 computers. Other computer manufacturers have used different techniques for addressing operands; some of these will be discussed in Chapter 3.

The programming examples included in this chapter were chosen to illustrate the basic types of operations that must be implemented by the instruction set of any computer. Moving instructions and operands to and from the main memory was discussed first, followed by a discussion of program branching. The elements of simple I/O operations were discussed with respect to transferring characters between a video terminal and the CPU. The subroutine concept and the instructions needed to implement it were also discussed. Subroutine linkage methods provided an example of the application of the stack data structure, which is also important in other situations. Indeed, it will be seen in Chapter 3 that stacks have been incorporated into the design of some computers in a basic way.

We should emphasize that this chapter is by no means complete in the sense of introducing the full range of instructions that are needed in an instruction set. Representative instructions of each of the major operational types were presented. However, there has been little mention of one important class of instructions that are found in most computers. These are the *shift* and *rotate* instructions that are used to shift the binary pattern in a byte or a word either to the right or left by some specified number of positions. The main applications for these instructions arise in implementing arithmetic routines, which will be discussed in Chapter 7. Appendices B and C contain a summary of the full instruction sets of the PDP-11 and 68000 computers, respectively.

The remainder of the book is concerned with computer design. Major subsystems will be described, namely, the CPU, the main memory, I/O device interfaces and controllers, and peripheral devices.

2.12   PROBLEMS

2.1. Assume that

$$\text{Multiply} \qquad \text{A,R}_i$$

is a Multiply instruction in a computer that has a $1\frac{1}{2}$-address format for instructions that need to reference two operands. The execution of this instruction is similar to that of the instruction

$$\text{Add} \qquad \text{A,R}_i$$

Also assume that the computer has a few general-purpose CPU registers and that it has other instructions and addressing modes (like those described in Sections 2.3 and 2.4 and used in the programs of Figures 2.3 to 2.6).

A program on this computer is required for the computation

$$C \leftarrow A_1 \times B_1 + A_2 \times B_2 + A_3 \times B_3$$

on the contents of main memory locations C, A_1, B_1, A_2, B_2, A_3, and B_3. None of the contents of the locations A_i or B_i are to be destroyed.

(*a*) Write a straight-line program for this task on the above-described computer.

(*b*) Write a loop program for the same task on the same computer.

(c) Calculate the number of main memory accesses (Read or Write operations) required for each of the programs in (a) and (b). Include all accesses required for fetching and executing the instructions. For example, the instruction

$$\text{Load} \quad \text{A,R}_i$$

requires two memory accesses: one for reading the instruction from the main memory into the CPU and one for reading the operand from main memory location A into the CPU.

2.2. A program is required for the task

$$C \leftarrow \sum_{i=1}^{n} A_i \times B_i$$

(a) Write a loop program for this task on the computer described in Problem 2.1. Assume that variables C, A_i, and B_i are located in the main memory and that the value n is stored in main memory location N. The contents of N, A_i, and B_i are not to be destroyed by executing the program.

(b) Would the two-address instruction format have been any better than the assumed $1\frac{1}{2}$-address format for the above program or for either of the programs in Problem 2.1?

(c) Calculate the values of the constants k_1 and k_2 in the expression $k_1 + k_2 n$, which represents the number of main memory accesses required to execute your program for part (a) of this problem.

2.3. Write a program for evaluating the polynomial

$$P(x) = a_n x^n + a_{n-1} x^{n-1} + \cdots + a_1 x + a_0$$

on the computer defined in Problem 2.1. The coefficients a_i, the argument x, and the value n are all stored in the main memory. The computed value $P(x)$ is to be stored in main memory location P, and none of the other operand values are to be destroyed by execution of the program. *Hint:* Consider the alternative formula $P(x) = ((\cdots(a_n x + a_{n-1})x + \cdots + a_2)x + a_1)x + a_0$ for polynomial evaluation.

2.4. Consider the following state of the PDP-11

Register R_1 contains 1000.
Register R_2 contains 2000.
Memory location 1000 contains 2000.
Memory location 2000 contains 3000.
Memory location 3000 contains 1000.
All numbers are in octal (base 8) notation.

For the following three instructions, each executed from the above initial state, what is the effect of executing each instruction? How many words does each instruction occupy? How many memory accesses does the fetching and execution of each instruction require?

(a)   ADD   R1,@R2
(b)   ADD   1000(R1),@R2
(c)   ADD   #2000,@R2

	Contents of locations					
Time	R_0	R_1	R_2	N	NUM	SUM
After first execution of ADD						
After second execution of ADD						
After third execution of ADD						
After fourth execution of ADD						
After execution of last MOV						

FIGURE P2.1
Format for the program trace in Problem 2.5.

2.5. A *program trace* is a tabular listing of the contents of certain registers and memory locations at different times during the execution of a program.

(*a*) Using the tabular format outlined in Figure P2.1, complete the trace for the PDP-11 program of Figure 2.20, assuming the following initial decimal values

$$[R_0] = \cdots \qquad [SUM] = \cdots$$

$$[R_1] = \cdots \qquad [1000] = 17$$

$$[R_2] = \cdots \qquad [1002] = -723$$

$$[N] = 4 \qquad [1004] = -519$$

$$NUM = 1000 \qquad [1006] = 184$$

(*b*) Using a tabular format similar to that used in part (*a*) of this problem, construct a trace for the sorting program of Figure 2.21*b*. Assume that a list of 5 bytes is to be sorted. The address LIST of the first byte of the list is 1000, and the decimal values of the bytes in the list are

$$[1000] = 200$$

$$[1001] = 213$$

$$[1002] = 196$$

$$[1003] = 227$$

$$[1004] = 213$$

The trace should show the contents of all list positions and the CPU registers R_1, R_2, and R_3 immediately after each execution of the instruction BLOS OUTER.

2.6. Consider two PDP-11 programs given in Figure P2.2. The labels X, N, M, and RESULT refer to main memory locations. Memory locations N and M contain the values n and $2n$, respectively.

(*a*) Do the programs accomplish the same task?

(*b*) What task(s) do they accomplish?

(*c*) Which program executes faster? Why?

(*d*) How many 16-bit words are required to represent each program in the main memory?

Program 1			Program 2		
	CLR	R0		CLR	R0
	MOV	M,R1		MOV	#X,R1
	SUB	#2,R1		MOV	N,R2
LOOP:	ADD	X(R1),R0	LOOP:	ADD	(R1)+,R0
	SUB	#2,R1		DEC	R2
	BGE	LOOP		BGT	LOOP
	MOV	R0,RESULT		MOV	R0,RESULT
	HALT			HALT	

FIGURE P2.2
Programs for Problem 2.6.

2.7. Consider the following PDP-11 program

```
                MOV       N,R0
                MOV       #1000.,R1
                MOV       #2000.,R2
                MOV       #3000.,R3
                JSR       R7,ROUTINE
                HALT
     ROUTINE:   MOV       (R1)+,R4
                ADD       -(R2),R4
                MOV       R4,(R3)+
                INC       R0
                BLT       ROUTINE
                RTS       R7
     N:         .WORD     -25.
```

(*a*) What does this program do?
(*b*) How many 16-bit words do the instructions require for their representation in the main memory?
(*c*) How many main memory cycles are required to fetch and execute the first five instructions?

2.8. Consider the following PDP-11 program

```
                CLR       SUM
                MOV       N,R0
                MOV       #X,R1
                MOV       #Y,R2
     LOOP:      MOV       (R1)+,R3
                MOV       (R2)+,R4
                JRS       R7,SUB
                ADD       R4,SUM
                DEC       R0
                BGT       LOOP
                HALT
```

```
SUB:            CMP   R3,R4
                BEQ   EXCEPTION
                RTS   R7
EXCEPTION:      CLR   R4
                RTS   R7
```

(a) What does this program do?

(b) How many 16-bit words do the instructions require for their representation in the main memory?

(c) Give an expression for the execution time of the whole program in terms of the number of main memory accesses required. The expression should follow the form $T = a + bn$, where $[N] = n$. Use the "worst case" path through the subroutine in calculating the constants in the expression.

2.9. Each of the following four PDP-11 assembly language program segments will cause errors at either the assembly or execution stages. What are the errors?

(a)
```
                MOV     #1000,R1
                MOVB    (R1)+,R0
                MOV     @R1,R2
```

(b)
```
                JSR     R7,READ
                HALT
                . . .
READ:           TSTB    STATUS
                BPL     READ
                MOVB    DATAIN,-(R6)
                RTS     R7
```

(c)
```
                . =     1000
                MOV     #1000,R5
                MOV     #7,R0
A:              MOV     R0,(R5)+
                DEC     R0
                BNE     A
```

(d)
```
                . =     1000.
                BR      A
                . =     1500.
A:              HALT
```

2.10. Describe what happens when the instruction

$$\text{JRS} \qquad \text{R7},@(R6)+$$

is executed. Assume that the instruction is stored at main memory location 2050, and that before it is executed, $[R6] = 950$ and memory location 950 contains 3000. What happens if the same instruction is executed by a subroutine?

2.11. Write PDP-11 programs for the tasks in Problems 2.1 to 2.3. Assume that only single-length products are required in all these programs.

2.12. (a) In the byte-sorting program shown in Figure 2.21b, the address value LIST and the value n are fixed in the program code at assembly time. Rewrite the program as a

PDP-11 subroutine under the assumption that the values LIST and *n* are contained in main memory locations whose addresses are placed immediately after the JSR instruction in a calling program.

(*b*) The execution-time efficiency of the byte-sorting subroutine of part (*a*) can be improved by keeping track of the address of the smallest byte of a sublist LIST(j) to LIST($n-1$) and performing, at most, one swap at the end of the sublist search. Rewrite the part (*a*) subroutine to achieve this efficiency and estimate the improvement. What happens to code space requirements when time efficiency is improved?

2.13. Consider the following PDP-11 program.

```
                 MOV      N,R0
                 MOV      R0,R2
                 MOV      #2000.,R1
        LOOP:    JSR      R7,ROUTINE
                 DEC      R0
                 DEC      R0
                 BGT      LOOP
                 HALT
        ROUTINE: MOVB     @R1,R4
                 MOVB     2000.(R2),(R1)+
                 MOVB     R4,2000.(R2)
                 DEC      R2
                 RTS      R7
```

(*b*) What does this program do?

(*c*) For each of the instructions answer the following questions.

   i. How many 16-bit words are required to represent the instruction in main memory?

   ii. How many main memory accesses are required to fetch and execute the instruction?

   iii. Give an expression for the execution time, as in Problem 2.8, part (*c*).

2.14. The PDP-11 program in Figure P2.3 transfers a sequence of bytes from the main memory to an output device.

(*a*) If a main memory access takes 0.5 μs, and if the device is ready, how long does it take to execute the "LOOP" once?

(*b*) If the device can only accept bytes at the rate of one every millisecond, approximately how many times is the BPL WAIT instruction executed for every byte transferred?

```
                 MOV      #LOC,R0
                 MOV      N,R1
        WAIT:    TSTB     DEVSTATUS
                 BPL      WAIT
"LOOP"           MOVB     (R0)+,DEVOUT
                 DEC      R1
                 BGT      WAIT
                 HALT
```

FIGURE P2.3
Program for Problem 2.14.

2.15. (*a*) For the following PDP-11 program, record the number of 16-bit words needed to represent each of the instructions in the main memory. Also record the number of main memory accesses needed to fetch and execute each instruction.

```
                CLR     R0
                MOV     #XLIST,R1
                MOV     #YLIST,R2
                MOV     N,R3
        LOOP:   MOV     @R1,R4
                MOV     @R2,R5
                ADD     R4,R5
                ADD     R5,R0
                ADD     #2,R1
                ADD     #2,R2
                DEC     R3
                BNE     LOOP
                MOV     R0,SUM
                HALT
```

(*b*) Calculate the values a and b in the expression $T = a + bn$, where T is the number of main memory accesses required to execute the program. The value n is the positive integer stored at location N.

(*c*) Rewrite the program using as few instructions and registers as you can. You should still perform the same overall computation, however, ending with the same answer in location SUM without changing the values in any other main memory location.

(*d*) Recalculate a and b in the T expression for your new program.

2.16. Consider the following state of the 68000 microprocessor.

Register D_0 contains $1000.

Register A_0 contains $2000.

Register A_1 contains $1000.

Memory location $1000 contains the long word $2000.

Memory location $2000 contains the long word $3000.

For the following instructions, each executed from the preceding initial state, what is the effect of executing each instruction? How many bytes does each instruction occupy? How many memory accesses does the fetching and execution of each instruction require?

(*a*)	ADD.L	D0,(A0)
(*b*)	ADD.L	(A1,D0),D0
(*c*)	ADD.L	#$2000,(A0)

2.17. Find the syntax errors in the following 68000 instructions

(*a*)	ADDX	−(A2),D3
(*b*)	LSR.L	#9,D2
(*c*)	MOVE.B	520(A0,D2)
(*d*)	SUBA.L	12(A2,PC),A0
(*e*)	CMP.B	#254,$12(A2,D1.B)

2.18. Consider Problem 2.5 in the 68000 environment.

(a) Complete the trace for the program of Figure 2.30. Replace R_0, R_1, and R_2 with D_0, D_1, and A_2 in Figure P2.1.

(b) Do the trace for the program of Figure 2.32, using the same parameters as in Problem 2.5(b). The trace should show the contents of all list positions and processor registers D_1, D_2, and D_3 immediately after each execution of the instruction BGT OUTER.

2.19. How many bytes of main memory are needed to store the program in Figure 2.33? How many memory accesses are needed during execution of this program?

2.20. Consider the two 68000 programs given in Figure P2.4.

(a) Do these programs leave the same value in location RSLT?

(b) What task(s) do they accomplish?

(c) How many bytes of memory are needed to store each program?

(d) Which program executes faster, assuming that the speed is directly proportional to the number of memory accesses needed?

(e) What are the advantages and disadvantages of these programs? Make some critical comments.

2.21. Consider the following 68000 program.

```
        MOVEA.L   MEM1,A0
        MOVEA.L   MEM2,A1
        ADDA.L    A0,A1
        MOVEA.L   A0,A2
        MOVE.B    (A0)+,D0
LOOP    CMP.B     (A0)+,D0
        BLE       NXT
        LEA       -1(A0),A2
        MOVE.B    (A2),D0
NXT     CMPA.L    A0,A1
        BGT       LOOP
        MOVE.L    A2,DESIRED
```

(a) What does this program do?

(b) How many 16-bit words are needed to store this program in the main memory?

Program 1		Program 2	
	CLR.L D0		MOVE.W #$FFFF,D0
	MOVEA.L #LIST,A0		MOVEA.L #LIST,A0
LOOP	MOVE.W (A0),D1	LOOP	LSL.W (A0)
	BGE LOOP		BCC LOOP
	ADDQ.L #1,D0		LSL.W #1,D0
	CMPI #17,D0		BCS LOOP
	BLT LOOP		MOVE.W -2(A0),RSLT
	MOVE.W -2(A0),RSLT		

FIGURE P2.4
Programs for Problem 2.20.

(c) Give an expression for the execution time of this program in terms of the number of main memory accesses required. The expression should be of the form $T = a + bn + cm$, where n is the number of times the loop is executed and m is the number of times the branch to NXT is not taken.

2.22. Write a 68000 program to reverse the order of bits in register D_2. For example, if the starting pattern in D_2 is $1110 \cdots 0100$, the result left in D_2 should be $0010 \cdots 0111$.

2.23. Write a PDP-11 or a 68000 subroutine that compares corresponding bytes of two lists of bytes and places the larger byte in a third list. The two lists start at byte locations X and Y, and the "larger byte" list starts at LARGER. The length of the lists is stored in main memory location N.

2.24. Write a PDP-11 or a 68000 subroutine that reads n characters from the keyboard of a video terminal and echoes them back to the display screen. The characters must be pushed onto a stack as they are read. Use R_0 in the PDP-11 or A_0 in the 68000 as the stack pointer.

2.25. A PDP-11 or 68000 program is required for the following character manipulation task. A string of n characters is stored in the main memory in consecutive byte locations beginning at location STRING. Another shorter string of m characters is stored in consecutive byte locations beginning at location SUBSTRING. The program must search the string stored beginning at STRING to determine whether or not it contains a contiguous substring identical to the string stored beginning at SUBSTRING. The length parameters n and m ($n > m$) are stored in main memory locations N and M, respectively. The result of the search is to be stored in register R_0: if a matching substring is found, the address of its first byte is to be stored in register R_0; otherwise, the contents of R_0 are to be cleared to 0. The program does not need to determine multiple occurrences of the substring. The address of the first matching substring only is required.

2.26. Write a PDP-11 or a 68000 program to accept three decimal digits from a keyboard. Each digit is represented in the ASCII code. Assume that these three digits represent a decimal integer in the range 0 to 999 and convert the integer into a binary number representation. The high-order digit is received first. To aid in this conversion, two tables of words are stored in the main memory. Each table has 10 entries. The first table, starting at word location TENS, contains the binary representations for the decimal values 0, 10, 20, . . . , 90. The second table starts at word location HUNDREDS and contains the decimal values, 0, 100, 200, . . . , 900 in binary representation.

2.27. Write a PDP-11 or a 68000 program that generates the first n numbers of the Fibonacci series. In this series the first two numbers are 0 and 1, and each subsequent number is generated by adding the preceding two numbers. For example, for $n = 8$, the series is

$$0, 1, 1, 2, 3, 5, 8, 13$$

Your program should store the numbers in byte memory locations starting at MEMLOC. Assume that the value n is found in location N. What is the largest n that your program can handle?

2.28. The concept of last-in first-out (LIFO) stacks was discussed in Section 2.9. The purpose of this question is to investigate the implementation of first-in first-out (FIFO) queues. These types of data structures can serve as data buffers during input or output operations.

A FIFO queue of bytes is to be implemented in the main memory, occupying a fixed region of k bytes. You will need two pointers, an IN pointer and an OUT pointer. The IN pointer keeps track of the location where the next byte is to be appended to the queue; and the OUT pointer keeps track of the location containing the next byte to be removed from the queue. The state of the queue, which can be full, empty, or partly filled, also must be known in order to correctly perform the append and remove operations.

Write APPEND and REMOVE subroutines for the PDP-11 or 68000 processor. Be careful to inspect and update the state of the queue and the pointers each time an operation is attempted and performed.

2.29. (a) Formulate the decimal to binary conversion program of Problem 2.26 as two nested subroutines. Any calling program that invokes the first subroutine passes two parameter addresses to it through main memory locations following the JSR instruction. The first of these is the address of a 3-byte main memory buffer area that the subroutines are to use for storing the input decimal digit characters. The second address is the location for the converted binary value.

The task of the first subroutine is to read in the three decimal digit characters from the keyboard. It then calls a second subroutine to perform the actual conversion. The necessary parameters are passed to this subroutine via the processor registers. Both subroutines must save the contents of any registers that they use on the processor stack.

(b) Give the contents of the processor stack immediately after the execution of the instruction that calls the second subroutine.

2.30. Write 68000 programs for the tasks in Problems 2.1 to 2.3. Assume that only 16-bit operands are involved.

2.31. Write a 68000 program to subtract two 16-digit BCD (binary coded decimal) numbers, P and Q. Both numbers are stored in a format that uses one byte for each BCD digit, and the most significant digit of each number occupies the lowest-address byte. The difference P−Q is to overwrite the number P in the memory.

Hint: An example of BCD subtraction is shown in Figure 10.5.

2.32. Repeat Problem 2.31, assuming that the numbers P and Q are stored in a "packed" format in which two BCD digits are stored in one byte.

2.33. Suppose that in a given computer the subroutine linkage is implemented in the following way. The Call-subroutine instruction stores the return address (that is, the address of the "next" instruction in the calling program) into the first location of the subroutine, and then branches to the second location where execution of the subroutine begins.

(a) Define a suitable instruction for returning from the subroutine.

(b) How would you pass parameters between the calling program and the subroutine?

(c) Would the above linkage method support subroutine nesting?

(d) Consider the nested call sequence Main program, SUB1, SUB2, ..., SUB*i*, SUB1. This type of nesting, in which a subroutine "calls itself," is referred to as *recursion*. Would the above linkage method support recursive calls?

(e) Would the stack linkage method discussed in Section 2.10.1 support recursive calls?

2.13 REFERENCES

1. Bell, C. G., J. C. Mudge, and J. E. McNamara, *Computer Engineering: A DEC View of Hardware Systems Design*, Digital Press, Bedford, MA, 1978.

CHAPTER
3

INSTRUCTION SETS

Chapter 2 introduced basic programming ideas and presented some simple examples of typical programs to illustrate the need for various machine instructions and different addressing modes. We introduced the instruction sets of the PDP-11 and 68000 computers to give examples in the context of real computers.

In this chapter we will discuss some features of the VAX-11,[*] IBM 370,[†] and HP3000[‡] instruction sets. The VAX-11 illustrates the evolution of the relatively simple PDP-11 instructions to a powerful instruction set more closely related to high-level language constructs. As we will see, there are a number of similarities between the 68000 and the VAX-11, particularly in their addressing modes. The differences between the 68000 and its successors, the 68020, 68030, and 68040, will be examined in Chapter 10. The IBM 370 instruction set provides another example of instruction set design for a high-performance, multiple-register machine. Finally, the HP3000 shows how an instruction set can be organized for a machine that has computation facilities designed around a hardware stack for holding data operands.

Having observed that a typical computation, or digital processing in general, involves a number of functionally different steps, we can assume that a corresponding number of different classes of instructions should be available. In the previous chapter, we showed that these classes involve data transfers between the main memory and

---

[*] Manufactured by Digital Equipment Corporation.

[†] Manufactured by International Business Machines Corporation.

[‡] Manufactured by Hewlett-Packard Company.

the CPU registers, arithmetic and logic operations on data, program-sequencing control, input-output transfers, and machine control functions. Another important aspect of instruction sets is their ability to support high-level language features. A large instruction set makes it easier to write programs, although there are obviously practical limits to the number of instructions that can be provided. Implementation of a large instruction set involves more complicated control and possibly higher cost. Cost is only one factor, however, that influences the size of the instruction set. Other factors related to organization of the memory and the number of bits in a word will be considered in our discussion.

We should note that a completely different approach to instruction set design has developed in recent years. Instead of replacing simple instruction sets like that of the PDP-11 with more complex sets like the 68000 or VAX-11, the new approach retains low complexity. It has been shown that machines based on such simple instruction sets are conducive to efficient implementation in the VLSI environment and result in high execution rates. These Reduced Instruction Set Computers (RISCs) will be discussed in detail in Chapter 11.

3.1   THE PDP-11

The basic operating principles follow the same general pattern for all computers, large and small. Many design features are independent of the size of the machine, but some are strongly influenced by it. The instruction set of a given computer reflects the effects of the word length, the maximum size of the main memory, and the versatility of the operations that can be performed.

The machine instructions and addressing modes of the PDP-11 were introduced in Chapter 2 in the programming examples. That discussion, in conjunction with the complete detailed listing of the instruction set in Appendix B, is sufficient to give the reader an adequate picture of the number, structure, meaning, and usefulness of the available instructions. In this section, we will extend the discussion of the PDP-11 instruction set in order to identify some of the constraints imposed by a 16-bit word length.

Word length is a basic constraint in the design of instruction sets. The number of available bits strongly affects the size of the addressable space as well as the number of available codes that can be used to encode instructions. Word length limitations can be overcome by using more than one word per instruction as we have already seen in Chapter 2.

Instructions are encoded as bit patterns within the provided bit space. Most instructions consist of an OP code and some addressing data, which are usually formatted in separate fields. However, an instruction consisting of a particular OP code and specific addressing data is really just one of the many (2^{16}) possible codes. It is not an essential requirement that OP codes and addressing data be represented in nicely partitioned fields. They can be encoded in a random fashion as long as the control circuits are able to decode them properly.

Partitioning of instructions into well-defined fields is found in the PDP-11 and many other machines because it simplifies the interpretation of the encoded information. For example, in a 6-bit field that specifies the address of an operand, bit position 3 is used to indicate indirect addressing. If indirect addressing is wanted, b_3 is set to 1; otherwise, it is set to 0. This is the case in all addressing modes. It is easy to see that dedicating 1 bit to such a specific purpose simplifies the encoding and decoding tasks, but it may also result in wasting a part of the available bit space. Two of the modes created by the use of a separate bit for specifying indirection are seldom found in real programs. These are the index indirect and the autodecrement indirect modes. Consider, for example, the autodecrement indirect mode (see Table 2.1). The operand address is $A_{effective} = [[R_n]]$ after R_n has been decremented. This mode would be useful if one wanted to go through a list of operand addresses in the "backward" direction, that is, from high to low memory addresses. Such a requirement is not likely to arise very often, and it can be argued that the mode is really a waste of bit space. This mode can be specified in conjunction with any of the registers R_0 through R_7, requiring eight of the available 2^6 codes. Extending this argument to two-operand instructions, we can easily see that 64 codes are not likely to be used in programs. We may also recall that the autodecrement mode makes no sense at all when $R_n = $ PC, hence its indirect version is equally useless. These examples illustrate the trade-off between full utilization of the bit space, which is likely to result in some codes being assigned in random fashion, and partitioning of instruction words into easily interpretable fields, which potentially wastes bit space.

The OP-code field in two-operand instructions consists of 4 bits (see Figure 3.1), allowing 16 distinct valuations. However, it is obviously not possible to assign all these codes to two-operand instructions. At least one of them must be used to denote the remaining instructions. It is interesting to see how this problem is resolved in the PDP-11. Five two-operand instructions — MOV(B), CMP(B), BIT(B), BIS(B), and

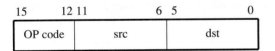

(a) General two-operand instructions

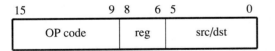

(b) Two-operand instructions with one operand restricted

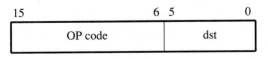

(c) One-operand instructions

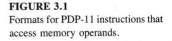

FIGURE 3.1
Formats for PDP-11 instructions that access memory operands.

BIC(B) — have both word and byte versions. This accounts for 10 of the 16 available codes. The ADD and SUB instructions are provided only in the word version and need another two codes. Other two-operand instructions can be useful too, such as XOR (Exclusive-OR), MUL (Multiply), and DIV (Divide). If they were assigned distinct 4-bit OP codes, insufficient bit space would be left to accommodate the rest of the instruction set. The solution used in the PDP-11 is to limit the scope of these two-operand instructions by allowing the full addressing range for one operand and restricting it for the other operand. The latter must be in one of the CPU registers, which requires 3 bits to specify the particular register. As a result, one code for bits b_{15} to b_{12} is sufficient to represent a number of instructions including XOR, MUL, and DIV. The particular code used is $b_{15}b_{14}b_{13}b_{12} = 0111$. The format of these instructions is given in Figure 3.1b.

In total, the two-operand instructions utilize 13 valuations of bits b_{15} to b_{12}. A large group of instructions require only one operand and present significantly less demanding requirements on the available bit space because only six bits are taken by the operand address. Thus, if we take one valuation of bits b_{15} to b_{12} that is not used by the two-operand instructions and combine it with the remaining six bits, it becomes possible to provide as many as 64 one-operand instructions in the format shown in Figure 3.1c.

The easiest instructions to accommodate are those that do not require any operands. These are instructions of a purely control nature, such as HALT, WAIT, and RESET. Because no operands are needed, all 16 bits of the instruction can be used as an OP code. Control and one-operand instructions use two codes in bits b_{15} to b_{12}; this accounts for all but one code.

Until now we have considered an instruction set intended primarily for operation on data represented in *integer* format, where the operand is interpreted as a signed integer with the most significant bit being the sign. Chapter 7 will discuss another useful method for representing data in which each operand consists of a sign, an exponent, and a fraction. This is the *floating-point* representation. Such data should have a longer word length, preferably some multiple of the integer word length. To process these data efficiently, a set of floating-point instructions is desirable. In the PDP-11, a distinct set of floating-point instructions is provided by use of the code $b_{15} \ldots b_{12} = 1111$ to designate the entire set.

3.1.1 Program Status Control

Individual processing steps carried out by separate instructions are seldom unrelated. During the discussion of branch instructions in Chapter 2, it was pointed out that condition code bits are provided to support conditional branching. These bits are stored in the CPU and form a part of the vital "processor status" information.

Execution of a given program may be interrupted by requests for service from peripheral devices. When this happens, the CPU saves the necessary processor status information and executes an appropriate interrupt service routine. Upon completion of this routine, the CPU must resume processing the original program, which clearly

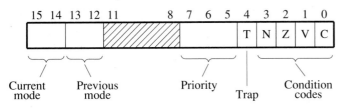

FIGURE 3.2
Processor status word in PDP-11.

requires the ability to restore the processor status information. Interrupt-handling techniques will be discussed in detail in Chapter 6. Here, we will only give a simple representation of the processor status information.

Many computers have a special register that contains the *processor status word* (PSW), which Figure 3.2 shows for the PDP-11. In addition to the condition codes, the PSW contains other status information. Bits b_7 to b_5 indicate the CPU interrupt priority, which will be discussed in Chapter 6. The trap bit (T) indicator causes a processor trap (interrupt) at the end of execution of an instruction, which will be discussed in Chapter 6 as a useful aid in program debugging. Bits b_{15} to b_{12} show the current and previous operational modes of the processor. In larger models of PDP-11 computers there are two basic operational modes for the processor, called supervisor and user. The supervisor mode grants the program control of all functions of the machine, but the user mode does not permit execution of certain instructions and may restrict direct access to peripherals. This feature is useful in preventing a user program from causing a failure of the entire system. In a multiuser environment, it allows each program to be protected against undesirable interference from other programs.

3.2 LIMITATIONS OF SHORT WORD-LENGTH MACHINES

Let us summarize the limitations imposed by the 16-bit word length of the PDP-11 that were discussed in the previous section. An address length of 16 bits allows a total of only 64K addressable locations in the main memory space. The size of this space has proved to be restrictive for many large application programs because the programs must be broken down into a number of segments. These segments must be repeatedly moved into the main memory from secondary disk storage as they are required for execution, and this causes significant time delays.

A second limitation of the 16-bit word length relates to the encoding of instructions and data. The small number of bits that can be allotted to OP codes and addressing modes results in small instruction sets and limited addressing capabilities, so many instructions are required to implement relatively simple program tasks. Also, the range of numbers that can be represented in a single word is too small for many applications. Both of these problems can be eliminated if the machine uses multiple words to represent an expanded instruction set and larger number ranges, as the 68000 does. However, there is an obvious performance loss in this approach because several main memory cycles are required to fetch an instruction or move a data item between the CPU and the main memory.

As we will see later in the chapter, longer word lengths can often remove these limitations as in the case of VAX-11 and IBM 370 computers.

3.3 HIGH-LEVEL LANGUAGE CONSIDERATIONS

Most programs are written in high-level languages, independent of the size or power of the computer used. Many early minicomputers and microcomputers needed a large number of instructions to implement computing tasks that have quite short expressions in high-level languages because those machines usually only provided simple instructions.

Consider, for example, the problem of matrix multiplication. Two $n \times n$ matrices, A and B, are to be multiplied, and the product is to be stored in matrix C. A program for this calculation, written in Pascal-like notation, is shown in Figure 3.3.

Let us consider a PDP-11 program for this task. In order to keep the program simple, the size of the numbers will be restricted. All three of the arrays are assumed to consist of 16-bit integers, and all products and sums involved in the calculation are assumed to fit into 16-bit words. Array subscripts run from $(0,0)$ to $(n-1, n-1)$, and the value n is assumed to be stored in main memory location N. The elements of each array are stored in consecutive word locations beginning with element $(0,0)$ and continuing in column order. That is, element $A(0,0)$ is stored in the main memory at byte address A, element $A(1,0)$ is stored at byte address $A + 2$, and so on.

A possible PDP-11 program for this task is given in Figure 3.4. This program is organized in a straightforward manner to follow the sequence of operations given

```
for i: = 0 to n-1 do

   begin

   for j: = 0 to n-1 do

      begin

      C(i,j): = 0;

      for k: = 0 to n-1 do

         C(i,j): = C(i,j) + A(i,k) × B(k,j)

      end

   end
```

FIGURE 3.3
A matrix multiplication program.

	CLR	R0	i loop control variable in R_0.
LOOPI:	CLR	R2	j loop control variable in R_2.
LOOPJ:	MOV	R2,R1	Compute relative address of
	MUL	N,R1	$\quad$ C(i,j) in R_1.
	ADD	R0,R1	
	ASL	R1	
	CLR	C(R1)	Clear C(i,j).
	CLR	R4	k loop control variable in R_4.
LOOPK:	MOV	R4,R3	Compute relative address of
	MUL	N,R3	$\quad$ A(i,k) in R_3.
	ADD	R0,R3	
	ASL	R3	
	MOV	A(R3),R3	Move A(i,k) to R_3.
	MOV	R2,R5	Compute relative address of
	MUL	N,R5	$\quad$ B(k,j) in R_5.
	ADD	R4,R5	
	ASL	R5	
	MUL	B(R5),R3	$R_3 \leftarrow A(i,k) \times B(k,j)$.
	ADD	R3,C(R1)	$C(i,j) \leftarrow C(i,j) + [R_3]$.
	INC	R4	Termination of k loop.
	CMP	R4,N	
	BLT	LOOPK	
	INC	R2	Termination of j loop.
	CMP	R2,N	
	BLT	LOOPJ	
	INC	R0	Termination of i loop.
	CMP	R0,N	
	BLT	LOOPI	

FIGURE 3.4
Matrix multiplication in a PDP-11.

in Figure 3.3. First, consider the implementation of the for-loop structure. The loop control variables i, j, and k are initialized to 0 and stored in registers R_0, R_2, and R_4, respectively. The outer loop is controlled by the value of i in R_0. Register R_0 is incremented and tested by the INC and CMP instructions at the end of the program. If i is less than n, the loop is repeated; otherwise, the program is finished. Three machine instructions, INC, CMP, and BLT, are required to implement loop termination control for each loop.

$\qquad$ Next, consider the way in which array elements are addressed. Recall that the arrays are stored in the main memory in column order. The byte address of element (i, j) of an array, relative to the address of the first element, is given by the expression $2(n \times j + i)$, where the factor of 2 is required because each word element consists of 2 bytes. For example, suppose $n = 10$. Then element $C(5,3)$ is stored at main memory location C + 2(10 × 3 + 5) = C + 70. In the first part of the program, four instructions compute the address of $C(i,j)$ relative to C. Note that an arithmetic left-shift instruction is used to perform multiplication by 2. Similar four-instruction sequences are used to compute the addresses of $A(i,k)$ and $B(k,j)$.

Some general observations can now be made about the PDP-11 implementation of the matrix multiplication operation. Loop termination control consists of the following functions. The loop control variable is incremented, and its new value is compared to the upper limit. If the upper limit has not been exceeded, a branch back to the beginning of the loop is taken; otherwise, the loop has been completed, and execution of the next part of the program proceeds. Note that individual instructions are used for each of these functions in the program of Figure 3.4. The calculation of the address of an array element from its two subscripts is done by a sequence of four instructions. Clearly, it would be useful if the instruction set allowed a more concise implementation for such tasks.

In the preceding example, the array elements were assumed to be 16-bit numbers. Suppose we wish to solve the same problem with larger integers. The program would become much more complex because multiple words are needed to represent the larger numbers. A sequence of instructions is required to generate partial products and handle the associated carries so that multiple-word products can be accumulated. An analogous task involving floating-point numbers is even more difficult.

This discussion of the implementation of matrix multiplication on a short word-length computer suggests three requirements that instruction sets of larger computers should satisfy if they are to facilitate the implementation of high-level language programs more directly.

The first and most obvious requirement is to provide support for a number of *data types*. By data types we mean integers, floating-point numbers, and character strings for the representation of names and text. In addition to the usual binary number representation schemes, it is also very useful in business applications to have a direct representation for decimal numbers. Two important aspects of numeric data types must be considered. First, the size of numbers that can be handled must encompass the range of values encountered in scientific and business calculations. Second, the instruction set must include instructions for each of the basic arithmetic operations on each number type. In the case of character strings, the instruction set should facilitate common operations such as translation between different character representations.

The second requirement is to include addressing modes and possibly even some specialized instructions to handle arrays. In this respect, a basic task is the calculation of main memory addresses of multidimensional array elements from their subscripts.

Finally, it would be convenient to have the three operations involved in loop termination control — loop-control variable manipulation, testing, and branching — provided in a single instruction.

We have considered only a few specific examples of the ways in which machine instruction sets can support high-level languages. Other features are also useful, such as

- Efficient procedure (subroutine) call instructions, including parameter passing and register save and restore operations
- Efficient representation and manipulation of stacks for the support of nested procedure calls
- Implementation of common tasks in single instructions, such as searching for a given pattern in a string of characters

The machines discussed in this chapter provide examples of support for such features.

3.4 THE VAX-11

The VAX-11 is a 32-bit computer. All addresses and data paths are 32 bits wide, and the main memory space is byte-addressable. A 32-bit address reaches a total of 2^{32} bytes (4 gigabytes), which is more than adequate for most programming tasks; indeed, the physical main memory provided in most implementations of the VAX-11 is considerably smaller. The mechanisms for mapping from the large programmer space provided by 32-bit addresses to a smaller physical memory space will be discussed in Chapter 8.

There are sixteen 32-bit CPU registers named R_0 through R_{15}. Registers R_0 through R_{11} are general-purpose registers that can be used to hold data or addresses. Register R_{14} is the stack pointer (SP) and R_{15} is the program counter (PC). Registers R_{12} and R_{13} have special roles in conjunction with handling procedure calls and parameter passing. Their use will be discussed later.

The VAX-11 supports many different data types. Signed integers in byte, word (2 bytes), long-word (4 bytes), and quad-word (8 bytes) sizes are handled by the instruction set. Floating-point numbers in both long-word and quad-word sizes are also included. All of these numeric data types can be stored in the main memory beginning at an arbitrary byte address. There are no word, long-word, or quad-word boundary restrictions on the location of the multiple-byte types. Some typical examples are shown in Figure 3.5. Note that the least significant byte of multiple-byte integers is stored in the lowest address location. Other formats are provided for representing binary-coded decimal (BCD) numbers, character strings, and bit strings.

The instruction set in the VAX-11 is extensive in comparison with the PDP-11. Numerous instructions are provided for operating directly on the various data types. In addition to the basic instructions, which include arithmetic and logic operations, tests, branches, and subroutine calls, a number of more complex machine instructions facilitate the implementation of high-level language constructs. Some specific examples, including those related to the matrix multiplication task of Figure 3.3, will be discussed in Section 3.4.3.

The addressing modes provided in the VAX-11 include the PDP-11 modes and other modes for efficient access to data arrays and compact representation for short immediate data.

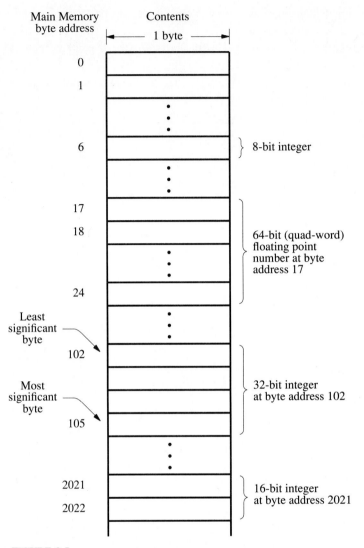

FIGURE 3.5
Examples of numeric data types in the VAX-11.

3.4.1   Instruction Formats

Instructions in the VAX-11 consist of a variable number of bytes and can begin at any byte address. The operation code (OP code) is contained in the first byte of an instruction, and the addressing information needed to access operands is placed in the bytes that follow. The term *operand specifier* is used to refer to the addressing information for an individual operand.

The general format of a single-operand instruction is shown in Figure 3.6a. The operand specifier consists of one or more bytes. Although most specifiers require one

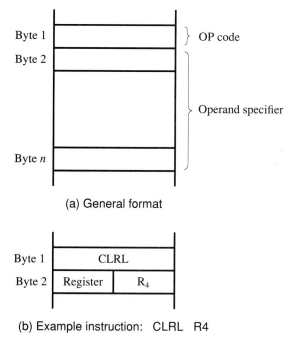

(a) General format

Byte 1 | CLRL
Byte 2 | Register | R$_4$

(b) Example instruction: CLRL   R4

FIGURE 3.6
VAX-11 one-operand instruction format.

to five bytes, up to ten bytes may be needed. A simple example of a one-operand in-struction that requires only one byte for the operand specifier is a Clear Long-word in-struction that clears the contents of register R$_4$. It is written in assembler notation as

CLRL   R4

The representation of this instruction in the main memory is shown in Figure 3.6b. Note that the instruction details are given as a vertical listing of its individual byte contents. This style is particularly convenient when two or more operand specifiers are involved. Full details on the format of an operand specifier, including the addressing modes available, are given in the next subsection.

The general multiple-operand instruction format is shown in Figure 3.7. Instruc-tions with up to six operands are included in the VAX-11 instruction set. Consider an example of a three-operand instruction that adds the words (2 bytes each) at main memory locations LOC1 and LOC2 and places their sum in the low-order half of register R$_0$. It is written in assembler notation as

ADDW3   LOC1,LOC2,R0

The fact that this is a three-operand operation involving 16-bit words is specified in the OP code by the descriptors 3 and W. As we shall see later in the discussion of addressing modes, each of the first two operand specifiers in this instruction requires several bytes for its representation.

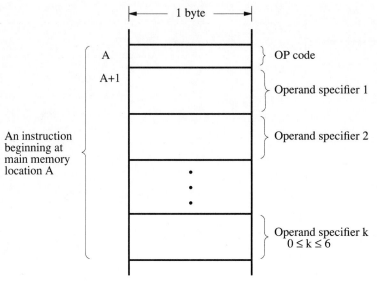

FIGURE 3.7
VAX-11 general instruction format.

3.4.2 Addressing Modes

We will now discuss the addressing modes used in the VAX-11. A 32-bit address is needed to specify the location of a main memory operand, and this address may be contained in a CPU register or in the instruction itself. Operands may also be held in CPU registers or included as immediate data directly in an instruction. In addition to these basic modes, the VAX-11 includes a very flexible index mode. It facilitates access to elements of data arrays in a way that is compatible with the use of subscripts in high-level languages.

Each operand specifier in an instruction begins with a mode byte whose bit format is shown in Figure 3.8. The high-order half, bits b_7 through b_4, specifies the mode. A CPU register is usually involved in the generation of the address of the operand. The register, one of R_1 through R_{15}, is specified in the low-order four bits of the mode byte.

A complete listing of the VAX-11 addressing modes is given in Tables 3.1 and 3.2. Modes 5 through 9, including the cases where R_n = PC in modes 8 and 9, are the same as the modes with the corresponding names in the PDP-11 (see Tables 2.1 and 2.2 in Chapter 2). Two examples of the use of these modes are given in Figure 3.9. The first example uses the autoincrement mode. The register that contains the

Mode			R_n		
7	6	5	4	3	2	1	0

FIGURE 3.8
Operand specifier mode byte in the VAX-11.

TABLE 3.1 VAX-11 addressing modes

$b_7\,b_6\,b_5\,b_4$	Decimal equivalent	Name	Assembler syntax	Meaning
0 0 X X	"0"	Literal	S↑#Value	Bits b_{5-0} of mode byte specify operand
0 1 0 0	4	Index	$\left\{\begin{array}{l}\text{Indexable}\\\text{mode}\end{array}\right\}$[Ri]*	$A_{\text{effective}} = A + k \times [R_i]$, where A is generated by the indexable mode, and k is determined by the operand length in bytes
0 1 0 1	5	Register	Rn	$A_{\text{effective}} = R_n$
0 1 1 0	6	Register indirect	(Rn)	$A_{\text{effective}} = [R_n]$
0 1 1 1	7	Autodecrement	–(Rn)	Decrement R_n; $A_{\text{effective}} = [R_n]$
1 0 0 0	8	Autoincrement	(Rn)+	$A_{\text{effective}} = [R_n]$; Increment R_n
1 0 0 1	9	Autoincrement indirect	@(Rn)	$A_{\text{effective}} = [[R_n]]$; Increment R_n
1 0 1 0 1 1 0 0 1 1 1 0	10 12 14	Displacement	$\left\{\begin{array}{l}\text{B↑}\\\text{W↑}\\\text{L↑}\end{array}\right\}$D(Rn)	$A_{\text{effective}} = D + [R_n]$
1 0 1 1 1 1 0 1 1 1 1 1	11 13 15	Displacement indirect	@$\left\{\begin{array}{l}\text{B↑}\\\text{W↑}\\\text{L↑}\end{array}\right\}$D(Rn)	$A_{\text{effective}} = [D + [R_n]]$

*The indexable modes are modes 6 through 15.
  R_i = R0, R1, ..., R14.

address of the operand is R_9. In this case, no other bytes are needed in the operand specifier. The instruction clears the long word at the memory location specified in R_9. R_9 is then incremented by four because the operand is four bytes long. The second example, shown in Figure 3.9*b*, involves a Move-byte (MOVB) instruction that uses the immediate mode to specify the first operand and the register mode to specify the second operand. This instruction moves the value 53, which is stored in the byte immediately following the mode byte in the first operand specifier, into register R_2. The symbol I↑, which precedes the immediate data specification #53, is an example of a general prefix that consists of a single letter followed by ↑. The letter is used

TABLE 3.2 VAX-11 addressing modes with R_n = PC (R_{15})

$b_7\,b_6\,b_5\,b_4$	Decimal equivalent	Name	Assembler syntax	Meaning
1 0 0 0	8	Immediate (autoincrement)	I↑#Value	$A_{effective} = [PC]$; Increment PC
1 0 0 1	9	Absolute (autoincrement indirect)	@#A	$A_{effective} = [[PC]] = A$; $PC \leftarrow [PC] + 4$
1 0 1 0 1 1 0 0 1 1 1 0	10 12 14	Relative (displacement)	$\left.\begin{array}{c} B\uparrow \\ W\uparrow \\ L\uparrow \end{array}\right\} A$	$A_{effective} = D + [PC] = A$
1 0 1 1 1 1 0 1 1 1 1 1	11 13 15	Relative indirect (displacement indirect)	$@\left\{\begin{array}{c} B\uparrow \\ W\uparrow \\ L\uparrow \end{array}\right\} A$	$A_{effective} = [D + [PC]] = [A]$

to describe the length of the immediate operand or address displacement (described below) that is contained in the operand specifier.

The displacement and displacement indirect modes (numbered 10 through 15) are functionally the same as the index and index indirect modes in the PDP-11. The 16-bit index value X in the PDP-11 modes (see Table 2.1) is replaced by a displacement D. The value D may be a byte, word, or long word, denoted by the prefixes B↑, W↑, or L↑, respectively. When R_n = PC in the displacement modes, the resulting relative modes are the same as the relative modes in the PDP-11.

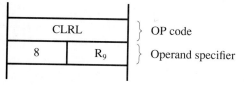

(a) CLRL (R9)+

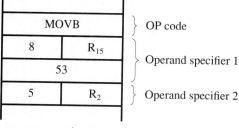

(b) MOVB I↑#53,R2

FIGURE 3.9
VAX-11 addressing mode examples.

Examples of the use of displacement and relative indirect modes are shown in Figure 3.10. The byte displacement mode is used in the Clear-word (CLRW) instruction in part (a) of the figure. In part (b), the relative indirect mode in the Move Long-word (MOVL) instruction generates the effective address 200. The four bytes starting at this location are moved into register R_0. In the example depicted in the figure, the value of this long word is -327. The instruction begins at byte address 1000. The PC has been incremented to contain the value 1004 at the time that the displacement value 1146 is added to it to generate the address 2150. This is the address POINTER. The effective address, $A_{effective}$, is the 32-bit value 200 stored at location POINTER. Note that the name POINTER is used in the instruction. The assembler program computes the displacement value 1146 at assembly time. The instruction

$$\text{MOVL} \qquad @W\uparrow1146(R15),R0$$

is equivalent to the instruction shown in the figure.

It should now be apparent that the functional capability of the PDP-11 addressing modes is included in the corresponding modes of the VAX-11. The one exception is that the VAX-11 does not have the autodecrement indirect mode. Experience with PDP-11 programs has shown that this is not a very useful mode. The two VAX-11 modes that remain to be described are the literal and index modes. Both of them are motivated by high-level language considerations.

The literal mode provides for a short, 6-bit, unsigned integer to be included as an immediate data operand directly in the mode byte itself. Many studies have indicated that small constants appear quite often in a wide variety of application programs. Therefore, their inclusion in a 1-byte operand specifier should lead to reduced program storage space and improved execution time. Longer constants can be specified by the immediate mode discussed earlier. The literal mode is indicated by setting the leftmost two bits of the mode byte to 0. The next 2 bits of the mode field, b_5 and b_4, along with bits b_3 through b_0, are used to specify the 6-bit immediate value. No register is involved in this mode. The decimal equivalent of the 4-bit mode field value thus varies from 0 to 3 in the literal mode, depending upon the high-order 2 bits of the constant being represented. We have simply shown the decimal equivalent of this mode as "0" in Table 3.1. The constant is represented by "Value" in the table, preceded by the # sign. The prefix $S\uparrow$ indicates that short immediate data are to be used (the literal mode) to distinguish it from the immediate mode indicated by the $I\uparrow$ prefix, which is used for longer immediate data.

Figure 3.11 shows the use of the literal mode in loading the value 23 into register R_1. Because a Move Long-word instruction is used, the 6-bit operand is padded out with zeroes to the left to form a 32-bit value, which is then loaded into R_1. It should be noted that short, floating-point constants can also be represented in the 6-bit data field of the literal mode. The OP code determines how the field is to be interpreted.

The VAX-11 index mode is intended for accessing individual elements in an array of fixed-length data elements. Suppose an array of integers is stored in consecutive main memory locations beginning at location ARRAY. In a high-level language program, the array elements may be referenced as ARRAY(0), ARRAY(1),

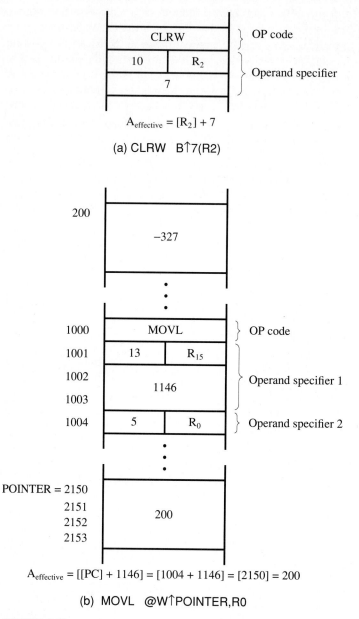

$A_{\text{effective}} = [R_2] + 7$

(a) CLRW B↑7(R2)

$A_{\text{effective}} = [[PC] + 1146] = [1004 + 1146] = [2150] = 200$

(b) MOVL @W↑POINTER,R0

FIGURE 3.10
VAX-11 displacement addressing mode examples.

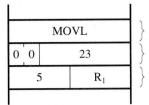

MOVL S↑#23,R1

FIGURE 3.11
VAX-11 literal mode example.

and so on. In machine instructions that refer to these elements, it is convenient if the starting address ARRAY can be specified in any of the usual addressing modes. Some simple way is then needed to specify the subscript. A CPU register R_i can be used for this purpose. If the OP code specifies the length of any array element, then the actual address of the desired element can be computed during instruction execution. For example, if the elements are 4-byte integers in a byte-addressable machine, then the address of ARRAY(j) is computed as ARRAY $+ [R_i] \times 4$, where $[R_i] = j$. This is how the VAX-11 index mode is used.

The VAX-11 index mode is named in the first byte of an operand specifier. This byte also specifies a register R_i, $0 \le i \le 14$, to be used as the index register. The index mode is always used in conjunction with another addressing mode, which can be any of the modes 6 through 15, and it is named in the second byte of the operand specifier. Suppose that this mode specifies the main memory address LOC. If the instruction OP code indicates that the operand length is n bytes, then the address generated by the complete operand specifier is

$$A_{\text{effective}} = \text{LOC} + [R_i] \times n$$

An example using the index mode is shown in Figure 3.12. A Clear-word instruction is used to clear the fourth element of a one-dimensional array whose first element is stored at main memory location ARRAY. The subscript defining the element to be cleared is stored in register R_6. The index mode is indicated by the code 4 in the first byte of the operand specifier, which also names R_6 as the index register. The address ARRAY $= 1050$ is generated by the relative mode with a byte displacement of 46 added to the current PC value of 1004. The subscript value 3 (specifying the fourth element) in register R_6 is multiplied by 2 because the OP code specifies that word data is involved. The value 1056 is thus generated as the address of the word to be cleared.

As a further example of the usefulness of the VAX-11 index mode, let us suppose that the address 200 in location POINTER in Figure 3.10b is the starting address of an array of long-word integers. If register R_0 is used to hold an index into this array, then the address specification @POINTER[R0] can be used to access individual array elements. This is an example of an addressing mode in which indexing is applied after indirection. Such a technique is useful in accessing an array whose starting address (200 in our example) is stored in the main memory. This is the case if one routine passes the starting address of an array to other routines as a parameter through a designated memory location (POINTER in our example). Note that this

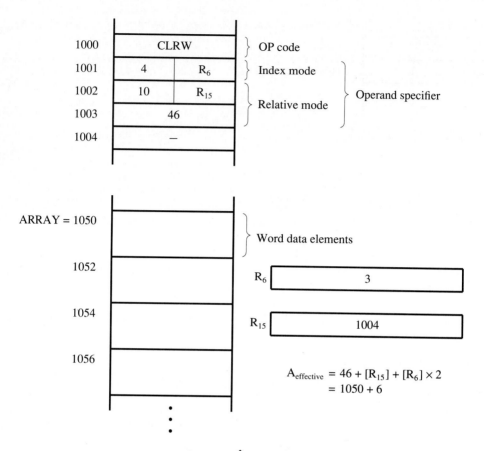

CLRW B↑ARRAY[R6]

FIGURE 3.12
VAX-11 index mode example.

style of addressing is not available in the PDP-11, where indirection is applied after indexing in the index indirect mode.

3.4.3 Instructions

The general format of VAX-11 instructions has already been discussed in Section 3.4.1. The instruction set is large, using most of the available 256 codes provided by the 8-bit OP code in the first byte of each instruction. In addition to the usual operations found in most computers, such as arithmetic and logic operations, data transfers, tests, and branches, the VAX-11 instruction set contains a number of more complex instructions. These instructions are intended to facilitate implementation of basic constructs that are common in high-level languages. This section will discuss examples of complex instructions as well as the usual, simpler instructions.

ARITHMETIC AND LOGIC. The operations of addition, subtraction, multiplication, and division are available for byte, word, and long-word integers, and also for long-word and quad-word floating-point numbers. Each operation is provided in both two- and three-operand formats. An example of the two-operand format is the instruction

$$\text{ADDW2} \qquad \text{op1,op2}$$

This instruction performs the operation

$$\text{op2} \leftarrow [\text{op1}] + [\text{op2}]$$

The three-operand format implements the three-address instructions discussed in Section 2.3. For example, the instruction

$$\text{ADDW3} \qquad \text{op1,op2,op3}$$

performs the operation

$$\text{op3} \leftarrow [\text{op1}] + [\text{op2}]$$

Note that the combination of the four basic arithmetic operations, five data types, and two formats uses 40 of the 256 available OP codes.

In addition to providing for the standard operations on integer and floating-point numbers in binary representations, the VAX-11 instruction set includes arithmetic operations on signed integers in packed decimal representation, which are useful in business applications. In this representation, decimal digits are stored in consecutive 4-bit fields, two per byte, with high-order digits first. An instruction referring to such a number must specify the address of the high-order byte and the length (in digits) of the number.

A full range of logical operations in both two- and three-operand formats is available.

DATA TRANSFERS AND CONVERSIONS. Move instructions are used to transfer operands between CPU registers and the main memory or from one area of the main memory to another. In any computer that supports a large number of data types, it is convenient, if not essential, to support conversions between the data types directly in the instruction set. The VAX-11 does this. For example, it implements conversions from integer to floating-point format and vice versa.

TESTS AND BRANCHES. Comparisons between two operands and tests on individual operands are used to set condition codes so that data-dependent branching can be done. A full set of conditional branches is included in the instruction set. An 8-bit signed offset value follows the OP-code byte in the simplest form of a conditional branch instruction. Since such instructions allow branching only within a limited range, they are supplemented by a jump instruction that enables branching to any location in the address space. Some specialized instructions combine counter manipulation, testing, and branching operations, which make them convenient for loop termination control.

MORE POWERFUL INSTRUCTIONS. The VAX-11 has a number of instructions that are considerably more powerful than the types of instructions found in PDP-11 computers. These instructions implement sequences of simple machine operations that occur as common high-level language operations. Typical examples are calculations involving array subscripts and procedure calls that pass parameters on a stack. We will discuss a few of these instructions because they are representative of instruction sets in modern computers that have been designed with high-level languages in mind.

Loop termination. The VAX-11 has a three-operand instruction AOBLEQ (Add One and Branch on Less than or EQual) that is useful for loop-termination control. It increments the loop-control variable, compares it to a specified upper limit, and branches to the beginning of the loop if the limit has not been exceeded. The first operand specifies the upper limit, the second names the loop-control variable, and the third operand is the branch offset. Versions of this instruction that allow options such as decrementing the loop-control variable and using different termination conditions are also available.

Case structure. A number of programming languages use a Case structure that consists of blocks of instructions. The first statement in the structure is the Case statement, which names a Case variable. The value of the Case variable determines which block is to be executed.

In the VAX-11, a three-operand instruction with the OP code CASE is provided. The operands specify the Case variable and its range. Address displacements to the beginning of the blocks are placed immediately after the CASE instruction. Execution of this instruction causes a branch to the beginning of the block selected by the Case variable.

Array indexing. Multidimensional arrays are commonly used data structures. The j'th element in the i'th row in a two-dimensional array might be referenced as ARRAY(i,j). Suppose the array is placed in the main memory in column order with the first element, ARRAY(0,0), in memory location ARRAY. Then, the element ARRAY(i,j) is found at memory location

$$\text{ARRAY} + j \times m + i$$

where m is the number of rows (that is, the number of elements in each column). The index expression added to ARRAY is called an address polynomial. Generalizing to three dimensions with the use of a third subscript, k, we have the address polynomial

$$k \times n \times m + j \times m + i$$

where n is the number of columns.

A more convenient computational form for the three-dimensional array address polynomial is

$$((k \times n) + j)m + i$$

This form leads to an iterative calculation in which each individual step is: "add next subscript to the incoming accumulated index value and multiply by size." A VAX-11 instruction, with the OP code INDEX, is provided for this basic step. It has six operands:

Operand 1	subscript
Operand 2	low limit
Operand 3	high limit
Operand 4	size
Operand 5	incoming accumulated index value
Operand 6	outgoing accumulated index value

The operation of this instruction is as follows. The subscript value is checked to verify that it is in the range defined by the low and high limits; if it is not, an error condition is indicated. Otherwise, the subscript value is added to the incoming accumulated index value and multiplied by the size operand. The result is placed in the outgoing accumulated index value location.

Consider a three-dimensional array $ARRAY(i,j,k)$, where each element is a word and the subscripts range from 0 to $m - 1$, $n - 1$, and $p - 1$, respectively. Let R_0 be used to accumulate the index value. The operation $ARRAY(i, j, k) \leftarrow 250$ can be implemented by the instruction sequence

```
INDEX    K,#0,#p−1,#n,#0,R0
INDEX    J,#0,#n−1,#m,R0,R0
INDEX    I,#0,#m−1,#1,R0,R0
MOVW     #250,ARRAY[R0]
```

It is easy to use the INDEX instruction in cases where the lower and upper limits are more general.

Procedure calls. The efficiency of executing procedure calls is an important factor in evaluating the instruction set of a computer. The reason is that modern programming style emphasizes the use of procedures in organizing large programs into smaller, more manageable units that can be easily understood.

Two important aspects of executing procedure calls are (1) the way in which parameters are passed from the calling program to the called procedure and (2) the way in which CPU register contents are saved on entry to the called procedure and restored on return to the calling program. The VAX-11 allows two methods for handling procedure calls. They differ in the way in which parameters are passed. In the first method, parameters are placed in a main memory block, and a pointer to this block is named in the Procedure-call instruction. In the second method, parameters are passed via the processor stack. We will describe this second method in more detail.

The sequence of operations in calling a procedure is as follows. First the parameters are pushed onto the stack. Then, the Procedure-call instruction is executed.

This instruction saves the contents of the CPU registers used by the procedure on the stack. The old PC and PSW values are then pushed onto the stack, and a branch is executed to the first instruction of the procedure. When execution of the procedure is completed, the Return instruction reverses the above sequence of steps by restoring the saved state of the CPU and eliminating the parameters from the stack. The saved state consists of all CPU registers saved on the stack.

A number of details have been omitted from the above general description of the VAX-11 Procedure-call and Return instructions. In order to describe the complete process, it is necessary to introduce the use of registers R_{12} and R_{13} into the discussion. Register R_{12} is the argument pointer (AP) and R_{13} is the frame pointer (FP). The AP register is used as a pointer to the parameter list, and the FP register is used as a pointer to the saved state, called a frame in the VAX-11 literature. The parameter list and the saved state are blocks of long words stored on the stack. The AP and FP registers are set as part of the execution of the Procedure-call instruction. Since the old contents of these two registers are a part of the saved state, nesting of procedure calls is possible.

The Procedure-call instruction CALLS has two operands. The first operand, n, specifies the number of long-word parameters that were previously pushed onto the stack. The second operand is the address of the called procedure. After execution of the instruction

$$\text{CALLS} \qquad \text{\#n,PROC}$$

the stack contents are as shown in Figure 3.13. The AP and FP registers have been loaded with the addresses of the beginning of the parameter list and frame, respectively, and the value n has been placed at the beginning of the parameter list. It is used during the execution of the Return instruction in eliminating the parameters from the stack. The long word 0 at the beginning of the frame is a reserved space used under some special conditions.

The first word of the called procedure is a register mask that specifies the CPU registers to be used by the procedure. If bit b_i of the mask is 1, then register R_i will be used and its old contents will be saved on the stack. This mask is pushed onto the stack so that the CPU can determine which registers should be restored from the stack during execution of the Return instruction.

During execution of the called procedure, the n parameters on the stack will be accessed and used according to the calculation to be performed by the procedure. In order to further illustrate the flexibility of the VAX-11 addressing modes, we will briefly consider how parameters are accessed by the called procedure through the AP register, R_{12}. Suppose PARAM2, the second parameter in the list shown in Figure 3.13, is an operand that is to be moved into register R_0. Because each parameter is a long word, the displacement of the address of PARAM2 from the address in AP is 8. Thus, the instruction

$$\text{MOVL} \qquad \text{8(AP),R0}$$

will achieve the desired operation. If PARAM2 is the address of the operand, the operand can be accessed using the addressing mode @8(AP). Finally, if PARAM2 is the starting address of an array, the ith item of this array can be addressed by

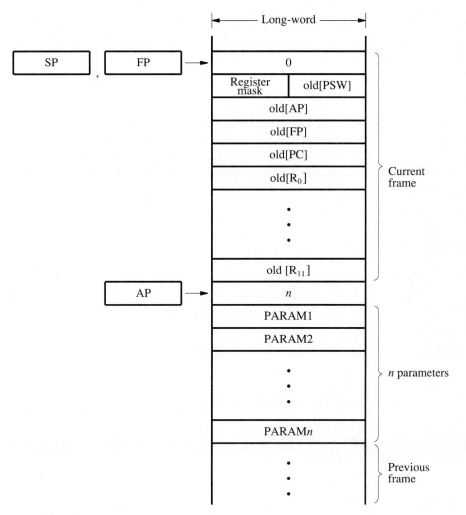

FIGURE 3.13
VAX-11 stack after execution of   CALLS #n,PROC.

@8(AP)[Rj]. In this case, the offset i is the content of index register R_j. This last possibility illustrates the usefulness of an addressing mode that involves two registers (AP and R_j) and shows the motivation for performing indexing after indirection.

When execution of the called procedure is completed, the frame information on the stack is used to restore the contents of the CPU registers. Note that restoring AP and FP returns the CPU to the previous procedure.

3.4.4 Programming Examples

This section discusses two VAX-11 programs that illustrate the instructions and the addressing modes in the context of sorting and matrix multiplication.

BYTE SORTING. A byte-sorting routine for the PDP-11 was discussed in Section 2.6.6. A list of unsigned byte integers is stored in the main memory, beginning at location LIST. The number of bytes in the list is n, and the bytes are to be sorted in increasing numerical order.

A VAX-11 program for this task that corresponds to the PDP-11 program in Figure 2.21 is shown in Figure 3.14. The first two instructions of the VAX-11 program initialize the j and k loop-control variables stored in registers R_1 and R_2. The next five instructions perform the basic sorting step of comparing two entries and interchanging them if necessary. Note that the Compare and Move instructions use the index mode in selecting list elements. In each case, the other mode used to generate the address LIST is the relative mode. Finally, the single instruction AOBLEQ is used to terminate each loop. This contrasts with the Increment, Compare, and Branch instruction sequence used in the PDP-11 program.

MATRIX MULTIPLICATION. A Pascal-like program for multiplication of two $n \times n$ matrices A and B was given in Figure 3.3, with a PDP-11 implementation in Figure 3.4. Recall that the array entries are assumed to consist of 16-bit integers.

A VAX-11 program that accomplishes the same task under the same conditions is shown in Figure 3.15. This program has the same structure as the PDP-11 program. Registers R_0 through R_5 are used the same way in both programs. The INDEX and AOBLSS instructions in the VAX-11 reduce the number of machine instructions required. A pair of INDEX instructions, for example, replaces four PDP-11 instructions in the calculation of each array index.

An obvious advantage of the availability of powerful instructions is that it simplifies the implementation of common programming constructs.

	CLRL	R1	Initialize outer loop-control variable j to 0 in R_1.
OUTER:	ADDL3	S↑#1,R1,R2	Initialize inner loop-control variable k to j + 1 in R_2.
INNER:	CMPB	LIST[R1],LIST[R2]	Compare LIST(j) to LIST(k) and interchange if LIST(j)>LIST(k).
	BLEQU	ENDINNER	
	MOVB	LIST[R1],R3	
	MOVB	LIST[R2],LIST[R1]	
	MOVB	R3,LIST[R2]	
ENDINNER:	AOBLEQ	#n−1,R2,INNER	Increment k and branch back if k ≤ n −1.
	AOBLEQ	#n−2,R1,OUTER	Increment j and branch back if j ≤ n −2.

FIGURE 3.14
VAX-11 byte-sorting program.

	MOVL	N,R6	Load high limit of array
	DECL	R6	subscripts into R_6.
	CLRL	R0	i and j loop-control variables
LOOPI:	CLRL	R2	initialized to 0 in R_0 and R_2.
LOOPJ:	INDEX	R2,#0,R6,N,#0,R1	Compute relative address of
	INDEX	R0,#0,R6,#1,R1,R1	C(i,j) in R_1.
	CLRW	C[R1]	Clear C(i,j).
	CLRL	R4	k loop variable set to 0 in R_4.
LOOPK:	INDEX	R4,#0,R6,N,#0,R3	Compute relative address of
	INDEX	R0,#0,R6,#1,R3,R3	A(i,k) in R_3.
	MOVW	A[R3],R3	Move A(i,k) into R_3.
	INDEX	R2,#0,R6,N,#0,R5	Compute relative address of
	INDEX	R4,#0,R6,#1,R5,R5	B(k,j) in R_5.
	MULW2	B[R5],R3	$R_3 \leftarrow A(i,k) \times B(k,j)$.
	ADDW2	R3,C(R1)	$C(i,j) \leftarrow C(i,j) + [R_3]$.
	AOBLSS	N,R4,LOOPK	Termination of k loop.
	AOBLSS	N,R2,LOOPJ	Termination of j loop.
	AOBLSS	N,R0,LOOPI	Termination of i loop.

FIGURE 3.15
Matrix multiplication in a VAX-11.

3.5 THE IBM 370

Mid-size computers like the VAX-11 and large computers like those at the upper end of the IBM 370 line are characterized by a large main memory space, an extensive repertoire of instructions, fast operations, and considerable cost. All these characteristics are closely linked to the fundamental design decisions that determine the word length. In the last section we discussed the 32-bit VAX-11 computer in some detail. In this section we will briefly discuss some of the instruction set and addressing mode aspects of the IBM 370 family of computers, which also has a 32-bit word length.

Let us start by considering the generation of addresses for operands in the main memory. Like the VAX-11, the IBM 370 starts with the contents of some register. IBM 370 computers have sixteen 32-bit general-purpose registers that may be used for this function. Consider first a general form of indexed addressing provided by a *base register* R_b, an *index register* R_x, and an offset called a *displacement* D. The effective address of the operand then becomes

$$A_{\text{effective}} = [R_b] + D + [R_x]$$

Registers R_b and R_x can be any two of the general-purpose registers other than register 0. A zero specification for a base or index register indicates that no base or index register is involved, respectively. The value $[R_b] + D$ may be regarded as the address of the first location of an array. The contents of index register R_x represent the distance between this location and the location of the operand. This is similar to one of the index modes in the VAX-11.

An additional degree of freedom is introduced through inclusion of the base register R_b. It, in effect, serves as a second index register whose main purpose is to allow *relocatability* of programs. In a large computer, it is common to have several programs residing in the main memory at the same time. In this environment it is desirable that a program and its associated data can be moved into any available space in the memory. An effective way of doing this is to specify a base register as part of each instruction that refers to storage operands. Then, a complete program can be located anywhere in the memory and executed correctly, simply by loading an appropriate address value into the base register. The contents of the base register remain unaltered during the computation of addresses. Thus, the value of R_b needs to be set only once at the start of each program. This means that R_b must not be used by the program as a general-purpose register in a way that changes its contents.

The requirement for relocating programs implies that the base register should be involved in all addressing modes for operands in the main memory. There are situations where this may not be true. In particular, an assembly language program can be written in such a way that absolute addresses, called *address constants*, are generated at assembly and initial load time. For example, one of the ways in which a subroutine call can be implemented involves loading the absolute address of the subroutine entry point into a register. Then a Branch instruction is executed which takes the contents of that register as the destination of the branch. In this case, the program will be executed correctly only if it is loaded in the main memory area for which it was originally assembled and loaded. If the program is loaded in a different position with a different value in the base register R_b, all references to main memory that are relative to R_b will operate correctly. But absolute references, such as the subroutine entry point mentioned above, will not be handled correctly because they are not specified relative to R_b. It is possible to explicitly manipulate such absolute references in the program to take into account the contents of R_b. However, this is not a desirable programming style.

A possible solution to the above problem involving address constants is to make all memory references relative to the contents of the base register. All programs in a computer that uses this approach will be relocatable. In this case, the programmer has no need to access the contents of the base register. In fact, it should not be permissible to include user instructions which access that register. Many computers incorporate mechanisms to enforce such restrictions. This stops users from accidentally or intentionally damaging other users' programs.

Another possible way to handle address constants is to adjust their values every time the program is loaded into a new position in the main memory. This is usually implemented by a program called a relocating loader. A more elegant solution to the relocatability problem is provided in computer systems that have a virtual memory feature. This topic will be treated in detail in Chapter 8.

The preceding discussion indicates that 8 bits are needed to specify R_b and R_x. The displacement D is allocated 12 bits. Another design decision resulted in a fixed OP-code field of 8 bits for all instructions, which allows 256 distinct functions to be indicated $(256 = 2^8)$. This means that in a two-operand instruction in which one operand is to be specified in the index address mode, a total of 28 bits must be dedicated to this operand and the OP code. Therefore, if the instruction is to fit within a 32-bit word, the second operand must be in one of the registers. This corresponds to the RX (register and indexed storage) format shown in Figure 3.16.

If we accept the base register as a desirable part of all memory reference address modes, it follows that the simplest and most direct access mode will involve R_b and D, where $A_{effective} = [R_b] + D$. This requires a total of 16 bits. Since an 8-bit OP code is also part of each instruction, there are 8 bits left that can be used to specify a second operand or some control information. Figure 3.16 shows two ways of assigning these bits. In the SI (immediate data and storage) format they are used as immediate data. We should reemphasize that immediate data must be an integral part of the instruction. It is not a significant drawback for the immediate operands to

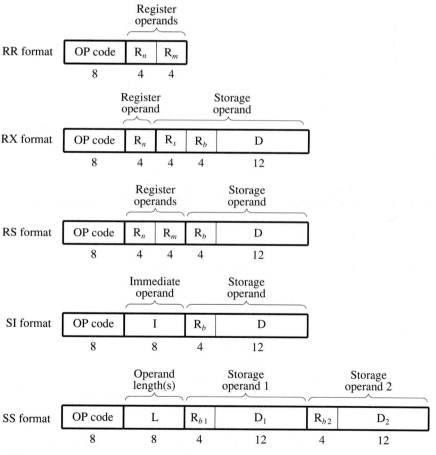

FIGURE 3.16
Instruction formats in IBM 370 computers.

have only 8 bits, because in many cases such operands are characters or small number constants that can fit in the available 8-bit space. The RS (register and storage) format makes use of the same field to specify two general-purpose registers. These registers, R_n and R_m, indicate the range of the registers to be affected by the instruction. In the case of a Load Multiple instruction, for example, registers are loaded from the main memory location given by the storage operand field. The registers are loaded in ascending order starting with the register specified in the R_n field and ending with the register specified as R_m. This illustrates the most general application of the RS format, but instructions in this group are rather diverse in nature.

Having presented the instruction formats that use 32-bit words, we should consider other instruction lengths. It is quite common, for example, to have two-operand instructions in which both operands are in registers. Such an instruction can be specified using an 8-bit OP code and 4 bits for each of the registers, as shown in the RR (register to register) format in Figure 3.16.

At the other extreme, it is desirable to have two-operand instructions in which both operands are in the main memory. This implies the existence of two address fields, each consisting of a base register and a displacement field. Thus, at least 40 bits must be available for the address fields and the OP code. Clearly, instructions of this type cannot fit into a single word. This may be solved by extending the instruction and using the SS (storage to storage) format shown in Figure 3.16. The L field is introduced to allow specification of operand length. An instruction of this type, for example, may be used to move character strings of up to 256 bytes in length from the memory location specified as the second operand to the location specified as the first operand.

These five formats constitute the full set of instruction formats used in IBM 370 computers. The instructions have variable lengths that require 2, 4, or 6 bytes. The 8-bit OP-code field provides sufficient bit space to implement a versatile set of instructions including a full set of decimal and floating-point operations. Decimal operations are particularly useful in business data processing applications.

Comparing the IBM 370 instruction set to that of the PDP-11, we can observe some interesting differences. The IBM 370 set benefits from longer word length, so that the instructions, except for the SS format, fit into a single 32-bit word. This means that fewer words have to be fetched from the main memory to execute comparable programs. The instruction set is extensive, and, like the instruction set in the VAX-11, it includes many powerful instructions that have no PDP-11 counterparts. For example, a single instruction in the IBM 370 machines can move a string of characters from one memory area to another. The simple mechanism for relocatability, which permits efficient implementations of multiprogram systems, gives the 370 a significant advantage. However, some interesting features of the PDP-11 and VAX-11 are completely absent in the IBM 370 machines. Indirect addressing does not exist, although indexed addressing can normally substitute for the indirect mode. There is also no equivalent to autoincrement and autodecrement address modes. As a result, stack manipulation is not as simple, and subroutine linkage is somewhat cumbersome.

3.6 THE HP3000

Section 2.9 introduced stacks as useful data structures for digital processing. It showed how a stack may be implemented in the main memory and accessed by the autoincrement and autodecrement addressing modes. This is the mechanism employed in the PDP-11 and 68000 computers. Many other computers allow similar implementations of stacks. It is a commonly used technique to dedicate one hardware register to serve as a stack pointer (SP) containing the memory address of the top word in the stack. In addition, stack instructions PUSH and POP are provided. The PUSH instruction causes data to be pushed onto the top of the stack. Conversely, the POP instruction transfers the top element on the stack into the location specified in the instruction. Both PUSH and POP instructions automatically update the contents of the SP.

The capability of establishing a stack data structure in the main memory has become a common feature in both large and small modern computers. Despite its importance, however, the stack feature is usually not the dominant characteristic of a typical computer. This leads to an interesting question. Is it worthwhile to design computers that are stack-oriented to a greater extent? Might it be advantageous to have a machine in which the stack structure is the dominant feature? A simple answer to these questions cannot be given because expert opinions lack consensus. The stack data structure naturally leads to efficient implementation of some computational tasks, and several commercially successful "stack computers" have been developed. The best known examples are Burroughs Corporation's B5500, B6500, and B6700 computers. These are large, general-purpose computers. A notable smaller stack machine is Hewlett-Packard Company's HP3000 computer.

Let us explore some possibilities for the organization of a stack computer. Its key component is the stack, which we already know can reside in the main memory. An alternative way to implement a stack is to use a set of registers. Let us assume that a stack capable of storing n-bit words is needed and that the required capacity of the stack is k words. Figure 3.17a shows a configuration in which k registers of n bits each realize the desired stack. The registers are connected so that a Push signal transfers the contents of all registers downward by one position. The contents of register i are transferred into register $i + 1$. The n-bit word is pushed onto the stack by loading it into register 0. Similarly, a Pop signal transfers the contents of all registers upward by one position. Thus, the contents of register i are transferred into register $i - 1$. The original contents of register 0 are the data popped off the stack.

Another possibility is to use n shift registers, each with a capacity of k bits, as indicated in Figure 3.17b. The shift registers must be capable of shifting their contents in either direction, one bit position at a time. Under a Push signal, the ith word in the stack, which occupies the ith bit position in all n registers, is shifted into the $(i + 1)$ position. Bit position 0 is loaded with the n-bit word that is being pushed onto the stack. A similar operation is performed under the Pop signal. In this case, the contents in bit position 0 are shifted out of the registers as the n-bit word is popped off the stack.

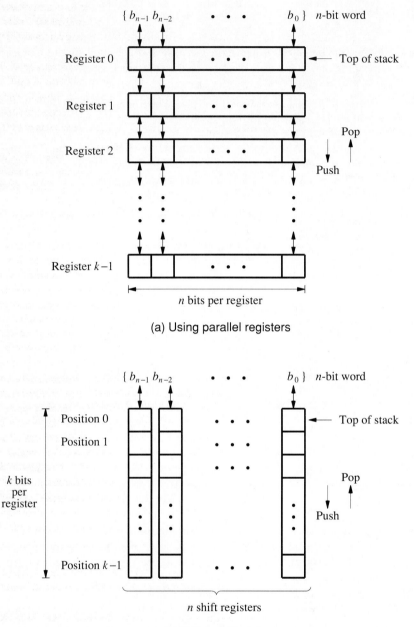

(a) Using parallel registers

(b) Using shift registers

FIGURE 3.17
Register implementation of a stack.

The main disadvantage of these schemes is the cost of the needed hardware. The stack depth k may be large ($k > 1000$), which implies the usage of either many relatively short n-bit registers or a few long shift registers.

In practice, neither of the preceding schemes has found much favor. The alternative of using the main memory to implement the stack remains the most cost-effective approach used in commercial stack computers. These machines rely heavily upon a set of hardware registers that are used as pointers to the stack in the memory. However, they do not normally contain general-purpose registers of the type found in conventional computers. To give the reader an idea of how a stack computer may be organized, we will consider a few of the features of the HP3000 computer.

3.6.1   Stack Structure of the HP3000 Computer

The HP3000 is a 16-bit computer that exhibits a number of features more often found in larger machines. However, since the aim of this section is to evaluate the stack mechanism, our discussion will concentrate only on the features that characterize the stack organization of this computer.

The main memory of the HP3000 contains program instructions and data in separate domains. Instructions and data cannot be intermixed except for immediate data that may be used in programs. Hardware registers are used as pointers to the program and data segments as shown in Figure 3.18.

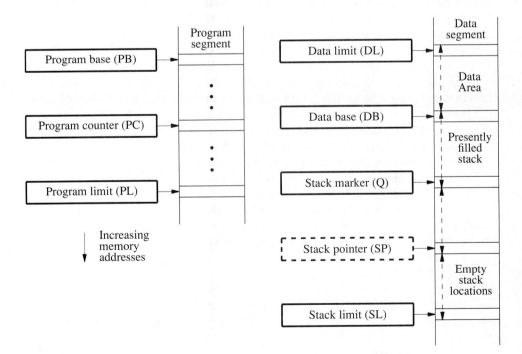

FIGURE 3.18
Program and data segment organization in the HP3000.

Three registers specify the program segment. The program base (PB) and the program limit (PL) registers indicate the memory area occupied by the program, and the program counter (PC) has the usual function of pointing to the current instruction. Each of these registers contains the appropriate 16-bit address.

The data segment is divided into two parts: the stack and the data area. Five 16-bit pointers are used to delineate and access these memory locations. The contents of the data base (DB) register denote the starting location of the stack. The stack grows in the higher-address direction. If the top element of the stack is at location i, then the next element pushed onto the stack will be at location $i + 1$. This contrasts with PDP-11 and 68000 stacks, which expand in the direction of decreasing addresses as explained in Section 2.9. The address of the top element in the stack, also called the top of stack (TOS), is stored in the 16-bit stack pointer (SP). The SP is not a single hardware register, as will be explained shortly, but it can be thought of that way. It is incremented or decremented when data elements are pushed onto or popped off the stack. From the user's point of view, it functions as any other 16-bit pointer register. The upper limit of the stack is defined by the contents of the stack limit (SL) register. Therefore, the stack is allowed to grow until [SP] = [SL]. Any attempt to extend the stack past the limits defined by DB and SL is prevented by the hardware. The data area extends from the location immediately preceding the location pointed to by the DB register to the limit specified in the data limit (DL) register.

The pointer registers specify the stack's current size, maximum size, and location in memory. The stack is thus a dynamic structure that can be easily changed. Figure 3.18 shows one other pointer that has not yet been discussed, the stack marker (Q) register, which is used to denote the starting point for the data of the current procedure. Actually, Q points to the fourth word of a four-word entry in the stack, called the stack marker, that facilitates passing control between procedures. If processing has to be suspended so that a new procedure (for example, an interrupt-handling routine) can be initiated, the machine must temporarily store the information that will be needed to allow proper return to the suspended procedure. This information is placed onto the stack in the form of a stack marker. The first word stores the current contents of an index register, and the second word contains the return address. This information is actually stored as the difference between the value in the PC, which points to the next instruction that is to be executed in the current procedure, and the contents of the PB register. Note that storing this difference, instead of storing the absolute value of the PC, allows programs to be moved out of the memory and later to be returned to a different place in the memory. Programs can therefore be dynamically relocated by changing the value in the PB register. The third word saves the status information contained in the status register, and the fourth word stores the distance between this stack marker and the one immediately preceding it. Figure 3.19 shows one stack marker that corresponds to the current procedure (Procedure$_k$) and another that is placed onto the stack when a new procedure (Procedure$_{k+1}$) is initiated. When the new procedure is completed, the machine transfers control to the previous procedure using the data in the stack marker $k + 1$. At that time, the Q register must be set to point to the fourth word of stack marker k. This is readily accomplished because the distance between the stack markers is stored as a part of each marker.

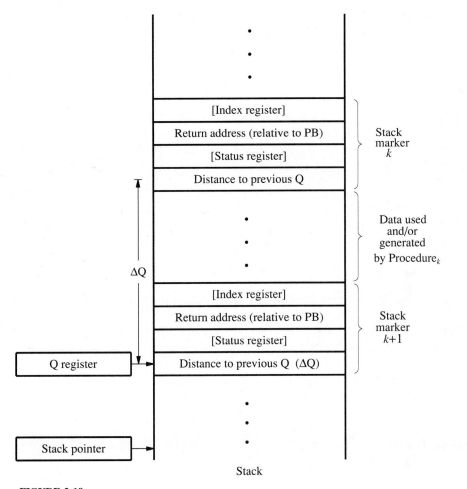

FIGURE 3.19
Stack markers in HP3000.

Also, the SP is set to point to the location immediately preceding stack marker $k + 1$. The SP, then, points to the top of the stack used by Procedure$_k$. This restores the situation that existed at the time Procedure$_{k+1}$ was invoked. This technique can be used to nest any number of procedures. Note that we have simplified our discussion by leaving out the parameter-passing protocols, which also make use of the stack.

In addition to the pointer registers, HP3000 computers have other hardware registers used to facilitate the internal organization of the machine. The only two of these that are visible to the programmer are the index and status registers, which function in essentially the same way as equivalently named registers in most other computers. We should note, however, that there are no general-purpose registers available to the programmer. Instead, data are manipulated using the stack as temporary storage, as will be shown in an example in the next section.

3.6.2 Stack Instructions in the HP3000

As a basic strategy, stack computers attempt to perform most operations on the data that occupy the top few locations of the stack. Many instructions will therefore use operands that are already in these locations. Furthermore, the results generated are left on the stack. This assumes the existence of instructions that can move data between the stack and other main memory locations.

The HP3000 has a variety of instructions that are all 16 bits long. Most of the instructions involve the stack in some way, and typically either the operands, operand addresses, or other relevant parameters reside in the stack. This allows great flexibility in using the 16-bit code space of the instructions.

There are 13 major classes of instructions. Instead of describing the full HP3000 instruction set, we will restrict our attention to the classes that illustrate the stack organization of the machine. Let us first consider the "Memory Address" instructions, whose format is shown in Figure 3.20. Eleven valuations of the 5-bit OP-code field are used to specify this class of instructions, including

LOAD	Push a specific memory word onto the stack.
STOR	Pop the top word of the stack (TOS) into a specified memory location.
ADDM	Add a specified memory word to TOS and replace the TOS operand with the resultant sum.
MPYM	Multiply a specified memory word with TOS and replace the TOS operand with the least significant word of the product.
INCM	Increment a specified memory word.

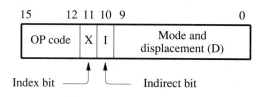

15	12 11	10 9		0
OP code	X	I	Mode and displacement (D)	

Index bit — Indirect bit

		Bit pattern	
Mode		$b_9 b_8 b_7 b_6 b_5 b_4 b_3 b_2 b_1 b_0$	Effective memory address
PC+	relative	0 0 ←—— D ——→	[PC] + D
PC–	relative	0 1 ←—— D ——→	[PC] – D
DB+	relative	1 0 ←—— D ——→	[DB] + D
Q+	relative	1 1 0 ←—— D ——→	[Q] – D
Q–	relative	1 1 1 0 ←— D ——→	[Q] – D
SP–	relative	1 1 1 1 ←— D ——→	[SP] – D

FIGURE 3.20
"Memory Address" instruction format in HP3000.

These instructions specify the memory operand in the relative address mode, in which addresses are given relative to the contents of the PC, DB, Q, or SP registers. The 10-bit mode and displacement field indicates the mode and the magnitude of the displacement as shown in the figure. Note that the range of the displacement is not the same in all modes, since the displacement field varies from 6 to 8 bits. Index and indirect bits are used to specify that indexed and/or indirect addressing are to be performed. We should mention that these are the only addressing modes that can be used to address operands in the data area of Figure 3.18.

The second class of instructions that reference either one or two memory operands are the Move instructions. These instructions can move words or bytes from one memory location to another, compare two strings of bytes in the memory, or scan a byte string until a particular byte is found. In this class of instructions, the memory addresses are again computed in the relative mode. The displacement is not given explicitly within the instruction, however, but is included as data in the stack. Moreover, the relative addresses can only be specified relative to the program or data bases (the contents of the PB or DB registers). A good example of this class of instructions is the basic MOVE instruction. It transfers k words from the source memory locations into the destination memory locations, in which

- The first stack element (TOS) specifies k.
- The contents of the second stack element give the address of the first source memory location relative to either PB or DB.
- The contents of the third stack element give the address of the first destination memory location relative to DB.

This instruction can be represented within a 16-bit code space because most of the addressing data and the length parameter are defined in implicitly specified stack locations. This data must be loaded onto the stack before instructions like MOVE can be executed.

Next, we will consider the "Stack" instructions whose format is shown in Figure 3.21. This class of instructions is identified by four 0s in the high-order bit positions. The remaining 12 bits are available to specify particular instructions and are split into two 6-bit fields, each of which may be used to specify a distinct operation. Six bits allow 64 distinct valuations, so as many as 64 distinct stack operations may be defined in this manner. This number is large enough to accommodate a variety of stack operations. An instruction specifying one stack operation uses 10 bits (main OP code plus the stack OP code A) and disregards the remaining 6 bits. However, the remaining bits may be used to specify a second stack operation (stack

15 12	11 6	5 0
0 0 0 0		

Main OP code   Stack OP code A   Stack OP code B

FIGURE 3.21
Format for "Stack" instructions in HP3000.

OP code B) that will be performed after the completion of the first operation. In this way, two stack operations may be packed within a single instruction. Such efficient utilization of the instruction code space is possible only because addressing data and operands are not included explicitly as part of an instruction.

Some examples of Stack instructions are

ADD   Add the contents of the top two words on the stack, delete them from the stack, and push the sum onto the stack.

CMP   Compare the contents of the top two words on the stack, set the condition codes accordingly, and delete both words from the stack.

DIV   Divide the integer in the second word of the stack by the integer in TOS. Replace the second word with the quotient and the word in TOS with the remainder.

DEL   Delete the top word of the stack.

Many instructions of this type are provided, although some are more complicated. A Divide Long instruction (DIVL), for example, divides a double-word integer in the second and third elements of the stack by the integer in the first element. Then, these three words are deleted, and the remainder and quotient are pushed onto the stack to become the first and second elements, respectively. We have used the term "instruction" somewhat loosely in this discussion. It would have been more rigorous to refer to Add and Divide operations, since these two operations can be specified within a single instruction. However, it is more customary to speak in terms of instructions when describing such action. Indeed, it is appropriate to describe the above technique as packing two instructions into one.

The OP-code field B for specifying a second stack operation can only be used to advantage when two consecutive stack operations are to be performed. In other cases this part of the instruction remains unused. So far we have emphasized only one advantage of compressing instructions, the low code-space requirements, but there are other benefits. Another advantage stems from the reduced number of memory accesses, because effectively, two instructions are fetched as part of one 16-bit word. Of course, we must remember that during execution of a stack instruction it is necessary to access operands in the stack, and this requires memory accesses if the stack resides in the main memory.

To illustrate the role of the stack as temporary storage for intermediate results in arithmetic processing, we can consider a simple example. Figure 3.22 shows how the arithmetic expression

$$w = (a + b)/[c/d + (e \times f)/(g + h)]$$

is evaluated. We will assume that the values of the variables $a, b, \ldots,$ and h are not available at the top of the stack. They are stored in memory locations with addresses A, B, . . . , and H, and may be accessed with the addressing mechanism given in Figure 3.20. Furthermore, let all operands be integers whose range is such that only single-length products need to be considered. The figure shows 13 processing steps that must be performed. The required operations follow the order obtained by

Step	Operation performed	Machine instruction	
1	S ← [A]	LOAD	A
2	S ← [S] + [B]	ADDM	B
3	S ← [C]	LOAD	C
4	S ← [D]	LOAD	D
5	S ← [S − 1] / [S]	DIV DEL	} combined
6	S ← [E]	LOAD	E
7	S ← [S] × [F]	MPYM	F
8	S ← [G]	LOAD	G
9	S ← [S] + [H]	ADDM	H
10	S ← [S − 1] / [S]	DIV DEL	} combined
11	S ← [S − 1] + [S]	ADD	
12	S ← [S − 1] / [S]	DIV DEL	} combined
13	W ← [S]	STOR	W

(a) Operations to be performed and the necessary machine instructions

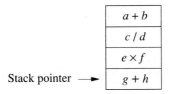

(b) Temporary results stored in the stack after step 9

FIGURE 3.22
Stack usage in processing of the expression $w = (a + b)/[c/d + (e \times f)/(g + h)]$.

scanning the expression left to right. In our notation, the top element of the stack (TOS) is denoted as S. Thus, the operation S ← [S] + [B] means that the contents of TOS and the operand B are added, and the sum replaces the value in TOS. The operation S ← [S − 1]/[S] indicates that the contents of the second element in the stack are divided by the contents of TOS. The two operands are deleted from the stack and the quotient and remainder are pushed onto the stack. The HP3000 machine instructions needed to perform the necessary computation are also shown in the figure. Their functional description was given earlier in this section. Most steps can be implemented with a single instruction except for the division operation. The DIV instruction replaces the dividend and the divisor with the quotient and the remainder, respectively. Because we are only interested in the quotient, we must use the DEL instruction to delete the remainder from the stack. Note that whenever two consecutive Stack instructions are encountered, they can be combined into one 16-bit instruction, as we explained previously. All intermediate results are stored on the stack. Figure 3.22b shows the top elements of the stack after the completion of step 9.

3.6.3 Hardware Registers in the Stack

Accessing main memory locations is one of the most critical time constraints in a computer. The time needed to read an operand from the main memory tends to be long in comparison with the time required to transfer data or perform operations within the CPU. This is the main argument for inclusion of general-purpose registers in the CPU. In the case of stack computers, the temporary storage function of the general-purpose registers is provided through the stack mechanism. If the stack is implemented strictly in the main memory, it will be necessary to make frequent memory accesses because all temporary storage locations are part of the stack. The time spent on such accesses makes it unlikely that a stack machine of this type will compare favorably with a standard computer that has a set of hardware registers for general-purpose use.

In Section 3.6 we considered the possibility of implementing the entire stack with hardware registers, but had to acknowledge that this is an expensive and somewhat inflexible approach. A compromise between the all-register and all-memory implementations of the stack is possible, however, if most of the stack is located in the main memory and its top few elements are held in hardware registers in the CPU. The time to access the stack would then be shortened because most accesses only involve the top few elements and would therefore only require register transfers within the CPU. How many registers should be provided as part of the stack? The number should clearly be small. In the HP3000 computer four registers contain the top four elements of the stack.

Including hardware registers in the stack implies that the true top of the stack (TOS) will often be one of the registers. This means that the SP does not necessarily point to a memory location. To keep track of the actual situation at any given time, the SP function is implemented by two registers. A 16-bit stack in memory (SM) register contains the address of the highest memory location presently occupied by the stack, and a 3-bit register (SR) is used to indicate whether zero, one, two, three, or four top elements of the stack are presently contained in the hardware registers. Thus, the value [SP] is

$$[SP] = [SM] + [SR]$$

The value [SP] is equal to the address in the main memory where the top element of the stack would be if all elements of the stack were in the main memory. This structure is illustrated in Figure 3.23.

The programmer does not have to be aware of the inclusion of hardware registers in the stack. For the programmer's purpose, only one relevant pointer, the stack pointer, appears to be an actual pointer register. Hardware stack registers reduce the number of memory references required and so speed up the operation of the computer.

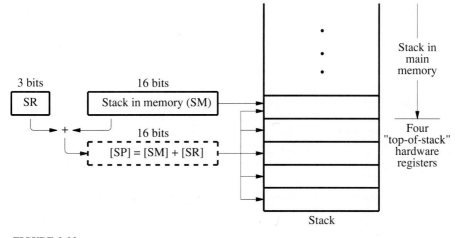

FIGURE 3.23
Top-of-stack structure in the HP3000.

3.7 CONCLUDING REMARKS

One of our main objectives in this chapter was to impress upon the reader the fact that considerable differences exist among computers. The fundamental principles of operation of digital machines that execute programs stored in a main memory are essentially the same for all computers. The more detailed characteristics vary from machine to machine, however, because they are dependent upon the size and structure of the machine. The differences are readily understood when one understands the common basic principles.

Let us summarize some of the ideas discussed in this chapter. A key feature of any computer is its mechanism for addressing operands in the main memory. The addressing scheme is inevitably dependent upon the word length of a given machine: the longer the word length, the more bits that can be dedicated for addressing purposes. A larger number of memory locations can therefore be addressed and the addressing mechanism may be simplified. Maximum size of the main memory is an important factor in many applications. A 16-bit computer such as the PDP-11 cannot easily provide more memory than the "natural" maximum of 64K bytes, but larger word-length machines such as the VAX-11 or the IBM 370 have no difficulty in providing sufficient memory space.

Instruction sets are also heavily dependent upon the word length. The number and variety of instructions that can be provided depend upon the utilization of the bit space within each instruction. It is often necessary to use more than one word to implement some instructions. This problem is obviously more pronounced in short word-length machines. The instruction set of the computer, however, can be designed to have many implicitly specified operands, as is the case in stack computers. This way, a wide variety of instructions can be provided using a single word per instruction.

In a multiuser environment, it is important to be able to easily relocate programs anywhere in the main memory. Computers in which all memory references are computed relative to the contents of certain registers are best suited for such applications. In our discussion of the IBM 370 computers, we saw that the inclusion of a base register in addressing of memory operands serves this purpose. Relocation of programs is also easily achieved in the HP3000 computer, because all memory references are made relative to the pointer registers.

We also discussed how instruction sets can provide support for high-level languages. Using the VAX-11 instruction set as an example, we illustrated a few of the ways that specialized, complex instructions can be used to implement certain constructs common to high-level languages.

3.8 PROBLEMS

3.1. A given computer has 16-bit instructions. Operand addresses are specified using 6-bit fields. There are K two-operand instructions (for example, Compare) and L zero-operand instructions (for example, Return-from-Subroutine) required. What is the maximum number of one-operand instructions that can be provided in this computer?

3.2. It is desirable to add a new instruction to the PDP-11 instruction set. This instruction, called INSERT, is supposed to achieve the combined effect of the instructions BIC and BIS as used in the example of Figure 2.22. Assume that an arbitrary pattern of bits can be inserted into a destination operand that may be specified in any of the eight address modes. The instruction INSERT may affect an arbitrary number of bit positions of the destination operand, while the remaining bit positions are not affected.

  (a) Show how this instruction may be implemented using the format of Figure 3.1b.

  (b) How could the instruction be implemented using the format of Figure 3.1c?

  (c) How do execution time (in terms of memory accesses required) and memory space requirements of this instruction compare with the BIC, BIS sequence that implements the same function?

3.3. Show how an instruction INSERT similar to that of Problem 3.2 may be implemented for the IBM 370 computers. In this case, the instruction can insert one or more BCD (binary-coded decimal) digits into any of the eight 4-bit fields of a 32-bit destination operand. Which of the formats of Figure 3.16 are suitable for implementation of this instruction?

3.4. Discuss the relative merits of addressing modes in the PDP-11, Motorola 68000, VAX-11, and IBM 370 computers. In particular, discuss how the addressing modes in each machine facilitate relocatability, implementation of a stack, accessing an operand list, and manipulating character strings.

3.5. IBM 370 computers do not have indirect addressing. Assume that an address of an operand is stored in the main memory. How would you access this operand?

3.6. Discuss the ease of relocating programs in the PDP-11, Motorola 68000, VAX-11, IBM 370, and HP3000 computers. How would you rank these computers with respect to this facility?

3.7. Write a PDP-11 program to evaluate the arithmetic expression in Figure 3.22. How does your program compare with the one given in the figure with respect to the number of memory locations and memory accesses required?

3.8. Show how the expression

$$w = a\{(bc + de) + fg/hi\}$$

can be evaluated in an HP3000 computer. How many memory words are needed for the program?

3.9. In an HP3000 computer, Procedure$_i$ generates eight words of data DI$_1$, . . . , DI$_8$, which are stored in the stack. After these words are placed in the stack, but before the completion of Procedure$_i$, a new Procedure$_j$ is called. It generates 10 words of data, DJ$_1$, . . . , DJ$_{10}$, which are also stored in the stack. Then, another Procedure$_k$ is called, which places three words of data in the stack.

Show the contents of the top words of the stack at this time.

3.10. (*a*) In the byte-sorting program shown in Figure 3.14, the address value LIST and the value *n* are fixed in the program code at assembly time. Rewrite the program as a VAX-11 procedure under the assumption that addresses of memory locations containing these values are passed on the stack from a calling program. See Figure 3.13 for the stack format.

(*b*) The execution-time efficiency of the byte-sorting procedure of part (*a*) can be improved by keeping track of the address of the smallest byte of a sublist LIST(*j*) to LIST(*n* − 1) and by performing, at most, one swap at the end of a sublist search. Rewrite the part (*a*) procedure to achieve this efficiency and estimate the improvement. What happens to code-space requirements when time efficiency is improved?

3.11. Using the VAX-11 INDEX instruction and other instructions as necessary, give a program segment that clears the word at array location A(*i*,*j*,*k*) in the case in which the subscript ranges are

$$i: \quad if, if+1, . . . , il$$
$$j: \quad jf, jf+1, . . . , jl$$
$$k: \quad kf, kf+1, . . . , kl$$

3.12. Show how the expression

$$w = (a + b)(c + d) + d \times e$$

can best be evaluated on the HP3000, PDP-11, and Motorola 68000 computers. The values of variables *w*, *a*, *b*, *c*, *d*, and *e* are stored in memory locations and the following assumptions are made. The addresses do not reference successive locations. Direct memory addressing in the DB + relative mode is used in the HP3000. Absolute memory addressing is used in the PDP-11 and the 68000. All products are single length and the PDP-11 has a MULT instruction in the double-operand class with the restriction that the destination operand must be in a CPU register.

3.13. Although there are fewer instructions in Figure 3.15 than in Figure 3.4, what is the total number of bytes needed to represent each program? Also, how many main memory accesses are needed to execute each program? Assume that the PDP-11 reads or writes 16 bits (a word) per access and that the VAX-11 can access up to 32 bits (a long word) at a time. (Also assume that when fetching instructions, the VAX-11 always fetches 32 bits at a time.)

3.14. Repeat Problem 3.13 for the programs in Figures 2.21 and 3.14.

3.15. Repeat Problem 3.7 for the 68000 microprocessor.

3.16. Repeat Problem 3.8 for the PDP-11 and 68000.

3.17. How does the 68000 byte-sorting program in Figure 2.32*b* compare to the VAX-11 program in Figure 3.14 from the standpoint of memory space requirements? Is this a fair comparison? If not, explain.

3.18. What is the largest number of stack locations occupied during execution of the program in Figure 3.22?

3.19. Repeat Problem 3.18 for the HP3000 programs of Problems 3.8 and 3.12.

3.20. (*a*) Write a 68000 program for the matrix multiply routine shown in Figure 3.3. Use the same assumptions as used for the VAX-11 program shown in Figure 3.15.

(*b*) Compare your solution to the solution given in Figure 3.15 in terms of the number of bytes needed to represent the programs and the number of main memory accesses needed to execute the programs. Recall that the 68000 reads or writes 16 bits (one word) per access.

3.21 Which addressing modes in the 68000 compare to the indexed displacement modes in the VAX-11? Comment on which machine implements such modes in the most flexible or general way.

CHAPTER

4

THE PROCESSING UNIT

In the previous chapters, the reader was introduced to a reasonably detailed picture of the computer as seen by the programmer. We will now turn our attention to the organization and operation of the different building blocks that constitute a computer system.

In its simplest form, a computer system has one unit that executes program instructions. This unit communicates with and often controls the operation of other subsystems within the computer. Because of the central role of such a unit, it is known as a *central processing unit,* or CPU. In many computers, a subsystem within the computer, such as an input unit or a mass storage device, may incorporate a processing unit of its own. Such a processing unit, while being central to its own subsystem, is clearly not central to the computer system as a whole. However, the principles involved in the design and operation of a CPU are independent of its position in a computer system. In this chapter we will deal with the organization of the hardware that enables a CPU to perform its main function: to fetch and execute instructions.

The solution algorithm for any problem consists of a number of steps that have to be carried out in a specific sequence. To implement such an algorithm on a computer, these steps are broken down into a number of smaller steps, where each of the smaller steps represents one machine instruction. The resulting sequence of instructions is a machine language program representing the algorithm. The same general approach is used to enable the computer to perform the functions specified by individual machine instructions; that is, each of these instructions is executed by carrying out a sequence of more rudimentary operations. These operations and the means by which they are generated will be the main topic of discussion in this chapter.

4.1 SOME FUNDAMENTAL CONCEPTS

The instructions constituting a program to be executed by a computer are loaded in sequential locations in the main memory. To execute this program, the CPU fetches one instruction at a time and performs the functions specified. Instructions are fetched from successive memory locations until the execution of a branch or a jump instruction. The CPU keeps track of the address of the memory location where the next instruction is located through the use of a dedicated CPU register, referred to as the program counter (PC). After fetching an instruction, the contents of the PC are updated to point to the next instruction in sequence.

Let us assume, for simplicity, that each instruction occupies one memory word. Therefore, execution of one instruction requires the following three steps to be performed by the CPU:

1. Fetch the contents of the memory location pointed to by the PC. The contents of this location are interpreted as an instruction to be executed. Hence, they are loaded into the instruction register (IR). Symbolically, this can be written as

$$IR \leftarrow [[PC]]$$

2. Increment the contents of the PC by 1, that is,

$$PC \leftarrow [PC] + 1$$

3. Carry out the actions specified by the instruction in the IR.

Note that in cases where an instruction occupies more than one word, steps 1 and 2 can be repeated as many times as necessary to fetch the complete instruction. These two steps are usually referred to as the *fetch phase*; step 3 constitutes the *execution phase*.

Before proceeding to study the above operations in detail, we will examine the structure of the main data paths inside the CPU. Most of the building blocks of the CPU were introduced in Figure 1.8. These blocks can be organized and interconnected in a variety of ways. One such organization is shown in Figure 4.1. In this case, the arithmetic and logic unit (ALU) and all CPU registers are connected via a single common bus. This bus, of course, is internal to the CPU and should not be confused with the external bus or buses connecting the CPU to the memory and I/O devices. The external memory bus is shown in Figure 4.1 connected to the CPU via the memory data and address registers, MDR and MAR. The number and function of registers R0 to $R(n-1)$ vary considerably from one machine to another. They may be provided for

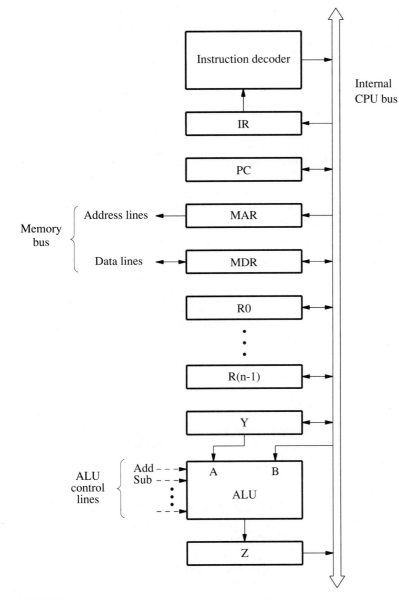

FIGURE 4.1
Single-bus organization of the data paths inside the CPU.

general-purpose use by the programmer; alternatively, some of them may be dedicated as special-purpose registers, such as index registers or stack pointers.

Two registers in Figure 4.1, registers Y and Z, have not been mentioned before. These registers are transparent to the programmer. That is, the programmer need not be concerned with their existence, because they are never referenced directly by any instruction. They are used only by the CPU for temporary storage during execution of some instructions. However, they are never used for storing data generated by one instruction for later use by another instruction.

With few exceptions, most of the operations in steps 1 to 3 mentioned above can be carried out by performing one or more of the following functions in some prespecified sequence:

1. Fetch the contents of a given memory location and load them into a CPU register.
2. Store a word of data from a CPU register into a given memory location.
3. Transfer a word of data from one CPU register to another or to the ALU.
4. Perform an arithmetic or logic operation and store the result in a CPU register.

Let us now consider in some detail the way in which each of the above functions is implemented in a typical computer.

4.1.1   Fetching a Word from Memory

To fetch a word of information from memory, the CPU has to specify the address of the memory location where this information is stored and request a Read operation. This applies whether the information to be fetched represents an instruction in a program or a word of data (operand) specified by an instruction. Thus, to perform a memory fetch, the CPU transfers the address of the required information word to the memory address register (MAR). As shown in Figure 4.1, the MAR is connected to the address lines of the memory bus. Hence the address of the required word is transferred to the main memory. Meanwhile, the CPU uses the control lines of the memory bus to indicate that a Read operation is required. Normally, after issuing this request the CPU waits until it receives an answer from the memory, informing it that the requested function has been completed. This is accomplished through the use of another control signal on the memory bus, which will be referred to as Memory-Function-Completed (MFC). The memory sets this signal to 1 to indicate that the contents of the specified location in the memory have been read and are available on the data lines of the memory bus. We will assume that as soon as the MFC signal is set to 1, the information on the data lines is loaded into MDR and is thus available for use inside the CPU. This completes the memory fetch operation.

As an example, assume that the address of the memory location to be accessed is in register R1 and that the memory data is to be loaded into register R2. This is achieved by the following sequence of operations:

1. MAR ← [R1]
2. Read
3. Wait for the MFC signal
4. R2 ← [MDR]

The duration of step 3 depends on the speed of the memory used. Usually, the time required to read a word from the memory is longer than the time required to perform any single operation within the CPU. Therefore, the overall execution time of an instruction can be decreased if the sequence of operations is organized such that a useful function is performed within the CPU while waiting for the memory to respond. Obviously, only functions that do not require the use of MDR or MAR can be carried out during this time. Such a situation arises during the fetch phase. As we will see shortly, the PC can be incremented while waiting for the Read operation to be completed.

In the above discussion, we have shown how data transfer can take place between two devices, namely, the CPU and the main memory. The transfer mechanism where one device initiates the transfer (Read request) and waits until the other device responds (MFC signal) is referred to as an *asynchronous* transfer. This mechanism enables transfer of data between two independent devices that have different speeds of operation. An alternative scheme found in many computers uses *synchronous* transfers. In this case, one of the control lines of the bus carries pulses from a continuously running clock of a fixed frequency. These pulses provide common timing signals to the CPU and the main memory. A memory operation can be completed during one clock cycle. The synchronous bus scheme leads to a simpler implementation. However, it cannot accommodate devices of widely varying speed, except by reducing the speed of all devices to that of the slowest one. In the remainder of the discussion of the operation of the CPU, we will assume that an asynchronous memory bus is used.

4.1.2 Storing a Word into Memory

The procedure for writing a word into a given memory location is as follows. After the address is loaded into the MAR, the data word to be written is loaded into MDR before or at the same time as the Write command is issued. If we assume that the data word to be stored in the memory is in R2 and that the memory address is in R1, the Write operation requires the following sequence:

1. MAR ← [R1]
2. MDR ← [R2], Write
3. Wait for MFC

It is interesting to note that steps 1 and 2 can be carried out simultaneously if this is allowed by the architecture, that is, if the two transfers do not use the same data path. Of course, this is not possible in the single-bus organization of Figure 4.1. Also, as in the case of the Read operation, the wait period in step 3 may be overlapped with other operations, provided that such operations do not involve registers MDR or MAR.

4.1.3 Register Transfers

To enable data transfer between various blocks connected to the common bus in Figure 4.1, input and output gating must be provided. This is represented symbolically in Figure 4.2. The input and output gates for register Ri are controlled by the signals Ri_{in} and Ri_{out}, respectively. Thus, when Ri_{in} is set to 1, the data available on the

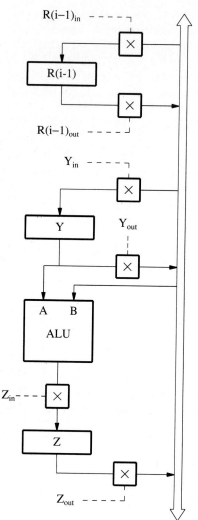

FIGURE 4.2
Input and output gating for the registers in Figure 4.1.

common bus is loaded into Ri. Similarly, when Ri_{out} is set to 1, the contents of register Ri are placed on the bus. While Ri_{out} is equal to 0, the bus can be used for transferring data from other registers. The details of implementation of input and output gating will be discussed in Section 4.1.5.

Let us now consider data transfer between two registers. For example, to transfer the contents of register R1 to register R4, the following actions are needed:

- Enable the output gate of register R1 by setting $R1_{out}$ to 1. This places the contents of R1 on the CPU bus.
- Enable the input gate of register R4 by setting $R4_{in}$ to 1. This loads data from the CPU bus into register R4.

4.1.4   Performing an Arithmetic or Logic Operation

The ALU, which performs arithmetic and logic operations, is a combinational circuit that has no internal storage. Therefore, to perform an addition, the two numbers to be added have to be made available at the two inputs of the ALU simultaneously. Register Y in Figures 4.1 and 4.2 is provided for this purpose. It is used to hold one of the two numbers while the other number is gated onto the bus. The result is stored temporarily in register Z. Therefore, the sequence of operations to add the contents of register R1 to register R2 and store the result in register R3 may be as follows:

Step	Action
1	$R1_{out}$, Y_{in}
2	$R2_{out}$, Add, Z_{in}
3	Z_{out}, $R3_{in}$

The signals whose names are given in any step are activated, or set to 1, for the duration of the clock cycle corresponding to that step. All other signals are inactive. Hence, in step 1, the output gate of register R1 and the input gate of register Y are enabled, causing the contents of R1 to be transferred to Y. In step 2, the contents of register R2 are gated onto the bus and hence to input B of the ALU. The contents of register Y are always available at input A. The function performed by the ALU depends on the signals applied to the ALU control lines. In this case, the Add line is set to 1, causing the output of the ALU to be the sum of the two numbers at inputs A and B. This sum is loaded into register Z, because its input gate is enabled (Z_{in}). In step 3, the contents of register Z are transferred to the destination register, R3. Obviously, this last transfer cannot be carried out during step 2, because only one register output can be meaningfully connected to the bus at any given time.

4.1.5   Register Gating and Timing of Data Transfers

Before proceeding to discuss the execution of machine instructions, we will present some of the implementation details required for gating data to and from the common bus in Figure 4.1. We will also present a brief overview of the required timing for the control signals involved in transferring data between registers.

Let us consider the case where each bit of the registers in Figures 4.1 and 4.2 consists of a flip-flop like the one shown in Figure 4.3 (see also Appendix A). The flip-flop shown is assumed to be one of the bits of register Z. While the control input Z_{in} is equal to 1, the state of the flip-flop changes to correspond to the data on the bus. Following a 1 to 0 transition at the Z_{in} input, the data stored in the flip-flop immediately before this transition is locked in until Z_{in} is again set to 1. Thus, the two input gates of the flip-flop perform the function of the input control switch in Figure 4.2.

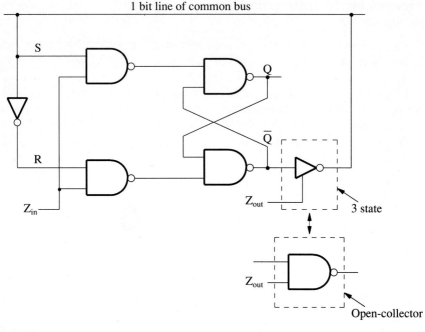

FIGURE 4.3
Input and output gating for one register bit.

Conceptually, the output switches in Figure 4.2 act as mechanical on/off switches. When a switch is in the on state, it transfers the contents of its corresponding register to the bus. When it is in the off state, the register output is electrically disconnected from the bus, thus allowing another register to place data on the bus. In other words, the output of the register-switch circuit can be in one of the three states 1, 0, or open circuit.

In actual implementations, electronic switches are used. The output gate of a register is capable of being electrically disconnected from the bus or of placing a 0 or a 1 on the bus. Because it supports these three possibilities, such a gate is said to have a *three-state* output. A separate control input is used to either enable the gate output to drive the bus to 0 or 1 or to put it in a high-impedance (electrically disconnected) state. The latter corresponds to the open-circuit state of a mechanical switch.

We should note that neither the TTL nor the CMOS logic gate circuits given in Appendix A are suitable for direct connection to a bus. Connecting the outputs of two such circuits in parallel constitutes a short circuit, which will lead to improper operation and may damage the gates involved. These circuits may be modified for three-state operation by arranging for a control input to turn off all transistors of the output stage shown in Figures A.16 and A.18.

An alternative design for the common bus of Figure 4.2 that does not require the output switches shown makes use of open-collector (for bipolar) or open-drain

Power supply

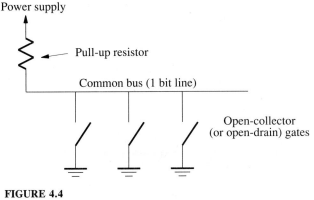

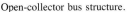

FIGURE 4.4
Open-collector bus structure.

(for MOS) gates. The output of such a gate is equivalent to a switch to ground. The switch is open when the gate output is in the 1 state and closed when it is in the 0 state. The structure of an open-collector bus is represented symbolically in Figure 4.4. When idle, the bus is maintained in the 1 state by the *pull-up* resistor shown. Thus, as long as all gate output switches are open (that is, all outputs are in the 1 state), the bus remains in the 1 state. If any gate output changes to the 0 state, the corresponding output switch is closed, and the bus is *pulled down* to the 0 state. In other words, the bus performs an AND function on all gate outputs connected to it. Hence, an open-collector bus is sometimes referred to as a *wired-AND* connection. If an open-collector arrangement is used, the three-state output gate of Figure 4.3 is replaced by an open-collector NAND gate, as shown. When Z_{out} is high (1), the bit stored in the latch is fed to the bus; when Z_{out} is low (0), the bus is left in the 1, or idle, state, allowing data from another register to be transferred to the bus.

In general, the three-state design enables faster data transfers than the open-collector, or open-drain, approach. For this reason, it is much more commonly used in bus design. The main distinguishing feature of an open-collector bus is its wired-AND behavior. Hence, the open-collector arrangement is used primarily for bus lines where this is needed. For example, it is used for interrupt request lines, as will be described in Chapter 6.

Let us now discuss some aspects of the timing of data transfers inside the CPU. Consider the addition operation in step 2 in Section 4.1.4. After the signal $R2_{out}$ is set to 1, a finite delay is encountered for the gate to open and then for the data to travel along the bus to the input of the ALU. Further delay is introduced by the ALU adder circuits. For the result to be properly stored in register Z, data must be maintained on the bus for an additional period of time equal to the setup and hold times for this register (see Appendix A). This situation is depicted in the timing diagram given in Figure 4.5. The sum of the five delay times shown defines the minimum duration of the signal $R2_{out}$.

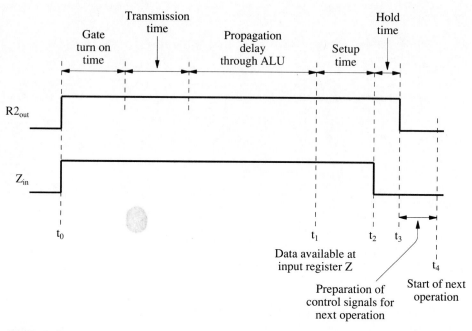

FIGURE 4.5
Timing of the control signals during the Add step.

4.1.6   Multiple-Bus Organization

The single-bus organization of Figure 4.1 represents only one of the possibilities for interconnecting different building blocks of the CPU. An alternative arrangement is the two-bus structure shown in Figure 4.6. All register outputs are connected to bus A, and all register inputs are connected to bus B. The two buses are connected through the bus tie G, which, when enabled, transfers the data on bus A to bus B. When G is disabled, the two buses are electrically disconnected. Note that the temporary storage register Z in Figure 4.1 is not required in this organization because, with the bus tie disabled, the output of the ALU can be transferred directly to the destination register. For example, the addition operation discussed earlier (R3 ← [R1] + [R2]) can now be performed as follows:

1. $R1_{out}$, G_{enable}, Y_{in}
2. $R2_{out}$, Add, ALU_{out}, $R3_{in}$

It is important to note that if the registers are simple latches as in Figure 4.3, the destination register in the above sequence must be different from R2, because the two operations $R2_{in}$ and $R2_{out}$ cannot be performed at the same time. The operation R2 ← [R1] + [R2] can still be performed, however, by interchanging $R1_{out}$

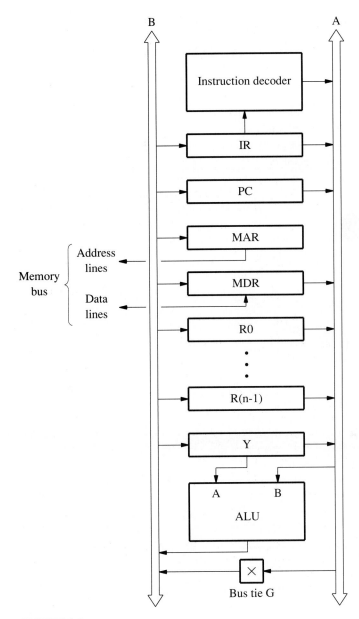

FIGURE 4.6
Two-bus structure.

and R2$_{out}$ and replacing R3$_{in}$ by R2$_{in}$ in step 2. The restriction that R2$_{out}$ and R2$_{in}$ cannot be performed in the same step may be removed through the use of edge-triggered flip-flops or a master-slave arrangement (see Appendix A).

Let us consider one more example of a CPU organization. Figure 4.7 illustrates a three-bus architecture, with each bus connected to only one output and a number of inputs. Two work registers, A and B, are provided. They may be loaded from either the input data bus or the register data bus. Because fewer components are connected to each of the buses in Figure 4.7, data can be transferred over these buses more quickly than in the case of Figure 4.6. Also, because there are three buses, three data transfers can take place simultaneously.

The general-purpose registers of the CPU in Figure 4.7 are shown as a single block. They are assumed to be implemented using a random-access memory unit (RAM). The internal organization of a RAM will be discussed in Chapter 8. We should emphasize that in this context the term RAM simply refers to the type of hardware used in the registers and should not be confused with the RAM that constitutes the main memory of the computer. The latter is connected to the external bus.

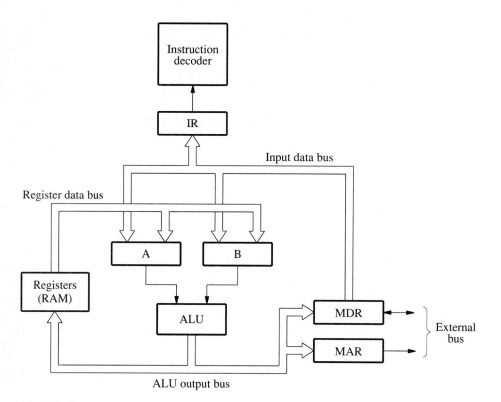

FIGURE 4.7
Three-bus structure.

4.2 EXECUTION OF A COMPLETE INSTRUCTION

Let us now try to put together the sequence of elementary operations required to execute one instruction. Consider the instruction "Add contents of memory location LOC to register R1." Let us assume, for simplicity, that the address LOC is given explicitly in the address field of the instruction. That is, location LOC is specified in the absolute mode. Executing this instruction requires the following actions:

1. Fetch the instruction.
2. Fetch the first operand (the contents of the memory location pointed to by the address field of the instruction).
3. Perform the addition.
4. Load the result into R1.

Figure 4.8 gives the sequence of control steps required to perform the above operations for the single-bus architecture of Figure 4.1. Instruction execution proceeds as follows. In step 1, the instruction fetch operation is initiated by loading the contents of the PC into the MAR and sending a Read request to the memory. While waiting for a response from the memory, the PC is incremented by 1 by setting one of the inputs to the ALU (register Y) to 0 and the other input (CPU bus) to the current value in the PC. At the same time, the carry-in to the ALU is set to 1, and an Add operation is specified. The updated value is moved from register Z back into the PC during step 2. Note that step 2 is started immediately after issuing the memory

Step	Action
1	PC_{out}, MAR_{in}, Read, Clear Y, Set carry-in to ALU, Add, Z_{in}
2	Z_{out}, PC_{in}, Wait for MFC
3	MDR_{out}, IR_{in}
4	Address-field-of-IR_{out}, MAR_{in}, Read
5	$R1_{out}$, Y_{in}, Wait for MFC
6	MDR_{out}, Add, Z_{in}
7	Z_{out}, $R1_{in}$, End

FIGURE 4.8
Control sequence for execution of the instruction "Add contents of a memory location addressed in absolute mode to register R1."

Read request without having to wait for completion of the memory function. Step 3, however, has to be delayed until the MFC signal is received. In step 3, the word fetched from the memory is loaded into the IR (instruction register). The instruction decoding circuit interprets the contents of IR at the beginning of step 4. This enables the control circuitry to choose the appropriate signals for the remainder of the control sequence, steps 4 to 7, which are referred to as the execution phase. Steps 1 through 3 constitute the instruction fetch phase of the control sequence. Of course, this portion is the same for all instructions.

In step 4, the address field of the IR, which contains the address LOC, is gated to the MAR, and a memory Read operation is initiated. Then the contents of R1 are transferred to register Y. When the Read operation is completed, the memory operand is available in register MDR. The addition operation is performed in step 6, and the result is transferred to R1 in step 7. The End signal in step 7 indicates that this is the last step of the current instruction and causes a new fetch cycle to be started by going back to step 1.

4.2.1   Branching

As described in Chapter 2, branching is accomplished by replacing the current contents of the PC by the branch address, that is, the address of the instruction to which branching is required. The branch address is usually obtained by adding an offset X, which is given in the address field of the branch instruction, to the current value of the PC. Figure 4.9 gives a control sequence for an unconditional branch using the single-bus organization of Figure 4.1. Processing starts as usual with the fetch phase, ending with the instruction being loaded into the IR in step 3 and decoded at the beginning of step 4. To execute the branch instruction, the contents of the PC are transferred to register Y in step 4. Then, the offset X is gated onto the bus, and the addition operation is performed. The result, which represents the branch address, is loaded into the PC in step 6.

Step	Action
1	PC_{out}, MAR_{in}, Read, Clear Y, Set carry-in to ALU, Add, Z_{in}
2	Z_{out}, PC_{in}, Wait for MFC
3	MDR_{out}, IR_{in}
4	PC_{out}, Y_{in}
5	Address-field-of-IR_{out}, ADD, Z_{in}
6	Z_{out}, PC_{in}, End

FIGURE 4.9
Control sequence for an unconditional branch instruction.

It is important to note that in this example the PC is incremented during the fetch phase, before knowing the type of instruction being executed. Thus, at the time the offset X is added to the contents of the PC (steps 4 and 5 in Figure 4.9) these contents have already been updated to point to the instruction following the Branch instruction in the program. Therefore, the offset X is the difference between the branch address and the address immediately following the Branch instruction. For example, if the Branch instruction is at location 1000, and it is required to branch to location 1050, the value of X must be 49.

Consider now the case of a conditional instead of an unconditional branch. The only difference between this case and that of Figure 4.9 is the need to check the status of the condition codes before loading a new value into the PC. For example, if the instruction decoding circuitry interprets the contents of the IR as a Branch on Negative (BRN) instruction, step 4 is replaced with

$$4. \ PC_{out}, \ Y_{in}, \ \text{If } \overline{N} \text{ then End}$$

As before, the contents of the PC are copied into register Y, just in case they will be needed to compute the branch address. Meanwhile, the N bit is checked. If it is equal to 0, the End signal is issued, terminating execution of that instruction. If $N = 1$, steps 5 and 6 are performed to complete the branch operation.

4.3   SEQUENCING OF CONTROL SIGNALS

To execute instructions, the CPU must have some means of generating the control signals discussed above in the proper sequence. Computer designers have used a wide variety of techniques to solve this problem. Most of these techniques, however, fall into one of two categories:

1. Hardwired control
2. Microprogrammed control

Hardwired control is discussed in this section, followed by a brief introduction to microprogrammed control. The latter will be discussed in detail in Chapter 5.

4.3.1   Hardwired Control

Consider the sequence of control signals given in Figure 4.8. Seven nonoverlapping time slots are required for execution of the instruction represented by this sequence. Each time slot must be at least long enough for the functions specified in the corresponding step to be completed. Let us assume, for the moment, that all time slots are equal in duration. Therefore, the required control unit may be based on the use of a counter driven by a clock signal, CLK, as shown in Figure 4.10. Each state, or count, of this counter corresponds to one of the steps in Figures 4.8 and 4.9. Hence the required control signals are uniquely determined by the following information:

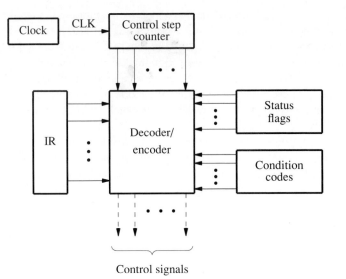

FIGURE 4.10
Control unit organization.

- Contents of the control counter
- Contents of the instruction register
- Contents of the condition code and other status flags

By status flags we mean the signals representing the state of various sections of the CPU and various control lines connected to it, such as the MFC status signal used in Figure 4.8.

In order to gain some insight into the structure of the control unit we will start by giving a simplified view of the hardware involved. The decoder-encoder block in Figure 4.10 is a combinational circuit that generates the required control outputs, depending on the state of all its inputs. By separating the decoding and encoding functions we obtain the more detailed block diagram in Figure 4.11. The step decoder provides a separate signal line for each step, or time slot, in the control sequence. Similarly, the output of the instruction decoder consists of a separate line for each machine instruction. That is, for any instruction loaded in the IR, one of the output lines INS_1 to INS_m is set to 1, and all other lines are set to 0. For design details of such decoders refer to Appendix A.

All input signals to the encoder block in Figure 4.11 should be combined to generate the individual control signals Y_{in}, PC_{out}, Add, End, and so on. The structure of the encoder is exemplified by the circuit given in Figure 4.12, which implements the logic function

$$Z_{in} = T_1 + T_6 \cdot \text{ADD} + T_5 \cdot \text{BR} + \cdots \tag{4.1}$$

That is, the control signal Z_{in}, which enables the input to register Z, is turned on

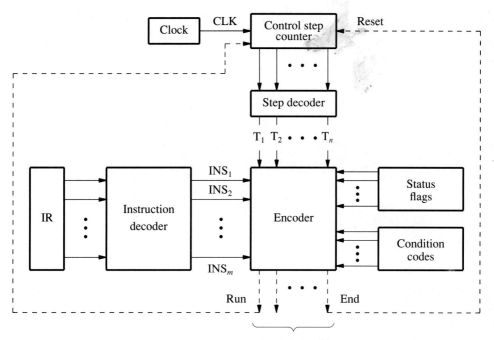

FIGURE 4.11
Separation of the decoding and encoding functions.

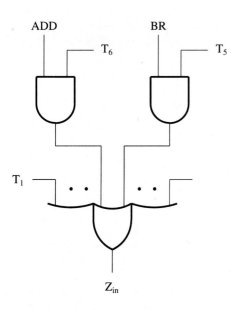

FIGURE 4.12
Generation of the Z_{in} control signal.

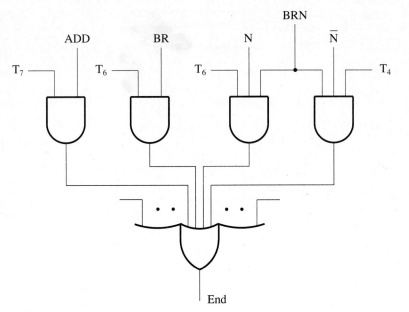

FIGURE 4.13
Generation of the End control signal.

during time slot T_1 for all instructions, during T_6 for an ADD instruction, and so on. This part of the Z_{in} function has been compiled from the control sequences in Figures 4.8 and 4.9. The term T_1 is common to all instructions, because it occurs during the fetch phase. Similarly, the End control signal, Figure 4.13, is generated from the logic function

$$\text{End} = T_7 \cdot \text{ADD} + T_6 \cdot \text{BR} + (T_6 \cdot N + T_4 \cdot \overline{N}) \cdot \text{BRN} + \cdots \quad (4.2)$$

Figure 4.11 shows how the End signal can be used to start a new instruction fetch cycle by resetting the control step counter to its starting value.

CPU-MEMORY INTERACTION. The interaction between the internal signals in the CPU and the external bus deserves special attention. In our earlier discussion we assumed that a Read or a Write control signal inside the CPU initiates a data transfer between the main memory and register MDR. The memory activates the MFC signal when the transfer operation is completed. Let us now examine this exchange in more detail.

Recall that the internal control signals generated during a given control step are active only for the duration of that step. Because the duration of the memory operation may extend over several clock cycles, the Read and Write control signals should be used to set flip-flops whose outputs are sent to the memory over the external bus to initiate the requested operation. The signals Memory Read request (MR) and Memory Write request (MW) in the circuit of Figure 4.14a perform this function. Figure 4.14b gives a timing diagram for a Read operation. The Read operation is

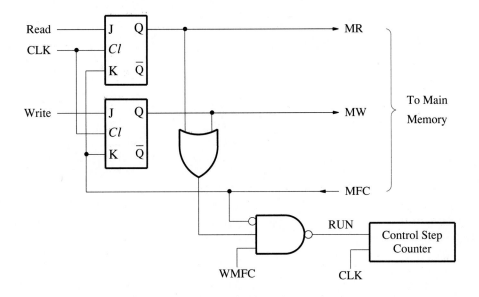

(a) Generation of read and write requests

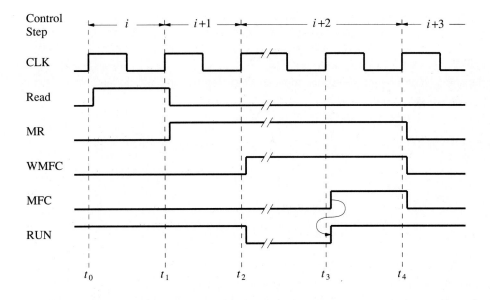

(b) Timing example for a Read operation

FIGURE 4.14
Control of external bus transfers.

requested in control step i. The next positive edge of the clock sets MR to 1 (t_1), thus starting a Read operation in the main memory. While the memory access is taking place, the CPU may perform internal operations such as incrementing the PC. In Figure 4.14b we have assumed that these internal operations require two control steps, $i + 1$ and $i + 2$. The WMFC signal is set to 1 during step $i + 2$ to delay step $i + 3$ until the MFC signal is received. This can be accomplished by inhibiting the advancement of the control step counter. Let us assume that the counter is controlled by a signal called RUN. The counter is advanced one step at the end of every clock cycle in which RUN is equal to 1, which is the usual case. If there is an outstanding memory access request at the time WMFC becomes equal to 1 (that is, if either MR or MW is active and MFC is still equal to 0), RUN is changed to 0. This action prevents the counter from being advanced. Sometime later, the MFC signal becomes active, causing RUN to change back to 1. At the next positive edge of the clock (t_4), the Memory Request flip-flop is reset, the step counter is advanced, and step $i + 3$ begins. Note that MR and MW have been included in the generation of the RUN signal to guarantee correct operation even in the case of a fast memory that completes the requested access before the WMFC signal is activated.

In Figure 4.14b, we have assumed that the main memory is controlled by the same clock as the CPU. The memory activates MFC at the positive edge of the clock signal and maintains it for one clock cycle. If the main memory is not controlled by the same clock as the CPU, the MFC response must be treated by the CPU as an asynchronous signal. This leads to two differences from the arrangement shown in Figure 4.14b. First, the MFC signal cannot be guaranteed to meet any setup requirements relative to clock transitions. It must be synchronized with CLK before being used to control any internal signals in the CPU. This may be done using a synchronizer circuit such as that shown in Figure 4.15. Flip-flop FF1 is set on the first positive edge of CLK after MFC becomes active. However, because MFC may change its state very close to that edge, the flip-flop may require an abnormally long time before its output reaches a stable state. For that reason, the output of FF1 is synchronized again one clock cycle later by a second flip-flop, FF2. The output of this flip-flop, MFCS, should be used in the circuit of Figure 4.14a instead of MFC. This synchronizer introduces a delay of one to two clock cycles between MFC and MFCS.

The second difference between the synchronous and asynchronous cases relates to the width of the MFC pulse. An asynchronous memory will normally maintain MFC active until the Memory Request signal becomes inactive. Because of propagation delays, MFC may not become inactive before the next clock edge. To prevent malfunc-

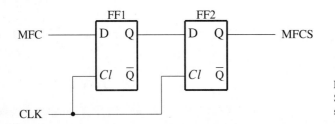

FIGURE 4.15
Synchronization of the MFC signal.

tion, the CPU must not issue a new memory request until the MFC signal belonging to the previous request has become inactive. The circuit in Figure 4.14 should be modified to implement this additional requirement (see Problem 4.28). In asynchronous interactions of this type, the Memory Request and MFC signals are said to perform a handshake. Data transfers controlled in this manner will be discussed further in Chapter 6.

PRACTICAL CONSIDERATIONS. The above discussion presented a simplified view of the way in which the sequence of control signals needed to fetch and execute instructions may be generated. The overall organization depicted in Figures 4.10 and 4.11 enables an arbitrary instruction set to be implemented. We will now consider some practical aspects of realizing such circuitry.

By necessity, the approach used in the design of a digital system must take into account the capabilities and limitations of the chosen implementation technology. The circuits of Figures 4.12 and 4.13 are easy to understand and to design; however, the complexity of the circuits may make this direct approach impractical. The implementation of modern computers is based on the use of very large scale integration (VLSI) technology. In VLSI chips, structures that involve regular interconnection patterns are much easier to realize than the random connections used in the circuits above. One such structure is a *programmable logic array* (PLA). As described in Appendix A, a PLA consists of an array of AND gates followed by an array of OR gates and can be used to implement combinational logic functions of several variables. The entire decoder-encoder block of Figure 4.10 can be implemented in the form of a single PLA. Thus, the control section of a CPU—or for that matter, of any digital system— may be organized as shown in Figure 4.16.

Before concluding the discussion on hardwired controllers, a few comments are in order. We have assumed that all control steps occupy equal time slots. This approach does not lead to efficient utilization of the CPU, because not all operations require the same amount of time. For example, a simple register transfer is usually

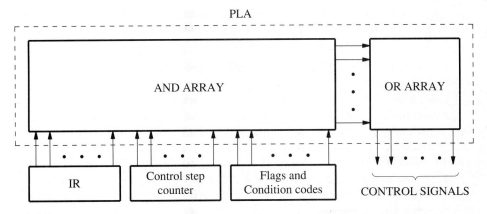

FIGURE 4.16
Implementation of a sequence controller on a VLSI chip.

much faster than an operation involving addition or subtraction. It is possible, at least in theory, to build a completely asynchronous control unit. In this case, the clock would be replaced by a circuit that advances the step counter as soon as the current step is completed. The main problem in such an approach is the incorporation of some reliable means to detect the completion of various operations. As it turns out, propagation delay in many cases is a function not only of the gates used but also of the particular data being processed. Some of the difficulties involved can be appreciated by studying the analysis of propagation delay in arithmetic circuits given in Chapter 7.

Some compromises are possible, however. For example, a maximum delay can be established for each operation, and the timing signals can be derived on that basis. It is also possible to use separate clocks for individual subsections of a circuit. Communication among various subsections can then be done asynchronously, in much the same way as for data transfers between the CPU and the main memory.

4.3.2   Microprogrammed Control

In Section 4.3.1, we saw how all the control signals required inside the CPU can be generated using a state counter and a PLA circuit. In the remainder of this chapter, we will discuss an alternative approach called *microprogrammed control*. Only a brief introduction is given below, followed by a more comprehensive treatment in Chapter 5. We will first introduce some frequently used terms.

Let us start by defining a *control word* (CW) as a word whose individual bits represent the various control signals in Figure 4.11. Therefore, each of the control steps in the control sequence of an instruction defines a unique combination of 1s and 0s in the CW. For example, the CWs corresponding to steps 5, 6, and 7 of Figure 4.8 are as shown in Figure 4.17. A sequence of CWs corresponding to the control sequence of a machine instruction constitutes the *microroutine* for that instruction. The individual control words in this microroutine are usually referred to as *microinstructions*.

Let us assume that the microroutines corresponding to the instruction set of a computer are stored in a special memory called the *microprogram memory*. The control unit can generate the control signals for any instruction by sequentially reading the CWs of the corresponding microroutine from the microprogram memory. This suggests organizing the control unit as shown in Figure 4.18. To read the control words sequentially from the microprogram memory a *microprogram counter* (μPC) is

Step	$R1_{in}$	$R1_{out}$	Y_{in}	Y_{out}	Z_{in}	Z_{out}	MDR_{in}	MDR_{out}	WMFC	Add	End
5	0	1	1	0	0	0	0	0	1	0	0
6	0	0	0	0	1	0	0	1	0	1	0
7	1	0	0	0	0	1	0	0	0	0	1

FIGURE 4.17
Example of microinstructions for Figure 4.8.

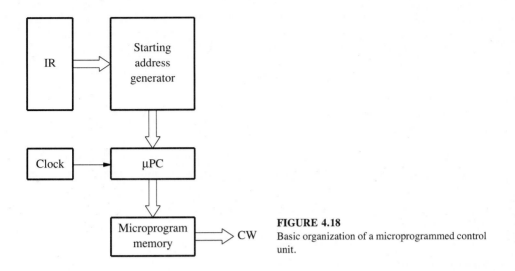

FIGURE 4.18
Basic organization of a microprogrammed control unit.

used. Every time a new instruction is loaded into the IR, the output of the block labeled "starting address generator" is loaded into the μPC. The μPC is then automatically incremented by the clock, causing successive microinstructions to be read from the memory. Hence the control signals will be delivered to various parts of the CPU in the correct sequence.

So far, one important function of the control unit has not been discussed and, in fact, cannot be implemented by the simple organization of Figure 4.18. This is the situation that arises when the control unit is required to check the status of the condition codes or status flags in order to choose between alternative courses of action. We have seen that in the case of hardwired control this situation is handled by including an appropriate logic function, as in Equation 4.2, in the encoder circuitry. An alternative approach in microprogrammed control is to use conditional branching. In this case, the microinstruction set is expanded to include some conditional branch microinstructions. In addition to the branch address, these microinstructions can specify which of the status flags, condition codes, or, possibly, bits of the instruction register should be checked as a condition for branching to take place. The instruction Branch on Negative may now be implemented by a microroutine such as that shown in Figure 4.19. After loading this instruction into IR, a branch microinstruction transfers control to the corresponding microtine, which is assumed to start at location 25 in the microprogram memory. This address is the output of the starting address generator block. At location 25, a conditional branch microinstruction tests the N bit of the condition codes. If this bit is equal to 0, a branch takes place to location 0 to fetch a new machine instruction. Otherwise, the microinstructions in locations 26 and 27 are executed to load a new value into the PC.

To support microprogram branching, the organization of the control unit should be modified as shown in Figure 4.20. The bits of the microinstruction word that specify the branch conditions and address are fed to the starting and branch address generator block. This block performs the function of loading a new address into the

Address	Microinstruction
0	PC_{out}, MAR_{in}, Read, Clear Y, Set carry-in to ALU, Add, Z_{in}
1	Z_{out}, PC_{in}, Wait for MFC
2	MDR_{out}, IR_{in}
3	Branch to starting address of appropriate microroutine.
. . . .	. . . .
25	PC_{out}, Y_{in}, if $\overline{N}$ then branch to 0
26	Address-field-of-IR_{out}, ADD, Z_{in}
27	Z_{out}, PC_{in}, End

FIGURE 4.19
Microroutine for the instruction Branch on Negative.

μPC when instructed to do so by a microinstruction. To enable the implementation of a conditional branch, inputs to this block consist of the status flags and condition codes as well as the contents of the instruction register. Therefore, the μPC is incremented every time a new microinstruction is fetched from the microprogram memory, except in the following situations:

1. When an End microinstruction is encountered, the μPC is loaded with the address of the first CW in the microroutine for the instruction fetch cycle (address = 0 in Figure 4.19).

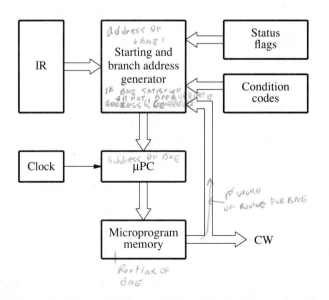

FIGURE 4.20
Organization of the control unit to enable conditional branching in the microprogram.

2. When a new instruction is loaded into the IR, the μPC is loaded with the starting address of the microroutine for that instruction.

3. When a Branch microinstruction is encountered and the branch condition is satisfied, the μPC is loaded with the branch address.

In conclusion, a few important points should be noted regarding microprogrammed control.

1. The microprogram defines the instruction set of the computer; hence it is possible to change the instruction set simply by changing the contents of the microprogram memory. This offers considerable flexibility to the designer of the computer.

2. Since the contents of the microprogram memory are changed very infrequently, if at all, a read-only type memory (ROM) is typically used for that purpose.

3. Execution of any machine instruction involves a number of fetches from the microprogram memory. Therefore, the speed of this memory plays a major role in determining the overall speed of the computer.

4. In the case where an entire CPU is fabricated as a single chip, the microprogram ROM is a part of that chip.

We have only introduced the basic features of microprogrammed control in this chapter. Various design alternatives and trade-offs will be discussed in more detail in Chapter 5.

4.4 CONCLUDING REMARKS

In this chapter, we presented an overview of the organization of the central processing unit of a computer. Many variations of the organizations presented here are encountered in commercially available machines. The choice of a particular organization involves trade-offs between speed of execution and cost of implementation. It is also influenced by a number of other factors, such as the technology used, flexibility for modification, or the desire to provide some special capabilities in the instruction set of the computer.

Two approaches were presented regarding the implementation of the control unit of a CPU: hardwired control and microprogrammed control. Microprogrammed control provides considerable flexibility in the implementation of instruction sets. It also facilitates the addition of new instructions to existing machines.

4.5 PROBLEMS

4.1. Why is the Wait for Memory Function Completed step needed when reading from or writing to the main memory?

4.2. Consider a computer system in which a memory Read or Write operation takes the same amount of time as any internal operation in the CPU. Is the WMFC signal needed in this case? Why?

4.3. The CPU of a computer uses a control sequence similar to that of Figure 4.8. Assume that a main memory read or write operation takes the same time as one internal CPU step and that both the CPU and the memory are controlled by the same clock. Rewrite the control sequence of Figure 4.8 for this machine.

4.4. Repeat Problem 4.3 for the case of a memory access time equal to twice the CPU clock period.

4.5. Assume that propagation delays along the bus and through the ALU of Figure 4.1 are 10 and 100 ns, respectively. The setup time for the registers is 8 ns, and the hold time is 0. What is the minimum time that must be allowed for performing each of the following operations?
(*a*) Transfer data from one register to another.
(*b*) Increment the program counter.

4.6. Write the sequence of control steps required for the bus structure of Figure 4.1 for each of the following three instructions.
(*a*) Add the number NUM to register R1.
(*b*) Add contents of memory location NUM to register R1.
(*c*) Add contents of the memory location whose address is at memory location NUM to register R1.

Assume that each instruction consists of two words and that each word occupies one address location. The first word of an instruction specifies the operation and the addressing mode, and the second word contains the number NUM.

4.7. Figure P4.1 gives a part of the internal organization of the CPU of a computer. All data transfers between the two buses go through the arithmetic and logic unit (ALU). Among other things, the ALU is capable of performing the following functions

$$F = A \qquad\qquad F = B$$
$$F = A + 1 \qquad\quad F = B + 1$$

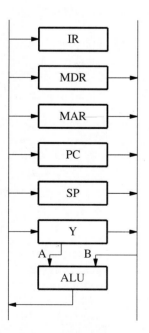

FIGURE P4.1
Internal organization of the CPU of Problem 4.7.

$$F = A - 1 \qquad F = B - 1$$

where A and B are the ALU inputs and F is the ALU output. Write the sequence of control steps required to fetch and execute the instruction Jump to Subroutine (JSR). In this machine, which is word-addressable, the JSR instruction occupies two words. The first word is the OP code, and the second word contains the starting address of the subroutine. The return address is saved in a stack, pointed to by a stack pointer, SP.

4.8. Consider the Add instruction that has the control sequence given in Figure 4.8. The CPU is driven by a continuously running clock, such that each control step is 100 ns in duration. How long will the CPU have to wait in steps 2 and 5, assuming that a memory read operation takes 0.4 μs to complete? What percentage of time is the CPU idle during execution of this instruction?

4.9. In a 16-bit byte-addressable machine, the PC should be incremented by 2 after fetching an instruction word from memory. Suggest some modification to Figure 4.1 to simplify this operation.

4.10. Assume that the flip-flops shown in Figure 4.3 are used to form the registers in Figure 4.6. What happens if the operation R2 ← [R1] + [R2] is attempted? What type of storage component is needed to allow such operations?

4.11. Assume that each register in Figure 4.6 consists of flip-flops of the type shown in Figure 4.3. Given one more register, how would you use it to enable the operation Ri ← [Ri] + [Y] to be carried out in a single clock cycle for any Ri? *Hint:* Study the operation of master-slave flip-flops in Appendix A.

4.12. Figure 4.6 gives the internal organization of the CPU of a computer, which we will use to emulate the operation of a PDP-11 computer. Give the control sequences required to fetch and execute the following instructions

(a)   CMP   (R1)+,X(R7)   (Compare)

(b)   RTS   R2   (Return from subroutine)

Recall that R7 is the PC and that register R6 is used as a pointer to the memory stack. Assume that a temporary storage register (TEMP) is available. It is connected to the two buses in the same way as registers R0 to R7.

4.13. The PDP-11 instruction JSR reg,dst is implemented by the five-step sequence

(1)   temp ← dst
(2)   SP ← [SP] − 2
(3)   [SP] ← [reg]
(4)   reg ← [PC]
(5)   PC ← [temp]

Why can't this be replaced by the sequence

(1)   SP ← [SP] − 2
(2)   [SP] ← [reg]
(3)   reg ← [PC]
(4)   PC ← dst

4.14. Consider a 2-bus CPU similar to that of Figure 4.6 and assume that inputs to the ALU, registers, and buses are 32 bits wide. The memory data bus, which is only 16 bits wide, is connected to MDRL, the low-order half of MDR. Input B of the ALU can be connected either to the bus as shown or to a constant value 2. Assume also that sufficient registers are available to implement the address and data registers of the 68000 microprocessor.

Explain what facilities are needed and give the control sequence for executing each of the following instructions
(a)   SUB.W   200(A3),D4
(b)   CMP.W   (A2)+,D1

4.15. The CPU of a computer has the two-bus structure of Figure 4.6. Like the 68000 microprocessor, its internal registers and data paths are 32 bits wide. However, its memory data bus has only 16 lines. The MDR register consists of two halves, MDRH and MDRL, both connected to the memory data lines. Two read operations are provided, RDH and RDL, which read data from the memory and load it into the high- and low-order halves of MDR, respectively. Register Y may be set to the value 2 or 4. A register may appear both as a source and a destination in the same control step, as in the control step

$$R2_{out}, \text{ Set } Y = 4, \text{ Add, } R2_{in}$$

which adds 4 to the contents of R2.
    Give the control steps needed to implement the following 68000 instructions on this CPU.
(a)   MOVE.W   #100,D1
(b)   ADD.W   (A2),D3
(c)   ADD.L   (A2),D3

4.16. Repeat Problem 4.15 for the instructions:
(a)   JSR $30A16
(b)   SUB.W $76C(A5),D0

4.17. The three-bus organization of Figure 4.7 allows a number of transfers to be carried out simultaneously (e.g., $A \leftarrow [MDR]$ and $B \leftarrow [R_i]$). Give a sequence of steps for implementing the PDP-11 or 68000 instruction:

$$ADD \qquad (R3),X(R4)$$

to take advantage of these possibilities. Assume that the data paths are 16 bits wide and that any constants needed in the implementation are stored in the register file. Register B can, if desired, be operated in a transparent mode. In this mode, data arriving at the input of the register appear at its output immediately, allowing data from the register file to be transferred to MAR or MDR or back to the register file in one control step.

4.18. Give a control step sequence for implementing the PDP-11 or 68000 instruction CMP #N,(R3)+ on the CPU of Figure 4.7, with the features described in Problem 4.17. Assume that the output of the ALU can be set to any of the following

$$A, \text{ B, } A+B+C_{in}, A+\overline{B}+C_{in}$$

Here C_{in} is the carry input to the ALU, which can be set to either 0 or 1.

4.19. The three instructions in Problem 4.6 have common control steps. However, these control steps occur at different counts of the control step counter. Show two different alternatives that exploit these common steps in reducing the complexity of the encoder block in Figure 4.11.

4.20. Consider a 16-bit byte-addressable machine that has the organization of Figure 4.1. Bytes at even and odd addresses are transferred on the high- and low-order 8 bits of the memory bus, respectively. Show a suitable gating scheme for connecting register MDR to the memory bus and to the internal CPU bus to enable byte transfers to take place. When a byte is being handled, it should always be in the low-order byte position inside the CPU.

4.21. Design an oscillator using an inverter and a delay element. Assuming that the delay element introduces a delay T, what is the frequency of oscillation?

Modify the oscillator circuit such that oscillations can be started and stopped under control of an asynchronous input RUN. When the oscillator is stopped, the width of the last pulse at its output must be equal to T, independent of the time at which RUN becomes inactive.

4.22. Refer to the timing diagram in Figure 4.14b. Assume that the positive pulses of CLK are of width T. It is required to generate a control step clock, CSCLK, that has one positive pulse of width T at the beginning of each control step, then remains in the low state until the beginning of the next control step. Design a circuit that generates the required signal from RUN and CLK.

4.23. Refer to the decoder and encoder blocks in Figure 4.11. Whenever the step counter is incremented, false signals may appear on the control lines while the gates within the decoder and encoder blocks settle to their new states. This may cause errors. Assume that some control signals are to be disabled for a short period after incrementing the control step counter. Give a design for a circuit to generate the CPU clock using a high-frequency oscillator and show how a gating signal may be generated for a period equal to one-eighth of the clock period.

4.24. To take advantage of the differences in the times required to perform various operations in the CPU, the duration of a control step may be extended when necessary to accommodate slow operations. Assume that one of the control signals generated by the encoder block of Figure 4.11 is called SHORT/LONG. When this line is equal to 1, the control step counter is advanced at successive positive edges of the clock. When the SHORT/LONG line is equal to 0, the length of the time slot is doubled. Assume that the counter has an Enable input and that it is advanced on the positive edge of the clock if Enable = 1. Give a suitable design for a circuit that generates the Enable signal to vary the size of the control steps as needed.

4.25. The output of a shift register is inverted and fed back to its input. This arrangement is known as a Johnson counter.

(a) What is the count sequence of a 4-bit Johnson counter, starting with the state 0000?

(b) Show how you can use a Johnson counter to generate the timing signals T_1, T_2, and so on in Figure 4.11, assuming there is a maximum of 10 timing intervals.

4.26. Consider the case in which control step $i + 2$ in Figure 4.14b contains a new Read command. The circuit in Figure 4.14a will fail to assert MR to start a new read operation. Modify this circuit such that MR goes to 0 before the end of control step $i + 2$, and MR is set to 1 again at the beginning of control step $i + 3$.

4.27. Consider a CPU in which the timing of control steps and memory transfer operations is similar to that depicted in Figure 4.14b. A control step in which MDR$_{out}$ is asserted transfers the contents of MDR, which were read from memory in a previous step, to another register. If Read is asserted, a memory transfer is initiated to load new data into MDR. Is there a conflict in asserting MDR$_{out}$ and Read in the same control step? Explain.

4.28. Refer to the timing diagram in Figure 4.14b. Consider a control sequence that involves two successive Memory Read operations. Can MAR$_{in}$ for the second operation be issued in the same control step as WMFC for the first operation (step $i + 2$)? Explain the conditions under which this might be possible.

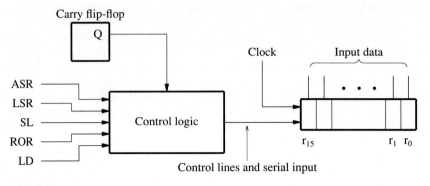

FIGURE P4.2
Organization of shift-register control for Problem 4.30.

4.29. It is required to implement the instruction ASL #n,R in a computer. This instruction results in shifting the contents of register R to the left *n* times, where $0 < n \le 4$. Show how to use multiplexers to replace the bus tie G in the organization of Figure 4.6 to implement this instruction and give the sequence of control steps for its execution.

4.30. A computer uses the shift register shown in Figure P4.2 to perform shift and rotate operations. Inputs to the control logic for this register consist of

ASR	Arithmetic Shift Right
LSR	Logic Shift Right
SL	Shift Left
ROR	Rotate Right
LD	Parallel Load

All shift and load operations are controlled by one clock input. The shift register is implemented with edge-triggered D flip-flops. Give a complete logic diagram for the control logic and for bits r_0, r_1, and r_{15} of the shift register.

4.31. A digital controller, Figure P4.3, has three outputs, X, Y, Z, and two inputs, A and B. It is externally driven by a clock. The controller is continuously going through the following sequence of events. At the beginning of the first clock period, line X is set to 1. At the beginning of the second clock period, either line Y or Z is set to 1, depending on whether line A is equal to 1 or 0, respectively. The controller then waits until line B

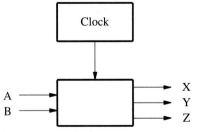

FIGURE P4.3
Digital controller in Problem 4.31.

is set to 1. On the following positive edge of the clock, the controller sets output Z to 1 for the duration of one clock period, then resets all output signals to 0 for one clock period. The sequence is repeated starting at the next positive edge of the clock. Give a suitable logic design for this controller.

4.32. The ALU of a computer is implemented in the form of a PLA (see Appendix A). It accepts two 2-bit numbers A and B, a carry input C_{in}, and a 2-bit function input F. The output of the ALU consists of a 2-bit result Y and a carry output C_{out}. The operation performed by the ALU is determined by the function inputs according to the following table

F_1	F_0	**Operation**	C_{out}
0	0	A + B	Carry output
0	1	A $\vee$ B	1
1	0	A $\wedge$ B	0
1	1	A $\vee$ $\overline{B}$	0

Design the required PLA by defining its product and sum terms. You should attempt to use as few product terms as possible.

CHAPTER

5

MICROPROGRAMMED CONTROL

Chapter 4 introduced the possibility of generating control signals in the CPU by software means, known as microprogrammed control. It dealt briefly with the general approach and some relative merits of such designs. In this chapter we will pursue this alternative to hardwired circuits in greater detail.

Let us start with the basic premise that microprogramming is a software approach that can be handled with hardware structures akin to those used to sequence ordinary programs. Assuming that microinstructions will be executed in sequential order from consecutive locations in the microprogram memory (also called the *control store*), it is natural to use a microprogram counter (μPC) to keep track of addresses. The μPC is incremented by one in order to fetch the next microinstruction. Because each machine instruction is executed by a corresponding microroutine, a starting address for the microroutine must be specified as a function of the contents of the instruction register (IR). The structure shown in Figure 4.20 fits these comments well. The means for branching within the microprogram is provided by a branch address generator, which supplements the incremental sequencing achieved by the μPC. Unconditional or conditional branching is possible, the latter as a result of tests on status flags and condition codes. This organization is remarkably similar to the basic sequencing hardware in the CPU, where the PC fetches instructions from the main memory. In normal operation, the PC is incremented to point to the next instruction unless branching is indicated.

5.1 MICROINSTRUCTIONS

Having looked at a possible scheme for sequencing microinstructions, we should take a closer look at the format of individual microinstructions. As we suggested in Chapter 4, a straightforward way to structure microinstructions is to assign one bit position to each control signal required in the CPU. A simple example of this is shown in Figure 4.17. To assess the usefulness of this approach, we will consider the example in Figure 4.8, which uses seventeen distinct control signals. As one programming option, we could assign one microinstruction bit per signal as indicated in Figure 5.1 and set each bit to 1 if the corresponding control signal is to be turned ON.

Seven timing steps were used in Figure 4.8, which suggests the need for seven microinstructions. A branch microinstruction is also needed to branch to the starting address of the routine that implements the required Add operation. Note that we have encountered the same use of the branch microinstruction in Figure 4.19.

A different problem arises with the Wait for Memory-function-completed (WM-FC) signal. This signal was used in Chapter 4 to synchronize the fast, hardwired-controlled CPU circuits with the slower main memory, but the need for such signals is less obvious in microprogrammed control. Microinstructions are fetched from the control store and are available at a rate determined by the access time of the store. If the control store had the same access time as the main memory, it may be argued that there would be no need for the WMFC signaling mechanism. However, control stores are usually relatively small, so it is feasible to speed up their cycle times with costly circuitry. This is often not an economical proposition with the main memories, which are normally considerably larger. Hence, main memory cycle times tend to be longer than those of the control store. To ensure that data read out of the main memory are valid, it is essential to wait for a signal from the memory that verifies the validity of the data in the MDR. This can be accomplished by a microinstruction test loop similar to the instruction loops used in Section 2.8 to test the status of ready flags in I/O devices. An alternative scheme, which was used in Chapter 4, delays the

Micro-instruction	..	PC_{in}	PC_{out}	MAR_{in}	Read	MDR_{out}	IR_{in}	Address out	Y_{in}	Clear Y	Carry-in	Add	Z_{in}	Z_{out}	$R1_{out}$	$R1_{in}$	WMFC	End	..
1		0	1	1	1	0	0	0	0	1	1	1	1	0	0	0	0	0	
2		1	0	0	0	0	0	0	0	0	0	0	0	1	0	0	1	0	
3		0	0	0	0	1	1	0	0	0	0	0	0	0	0	0	0	0	
4		0	0	1	1	0	0	1	0	0	0	0	0	0	0	0	0	0	
5		0	0	0	0	0	0	0	1	0	0	0	0	0	1	0	1	0	
6		0	0	0	0	1	0	0	0	0	0	1	1	0	0	0	0	0	
7		0	0	0	0	0	0	0	0	0	0	0	0	1	0	1	0	1	

FIGURE 5.1
An example of bit patterns for a microprogram corresponding to Figure 4.8.

execution of the next microinstruction until the Memory-function-completed (MFC) signal arrives. This signal is indicated by the WMFC bit in a microinstruction. Figure 4.8 shows the required WMFC delay as part of steps 2 and 5.

5.2   GROUPING OF CONTROL SIGNALS

The preceding scheme for microprogrammed control has one serious drawback. Assigning individual bits to each control signal is certain to lead to long microinstructions, because the number of required signals is normally fairly large. Moreover, only a few bits are set to 1 (to be used for active gating) in any given microinstruction, and this obviously results in poor utilization of the available bit space. Consider the CPU block diagram in Figure 4.1. Assume that it contains four general-purpose registers, R0, R1, R2, and R3, and three other registers called SOURCE, DESTIN, and TEMP. These latter are used for temporary storage within the CPU but are completely transparent to the programmer. Most computers have such registers for sequencing the movement of addresses and operands over a limited set of data paths. The augmented block diagram shown in Figure 5.2 indicates the control signals necessary to provide the transfers within the CPU. Note that some connections are permanent, such as the output of IR to the decoding circuits and both inputs to the ALU. There is a total of 24 gating signals in the diagram. A number of control signals not shown in the figure are also needed, as seen in the previous example. These include the Read, Write, Clear Y, Set Carry-in, WMFC, and End signals. Finally, it is necessary to specify the function to be performed by the ALU. Let us assume that 16 functions are provided in our example, including Add, Subtract, AND, and XOR. These functions depend upon the particular ALU used and do not necessarily show a one-to-one correspondence with the OP codes in machine instructions.

The discussion above indicates that 46 distinct signals are required, which would imply the existence of at least 46 bits in each microinstruction. Such poor utilization of bits is unattractive from the design point of view, but fortunately, the scheme can be easily improved. Most signals are not needed simultaneously, and many signals are mutually exclusive. For example, only one function of the ALU can be activated at a time. A source for data transfers must be unique, because it is not possible to gate the contents of two different registers onto the bus at the same time. Read and Write signals to the memory cannot be active simultaneously. This suggests the possibility of grouping the signals so that all mutually exclusive signals are placed in the same group. Thus, at most one *microoperation* per group is specified in any microinstruction. Then it is possible to use a binary coding scheme to represent given signals within a group. In the case of ALU functions, it is apparent that 4 bits suffice to represent the 16 available functions. Register output control signals can be placed in a group consisting of PC_{out}, MDR_{out}, Z_{out}, $Address_{out}$, $R0_{out}$, $R1_{out}$, $R3_{out}$, $SOURCE_{out}$, $DESTIN_{out}$, and $TEMP_{out}$. Any one of these can be selected by a unique 4-bit code.

Further natural groupings can be made for the remaining signals. Figure 5.3 shows a possible partial format for the microinstructions, in which each group occupies a field large enough to contain the required codes. Most fields must include

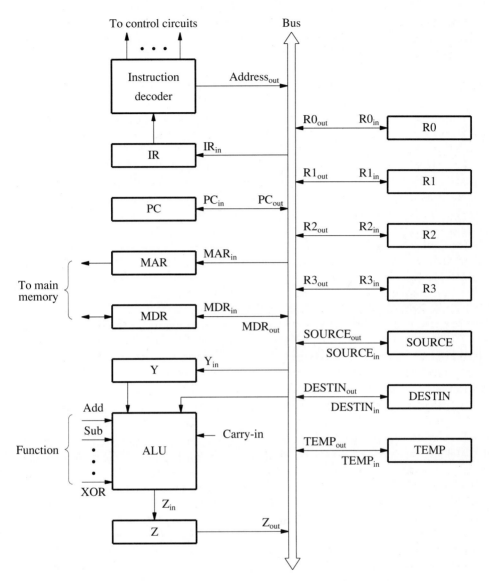

FIGURE 5.2
A single-bus CPU block diagram.

one inactive code for the case in which no action is required. This is not necessarily a requirement for all fields. For example, F5 contains 4 bits that specify one of the 16 operations performed in the ALU. Since no spare code is included, the ALU will be active during execution of every microinstruction. However, its activity is monitored by the rest of the machine through register Z, which is loaded only when the Z_{in} signal is present.

Microinstruction

...	F1	F2	F3	F4	F5
	F1 (4 bits)	F2 (3 bits)	F3 (2 bits)	F4 (2 bits)	F5 (4 bits)
	0000: No transfer	000: No transfer	00: No transfer	00: No transfer	0000: Add
	0001: PC_{out}	001: PC_{in}	01: MAR_{in}	01: Y_{in}	0001: Sub
	0010: MDR_{out}	010: IR_{in}	10: MDR_{in}	10: $SOURCE_{in}$	•
	0011: Z_{out}	011: Z_{in}	11: $TEMP_{in}$	11: $DESTIN_{in}$	•
	0100: $R0_{out}$	100: $R0_{in}$			•
	0101: $R1_{out}$	101: $R1_{in}$			1111: XOR
	0110: $R2_{out}$	110: $R2_{in}$			
	0111: $R3_{out}$	111: $R3_{in}$			16 ALU
	1000: $SOURCE_{out}$				functions
	1001: $DESTIN_{out}$				
	1010: $TEMP_{out}$				
	1011: $Address_{out}$				

F6	F7	F8	F9	F10	...
F6 (2 bits)	F7 (1 bit)	F8 (1 bit)	F9 (1 bit)	F10 (1 bit)	
00: No action	0: No action	0: Carry-in = 0	0: No action	0: Continue	
01: Read	1: Clear Y	1: Carry-in = 1	1: WMFC	1: End	
10: Write					

FIGURE 5.3
An example of a partial format for field-encoded microinstructions.

Grouping control signals into fields results in a small increase in the required hardware because decoding circuits must be used to translate the bit patterns of each field into actual control signals. The cost of additional hardware is more than offset by the reduced number of bits in microinstructions, however, which will result in a smaller control store. Note that in Figure 5.3 only 21 bits are needed to store the patterns for the 46 desired signals.

So far we have considered one level of grouping and encoding of the control signals. We can extend this idea by attempting to enumerate the required signals at all possible instances. Each combination of signals can then be assigned a distinct code that would be stored in microinstructions. Such full encoding is likely to further reduce the length of microwords, but it will also increase the complexity of the required decoder circuits.

Highly encoded schemes that use compact codes to specify only a small number of control functions in each microinstruction are often called the *vertical* organization. On the other hand, the minimally encoded scheme of Figure 5.1, where a large number of resources can be controlled with a single microinstruction, is called the *horizontal* organization. The latter approach is desirable when the operating speed of a computer is the critical factor and when the machine structure allows parallel usage of resources. The vertical approach results in considerably slower operating speeds because more microinstructions are needed to perform the desired control functions. However, fewer bits are required for each microinstruction. This obviously does not imply that the total number of bits in the control store is smaller. The significant factor is the reduced requirement for parallel hardware needed to handle the execution of microinstructions.

Horizontal and vertical organizations represent the two organizational extremes in microprogrammed control. Many intermediate schemes are also possible in which the degree of encoding is a design parameter. The layout of Figure 5.3 fits in this intermediate category. It is closer to the horizontal organization than vertical because it attempts to group only mutually exclusive microoperations in the same fields, which results in a considerable number of fields per microinstruction. Such *mixed* organizations are found in most practical computers, although it is common practice to describe their control structures as emphasizing either horizontal or vertical organization.

The example used in this chapter is based on the structure of Figure 5.2, which shows only the basic components. A number of details are not included in it, because they are not essential for understanding the principles of operation. Although we considered only a subset of the control signals needed in a typical machine, this subset is quite representative of actual requirements.

5.3 MICROPROGRAM SEQUENCING

The simple example of a microprogram in Figure 5.1 requires only straightforward sequential execution of microinstructions, except for the branch at the end of the fetch phase. If each machine instruction can be implemented by a microroutine of this kind, effective use can be made of the microcontrol structure suggested in Figure 4.20, in which a μPC governs the sequencing. Each microroutine can be accessed initially by decoding the machine instruction into the starting address to be loaded into the μPC. Some branching capability within the microprogram may be introduced through special branch microinstructions, which can specify the branch address as the corresponding machine branch instructions do.

We suggested at the beginning of this chapter that this approach is natural because it follows general patterns of computer organization and operation. Writing microprograms is likely to be fairly simple because standard software techniques can be used. However, these advantages are counterbalanced by two major disadvantages. Having a separate microroutine for each machine instruction requires using a large number of microinstructions and a large control store. Noting that most machine instructions involve several addressing modes, we can see that having a separate microroutine for each instruction combined with each addressing mode is not an appealing proposition, because many microroutines would show considerable duplication in parts. It is therefore more reasonable to organize the microprogram so that as many common parts as possible are shared by the microroutines. This requires a considerable number of branch microinstructions to transfer control among the various parts. Hence a second disadvantage arises, because execution time is lengthened by the time needed to carry out the required branches.

Let us consider a more complicated example of a complete machine instruction. In Chapter 2 we used the PDP-11 instruction set to illustrate some basic programming concepts. A typical two-operand instruction in that set is

$$\text{ADD} \qquad \text{src,dst}$$

which adds the contents of the source (src) and destination (dst) and places the sum into the destination location. Operand locations (both src and dst) can be specified in any of the eight allowable address modes. We will use this instruction in conjunction with the CPU structure detailed in Figure 5.2 to demonstrate a possible microprogrammed implementation. It is important to keep in mind that Figure 5.2 is a simplified block diagram and does not exactly represent any particular machine, although it represents a general structure used in many commercially available machines.

A suitable microprogram, presented in flowchart form for easier understanding, is shown in Figure 5.4. Each box in the chart corresponds to a microinstruction that controls the transfers and operations indicated within the box. The microinstruction is located at the address indicated by the octal number above the upper right-hand corner of the box. Most of the flowchart is self-explanatory, although some details warrant elaboration.

The microprogram in the figure is arranged so that each microinstruction controls transfers that can be performed simultaneously. It is possible to have a more compact microprogram if some of the microinstructions are combined. For example, after the initiation of the instruction fetch, the program must update (that is, increment) the contents of the PC. If the main memory is organized on a word-addressable basis, the PC must be incremented by 1. (In a 16-bit, byte-addressable machine, the PC would be incremented by 2, and in a 32-bit machine by 4.) This is indicated as

$$Z \leftarrow [PC] + 1$$
$$PC \leftarrow [Z]$$

The required action is to gate the contents of the PC onto the bus, set the carry-in signal, clear register Y, perform the addition, and gate the result into register Z. As the next step, the updated value must be transferred from Z to the PC. It is obvious that both steps cannot be carried out at the same time, because only one register can be gated onto the bus at any given time. However, it is not essential that the actions to be performed in these steps be specified in two separate microinstructions.

Consider the alternative of using a single microinstruction and a two-phase clock to sequence gating onto the bus in these two steps. During clock phase 1, the first step can be performed, at the end of which the updated contents of the PC are available in the Z register. Then, phase 2 can be used to transfer these contents into the PC, as required in the second step.

Other microinstructions can be combined in the same fashion. For example, single microinstructions can replace the pairs of microinstructions at the following

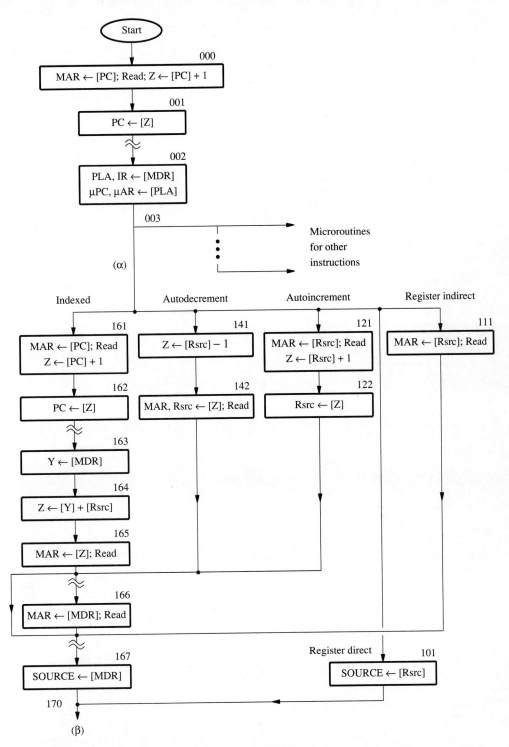

FIGURE 5.4

Flowchart of a microprogram for the ADD src,dst instruction.

189

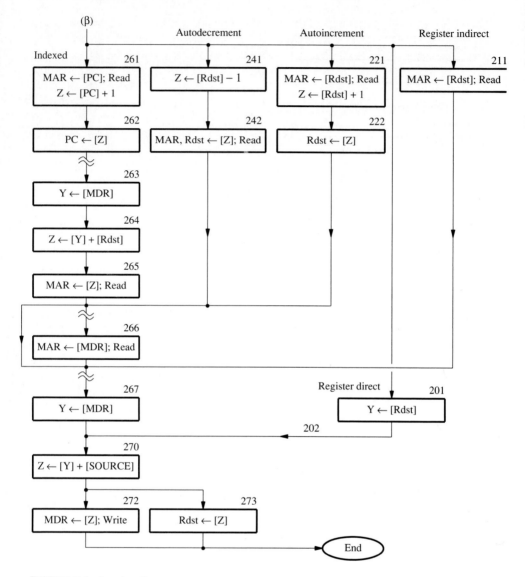

FIGURE 5.4   *(continued)*

addresses: (121, 122), (141, 142), (161, 162), (164, 165), (221, 222), (241, 242), (261, 262), and (264, 265). The transfers indicated in the first microinstruction of each pair can be performed during phase 1, and those in the second microinstruction can be carried out during phase 2.

The obvious advantages of controlling gating by means of a two-phase clock are the accompanying reduction in the size of the control store and faster execution because fewer microinstructions need to be fetched. The disadvantages are that some extra hardware is needed, and the flexibility in assigning codes to represent control signals in microinstructions is somewhat diminished. The latter point may be illustrated by the Z_{out} signal. When the contents of the PC are being updated, the Z_{out} signal must be asserted only during phase 2 (P2) of the clock. However, in the case of the microinstructions in locations 272 and 273, it is not necessary to wait until P2. Z_{out} could be asserted during phase 1 (P1), which would result in a somewhat faster operation. If speed is extremely important, two codes could be assigned to Z_{out} (in the microinstruction field F1), one corresponding to $Z_{out} \cdot P1$ and the other to $Z_{out} \cdot P2$.

5.3.1 Branch Address Modification

The microprogram in Figure 5.4 shows that branches are not always made to a single branch address. This is a direct consequence of the attempt to combine simple microroutines by sharing common parts. Consider the point labeled β in Figure 5.4. At this point, it is necessary to derive the destination (dst) operand address and fetch the operand. The figure shows five possible branches which, from left to right, correspond to indexed, autodecrement, autoincrement, register indirect, and register address modes. A straightforward but very inefficient way to generate the proper branch address would be to use four consecutive two-way conditional branch microinstructions. Alternatively, several fields could be included within the branch microinstruction, where each field is used to generate a particular branch address. There is a range of possibilities between these two extremes. An efficient technique is to arrange the microinstructions so that the five branch addresses differ in a few designated bits only (at least three in this case). A single branch microinstruction can then be used to specify the other bits, leaving the designated bits equal to zero, and can instruct the control circuitry to modify these bits on the basis of the address mode held in the IR. The necessary modification can be accomplished simply by ORing in the desired bits from the IR, or some decoded version of them, as will be illustrated in the example that follows.

A similar modification is required when computing the source address (point α in the flowchart), but this is a part of an even wider branch. Note that branch microinstructions are not shown explicitly in Figure 5.4 because their presence is implicit in the structure of the flowchart. However, addresses of some branch microinstructions are shown for the convenience of interpretation of a later example.

5.3.2 Wide-Branch Addressing

The above technique of modifying branch addresses results in increasingly more complex circuitry as the number of branches becomes larger. One complex case arises when the machine instruction fetch is completed and it is necessary to decide which microroutine corresponds to the instruction. It is not unusual to have 30 or more possible branches, depending upon organization of the microprogram.

A simple and inexpensive way to generate the required branch addresses is to use a programmable logic array (PLA). A description of PLA integrated circuits is given in Appendix A and an example of their use was shown in Chapter 4. In the case of wide-branch addressing, the OP code of a machine instruction must be translated into the starting address of the corresponding microroutine. This may be done by connecting the OP-code bits of the instruction register as inputs to the PLA, which acts as a decoder. The output of the PLA is the address of the desired microroutine. This approach is particularly attractive when the OP-code field is variable in length, because a considerable number of input variables (to the decoder) are needed to produce relatively few output addresses.

5.3.3   Detailed Example

Let us examine one path of the flowchart in Figure 5.4 in more detail. Before proceeding, recall that each microinstruction is assigned an address in the control store, indicated by the octal number above the upper right-hand corner of the box. It is assumed that all microinstructions require the same amount of time to be fetched from the control store, and that this time is shorter than the access time for the main memory. Therefore, in some instances, it is necessary to wait for completion of a main memory cycle. These situations are indicated in the figure by breaks in the flow lines.

As a particular example, consider a specific version of the general ADD instruction, where the source involves the autoincrement mode, and the destination is given in the register mode. We will look at the path (microroutine) needed to execute

$$\text{ADD} \qquad (\text{Rsrc}) +, \text{Rdst}$$

where Rsrc and Rdst are general registers in the machine. Figure 5.5 shows the detailed signals that are specified by the microinstructions in this path. Actual signals are shown, instead of encoded bit patterns, for ease of understanding. The corresponding codes may be those given in Figure 5.3.

The microroutine of Figure 5.5 contains two features that we have not used before. First, we have assumed that it is possible to issue WMFC in the same microinstruction that contains a Read or a Write request, as in the microinstruction at location 166. This would not be allowed with the simple circuit given in Figure 4.14. Second, an additional class of register transfer signals is required. Allowing specification of any general-purpose register as part of the address modes implies that gating functions involving a particular register cannot be indicated in the microinstructions. Instead, we must resort to a more general indication of src and dst registers. Thus, microinstructions contain codes for Rsrc_{out}, Rsrc_{in}, Rdst_{out}, Rdst_{in}. These microinstruction-generated signals must be translated into specific register transfer signals by the decoding circuitry connected to the src and dst address fields of the IR. Note that this involves a two-level decoding process. First, the microinstruction field must be decoded to determine that an Rsrc or Rdst register is involved. The decoded output is then used to gate the contents of the src or dst fields in the IR

Contents of IR :	0 1 1 0	0 1 0	Rsrc	0 0 0	Rdst
	15 12	11 9	8 6	5 3	2 0

Address (octal)	Microinstruction
000	PC_{out}, MAR_{in}, Read, Clear Y, Set carry-in, Add, Z_{in}
001	Z_{out}, PC_{in}, WMFC
002	MDR_{out}, IR_{in}
003	μBranch {μPC $\leftarrow$ [PLA]}
121	$Rsrc_{out}$, MAR_{in}, Read, Clear Y, Set carry-in, Add, Z_{in}
122	Z_{out}, $Rsrc_{in}$
123	μBranch {μPC $\leftarrow$ 166; μPC$_0$ $\leftarrow$ $\overline{[IR_9]}$}, WMFC
166	MDR_{out}, MAR_{in}, Read, WMFC
167	MDR_{out}, $SOURCE_{in}$
170	μBranch {μPC $\leftarrow$ 201; μPC$_{5,4}$ $\leftarrow$ $[IR_{5,4}]$; μPC$_3$ $\leftarrow$ $\overline{[IR_5]}$ $\cdot$ $\overline{[IR_4]}$ $\cdot$ $[IR_3]$}
201	$Rdst_{out}$, Y_{in}
202	μBranch {μPC $\leftarrow$ 270}
270	$SOURCE_{out}$, Add, Z_{in}
271	μBranch {μPC $\leftarrow$ 272; μPC$_0$ $\leftarrow$ $\overline{[IR_5]}$ $\cdot$ $\overline{[IR_4]}$ $\cdot$ $\overline{[IR_3]}$}
273	Z_{out}, $Rdst_{in}$, End

FIGURE 5.5

Microroutine for ADD (Rsrc)+,Rdst. *Note:* Microinstruction at location 166 is not executed in this specific example.

into a second decoder, which produces the gating signals for the actual registers R0 to R3.

The microprogram in Figure 5.4 is derived by combining a number of separate microroutines to save space in the control store, which results in a structure that necessitates many branch points. Our example in Figure 5.5 has five branch points, so five branch microinstructions are required. In each case, the expression in brackets indicates the branch address that is to be loaded into the μPC. The expression also shows how this address is modified according to the bit-ORing scheme discussed in Section 5.3.1. Consider the microinstruction in location 123 as an illustration. The action of its unmodified version causes a branch to the microinstruction in 166, which causes another fetch from the main memory corresponding to an indirect address mode. When a direct address mode appears, this fetch must be bypassed by branching directly to location 167. This bypass may be accomplished simply by ORing the inverse of the "indirect" bit in the src address field (that is, bit 9 in the IR) with the 0 bit position of the μPC.

An example of a multiple branch is presented by the microinstruction in location 170. In this case, the five branch addresses differ in the middle octal digit only. Therefore, the octal pattern 201 is loaded into the μPC, and the 3 bits to be ORed with the middle octal digit are supplied by the decoding circuitry connected to the dst address mode field (bits 3, 4, and 5 of the IR). Note that microinstruction addresses have been chosen to make this modification easy to implement. Bits 4 and 5 of the μPC are set directly from the corresponding bits in the IR. This suffices to select the appropriate microinstruction for all dst address modes except register indirect. This register is covered by setting bit 3 of the μPC to 1 using the AND gate $[\overline{IR_5}] \cdot [\overline{IR_4}] \cdot [IR_3]$.

5.4 MICROINSTRUCTIONS WITH NEXT-ADDRESS FIELD

One of the most striking features of the microroutine in Figure 5.5 is the relatively large number of branch microinstructions. These microinstructions constitute one-third of the total and present a serious constraint on the operating speed of the computer. The situation can become significantly worse when other microroutines are considered. The increase in branch microinstructions stems partly from limitations in the ability to assign successive addresses to all microinstructions that are generally executed in consecutive order. For example, in cases of wide branching with address modification, some addresses have to be assigned in a rather inflexible fashion, and this frequently leaves address spaces that are difficult to use efficiently.

This situation prompts a reevaluation of the sequencing technique built around an incrementable μPC. As an alternative, we may consider a scheme in which each microinstruction includes some branching capability. The simplest approach is to include an address field as a part of every microinstruction to indicate the location of the next microinstruction to be fetched. This means, in effect, that every microinstruction becomes a branch microinstruction, in addition to its other functions.

The major disadvantage of this approach is the need for additional bits for the address field. Its severity can be assessed as follows. In a typical computer, it is possible to design an adequate microprogram that governs most control functions with fewer than 4K microinstructions, employing perhaps 50 to 80 bits per microinstruction. This implies that an address field of 12 bits is required. Therefore, approximately one-sixth of the control store capacity must be devoted to addressing purposes. Even if more extensive microprograms are needed, the address field will become only slightly larger.

The most obvious advantage of this approach is the virtual elimination of separate branch microinstructions. Furthermore, there are few limitations in assignment of addresses to microinstructions. These advantages outweigh the negative attributes and make the scheme attractive from the practical point of view. In fact, versions of this approach are adopted in most commercially available computers that use microprogrammed control. This approach eliminates the need for an incrementable μPC. A simple *microinstruction address register* (μAR) can hold the address of the microinstruction to be fetched. This calls for a new control structure, and one possible organization is given in Figure 5.6. Note that the next-address bits are fed through the OR gates to the μAR. The address may be modified on the basis of the data in the IR, status flags, and condition codes. The decoding circuits include a PLA decoder that is used to generate the starting address of a given microroutine on the basis of the OP code in the IR.

Let us now reconsider the example of Figure 5.5 to see how a microroutine for the machine instruction

$$\text{ADD} \qquad (\text{Rsrc})+, \text{Rdst}$$

may be arranged in light of the ideas introduced in this section. Let us assume that the CPU has eight general-purpose registers. Otherwise, it is structured essentially the same as the block diagram in Figure 5.2. Furthermore, let its microprogrammed control follow the pattern of Figure 5.6.

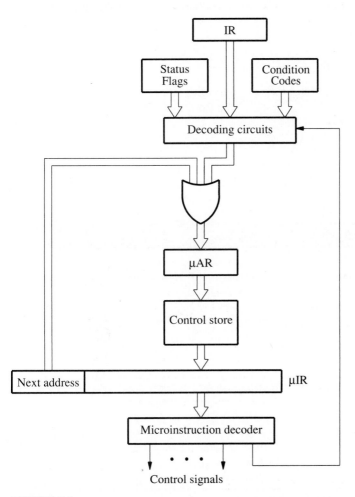

FIGURE 5.6
Microinstruction-sequencing organization.

A number of control signals that were not included in Figure 5.3 will be needed. Instead of referring to registers R0 to R7 explicitly, we will use the Rsrc and Rdst names, which can be decoded into the actual control signals with the data in the src and dst fields of the IR. Branching with the bit-ORing technique will require including the appropriate commands in the microinstructions. Let the bit ORing needed in microinstructions 123, 170, and 271 of Figure 5.5 be denoted by the signals OR_{indsrc}, OR_{dst}, and OR_{result}, respectively. For completeness, we will also include OR_{inddst}, which indicates indirect addressing for the destination operand. These signals will be

F0	F1	F2	F3
F0 (8 bits)	F1 (4 bits)	F2 (3 bits)	F3 (2 bits)
Address of next microinstruction	0000: No transfer 0001: PC_{out} 0010: MDR_{out} 0011: Z_{out} 0100: $Rsrc_{out}$ 0101: $Rdst_{out}$ 1000: $SOURCE_{out}$ 1001: $DESTIN_{out}$ 1010: $TEMP_{out}$	000: No transfer 001: PC_{in} 010: IR_{in} 011: Z_{in} 100: $Rsrc_{in}$ 101: $Rdst_{in}$	00: No transfer 01: MAR_{in} 10: MDR_{in} 11: $TEMP_{in}$

F4	F5	F6	F7
F4 (2 bits)	F5 (4 bits)	F6 (2 bits)	F7 (1 bit)
00: No transfer 01: Y_{in} 10: $SOURCE_{in}$ 11: $DESTIN_{in}$	0000: Add 0001: Sub ••• 1111: XOR	00: No action 01: Read 10: Write	0: No action 1: Clear Y

F8	F9	F10	F11
F8 (1 bit)	F9 (1 bit)	F10 (3 bits)	F11 (1 bit)
0: Carry-in = 0 1: Carry-in = 1	0: No action 1: WMFC	000: No action 001: OR_{dst} 010: OR_{indsrc} 011: OR_{inddst} 100: OR_{result}	0: No action 1: PLA_{out}

FIGURE 5.7
Format for microinstructions in the example of Section 5.4.

Octal address	F0	F1	F2	F3	F4	F5	F6	F7	F8	F9	F10	F11
0 0 0	0 0 0 0 0 0 0 1	0 0 0 1	0 1 1	0 1	0 0	0 0 0 0	0 1	1	1	0	0 0 0	0
0 0 1	0 0 0 0 0 0 1 0	0 0 1 1	0 0 1	0 0	0 0	0 0 0 0	0 0	0	0	1	0 0 0	0
0 0 2	0 0 0 0 0 0 1 1	0 0 1 0	0 1 0	0 0	0 0	0 0 0 0	0 0	0	0	0	0 0 0	0
0 0 3	0 0 0 0 0 0 0 0	0 0 0 0	0 0 0	0 0	0 0	0 0 0 0	0 0	0	0	0	0 0 0	1
1 2 1	0 1 0 1 0 0 1 0	0 1 0 0	0 1 1	0 1	0 0	0 0 0 0	0 1	1	1	0	0 0 0	0
1 2 2	0 1 1 1 0 1 1 0	0 0 1 1	1 0 0	0 0	0 0	0 0 0 0	0 0	0	0	1	0 1 0	0
1 6 6	0 1 1 1 0 1 1 1	0 0 1 0	0 0 0	0 1	0 0	0 0 0 0	0 1	0	0	1	0 0 0	0
1 6 7	1 0 0 0 0 0 0 1	0 0 1 0	0 0 0	0 0	1 0	0 0 0 0	0 0	0	0	0	0 0 1	0
2 0 1	1 0 1 1 1 0 0 0	0 1 0 1	0 0 0	0 0	0 1	0 0 0 0	0 0	0	0	0	0 0 0	0
2 7 0	1 0 1 1 1 0 1 0	1 0 0 0	0 1 1	0 0	0 0	0 0 0 0	0 0	0	0	0	1 0 0	0
2 7 3	0 0 0 0 0 0 0 0	0 0 1 1	1 0 1	0 0	0 0	0 0 0 0	0 0	0	0	0	0 0 0	0

FIGURE 5.8
Implementation of the microroutine of Figure 5.5, using a next-microinstruction address field. (See Figure 5.7 for encoded signals.)

encoded in a 3-bit field in the microinstructions. If a PLA is used to initially decode the instruction OP codes, one bit in a microinstruction will be used to indicate when the output of the PLA is to be gated into the μAR. Finally, each microinstruction will contain an 8-bit field that holds the address of the next microinstruction. Figure 5.7 shows a complete format for the assumed microinstructions, which is essentially an expanded version of the format in Figure 5.3.

Using such microinstructions we can implement the microroutine of Figure 5.5 as shown in Figure 5.8. In this case, fewer microinstructions are needed because most of the branch microinstructions are no longer required. The branch microinstructions at locations 123 and 271 have been combined with the microinstructions immediately preceding them. The branch microinstruction at 003 must remain separate, however, because it depends on the contents of IR that are loaded by the microinstruction at location 002. This microroutine does not terminate by producing the End signal. When microinstruction sequencing is controlled by a μPC, the End signal is used to reset the μPC to point to the starting address of the microinstruction that will fetch the next machine instruction to be executed. In our example, this starting address is 000_8. However, in an organization corresponding to Figure 5.8, the starting address is not specified by a resetting mechanism triggered by the End signal. Instead, it is specified explicitly in the F0 field.

Figure 5.9 gives a more detailed diagram of the control structure of Figure 5.6. It shows how control signals can be decoded from the microinstruction fields and used to control the sequencing. Detailed circuitry for bit-ORing is shown in Figure 5.10.

5.5 PREFETCHING MICROINSTRUCTIONS

The major drawback of microprogrammed control is the inherently slower operating speed of the computer. Fetching a microinstruction from the control store takes considerably longer than generating equivalent control signals using hardwired circuits.

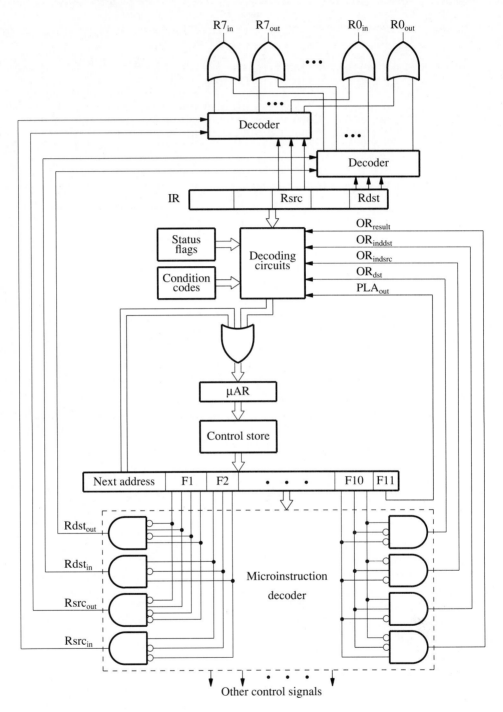

FIGURE 5.9
Some details of the control-signal-generating circuitry.

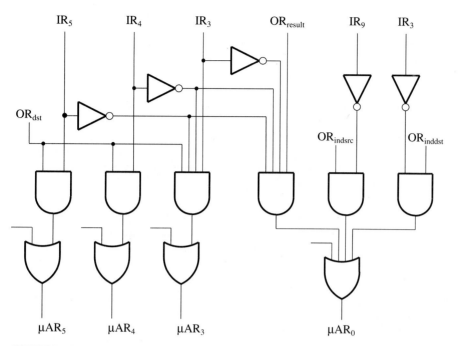

FIGURE 5.10
Control circuitry for bit-ORing (part of decoding circuits in Figure 5.9).

It is obvious that microprogrammed machines will never be able to match the speed of hardwired ones.

Having made a fundamental decision to use microprogramming, the designer may still desire to produce as fast a machine as possible; probably by choosing the fastest available control store, and using long microinstructions to simultaneously generate as many control signals as possible. But there is another option available. Instead of following the natural sequence of fetching a microinstruction, executing it, and then fetching the next one, it is possible to save time by prefetching the next microinstruction while the current one is being executed. In this way, most of the execution time can be overlapped with the fetch time. Thus the overall machine speed is essentially dependent upon the fetch times. Such techniques of overlapping operations to keep the hardware units as busy as possible are often referred to as "pipelining." The concept of pipelining will be discussed in detail in Chapter 11.

Prefetching microinstructions presents some organizational difficulties. It is sometimes necessary to use the status flags and the results of the currently executed microinstruction to determine the address of the next microinstruction. Thus, straightforward prefetching will occasionally prefetch a wrong microinstruction. In these cases it is necessary to repeat the fetch with the correct address, which requires more complex hardware. However, the disadvantages are minor and the prefetching technique is often found in practice.

5.6 EMULATION

The main function of microprogrammed control, as discussed previously, is to provide a means for simple, flexible, and relatively inexpensive control of a computer. However, it also offers other interesting possibilities. Its flexibility in handling resources within a machine allows implementation of diverse classes of instructions. Given a computer with a certain instruction set, it is possible to define additional machine instructions and implement them with extra microroutines.

An extension of the preceding idea leads to an even more attractive possibility. Suppose we add to the instruction repertoire of a given computer M_1 an entirely new set of instructions that is in fact the instruction set of a different computer M_2. Programs written in the machine language of M_2 can then be run on computer M_1. In this case, we say that M_1 *emulates* M_2. This is a very useful function because it can enable replacement of obsolete equipment with more up-to-date machines. If the replacement computer fully emulates the original one, then no software changes have to be made to run the existing programs. Thus, emulation facilitates transitions into new systems with a minimum of disruption.

Emulation is easiest when the machines involved have similar architectures. However, there have also been many successes in emulating computers using machines with totally different architectures.

Finally, we should note the possibility of designing a computer with a highly flexible structure that is controlled by a microprogram in RAM storage. Let us assume that the structure is flexible enough to permit easy reconfiguration of the machine through simple replacement of the microprogram. We may then use different microprograms for execution of different tasks. If a program written for a given class of machines, say, VAX-11, is to be executed, the computer would be configured to emulate VAX-11 machines by loading the corresponding microprogram into the control store. Another microprogram could be used to emulate the Motorola 68000 architecture, and so on. Thus a single computer could exhibit the characteristics of a number of distinct machines.

5.7 BIT SLICES

The flexibility attainable through microprogramming makes it possible to design the data path section of a processor (the ALU, registers, and internal connections), independently of its instruction set. Moreover, it is possible to design general-purpose microinstruction sequencing hardware that can be used in conjunction with a wide range of data path configurations and instruction sets. In other words, we can define building blocks that can be easily assembled into a computer that meets the needs of a given application class. The capabilities and the instruction set of such a computer are determined by the particular building blocks chosen, by the way they are interconnected, and of course by the microprogram.

The flexibility of this building block approach can be enhanced considerably if the blocks can be used to build processors that have arbitrary word lengths. This is the basis of the bit-slice idea. A *bit slice* is a "slice" through the data path of a typical processor. It contains all circuits necessary to provide ALU functions, register transfers, and control functions for only a few bits of the data path (typically 2, 4, or 8 bits). The connection patterns for the circuits on the slice are under microprogram control. The necessary control signals are provided by other building blocks.

A 4-bit slice provides the functions of an ALU and a number of registers for 4 bits of data. It also provides the signals necessary to interconnect a number of slices side by side to form a wider data path. Thus, it is possible to use four slices to form the basis of a 16-bit processor, or eight slices for a 32-bit processor.

The bit-slice building block is highly compatible with VLSI technology. Individual blocks are produced in the form of single chips. In order to illustrate the structure and use of bit slices, we will use the AMD 2900 family of chips, manufactured by Advanced Micro Devices, Inc. Two of the building blocks in this family are a 4-bit ALU chip (AMD 2903) and a microprogram control sequencer chip (AMD 2910). A computer implemented with these chips has a number of 2903s for its data path and uses a 2910 to generate the control store addresses.

The internal structure of the ALU chip is given in Figure 5.11. It consists of a 4-bit ALU, two 4-bit shifters, and a number of 4-bit registers. The ALU provides a full set of arithmetic and logic functions, and the shifters perform shift and rotate operations. The registers consist of 16 general-purpose registers and one register for temporary storage of operands (the Q register). The general-purpose registers are implemented in the form of a *two-port memory*. This is a random-access memory in which all addressing circuits are duplicated. Hence, two registers can be accessed at the same time using the two address inputs AA and AB. The contents of these two registers are then available at the data outputs A and B. Data fed to the DATA IN input of the register file is stored in the register pointed to by the AB address. The outputs A and B are fed to the ALU via two multiplexers. Data may also be fed to the inputs of the ALU from sources external to the chip, which allows additional registers to be used when implementing a processor with more than 16 registers. Of course, these inputs can also be used for connecting the ALU chip to the main memory bus.

Several ALU chips may be concatenated to form a wider data path, as illustrated in Figure 5.12. The address inputs to the register file are connected in parallel so that the corresponding registers are selected on all chips. The serial input-output terminals of the shifter are connected to implement a 16-bit shifter, and the carry inputs and outputs of the arithmetic and logic units are connected in a similar manner. Various aspects of dealing with carry signals will be discussed in Chapter 7.

The organization of the AMD 2910 microprogram control sequencer is illustrated in Figure 5.13. A control store address is generated at the output of the sequencer from one of four sources. A microprogram counter is used for sequential addresses. At any time, its output can be pushed onto a stack to allow subroutine calls within the microprogram. Branching is implemented by supplying a branch address to the input of the sequencer chip. A register/counter stores temporary addresses and simplifies the implementation of loops in the microprogram.

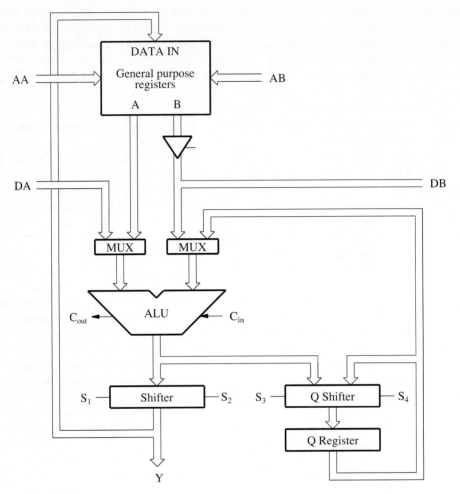

FIGURE 5.11
Internal organization of the AMD 2903 processing element.

A simple, 16-bit processor that uses four AMD 2903 chips and one AMD 2910 chip is shown in Figure 5.14. The bit slices are connected to the memory data and address buses via the MDR and MAR registers, respectively. Two MDR registers are used, one for each direction of transfer. The control section of the processor is organized in a manner similar to the scheme of Figure 5.6. The μBA input of the sequencer is connected to the output of a PLA, which provides the starting microprogram address for each machine instruction. It is also connected to one of the fields in the microinstruction register to allow branching in the microprogram.

The preceding example illustrates how bit slices can be used to implement a processor. This approach enables the design of a fully microprogrammable processor with arbitrary word length that can be tailored to meet any special requirements.

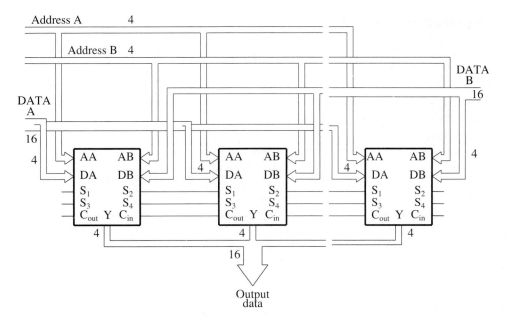

FIGURE 5.12
Concatenation of 4-bit slices to form a 16-bit data path.

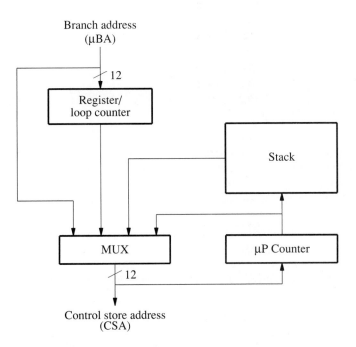

FIGURE 5.13
Organization of the AMD 2910 microprogram control sequencer.

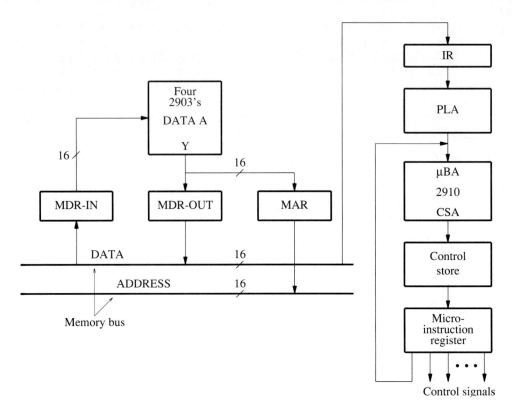

FIGURE 5.14
A 16-bit processor based on the AMD 2903 bit slice.

5.8 CONCLUDING REMARKS

Microprogrammed control is a powerful concept. It provides simple and efficient means for replacing hardwired control logic, not only in computers, but also in the most general class of digital control circuits.

Preparation of microprograms can be an arduous task. Optimization of microcode is often difficult to achieve. Consequently, there is great need for tools to help cope with these difficulties. Much work has been done in the development of high-level languages for microprogramming. Considerable progress has also been made in development of techniques for microcode optimization.

Microprogrammed processors are having a significant impact on many special-purpose applications. The bit-slice approach is particularly significant in this area.

5.9 PROBLEMS

5.1. Write a microroutine (such as the one shown in Figure 5.5) for the instruction

$$\text{MOV} \quad \text{X(Rsrc)},-(\text{Rdst})$$

where the source and destination operands are specified in indexed and autodecrement addressing modes, respectively.

5.2. A BGT (Branch if > 0) machine instruction has the expression $Z + (N \oplus V) = 0$ as its branch condition, where Z, N, and V are the zero, negative, and overflow condition flags, respectively. Write a microroutine that can implement this instruction. Show the circuitry needed to appropriately test the condition codes.

5.3. Write a combined microroutine that can implement the BGT (Branch if >0), BPL (Branch if Plus), and BR (Branch Unconditionally) instructions. The branch conditions for the BGT and BPL instructions are $Z + (N \oplus V) = 0$ and $N = 0$, respectively. What is the total number of microinstructions required? How many microinstructions will be needed if a separate microroutine is used for each machine instruction?

5.4. Figure 5.5 shows an example of a microroutine in which bit-ORing is used to accomplish the modification of microinstruction addresses. Write an equivalent routine, without the use of bit-ORing, in which conditional branch microinstructions are used. How many additional microinstructions are needed? Assume that the conditional branch microinstructions can test some of the bits in the IR.

5.5. In Figure 5.5, bit-ORing is used in conjunction with branch microinstructions. Can the same approach be used for the instruction

$$\text{ADD} \qquad \text{X(Rsrc),Rdst}$$

using the details given in Figure 5.4? What modification, if any, may be needed in the suggested approach?

5.6. Can the microprogram in Figure 5.4 be used to implement the general 68000 microprocessor instruction

$$\text{MOVE} \qquad \text{src,dst}$$

If not, how should it be modified? Show a detailed flowchart.

5.7. Is the microprogram in Figure 5.4 suitable for implementing the 68000 microprocessor instruction

$$\text{ADD} \qquad \text{src,dst}$$

If not, show how it should be modified.

5.8. Write a microroutine for the PDP-11 instruction ASH (Arithmetic Shift) defined in Appendix B. Assume that the ALU can shift the data word on one of its input ports one bit position to the right, under the control of the shift right signal. In this operation the most significant bit position remains unchanged and the least significant bit is shifted into the C bit. Note that the required shifting to the left can be accomplished by adding the given data word to itself (that is, multiplying it by 2). Is any additional hardware desirable in the implementation of this instruction?

5.9. Assuming similar conditions to those specified in Problem 5.8, write a microroutine for the PDP-11 instruction ASHC (Arithmetic Shift Combined), defined in Appendix B.

5.10. Suppose that the two-operand instructions of the PDP-11 minicomputer are to be implemented by using microprogrammed control patterned after Figure 5.4. Estimate the size of the control store that would be required to implement the following instructions (defined in Appendix B): MOVB, CMPB, BITB, ADD, SUB, and XOR.

5.11. Figure P5.1 gives a part of the microinstruction sequence corresponding to one of the machine instructions of a microprogrammed computer. Microinstruction B is followed by C, E, F, or I, depending upon bits b_6 and b_5 of the machine instruction register. Compare the three possible implementations described below.

(a) Microinstruction sequencing is accomplished by means of a microprogram counter. Branching is achieved by microinstructions of the form

$$\text{If } b_6 b_5 \text{ branch to X}$$

where $b_6 b_5$ is the branch condition and X is the branch address.

(b) Same as (a) except that the branch microinstruction has the form

$$\text{Branch to X}$$

where X is a base branch address. Branching is to be modified by bit ORing of bits b_5 and b_6 with the appropriate bits within X.

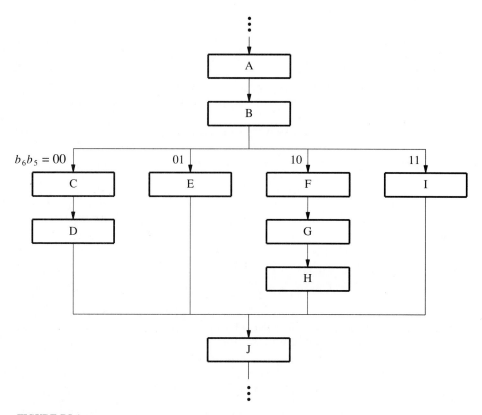

FIGURE P5.1
A microinstruction-sequence pattern.

(c) A field in each microinstruction specifies the address of the next microinstruction, which has bit-ORing capability.

Assign suitable addresses for all microinstructions in Figure P5.1 in each of the above implementations. Note that you may need to insert branch instructions in some cases. You may choose arbitrary addresses, as long as they are consistent with the method of sequencing used. For example, in case (a)

Address	Microinstruction
00010	A
00011	B
00100	If $b_6b_5 = 00$ branch to XXXXX
....	....
XXXXX	C

5.12. It is desired to reduce the number of bits needed to encode the control signals in Figure 5.3. Show a possible format for encoding these signals that requires a maximum of 18 bits, instead of the 21 in the figure. No two signals may be in the same field if they are likely to be specified in any one microinstruction.

5.13. Can the control signals in Figure 5.3 be encoded using only 12 bits in a microinstruction? If they can, what will be the effect of such encoding on microroutines corresponding to the ADD and BR machine instructions in Figures 4.8 and 4.9, respectively?

5.14. What are the relative merits of horizontal and vertical microinstruction formats? Relate your answer to the answers to Problems 5.12 and 5.13.

5.15. What are the advantages and disadvantages of hardwired and microprogrammed control?

5.16. Show how one could use the AMD 2903 bit slices to implement a Multiply operation. The operation is designed to multiply two unsigned 16-bit numbers in registers R1 and R2 and to leave the 32-bit result in registers R0 and R1. Make any necessary assumptions about the control signals needed to gate the data within a bit-slice element.

5.17. Consider the possibility of using the AMD 2903 bit slices to implement the PDP-11 instruction set.
(a) Is the arrangement of Figure 5.14 suitable for this objective?
(b) How would you implement the program counter and PSW register?
(c) How would the JSR instruction be implemented? Show a sequence of microinstruction steps needed to execute the instruction

$$\text{JSR} \quad \text{R5,@\#2000}$$

5.18. The 16 general-purpose registers in the AMD 2903 bit slice (see Figure 5.11) are addressed by means of the AA and the AB address lines.
(a) Indicate the circuitry required to generate the signals on these lines if a PDP-11 instruction set is to be implemented with these bit slices. In particular, consider the effects of the instruction fetching process, two- and one-operand instructions, and subroutine calls.
(b) Can your circuit support the execution of the MUL instruction defined in Appendix B? If not, what modifications are required?

5.19. Consider the possibility of using the AMD 2903 bit slices to implement the 68000 instruction set.

   (*a*) Is the structure suggested by Figure 5.14 suitable for this objective?

   (*b*) How would you implement the program counter and the status register?

   (*c*) How would the JSR instruction be implemented? Show a sequence of microinstruction steps needed to execute the instruction

JSR $2000

CHAPTER

6

INPUT-OUTPUT ORGANIZATION

One of the basic features of a computer is its ability to exchange data with other devices. This communication capability enables a human operator, for example, to enter a program and its associated data via the keyboard of a video terminal and receive results on a printer. A computer may be required to communicate with a variety of equipment such as video terminals, printers, and plotters, as well as magnetic disk and tape drives. In addition to these standard I/O devices, a computer may be connected to other types of equipment. For example, in industrial control applications, input to a computer may be the digital output of a voltmeter, a temperature sensor, or a fire alarm. Similarly, the output of a computer may be a digitally coded command to change the speed of a motor, open a valve, or cause a robot to move in a specified manner. In short, a general-purpose computer should have the ability to deal with a wide range of device characteristics in varying environments.

In this chapter we will consider in detail various ways in which I/O operations are performed. First, we will consider the problem from the point of view of the programmer. Then, we will present some of the hardware details associated with buses and I/O interfaces. The discussion in Sections 6.1 through 6.6 applies directly to small- and medium-sized computers. Larger machines use special-purpose units to handle I/O operations; the characteristics of these units will be treated in Section 6.7.

6.1 ACCESSING I/O DEVICES

Because more than one device is usually connected to a computer, some means have to be provided by which a particular device can be selected to participate in a given I/O operation. This can be accomplished through the use of an I/O bus arrangement, as shown in Figure 6.1. This bus, to which all I/O devices are connected, consists of three

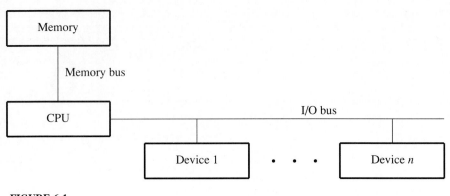

FIGURE 6.1
Use of I/O bus.

sets of lines used for transmission of address, data, and control signals. Each device is assigned an identifying code, or address, so that the CPU can select a device by placing its address on the address lines. Only the device that recognizes its address responds to the CPU commands issued on the control lines.

With I/O devices connected to a separate bus, special instructions are needed to perform I/O transfers. For example, an instruction such as

$$\text{OUT} \qquad \text{data,device}$$

may be used to transfer the data identified by the first operand to the device identified by the second operand. Execution of this instruction causes the CPU to start a write operation on the I/O bus, instead of the memory bus. Similarly, an input operation may be performed by an IN instruction.

In single-bus machines, the same bus serves both as a memory bus and as an I/O bus. In this case, I/O transfers may be distinguished from memory read and write operations by including a special I/O control line on the bus. This line is activated by the CPU during a read or a write operation that is intended for an I/O device. The memory unit responds to commands on the bus when the I/O line is inactive, and I/O devices respond when it is active.

An alternative arrangement for single-bus machines is to identify I/O devices by assigning them unique addresses within the memory address space of the computer. Thus, it becomes possible to access I/O devices in the same way as any other memory location. This arrangement is known as *memory-mapped I/O*. Neither the special IN and OUT instructions nor the I/O control lines on the bus are needed. Instead, any instruction that moves data to or from a memory location can be used to transfer data to or from an I/O device. For example, if INBUF is the address of the input buffer associated with the keyboard of a video terminal, the 68000 instruction

$$\text{MOVE.B} \qquad \text{INBUF,MEM}$$

reads one byte from INBUF and deposits it into memory location MEM.

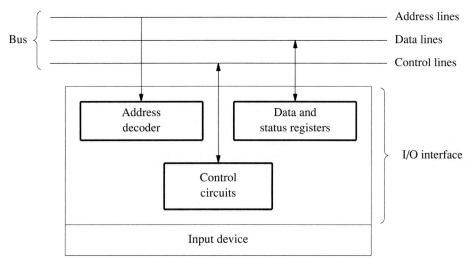

FIGURE 6.2
I/O interface for an input device.

The use of memory-mapped I/O offers considerable flexibility in handling I/O operations, because any machine instruction and addressing mode that can be used to deal with memory operands can also refer to an I/O device. It is customary, though not necessary, to assign a contiguous portion of the address space of the machine to I/O devices.

The PDP-11 and the 68000 use memory-mapped I/O. Intel microprocessors have special I/O instructions and a separate 16-bit address space for I/O devices. However, it is also possible to connect an I/O device to an Intel microprocessor in a memory-mapped fashion. This is done in many systems, including the popular IBM-PC computers.

Figure 6.2 illustrates the arrangement required to connect an I/O device to the bus of a computer. The address decoder enables the device to recognize its address when this address is placed on the address bus by the CPU. The data register is used to hold data to be transferred to the CPU from an input device or to receive data from the CPU for transfer to an output device. It was pointed out in Section 2.8 that I/O devices often have one or more status registers that contain information relevant to their operation. Such registers must also be connected to the data bus and assigned unique addresses. The address decoder, the data and status registers, and the control hardware required to coordinate I/O transfers constitute the device *interface circuit*.

6.2 DIRECT MEMORY ACCESS

In the discussion above, we assumed that machine instructions such as IN, OUT, or MOVE are used to transfer data to or from an I/O device. This is program-controlled I/O, which was introduced in Section 2.8. When large blocks of data need to be transferred at high speed, an alternative approach may be used. A special control unit may be provided to enable transfer of a block of data directly between an external device and the main memory, without continuous intervention by the CPU. This approach is called *direct memory access*, or DMA.

Program-controlled I/O is unsuitable for high-speed data transfer for two reasons:

1. In program-controlled I/O considerable overhead is incurred, because several program instructions have to be executed for each data word transferred between the external device and the main memory.
2. Many high-speed peripheral devices have a synchronous mode of operation. That is, data transfers are controlled by a clock of fixed frequency, independent of the CPU.

The overhead incurred in program-controlled I/O is illustrated by the examples given in Figure 6.3. They show PDP-11 and 68000 programs that transfer 80 characters from memory to a line printer, where the first character is in memory location LOC. Register R0 (A0) is used as a pointer to data characters in the memory, and register

			Memory Cyles	
	MOV	#LOC,R0	2	
	MOV	#−80.,R1	2	
WAIT:	TSTB	@#LPRSTATUS	3	Character transfer loop
	BPL	WAIT	1	
	MOVB	(R0)+,@#LPROUT	4	
	INC	R1	1	
	BNE	WAIT	1	

(a) A PDP-11 program

			Memory Cycles	
	MOVEA.L	#LOC,A0	3	
	MOVEQ	#79,D0	1	
WAIT	TST.B	LPRSTATUS	4	Character transfer loop
	BPL	WAIT	1	
	MOVE.B	(A0)+,LPROUT	5	
	DBRA	D0,WAIT	2	

(b) A 68000 program

FIGURE 6.3
Two programs to print 80 characters on a line printer.

R1 (D0) keeps track of the character count. The status and buffer registers of the printer are represented by the names LPRSTATUS and LPROUT, respectively. The memory cycles column gives the number of memory references required to execute each instruction. For example, the 68000 instruction

WAIT   TST.B   LPRSTATUS

requires four memory references. Three of these are needed to fetch the instruction and the addressing data for the operand. The fourth memory cycle is needed to fetch the operand itself (i.e., the contents of the status register) in order to perform the test. The need for so many instructions and memory cycles for each character transferred to the printer introduces a considerable overhead.

In many cases, synchronous data transfer is required because of the physical characteristics of the peripheral device. For example, a high-speed magnetic disk drive cannot be stopped after each character; data transfer to or from these devices takes place at rates on the order of several million bytes per second. This is of the same order of magnitude as the speed at which main memory fetches can be performed. The combination of high speed and the requirement for synchronism makes operation of these devices incompatible with program-controlled data transfer as given in Figure 6.3.

The problems encountered in operating high-speed devices can be overcome by incorporating all functions performed by the programs of Figure 6.3 in a hardwired controller. The purpose of this controller is to enable direct data transfer between the device and the main memory without involvement of the CPU. Inspection of Figure 6.3 suggests that such a DMA controller requires two counter registers, one for generating the memory address and the other for keeping track of the word count. A third register is needed to store a command specifying the function to be performed. For more complex devices, such as tape and disk drives, other registers may also be required to control their operation. Since controller registers must be accessible for initialization by the CPU under program control, they should be connected to the bus and assigned unique addresses, as in the case of any other I/O device interface.

Figure 6.4 shows an example of a DMA controller used in conjunction with two I/O devices, a disk drive and a high-speed printer. In this case, the controller is said to provide two DMA channels. The registers needed to store the memory address, the word count, and so on are duplicated, so that one set can be used with each device. A connection is also provided for each channel between the DMA controller and one of the I/O devices.

To start a DMA transfer of data between the disk and the main memory, a program writes the following information into the registers of the DMA channel assigned to the disk:

- Memory address
- Word count
- Address of data on the disk
- Function to be performed (Read or Write)

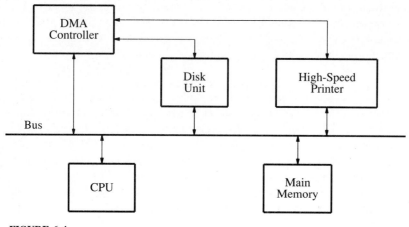

FIGURE 6.4
A 2-channel DMA controller.

The DMA controller then proceeds independently to implement the function specified. It uses its connection to the disk unit to synchronize its operation with that of the disk. When the DMA transfer is completed, this fact is recorded in the status register of the DMA controller. The status register will also contain information indicating whether the transfer took place correctly or errors were encountered.

   While the DMA transfer is taking place, the program that requested the transfer cannot continue. However, the CPU can be used to execute another program. After the DMA transfer is completed the CPU may switch back to the program that requested the transfer. As mentioned in Chapter 1, it is the responsibility of the operating system to suspend the execution of one program and to start another. It is also the operating system that initiates the DMA operation when requested to do so by a program. When the transfer is completed, the DMA controller informs the CPU by means of a control signal on the bus, called an interrupt request signal. The controller activates this signal at the same time it sets the Ready bit in its status register. The interrupt mechanism and the way it is used to coordinate DMA and other I/O operations will be discussed in the next section.

   Note that a conflict situation may arise if both the CPU and a DMA controller try to access the main memory at the same time. To resolve this conflict, a special circuit called the *bus arbiter* is provided to coordinate the activities of all devices requesting memory transfers. The arbiter implements a priority system, as will be described later. Memory accesses by the CPU and DMA controllers are interwoven, with top priority given to transfers involving synchronous, high-speed peripherals such as disk and tape drives. Considering that in most cases the CPU originates the majority of memory access cycles, the DMA controller can be regarded as "stealing" memory cycles from the CPU. Hence, this interweaving technique is usually referred to as *cycle stealing*. Alternatively, the DMA controller may be given exclusive access to the main memory to transfer a block of data without interruption. This is known as *burst* mode.

6.3 INTERRUPTS

A computer must have some means of coordinating its activities with those of the external devices connected to it. For example, when accepting characters from a keyboard, the computer needs to know when a new character has been typed. Similarly, during an output operation, it should not send a character to a printer until the printer is ready to accept it.

The current status of each input or output device connected to a computer is indicated by one or more bits of information. The most important of these bits, usually referred to as the Ready bit, is set whenever the device is ready to participate in a new transfer operation. A program should *poll* the device by testing its status bits before using an I/O instruction to transfer data.

In the examples of Figures 2.35, 2.36, and 6.3, the program enters a wait loop in which it repeatedly tests the device status. During this period, the CPU is not performing any useful computation. There are many situations where other tasks can be performed while waiting for an I/O device to become ready. To allow this to happen, we can arrange for the I/O device to alert the CPU when it becomes ready. It can do so by sending a hardware signal called an *interrupt* to the CPU. At least one of the bus control lines, called an *interrupt-request* line, is usually dedicated for this purpose. The CPU can instruct an I/O device to activate this line at the same time that it sets the Ready bit in its status register. Since the CPU is no longer required to continuously check the status of external devices, the waiting period can be utilized to perform other useful functions. Indeed, by using interrupts, such waiting periods can ideally be eliminated.

> **Example 6.1.** Consider a task that requires some computations to be performed and the results to be printed on a line printer. This is followed by more computations and output, and so on. Let the program consist of two routines, COMPUTE and PRINT. Assume that COMPUTE produces n lines of output, to be printed by the PRINT routine.
>
> The required task may be performed by repeatedly executing first the COMPUTE routine and then the PRINT routine. The printer accepts only one line of text at a time. Hence, the PRINT routine must send one line of text, wait for it to be printed, then send the next line, until all the results have been printed. The disadvantage of this simple approach is that the CPU spends a considerable amount of time waiting for the printer to become ready. If it is possible to overlap printing and computation, that is, to execute the COMPUTE routine while printing is in progress, a faster overall speed of execution will result. This may be achieved as follows. First, the COMPUTE routine is executed to produce the first n lines of output. Then, the PRINT routine is executed to send the first line of text to the printer. At this point, instead of waiting for the line to be printed, the PRINT routine may be temporarily suspended and execution of the COMPUTE routine continued. Whenever the printer becomes ready, it alerts the CPU by sending an interrupt-request signal. In response, the CPU interrupts execution of the COMPUTE routine and transfers control to the PRINT routine. The PRINT routine sends

the second line to the printer and is again suspended. Then the interrupted COMPUTE routine resumes execution at the point of interruption. This process continues until all n lines have been printed.

The PRINT routine will be restarted whenever the next set of n lines is available for printing. If COMPUTE takes longer to generate n lines than the time required to print them, the CPU will be performing useful computations all the time.

The example above is intended to introduce the concept of interrupts. The routine executed in response to an interrupt request is called the *interrupt-service routine*. This is the PRINT routine in our example. Interrupts bear considerable resemblance to subroutine calls. Assume that an interrupt request arrives during execution of instruction i in Figure 6.5. The CPU first completes execution of instruction i. Then, it loads the program counter with the address of the first instruction of the interrupt-service routine. For the time being, let us assume that this address is hardwired in the CPU. After execution of the interrupt-service routine, the CPU has to come back to instruction $i + 1$. Therefore, when an interrupt occurs, the current contents of the PC, which point at instruction $i + 1$, have to be put in temporary storage. A Return-from-interrupt instruction at the end of the interrupt-service routine reloads the PC from that temporary storage location, causing execution to resume at instruction $i + 1$. In most computers, the return address is saved on the processor stack.

We should note that as part of handling interrupts, the CPU must inform the device that its request has been recognized, so that it may remove its interrupt-request signal. This may be accomplished by means of a special control signal on the bus. An *interrupt-acknowledge* signal, used in some of the interrupt schemes to be discussed later, serves this function. A common alternative is to have the transfer of data between the CPU and the I/O device interface accomplish the same purpose. The execution of an instruction in the interrupt-service routine that accesses a status or data register in the device interface implicitly informs the device that its interrupt request has been recognized.

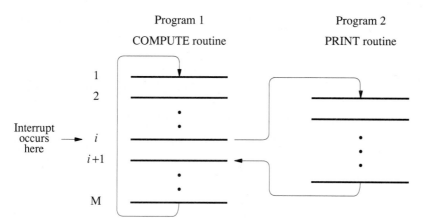

FIGURE 6.5
Transfer of control through the use of interrupts.

So far, treatment of an interrupt-service routine is very similar to that of a subroutine. An important departure from this similarity should be noted. A subroutine performs a function required by the program from which it is called. However, the interrupt-service routine may not have anything in common with the program being executed at the time the interrupt request is received. In fact, the two programs often belong to different users. Therefore, before starting execution of the interrupt-service routine, the CPU should save, along with the contents of the PC, any information that may affect execution after return to the interrupted program. In particular, the CPU should save the *status word* that includes the condition codes and any other status indicators at the time of interruption. Upon return from the interrupt-service routine, the CPU reloads the status word from its temporary storage location. This enables the original program to resume execution without being affected in any way by the occurrence of the interrupt, except, of course, for the time delay.

The contents of CPU registers other than the program counter and the processor status register may or may not be saved automatically by the interrupt-handling mechanism. If the CPU does save register contents before entering the interrupt-service routine, it must also restore them before returning to the interrupted program. The process of saving and restoring registers involves a number of memory transfers that create a time overhead for every interrupt accepted by the CPU. In a computer that does not automatically save all register contents following an interrupt, the interrupt-service routine should save the contents of any CPU register that it needs to use. The saved data should be restored to their respective registers before returning to the interrupted program. In order to minimize the interrupt overhead, some computers provide two types of interrupts. One saves all register contents, and the other does not. A particular I/O device may use either type, depending upon its response time requirements. An example of this approach is found in Motorola's 6809 microprocessor, which will be described in Chapter 10. Another interesting approach is to provide duplicate sets of CPU registers, so that a different set of registers can be used when servicing interrupt requests. This approach is found in the Z80 microprocessor* and in IBM Series 1 minicomputers.

An interrupt is more than a simple mechanism for coordinating I/O transfers. In a general sense, interrupts enable transfer of control from one program to another to be initiated by an event external to the computer. Execution of the interrupted program resumes after completion of execution of the interrupt-service routine. The concept of interrupts is useful in operating systems and in many control applications where processing of certain routines has to be accurately timed relative to external events. The latter type of application is generally referred to as *real-time processing*.

6.4   INTERRUPT HANDLING

The facilities in a computer should give the programmer complete control over the events that take place during program execution. The arrival of an interrupt request

---

*Manufactured by Zilog Corporation

from an external device causes the CPU to suspend the execution of one program and start the execution of another. Because interrupts can arrive at any time, they may alter the sequence of events from that envisaged by the programmer. Hence, they should be carefully controlled. A fundamental facility found in all computers is the ability to enable and disable the occurrence of program interrupts as desired. We will now examine such facilities in some detail.

6.4.1 Enabling and Disabling Interrupts

There are many situations in which the CPU should ignore interrupt requests. For example, in the case of the Compute-Print program of Figure 6.5, an interrupt request from the printer should be accepted only if there are output lines to be printed. After printing the last line of a set of n lines, interrupts should be disabled until another set becomes available for printing. In another case, it may be necessary to guarantee that a particular sequence of instructions is executed to the end without interruption, because the interrupt-service routine may change some of the data used by the instructions in question. For these reasons, some means for enabling and disabling interrupts must be available to the programmer. A simple way is to provide machine instructions, such as Interrupt-enable and Interrupt-disable, that perform these functions.

Let us consider in some detail the specific case of a single interrupt request from one device. When a device activates the interrupt-request signal, it keeps this signal activated until it learns that the CPU has accepted its request. This means that the interrupt-request signal will be active during execution of the interrupt-service routine, perhaps until an instruction is reached that accesses the device in question. It is essential to ensure that this active request signal does not cause a second interruption during this period. An erroneous interpretation of a single interrupt as multiple requests would cause the system to enter an infinite loop from which it could not recover. Several mechanisms are available to solve this problem. We will describe three simple possibilities here; other schemes that can handle more than one interrupting device will be presented later.

The first possibility is to have the CPU hardware ignore the interrupt-request line until the execution of the first instruction of the interrupt-service routine has been completed. Thus, by using an Interrupt-disable instruction as the first instruction in the interrupt-service routine, the programmer can ensure that no further interrupts will occur until an Interrupt-enable instruction is executed. Typically, this will be the last instruction in the interrupt-service routine before the Return-from-interrupt instruction. Again, the CPU must guarantee that execution of the Return-from-interrupt instruction is completed before further interruption can occur.

Another option, which is commonly encountered in practice, is to have the CPU automatically disable interrupts before starting the execution of the interrupt-service routine. That is, after saving the contents of the PC and the processor status (PS) on the stack, the CPU automatically performs the equivalent of executing an Interrupt-disable instruction. It is often the case that one bit in the PS register, the *interrupt mask*, indicates whether interrupts are enabled or disabled. The CPU sets this bit to disable interrupts before it starts execution of the interrupt-service routine. Similarly, the CPU may automatically enable interrupts when a Return-from-interrupt instruction is executed. This is one of the results of the restoration of the old contents of the PS register from the stack.

The third approach that can be used is to arrange the interrupt-handling circuit in the CPU such that it responds only to the leading edge of the interrupt-request signal. Only one such transition will be seen by the CPU for every request generated by the device. Such interrupt-request lines are said to be *edge-triggered*.

Before proceeding to study more complex aspects of interrupts, let us summarize the sequence of events involved in handling an interrupt request from a single device:

1. A program instruction enables interrupts in the CPU.
2. The device raises an interrupt request.
3. The CPU interrupts the program being executed at the time.
4. Interrupts are disabled.
5. The device is informed that its request has been recognized, and in response, it deactivates the interrupt-request signal.
6. The action requested by the interrupt is performed.
7. Interrupts are enabled.
8. Execution of the interrupted program is resumed.

6.4.2 Handling Multiple Devices

Let us now consider the situation where a number of devices capable of initiating interrupts are connected to the CPU. Because these devices are operationally independent, there is no definite order in which they will generate interrupts. For example, device X may request an interrupt while an interrupt caused by device Y is being serviced, or all devices may request interrupts at exactly the same time. This gives rise to a number of questions:

1. How can the CPU recognize the device requesting an interrupt?
2. Given that different devices are likely to require different interrupt-service routines, how can the CPU obtain the starting address of the appropriate routine in each case?
3. Should a device be allowed to interrupt the CPU while another interrupt is being serviced?
4. How should two or more simultaneous interrupt requests be handled?

The means by which the above problems are resolved vary considerably from one machine to another. The approach taken in any machine is an important consideration in determining its suitability for a given application. We will now discuss some of the more commonly used techniques.

6.4.3 Device Identification

Consider the case where an external device requests an interrupt by activating an interrupt-request line that is common to all devices. A single line may be used to

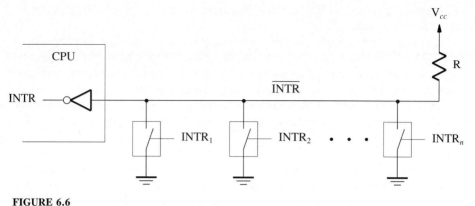

FIGURE 6.6
An equivalent circuit for an open-collector bus used to implement a common interrupt-request line.

serve several devices by means of the open-collector organization depicted in Figure 6.6. All n devices are attached to a common line via open-collector gates. As was stated in Chapter 4, an open-collector gate is equivalent to a switch to ground, which is closed when the gate's input is activated. If all interrupt-request signals $INTR_1$ to $INTR_n$ are inactive, that is, in the 0 state, the interrupt-request line will be maintained in the high-voltage state by resistor R. Hence, this should be interpreted as the inactive state of the line. When a device requests an interrupt, the corresponding switch is closed. This forces the line to the low-voltage or active state. The interrupt-request, INTR, received by the CPU is given by

$$INTR = INTR_1 + \cdots + INTR_n$$

It is customary to use the complemented form, $\overline{INTR}$, to name the interrupt-request signal on the common line, because this signal is low when active.

When a request is received over the common interrupt-request line of Figure 6.6, additional information is needed to identify the particular device that activated the line. The required information is available in the status registers of the devices. Hence, the interrupt-service routine should begin by polling the devices in some order. The first device encountered with its Ready bit set is the device that should be serviced, and an appropriate subroutine should be called to provide the requested service.

The polling scheme is very simple and easy to implement. Its main disadvantage is the time spent interrogating the status bits of all the devices that may not be requesting any service. An alternative approach is to use vectored interrupts, as we will describe next.

6.4.4 Vectored Interrupts

In order to reduce the overhead involved in the polling process, a device requesting an interrupt may identify itself directly to the CPU. Then, the CPU can immediately start executing the corresponding interrupt-service routine. The term *vectored interrupts* refers to all interrupt-handling schemes based on this approach.

A device requesting an interrupt may identify itself by sending a special code to the CPU over the bus. This technique enables identification of individual devices even if they share a single interrupt-request line. The code supplied by the device may represent the starting address of the interrupt-service routine for that device. In some cases, especially in smaller machines, only a few bits of the address are supplied, with the remainder of the address being fixed. This reduces the number of bits that need to be transmitted by the I/O device, thus simplifying the design of its interface circuit. However, having a code with only a few bits limits the number of devices that can be automatically identified by the CPU. For example, if four bits are supplied by the device, only 16 different devices can be recognized by the CPU. However, it is possible to assign each code to a group of devices; when a given code is received, the interrupt-service routine can identify the device that generated the interrupt by polling members of the group represented by that code.

The above arrangement implies that the interrupt-service routine for a given device must always start at the same location. The programmer may gain some flexibility by storing in this location an instruction that causes a jump or a branch to the appropriate routine. In many machines, this is done automatically by the interrupt-handling mechanism. The CPU uses the code received from the interrupting device as an indirect specification of the starting address of the interrupt-service routine. That is, this code is an address of a memory location that contains the required starting address. The contents of this location, which constitute a new value for the PC, are referred to as the *interrupt vector*. In some machines, the interrupt vector also includes a new value for the processor status register.

Some modifications to the hardware are required to support vectored interrupts. The key modification follows from the realization that the CPU may not respond immediately when it receives an interrupt request. The minimum delay in the CPU's response results from the requirement to complete execution of the current instruction. Further delays may occur if interrupts happen to be disabled at the time the request is received. Because the CPU may require the use of the bus during this delay, the interrupting device should not be allowed to put data on the bus until the CPU is ready to receive it. The necessary coordination can be achieved through the use of another control signal that may be termed *interrupt acknowledge* (INTA). As soon as the CPU is ready to service the interrupt, it activates the INTA line. This, in turn, causes the device interface to place the interrupt-vector code on the data lines of the bus and to turn off the INTR signal.

6.4.5 Interrupt Nesting

It was suggested in Section 6.4.1 that interrupts should be disabled during the execution of an interrupt-service routine. This ensures that an interrupt request from one device will not cause more than one interruption. The same arrangement is often used when several devices are involved, in which case execution of a given interrupt-service routine, once started, always continues to completion before a second interrupt request is accepted by the CPU. Interrupt-service routines are typically short, and the delay they may cause in responding to a second request is acceptable for most simple devices.

For some devices, however, a long delay in responding to an interrupt request may lead to erroneous operation. Consider, for example, a computer that keeps track of the time of day using a real-time clock. This is a device that sends interrupt requests to the CPU at regular intervals. For each of these requests, the CPU executes a short interrupt-service routine to increment a set of counters in the memory that keep track of time in seconds, minutes, and so on. Proper operation requires that the delay in responding to an interrupt request from the real-time clock be small in comparison with the interval between two successive requests. To ensure that this requirement is satisfied in the presence of other interrupting devices, it may be necessary to accept an interrupt request from the clock during the execution of an interrupt-service routine for another device.

The example of the real-time clock suggests that I/O devices should be organized in a priority structure. An interrupt request from a high-priority device should be accepted while the CPU is servicing another request from a lower-priority device.

A multiple-level priority organization means that during execution of an interrupt-service routine, interrupt requests will be accepted from some devices but not from others, depending upon the device's priority. In order to facilitate implementation of this scheme, it is useful to assign a priority level to the CPU that can be changed under program control. The priority level of the CPU is the priority of the program that is currently being executed. The CPU accepts interrupts only from devices that have priorities higher than its own. At the time the execution of an interrupt-service routine for some device is started, the priority of the CPU should be raised to that of the device. This action disables interrupts from devices at the same level of priority or lower. However, interrupt requests from higher-priority devices will continue to be accepted.

The CPU priority is usually encoded in a few bits of the processor status word. It may be changed by a program instruction that writes into the PS. Such instructions are usually privileged instructions, which are only executed by the operating system. Thus, a user program cannot accidentally or intentionally change the CPU priority and disrupt the system's operation.

From the hardware point of view, a multiple-priority scheme can be implemented easily by using separate interrupt-request and interrupt-acknowledge lines for each device. Such an arrangement is shown in Figure 6.7. Each of the interrupt-request lines is assigned a different priority level. Interrupt requests received over these lines are sent to a priority arbitration circuit in the CPU. A request is accepted only if it has a higher priority level than that currently assigned to the CPU.

6.4.6 Simultaneous Requests

Let us now consider the problem of simultaneous arrivals of interrupt requests from two or more devices. The CPU should have some means of arbitration by which only one request is serviced and the others are either delayed or ignored. In the pres-

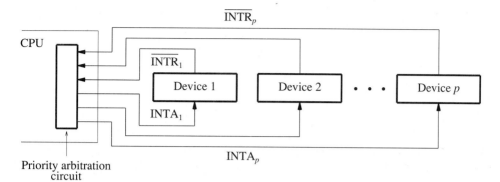

FIGURE 6.7
Implementation of interrupt priority using individual interrupt-request and acknowledge lines.

ence of a priority scheme such as that of Figure 6.7, the solution to this problem is straightforward. The CPU simply accepts the request having the highest priority. However, if several devices share one interrupt-request line, some other mechanism must be employed to assign relative priority to these devices.

When polling is used to identify the interrupting device, priority is automatically assigned by the order in which devices are polled. Therefore, no further treatment is required to accommodate simultaneous interrupt requests. In the case of vectored interrupts, the priority of any device is usually determined by the way in which it is connected to the CPU. A widely used scheme is to connect the devices to form a *daisy chain*, as shown in Figure 6.8a. The interrupt-request line ($\overline{INTR}$) is common to all devices. However, the interrupt-acknowledge line (INTA) is connected in a daisy-chain fashion, allowing its signal to propagate serially through the devices. When several devices issue an interrupt request and the $\overline{INTR}$ line is activated, the CPU responds, after some delay, by setting the INTA line to 1. This signal is received by device 1. Device 1 passes the signal on to device 2 only if it does not require any service. If device 1 has a pending request for interrupt, it blocks the acknowledgment signal and proceeds to put its identifying code on the data lines. Therefore, the daisy-chain arrangement results in the device that is electrically closest to the CPU having the highest priority. The second device along the chain has second highest priority, and so on.

The scheme of Figure 6.8a has the advantage that it requires considerably fewer wires than the individual connections of Figure 6.7. The main advantage of the latter scheme is that it makes it possible for the CPU to accept interrupt requests from some devices, but not from others, depending upon their priorities. The two schemes may be combined to produce the more general structure of Figure 6.8b. This organization is used in many computer systems, including the PDP-11 and 68000, which will be described in Sections 6.4.8 and 6.4.9.

We should note that the general organization of Figure 6.8b makes it possible for a device to be connected to several priority levels. At any given time, the device requests an interrupt at the priority level consistent with the urgency of the function

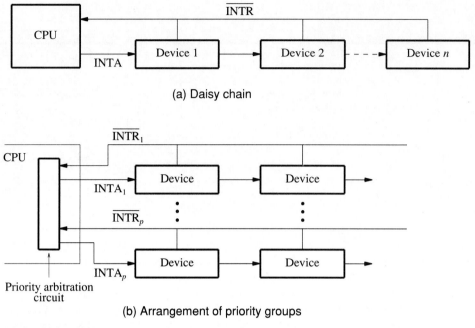

FIGURE 6.8
Interrupt priority schemes.

being performed. This approach offers additional flexibility; however, it requires more complex control circuitry in the device interface.

6.4.7 Controlling Device Requests

So far in our discussion of interrupts, we have assumed that an I/O device interface generates an interrupt request whenever it is ready for an I/O transfer, that is, whenever the Ready bit in its status register is equal to 1. It is important to ensure that interrupt requests are generated only by those I/O devices that are being used by a given program. Idle devices must not be allowed to generate interrupt requests even though they may be ready to participate in I/O transfer operations. Hence, a facility is needed to enable and disable interrupts in the interface circuit of individual devices, in order to control whether the device is allowed to generate an interrupt request. Such a facility is usually provided in the form of an Interrupt-enable bit in the devices's interface circuit, which may be set or cleared by the CPU. The Interrupt-enable bit may be a part of a control register into which the CPU can write. When this bit is set, the interface circuit generates an interrupt request whenever its Ready bit is set. If it is a 0, the interface circuit will not generate an interrupt request even if the Ready bit is set.

To summarize, there are two independent facilities that control interrupt requests. At the device end, an Interrupt-enable bit in a control register determines whether the device is allowed to generate an interrupt request. At the CPU end, a priority structure and an interrupt mask in the PS determine whether a given interrupt request will be accepted.

We have discussed the organizational aspects of interrupts in general. We will now describe the interrupt-handling mechanism of the PDP-11 and 68000 computers as examples.

6.4.8 PDP-11 Interrupt Structure

The PDP-11 uses vectored interrupts, with I/O devices organized in priority groups. There is provision for eight levels of priority; however, in most existing models only the top four of these levels are in actual use. Within each group, daisy-chain priority is used, as in Figure 6.8b. The CPU priority is determined by three bits in the processor status register, PS, as shown in Figure 6.9. An interrupt request is accepted when the I/O device has a priority higher than that of the CPU. The CPU sends an interrupt-acknowledge signal to which the device responds by turning off its interrupt request and sending the 16-bit address of its interrupt vector. After pushing the PS and PC registers on the processor stack, the CPU reads the first word of a two-word interrupt vector at the address obtained from the device, and loads it into the PC. It then loads the second word of the interrupt vector into the PS. This word includes three bits that determine the new priority of the CPU. The bits in the interrupt vector should be set by the programmer to give the CPU the same priority as the I/O device, so that interrupts from devices of equal or lower priority are automatically disabled. The interrupt-service routine ends with a Return-from-interrupt (RTI) instruction, which causes the return address and the old contents of the PS to be transferred from the stack into the PC and PS registers. The restoration of these registers sets the CPU priority back to its value prior to interruption and causes execution of the interrupted program to be resumed.

6.4.9 68000 Interrupt Structure

The 68000 has eight interrupt priority levels. The priority at which the processor is running at any given time is encoded in three bits of the processor status word, as shown in Figure 6.10, with level 0 being the lowest priority. I/O devices are connected

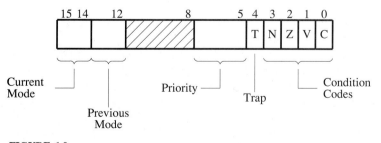

FIGURE 6.9
Processor status register in PDP-11.

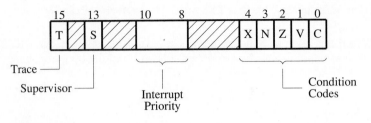

FIGURE 6.10
Processor status register in 68000.

to the 68000 using an arrangement similar to that in Figure 6.8*b*, where interrupt requests are assigned priorities in the range 1 to 7. A request is accepted only if its priority is higher than that of the processor, with one exception: An interrupt request at level seven is always accepted. It is called a *nonmaskable* interrupt. When the CPU accepts an interrupt request, the priority level indicated in the PS is automatically raised to that of the request, before the interrupt-service routine is executed. Thus, requests of equal or lower priority are disabled, except for level seven interrupts, which are always enabled.

The 68000 microprocessor uses vectored interrupts. When it accepts an interrupt request, it obtains the starting address of the interrupt-service routine from an interrupt vector stored in the main memory. There are 256 interrupt vectors, numbered 0 to 255. Each vector consists of 32 bits that constitute the required starting address. When a device requests an interrupt, it may point to the vector that should be used by sending an 8-bit vector number to the processor, in response to the interrupt acknowledge signal. As an alternative, the 68000 also provides an *autovector* facility. Instead of sending a vector number, the device may activate a special bus control line to indicate that it wishes to use the autovector facility. In this case, the CPU chooses one of seven vectors provided for this purpose, based on the priority level of the interrupt request.

6.4.10   An Example of an Interrupt Program

Let us now consider a simple example of an interrupt-service routine. At some point in a program MAIN it is necessary to read an input line from the keyboard of a video terminal. The input characters are to be stored in a buffer area in the main memory, starting at location LOC. Let us assume that the Ready bit is bit b_7 of register STATUS in the terminal interface. When set, it indicates that a character is available in the input data buffer INBUF. Bit b_6 of register STATUS is used for enabling interrupts. While b_6 is set, an interrupt request is generated by the interface whenever the Ready bit is set, that is, whenever a key is pressed causing an input character to be deposited in the INBUF register. The format of the STATUS register is shown in Figure 6.11. Figures 6.12 and 6.13 give two examples for reading an input line from the terminal's keyboard using interrupts, one for the PDP-11 and one for the 68000. In each case, the relevant parts of the main program, MAIN, are shown, together with the interrupt-service routine, READ. Let the interrupt vector be at location INTVEC in the main

Bit position	Function
7	Set when data is available in INBUF Cleared when a program instruction reads INBUF
6	Enables interrupts when set. Device generates an interrupt request when $b_6 = b_7 = 1$

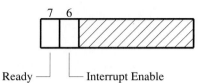

Ready — — Interrupt Enable

FIGURE 6.11
Bit assignment in register STATUS.

```
            INTVEC   = 60              Interrupt Vector address.
            INTEN    = 100             Keyboard interrupt enable
            INTDIS   = 0                and disable masks.
            PR4      = 200             Value of PS to set priority to 4.
            PS       = 177776          Address of PS register.
            CR       = 15             ASCII code for carriage return.

   MAIN:    MOV      #READ,@#INTVEC    Set interrupt vector.
            MOV      #PR4,@#INTVEC+2   .
            MOV      #LOC,PNTR         Initialize buffer pointer.
            MOV      #INTEN,@#STATUS   Enable keyboard interrupts.
            CLR      PS                Set CPU priority to 0.
            .
            .
            main program
            .
            .
   READ:    MOV      PNTR,R1           Load address pointer.
            MOVB     @#INBUF,(R1)+     Get input character.
            MOV      R1,PNTR           Update pointer.
            CMPB     #CR,-1(R1)        Check if carriage return.
            BNE      DONE
            MOV      #INTDIS,@#STATUS  Disable keyboard interrupts.
            JSR      LINE              Process input line.
   DONE:    RTI
   PNTR:    .WORD    0
```

FIGURE 6.12
A PDP-11 interrupt-service routine to read one line from a keyboard.

INTVEC	EQU	$64	Interrupt Vector address.
INTEN	EQU	$80	Keyboard interrupt enable
INTDIS	EQU	0	and disable masks.
PR0	EQU	$2000	Value of PS to set priority to 0.
CR	EQU	$0D	ASCII code for carriage return.
MAIN	MOVE.L	#READ,INTVEC	Set interrupt vector.
	MOVE.L	#LOC,PNTR	Initialize buffer pointer.
	MOVE.B	#INTEN,STATUS	Enable keyboard interrupts.
	MOVE.W	#PR0,SR	Set CPU priority to 0.
	⋮		
	main program		
	⋮		
READ	MOVEA.L	PNTR,A0	Load address pointer.
	MOVE.B	INBUF,(A0)+	Get input character.
	MOVE.L	A0,PNTR	Update pointer.
	CMPI.B	#CR,−1(A0)	Check if carriage return.
	BNE	DONE	
	MOVE.B	#INTDIS,STATUS	Disable keyboard interrupts.
	BSR	LINE	Process input line.
DONE	RTE		
PNTR	DC.L	0	

FIGURE 6.13
A 68000 interrupt-service routine to read one line from a keyboard.

memory. This location must be initialized to point to READ before program MAIN begins the input operation. In the case of the PDP-11, we have assumed that INTVEC = 60. This means that the value READ should be stored at location 60 and that a suitable value for the PS should be stored at location 62. The value 200 has been chosen for the PS, assuming that the keyboard has been assigned priority four, which is the lowest priority on the PDP-11 bus. For the 68000, we have chosen interrupt vector number 25, which is the autovector for priority one. Because the vector table in the 68000 starts at location 0, and each vector is four bytes long, the value assigned to INTVEC is four times the vector number. Only the starting address, READ, is stored at location INTVEC. The priority bits in the PS of the 68000 change automatically at the time an interrupt request is accepted.

In addition to setting the interrupt vector, program MAIN loads the address LOC into location PNTR in the main memory. The interrupt-service routine uses this location as a pointer for storing input characters in the memory buffer. Interrupts from the video terminal are enabled by setting b_6 of STATUS to 1. Finally, the PS is cleared, thus setting the CPU priority to 0.

Program MAIN may now proceed to perform other tasks. However, it should not change the contents of PNTR or use the contents of the main memory data buffer at LOC until a complete input line has been read. Whenever a key is pressed on the keyboard, program MAIN will be interrupted and READ will be executed to transfer the input character to the memory buffer. Unless the character is Carriage Return (CR), a Return-from-interrupt instruction is executed. This causes the PC and the PS to be restored from the stack. When a CR character is encountered, interrupts from the keyboard interface are disabled by clearing b_6 in the interface's status register, and subroutine LINE is called to process the input line in the memory data buffer. Note that in Motorola terminology, interrupts are called exceptions, and the return-from-interrupt instruction is called Return from exception, RTE.

Although we have shown program MAIN as the program that initializes the keyboard status register and the interrupt vector location, those tasks are usually performed by operating system software. Application programs such as MAIN do not interact directly with I/O devices. We will examine these issues later in Section 6.4.12.

6.4.11 Types of Interrupts

An interrupt is an event that causes the execution of one program to be suspended and another program to be executed. So far we have assumed that the occurrence of this event is caused by a request received from an I/O device in the form of a hardware signal over the computer bus. In fact, there are many uses for interrupts other than for controlling I/O transfers, some of which we will now describe.

RECOVERY FROM ERRORS. Computers use a variety of techniques to ensure that all hardware components are operating properly. For example, many computers include a parity check code in the main memory, which allows detection of errors in the stored data. If an error occurs, the control hardware detects it and informs the CPU by raising an interrupt.

The CPU may also interrupt a program if it detects an error or an unusual condition while executing the instructions of this program. For example, the OP-code field of an instruction may not correspond to any legal instruction, or some instruction may attempt a division by zero.

When an interrupt is initiated as a result of such causes, the CPU proceeds in exactly the same manner as in the case of an I/O interrupt request: it suspends the program being executed and starts an interrupt-service routine. The interrupt-service routine should take appropriate action to recover from the error, if possible, or inform the user about it. Recall that in the case of an I/O interrupt, the CPU completes execution of the instruction in progress before accepting the interrupt. However, when an interrupt is caused by an error, execution of the interrupted instruction cannot be completed, and the CPU begins servicing the interrupt immediately.

DEBUGGING. Another important use of interrupts is as an aid in debugging programs. System software usually includes a program called a debugger, which helps the programmer to find errors in a program. The debugger uses interrupts to provide two important facilities: trace and breakpoints.

A *trace* facility causes an interrupt to occur after execution of every instruction in a program that is being debugged. The interrupt-service routine for a trace interrupt starts the execution of the debugging routine, which allows the user to examine the contents of registers, memory locations, and so on. On return from the debugging routine, the next instruction is executed, then the debugging routine is activated again. During the execution of the debugging routine trace interrupts are disabled.

Breakpoints provide a similar facility, except that the program being debugged is interrupted only at specific points selected by the user. An instruction called Trap or Software-interrupt is usually provided for this purpose. Execution of this instruction results in exactly the same actions as when a hardware interrupt request is received. Thus, if the user wishes to interrupt a program after execution of instruction i, the debugging routine replaces instruction $i + 1$ with a software interrupt instruction. When the program is executed and reaches that point, it is interrupted and the debugging routine is activated. Later, when the user is ready to continue executing the program being debugged, the debugging routine restores the instruction that was at location $i + 1$ and executes a Return-from-interrupt instruction.

COMMUNICATION BETWEEN PROGRAMS. Software interrupt instructions are used by the operating system to communicate with and control the execution of other programs, as discussed in the next section.

6.4.12   Use of Interrupts in Operating Systems

The preceding discussion presented the details of interrupt mechanisms in modern computers. We concentrated on describing interrupt handling at the machine level. It is illustrative at this point to consider how interrupts are handled in an environment where application programs run under the control of an operating system.

As mentioned in Chapter 1, all activities within a computer are coordinated by the operating system. Among other things, the operating system performs all input and output operations. It incorporates interrupt-service routines for all devices connected to the computer. An application program requests an I/O operation by issuing a software interrupt. The operating system suspends the execution of that program temporarily and performs the steps necessary for the requested operation. When the operation is completed, the operating system transfers control back to the application program.

In a computer that has both a Supervisor and a User mode, the CPU switches its operation to Supervisor mode at the time it accepts an interrupt request. It does so by setting a bit in the processor status register after saving the old contents of that register on the stack. Thus, when an application program calls the operating system by a software interrupt instruction, the CPU automatically switches to Supervisor mode, giving the operating system complete access to the machine's resources. When the operating system executes a Return-from-interrupt instruction, the processor status word belonging to the application program is restored from the stack. As a result, the CPU switches back to the User mode.

To illustrate the interaction between application programs and the operating system, let us consider an example that involves multitasking. Figure 6.14 describes a

OSINIT	Set interrupt vectors
	Time-slice clock ← Scheduler
	Trap ← OSSERVICES
	VDT interrupts ← IOData
	$\vdots$
OSSERVICES	Examine stack to determine requested operation.
	Call appropriate routine.
SCHEDULER	Save current context.
	Select a runnable process
	Restore saved context of new process.
	Push new values for PS and PC on stack.
	Return from interrupt

(a) OS initialization, services and scheduler

IOINIT	Set process status to Blocked
	Initialize memory buffer address pointer and counter
	Call device driver to initialize device
	and enable interrupts in the device interface
	Return from subroutine
IODATA	Poll devices to determine source of interrupt
	Call appropriate driver
	If END = 1 then set process status to Runnable
	Return from interrupt

(b) I/O routines

VDTINIT	Initialize device interface (select baud rate, etc.)
	Enable interrupts
	Return from subroutine
VDTDATA	Check device status
	If ready then transfer character
	If character = CR then set END = 1
	else set END = 0
	Return from subroutine

(c) VDT driver

FIGURE 6.14
A few operating system routines.

few routines needed to implement some of the essential functions in this environment. We will assume that the operating system uses a technique called *time slicing* to enable several programs to be executed in parallel. With this technique, each program runs for a short period called a time slice (τ), then another program runs for its time slice, and so on. The period τ is determined by a continuously running hardware clock, which generates an interrupt every τ seconds and causes an OS scheduling routine, called SCHEDULER in Figure 6.14, to be executed. The starting address of this routine is stored in the corresponding interrupt vector by the OSINIT routine at the time the operating system is started. The scheduler routine saves all information relating to the program that was just interrupted, say program A. The information saved, which is called the *program state*, includes the general register contents, the processor status word, and so on. The scheduler selects for execution another program, B, that was suspended earlier.

A program, together with any information that describes its current state, is regarded by the operating system as an entity called a *process*. A process can be in one of three states, Running, Runnable, or Blocked. The Running state means that the program is currently being executed. The process is Runnable if the program is ready for execution but is waiting to be selected by the scheduler. The third state, Blocked, means that the program is not ready to resume execution for some reason. For example, it may be waiting for completion of an I/O operation that it requested earlier.

Having selected program B, the scheduler restores all information saved at the time that program was suspended, including the contents of PS and PC, and executes a Return-from-interrupt instruction. As a result, program B resumes execution for τ seconds, at the end of which the clock raises an interrupt again, and a *context switch* to another runnable process takes place.

Consider now the case when program A wishes to read an input line from a video terminal. Instead of performing the operation itself, it requests that service from the operating system. The program uses the stack or the CPU registers to pass to the operating system information describing the required operation, the I/O device, and the address of a buffer in the program data area where the line should be placed. Then it executes a software interrupt instruction. The interrupt vector for this instruction points to the OSSERVICES routine in Figure 6.14. This routine examines the information on the stack and initiates the requested operation by calling an appropriate OS routine. In our example, it calls IOINIT in Figure 6.14*b*, which is a routine responsible for starting I/O operations.

While an I/O operation is in progress, the program that requested it cannot continue execution. Hence, the IOINIT routine sets the process represented by program A into the Blocked state, indicating to the scheduler that the program cannot resume execution at this time. Then, IOINIT starts the requested I/O operation. It carries out any preparations needed, such as initializing address pointers, byte count, and so on, then it calls a routine that starts operation of the desired I/O device.

Operating system designers strive to prepare all software pertaining to a particular device in the form of a self-contained module called the *device driver* so that these modules can be added or deleted easily. We have assumed that the device driver for the video terminal consists of two routines, VDTINIT and VDTDATA, as shown in Figure 6.14*c*. IOINIT calls VDTINIT to perform any initialization operations needed by the device or its interface circuit, such as selecting the data transmission format or baud rate. Then, VDTINIT enables interrupts in the interface circuit by setting the appropriate bit in its status register. Once these actions are completed, the device becomes ready to participate in a data transfer operation. It will generate an interrupt request whenever a character is entered at the keyboard.

Following the return to OSSERVICES, the SCHEDULER routine selects a user program to run. Of course, the scheduler will not select program A, because that program is now in the Blocked state. The Return-from-interrupt instruction that causes the selected user program to begin execution will also lower the CPU's priority to the user level. Thus, an interrupt request generated by the video terminal's interface will be accepted. The interrupt vector for the terminal points to an operating system routine called IODATA. Because there could be several devices connected to the same interrupt request line, this routine begins by polling these devices to determine the one requesting service. Then, it calls the appropriate device driver to service the request. In our example, the driver called will be VDTDATA, which will transfer one character of data. If the character is a carriage return, it will also set to 1 a flag called END, which informs IODATA that the requested I/O operation has been completed. At this point, the IODATA routine changes the state of program A from Blocked to Runnable, so that the scheduler will select it for execution in some future time slice.

6.5   I/O INTERFACES

The function of an I/O interface is to coordinate the transfer of data between the CPU and an external device. As stated earlier in this chapter, such an interface should:

1. Store the device status for presentation to the computer when required using a *device status register*;
2. Provide storage space (the *data buffer register*) for at least one data character, or perhaps one word, to be used when transferring data to or from the computer;
3. Recognize the device address when this address appears on the I/O address lines; and
4. Provide appropriate timing and gating signals to accomplish the transfer of data or status information as required.

To illustrate the means by which these functions are implemented, we shall discuss a specific interface example. Although details may differ from one computer to another, the basic ideas are applicable to most interface designs. We shall start by studying the *protocols* used for data transfer on a bus.

6.5.1   Control of Data Transfer

A typical bus consists of three sets of lines: data lines, address lines, and control lines. A few control lines are required to coordinate data transfers over the bus, and hence they are used by all devices connected to the bus. Other control lines are needed for handling requests for interrupts and direct memory access (DMA) operations; these lines are used only by devices that have such capabilities. The remaining control lines may carry information related to detection of power failures, initialization of the system, and so on. In what follows, we will discuss the operation of the bus in the context of a computer with a single-bus organization. That is, we will assume that the CPU, the main memory, and all peripherals exchange data via a single common bus (see Figure 1.11).

Let us first consider the lines that are required for transferring data between the CPU and one of the I/O devices. The control signals involved in such transfers should be capable of specifying two types of information, namely, the nature of the transfer and its timing. The first of these, which we will refer to as the mode of the transfer, involves the specification of whether a Read or a Write operation is to be performed. A Read/Write line specifies Read when set to 1 and Write when set to 0. When several operand sizes are possible, such as byte, word, or long word, the required size of data should also be indicated.

The second component of the bus control signals carries timing information. These signals specify the times at which the CPU and the I/O devices may place data on the bus or receive data from the bus. A variety of schemes have been devised for the timing of data transfers over a bus. They may be broadly classified as either synchronous or asynchronous schemes.

In the case of a synchronous bus, all devices derive timing information from a common clock line. Equally spaced pulses on this line define equal time intervals, where each interval constitutes a "bus cycle," during which one data transfer may take place. Such a scheme is illustrated in Figure 6.15. Note that the address and data lines in this and subsequent figures are shown as high and low at the same time. This is intended to indicate that some lines are high and some low, depending on the particular address or data pattern being transmitted. The crossing points indicate

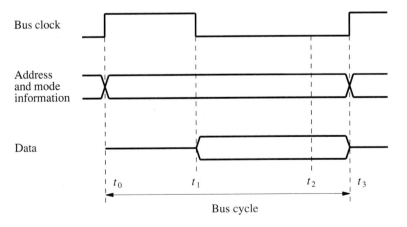

FIGURE 6.15
Timing of an input transfer on a synchronous bus.

the time at which these patterns change. A signal line in an indeterminate or high impedance state is represented by an intermediate level half-way between the low and high signal levels.

Let us consider the sequence of events during an input operation. At time t_0, the CPU places the device address on the address lines and sets the mode control lines to indicate an input operation. This information travels over the bus at a speed determined by its physical and electrical characteristics. The clock pulse width $t_1 - t_0$ should be chosen such that it is greater than the maximum propagation delay between the CPU and any of the devices connected to the bus. It should also be wide enough to allow all devices to decode the address and control signals so that the addressed device can be ready to respond at time t_1. The addressed device, recognizing that an input operation is requested, places its input data on the data lines at time t_1. After some further delay, $t_2 - t_1$, the CPU strobes the data lines and loads the data into its input buffer (MDR in Figure 4.1). As before, this delay should be greater than the maximum bus propagation time plus the setup time for the input buffer of the CPU. After t_2, all the bus lines are cleared in preparation for a new bus cycle.

The procedure for an output operation is similar to the input sequence. The CPU places the output data on the data lines when it transmits the address and mode information. At time t_1, the addressed device strobes the data into its data buffer.

The synchronous bus scheme described in the preceding discussion is very simple and results in a simple design for the device interface. The clock speed has to be chosen such that it accommodates the longest delays on the bus and the slowest interface. Furthermore, the CPU has no way of determining whether the addressed device has actually responded. It simply assumes that at t_2 the output data has been received or that the input data is available on the data lines. If as a result of a malfunction the device does not respond, the error will not be detected.

An alternative scheme for controlling data transfers on the bus is based on the use of a "handshake" between the CPU and the device being addressed. The common clock is eliminated, hence the resulting bus operation is asynchronous. The clock line is replaced by two timing control lines, which we will refer to as "Ready" and "Accept." In principle, a data transfer controlled by a handshake protocol proceeds as follows. The CPU places the address and mode information on the bus. Then, it indicates to all devices that it has done so by sending a pulse on the Ready line. When the addressed device receives the Ready signal, it performs the required operation, then transmits a pulse on the Accept line. The CPU waits for the Accept signal before it clears the bus and, in the case of an input operation, strobes the data into its input buffer.

An example of the timing of a data transfer using the handshake scheme is given in Figure 6.16, which depicts the following sequence of events.

t_0: The CPU places the address and mode information on the bus.

t_1: The CPU sets the Ready line to 1 to inform the I/O devices that the address and mode information is ready. The delay $t_1 - t_0$ is intended to allow for any *skew* that may occur on the bus. Skew refers to the situation where two

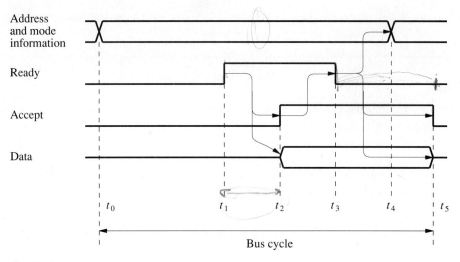

FIGURE 6.16
Handshake control of data transfer during an input operation.

signals simultaneously transmitted from one source arrive at the destination at different times. It arises from differences in the propagation speed on different lines of the bus. Thus, to guarantee that the Ready signal will not arrive at any device ahead of the address and mode information, the delay $t_1 - t_0$ should be larger than the maximum possible bus skew. (We should note that in the synchronous case bus skew is accounted for as a part of the maximum propagation delay.) When this address information arrives at any device, it is decoded by the interface circuitry. Sufficient time should be allowed for the interface circuitry to decode the address. This delay may be included in the period $t_1 - t_0$.

t_2: The interface of the addressed device receives the Ready signal, and having already decoded the address and mode information, it recognizes that it should perform an input operation. Hence it gates the data from its internal buffer to the data lines. At the same time, it sets the Accept signal to 1. If extra delays are introduced by the interface circuitry before placing the data on the bus, it must delay the Accept signal accordingly. The period $t_2 - t_1$ is dependent on the distance between the CPU and the device interface. It is also a function of the delays introduced by the interface circuitry. It is this variability that gives the bus its asynchronous nature.

t_3: The Accept signal arrives at the CPU, indicating that the input data is available on the bus. However, since it was assumed that the device interface transmits the Accept signal at the same time that it places the data on the bus, the CPU should allow for bus skew. After a delay equivalent to the maximum bus skew, the CPU strobes the data into its input buffer. At the same time, it drops the Ready signal, indicating that it has received the data.

t_4: The CPU removes the address and mode information from the bus. The delay between t_3 and t_4 is again intended to allow for bus skew. Erroneous addressing may take place if the address, as seen by some device on the bus, starts to change while the Ready signal is still equal to 1.

t_5: When the 1 to 0 transition of the Ready signal is received by the device interface, it removes the data and the Accept signal from the bus. This completes the input transfer.

The timing for an output operation is essentially the same as for an input operation. It is illustrated in Figure 6.17. In this case, the CPU places the output data on the data lines at the same time that it transmits the address and mode information. The addressed device strobes the data into its output buffer when it receives the Ready signal. It indicates that it has done so by setting the Accept signal to 1. The remainder of the cycle is identical to the input operation.

In the timing diagrams of Figures 6.16 and 6.17, it is assumed that the compensation for bus skew and address decoding is performed by the CPU. This simplifies the I/O interface at the device end, because the interface circuit can use the Ready signal directly to gate other signals to or from the bus.

The asynchronous scheme as described is often used in practice. An almost identical set of signals can be found on the Unibus of the PDP-11 computer, and similar signals are used in the 68000 microprocessor. Many alternatives that have some synchronous and some asynchronous features are also possible; for example, a fixed pulse width may be used for the Ready and Accept signals. The choice of a given design involves a trade-off between many factors. Some of the important considerations are

- Simplicity of the device interface
- Ability to accommodate device interfaces that introduce different amounts of delay

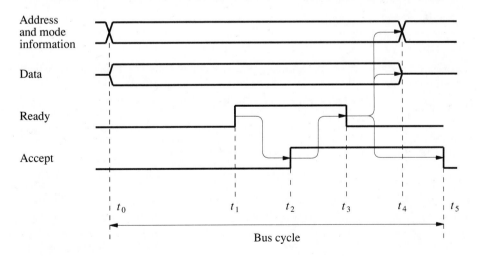

FIGURE 6.17
Handshake control of data transfer during an output operation.

- Total time required for a bus transfer
- Ability to detect errors resulting from addressing a nonexistent device or from an interface malfunction

The fully asynchronous scheme provides the highest degree of flexibility and reliability, but the device interface circuit is somewhat more complex. The error-detection capability is provided by interlocking the Ready and Accept signals. If the Accept signal is not received within a fixed time-out period after setting Ready to 1, the CPU assumes that an error has occurred. This may be used to cause an interrupt and execute a routine that alerts the operator to the malfunction or to take some other appropriate action.

6.5.2   Interface Design Example

The I/O interface consists of the circuitry required to transfer data between the computer bus and an I/O device. Therefore, on one side of the interface we have the bus signals: address, data, and control. On the other side we have a data path, with its associated controls, that enables transfer of data between the interface and the I/O device. This side is obviously device-dependent. However, it may be broadly classified as either a parallel or a serial interface. A parallel interface transfers data in the form of one or more bytes in parallel to or from the device. On the other hand, a serial interface transmits and receives data one bit at a time. Communication with the bus is the same for both formats; the conversion from the parallel to the serial format, and vice versa, takes place inside the interface circuit.

Before discussing a specific example, let us recall the functions of an I/O interface. According to the discussion in the previous section, an I/O interface:

1. Provides a storage buffer for one word of data (or one byte in the case of byte-oriented devices);
2. Contains status flags that can be accessed by the computer to determine whether the buffer is full (for input) or empty (for output);
3. Contains address-decoding circuitry to determine when it is being addressed by the computer;
4. Generates the appropriate timing signals as required by the bus control scheme used; and
5. Performs any format conversion that may be necessary to transfer data between the bus and the I/O device (for example, parallel-serial).

PARALLEL INTERFACE. We will present first an example of a parallel interface. A 16-bit, byte-addressable computer is assumed, where program-controlled I/O is used. The bus is the fully asynchronous type, and timing of bus transfers is the same as in Figures 6.16 and 6.17. We will further assume that the interface contains separate data buffers (DIN and DOUT) for input and output and that there is one status register associated with each buffer (SIN and SOUT). The two buffers and the two status registers are assigned four adjacent word addresses. These addresses differ only in the least significant three bits. Since only one status flag is required for each data buffer, only 1 bit of SIN and SOUT needs to be implemented; bit 7 is chosen for consistency with the example programs in Chapter 2 and Figure 6.3. A logic diagram for the required interface is shown in Figure 6.18.

The operation of the interface can be described as follows. For an input operation, one word (or one byte) of data is transferred from the input device to register

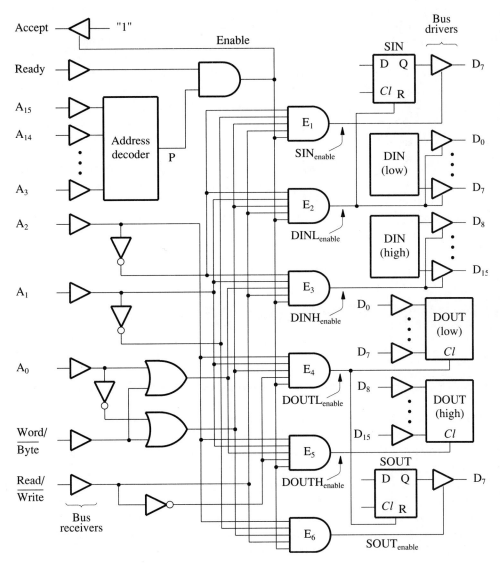

FIGURE 6.18
Logic diagram for a parallel I/O interface.

DIN, and flip-flop SIN is set to 1. The data and control lines required for this transfer are not shown in the figure, because this circuitry is internal to the device and not a part of the interface. The interface circuitry shown is responsible for transferring the contents of either SIN or DIN to the CPU whenever a Read request is received specifying these locations. The high-order 13 address lines, A_3 to A_{15}, are decoded by the address decoder block. Whenever these lines carry the address assigned to this interface, point P goes to the logic 1 state. Then, as soon as the Ready signal is received, the Enable line is set to 1. At the same time, bits A_0, A_1 and A_2, together with the mode control lines Read/Write and Word/Byte, select one of the six gates E_1 to E_6. This results in enabling the output gates corresponding to the addressed byte or word and placing its contents on the data lines. While the Enable line is in the 1 state, the output signal Accept is also set to 1. This constitutes the response of the interface to the Read request issued by the CPU. As soon as the Ready signal drops to 0, the Accept signal is removed, and all the bus driver gates are disabled. The reader should verify that this sequence will result in bus signals that are consistent with the timing diagram of Figure 6.16. Note that when the DIN buffer is addressed, the input status flag SIN is reset to 0. This is essential in order to guarantee that each item of input data is read by the computer only once.

An output operation proceeds in essentially the same way. When the Enable signal is set to 1, while DOUT is selected, the clock input to the output buffer is set. This results in loading the buffer, which is assumed to be positive edge-triggered, with the data on the data lines. At the same time SOUT is reset to 0. When the data in DOUT is transferred to the output device, SOUT is set to 1 to indicate that the interface is ready to accept a new output transfer.

SERIAL INTERFACE. A serial interface contains the same addressing and control circuitry as the parallel interface of Figure 6.18. In addition, some controls are needed to transfer data serially between registers DIN and DOUT and the I/O device. For example, the data and status registers in Figure 6.18 may be replaced by the circuit given in Figure 6.19. This circuit enables transmission in the asynchronous start-stop format, which is commonly used with low-speed serial devices such as video terminals. A discussion of this transmission format will be given in Chapter 9.

The example of Figure 6.19 is based on the use of a UART (universal asynchronous receiver transmitter) chip. This is an integrated circuit chip that contains all the logic circuitry for the required parallel-serial conversion. The two registers DIN and DOUT and the status flags SIN and SOUT are included on the chip. Thus they can be used to replace the corresponding registers in Figure 6.18. However, all address decoding and control circuits in the parallel interface remain unchanged. Note that in this case, only one byte is transferred at a time. Therefore, only the low-order bytes of DIN and DOUT are implemented.

In order to illustrate the operation of the UART, let us consider a UART connected to a video terminal. Input and output transfers can be described briefly as follows:

Input—When a key is depressed on the keyboard, the corresponding 8-bit character code is transmitted serially to the serial input (SI) pin of the UART and

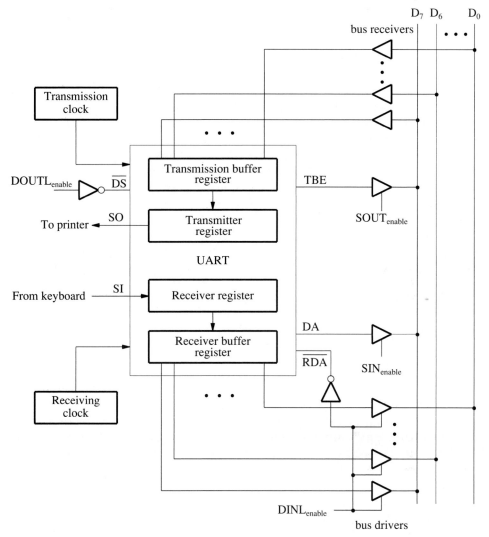

FIGURE 6.19
Serial to parallel conversion using a universal asynchronous receiver transmitter (UART).

shifted into the receiver register. At the end of transmission, the character is transferred to the receiver buffer register, and the output DA (data available) is set to 1. Hence, DA can be used as the status flag SIN. It is, therefore, gated to line D_7 of the data bus under control of the SIN_{enable} signal. Similarly, the contents of the receiver buffer register are gated to the low-order byte of the data bus under control of $DINL_{enable}$. The $DINL_{enable}$ signal is also inverted and connected to the $\overline{RDA}$ (reset data available) pin of the UART. When $\overline{RDA}$ is set to 0, it resets the DA output to 0. Thus, when a character is transferred from the receiver buffer register to the bus, the keyboard Ready flag is simultaneously reset to 0. It will be set to 1 again when a new character is entered at the keyboard.

Output—Serial transmission of one character to the video terminal is accomplished by serially shifting data out of the transmitter register in the UART to the SO (serial output) pin. The transmission buffer register can hold a second character waiting for transmission. Output data are loaded into the transmission buffer register when a 0 is applied to the $\overline{\text{DS}}$ (data strobe) pin. When transmission of the character in the transmitter register is completed, the contents of the transmission buffer register are transferred to it, and their transmission is started immediately. At the same time, the output TBE (transmitter buffer empty) is set to 1. Hence, the transmission buffer register can be used as the output data buffer DOUT, and TBE constitutes the output status flag SOUT, as shown in Figure 6.19.

The above interface example is applicable, with minor modifications, to a variety of devices that use the asynchronous serial-transmission format. In particular, such a scheme can be used for connection of a *modem* (*mod*ulator *dem*odulator) for transmission of data over telephone lines. Data transmission over telephone lines will be treated in more detail in Chapter 13.

6.5.3 Bus Scheduling

The discussion in the previous two sections concentrated on data transfer operations between the CPU and the I/O devices. The transfers were initiated by the CPU, which was implicitly assumed to be the only device with the capability to drive the address and the mode lines. However, the bus is used for other types of data transfer. For example, a device with DMA capability transfers data directly to and from the main memory without involvement of the CPU.

A DMA transfer uses the same data paths and control lines as the CPU. Therefore, some means have to be introduced to coordinate the use of these lines, to prevent two devices from initiating transfers at the same time. A bus controller, which may be part of the CPU, is used to perform the required scheduling function. During the discussion of interrupts, it was pointed out that simultaneous requests can be handled by means of a variety of priority structures. This requires the use of control lines such as interrupt-request and interrupt-acknowledge. An almost identical approach can be used to schedule the use of the bus. The control signals required for this purpose may be referred to as Bus Request and Bus Grant. Priorities for use of the bus may be established in the same way as for acknowledging interrupts.

When a Bus Grant signal is received from the bus controller, the device gains the right to initiate one or more bus transfers. It can then use the address, control, and data lines to transfer data to or from the main memory or any other device. While one device is performing data transfers, other devices may request the use of the bus. One of them is chosen by the bus controller as next in line and is so informed via a Bus Grant signal. When the current device completes its transfers, the next-in-line device gains control, and so on. A Bus Busy signal is set to 1 by the current user of the bus to prevent the next-in-line device from starting transmission prematurely.

This discussion is intended only to point out some key aspects in the design of a bus. Further details will not be given, because the principles involved are essentially the same as in the handling of interrupt requests discussed earlier in this chapter.

6.6   STANDARD I/O INTERFACES

In the previous sections, it was pointed out that there are a number of alternatives for the design of the bus of a computer. This variety means that I/O devices fitted with an interface circuit suitable for one computer may not be usable with other computers. A different interface may have to be designed for every combination of I/O device and computer, resulting in a need for a large number of different interfaces. A better alternative is to standardize interface signals and protocols.

It is difficult to define a uniform standard for the main bus of a computer, however. The structure of this bus is closely tied to the architecture of the computer; therefore, it can be expected to change from one computer to another. It is equally difficult to develop a standard that covers all computer peripherals because of the extremely wide range of transfer speeds and other requirements. A workable alternative is to define standards for certain classes of interconnection that are suitable for both computers and peripherals.

Figure 6.20 illustrates the way in which some commonly used standards may be incorporated into a computer system. The CPU is connected through its processor

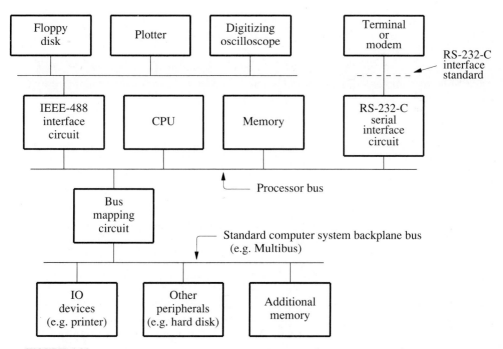

FIGURE 6.20
An example of a computer system showing different interface standards.

bus to the memory and I/O interfaces. The properties of this bus are determined by the structure of the computer in question, and more specifically, by the CPU signal lines. In fact, different computer models made by the same manufacturer often have different bus structures. For example, the Unibus serves as the main bus in PDP-11 computers. However, VAX computers, also made by Digital Equipment Corporation, use a different bus, known as SBI (Synchronous Backplane Interconnect). Because the processor bus itself cannot be made to conform to any particular standard, interface circuits are used to adapt the connection lines and signals to the requirements of a given standard. Three examples of this approach are shown in Figure 6.20. The Multibus[1] and IEEE-488[2] standards allow the interconnection of several devices via a bus. The third example, the RS-232-C[3], defines an interface for connecting a single device.

The word "interface" refers to the boundary between two circuits or devices. A standard for this interface comprises a set of specifications for the functional, electrical, and mechanical characteristics of all signal and power lines that cross the boundary. This means that it defines a connector and the signal lines used. The reader should be warned that an interface circuit is often referred to simply as an interface in the literature, and particularly so in the commercial literature. However, in the context of a standard, the word "interface" is used only in the more precise sense defined above. It is the task of the computer system designer to design a circuit that meets the requirements of a given interface standard.

Perhaps the most commonly used interface standard is RS-232-C, also known as CCITT Recommendation V.24. It is intended for the interconnection of devices that use serial transmission, either synchronous or asynchronous, and is widely available with computer peripherals such as video terminals and modems. This standard will be discussed in Chapter 13.

A number of bus standards have evolved. Some of these, such as VMEbus[4] and Multibus, implement a full complement of the functions normally supported by a computer bus. Hence, they can be used as an extension of a computer bus, as shown in Figure 6.20. They serve to provide a standard interface for connecting additional main memory modules, secondary storage units, or I/O devices. The existence of a standard bus connected in this manner is transparent to the CPU and hence to the programmer. The function of the bus-mapping circuit shown in Figure 6.20 is to translate one set of bus signals into the other and to provide any temporary buffering that may be needed because of differences in the timing of data transfers.

Another bus standard, IEEE-488, is intended for connecting laboratory instruments, plotters, floppy disks, and other low- to medium-speed peripherals to a computer or to some other appropriate controller. However, the manner in which data transfers are controlled on this bus and the speed of these transfers do not make it suitable for use as a computer bus in the same manner as the Multibus. Moreover, the interface circuit shown in the figure between the processor bus and the IEEE-488 bus cannot be designed so that it is transparent to the CPU. This circuit contains data and control registers that must be accessed explicitly by the software.

In what follows we discuss briefly the Nubus, the Multibus, and the IEEE-488 bus.

6.6.1 The Nubus

The Nubus[5] is a processor-independent, synchronous bus standard intended for use in 32-bit microprocessor systems. It defines a backplane into which up to 16 devices may be plugged, each in the form of a circuit board of standard dimensions. The Nubus was first proposed by researchers at MIT as a high-performance, low-cost bus for use in workstations and personal computers. After some refinement, it was adopted by the Institute of Electrical and Electronics Engineers as IEEE Standard No. 1196.

The Nubus was designed to provide only essential functions, in order to minimize the number of bus signals needed and the complexity of the device interface circuits. Since many workstations and personal computers make use of several microprocessors internally, the bus was also designed to meet the needs of multiprocessor systems. Any or all devices on the bus may have processing capability. A circuit board is connected to the bus via a 96-pin connector, which carries 51 bus signals. The remaining pins are used for ground and power supply connections. Bus lines are organized in four groups, as follows:

1. Data transaction
2. Arbitration
3. Utility
4. Power and ground

A listing of the bus lines in each group is given in Table 6.1. Note that in the nomenclature of IEEE standards, a signal name that ends in an asterisk (*) indicates that the signal is active (asserted) when in the low-voltage state. All Nubus signals are active when low.

The data transaction signals are used to transfer 8, 16, or 32 bits of data in parallel between two devices. Devices on the bus share a single, byte-addressable space consisting of 2^{32} bytes. To reduce the number of bus lines, address and data are time-multiplexed; that is, they are transmitted on the same lines, lines AD(31–0)*, but at different times. The other lines in the data transaction group are used by the two devices involved in a data transfer operation to coordinate their activities.

Timing of most activities on the bus is controlled by a 10-MHz clock signal, CLK*, which is one of the utility lines. The clock signal has a duty cycle of 25 percent; that is, it is active (low) 25 percent of the time. New information may be placed on the bus only at the rising edge of this signal, called the *driving edge*. The line signals are sampled by all devices at the falling edge of CLK*, called the *sample edge*, which occurs 75 nanoseconds later.

At any time, one device on the bus is designated the *bus owner*, or *bus master*. This is the only device that is allowed to issue read and write requests. Another device may become the bus owner by issuing a request on the arbitration lines. It may begin transferring data after it wins arbitration and becomes the new owner of the bus.

We will now discuss some of the salient features of the Nubus.

Data transactions. A read or write operation on the Nubus occupies at least two clock cycles, one to transmit the address and the other to transmit the data. If a

TABLE 6.1 Nubus lines.

Function	Name	Description	Number
Utility			8
	CLK*	Clock	
	RESET*	Reset1	
	PFW*	Power Fail	
	ID(3-0)*	Card slot identification	
	NMRQ*	Non-master request	
Data Transaction			38
	AD(31-0)*	Address and data	
	TM(1-0)*	Transfer mode	
	SP*	System parity	
	SPV*	System parity valid	
	START*	Start signal	
	ACK*	Transfer acknowledge	
Arbitration			5
	RQST*	Request for bus ownership	
	ARB(3-0)*	Arbitration signals	
Power supply	+5V, –5.2V		45
	±12V, and GND		
		Total	96

device requires additional time, a data transaction may be extended to several clock periods. The sequence of events for a read operation is illustrated in Figure 6.21. Starting at driving edge d_1, the bus master transmits the address and maintains it on the bus for one clock cycle. At the same time, it sends an appropriate code on the Transfer Mode lines, TM(1–0)*, to specify the size of the operand and to indicate whether it is requesting a read or a write operation. It also asserts the START* signal to mark this clock cycle as the beginning of a data transaction. All devices on the bus read this information at the next sampling edge, s_1. If the addressed slave is fast enough to provide the requested data at d_2, it does so. Otherwise, it delays its response for one or more clock cycles. At d_n, the slave places the requested data on the AD lines for one clock cycle. It uses the TM lines to send a 2-bit status code, indicating whether the transfer was completed correctly or whether an error was detected. It also asserts the acknowledgment line, ACK*. If no slave responds within 256 clock cycles, a special device on the bus responds instead, using the TM lines to indicate a timeout error.

A write operation proceeds in a similar manner. The bus master transmits the data beginning at d_2, and maintains it on the AD lines until the end of the clock cycle in which it receives the acknowledgement signal.

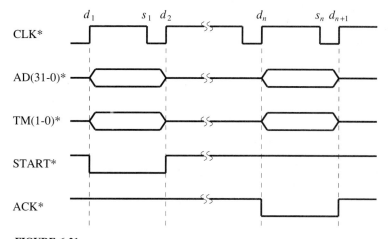

FIGURE 6.21
A read operation on the Nubus.

The Nubus protocol allows block transfers, in which two, four, eight, or sixteen words may be transferred in a single bus transaction. Also, in any data transaction, whenever a device places either address or data on the AD lines, it may transmit a parity bit on line SP*. It should always indicate on line SPV* whether it has used this option. Parity enables the device receiving the information to determine whether an error has occurred during the bus transfer.

Arbitration. When a device that is not currently the bus master wishes to perform read or write operations, it must first request and obtain bus ownership. It requests bus ownership by asserting the RQST* line, beginning at the driving edge of some clock cycle. Since more than one device may request the bus at the same time, the assertion of RQST* marks the beginning of an *arbitration contest* occupying two clock cycles. There is no single arbiter on the bus, which issues bus grant signals in the manner described in Section 6.5.3. Instead, the arbitration circuitry is distributed across all device interfaces, as will be described shortly.

The winner of the arbitration contest immediately becomes the new bus master if there is no data transaction in progress. Otherwise, it must wait for the acknowledgment signal, which marks the end of the transaction. The current master releases the bus at the end of that transaction, because the RQST* line is asserted. The new master claims the bus by asserting the STRT* signal. Then, the devices that lost the arbitration contest, if any, begin a new competition to select another winner. Note that in order to minimize overhead, arbitration can take place concurrently with data transfers.

The arbitration rules of the Nubus are intended to provide for fair sharing of the bus among its possible masters. If all devices request the bus continuously, bus ownership will move from one device to the next in a round-robin fashion, giving each device a chance to perform one bus transaction. Fairness is guaranteed by the simple rule that no device can request bus ownership if the RQST* line is already asserted. When a device becomes the bus master, it releases the RQST* line, giving other devices a chance to compete for bus ownership. That device will not be able to request the bus again until all other devices have used it.

We will now describe the way in which arbitration takes place when several devices simultaneously request bus ownership. Each device on the bus is assigned a 4-bit identification number based on its physical location. This number is hardwired in the bus connectors using pins ID(3–0)*. In the case of multiple requests, devices are selected according to the order of their identification numbers, starting with the highest-numbered contender.

The arbitration contest takes place over four lines, ARB(3–0)*. A winner is selected as a result of interaction among the signals transmitted over these lines by all contestants. The net outcome of this interaction is that the code on the four lines represents the request having the highest ID number. We will illustrate the mechanism by which this is accomplished using a simple example. Consider two devices, A and B, that are requesting the use of the bus; let their ID numbers be 5 and 6, respectively. Each device is connected to the arbitration lines as shown in Figure 6.22. A device requesting the bus attempts to place its 4-bit ID code on the arbitration lines. Device A transmits the pattern 0101, and device B the pattern 0110. Because the arbitration lines are active when low (i.e., a logic 1 drives the line low), and open-collector driver gates are used in the device interfaces, the code seen by either of the two devices will be 0111. Each device continually compares the pattern on the ARB lines to its own ID, starting from the most significant bit. If it detects a difference at any

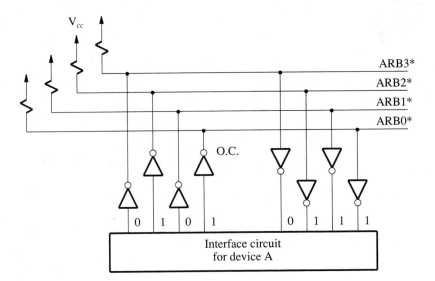

FIGURE 6.22
Connection of device interface circuit to priority arbitration lines.

bit position, it disables its bus drivers for the corresponding line and for all lower-order lines. In the case of our example, device A detects a difference on line ARB1*. Hence, it disables its drivers for lines ARB1* and ARB0*. This causes the pattern on the arbitration lines to change to 0110, which means that B has won the contest. Note that since for a short period the code on the priority lines is 0111, device B may temporarily disable its driver for line ARB0*. However, it will enable it again once device A has disabled its drivers. The specifications of the Nubus require the arbitration circuitry to reach the final decision within two clock cycles.

It was mentioned earlier that the bus master is not allowed to start a new data transaction if it sees the RQST* line asserted. To allow for critical operations in which several transactions may be needed without interruption, the bus master is allowed to *lock* a particular resource or the entire bus. While the bus is locked, the bus master ignores requests from other devices and continues using the bus for several bus transactions. An example of the use of this feature is in the implementation of the *test-and-set* operation needed in multiprocessor systems, which will be described in Chapter 12.

Interrupts. A backplane bus must provide a mechanism for one device to send an interrupt signal to another. There are two such mechanisms in the Nubus protocol. The first is intended for use by devices that are capable of becoming bus masters. In order for such a device, say A, to send an interrupt request to another device, B, it simply performs a write operation into a register in the interface of that device. The circuitry in the interface of device B should then generate an interrupt request on the bus of its local processor. This simple mechanism obviates the need for any special signals on the bus to handle interrupts. Also, such details as interrupt priorities and the transfer of interrupt vector addresses are left to the device interface designer. Since they are processor-dependent, they may differ from one device to another.

The interrupt mechanism just described can be used only by devices that are capable of acquiring bus ownership and performing write operations. In the application environments of the Nubus, most devices are of this type. However, the circuitry needed to provide bus ownership capability may be too costly for the interface of a simple device, such as a video terminal. The Nonmaster request line, NMRQ*, is provided to serve as a simple interrupt request line for such devices, and one of the processors connected to the bus should be responsible for servicing these requests. There is no provision for interrupt acknowledgment or for a device to identify itself to the processor at the time the interrupt request on NMRQ* is accepted.

Power failure. Two of the utility signals of the Nubus have not been discussed yet. These are RESET* and Power Fail (PFW*). The RESET* signal is used to put all devices on the bus in their starting state. It can be activated at any time by any device to restart the system's operation after a failure. The RESET* signal is also used in conjunction with PFW* to ensure proper functioning of the system at the time power is turned on and enable an orderly shut-down when power is interrupted. The latter case typically involves saving essential data in the main memory by transferring them to a nonvolatile device such as a disk.

The power supply of a computer includes large capacitors, which require several milliseconds to be charged or discharged. Hence, when power is first applied, the DC output of the power supply rises slowly from 0. The RESET* signal is activated by the power supply during this period, because logic circuitry may produce erroneous outputs when the DC voltages are below their rated values. When AC power is interrupted, the power supply is capable of maintaining the DC voltages at their rated values for several milliseconds. The power supply must activate the PFW* line immediately, to alert all devices on the bus to the imminent loss of power. Device interfaces may arrange for the activation of PFW* to cause an interrupt, so that a service routine can be executed to save essential data by transferring them to disk. The power supply must activate RESET* before the DC voltages drop below their minimum acceptable values, but no sooner than two milliseconds after activating PFW*.

6.6.2 The Multibus

The Multibus was originally developed for use in Intel's Microcomputer Development System (MDS). It has now evolved into two recommended IEEE Standards, numbers 796[1] and 1296[6]. Both standards give a full functional, electrical, and mechanical specification for a backplane bus through which a number of circuit boards may be interconnected. A full range of devices may be involved, including computers, memory boards, I/O devices, and other peripherals.

Standard 796 defines a bus with a 16-bit data path. Its successor, defined in Standard 1296, is also known as Multibus II. It has a 32-bit data path and provides many features to support multiprocessor systems. In what follows, we will restrict the discussion to the basic features of Multibus as given in Standard 796. This bus consists of the 86 signals given in Table 6.2. We will discuss some of its distinguishing features below. For full details, interested readers should consult the IEEE Standard 796-1983 document.

Data transfers over the Multibus are controlled by an asynchronous handshake similar to that of Figures 6.16 and 6.17. The main difference is that the two signals, Read/Write and Ready, are replaced by MRDC* (Memory Read Command) and MWTC* (Memory Write Command). As in the case of Nubus, a signal whose name ends with a * is active when low. During a memory read operation the MRDC* signal is activated, and for a write operation the MWTC* signal is used, as shown in Figure 6.23. The slave uses the XACK* (Transfer Acknowledge) signal to indicate that it has accepted the command.

In computer systems that use memory-mapped I/O, the MRDC* and MWTC* signals suffice for all data transfers. When used in conjunction with computers that have separate I/O instructions, such as Intel microprocessors, these two commands are replaced by IORC* and IOWC* during I/O transfers.

The Multibus supports both 8-bit and 16-bit data transfers. It also allows an 8-bit computer to exchange data with a 16-bit computer, one byte at a time. The BHEN*

TABLE 6.2 IEEE 796 bus (Multibus) signals.

Function	Name	Description	Number
Data transfer			44
	D0* to D15*	8- or 16-bit data	
	A0* to A19*	Byte address	
	MRDC*	Memory read cmd.	
	MWTC*	Memory write cmd.	
	IORC*	I/O read cmd.	
	IOWC*	I/O write cmd.	
	XACK*	Transfer acknowledge	
	BHEN*	Byte high enable	
	INH1*,INH2*	Inhibit	
Scheduling			6
	CBRQ*	Common bus request	
	BREQ*	Bus request	
	BPRN*	Bus priority in	
	BPRO*	Bus priority out	
	BUSY*	Bus busy	
	BCLK*	Bus clock	
Interrupts			9
	INT0* to INT7*	Interrupt requests	
	INTA*	Interrupt acknowledge	
Misc.			2
	CCLK*	Constant clock	
	INIT*	Initialize	
Power supply	+5,±12,GND		20
Reserved		For future use	5
		Total	86

(Byte High Enable) signal is used during these transfers to indicate whether the high-order data lines, D8 to D15, carry valid data.

Another interesting facility is provided by the Inhibit lines, INH1* and INH2*. In order to illustrate the use of these lines, let us consider a typical example. Most of the address space of a computer is filled with RAM locations. However, small portions of this space are occupied by memory-mapped I/O devices and by ROM. The latter may be needed, for example, to store a short power-up routine. This arrangement of the address space may be realized by designing the address decoder of the RAM in such a way that it responds to memory read and write commands only when they are outside the regions occupied by the ROM or the I/O devices. The Inhibit lines offer an alternative approach. When the interface for the ROM or for

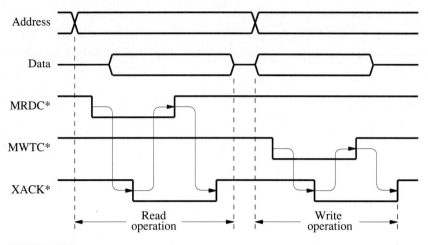

FIGURE 6.23
Multibus handshake signals.

one of the I/O devices recognizes its address, it asserts one of the Inhibit lines. At the same time, the RAM interface responds to all addresses, provided that neither of the two Inhibit lines is asserted. Whenever one of the Inhibit lines is active, the RAM interface turns off all its bus drivers and does not participate in the bus operation.

Figure 6.24 shows the sequence of events for a memory read cycle involving the use of the inhibit feature. At the beginning of the cycle, the bus master places a new address on the bus and asserts MRDC*. This may result in two devices being selected, a RAM and a ROM. As soon as the ROM interface is selected, it activates the INH1* line, which forces the RAM interface to be deselected. After a short delay to allow for signal propagation, the ROM interface enables its output drivers to place its data on the bus, and then asserts XACK*. The remainder of the cycle proceeds in the normal manner.

The existence of two Inhibit lines makes it possible to implement a hierarchy among three classes of devices, A, B, and C. Addressing device B inhibits the operation of device A, while addressing device C inhibits both A and B.

The use of the Inhibit lines offers considerable flexibility in the allocation of the memory address space to different devices. In particular, it makes it possible to assemble independently designed circuit boards into a single system. For example, all RAM circuit boards for the system of Figure 6.20 can be designed without any knowledge of the addresses to be allocated to the ROM and the I/O devices. On the other hand, devices that use the inhibit facility cannot operate at the maximum speed of the bus. Sufficient time must be allowed for a device to recognize its address and then inhibit other devices at a lower level in the addressing hierarchy. As a result, the use of the Inhibit feature in a device slows down all data transfers involving that device.

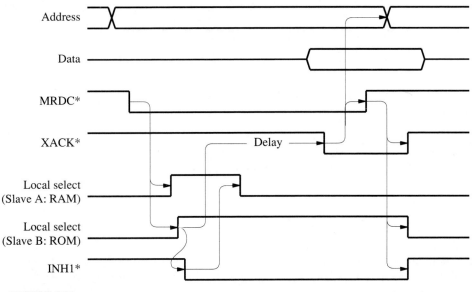

FIGURE 6.24
Use of the Inhibit signals of the Multibus.

Scheduling. Six signals are used for scheduling the use of the bus (see Table 6.2). They allow either parallel or daisy-chain priority or both. The Bus Clock signal, BCLK*, provides a timing reference for the operation of all bus scheduling circuitry. Interested readers are referred to the IEEE Standard document for details.

Interrupts. The interrupt-request lines, INT0* through INT7*, provide eight levels of priority, with INT0* having the highest priority. Each of these lines is an open-collector line to which several devices may be connected. In order to support computer systems in which the interrupting device sends an interrupt-vector address to the CPU, an interrupt-acknowledge line INTA* is provided.

Though there are eight interrupt-request lines, there is only one INTA* line. When INTA* is activated, the number of the interrupt request being acknowledged is transmitted on three of the address lines. Figure 6.25 illustrates the sequence of events leading to the transfer of an interrupt-vector address from the highest priority device requesting an interrupt to the CPU. Following the arrival of an interrupt request, the CPU activates the INTA* line for a short period. This is interpreted by all devices on the bus as a command to freeze the state of the interrupt-request logic; that is, no device is allowed to change the state of its interrupt-request line after receiving this pulse. The CPU uses this quiet period to select the highest-priority line among those that may be simultaneously active. Then, it places the number of this line on the address bus and activates the INTA* line a second time. The combination of the INTA* line and the priority-level information on the address lines has exactly the same effect as the multiple INTA lines in Figure 6.8b. The highest-priority device

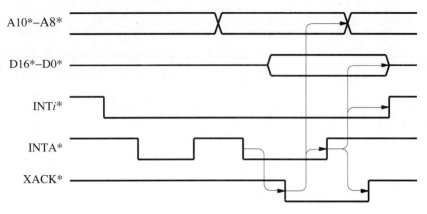

FIGURE 6.25
Timing for a vectored interrupt operation.

responds to the second activation of the INTA* line by placing its interrupt-vector address on the data lines and activating XACK* in the same manner as for a Read operation.

6.6.3   The IEEE-488 bus

As pointed out earlier, this bus is intended for laboratory instrumentation. For example, it may be used for connecting a number of measuring devices, a digital oscilloscope, a plotter, and a printer to a desktop computer. The standard defines a bus that enables interconnection of up to 15 devices. Data transfer takes place in a byte-parallel format, at rates of up to 250,000 bytes per second over a distance of 20 meters. A transfer rate of 1 Mbyte per second is possible over shorter distances. The bus consists of eight data lines and eight control lines, as shown in Figure 6.26. The eight data lines may be used to carry either data or commands to the device interfaces. The eight control lines are used to carry timing and other control information.

The interface of any device connected to the bus has the capability to assume one or more of three modes of operation; namely, it may be a *listener*, a *talker*, or a *controller*. The operations that a device interface can perform in each of these modes are as follows:

1. When the interface is in the listener mode it can receive data from the bus. This is the mode required for the interface of an output device or for an instrument that receives data from other devices.
2. A talker interface transfers data from an input device to the bus.
3. The controller interface controls the bus. It has the ability to place any device interface in either the listener or the talker mode.

To illustrate the operation of the instrumentation bus, let us consider the following situation. A computer acts as the controller for the bus and is about to start reading

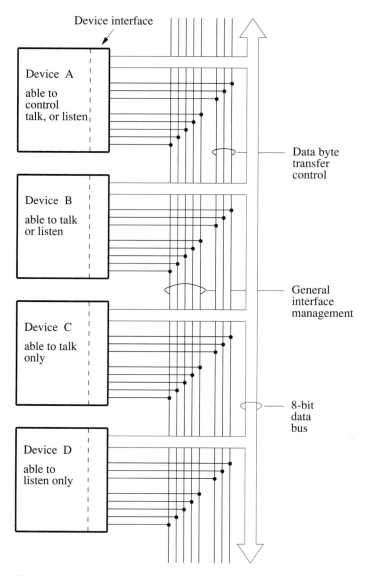

FIGURE 6.26
IEEE standard instrumentation bus.

data from one of the instruments connected to it. To read data from the instrument, the computer places the instrument interface in the talker mode by sending a command addressed to this interface. As soon as the device interface assumes the talker mode, it starts data transmission. The controller assumes the listener mode in order to receive the data transmitted by the talker. Before proceeding to consider this process in more detail, let us first examine the mechanism by which a byte of data is transferred over the bus.

Data transfer over the bus is controlled by an asynchronous handshake protocol. The main difference between this protocol and the scheme of Figures 6.16 and 6.17 is that one source can transfer data to a number of acceptors simultaneously. Three control signals, Data Valid (DAV), Ready for Data (RFD), and Data Accepted (DAC), are used instead of the Ready and Accept signals in the previous figures. The functions of the DAV and DAC signals are identical to the Ready and Accept signals, respectively. The RFD signal informs the source when the acceptor is ready to receive a new byte of data.

Transfer of data takes place as shown in Figure 6.27a. Let us consider first the case of one acceptor. The source starts by placing a data byte on the data lines (t_0), then waits until the data lines settle (t_1). If at time t_1 the RFD signal is equal to 0,

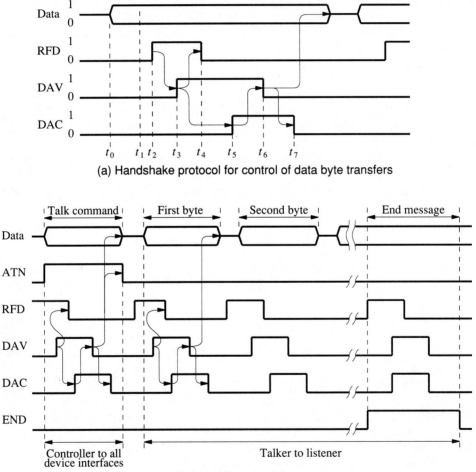

(a) Handshake protocol for control of data byte transfers

(b) A multibyte transfer

FIGURE 6.27
Timing of data transfer over the instrumentation bus.

indicating that the acceptor is not ready to receive data, the source waits until RFD changes to 1 (t_2). Then it sets DAV to 1 (t_3). In response, the acceptor drops RFD to 0 (t_4), strobes the data into an internal buffer, and then sets DAC to 1 (t_5). As a result, the source removes the DAV signal (t_6). Then, after some delay to allow for bus skew, it starts changing the data to place a new byte on the data lines. When DAV = 0 is detected by the acceptor, it resets DAC to 0 (t_7). The acceptor interface does not set RFD to 1 until it is ready to accept a new byte of data.

Let us now consider the case where there is more than one acceptor on the bus. The instrumentation bus is an open-collector bus (see Section 4.1.5). Therefore, the RFD line will be in the 1 state only when all acceptors on the bus are ready for receiving data. Similarly, the DAC line goes to the 1 state when all acceptors have accepted the data. This means that the handshake protocol of Figure 6.27a enables proper transfer of data, irrespective of the number of acceptors receiving the data. Because of electrical limitations, no more than 15 devices should be connected to the instrumentation bus, out of which up to 14 devices may be accepting data simultaneously.

The eight data lines of the bus are used to carry both commands to the device interfaces (for example, to place an interface in the talker or listener mode) and data. Some means have to be provided for identifying these two types of information. An interface management line referred to as the Attention line (ATN) is provided for this purpose. Whenever ATN = 1, all interfaces connected to the bus monitor the data lines and interpret the 8-bit byte on these lines as a command. Commands carry a 5-bit address that selects either a single device or a group of devices. One address is reserved for broadcast commands, which are intended for all devices on the bus.

Let us now return to the input operation discussed earlier. The sequence of signals for this operation is shown in Figure 6.27b. To place the input device interface in the talker mode, the controller starts by placing a command on the data lines and setting ATN to 1. The command contains the device address and specifies that the device should be set in the talker mode. This information is transferred to the device interface under control of the DAV, RFD, and DAC lines, as previously described. As soon as ATN drops to 0, the device interface assumes the talker mode and begins transmitting data. Transmission of each byte is under control of the handshake protocol between the talker and the listener. When all data bytes have been transferred, the talker indicates this by sending an END message. This is accomplished by setting the END control line (one of the control lines for interface management) to 1 and transferring this information to the listener, using the handshake protocol.

In the preceding example, it was assumed that the controller was also a listener. The controller may, if required, assign the listener mode to one or more other devices, either in addition to or instead of itself. In such a case, the talker command of Figure 6.27b should be preceded by a listener command (or commands) addressed to the desired device interfaces. Such a procedure allows the computer to read data from an instrument, for example, and at the same time to have this data transferred to a printer or a plotter.

The instrumentation bus provides a high degree of flexibility. It offers many capabilities in addition to the simple transfers described above. For example, a device may request the attention of the controller at any time. The controller may simultaneously check the status of a number of devices. A full description of these capabilities is beyond the scope of this text. Interested readers should refer to the documentation on the IEEE or ANSI standards.

6.7 I/O CHANNELS

So far, we have seen two methods for implementing I/O data transfers, namely, program-controlled I/O and direct memory access. The main features of these two approaches can be summarized as follows:

1. Program-controlled I/O requires continuous involvement of the CPU. However, only a minimal amount of external hardware is needed to connect peripheral devices to the computer.
2. Direct memory access relieves the CPU of all I/O functions, except for the initialization of the transfer parameters. An external controller is required to control the actual transfer of data.

These two mechanisms are adequate for fulfilling all I/O requirements of many machines. Program-controlled I/O is normally used with low-speed devices, and high-speed devices are served by a DMA facility. The economics of operating large single-CPU computers, however, gives rise to slightly different requirements. The size of the system and the cost of the CPU justify considerable effort to use CPU time as efficiently as possible. The overhead incurred with program-controlled I/O makes this approach highly undesirable with large machines. Therefore, some sort of DMA arrangement should be used for all I/O operations. This gives rise to the idea of using a specialized processor that acts as a shared DMA facility for a number of devices. In some computers, particularly those manufactured by the IBM Corporation, the I/O processor is called an I/O channel. The discussion below reflects the approach taken in some IBM computers.

Figure 6.28 gives a possible organization of a computer using two I/O channels. A memory controller serves to coordinate access to the main memory by the CPU and the two channels. This enables the implementation of the cycle-stealing feature, which is necessary to perform direct memory access. Each I/O device is connected to a channel via a control unit. The function of the control unit is to communicate with the channel and issue the appropriate control signals to the device. One control unit may be used for a number of similar devices, provided only one of these devices is active at any given time. The control unit is equivalent to the interface block in Figure 6.2.

There are three types of channels: Multiplexer, Selector, and Block multiplexer. We will describe each of them briefly.

Multiplexer channels. A multiplexer channel is used for connecting a number of slow- and medium-speed devices. The channel-to-memory link is capable of transferring data at rates much faster than that of the individual devices connected to the channel. Therefore, it is possible to operate a number of I/O devices simultaneously.

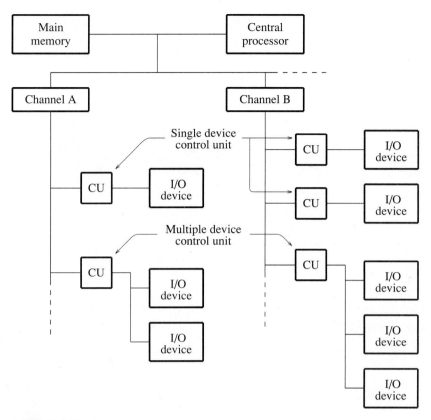

FIGURE 6.28
Use of channels for performing I/O operations.

Operation of the multiplexer channel can take place in either of two modes, namely, the *byte-interleave* and the *burst* modes. In the byte-interleave mode, channel operation is divided into short segments of time. During each of these time segments the channel services one of the devices that are currently ready for an I/O operation. Information transferred during this time may consist of a byte of data, control, or status information. The device is logically connected to the channel only for the duration of this transfer. However, if the transfer takes more than some prespecified limit, the logical connection to the I/O device is maintained until all the requested data have been transferred. The channel uses a time-out mechanism to determine its mode of operation with any device. If data transfer requests from the device cause the logical connection to be maintained longer than a preset period, the channel switches to the burst mode. Otherwise it continues operation in the byte-interleave mode.

Figure 6.29 indicates the organization of a multiplexer channel. The multiplexing arrangement allows the channel to handle a large number of devices at the same time. Parameters relating to the operation of each of these devices, for example, byte count and memory data addresses, are usually kept in fixed locations in the main memory. Whenever the channel addresses a device, it fetches the appropriate param-

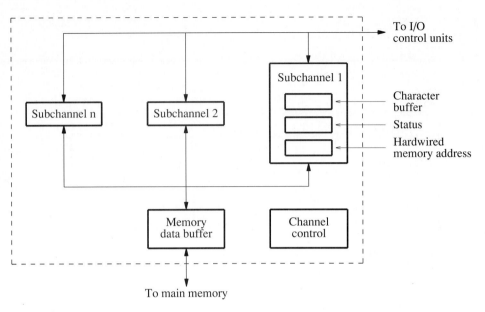

FIGURE 6.29
Organization of a multiplexer channel.

eters from memory. At the time that the device is disconnected the updated values of the parameters replace the old values in the memory. However, the channel still requires some hardware that can be dedicated to each I/O operation in progress. This part of the channel hardware is referred to as a *subchannel*. Each subchannel must have sufficient storage capacity for at least one byte of information and a few status flags. The relevant data transfer parameters for each subchannel are stored at a fixed address in the main memory.

Selector channels. High-speed devices such as magnetic disks require data transfer at such high rates that they cannot be easily multiplexed with other devices by means of a multiplexer channel. Instead, it is necessary to use a separate channel to handle such devices one at a time. A selector channel serves this purpose. It is similar to a multiplexer channel operating in a burst mode, but it operates at a higher speed.

The organization of a selector channel is shown in Figure 6.30. It contains hardware registers that hold the parameters needed in I/O transfers. These include the address of the next main memory location to or from which data is to be transferred and the byte count, which is the number of bytes that remain to be transferred as part of a particular I/O operation. Transfers between the selector channel and the main memory usually involve 16, 32, or 64 bits in parallel. Because most I/O devices are byte-oriented, the channel includes the circuitry necessary to assemble serially received bytes into larger units for parallel transfer to the memory, and vice versa.

When an I/O operation is initiated by means of a selector channel, the channel remains dedicated to that task for the duration of the entire operation. It cannot be used for another I/O operation until the current one is completed.

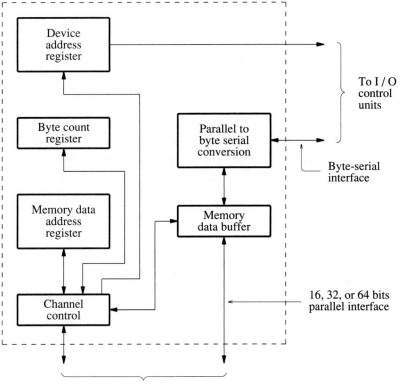

FIGURE 6.30
Organization of a selector channel.

Block multiplexer channels. This type of channel combines the features of both the multiplexer and selector channels. It allows multiplexing of a number of high-speed I/O operations on a block-by-block basis. Thus, it corresponds to a high-speed multiplexer channel that operates only in the burst mode. The advantages gained from the use of block multiplexer channels rather than selector channels stem from the nature of operation of I/O devices such as magnetic disks and tapes. A typical transaction with a disk drive may require the following sequence of commands (see Chapter 9):

1. Seek (Move Read/Write head to a given track).
2. Search for a particular record.
3. Start reading the data in the record.

Because of the considerable mechanical delay involved in the first two operations, it is not appropriate to tie up the entire channel throughout this sequence, which would be the case with a selector channel. A block multiplexer channel can send the Seek command to the disk drive and then disconnect so it can service other I/O devices. When the Seek operation is completed, the channel reconnects, sends the Search command, and disconnects once more. On completion of the Search, the channel begins the transfer of the desired record and stays connected until the I/O operation is terminated. Using a block multiplexer channel in this way results in substantially improved throughput in comparison with selector channels.

In the simple DMA controller discussed in Section 6.2, the CPU is responsible for loading the parameters relating to any data transfer in the appropriate registers of the DMA controller. In the case of an I/O channel, all the information relating to a particular I/O operation is stored in the main memory in the form of a *channel program*. The channel accesses the main memory on a cycle-stealing basis and is capable of executing a limited set of instructions, referred to as *channel commands*. These commands specify the parameters needed by the channel to control the I/O devices and perform data transfer operations. A sequence of these commands constitutes a channel program. The CPU initiates execution of a channel program by issuing a special command to the channel, which causes the channel to start fetching and executing the commands that perform the desired sequence of I/O operations.

6.8   CONCLUDING REMARKS

In this chapter we discussed three basic approaches to I/O transfers. The simplest technique is programmed I/O, where the CPU performs all the necessary control functions. When speed becomes a problem, one may turn to the DMA approach, which requires additional hardware. In large computers, it is reasonable to dedicate a separate peripheral processor, sometimes called a channel, to I/O tasks.

A key concept presented in the chapter is that of interrupts. In many computer applications it is essential to be able to interrupt the normal execution of programs in order to service higher-priority requests that require urgent attention. Most computers, both large and small, have a mechanism for dealing with such situations. However, the complexity and sophistication of interrupt-handling schemes vary from one computer to another.

6.9   PROBLEMS

6.1. Assume the existence of a machine with a vectored-interrupt capability, in which an I/O device supplies the starting address of the interrupt-service routine at the time the interrupt is acknowledged. The processor status is saved on a memory stack. Describe in point form the sequence of events from the time the device requests an interrupt until execution of the interrupt-service routine is started. If machine instructions require one to five memory cycles to execute, estimate the maximum number of memory cycles that may occur before execution of the interrupt-service routine is started.

6.2. The following questions apply to either the PDP-11 or the 68000.

    (*a*) Describe the sequence of steps that takes place when an interrupt is received and give the number of bus transfers required during each of these steps. (Do not give details of bus signals or the microprogram.)

(b) Estimate the maximum possible number of memory cycles that can be used to fetch and execute an instruction. Name the data read from or written into the main memory in each cycle.

(c) Estimate the number of bus transfers that may occur from the instant a device requests an interrupt until the first instruction of the interrupt-service routine is fetched for execution.

6.3. The CPU of a computer, which has the internal structure given in Figure 4.1, inspects the interrupt lines at the end of the execution phase of each instruction. If an I/O device is requesting an interrupt, the CPU performs all the necessary functions for accepting the interrupt vector address, storing the processor status register and program counter on a memory stack, and branching to the interrupt-service routine. Assume that the sequence of events is identical to that in the PDP-11 or 68000. Give the controls steps (as in Figure 4.8) required for this function. Make any necessary additions to Figure 4.1.

6.4. Two magnetic disk units, a real-time clock, and a number of video terminals are some of the I/O devices connected to a PDP-11 computer. All devices are serviced via interrupts. The real-time clock interrupts the CPU at regular time intervals (for example, every $1/60$ seconds) for time-keeping purposes, and the disk interrupts the CPU when it has completed an operation and is ready to receive a new command. Servicing of disk interrupts should take priority over terminal interrupts, with the real-time clock having the highest priority. Suggest suitable numerical values for the priorities of the above devices and specify the interrupt vector associated with each. (Refer to Figure 6.9 for details of the PS word.)

6.5. A logic circuit is needed for implementation of the priority network shown in Figure 6.8b. The network handles three interrupt request lines. When a request is received on line $INTR_i$, the network generates an acknowledgment on line $INTA_i$. If more than one request is received, only the highest-priority request is acknowledged, where the ordering of priorities is

$$\text{Priority of } INTR_1 > \text{priority of } INTR_2 > \text{priority of } INTR_3$$

(a) Give a truth table for each of the outputs $INTA_1$, $INTA_2$, $INTA_3$.

(b) Give a logic circuit for implementing this priority network.

(c) Can your design be easily extended for more interrupt-request lines?

(d) By adding inputs DECIDE and RESET, modify your design such that $INTA_i$ is set to 1 when a pulse is received on the input DECIDE and is reset to 0 when a pulse is received on the input RESET.

6.6. The 68000 microprocessor has a set of three lines called IPL2-0 that are used to signal interrupt requests. The 3-bit binary number on these lines is interpreted by the microprocessor as representing the highest priority device requesting an interrupt. Design a priority encoder, a circuit that accepts interrupt requests from as many as 7 devices and generates a 3-bit code representing the request with the highest priority.

6.7. A computer is required to accept characters from 20 video terminals. All terminals use the same interrupt vector, INTVEC, in the main memory. The main memory area to be used for storing data for each terminal is pointed to by a pointer PNTRn ($n = 1$ to 20). Input data must be collected from the terminals while another program PROG is being executed. This may be accomplished in one of two ways:

(a) Every T seconds the program PROG calls a subroutine DEVSUB. This subroutine checks the status of each of the 20 terminals in sequence and transfers any input characters to the memory. Then it returns to PROG.

(b) Whenever a character is ready in any of the interface buffers of the terminals, an interrupt is generated. This causes the interrupt routine DEVINT to be executed. After polling the status registers, DEVINT transfers the input character and then returns to PROG.

Write the routines DEVSUB and DEVINT for either the PDP-11 or 68000 computer. Let the maximum character rate for any terminal be c characters per second, with an average rate equal to rc, where $r \leq 1$. In method (a), what maximum value of T can guarantee that no input characters will be lost? What is the equivalent condition for method (b)? Estimate, on the average, the percentage of time spent in servicing the terminals for methods (a) and (b) for $c = 100$ characters per second and $r = 0.01, 0.1, 0.5$, and 1. Assume that each bus transfer requires $0.3\mu s$.

6.8. Consider a computer in which several devices are connected to a common interrupt-request line, as shown in Figure 6.8a. Assume that each device has a separate interrupt vector that points to an appropriate interrupt-service routine. Explain how you would arrange for interrupts from device j to be accepted before the execution of the interrupt-service routine for device i is completed. Comment in particular on the times at which interrupts must be enabled and disabled at various points in the system.

6.9. Consider the daisy chain arrangement in Figure 6.8a. Assume that after a device generates an interrupt request, it turns off that request as soon as it receives the interrupt acknowledge signal. Is it still necessary to disable interrupts in the CPU before entering the interrupt service routine? Why?

6.10. Successive data blocks of N bytes each are to be read from a character-oriented input device, and program PROG is to perform some computation on each block of data. Write a control program, CNTRL, for the PDP-11 or 68000, which will perform the following functions.

(a) Read data block 1.
(b) Activate PROG and point it to the location of block 1 in the main memory.
(c) Read block 2 using interrupts while PROG is performing computations on block 1.
(d) Start PROG on block 2 and meanwhile start reading block 3, and so on.

Note that CNTRL must maintain correct buffer pointers, keep track of the character count, and correctly transfer control to PROG, whether PROG takes more or less time than block input.

6.11. In most computers, interrupts are not acknowledged until the end of execution of the current machine instruction. Consider the possibility of suspending operation of the CPU in the middle of execution of an instruction in order to acknowledge an interrupt. Discuss the difficulties that may arise.

6.12. Figure P6.1 shows a possible arrangement of the Bus Request (BR) and Bus Grant (BG) signals in a decentralized bus assignment scheme. Describe how device i should generate BR_i, interpret BG_i, and generate BG_{i+1}. Specify the timing for the rising and falling

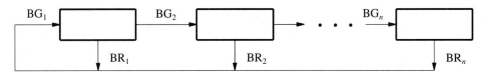

FIGURE P6.1
A decentralized bus assignment scheme.

edges of each signal and the priority of each device. What happens in your scheme when one or more devices request the use of the bus while another device is actively using the bus?

6.13. Design the logic circuitry required in each device interface to implement the bus assignment scheme you have devised in Problem 6.12.

6.14. (This problem is suitable for use as a laboratory experiment.) Given a video terminal connected to a PDP-11 or 68000 computer, complete the following two assignments.

(a) Write a programmed I/O routine that prints letters in alphabetical order. It prints two lines as follows:

$$ABC \cdots YZ$$
$$ABC \cdots YZ$$

then stops.

(b) Write a programmed I/O routine that prints the numeric characters 0 to 9 in increasing order three times. Its output should have the following format:

$$012 \cdots 9012 \cdots 9102 \cdots 9$$

Use program (a) as the main program and program (b) as an interrupt-service routine whose execution is initiated by entering any character at the keyboard. Execution of program (b) may also be interrupted by entering another character at the keyboard. Upon completion of program (b), execution of the most recently interrupted program should be resumed at the point of interruption. Thus the printed output may appear as follows:

```
ABC
012 · · · 901
012 · · · 9012 · · · 9012 · · · 9
2 · · · 9102 · · · 9
DE · · · YZ
```

Show how you can use the processor priority to either enable or inhibit interrupt nesting.

6.15. (This problem is suitable for use as a laboratory experiment.) Write a program (c) in addition to programs (a) and (b) of Problem 6.14. Program (c) should perform the carriage control functions required to put the printed output in the following format:

```
ABC
012 · · · 901
012 · · · 9012 · · · 9012 · · · 9
              2 · · · 9012 · · · 9
        DE · · · YZ
```

6.16. (This problem is suitable for use as a laboratory experiment.)

(a) Given a video terminal and a stopwatch, devise a scheme to measure the execution time of any machine instruction. Use your technique to measure the execution time of the instruction

$$\text{ADD} \qquad \text{R0,R1} \qquad \text{(PDP-11)}$$

or

ADD.W   D0,D1   (68000)

(*b*) Repeat your experiment for two Add instructions in sequence. Do you obtain the same time per instruction? Comment on the difference, if any.

6.17. Three devices A, B, and C are connected to the bus of a computer. I/O transfers for all three devices use interrupt control. Interrupt nesting for devices A and B is not allowed, but interrupt requests from C may be accepted while either A or B is being serviced. Suggest different ways in which this can be accomplished in each of the following cases.

(*a*) The computer has one interrupt-request line and no vectored-interrupt capability.

(*b*) Two interrupt-request lines $INTR_1$ and $INTR_2$ are available, with $INTR_1$ having higher priority.

Specify when and how interrupts are enabled and disabled in each case.

6.18. An industrial plant uses a number of limit sensors for monitoring temperature, pressure, and other factors. The output of each sensor consists of an ON/OFF switch, and eight such sensors must be connected to the bus of a small computer. Design an appropriate interface so that the state of all eight switches can be read simultaneously as a single byte at address 177020_8 ($FE10_{16}$). Assume a synchronous bus that uses the timing sequence of Figure 6.15.

6.19. Repeat Problem 6.18 for an asynchronous bus that uses the handshake control scheme of Figure 6.16.

6.20. Design an appropriate interface for connecting a seven-segment display as an output device on a synchronous bus. (See Section A.10 for a description of a seven-segment display.)

6.21. The address bus of a computer has 16 address lines, A_{15-0}. If the address assigned to one device is $6AB4_{16}$ and the address decoder for that device ignores lines A_4 and A_5, what are all the addresses to which this device will respond?

6.22. Two devices A and B exchange data over an asynchronous bus, with A as the bus master and B as a slave. Redraw the timing diagram of Figure 6.16 and replace each signal with two signals, one as seen by A and the other as seen by B.

6.23. Consider a data transfer operation in which all delays are negligible except the end-to-end propagation delay, P, on the bus. Estimate the maximum data transfer rate achievable in the cases of Figures 6.15 to 6.17.

6.24. Consider the interface of Figure 6.18. Assume that the propagation delay through each gate varies between 5 and 15 ns and that the address decoder is equivalent to three gate delays. Flip-flops require minimum setup and hold times of 20 and 3 ns, respectively. Three-state gates require a maximum of 30 ns to change from the high impedance state to the enabled state. Assume also that propagation over the bus, including delays through the bus drivers and receivers in the CPU, is in the range of 5 to 25 ns.

(*a*) What is the maximum bus skew?

(*b*) Suggest suitable values for the fixed delays introduced by the bus master in the timing diagram of Figure 6.16.

(*c*) Estimate the duration of a Read operation and a Write operation.

6.25. Estimate the bus cycle time for a synchronous bus using the timing diagram of Figure 6.15. Modify Figure 6.18 as appropriate and assume the same delay parameters as given in Problem 6.24.

6.26. An interrupt-request line must be added to the interface of Figure 6.19. An interrupt request should be generated whenever an input character is available or when the transmission buffer is empty. Bit b_6 of the input and output status registers of this interface should enable interrupts when set to 1 under program control. Design a suitable circuit.

6.27. Bus extenders are sometimes used to increase the number of devices that can be connected to a bus. A bidirectional bus driver, consisting of two 3-state or open-collector gates connected in opposite directions, may be used for this purpose. Consider the Address, Data, Ready, and Accept signals on an asynchronous bus. In which direction should the bidirectional buffers point during Read and Write operations initiated by the CPU? Consider two cases:

(*a*) The addressed device is on the CPU side of the bus.

(*b*) The addressed device is on the opposite side of the bus.

6.28. Design a logic circuit to control the extender gates for the address and data lines in Problem 6.27.

6.29. Consider the section of a bus interface circuit that handles the daisy-chain signals for device *i* in Figure 6.8*a*. This circuit receives an Interrupt Acknowledge signal, $INTA_i$, from the interface of device $i - 1$ and generates $INTA_{i+1}$ for device $i + 1$. Let REQUEST and READY be handshake signals that are used for communication between device *i* and the daisy-chain circuit in its bus interface. When the device requires service, it asserts REQUEST. The daisy-chain circuit activates the $\overline{INTR}$ line, and when it receives $INTA_i$ it asserts READY. Show how you can use an edge-triggered D flip-flop and some logic gates to implement the daisy-chain circuit.

6.30. (*a*) The daisy-chain circuit of Problem 6.29 can be designed as an asynchronous sequential machine. Give a state diagram representing the operation of this circuit and derive the smallest number of states needed. Use asynchronous circuit design techniques to obtain a suitable implementation.

(*b*) The implementation in Problem 6.29 uses one flip-flop. Compare this to the number of states obtained in part (*a*) and comment.

6.31. In some computers, the CPU responds only to the leading edge of the interrupt-request signal on one of its interrupt-request lines. What happens if two independent devices are connected to this line?

6.32. Draw a timing diagram that illustrates the sequence of events during priority arbitration in the example described in conjunction with Figure 6.22. Assume that the two devices, A and B, are at opposite ends of the bus.

6.33. Consider the arbitration circuit shown in Figure 6.22, which is used on the Nubus. Assume that the priority code for a device is generated by four ON/OFF switches. Design a circuit to connect these switches to the bus to implement this arbitration scheme. Arbitration should begin when a signal called Compete is asserted. A little later, the arbitration circuit should activate an output called Winner if it wins the arbitration cycle.

6.34. The Multibus timing diagram in Figure 6.25 shows that the processor activates the interrupt acknowledge line, $INTA^*$, twice during the interrupt acknowledge cycle. Explain how an error could occur if the first pulse is omitted.

6.35. Referring to the Multibus timing diagram in Figure 6.24, design the part of the circuit that generates $XACK^*$ in the interface of device A.

6.36. The Data Accepted line, DAC, on the IEEE-488 bus becomes active only after all listeners have received the data (see Figure 6.27*a*). Why is the Ready-for-Data (RFD) line needed?

6.37. A 32-bit computer has two selector channels and one multiplexer channel. Each selector channel supports two magnetic disks and two magnetic tape units. The multiplexer channel has two line printers and 10 video terminals connected to it. Assume that the transfer rates for these peripherals are as follows:

Disk Drive	800K	bytes/s
Magnetic tape drive	200K	bytes/s
Line printer	6.6K	bytes/s
Video terminal	1K	bytes/s

Estimate the maximum aggregate I/O transfer rate in this system.

6.10 REFERENCES

1. IEEE Standard Microcomputer System Bus, *IEEE* Standard 796-1983.
2. IEEE Standard Digital Interface for Programmable Instrumentation, *ANSI/IEEE* Standard 488-1978.
3. Interface between Data-Terminal Equipment and Data Circuit-Terminating Equipment Employing Serial Binary Data Interchange, *Electronics Industries Association* Standard RS-232-C, Oct. 1969.
4. IEEE Standard for a Versatile Backplane Bus: VMEbus, *ANSI/IEEE* Standard 1014-1987.
5. Simple 32-Bit Backplane Bus: Nubus, *ANSI/IEEE* Standard 1196-1987.
6. High-Performance Synchronous 32-Bit Bus: MULTIBUS II, *ANSI/IEEE* Standard 1296-1987.

CHAPTER

7

ARITHMETIC

A basic operation in all digital computers is the addition or subtraction of two numbers. Such operations are provided at the machine instruction level. They are implemented, along with basic logic functions such as AND, OR, NOT, and EXCLUSIVE-OR, in the arithmetic and logic unit (ALU) subsystem of the processor, as mentioned in Chapters 1 and 4. These functions are normally performed by combinational logic circuitry. The operands are presented to the ALU as the outputs of two registers, possibly via an internal processor bus. A typical arrangement was shown in Figure 4.1. The result is usually routed to another register after an amount of time that permits the combinational logic to complete the computations. These operations can be executed within the time allotted for a basic step in a hardwired control sequencer or within the execution time of a microinstruction in a processor implemented with microprogrammed control. Usually, an ALU operation is faster than a memory access operation. This means that an instruction that involves an ALU operation on operands that must be brought from memory does not require much more execution time than an instruction that only moves the contents of one memory location to another memory location.

Multiply and divide operations are comparatively more complex than either addition or subtraction. These operations are usually included in the basic instruction set. However, their execution times may be significantly slower than simpler instructions such as Add, Move, and so on. This is because they are implemented as a sequence of addition, subtraction, and shift steps through the ALU, controlled by a microprogram. In high-performance computers, hardware multipliers and dividers are often used to increase the speed of arithmetic operations. Of course, as long as Add, Subtract, and Shift are available as machine instructions, both multiply and divide operations can be supplied as software routines.

Compared with arithmetic operations, logic operations are simple from the combinational circuit viewpoint. They require only independent Boolean operations on individual bit positions of the operands, whereas carry/borrow lateral signals are required in arithmetic operations.

Before discussing details of the implementation of computer arithmetic, we will first need to discuss number representation schemes.

7.1   NUMBER REPRESENTATIONS

The binary number system is the most conventional internal representation for numbers in digital computers. Consider an n-bit vector

$$B = b_{n-1} \cdots b_1 b_0$$

where $b_i = 0$ or 1 for $0 \le i \le n - 1$. This vector can represent positive integer values V in the range 0 to $2^n - 1$, where

$$V(B) = b_{n-1} \times 2^{n-1} + \cdots + b_1 \times 2^1 + b_0 \times 2^0$$

There are three widely used systems for representing both positive and negative numbers:

- Sign-and-magnitude
- 1's-complement
- 2's-complement

In all three systems, the leftmost bit is 0 for positive numbers and 1 for negative numbers. Figure 7.1 illustrates all three representations using 4-bit numbers. Positive values have identical representations in all systems, though variations occur in the representation of negative values. In the sign-and-magnitude case, negative values are represented by changing b_3 to 1 in the B vector of the corresponding positive value. For example, $+5$ is represented by 0101, and -5 is represented by 1101. In the 1's-complement representation, negative values are obtained by complementing each bit of the corresponding positive number. Thus, the representation for -3 is obtained by bit complementing the vector 0011 to yield 1100. The operation of obtaining the 1's complement of a number is equivalent to subtracting the number from $2^n - 1$, that is, from 1111 in the case of 4-bit numbers in Figure 7.1. Finally, in the 2's-complement system, a negative number is obtained by subtracting the corresponding positive number from 2^n. Hence, the 2's-complement representation can be obtained by adding 1 to the 1's-complement representation.

Some final comments are pertinent before we proceed to show how to perform addition or subtraction in these representations. There are distinct $+0$ and -0 representations in both the sign-and-magnitude and 1's-complement systems, but there is only a $+0$ representation in the 2's-complement system. For 4-bit numbers, the value -8 is representable in the 2's-complement system and not in the other systems. The sign-and-magnitude system seems the most natural, because we deal with sign-and-magnitude decimal values in hand computations. The 1's-complement system

B	Values represented		
$b_3b_2b_1b_0$	Sign and magnitude	1's complement	2's complement
0 1 1 1	+7	+7	+7
0 1 1 0	+6	+6	+6
0 1 0 1	+5	+5	+5
0 1 0 0	+4	+4	+4
0 0 1 1	+3	+3	+3
0 0 1 0	+2	+2	+2
0 0 0 1	+1	+1	+1
0 0 0 0	+0	+0	+0
1 0 0 0	−0	−7	−8
1 0 0 1	−1	−6	−7
1 0 1 0	−2	−5	−6
1 0 1 1	−3	−4	−5
1 1 0 0	−4	−3	−4
1 1 0 1	−5	−2	−3
1 1 1 0	−6	−1	−2
1 1 1 1	−7	−0	−1

FIGURE 7.1
Binary, signed-integer representations.

is easily related to this system, and the 2's-complement system seems unnatural. However, we will soon see that the 2's-complement system yields the most efficient logic circuit implementation (and the one most often used in computers) of both the add and subtract operations.

7.2 ADDITION OF POSITIVE NUMBERS

In this section and in the next, we will be concerned only with unsigned numbers. Consider adding two 1-bit numbers. The results are shown in Figure 7.2. The sum of 1 and 1 requires the 2-bit vector 10 to represent the value 2. We say that the *sum* is

```
   0        1        0        1
 + 0      + 0      + 1      + 1
 ---      ---      ---      ----
   0        1        1       10
```

FIGURE 7.2
Addition of 1-bit numbers.

0 and the *carry-out* is 1. The operation is analogous to the usual hand computation with decimal numbers. We add bit pairs starting from the low-order (right) end of the bit vectors, propagating carries toward the high-order (left) end. The truth table for the sum and carry-out functions for adding two equally weighted bits x_i and y_i in vectors X and Y is shown in Figure 7.3. The figure also gives two-level AND-OR logic expressions for these functions, along with an example of addition. Note that each stage of the addition algorithm must be able to accommodate a *carry-in* bit. We shall use c_i to represent the carry-in to the ith stage and the carry-out from the $(i - 1)$st stage.

A combinational logic implementation of the truth table for addition is shown in Figure 7.4a, along with a convenient symbol for an adder to be used in the subsequent discussion. Other logic circuits can be used to realize these functions; for example, either NAND or NOR gates can be used. A cascaded connection of n ADDER blocks, as shown in Figure 7.4b, can be used to add two n-bit numbers. Since the carries propagate, or ripple, through this cascade, the configuration is called an *n-bit ripple-carry adder*. When the carry-out c_n from the *most significant bit* (MSB) position is equal to 1, there is an *overflow* from the operation. This means that the result cannot be represented in n bits. The carry-in c_0 into the *least significant bit* (LSB) position provides a convenient means for adding 1 to a number. For instance, in the previous section we stated that forming the 2's-complement of a number involves

x_i	y_i	Carry-in c_i	Sum s_i	Carry-out c_{i+1}
0	0	0	0	0
0	0	1	1	0
0	1	0	1	0
0	1	1	0	1
1	0	0	1	0
1	0	1	0	1
1	1	0	0	1
1	1	1	1	1

$$s_i = \overline{x_i}\,\overline{y_i}c_i + \overline{x_i}y_i\overline{c_i} + x_i\overline{y_i}\,\overline{c_i} + x_iy_ic_i$$
$$c_{i+1} = y_ic_i + x_ic_i + x_iy_i$$

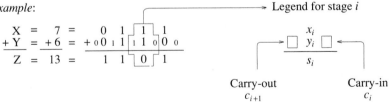

FIGURE 7.3
Logic specification for a stage of binary addition.

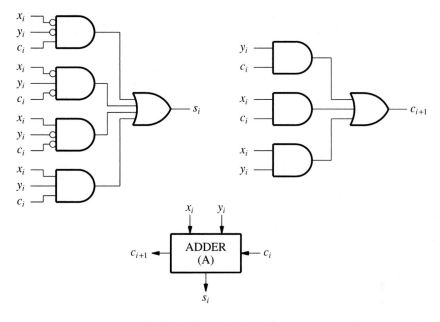

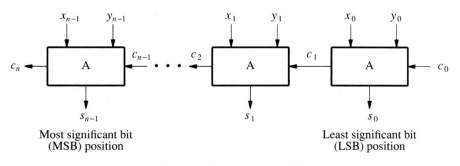

(a) Logic for a single stage

(b) An n-bit ripple-carry adder

Most significant bit
(MSB) position

Least significant bit
(LSB) position

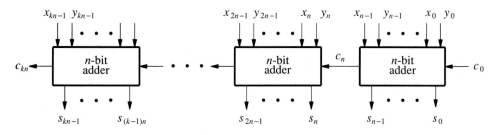

(c) Cascade of k n-bit adders

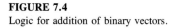

FIGURE 7.4
Logic for addition of binary vectors.

adding 1 to the 1's-complement of the number. The carry signals are also useful for interconnecting k n-bit adders to form an adder capable of handling input numbers of length kn bits, as shown in Figure 7.4c.

7.3 LOGIC DESIGN FOR FAST ADDERS

The n-bit ripple-carry adder shown in Figure 7.4b may have too much delay in developing its outputs c_n, s_{n-1}, . . . , s_1, and s_0. Whether the delay associated with any particular implementation technology is acceptable can be decided only in the context of the speed of other processor components and the main memory cycle time. Delay through a network of logic gates is dependent on the electronic technology (see Appendix A) used in fabricating the basic gates and on the number of gates in the paths from inputs to outputs. After a particular technology is chosen, the delay associated with any combinational logic network constructed from gates in that technology can be determined by adding up the number of logic-gate delays along the longest path through the network. In the case of the ripple-carry adder, the longest signal propagation is from inputs x_0, y_0, and c_0 at the LSB position to outputs c_n and s_{n-1} at the MSB position.

In the introductory remarks of this chapter, it was suggested that addition can be performed within the execution time of a microinstruction. Suppose this time is in the range 50 to 100 nanoseconds in a 16-bit word-length computer. Now consider the delay of the n-bit ripple-carry adder of Figure 7.4b. Suppose that the delay from c_i to c_{i+1} of any ADDER block is 10 ns. An n-bit addition can be performed in the time it takes the carry signal to reach the c_{n-1} position, followed by the delay in developing s_{n-1}. Assuming this last delay is 15 ns, a 16-bit addition takes $15 \times 10 + 15 = 165$ ns.

There are two approaches that can be taken to reduce this 165-ns delay to the desired 50- to 100-ns range. The first approach, which is suggested by our earlier discussion, is to use faster electronic circuit technology in implementing the same ripple-carry logic design of Figure 7.4b. The second approach is to use a logic network structure different from that shown in Figure 7.4b.

Logic structures for fast adder design must address the problem of speeding up the generation of the carry signals. The logic expressions for s_i (sum) and c_{i+1} (carry-out) of stage i (see Figure 7.3) are

$$s_i = \bar{x}_i \bar{y}_i c_i + \bar{x}_i y_i \bar{c}_i + x_i \bar{y}_i \bar{c}_i + x_i y_i c_i$$

and

$$c_{i+1} = y_i c_i + x_i c_i + x_i y_i$$

Factoring the second of these into

$$c_{i+1} = x_i y_i + (x_i + y_i) c_i$$

we can write

$$c_{i+1} = G_i + P_i c_i$$

where

$$G_i = x_i y_i$$

and

$$P_i = x_i + y_i$$

The expressions G_i and P_i are called the *generate* and *propagate* functions for stage i. The generate function produces an output carry from stage i when both x_i and y_i are 1; the propagate function causes an output carry when there is an input carry and either x_i is 1 or y_i is 1. All G_i and P_i functions for $0 \le i \le n - 1$ can be formed independently and in parallel in one logic-gate delay after the X and Y vectors are available as parallel inputs to the n-bit adder. Expanding c_i in terms of $i - 1$ subscripted variables and substituting into the c_{i+1} equation, we obtain

$$c_{i+1} = G_i + P_i G_{i-1} + P_i P_{i-1} c_{i-1}$$

Continuing with this type of expansion, the final expression for any carry variable is

$$c_{i+1} = G_i + P_i G_{i-1} + P_i P_{i-1} G_{i-2} + \cdots + P_i P_{i-1} \cdots P_1 G_0 + P_i P_{i-1} \cdots P_0 c_0$$

Thus, all carries can be obtained three logic-gate delays after the input operands X, Y, and c_0 are available, because only one gate delay is needed to develop all P_i and G_i signals, followed by two gate delays in the AND-OR circuit for c_{i+1}. After another three gate delays (one delay to invert the c_i's and two delays to form s_i as shown earlier), all sum bits are available. Therefore, independent of n, the n-bit addition process requires only six levels of logic.

A practical problem with this approach are gate fan-in constraints. The expression for c_{i+1} requires $i + 2$ inputs to the largest AND term and $i + 2$ inputs to the OR term. Due to electronic circuit considerations, logic gate fan-in is usually restricted to about eight or less. Let us consider the design of a 4-bit adder as a basic unit. The function

$$c_4 = G_3 + P_3 G_2 + P_3 P_2 G_1 + P_3 P_2 P_1 G_0 + P_3 P_2 P_1 P_0 c_0$$

requires a fan-in of five for the basic gates and needs two gate delays after the G_i and P_i functions are available. Using four of these connected as in Figure 7.4c (with $n = 4$), a 16-bit adder is obtained that requires an amount of time equal to 12 gate delays. This total is composed of one delay for G_i and P_i information, two each for c_4, c_8, c_{12}, and c_{15}, and a final three for s_{15}. All other sum bits and c_{16} are available at or before the time for s_{15}. In our earlier discussion involving absolute time values, an implied gate delay of 5 ns was used. With this value, the above 16-bit adder requires 60 ns to develop all outputs, rather than the 165 ns required by the original design in Figure 7.4b. This is well within the previously stated 50- to 100-ns objective for the addition operation. Fast adders that form carry functions as in this simple example are called *carry lookahead adders*. Note that in the preceding 16-bit adder example we have assumed that the carries inside each block are formed by lookahead circuits. However, they still ripple between blocks.

For longer word lengths and in higher-performance computers, it is necessary to speed up the addition operation even further. This may be done by applying the lookahead technique to the carry signals between blocks; thus, a second level of lookahead is employed. We will illustrate this procedure by redesigning the above 16-bit adder. Suppose that each of the 4-bit adder blocks provides two new output functions defined as G_k^I and P_k^I, where $k = 0$ for the first 4-bit block, $k = 1$ for the second 4-bit block, and so on. In the first block,

$$P_0^I = P_3 P_2 P_1 P_0$$

and

$$G_0^I = G_3 + P_3 G_2 + P_3 P_2 G_1 + P_3 P_2 P_1 G_0$$

In words, if we say that G_i and P_i determine whether bit stage i generates or propagates a carry, then G_k^I and P_k^I determine whether block k generates or propagates a carry. With these new functions available, it is not necessary to wait for carries to ripple through blocks. For example, c_{16} can be formed as

$$c_{16} = G_3^I + P_3^I G_2^I + P_3^I P_2^I G_1^I + P_3^I P_2^I P_1^I G_0^I + P_3^I P_2^I P_1^I P_0^I c_0$$

using gates with a fan-in of five. The delay in developing c_{16} is two gate delays more than the time needed to develop the G_k^I and P_k^I functions. The latter require two and one gate delays, respectively, after the generation of G_i and P_i. Therefore, c_{16} is available five gate delays after X, Y, and c_0 are applied as inputs. Earlier, using only G_i and P_i functions, c_{16} required nine gate delays.

Now consider that longer adders are constructed by cascading 16-bit basic blocks built using G_k^I and P_k^I functions as well as G_i and P_i functions. The total adder delay will be about half what it would have been if the longer adders had been built by cascading 4-bit basic blocks using only G_i and P_i functions.

7.4   ADDITION AND SUBTRACTION

In Section 7.1 we discussed three systems for representing positive and negative numbers, hereafter simply called signed numbers. These systems differ only in the way in which they represent negative values. Their relative merits from the standpoint of ease of implementation of arithmetic operations can be determined through a few simple examples. The conclusions that can be drawn are as follows. The sign and magnitude system is the simplest representation but also the most awkward for addition and subtraction operations. The 1's-complement method is somewhat better. However, the 2's-complement system, which seems rather unnatural from a representation standpoint, is actually the best method in terms of implementation of addition and subtraction operations.

Why is the 2's-complement representation a good choice? First, consider addition modulo N (mod N). A helpful graphical device for the description of addition mod N of positive integers is a circle with the N values 0 through $N - 1$ marked along its perimeter, as shown in Figure 7.5a. To treat some specific examples, we will choose $N = 16$. The operation $(7 + 4)$ mod 16 yields the value 11. To perform

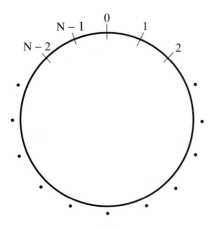

(a) Circle representation of integers mod N

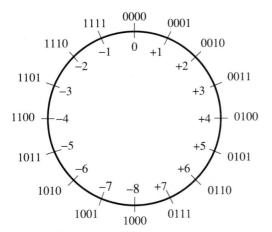

(b) Mod 16 system for 2's-complement numbers

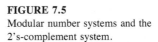

FIGURE 7.5
Modular number systems and the
2's-complement system.

this operation graphically, locate 7 mod 16 = 7 on the circle and then step off 4 units
in the clockwise direction to arrive at the answer 11. As a second example, consider
$(9 + 14)$ mod 16 = 7, which is modeled on the circle by locating 9 mod 16 = 9
and stepping off 14 units in the clockwise direction to arrive at the answer 7. This
graphical technique works for the computation of $(a + b)$ mod 16 for any positive
numbers a and b; that is, locate a mod 16 and step off b units in the clockwise
direction to arrive at $(a + b)$ mod 16.

Now consider a different interpretation of the mod 16 circle. Let the values
0 through 15 be represented by the 4-bit binary vectors 0000, 0001, . . . , 1111,
according to the binary number system, and then reinterpret these binary vectors to
represent signed numbers in the range -8 through $+7$ in the 2's-complement method
(see Figure 7.1), as shown in Figure 7.5b.

Let us apply the mod 16 addition technique discussed above to the simple example of adding $+7$ to -3. The 2's-complement representation for these numbers is 0111 and 1101, respectively. To add these numbers, locate 0111 on the circle of Figure 7.5b. Then step off 1101 (13 steps) in the clockwise direction to arrive at 0100, which yields the correct answer of $+4$. If we use one of the adder circuits, discussed earlier, we obtain

$$
\begin{array}{cccc}
 & 0 & 1 & 1 & 1 \\
+ & 1 & 1 & 0 & 1 \\
\hline
1 & 0 & 1 & 0 & 0 \\
\end{array}
$$

↑

Carry-out

Note that if we ignore the carry-out from the fourth bit position in this addition, we obtain the correct answer. In fact, this is always the case.

We now state the rules governing addition and subtraction of n-bit signed numbers using the 2's-complement representation system.

1. To perform *addition* of two numbers, add their representations in an n-bit adder, ignoring the carry-out signal from the MSB position. The sum will be the algebraically correct value in the 2's-complement representation as long as the answer is in the range -2^{n-1} through $+2^{n-1} - 1$.

2. To perform *subtraction* of two numbers X and Y, that is, to perform $X - Y$, form the 2's complement of Y and then add it to X as in rule 1. Again, if the answer is in the range -2^{n-1} through $+2^{n-1} - 1$, the result will be the algebraically correct value in the 2's-complement representation system.

Figure 7.6 shows some examples of addition and subtraction. In all these 4-bit examples the answers fall into the representable range of -8 through $+7$. When answers do not fall within the representable range, we say that an *arithmetic overflow* has occurred. Section 7.4.1 will deal with such situations. The four addition operations (a) through (d) in Figure 7.6 follow rule 1 above, and the six subtraction operations (e) through (j) follow rule 2. Note that the subtraction operation requires the subtrahend (bottom) value to be 2's complemented before the addition is performed. In the logic circuit implementation of subtraction, this complementation can be combined with the addition operation as shown in Figure 7.7. The ADD/SUB control wire is set to 0 for addition. This allows the Y vector to be applied unchanged to one of the adder inputs along with a carry-in signal c_0 of 0. When the ADD/SUB control wire is set to 1, signifying subtraction, the Y vector is 1's complemented (that is, bit complemented) by the EX-OR gates, and c_0 is set to 1 to complete the 2's complementation of Y. Note that 2's complementing a negative value, as in Figure 7.6e, is done in exactly the same manner as 2's complementing a positive value.

The logical simplicity and speed of performing either addition or subtraction of signed numbers in 2's-complement representation is the reason why this number representation is used in the ALU subsystems of most modern computers. It might seem

(a)	0 0 1 0	(+2)	(b)	0 1 0 0	(+4)
	+ 0 0 1 1	(+3)		+ 1 0 1 0	(−6)
	0 1 0 1	(+5)		1 1 1 0	(−2)

(c)	1 0 1 1	(−5)	(d)	0 1 1 1	(+7)
	+ 1 1 1 0	(−2)		+ 1 1 0 1	(−3)
	1 0 0 1	(−7)		0 1 0 0	(+4)

(e)

1 1 0 1	(−3)	$\Longrightarrow$	1 1 0 1	
− 1 0 0 1	(−7)		+ 0 1 1 1	
			0 1 0 0	(+4)

(f)

0 0 1 0	(+2)	$\Longrightarrow$	0 0 1 0	
− 0 1 0 0	(+4)		+ 1 1 0 0	
			1 1 1 0	(−2)

(g)

0 1 1 0	(+6)	$\Longrightarrow$	0 1 1 0	
− 0 0 1 1	(+3)		+ 1 1 0 1	
			0 0 1 1	(+3)

(h)

1 0 0 1	(−7)	$\Longrightarrow$	1 0 0 1	
− 1 0 1 1	(−5)		+ 0 1 0 1	
			1 1 1 0	(−2)

(i)

1 0 0 1	(−7)	$\Longrightarrow$	1 0 0 1	
− 0 0 0 1	(+1)		+ 1 1 1 1	
			1 0 0 0	(−8)

(j)

0 0 1 0	(+2)	$\Longrightarrow$	0 0 1 0	
− 1 1 0 1	(−3)		+ 0 0 1 1	
			0 1 0 1	(+5)

FIGURE 7.6
2's-complement ADD and SUBTRACT operations.

that the 1's-complement representation would be just as good as the 2's-complement system for use in a combined addition-subtraction logic network. However, although complementation is easy, the result obtained after the add operation is not always correct. In fact, the carry-out c_n cannot be ignored. If $c_n = 1$, then 1 must be added to the result to make it correct. If $c_n = 0$, the result as obtained is correct. The requirement for this correction cycle, which is conditional on the carry-out from the add operation, means that addition and subtraction cannot be implemented as conveniently in the 1's-complement system as in the 2's-complement system.

7.4.1 Overflow in Integer Arithmetic

When adding unsigned numbers, the carry-out c_n serves as the overflow indicator. However, the case of signed numbers is slightly more involved. If we try to add the numbers +7 and +4 in a 4-bit adder, the output vector S will be 1011, which is the

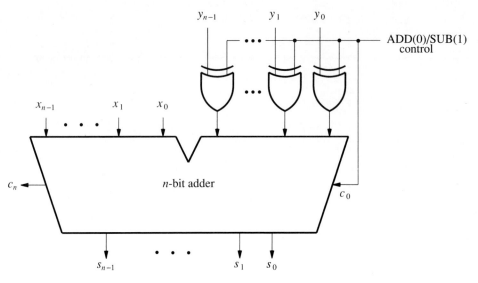

FIGURE 7.7
Binary addition-subtraction logic network.

code for -5, an obviously wrong result. The carry-out signal from the MSB position will be 0. Similarly, if we try to add -4 and -6, we get $S = +6$, another obvious error, and in this case the carry-out signal is 1. Clearly, the addition of numbers with different signs cannot cause overflow, because the absolute value of the sum will always be smaller than the larger absolute value of the two summands. The above discussion leads to the following conclusions:

1. Overflow can occur only when adding two numbers that have the same sign.
2. The carry-out signal from the sign-bit position is not a sufficient indicator of overflow in the case of signed-number addition.

It is readily seen that an overflow has occurred whenever the sign of S does not agree with the signs of X and Y and the signs of X and Y are the same. In an n-bit adder, we can define a signal Overflow by the logical expression

$$\text{Overflow} = x_{n-1} y_{n-1} \overline{s}_{n-1} + \overline{x}_{n-1} \overline{y}_{n-1} s_{n-1}$$

For the case of a combined addition-subtraction unit, such as that of Figure 7.7, the variable y_{n-1} in the Overflow expression should be taken from the output of the leftmost EX-OR gate. This will lead to the correct indication of overflow from either addition or subtraction.

Occurrence of an overflow is an important condition to detect in a computer. It is customary to dedicate a condition code flag as its indicator. It is possible to have this flag cause an interrupt when an add or subtract instruction results in an overflow. It is the programmer's responsibility to decide on remedial action.

7.5 ARITHMETIC AND BRANCHING CONDITIONS

We have now discussed addition of unsigned numbers, as well as addition and subtraction of signed numbers in the 2's-complement representation. At this point it is useful to return to the discussion of condition codes and conditional branches presented in Chapter 2, Sections 2.6.5, 2.6.6 (PDP-11), and 2.7.5 (68000).

In both the PDP-11 and the 68000, the four condition code flags N, Z, V, and C are set and cleared by arithmetic operations as follows:

N   Set to 1 if the result is negative; otherwise, cleared to 0.

Z   Set to 1 if the result is 0; otherwise, cleared to 0.

V   Set to 1 if arithmetic overflow occurs; otherwise, cleared to 0.

C   For an add operation, C is set to 1 if a carry-out results; otherwise, it is cleared to 0. For a subtract operation, C is set to 1 if no carry-out results; otherwise, it is set to 0.

For purposes of this discussion, it can be assumed that addition and subtraction are performed as indicated by the logic unit of Figure 7.7. The carry-out signal referred to in the definition of the C flag is synonymous with the signal c_n in that figure. The V flag is set according to the Overflow expression given in Section 7.4.1.

Let us now consider how conditional branch instructions make use of the condition code flags. The examples we will use apply to the conditional branch instructions in the 68000. Similar arguments apply to the PDP-11.

In some branch instructions, the branch condition is determined by the value of a single flag. For example, the instructions BNE (Branch if Not Equal to 0) and BEQ (Branch if EQual to 0) test the Z flag in an obvious way. Other instructions involve the testing of two or more flags. Consider the BLS (Branch if Lower or Same) instruction. It is normally used after a Compare instruction, which compares two unsigned integers. The branch is taken if the destination operand is less than or equal to the source operand. The comparison is done by subtracting the source operand from the destination operand. The C flag is set to 1 if no carry occurs in the subtraction operation. A few examples will clearly demonstrate that no carry occurs when the source operand is larger than the destination and a carry does occur when the source operand is smaller. When both operands are the same, a carry occurs, but then the Z flag is set to 1 because the result is 0. Therefore, the required branch condition is $C + Z = 1$.

Consider now a similar comparison dealing with signed numbers. In this case, the BLE (Branch if Less than or Equal) instruction should be used instead of BLS. The result of the comparison will be negative if the destination operand is less than the source. This is one of the conditions for which the branch should occur. Therefore, it would seem that $N + Z = 1$ is the branch condition for the BLE instruction. This is sufficient if arithmetic overflow does not occur when the subtraction operation is performed. However, if overflow occurs, the sign of the result will be opposite to what it should be. To obtain the proper branch condition in this case, the complement of the N flag should be tested. Therefore, the complete branch condition for the BLE instruction is $(N \oplus V) + Z = 1$.

Another important aspect of condition code flags is the role of the C flag in performing multiple-precision arithmetic. Consider the task of adding two operands, each occupying several words in memory. The required addition can be done by a program loop that adds individual words in successive iterations. The C flag must be preserved from one iteration to the next in order to propagate the carries through the complete addition operation. A problem arises if the C flag is altered by instructions other than the Add instruction in the loop. In the 68000, a fifth condition code flag, X, is added. It is set in the same way as the C flag, but it is not affected by as many instructions. Therefore, the X flag serves the role of preserving the value of the carry flag for use in multiple-precision arithmetic routines.

7.6 MULTIPLICATION OF POSITIVE NUMBERS

The usual "paper-and-pencil" algorithm for multiplication of integers represented in any positional number system is illustrated in Figure 7.8a for the binary system, assuming positive 4-bit operands. The product of two n-digit numbers can be accommodated in $2n$ digits, so the product in this example fits into 8 bits, as shown. In the binary system, multiplication of the multiplicand by 1 bit of the multiplier is easy. If the multiplier bit is 1, the multiplicand is entered in the appropriately shifted position to be added with other shifted multiplicands to form the product. If the multiplier is 0, then 0s are entered as in the third row of the example.

It is possible to implement positive operand binary multiplication in a purely combinational two-dimensional logic array, as shown in Figure 7.8b. The main component in each cell is an adder circuit. The AND gate in any cell determines whether a multiplicand bit m_j is added to the incoming partial-product bit, based on the value of the multiplier bit q_i. Each row i, where $0 \le i \le 3$, adds the multiplicand (appropriately shifted) to the incoming partial product PPi to generate the outgoing partial product PP$(i + 1)$ if $q_i = 1$. If $q_i = 0$, PPi is passed vertically downward unchanged. PP0 is obviously all 0s, and PP4 is the desired product. The multiplicand is shifted left one position per row by the diagonal signal path.

Although the above combinational multiplier is quite easy to understand, it may be impractical to use when dealing with long numbers, because it uses a large number of gates and performs only one function. Many computers that provide multiplication in the basic machine instruction set do so through a sequence of operations similar to those shown in Figure 7.9. The block diagram in Figure 7.9a describes a possible hardware arrangement. This circuit performs multiplication by using a single adder n times to implement the addition being performed spatially by the n rows of ripple-carry adders of Figure 7.8b. The combination of registers A and Q holds PPi during the time that multiplier bit q_i is used to generate the signal ADD/NOADD. This signal controls the addition of the multiplicand M to PPi to generate PP$(i + 1)$. There are n cycles needed to compute the product. The partial product grows in length by 1 bit per cycle from the initial vector (PP0) of n 0s in register A. The carry-out from

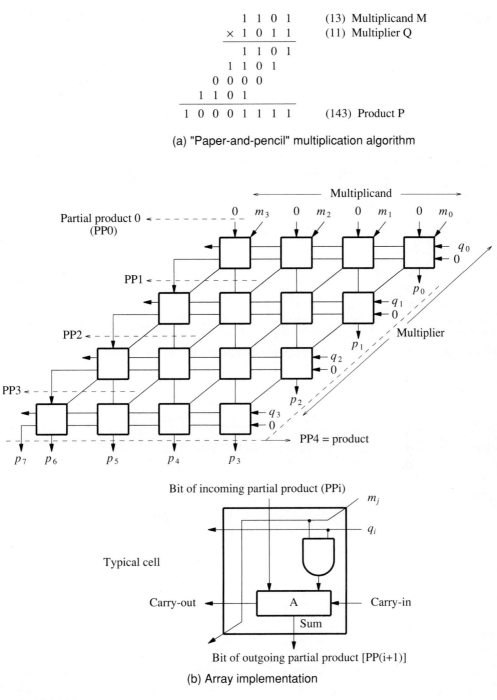

$$
\begin{array}{r}
1\ 1\ 0\ 1 \\
\times\ 1\ 0\ 1\ 1 \\
\hline
1\ 1\ 0\ 1 \\
1\ 1\ 0\ 1 \\
0\ 0\ 0\ 0 \\
1\ 1\ 0\ 1 \\
\hline
1\ 0\ 0\ 0\ 1\ 1\ 1\ 1
\end{array}
$$

(13) Multiplicand M
(11) Multiplier Q

(143) Product P

(a) "Paper-and-pencil" multiplication algorithm

(b) Array implementation

FIGURE 7.8

Array multiplication of positive binary operands.

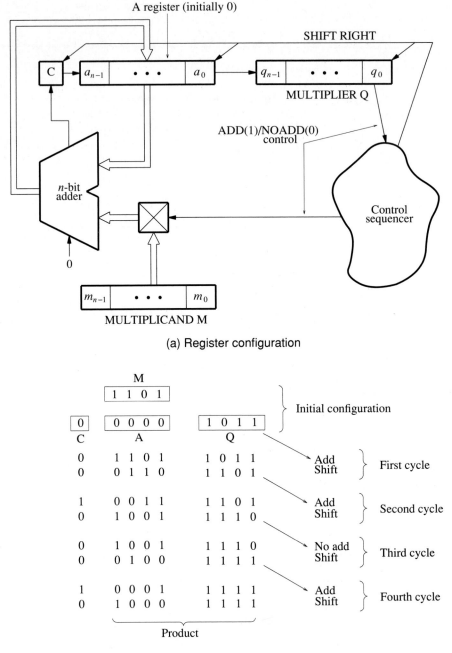

(a) Register configuration

(b) Multiplication example

FIGURE 7.9
Sequential circuit binary multiplier.

the adder is stored in flip-flop C shown at the left end of register A. At the start, the multiplier is loaded into register Q, the multiplicand into register M, and C and A are set to 0. At the end of each cycle, C, A, and Q are shifted right one bit position to allow for growth of the partial product as the multiplier is shifted out of register Q. Because of this shifting, multiplier bit q_i appears at the LSB position of Q to generate the ADD/NOADD signal at the correct time, starting with q_0 during the first cycle, q_1 during the second, and so on. After use, the multiplier bits can be discarded. This is accomplished by the right-shift operation. Note that the carry-out from the adder is the leftmost bit of PP($i + 1$), and it must be held in the C flip-flop to be shifted right with the contents of A and Q. After n cycles, the high-order half of the product is held in register A and the low-order half is in register Q. The multiplication example of Figure 7.8*a* is shown in Figure 7.9*b* as it would be performed by this hardware arrangement.

We can now relate the components of Figure 7.9*a* to Figure 4.1. The relevant parts of that figure are reproduced in Figure 7.10. Assume that the multiply sequence is to be hardwired as a machine instruction. Furthermore, assume that the multiplier and multiplicand are in registers R2 and R3, respectively, and that the two-word

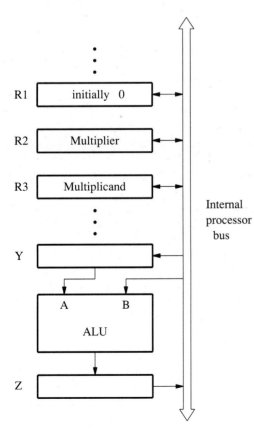

FIGURE 7.10
Computer processor arrangement for multiplication.

product is to be left in R1 and R2. First, the multiplicand is moved into register Y. Thus, register Y corresponds to M in Figure 7.9a, and R1 and R2 correspond to A and Q. Connections must be made so that R1 and R2 can be shifted right as a two-word combination. A transfer from Z to R1 is made after each cycle. The C bit in Figure 7.9a is actually the carry flag in the condition codes. It must be possible to connect it to R1 for shifting operations as in Figure 7.9a. We will not give the register transfer sequencing for multiplication at the level used in Chapter 4; it should now be reasonably clear how it can be done.

Because we assumed that the multiply operation is hardwired, the component called Control Sequencer is implemented by the general instruction execution sequencer, as shown in Chapter 4. This results in a relatively complicated single machine instruction. If the adder has a delay of about 50 ns and the control settings and shift operations associated with each cycle take another 50 ns, then a hardwired multiply operation in a 16-bit word-length computer might take 1.5 to 2 μs.

7.7 SIGNED-OPERAND MULTIPLICATION

Multiplication of signed operands generating a double-length product in the 2's-complement number system requires a few further remarks about that representation scheme. We will not discuss multiplication in the other representations because it reduces to the multiplication of positive operands already discussed. The accumulation of partial products by adding versions of the multiplicand as selected by the multiplier bits is still the general strategy.

Let us first consider the case of a positive multiplier and a negative multiplicand. When we add a negative multiplicand to a partial product, we must extend the sign-bit value of the multiplicand to the left as far as the extent of the eventual product. Consider the example shown in Figure 7.11, where the 5-bit signed operand -13 (multiplicand) is multiplied by $+11$ (multiplier) to get the 10-bit product -143. The sign extension of the multiplicand is shown underlined. To see why this sign-extension operation is correct, consider the following argument. The extension of a positive number is obviously achieved by the addition of zeros at the left end. For the case of negative numbers, scan around the mod 16 circle of Figure 7.5 in the counterclockwise direction, starting from the code for 0. If negative numbers of more bits (5-bit, 6-bit, 7-bit, etc.) were written out, they would be derived correctly by extending the

```
                1  0  0  1  1   (−13)
            ×  0  1  0  1  1   (+11)
 1  1  1  1  1  1  0  0  1  1
 ─────────────────────────────
 1  1  1  1  1  0  0  1  1
 0  0  0  0  0  0  0  0
 1  1  1  0  0  1  1
 ─────────────────────────────
 0  0  0  0  0  0
 ─────────────────────────────
 1  1  0  1  1  1  0  0  0  1   (−143)
```

FIGURE 7.11
Sign extension of negative multiplicand.

given 4-bit codes by 1s to the left. Therefore, to obtain the representation for a given positive or negative number using a larger number of bits, we simply repeat the sign bit as many times as needed to the left. This operation is called *sign extension*. Sign extension must be done by any hardware or software implementation of the multiply operation.

We will now consider the case of negative multipliers. A straightforward solution is to form the 2's complement of both the multiplier and the multiplicand and proceed as in the case of a positive multiplier. This is possible, of course, since complementation of both operands does not change the value or the sign of the product. Another technique that works correctly for negative numbers in 2's-complement representation is to add shifted versions of the multiplicand, properly sign-extended, just as in the case of positive multipliers, for all 1 bits of the multiplier to the right of the sign bit. Then add $-1\times$ multiplicand, properly shifted, if there is a 1 in the sign-bit position of the multiplier. The sign position is thus viewed in the same way as the other positions, except that it has a negative weight. The general version of this property of the 2's-complement representation will be used in the next section describing the Booth algorithm.

Booth Algorithm. A powerful algorithm for signed-number multiplication is the Booth algorithm. It generates a $2n$-bit product and treats both positive and negative numbers uniformly. Consider a multiplication operation in which the multiplier is positive and has a single block of 1s, for example, 0011110. To derive the product, we could add four appropriately shifted versions of the multiplicand as in the standard procedure. However, the number of required operations can be reduced by observing that this multiplier can be regarded as the difference between two numbers:

$$
\begin{array}{ll}
0100000 & (32) \\
-\ 0000010 & (2) \\
\hline
0011110 & (30)
\end{array}
$$

This suggests that the product can be generated by adding $2^5 \times$ multiplicand and the 2's complement of $2^1 \times$ multiplicand. For convenience, the sequence of required operations can be described by recoding the multiplier above as 0 +1 0 0 0 −1 0.

In general, in the Booth scheme, $-1\times$(shifted multiplicand) is selected at $0 \rightarrow 1$ boundaries, and $+1\times$(shifted multiplicand) is selected at $1 \rightarrow 0$ boundaries as the multiplier is scanned from right to left. Figure 7.12 illustrates the normal and the Booth schemes. The Booth algorithm clearly extends to any number of blocks of 1s in a multiplier including the situation where a single 1 is considered to be a block. See Figure 7.13 for another example.

Until now we have used positive multipliers. Since there is at least one 0 at the left end of any multiplier, a +1 operation can be matched to the left of every −1 operation to preserve the correctness of the method. It is also true that if we apply the method to a negative multiplier, we get the correct answer (an example is given in Figure 7.14). To see the correctness of this technique in general, we use a property of negative-number representations in the 2's-complement system. If the leftmost zero of a negative number is at bit position k, that is, if

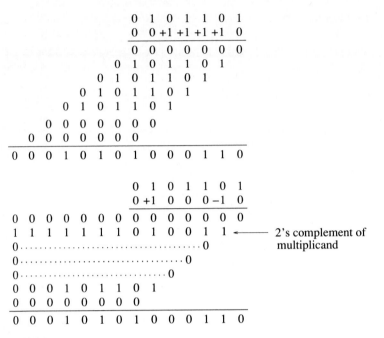

```
                          0   1   0   1   1   0   1
                          0   0  +1  +1  +1  +1   0
                         ─────────────────────────────
                          0   0   0   0   0   0   0
                    0   1   0   1   1   0   1
                0   1   0   1   1   0   1
            0   1   0   1   1   0   1
        0   0   0   0   0   0   0
    0   0   0   0   0   0   0
  ─────────────────────────────────────────────────────
    0   0   0   1   0   1   0   1   0   0   0   1   1   0


                          0   1   0   1   1   0   1
                          0  +1   0   0   0  -1   0
    0   0   0   0   0   0   0   0   0   0   0   0   0   0
    1   1   1   1   1   1   1   0   1   0   0   1   1   ◄──── 2's complement of
    0 · · · · · · · · · · · · · · · · · · · · · · · · 0        multiplicand
    0 · · · · · · · · · · · · · · · · · · · · · · 0
    0 · · · · · · · · · · · · · · · · · · 0
    0   0   0   1   0   1   1   0   1
    0   0   0   0   0   0   0   0
  ─────────────────────────────────────────────────────
    0   0   0   1   0   1   0   1   0   0   0   1   1   0
```

FIGURE 7.12
Normal and Booth multiplication schemes.

$$X = 11 \ldots 10x_{k-1} \ldots x_0$$

is an n-bit negative number, its value is given by

$$V(X) = -2^{k+1} + x_{k-1} \times 2^{k-1} + \cdots + x_0 \times 2^0$$

This can be checked by applying it to some of the codes in Figure 7.1. For example,

$$V(1011) = -2^3 + 0 + 2^1 + 2^0 = -5$$

and

$$V(1110) = -2^1 + 0 = -2$$

Now consider that X is a multiplier. If X has no zeros, then $X = 11 \cdots 11$, and
$V(X) = -1$. Applying the Booth scheme, we recode the multiplier as $00 \cdots 0\, -1$.
The product is computed as $-1 \times$ multiplicand, which is correct. On the other hand, if
X has at least one 0, let the leftmost 0 be in the x_k position as above. Perform the
multiplication using the recoded multiplier in the same way as for positive multipliers.

```
0    0    1    0    1    1    0    0    1    1    1    0    1    0    1    1    0    0
                              ⇓⇓
0   +1   -1   +1    0   -1    0   +1    0    0   -1   +1   -1   +1    0   -1    0    0
```

FIGURE 7.13
Booth recoding of a multiplier.

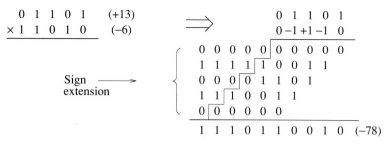

FIGURE 7.14
Booth multiplication with a negative multiplier.

This will result in adding $-1 \times 2^{k+1} \times$ multiplicand to the versions of the multiplicand selected by the rightmost $k + 1$ bits of the recoded multiplier. It is easy to see from the expression for $V(X)$ that this generates the correct product.

The Booth technique for recoding multipliers is summarized in Figure 7.15.

7.8 FAST MULTIPLICATION

The basic transformation $011 \ldots 110 \Rightarrow +100 \ldots 0 -10$ that is fundamental to the Booth algorithm has been called the *skipping over 1s* technique. The motivation for this term is that in cases where the multiplier has its 1s grouped into a few contiguous blocks, only a few versions of the multiplicand (summands) need to be added to generate the product. If only a few summands need to be added, the multiplication operation can potentially be speeded up. However, in the worst case—that of alternating 1s and 0s in the multiplier—each bit of the multiplier selects a summand. In fact, this results in more summands than if the Booth algorithm is not used. A 16-bit "worst-case" multiplier, a more "normal" multiplier, and a "good" multiplier are shown in Figure 7.16.

The Booth algorithm has two attractive features. First, it handles both positive and negative multipliers uniformly. Second, it achieves some efficiency in the number of additions required when the multiplier has a few large blocks of 1s. The speed gain possible by skipping over 1s is clearly data dependent. On average, the speed of doing multiplication is the same as with the normal algorithm.

Multiplier		Version of multiplicand selected by bit i
Bit i	Bit $i-1$	
0	0	$0 \times M$
0	1	$+1 \times M$
1	0	$-1 \times M$
1	1	$0 \times M$

FIGURE 7.15
Booth multiplier recoding table.

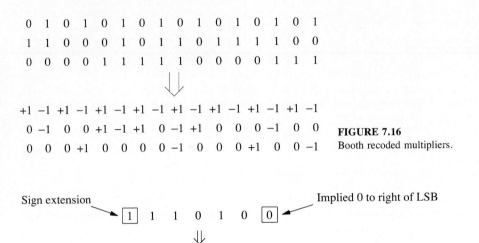

+1	−1	+1	−1	+1	−1	+1	−1	+1	−1	+1	−1	+1	−1	+1	−1
0	−1	0	0	+1	−1	+1	0	−1	+1	0	0	0	−1	0	0
0	0	0	+1	0	0	0	0	−1	0	0	0	+1	0	0	−1

FIGURE 7.16
Booth recoded multipliers.

Sign extension ← ⬚1 1 1 0 1 0 ⬚0 ← Implied 0 to right of LSB

⇓

0 0, −1 +1, −1 0,

0   −1   −2

(a) Example of bit-pair recoding derived from Booth recoding

Multiplier bit-pair		Multiplier bit on the right	Multiplicand
$i+1$	i	$i-1$	selected at SPi
0	0	0	$0 \times M$
0	0	1	$+1 \times M$
0	1	0	$+1 \times M$
0	1	1	$+2 \times M$
1	0	0	$-2 \times M$
1	0	1	$-1 \times M$
1	1	0	$-1 \times M$
1	1	1	$0 \times M$

(b) Table of multiplicand selection decisions

FIGURE 7.17
Multiplier bit-pair recoding.

We now describe a multiplication speedup technique that guarantees that an n-bit multiplier will generate at most $n/2$ summands and that uniformly handles the signed-operand case. This is twice as fast as the worst-case Booth algorithm situation.

The new technique is derived directly from the Booth technique. Recall that in the Booth technique multiplier bit q_i selects a summand as a function of the bit q_{i-1} on its right. The summand selected is shifted i binary positions to the left of the LSB position of the product before the summand is added. Let us call this summand position i (SPi). The basic idea of the speedup technique is to use bits $i + 1$ and i to select one summand, as a function of bit $i - 1$, to be added at SPi. To be practical, this summand must be easily derivable from the multiplicand. The $n/2$ summands are thus selected by bit pairs (x_1, x_0), (x_3, x_2), (x_5, x_4), and so on. The technique is called the bit-pair recoding method. Consider the multiplier of Figure 7.14, which is repeated in Figure 7.17a. Grouping the Booth-recoded selectors in pairs, we obtain a single, appropriately shifted summand for each pair as shown. The rightmost Booth pair, $(-1, 0)$, is equivalent to $-2 \times$(multiplicand M) at SP0. The next pair, $(-1, +1)$, is equivalent to $-1 \times$M at SP2; finally, the leftmost pair of zeros is equivalent to $0 \times$M at SP4. Restating these selections in terms of the original multiplier bits, we have the cases (1,0) with 0 on the right selecting $-2 \times$M; (1,0) with 1 on the right selecting $-1 \times$M; and (1,1) with 1 on the right selecting $0 \times$M. The complete set of eight cases is shown in Figure 7.17b; the multiplication example of Figure 7.14 is shown again in Figure 7.18 as it would be computed using the bit-pair recoding method.

The preceding discussion is intended to give the reader some grasp of the algorithms that have been used in commercially available MSI and LSI circuits intended for high-performance signed-integer multiplication. Single-chip multiplier circuits are available; these circuits use techniques similar to those described, as well as further enhancements, such as those discussed in Problems 7.24 and 7.25. These circuits can be used in both general-purpose computers and special-purpose systems, such as signal processors, where high-speed arithmetic operations are essential.

7.9   INTEGER DIVISION

In Section 7.6 we discussed positive-number multiplication by relating the way in which the multiplication operation can be done on paper to the way a logic circuit can do it. It is instructive to follow the same strategy here. We will discuss only positive-number division in detail. Some general comments on the signed-operand case will be made later.

Figure 7.19 shows an example of decimal division along with the binary-coded division of the same values. Consider the decimal version. The 2 in the quotient is determined by the following reasoning. We first try 13 divided into 2 and it "doesn't go." Next we try 13 divided into 27. We go through the trial exercise of multiplying 13 by 2 to get 26, and knowing that $27 - 26 = 1$ is less than 13, we enter 2 as the quotient and perform the required subtraction. The next digit of the dividend, 4, is "brought down," and we finish by deciding that 13 goes into 14 once, with the remainder being determined as 1. A similar discussion can be given for the binary

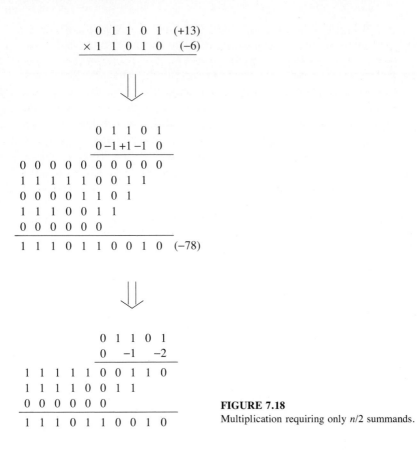

```
        0  1  1  0  1   (+13)
     ×  1  1  0  1  0    (−6)
```

```
            0  1  1  0  1
            0 −1 +1 −1  0
  0  0  0  0  0  0  0  0  0  0
  1  1  1  1  1  0  0  1  1
  0  0  0  0  1  1  0  1
  1  1  1  0  0  1  1
  0  0  0  0  0  0
  ───────────────────────────
  1  1  1  0  1  1  0  0  1  0  (−78)
```

```
            0  1  1  0  1
            0    −1    −2
  1  1  1  1  1  0  0  1  1  0
  1  1  1  1  0  0  1  1
  0  0  0  0  0  0
  ───────────────────────────
  1  1  1  0  1  1  0  0  1  0
```

FIGURE 7.18
Multiplication requiring only $n/2$ summands.

case, with the simplification that the only possibilities for the quotient bits are 0 and 1.

The important point to conclude from the "longhand" division algorithm is that the process of trial determination of the quotient digits is more difficult to automate in a logic circuit than the selection and addition of summands in the multiplication case. The simplest circuit that implements binary division must methodically position the divisor with respect to the dividend and perform a subtraction. If the remainder is zero or positive, a quotient bit of 1 is determined, the remainder is extended by another

```
        21                        10101
  13 ) 274             1101 ) 100010010
        26                       1101
      ────                     ──────
        14                       10000
        13                        1101
      ────                      ──────
         1                        1110
                                  1101        FIGURE 7.19
                                ──────        "Longhand" division examples.
                                     1
```

bit of the dividend, the divisor is repositioned, and another subtraction is performed. On the other hand, if the remainder is negative, a quotient bit of 0 is determined, the dividend is restored by adding back the divisor, and the divisor is repositioned for another subtraction.

Figure 7.20 shows a logic circuit arrangement that implements the above *restoring-division* technique. Note its similarity to the structure for multiplication that was shown in Figure 7.9. An n-bit positive divisor is loaded into register M and an n-bit positive dividend is loaded into register Q at the start of the operation. Register A is set to 0. After the division is complete, the n-bit quotient will be in register Q and the remainder in A. The required subtractions are facilitated by using 2's-complement arithmetic. The extra bit position at the left end of both A and M is for the sign bit for the subtractions.

The following algorithm performs the division:

S1:   Do n times

Shift A and Q left one binary position.

Subtract M from A, placing the answer back in A.

If the sign of A is 1, set q_0 to 0 and add M back to A (restore A); otherwise, set q_0 to 1.

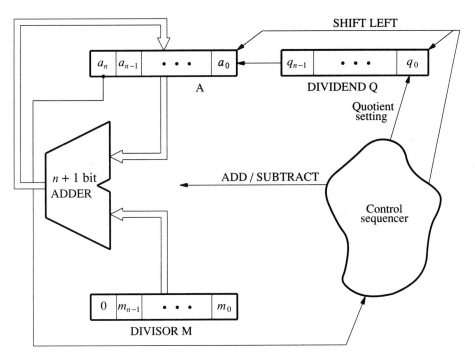

FIGURE 7.20
Circuit arrangement for binary division.

$$
\begin{array}{r}
1\,0 \\
11\,\overline{)\,1\,0\,0\,0} \\
1\,1 \\
\hline
1\,0
\end{array}
$$

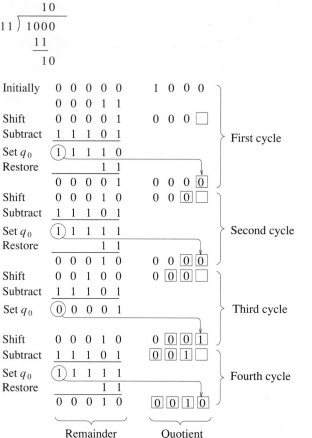

Remainder   Quotient

FIGURE 7.21
A restoring division example.

Figure 7.21 shows a 4-bit example as it would be processed by the circuit in Figure 7.20.

It is possible to improve on this algorithm by avoiding the need for restoring A after an unsuccessful subtraction (we define a subtraction to be unsuccessful if the result is negative). Consider the sequence of operations that takes place after the subtraction operation in the above algorithm. If A is positive, we shift left and subtract M; that is, we perform $2A - M$. If A is negative, we restore it by performing $A + M$, and then we shift it left and subtract M. This is equivalent to performing $2A + M$. The q_0 bit is appropriately set to 0 or 1 after the correct operation has been performed. We can summarize this into the following *nonrestoring-division* algorithm:

S1:   Do *n* times

      If the sign of A is 0, shift A and Q left one binary position and subtract M from A; otherwise, shift A and Q left and add M to A.

      If the sign of A is 0, set q_0 to 1; otherwise, set q_0 to 0.

S2:   If the sign of A is 1, add M to A.

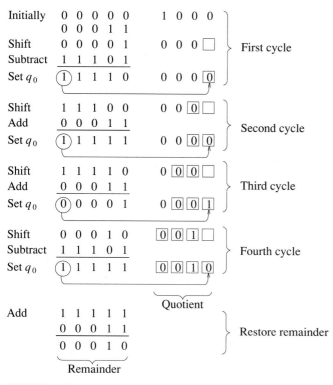

FIGURE 7.22
A nonrestoring-division example.

The S2 step is needed to leave the proper positive remainder in A at the end of n cycles. It is clear that the logic circuitry of Figure 7.20 can also be used to perform this algorithm as well as the original one. Note that the restore operations are not used and that exactly one add or subtract operation is performed per cycle. Figure 7.22 shows how the division example of Figure 7.21 is executed by the nonrestoring-division algorithm.

There are no simple algorithms for performing signed division that are comparable to the multiplication situation. In division, preprocessing of the operands and/or postprocessing of the results are usually required. These extra operations depend on the sign of the operands in conjunction with the desired signs of the results, and complementation of one or more numbers is usually involved. We will not discuss these possibilities in detail. However, it is useful to note that we can always transform the operands to positive values, use one of the algorithms discussed above, and transform the results to the correct signed values as necessary.

7.10 FLOATING-POINT NUMBERS AND OPERATIONS

Until now in this chapter we have been exclusively concerned with signed, fixed-point numbers. It has been convenient to consider them as integers, that is, with an implied binary point at the right end of each number. It is just as easy to assume that the binary point is just to the right of the sign bit, thus representing fractions. In the 2's-complement system, the signed value F, represented by the n-bit binary fraction

$$B = b_0.b_{-1}b_{-2} \ldots b_{-(n-1)}$$

is given by

$$F(B) = -b_0 \times 2^0 + b_{-1} \times 2^{-1} + b_{-2} \times 2^{-2} + \cdots + b_{-(n-1)} \times 2^{-(n-1)}$$

where the range of F is

$$-1 \le F \le 1 - 2^{-(n-1)}$$

Consider the range of values representable in a 16-bit fixed-point format. Interpreted as integers, the value range is $-32,768 \, (= -2^{15})$ to $+32,767 \, (= +2^{15} - 1)$. If we consider them to be fractions, the range is approximately $\pm 3 \times 10^{-5}$ ($\approx \pm 2^{-15}$) to ± 1. Neither of these ranges is sufficient for scientific calculations, which might involve parameters like Avogadro's number ($6.0247 \times 10^{23} \, \text{mole}^{-1}$) or Planck's constant ($6.6254 \times 10^{-27} \, \text{erg·s}$). Hence, there is a need to easily accommodate both very large integers and very small fractions. This means that a facility should be provided for both representing numbers and operating on numbers so that the position of the binary point is variable and is automatically adjusted as computation proceeds. In such a case, the binary point is said to float, and the numbers are called *floating-point numbers*. This distinguishes them from fixed-point numbers, whose binary point is always in the same position.

Because the position of the binary point in a floating-point number is variable, it must be given explicitly in the floating-point representation. For example, in the familiar decimal scientific notation, numbers may be written as 6.0247×10^{23}, 6.6254×10^{-27}, -1.0341×10^2, -7.3000×10^{-14}, and so on. These numbers are said to be given to five *significant digits*. The *scale factors* (10^{23}, 10^{-27}, etc.) indicate the position of the decimal point with respect to the significant digits. By convention, when the decimal point is placed to the right of the first (nonzero) significant digit the number is said to be *normalized*. Note that the base 10 in the scale factor is fixed and does not need to appear explicitly in the machine representation of a floating-point number. The sign, the significant digits, and the exponent in the scale factor constitute the representation. We are thus motivated to define a floating-point number representation as one in which a number is represented by its sign, a string of significant digits (commonly called a *mantissa*), and an *exponent* to an implied base. Let us state a general form for such numbers in the decimal system and then relate the form to a comparable binary representation. A widely used form is

$$\pm X_1.X_2X_3X_4X_5X_6X_7 \times 10^{\pm Y_1Y_2}$$

where X_i and Y_i are decimal digits. This is sufficient for a wide range of scientific calculations. As we shall see, it is possible to approximate this range and mantissa precision in a binary representation that occupies 32 bits. A 24-bit number can approximately represent a seven-digit decimal number. Therefore, 24 bits are assigned to represent the mantissa in the binary representation. One bit is needed for the sign of the number, leaving seven bits for a signed exponent.

A specific binary format for floating-point numbers is shown in Figure 7.23a. Let us first assume that the implied base is 2 and that the 7-bit signed exponent is expressed as a 2's-complement integer. The 24-bit mantissa is considered to be a fraction with the binary point at its left end and the sign of the number is given in the leftmost bit of the format. To retain as many significant bits as possible, the fractional mantissa is kept in a normalized form in which, for nonzero values, its leftmost bit is always 1. Thus the magnitude of the mantissa M is either 0 or lies in the range of $1/2 \le M < 1$. A number that is not in this form can always be put in normalized form by shifting the fraction and adjusting the exponent, assuming that exponent overflow/underflow does not occur. Figure 7.23b shows an unnormalized value, $0.001 \ldots \times 2^9$, and its normalized version, $0.1 \ldots \times 2^7$. A 7-bit, 2's-complement exponent has a range of -64 to $+63$, which means that the scale factor has a range of 2^{-64} to 2^{63}, which is smaller than the desired scale factor range of 10^{-99} to 10^{99}. If we reduce the size of the mantissa to allocate more bits to the exponent, then we will not be able to approximate the desired seven-decimal-digit accuracy. The solution that has been used in a number of computers is to change the value of the implied base in the scale factor. The base should be of the form 2^q so that a right or left shift of the mantissa by q binary positions with respect to its binary point corresponds to a

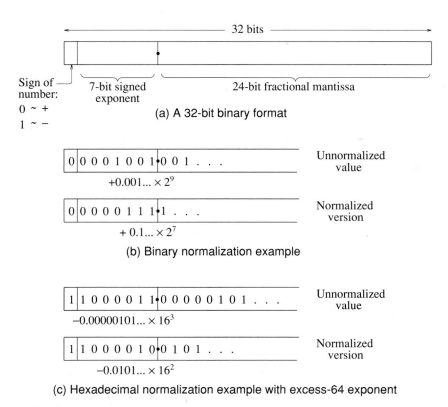

(a) A 32-bit binary format

(b) Binary normalization example

(c) Hexadecimal normalization example with excess-64 exponent

FIGURE 7.23
Floating-point format.

decrease or increase of 1 in the exponent of the scale factor, respectively. If we let the implied base be 16, then the range of the scale factor becomes 16^{-64} to 16^{63}, which corresponds approximately to the decimal range 10^{-76} to 10^{76}. This representation for floating-point numbers has both an adequate range and number of bits in the mantissa. (However, as we shall see later, a floating-point standard has been developed in which a significantly larger range and mantissa accuracy are provided.) Because the base is now 16, shifting the mantissa to perform normalization must take place in steps of 4-bit shifts. This corresponds to the smallest change (±1) in the exponent. A representation is now considered to be normalized if any of the leading 4 bits of its mantissa is 1. This is often called *hexadecimal normalization*.

It should be pointed out that the gain in range achieved by using a base of 16 in the scale factor may result in a less precise mantissa. Even though 24 bits are still used for the mantissa, hexadecimal normalization allows the leading three bits of a mantissa to be 0s. Thus, in some cases, only 21 significant bits are retained in the mantissa. This differs from the use of the base 2 in the scale factor, where 24 bits of precision are always maintained.

Another change in the format of a floating-point number is useful. Instead of representing the exponent in a signed 2's-complement integer format, we represent it in *excess*-64 format. In this format, an exponent having the signed value E is represented by the value $E' = E + 64$. Since the desired range for E is $-64 \leq E \leq 63$, the excess-64 value E' will be in the range $0 \leq E' \leq 127$. The smallest scale factor, 16^{-64}, is then represented by seven 0s, and the largest scale factor, 16^{+63}, by seven 1s. This simplifies the circuitry needed for determining the relative size of two floating-point numbers. An unnormalized value and its corresponding normalized version in the excess-64, base-16 scale factor scheme are shown in Figure 7.23c. The value 0 is represented by all zeros.

As computations proceed, a number that does not fall in the representable range may be generated. This means that its normalized representation requires an exponent less than -64 or greater than $+63$. In the first case, we say that *underflow* has occurred, and in the second case, we say that *overflow* has occurred. Events like these are generally called arithmetic *exceptions*. A uniform way to handle exceptions in a computer system is to raise an interrupt when they occur. The interrupt-service routine can then take action as specified by the user or by a system convention. For example, on underflow the decision might be to set the value to 0 and proceed. A further discussion of exception handling is beyond the scope of our presentation.

To see the gain in range that has been achieved by using the floating-point representation, we should note the range provided by fixed-point 32-bit formats. A 2's-complement, 32-bit integer format has a range of approximately -2.15×10^9 to 2.15×10^9 and a corresponding fractional range of $\pm 4.66 \times 10^{-10}$ to ± 1. Of course, the gain in range is achieved at the expense of a loss of significant bits. A large number range is a significant feature of a floating-point system; however, the user convenience provided by automatic handling of the variable position of the binary point with respect to the significant bits is the most important feature of such systems.

7.10.1 Arithmetic Operations on Floating-Point Numbers

In this section we will discuss the general procedures for addition, subtraction, multiplication, and division of floating-point numbers. The rules we will give apply to hexadecimal-normalized, 24-bit fraction mantissas and scale factors that have an implied base of 16 and an explicit 7-bit signed exponent in excess-64 format. This format was discussed in the previous section, and an example is shown in Figure 7.23c. The rules specify only the major steps needed in performing the four operations; further detail is not pursued here. For example, the possibility that overflow or underflow might occur is not handled. Furthermore, intermediate results for both mantissas and exponents might require more than 24 and 7 bits, respectively, for their representation. Both of these aspects of the operations need to be carefully considered in the design of an arithmetic processor. While we do not provide that level of detail in specifying the rules, some considerations will be given to these implementation aspects, including rounding, in later sections.

If their exponents differ, mantissas must be shifted with respect to each other before they are added or subtracted. Consider a decimal example in which we wish to add 2.9400×10^2 to 4.3100×10^4. We rewrite 2.9400×10^2 as 0.0294×10^4 and then perform addition of the mantissas to get 4.3394×10^4. A general rule for addition and subtraction may be stated as follows:

ADD/SUBTRACT RULE

1. Choose the number with the smaller exponent and shift its mantissa right (in 4-bit steps) a number of steps equal to the difference in exponents.
2. Set the exponent of the result equal to the larger exponent.
3. Perform addition/subtraction on the mantissas and determine the sign of the result.
4. Normalize the resulting value if necessary and use the first 24 bits after the binary point (truncated, as discussed later) as the mantissa of the result.

Multiplication and division are somewhat easier than addition and subtraction in that no alignment of mantissas is needed.

MULTIPLY RULE

1. Add the exponents and subtract 64.
2. Multiply the mantissas and determine the sign of the result.
3. Normalize the resulting value if necessary and use the first 24 bits after the binary point (truncated) as the mantissa of the result.

DIVIDE RULE

1. Subtract the exponents and add 64.
2. Divide the mantissas and determine the sign of the result.
3. Normalize the resulting value if necessary and use the first 24 bits after the binary point (truncated) as the mantissa of the result.

The addition or subtraction of 64 in the above two rules is a result of using the excess-64 notation for exponents.

7.10.2 Guard Bits and Rounding

Before we discuss the implementation of floating-point operations, we should consider some details associated with the steps in the above algorithms. Although the mantissas of initial operands and final results are limited to 24 bits, it is important to retain extra bits, often called *guard* bits, during the intermediate steps. This yields maximum accuracy in the results.

The operation of removing guard bits in generating final results raises an important issue, however. The problem is that a binary fraction must be *truncated* to give a fraction that is a shorter approximation to the longer value. This problem also arises in other situations, for instance, in the conversion from decimal to binary fractions.

There are a number of ways to truncate. The simplest way is to remove the guard bits and make no changes in the retained bits. This is called *chopping*. Suppose we wish to truncate a fraction from six to three bits by this method. All fractions in the range $0.b_{-1}b_{-2}b_{-3}000$ to $0.b_{-1}b_{-2}b_{-3}111$ will be truncated to $0.b_{-1}b_{-2}b_{-3}$. The error in the 3-bit result obviously ranges from 0 to 0.000111. It is more convenient to say that, in general, the error in chopping ranges from 0 to almost 1 in the least significant position of the retained bits. In our example, this is the b_{-3} position. The result of chopping is called a *biased* approximation, because the error range is not symmetrical about 0.

The next simplest method of truncation is *Von Neumann rounding*. If the bits to be removed are all zeroes, they are simply dropped, with no changes to the retained bits. However, if any of the bits to be removed are 1, the least significant bit of the retained bits is set to 1. In our 6-bit to 3-bit truncation example, all 6-bit fractions with $b_{-4}b_{-5}b_{-6}$ not equal to 000 will be truncated to $0.b_{-1}b_{-2}1$. It is easy to see that the error in this truncation method ranges between -1 and $+1$ in the LSB position of the retained bits. Although the range of error is larger with this technique than it is with chopping, the maximum magnitude is the same, and the approximation is *unbiased* because the error range is symmetrical about 0.

It is advantageous to use unbiased approximations if a large number of operands and operations are involved in generating a few results and if it can be assumed that the individual errors are approximately symmetrically distributed over the error range. In this case, positive errors should tend to offset negative errors as the computation proceeds. From a statistical standpoint, we might then expect the results to have a high probability of being very accurate.

The third truncation method is a *rounding* procedure. It achieves the closest approximation to the number being truncated and is an unbiased technique. The procedure is as follows. A 1 is added to the LSB position of the bits to be retained if there is a 1 in the MSB position of the bits being removed. Thus, $0.b_{-1}b_{-2}b_{-3}1\cdots$ rounds to $0.b_{-1}b_{-2}b_{-3} + 0.001$, and $0.b_{-1}b_{-2}b_{-3}0\cdots$ rounds to $0.b_{-1}b_{-2}b_{-3}$. This provides the desired approximation, except for the case where the bits to be removed are $10\cdots0$. This case is a tie situation: The longer value is halfway between the two closest truncated representations. In order to break the tie in an unbiased way, one possibility is to choose the retained bits to be the nearest even number. In terms of our 6-bit example, the value $0.b_{-1}b_{-2}0100$ is truncated to the value $0.b_{-1}b_{-2}0$, and $0.b_{-1}b_{-2}1100$ is truncated to $0.b_{-1}b_{-2}1 + 0.001$. The descriptive phrase "round to the nearest number, or nearest even number in case of a tie" is sometimes used to refer to this truncation technique. The error range is approximately $-\frac{1}{2}$ to $+\frac{1}{2}$ in the LSB position of the retained bits. Clearly, this is the best method. However, it is also the most costly to implement, because it requires an addition operation and a possible renormalization. This rounding technique is used in the IEEE floating-point standard that is described in Section 7.10.4.

This discussion of errors that are introduced when guard bits are removed by truncation has treated the case of a single truncation operation. When a long series of calculations involving floating-point numbers is performed, the analysis that determines error ranges or bounds for the final results can be quite a complicated study. We will not dwell further on this aspect of numerical computation.

7.10.3 Implementation of Floating-Point Operations

The provision of floating-point arithmetic in both large and small computers is a tremendous convenience for many users. Aside from any consideration of the expanded range of values, the flexibility in location of the binary point is an important aspect. The user (programmer) does not need to worry about manipulating scale factors, aligning binary points, and so on. Fractions and mixed numbers can be used as easily as integers at the programming level.

The hardware implementation of floating-point operations involves considerable circuitry. These operations may also be implemented by software routines. In either case, provision must be made for input and output conversion to and from the user's decimal representation of numbers. In many computers, floating-point operations are available at the basic machine instruction level. Hardware implementations range from serial through highly parallel forms, analogous to the range of hardware multipliers discussed earlier.

As an example of the implementation of floating-point operations, let us consider the block diagram for a hardware implementation of addition and subtraction on 32-bit floating-point operands that have the format shown in Figure 7.23c. Let the signs, exponents, and mantissas of operands A and B be represented by S_A, E_A, M_A and S_B, E_B, M_B, respectively. Following the ADD/SUBTRACT rule given in Section 7.10.1, we see that the first step is to compare exponents to determine how far to shift the mantissa of the number with the smaller exponent. This shift-count value, n, is determined by the 7-bit subtractor circuit in the upper left corner of Figure 7.24. The magnitude of the difference $E_A - E_B$, which is n, is sent to the SHIFTER unit. The range of n is restricted to 0, 1, . . . , 7, where $n = 7$ if $|E_A - E_B| \geq 7$; otherwise, $n = |E_A - E_B|$. If $n = 7$, it is possible to determine the result immediately as being equal to the larger operand (or its negative). However, this option is not explicitly shown in Figure 7.24. The sign of the difference resulting from the exponent comparison

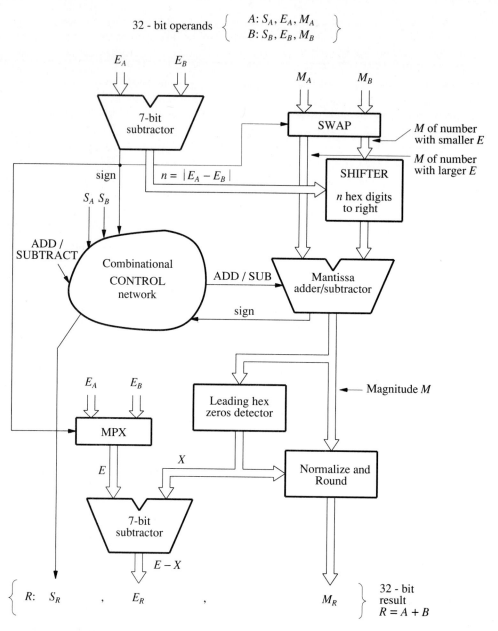

FIGURE 7.24
Floating-point addition-subtraction unit.

determines which mantissa is to be shifted. Therefore, the sign is sent to the SWAP network in the upper right corner of this figure. If the sign is 0, then $E_A \geq E_B$, and the mantissas M_A and M_B are sent straight through the SWAP network. This results in M_B being sent to the SHIFTER, to be shifted n hex positions to the right. The other mantissa, M_A, is sent directly to the mantissa adder-subtractor. If the sign is 1, then $E_A < E_B$, and the mantissas are swapped before being sent to the SHIFTER.

Step 2 is performed by the two-way multiplexer, MPX, in the bottom left corner of the figure. The exponent of the result, E, is tentatively determined as E_A if $E_A \geq E_B$, or E_B if $E_A < E_B$. This is determined by the sign of the difference resulting from the exponent comparison operation in step 1.

Step 3 involves the major component, the mantissa adder-subtractor in the middle of the figure. The CONTROL logic determines whether the mantissas are to be added or subtracted. This is decided by the signs of the operands (S_A and S_B) and the operation (Add or Subtract) that is to be performed on the operands. The CONTROL logic also determines the sign of the result, S_R. For example, if A is negative ($S_A = 1$), B is positive ($S_B = 0$), and the operation is $A - B$, then the mantissas are subtracted. The sign of the result S_R now depends on the mantissa subtraction operation. For instance, if $E_A > E_B$, then $M_A -$ (shifted M_B) will be positive and the result will be positive. But if $E_B > E_A$, then $M_B -$ (shifted M_A) will be positive and the result will be negative. This example shows that the sign from the exponent comparison is also required as an input to the CONTROL network. When $E_A = E_B$ and the mantissas are subtracted, the sign of the mantissa adder-subtractor output is crucial in determining the sign of the result. The reader should now be able to construct the complete truth table for the CONTROL network.

Step 4 of the ADD/SUBTRACT rule is the normalization of the result mantissa M produced by step 3. The number of leading zeros in M determines the number X of hex digit shifts to be applied to M. Then, the normalized value is truncated to generate the 24-bit mantissa, M_R, of the result. The value X is also subtracted from the tentative result exponent E to generate the true result exponent, E_R. We should note that it is possible that a single hex digit right shift might be needed to normalize the result. This would be the case if two mantissas of the form $0.1xx \ldots$ are added. The vector M would then have the form $1.xxx \ldots$. This would correspond to an X value of -1 in the figure.

We have not given any details on the guard bits that need to be carried along with intermediate mantissa values. In general, only a few bits are needed, depending on the truncation technique used to generate the 24-bit normalized mantissa of the result.

A few comments are in order about the actual hardware that might be used to implement the blocks in Figure 7.24. The two 7-bit subtractors and the mantissa adder-subtractor can be implemented by combinational logic as discussed earlier in this chapter. Because their outputs must be in sign-and-magnitude form, some modifications to our earlier discussions need to be made—a combination of 1's-complement arithmetic and sign-and-magnitude representation is often used. There is considerable flexibility in the implementation of the SHIFTER and the output normalization operation. To make these parts inexpensive, they should be constructed as shift registers. However, if speed of execution is important, they can be built in a more combinational manner. Figure 7.24 is organized along the lines of part of the floating-point hardware used in some IBM computers.

A modern approach is to implement floating-point operations in a VLSI chip that can be used as a peripheral device with general-purpose processors. Several such chips are commercially available. Typical examples are the Intel 8231[1] and the AMD 9511.[2] As well as performing the four basic floating-point operations of add, subtract, multiply, and divide, they are capable of computing square roots and trigonometric, logarithmic, and exponential functions. Both of these chips use a 32-bit, floating-point format with a 24-bit, binary-normalized mantissa. A processor usually communicates with these chips through a parallel I/O port. A string of bytes consisting of operands and an encoded operation are sent to the arithmetic chip. The processor either enters a polling loop or awaits an interrupt until the chip completes the operation. A string of bytes encoding the result is then returned to the processor or the main memory.

One of the best-known floating-point chips is Intel's 8087.[3] It is intended for use with the Intel 8086 microprocessor. It does not operate as a peripheral device, as is the case with the two chips just described; rather, the 8087 is closely synchronized with the 8086 CPU chip. It executes the floating-point instructions directly as they are fetched from the main memory and is referred to as a *coprocessor*. It has a register file for operands and the required arithmetic circuitry. The data formats used in the 8087 conform to the IEEE standard that will be discussed in Section 7.10.4. The 8087 evaluates trigonometric, logarithmic, and exponential functions, as well as performing the four basic floating-point operations.

7.10.4   The IEEE Floating-Point Standard

The IEEE Computer Society has developed a standard for binary floating-point arithmetic.[4] The main motivation for such a standard was an interest in facilitating the portability of numerically oriented programs from one computer system to another and encouraging the development of high-quality numerical software.

The standard consists of three aspects: the format of the data types, the arithmetic operations, and exception handling for errors (overflow/underflow, divide by 0, etc.). We will only discuss the first of these in detail.

The basic format sizes are 32 bits (single precision) and 64 bits (double precision). These sizes are easily addressable in 8-, 16-, or 32-bit computers. The main criterion used in formulating the 32-bit, single-precision format was to maximize precision (significant bits) in the mantissa while maintaining a sufficiently large range (determined by the number of bits in the exponent). This leads to a choice of binary normalization (as opposed to octal or hexadecimal) for the mantissa and an implied base of 2 for the exponent. In order to provide as many bits as possible for the mantissa, the exponent must be kept as small as possible. A field of 8 bits is assigned to the exponent. The complete format is shown in Figure 7.25a. The exponent, denoted as E' in the figure, is represented in the excess-127 representation. The end values of E', namely 0 and 255, are used to indicate special values such as exact 0 and infinity. Thus, the range of E' for normal values is $0 < E' < 255$. This means that

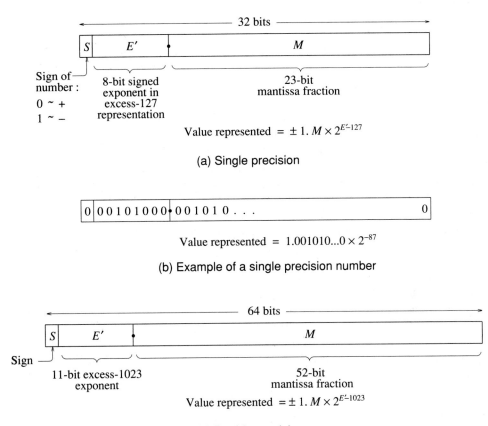

Value represented $= \pm 1. M \times 2^{E'-127}$

(a) Single precision

Value represented $= 1.001010...0 \times 2^{-87}$

(b) Example of a single precision number

Value represented $= \pm 1. M \times 2^{E'-1023}$

(c) Double precision

FIGURE 7.25
IEEE standard floating-point formats.

the actual exponent E is in the range $-126 \leq E \leq 127$. Since binary normalization is used, the most significant bit of the mantissa is always equal to 1. This bit is not explicitly represented; it is assumed to be to the immediate left of the binary point. The 23 bits stored in the M field represent the fractional part of the mantissa, that is, the bits to the right of the binary point. An example of a single-precision floating-point number is shown in Figure 7.25b.

If we compare the single-precision format of the IEEE standard to the format given earlier in Figure 7.23c, we observe that both formats use 24 bits of significance. Note that the bit position saved by using the previously described implicit mantissa bit has been added to the exponent field in the standard. The scale factor in the standard has the range 2^{-126} to 2^{+127} (approximately $10^{\pm 38}$). This should be compared to the larger scale factor range of 16^{-64} to 16^{63} (approximately $10^{\pm 76}$) of the earlier format. On the other hand, the standard provides more precision because it uses binary normalization.

The double-precision format has increased exponent and mantissa ranges. This 64-bit format is shown in Figure 7.25c. The excess-1023 exponent E' is in the range $0 < E' < 2047$ for normal values, with 0 and 2047 being used to indicate special values, as before. Thus, the actual exponent E is in the range $-1022 \leq E \leq 1023$, providing scale factors of 2^{-1022} to 2^{1023} (approximately $10^{\pm 308}$).

An implementation must provide at least single precision to conform to the standard. The provision of double precision is optional. The standard also specifies certain optional extended forms of both of these formats. The extended formats are intended to provide increased precision and increased exponent range in the representation of intermediate values in a sequence of calculations. For example, the dot product of two vectors of numbers can be computed by accumulating the sum of products in extended precision. The inputs are given in a standard precision (single or double), and the answer is truncated to the same precision. The use of extended formats helps to reduce the size of the accumulated round-off error in a sequence of calculations. The accuracy of evaluation of elementary functions (sin, cos, etc.) is also enhanced by use of the extended formats.

In addition to the four basic arithmetic operations, the standard requires that the operations of remainder, square root, and conversion between binary and decimal representations be provided. Results of single operations must be computed to be accurate within half a unit in the LSB position. In general, this requires that rounding be used as the truncation method, as described in Section 7.10.2. The implementation of this rounding scheme requires only three guard bits to be carried along during the intermediate steps in performing the above operations. The first two of these bits are the two most significant bits of the section of the mantissa to be removed. The third bit is the logical OR of all bits beyond the above mentioned two bits in the full representation of the mantissa. This bit is relatively easy to maintain during the intermediate steps of the operations to be performed. It should be initialized to 0. If a 1 is shifted through this position, the bit becomes 1 and retains that value. Hence, it is usually called the *sticky bit*.

A few brief comments on exceptions will complete our discussion. The standard specifies the action to be taken when operations produce results that fall outside the range of normalized floating-point numbers. In general, these exceptions should cause a trap (software interrupt) whose action is under user control. Five exceptions are to be detected: invalid operation, division by 0, overflow, underflow, and inexact. A simple example of an invalid operation is an attempt to take the square root of a negative number. A division by 0 exception is signaled when the divisor is 0 and the numerator is a finite, nonzero number. The result is infinity, which has a representation as mentioned earlier. The handling of overflow and underflow exceptions, and the results produced, are also given in the standard; it is beyond the scope of this discussion to give the details. One interesting aspect of the standard in this area is that it defines a class of *denormalized* numbers: nonzero numbers whose magnitude is smaller than the magnitude of the smallest normalized number. These numbers may be used to handle underflow. Finally, an inexact exception is signaled if the rounded result of an operation is not exact.

7.11 CONCLUDING REMARKS

There is a great deal known about computer arithmetic. This subject is the source of a number of interesting logic design problems. The main theme in this chapter has been to discuss some of the design techniques that have proven useful in the design of binary arithmetic units. Carry lookahead techniques were discussed as the major idea involved in high-performance adder design. In the design of fast multipliers, the method of bit pairing in the multiplier was shown to lead to a reduction of the number of summands that must be added to generate the product.

The floating-point number representation system was described, including a set of rules for performing the four standard operations. To provide an appreciation for the circuit complexity required in such an implementation, we sketched the block diagram of an addition-subtraction unit. Finally, the IEEE floating-point standard was outlined. The adoption of this standard by manufacturers has greatly enhanced the portability and quality of numerical software.

7.12 PROBLEMS

7.1. Represent the decimal values 26, -37, 497, and -123 as signed, 10-bit numbers in the following binary formats:
(*a*) sign-and-magnitude
(*b*) 1's-complement
(*c*) 2's-complement
(See Appendix D for decimal-to-binary integer conversion.)

7.2. Binary fractions were discussed briefly in Section 7.10.
(*a*) Express the decimal values 0.5, -0.123, -0.75, and -0.1 as signed 6-bit numbers in the binary formats of Problem 7.1. (See Appendix D for decimal-to-binary fraction conversion.)
(*b*) What is the maximum representation error e involved in using only 5 significant bits after the binary point?
(*c*) Calculate the number of bits needed after the binary point so that (1) $e < 1/10$; (2) $e < 1/100$; (3) $e < 1/1000$; and (4) $e < 1/10^6$.

7.3. The 1's-complement and 2's-complement binary representation methods are special cases of the $(b-1)$'s-complement and b's-complement representation techniques in base b number systems. For example, consider the decimal system. The sign-and-magnitude values $+527$, $+3219$, -382, and -1999 have four-digit signed-number representations in each of the complement systems as shown in Table P7.1. The 9's-complement is formed by taking the complement of each digit position with respect to 9. The 10's-complement is formed by adding 1 to the 9's-complement. In each of the latter two representations, the leftmost digit is < 5 for a positive number and ≥ 5 for a negative number.

Now consider the base 3 (ternary) system, where the unsigned five-digit number $t_4 t_3 t_2 t_1 t_0$ has the value $t_4 \times 3^4 + t_3 \times 3^3 + t_2 \times 3^2 + t_1 \times 3^1 + t_0 \times 3^0$, with $0 \leq t_i \leq 2$. Express the ternary sign-and-magnitude numbers $+11011$, -10222, $+2120$, -1212, $+10$, and -201 as five-digit, signed, ternary numbers in the 3's-complement system. Note that the largest positive number representable in this system is 11111.

TABLE P7.1 Signed numbers in base 10.

Representation	Examples			
Sign and magnitude	+0527	−0382	+3219	−1999
9's complement	0527	9617	3219	8000
10's complement	0527	9618	3219	8001

7.4. Represent each of the decimal values 26, −37, 222, and −123 as signed 6-digit numbers in the following ternary formats:
(a) sign-and-magnitude
(b) 3's-complement
See Problem 7.3 for a definition of the ternary number system and use a technique analogous to that given in Appendix D for decimal-to-ternary integer conversion.

7.5. Consider the binary numbers in the following addition and subtraction problems to be signed 6-bit values in the 2's-complement representation. Perform the operations indicated, specify whether overflow occurs, and check your answers by converting operands and results to decimal sign-and-magnitude representation.

$$
\begin{array}{ccc}
010110 & 101011 & 111111 \\
+001001 & +100101 & +000111 \\
\hline
\end{array}
$$

$$
\begin{array}{ccc}
011001 & 110111 & 010101 \\
+010000 & +111001 & +101011 \\
\hline
\end{array}
$$

$$
\begin{array}{ccc}
010110 & 111110 & 100001 \\
-011111 & -100101 & -011101 \\
\hline
\end{array}
$$

$$
\begin{array}{ccc}
111111 & 000111 & 011010 \\
-000111 & -111000 & -100010 \\
\hline
\end{array}
$$

7.6. Using "paper-and-pencil" methods, perform the operations $A \times B$ and $A \div B$ on the 5-bit unsigned numbers $A = 10101$ and $B = 00101$.

7.7. Show how the multiplication and division operations in Problem 7.6 would be performed by the hardware in Figures 7.9a and 7.20, respectively, by constructing the equivalent of Figures 7.9b and 7.22.

7.8. Multiply each of the following pairs of signed 2's-complement numbers using the Booth algorithm. In each case, assume that A is the multiplicand and B is the multiplier.
(a) $A = 010111$
    $B = 110110$
(b) $A = 110011$
    $B = 101100$
(c) $A = 110101$
    $B = 011011$

(d) $A = 1111$
 $B = 1111$

7.9. Repeat Problem 7.8 using bit-pairing of the multipliers.

7.10. Derive logic equations that specify the ADD/SUB and S_R outputs of the combinational CONTROL network in Figure 7.24.

7.11. Show a microroutine that can implement the MUL (Multiply) instruction defined in Appendix B. Assume that the basic structure of Figure 5.2 and eight general-purpose registers are used. What other hardware, if any, would be useful to have?

7.12. Write either a PDP-11 or 68000 program for integer division based on the non-restoring division algorithm. Assume that both operands are positive; that is, the leftmost bit is zero for both the dividend and the divisor. Do not use the Divide instruction that is available in either machine.

7.13. In Section 7.10.1, we used a practical-size 32-bit format for floating-point numbers. In this problem we will use a shortened format that retains all the pertinent concepts but is manageable for working through numerical exercises. Consider that floating-point numbers are represented in a 12-bit format as shown in Figure P7.1. The scale factor has an implied base of 4 and a 5-bit, excess-16 exponent. The 6-bit mantissa is normalized.

(a) What does "normalized" mean in the context of this format?

(b) Represent the numbers $+1.7$, -0.012, $+19$, and $\frac{1}{8}$ in this format.

(c) What are the smallest and largest numbers representable in this format?

(d) How does the range calculated in (c) compare to the ranges of a 12-bit signed integer and a 12-bit signed fraction?

(e) Perform Add, Subtract, Multiply, and Divide operations on the operands

$$A = \boxed{0}\,\boxed{1\,0\,0\,0\,1}\,\boxed{0\,1\,1\,0\,1\,1}$$

$$B = \boxed{1}\,\boxed{0\,1\,1\,1\,1}\,\boxed{1\,0\,1\,0\,1\,0}$$

7.14. The IBM 370 32-bit floating-point format is described in Section 7.10.

(a) Represent the following decimal numbers in this format.

(1)	0	(6)	3.92×10^2
(2)	-1	(7)	-0.000125
(3)	0.5	(8)	500
(4)	10	(9)	-1.0×10^5
(5)	4096	(10)	1.1×10^{-4}

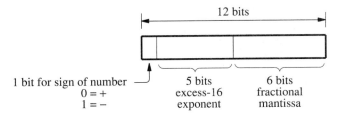

FIGURE P7.1
Floating-point format.

(b) What problems do you encounter when trying to convert the following decimal numbers into this format?

(1) 7.1239×10^{51}
(2) -1.4325×10^{-27}

(c) Propose some solution to the problem encountered in part (b). Your solution should be programmable on a machine that has the four arithmetic operations on the 32-bit internal format that you must use. You may also use the machine's 32-bit integer facilities if it helps your conversion.

7.15. Consider the representation of the decimal number 0.1 as a signed, 8-bit, binary fraction in the representation discussed at the beginning of Section 7.10. If the number does not convert exactly into this 8-bit format, give the approximations to it that are developed by all three of the truncation methods discussed in Section 7.10.2.

7.16. Write a PDP-11 or 68000 program to transform a 16-bit positive binary number into a five-digit decimal number in which each digit of the number is coded in the binary-coded decimal (BCD) code. These BCD digit codes are to occupy the low-order 4 bits of five successive byte locations in the main memory. Use the conversion technique based on successive division by 10. This method is analogous to successive division by 2 when converting decimal-to-binary as discussed in Appendix D. Consult Appendix B or C for the format and operation of the Divide instruction.

7.17. A modulo 10 adder must be built for adding BCD digits. Modulo 10 addition of two BCD digits $A = A_3A_2A_1A_0$ and $B = B_3B_2B_1B_0$ can be achieved as follows. Add A to B (binary addition). Then, if the result is an illegal code that is greater than or equal to 10_{10}, add 6_{10}. (Ignore overflow from this addition.)
(a) When is the output carry equal to 1?
(b) Show that the above algorithm will give correct results for

(1) $A = 0101$ $B = 0110$
(2) $A = 0011$ $B = 0100$

(c) Design a BCD digit adder using logic gates and a 4-bit version of the binary adder of Figure 7.7. The inputs are $A_3A_2A_1A_0$, $B_3B_2B_1B_0$, and a carry-in. The outputs are the sum digit $S_3S_2S_1S_0$ and the carry-out. A cascade of such blocks can form a ripple-carry BCD adder.

7.18. If gate fan-in is limited to four, how can the hex digit SHIFTER in Figure 7.24 be implemented combinationally?

7.19. (a) Sketch a logic-gate network that implements the multiplexer MPX in Figure 7.24.
(b) Relate the structure of the SWAP network in Figure 7.24 to your solution to part (a).

7.20. How can the "leading hex zeros detector" of Figure 7.24 be implemented combinationally?

7.21. The mantissa adder-subtractor in Figure 7.24 operates on positive, unsigned binary fractions and must produce a sign-and-magnitude result. In the discussion accompanying Figure 7.24, we stated that 1's-complement arithmetic is convenient because of the required format for input and output operands. When adding two signed numbers in 1's-complement notation, the carry-out from the sign position must be added to the result to obtain the correct signed answer. This is called "end-around carry" correction. Consider the two examples in Figure P7.2, which illustrate addition using signed, 4-bit encodings of operands and results in the 1's-complement system.

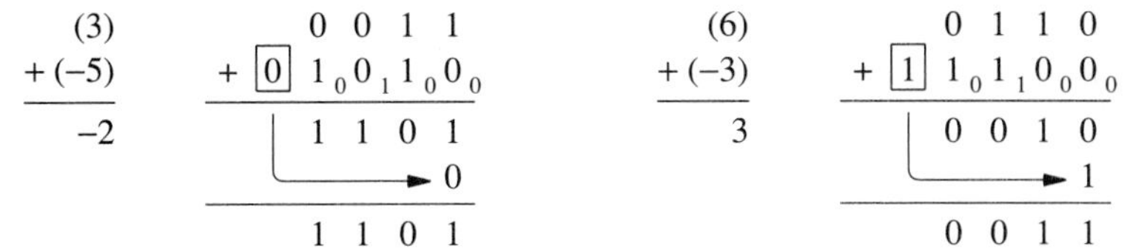

$$
\begin{array}{rl}
(3) & \quad 0\ 0\ 1\ 1 \\
+(-5) & \quad +\ \boxed{0}\ 1\ {}_0 0\ {}_1 1\ {}_0 0\ {}_0 \\
\hline
-2 & \quad \ \ 1\ 1\ 0\ 1 \\
& \quad \ \ \rule{0pt}{0pt} \to 0 \\
\hline
& \quad 1\ 1\ 0\ 1
\end{array}
\qquad
\begin{array}{rl}
(6) & \quad 0\ 1\ 1\ 0 \\
+(-3) & \quad +\ \boxed{1}\ 1\ {}_0 0\ {}_1 1\ {}_0 0\ {}_0 \\
\hline
3 & \quad \ \ 0\ 0\ 1\ 0 \\
& \quad \ \ \rule{0pt}{0pt} \to 1 \\
\hline
& \quad 0\ 0\ 1\ 1
\end{array}
$$

FIGURE P7.2
1's-complement addition.

The 1's-complement arithmetic system is convenient when a sign-and-magnitude result is to be generated, because a negative number in 1's-complement notation can be converted to sign and magnitude by complementing the bits to the right of the sign-bit position. Using 2's-complement arithmetic, addition of $+1$ is needed for conversion of a negative value into sign-and-magnitude notation. If a carry lookahead adder is used, it is possible to incorporate the end-around carry operation required by 1's-complement arithmetic into the lookahead logic. With the above discussion as a guideline, give the complete design of the 1's-complement adder-subtractor required in Figure 7.24.

7.22. Give a complete design for the adder shown in Figure 7.7 for $n = 4$. Carry lookahead logic is to be used for all the internal carries c_1, c_2, and c_3 as well as for the block output c_4. Your answer can be in the form of a sketch of the logic-gate network required or a listing of logic equations that describe the network.

7.23. Four of the 4-bit adder circuits shown in Figure 7.7 can be cascaded to form a 16-bit adder. In this cascade, the output c_4 from the low-order circuit is connected as the carry-in to the next circuit. Its carry-out, c_8, is connected as the carry-in to the third circuit, and so on.

(a) A faster adder can be constructed by using external logic to generate the carry-in variables for the three high-order circuits. Give the logic design for a carry lookahead circuit that has outputs c_4, c_8, and c_{12}. Its inputs are c_0, P_0^I, G_0^I, P_1^I, G_1^I, P_2^I, and G_2^I. Assume that the network in Figure 7.7 produces the variables P^I and G^I. Estimate the increase in adder speed achievable by using this circuit in conjunction with the four 4-bit adder circuits—as opposed to using a cascade of the adder circuits—in building a 16-bit adder.

(b) Extend your design by assuming that the carry lookahead chip has P_3^I and G_3^I as additional inputs and that it provides additional outputs P_0^{II} and G_0^{II}. These higher-level propagate-and-generate functions are defined by

$$
P_0^{II} = P_3^I P_2^I P_1^I P_0^I
$$

$$
G_0^{II} = G_3^I + P_3^I G_2^I + P_3^I P_2^I G_1^I + P_3^I P_2^I P_1^I G_0^I
$$

(c) Design a 64-bit adder that uses sixteen 4-bit adder circuits, carry lookahead circuits as defined in part (b), and additional logic to generate c_{16}, c_{32}, and c_{48} from c_0 and the P_i^{II} and G_i^{II} variables. What is the relationship of the additional logic to the logic inside each lookahead circuit?

7.24. Figure P7.3 shows a two-dimensional array of combinational logic cells for 3×3 positive-number multiplication. This cellular logic arrangement is the basis for some of the VLSI multiplier chips that are commercially available. Analyze these cells and the data flow to verify that the circuit computes the product correctly.

(a) Compare the total delay in developing the product in this type of array with that of Figure 7.8 as a function of the input operand length n.

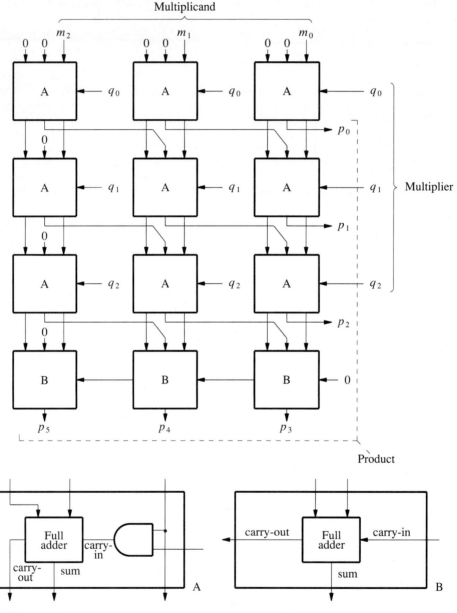

FIGURE P7.3
Array multiplier.

(b) Which of the cells in Figure P7.3 and its $n \times (n + 1)$ extension perform no useful function?

7.25. The array described in Problem 7.24 is an example of the application of the principle of *carry-save addition*. This principle can be applied in any situation in which a number of summands need to be added. The simplest example is the case of adding three numbers

W, X, and Y. The straightforward way to do this is to add W to X and then add the resulting sum to Y to generate the answer. An alternative method, using carry-save addition, combines the three operands with n full adders to generate two numbers, S (sum bits) and C (carry bits), which are then added in a ripple-carry adder to generate the desired sum. This process is shown in Figure P7.4.

(a) Apply this idea to the multiplication of two n-bit positive numbers. Start by considering the problem as one of adding n summands, appropriately shifted, as in the paper-and-pencil method. Reduce these n summands to $\frac{2}{3}n$ numbers by performing carry-save additions on them in parallel groups of three. Then reduce the results until only two numbers remain. These are finally added to generate the desired product. This principle is used in many high-performance computers.

(b) Compare the speed and cost of this type of multiplier with that of Problem 7.24 or Figure 7.8.

(c) Can bit grouping of the multiplier be combined with carry-save addition to configure a faster and/or less expensive multiplier?

7.26. Write a PDP-11 or 68000 program to implement the Booth algorithm for signed-number multiplication.

7.27. Assume that four BCD digits, representing a decimal integer in the range 0 to 9999, are packed into the 16-bit word at main memory location DECIMAL. Write a PDP-11 or 68000 subroutine to convert the decimal integer stored at DECIMAL into binary representation and to store it in main memory location BINARY.

7.28. In the discussion in Section 7.10.4 of rounding in association with the IEEE floating-point standard, it was claimed that 3 guard bits are sufficient to implement rounding as defined in Section 7.10.2. Construct an example that shows that all 3 guard bits are needed to produce the correct answer. *Hint:* Consider the subtraction of two positive numbers.

7.29. Repeat Problem 7.14 for the IEEE standard single-precision floating-point format.

7.30. Consider a 16-bit floating-point number in a format similar to that shown in Figure P7.1 with a 6-bit exponent and a 9-bit normalized fractional mantissa. The base of the scale factor is 8 and the exponent is represented in excess-32 format.

(a) Add the numbers

$$A = 0 \quad 100001 \quad 111111110$$

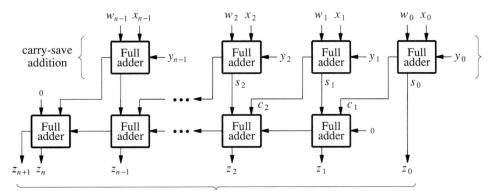

$$Z = W + X + Y$$

FIGURE P7.4
Carry-save addition principle.

and

$$B = 0 \quad 011111 \quad 101010101$$

which are expressed in the preceding format, giving the answer in normalized form. Use rounding when producing the final normalized 9-bit mantissa.

(b) Using decimal numbers w, x, y, and z, express the magnitude of the largest and smallest (nonzero) values representable in the preceding normalized floating-point format, in the form

$$\text{Largest} = w \times 8^x$$

$$\text{Smallest} = y \times 8^{-z}$$

7.31. Show how to modify the circuit diagram of Figure 7.9 to implement multiplication of signed, 2's-complement, n-bit numbers using the Booth algorithm.

7.32. Which of the four 6-bit answers to Problem 7.2(a) are not exact? For each of these cases, give the three 6-bit values that correspond to the three types of truncation defined in Section 7.10.2.

7.33. Write a PDP-11 program for the multiplication of two 16-bit unsigned numbers that is patterned after the technique used in Figure 7.9. Assume that the multiplier and multiplicand are in registers R_2 and R_3, respectively. The product is to be developed in registers R_1 (high-order half) and R_2 (low-order half). *Hint:* Use a combination of shift and rotate operations for a double-register shift.

7.34. Write a 68000 program for the multiplication of two 16-bit unsigned numbers located in the lower halves of two 32-bit data registers. The 32-bit product is to be developed in one data register. Do not use the machine's Multiply instruction. Use combinations of Shift and Add instructions.

7.35. If the product of two n-bit signed numbers in the 2's-complement representation can be represented in n bits, the paper-and-pencil algorithm shown in Figure 7.8a can be used directly, treating the sign bits the same as the other bits. Try this on the 4-bit signed numbers

$$A = 1110 \quad \text{(multiplicand)}$$

and

$$B = 1101 \quad \text{(multiplier)}$$

and

$$C = 0010$$

and

$$D = 1110$$

Why does this work correctly?

7.13 REFERENCES

1. "The Intel 8231 Arithmetic Processing Unit," Intel Corporation, Santa Clara, CA, January 1980.
2. "The Advanced Micro Devices Am9511 Floating-Point Processor," Advanced Micro Devices, Inc., Sunnyvale, CA, 1979.
3. "The Intel 8087 Numeric Data Processor," Intel Corporation, Santa Clara, CA, May 1980.
4. A Proposed Standard for Floating-Point Arithmetic, *Computer*, 14, no. 3: 51–62, March 1981.

CHAPTER
8

THE MAIN MEMORY

Programs and the data they operate on are held in the main memory (MM) of the computer during execution. In this chapter, we will discuss the way in which this vital part of the computer operates. By now, the reader appreciates the fact that the execution speed of instructions is highly dependent upon the speed with which data can be transferred to or from the MM. Thus it is not surprising that memory design is an important topic in computer development.

In most modern computer systems, the physical MM is not as large as the address space spanned by an address issued by the processor. When a program does not totally fit into the MM, the parts of it not currently being executed are stored on secondary storage devices such as magnetic disks. Of course, all parts of a program that are eventually executed are first brought into the MM. When a new segment of a program is to be moved into a full MM, it must replace another segment already in the MM. Modern computers can manage such operations automatically, so that the programmer need not be concerned with their details. These memory management techniques will be discussed in this chapter.

8.1 SOME BASIC CONCEPTS

The maximum size of the MM that can be used in any computer is determined by the addressing scheme. For example, a 16-bit computer that generates 16-bit addresses is capable of addressing up to 2^{16} (64K) memory locations. Similarly, a machine whose instructions generate 32-bit addresses can utilize an MM that contains up to 2^{32} (4G) memory locations. This number represents the size of the address space of the computer.

In some computers, the smallest addressable unit of information is a memory word. Memory addresses refer to successive memory words, and the machine is called *word-addressable*. Alternatively, individual memory bytes may be assigned distinct addresses, yielding a *byte-addressable* computer. In such a case, a memory word contains one or more memory bytes that can be addressed individually. For example, in a byte-addressable 32-bit computer, each memory word contains 4 bytes. Figure 8.1 shows possible address assignment in this case. The address of a word is that of its high-order byte; thus, word addresses are always integer multiples of 4. It should be noted that in some machines, including the PDP-11, byte-address assignment within a word is opposite to that shown in Figure 8.1 (see Figure 2.7).

The MM is usually designed to store and retrieve data in word-length quantities. In fact, the number of bits actually stored or retrieved in one MM access is the most common definition of the word length of a computer. Consider, for example, a byte-addressable computer with the addressing structure of Figure 8.1, whose instructions generate 32-bit addresses. When a 32-bit address is sent from the CPU to the MM unit, the high-order 30 bits determine which word will be accessed. If a byte quantity is specified, the low-order 2 bits of the address specify which byte location is involved. In the case of a Read operation, other bytes may be fetched from the MM, but they are ignored by the CPU. If the byte operation is a Write, however, the control circuitry of the MM must ensure that the contents of other bytes of the same word are not changed.

From the system standpoint, we can view the MM unit as a "black box." Data transfer between the MM and the CPU takes place through the use of two CPU registers, usually called MAR (memory address register) and MDR (memory data register). If MAR is k bits long and MDR is n bits long, then the MM unit may contain up to 2^k addressable locations. During a "memory cycle," n bits of data are transferred between the MM and the CPU. This transfer takes place over the *processor bus*, which has k address lines and n data lines. The bus also includes the control lines Read, Write, and Memory Function Completed (MFC) for coordinating data transfers. In the case of byte-addressable computers, another control line may be added to indicate when only a byte, rather than a full word of n bits, is to be transferred. The connection between the CPU and the MM is shown schematically in Figure 8.2. As Chapter 4 describes, the CPU initiates a memory operation by loading the appropriate data into registers MDR and MAR, then setting either the Read or Write memory control line to 1. When the required operation is completed, the memory control circuitry indicates this to the CPU by setting MFC to 1. The details of bus operation were presented in Chapter 6.

A useful measure of the speed of memory units is the time that elapses between the initiation of an operation and the completion of that operation (for example, the time between Read and MFC). This is referred to as the *memory access time*. Another

Word address	Byte address			
0	0	1	2	3
4	4	5	6	7
8	8	9	10	11

FIGURE 8.1

Organization of the main memory in a 32-bit byte-addressable computer.

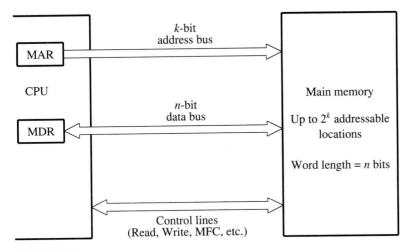

FIGURE 8.2
Connection of the main memory to the CPU.

important measure is the *memory cycle time*, which is the minimum time delay required between the initiation of two successive memory operations (for example, the time between two successive Read operations). The cycle time is usually slightly longer than the access time, depending upon the implementation details of the memory unit.

Recall that a memory unit is called a *random-access memory* (RAM) if any location can be accessed for a Read or Write operation in some fixed amount of time that is independent of the location's address. Main memory units are of this type. This distinguishes them from serial, or partly serial, access storage devices such as magnetic tapes and disks, which will be discussed in Chapter 9. Access time on the latter devices depends upon the address or position of the data.

The basic technology for the implementation of main memories uses semiconductor integrated circuits. The sections that follow will present some basic facts about the internal structure and operation of such memories. We will then discuss some of the techniques used to increase the effective speed and size of the main memory.

The CPU of a computer can usually process instructions and data faster than they can be fetched from a compatibly priced main memory unit. The memory cycle time, then, is the bottleneck in the system. One way to reduce the memory access time is to use a *cache memory*. This is a small and fast memory that is inserted between the larger, slower main memory and the CPU. It holds the currently active segments of a program and its data. Another technique, called *memory interleaving*, divides the system into a number of memory modules and arranges addressing so that successive words in the address space are placed in different modules. If requests for memory access tend to involve consecutive addresses, as when executing straight-line program segments, then the accesses will be to different modules. Since parallel access to these modules is possible, the average rate of fetching words from the MM can be increased.

Virtual memory is another important concept related to memory organization. So far, we have assumed that the addresses generated by the CPU directly specify physical locations in the MM. This may not always be the case. For reasons that will become apparent later, data may be stored in physical memory locations that have addresses different from those specified by the program. The memory control circuitry translates the address specified by the program into an address that can be used to access the physical memory. In such a case, an address generated by the CPU is referred to as a *virtual* or *logical address*. The virtual address space is mapped onto the physical memory where data is actually stored. The mapping function is implemented by a special memory control circuit, often called the *memory management unit*. This mapping function may be changed during program execution according to system requirements.

Virtual memory can be used to increase the effective size of the MM. Data are addressed in a virtual address space that can be as large as the addressing capability of the CPU, but at any given time, only the active portion of this space is mapped onto locations in the physical main memory. The remaining virtual addresses are mapped onto the bulk storage devices used. As the active portion of the virtual address space changes during program execution, the memory management unit changes the mapping function and transfers data between the bulk storage and the main memory. Thus, during every memory cycle, an address-processing mechanism (hardware or software) determines whether the addressed information is in the physical MM unit. If it is, then the proper word is accessed and execution proceeds. If it is not, a contiguous block of words containing the desired word is transferred from the bulk storage to the MM, displacing some block that is currently inactive. Because of the time required for movement of blocks between bulk storage and the MM, there is a speed degradation in this type of a system. By judiciously choosing which block to replace in the MM, however, there may be reasonably long periods during which the probability is high that the words accessed by the CPU are in the physical MM unit.

This section has briefly introduced a number of organizational features of memory systems. These features have been developed to help provide a computer system with as large and as fast an MM component as can be afforded in relation to the overall cost of the system. We do not expect the reader to have grasped all the ideas or their implications. More detail will be given later. We have introduced these terms together to establish the notion that they are related, because a study of their interrelationships is as important as a detailed study of their individual features.

8.2 SEMICONDUCTOR RAM MEMORIES

Semiconductor memories are available in a wide range of speeds. Their cycle times range from a few hundred nanoseconds to a few tens of nanoseconds. When first introduced in the late 1960s, they were much more expensive than the magnetic-core memories they replaced. Because of the rapid advances in VLSI (very large scale integration) technology, however, the cost of semiconductor memories has dropped dramatically. As a result, they are now used almost exclusively in the implementation of main memories.

Semiconductor memories may be divided into bipolar and MOS (metal-oxide semiconductor) types. We will present a configuration for a storage cell in each of these technologies in the following sections, but we should note that these are by no means the only possibilities. The purpose of this discussion is to point out the major characteristics of semiconductor memories and their impact on the performance of the MM unit of a computer. We will start by introducing the way that a number of memory cells are organized inside a chip.

8.2.1 Internal Organization of Memory Chips

Memory cells are usually organized in the form of an array, in which each cell is capable of storing one bit of information. One such organization is shown in Figure 8.3. Each row of cells constitutes a memory word, and all cells of a row are connected to a common line referred to as the *word line*, which is driven by the address decoder on the chip. The cells in each column are connected to a Sense/Write circuit by two lines known as *bit lines*. The Sense/Write circuits are connected to the data input/output lines of the chip. During a Read operation, the Sense/Write circuits sense, or read, the information stored in the cells selected by a word line and transmit this information to the output data lines. During a Write operation, they receive input information and store it in the cells of the selected word.

Figure 8.3 shows a memory chip consisting of 16 words of 8 bits each, which is usually referred to as a 16×8 organization. The data input and the data output of

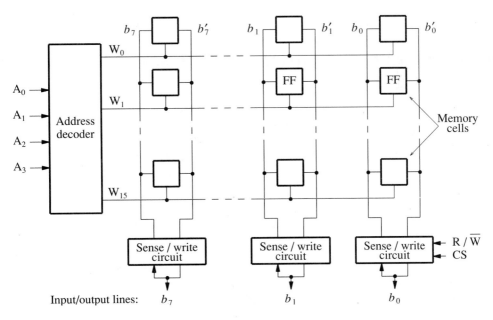

FIGURE 8.3
Organization of bit cells in a memory chip.

each Sense/Write circuit are connected to a single bidirectional data line in order to reduce the number of pins required. Two control lines, $R/\overline{W}$ and CS, are provided in addition to address and data lines. The $R/\overline{W}$ (Read/Write) input is used to specify the required operation, and the CS (Chip Select) input is needed to select a given chip in a multichip memory system. This will be discussed in Section 8.3.

The memory circuit of Figure 8.3 stores 128 bits and requires 14 external connections. Thus, it can be manufactured in the form of a 16-pin chip, allowing 2 pins for power supply and ground connections. We will now consider a slightly larger memory circuit, one that has 1K (1024) memory cells. This circuit can be organized as a 128×8 memory chip, requiring a total of 19 external connections. A 20-pin chip may be used, leaving 1 pin unused. Alternatively, the same number of cells can be organized into a $1K \times 1$ format. This makes it possible to use a 16-pin chip, even if separate pins are provided for the data input and data output lines. Figure 8.4 shows such an organization. The required 10-bit address is divided into two groups of 5 bits each to form the row and column addresses for the cell array. A row address selects a row of 32 cells, all of which are accessed in parallel. However, according to the column address, only one of these cells is connected to the external data lines by the input and output multiplexers.

We should note that commercially available chips contain a much larger number of memory cells than those shown in Figures 8.3 and 8.4. We have chosen to use small memory cell arrays as examples to make these figures simple and easy to understand. Larger arrays have essentially the same organization as that shown in Figure 8.4.

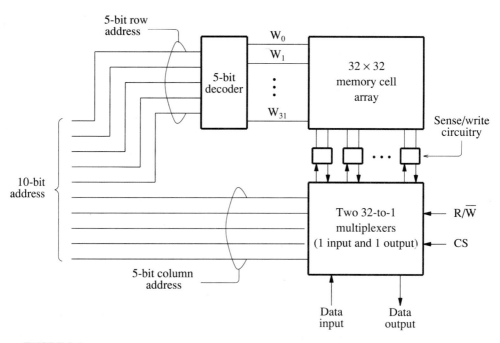

FIGURE 8.4
Organization of a $1K \times 1$ memory chip.

8.2.2 Bipolar Memory Cell

A typical bipolar storage cell is shown in Figure 8.5. Two transistor inverters (see Appendix A) are connected to implement a basic flip-flop. The cell is connected to one word line and two bit lines as shown. Normally, the bit lines are kept at about 1.6 V, and the word line is kept at a slightly higher voltage of about 2.5 V. Under these conditions, the two diodes D_1 and D_2 are reverse biased. Thus, because no current flows through the diodes, the cell is isolated from the bit lines.

READ OPERATION. Let us assume that a 1 is stored in the cell when Q_1 is conducting and Q_2 is off, and a 0 is stored when Q_2 is conducting and Q_1 is off. To read the contents of a given cell, the voltage on the corresponding word line is reduced from 2.5 V to approximately 0.3 V. This causes one of the diodes D_1 or D_2 to become forward-biased, depending on whether transistor Q_1 or Q_2 is conducting. As a result, current flows from bit line b when the cell is in the 1 state and from bit line b' when the cell is in the 0 state. The Sense/Write circuit at the end of each pair of bit lines monitors the current on lines b and b' and sets the output bit lines accordingly.

WRITE OPERATION. While a given row of bits is selected, that is, while the voltage on the corresponding word line is 0.3 V, the cells can be individually forced to either the 1 state by applying a positive voltage ($\approx$ 3 V) to line b' or to the 0 state by driving line b. This function is performed by the Sense/Write circuit.

8.2.3 MOS Memories

MOS technology is used extensively in MM units. Two important advantages of MOS devices, in comparison with bipolar devices, are the higher bit densities that they

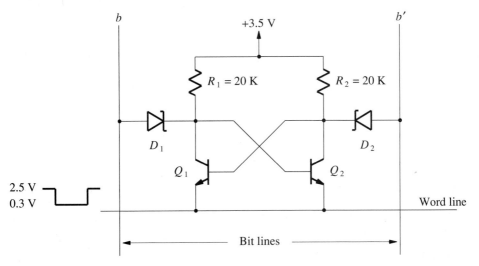

FIGURE 8.5
A bipolar memory cell.

allow on integrated circuit chips and their simpler manufacturing process. MOS transistors are also higher-impedance devices; they yield circuits that have lower power dissipation. Their disadvantage is their slower speed of operation.

As in the case of bipolar memories, many MOS cell configurations are possible. The simplest of these is the flip-flop circuit of Figure 8.6. Operation of the circuit is similar to its bipolar counterpart: transistors T_3 and T_4 perform the same function as resistors R_1 and R_2 in Figure 8.5, and transistors T_5 and T_6 correspond to diodes D_1 and D_2. These transistors act as switches that can be opened or closed under control of the word line. When these two switches are closed, the contents of the cell are transferred to the bit lines. As in the case of the bipolar memory, when a given cell is selected, its contents can be overwritten by applying appropriate voltages on the bit lines.

Both the bipolar cell in Figure 8.5 and its MOS counterpart in Figure 8.6 require continuous flow of current from the power supply through one of the branches of the flip-flop. If this current flow is maintained, both cells are capable of storing information indefinitely. Hence, they are referred to as *static memories*.

The high impedance attainable in MOS technology allows construction of a different type of memory known as *dynamic memory* (DRAM). A dynamic memory is based on simple cells that allow higher bit density and have lower power consumption relative to static configurations.

DYNAMIC MEMORIES. The basic idea of a dynamic memory is very simple. Information is stored in the form of a charge on a capacitor. If the capacitor discharges

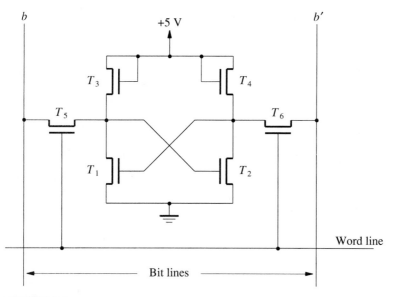

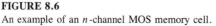

FIGURE 8.6
An example of an n-channel MOS memory cell.

very slowly, the stored information will be retained for some time. These memories are capable of storing information for only a few milliseconds. Each cell is usually required to store the information for a longer time, however, so its contents must be periodically refreshed by restoring the capacitor charge to its full value.

An example of a dynamic memory cell that consists of a capacitor C and a transistor T is shown in Figure 8.7. In order to store information in this cell, transistor T is turned on and an appropriate voltage is applied to the bit line. This causes a known amount of charge to be stored on the capacitor.

After the transistor is turned off, the capacitor begins to discharge. This is caused by the capacitor's own leakage resistance and by the fact that the transistor continues to conduct a small amount of current, measured in picoamperes, after it is turned off. Hence, the information stored in the cell can be retrieved correctly only if it is read before the charge on the capacitor drops below some threshold value. During a Read operation, the bit line is placed in a high-impedance state, and the transistor is turned on. A sense circuit connected to the bit line is used to determine whether the charge on the capacitor is above or below the threshold value. Because this charge is small, the Read operation is an intricate process whose details are beyond the scope of this text. However, we should note one important feature. During the process of reading the contents of the cell, the charge on the capacitor is restored to its original value. A memory cell is therefore refreshed every time its contents are read.

A typical organization of a 64K $\times$ 1 dynamic memory chip is shown in Figure 8.8. The cells are organized in the form of a square array such that the high- and low-order 8 bits of the 16-bit address constitute the row and column addresses of a cell, respectively. In order to reduce the number of pins needed for external connections, the row and column addresses are multiplexed on eight pins. During a Read or a Write operation, the row address is applied first. It is loaded into the row address latch in response to a signal pulse on the Row Address Strobe (RAS) input of the chip. Then, a Read operation is initiated in which all cells on the selected row are read and refreshed. Shortly after the row address is loaded, the column address is applied to the address pins and loaded into the column address latch under control of the Column Address Strobe (CAS) signal. The information in this latch is decoded and the appropriate Sense/Write circuit is selected. If the R/$\overline{\text{W}}$ control signal indicates a Read operation, the output of the selected circuit is transferred to the data output,

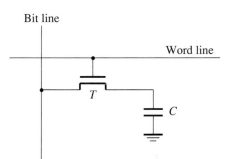

FIGURE 8.7
A single-transistor dynamic memory cell.

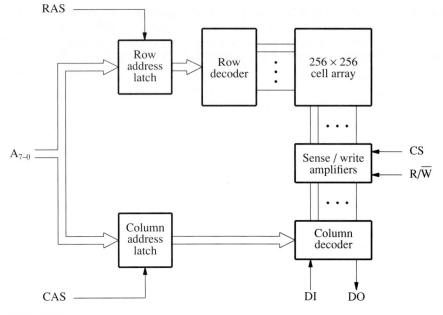

FIGURE 8.8
Internal organization of a 64K × 1 dynamic memory chip.

DO. For a Write operation, the information at the data input DI is transferred to the selected circuit. This information is then used to overwrite the contents of the selected cell in the corresponding column.

It is important to emphasize that the application of a row address causes all cells on the corresponding row to be read and refreshed during both Read and Write operations. To ensure that the contents of a dynamic memory are maintained, each row of cells must be addressed periodically, typically once every two milliseconds. A *Refresh circuit* usually performs this function automatically. Some dynamic memory chips incorporate a Refresh facility within the chips themselves. In this case, the dynamic nature of these memory chips is almost completely invisible to the user. Such chips are often referred to as pseudostatic.

Because of their high density and low cost, dynamic memories are widely used in the main memory units of computers. Available chips range in size from 1K to 4M bits, and even larger chips are being developed. To provide flexibility in designing memory systems, these chips are manufactured in different organizations: for example, a 64K chip may be organized as 64K × 1 or as 16K × 4. The latter differs from Figure 8.8 in that four data lines are provided. In this case, corresponding input and output lines are usually combined to reduce the number of pins needed.

A useful feature that is available on many dynamic memory chips should be mentioned at this point. Consider an application in which a number of memory locations at successive addresses are to be accessed, and assume that the cells involved are all on the same row inside a memory chip. Because row and column addresses are loaded separately into their respective latches, it is only necessary to load the row address once. Different column addresses can then be loaded during successive memory cycles. The rate at which such block transfers can be carried out is typically double that for transfers involving random addresses. The faster rate attainable in block transfers can be exploited in specialized machines in which memory accesses follow regular patterns, such as in graphics terminals. This feature can also be beneficial in general-purpose computers for the transfer of data blocks between the main memory and a cache, as will be explained later.

8.3 MEMORY SYSTEM CONSIDERATIONS

The choice of a RAM chip for a given application depends on several factors. Foremost among these factors are the speed, power dissipation, and size of the chip. In certain situations, other features such as the availability of block transfers may be important.

Bipolar memories are generally used only when very fast operation is the primary requirement. High power dissipation in bipolar circuits makes it difficult to achieve high densities. Hence, a memory implemented with bipolar memory chips requires a relatively large number of chips.

Dynamic MOS memory is the predominant technology used in computer main memories. The high densities achievable in this technology make the implementation of large memories economically attractive. Static MOS memory chips have higher densities and slightly longer access times than bipolar chips. They have lower densities than dynamic memories, but are easier to use because they do not require refreshing.

We will now discuss the design of memory subsystems using static and dynamic chips. Consider first a small memory consisting of 64K (65,536) words of 16 bits each. Figure 8.9 gives an example of the organization of this memory using 16K × 1 static memory chips. Each column in the figure consists of four chips, which implement one bit position. Sixteen of these sets provide the required 64K × 16 memory. Each chip has a control input called Chip Select. When this input is set to 1, it enables the chip to accept data input or to place data on its output line. The data output for each chip is of the three-state type (see Section 4.1.5). Only the selected chip places data on the output line, while all other outputs are in the high-impedance state. The address bus for this 64K memory is 16 bits wide. The high-order 2 bits of the address are decoded to obtain the four Chip Select control signals, and the remaining 14 address bits are used to access specific bit locations inside each chip of the selected row. The R/$\overline{\text{W}}$ inputs of all chips are also tied together to provide a common Read/Write control (not shown in the figure).

Next let us consider a large dynamic memory. The organization of this type of memory is essentially the same as the memory shown in Figure 8.9. However, the control circuitry differs in three respects. First, the row and column parts of the address for each chip usually have to be multiplexed. Second, a Refresh circuit is needed. Finally, the timing of various steps of a memory cycle must be carefully controlled.

An example of a dynamic memory unit is given in Figure 8.10, which depicts an array of dynamic memory chips and the required control circuitry. We assumed that the memory chips are arranged in a 4 × 16 array in exactly the same format as shown in

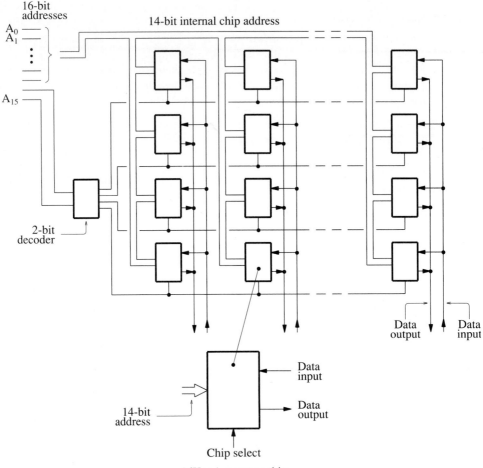

16-bit addresses

14-bit internal chip address

A_0
A_1

A_{15}

2-bit decoder

Data output   Data input

14-bit address

Data input

Data output

Chip select

16K × 1 memory chip

FIGURE 8.9
Organization of a 64K × 16 memory using 16K × 1 static memory chips.

Figure 8.9. Thus, if individual chips have a 64K × 1 organization, the array has a total storage capacity of 256K words of 16 bits each. The control circuitry provides the multiplexed address and Chip Select inputs and sends the Row and Column Address Strobe signals (RAS and CAS) to the memory chip array. It is also responsible for generating Refresh cycles as needed. The memory unit is assumed to be connected to an asynchronous memory bus that has 18 address lines ($ADRS_{17-0}$), 16 data lines ($DATA_{15-0}$), two handshake signals (Memory Request and MFC), and a Read/$\overline{Write}$ line to indicate the type of memory cycle requested.

In order to understand the operation of the control circuitry displayed in Figure 8.10, let us start by examining a normal memory read cycle. The cycle begins when the CPU activates the address, the Read/$\overline{Write}$, and the Memory Request lines. The access

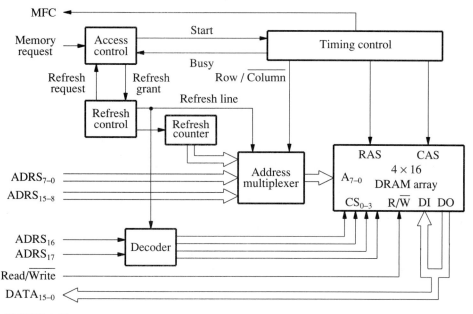

FIGURE 8.10
A block diagram of a 256K × 16 dynamic memory unit.

control block recognizes the request when the Memory Request signal becomes active, and it sets the Start signal to 1. The timing control block responds immediately by activating the Busy signal, in order to prevent the access control block from accepting new requests until the cycle ends. The timing control block then loads the row and column addresses into the memory chips by activating the RAS and CAS lines. During this time, it uses the Row/Column line to select first the row address, $ADRS_{15-8}$, followed by the column address, $ADRS_{7-0}$. The decoder block performs exactly the same function as the decoder in Figure 8.9. It decodes the 2 most significant bits of the address, $ADRS_{17,16}$, and activates one of the Chip Select lines, CS_{0-3}.

Having obtained the row and column parts of the address, the selected memory chips place the contents of the requested bit cells on their data outputs. This information is transferred to the data lines of the memory bus via appropriate drivers. The timing control block then activates the MFC line, indicating that the requested data is available on the memory bus. At the end of the memory cycle, the Busy signal is deactivated, and the access unit becomes free to accept new requests. The timing unit is responsible throughout the process for ensuring that various signals are activated and deactivated in accordance with the specifications of the particular type of memory chips used.

Consider now a Refresh operation. The Refresh control block periodically generates Refresh requests, causing the access control block to start a memory cycle in the normal way. The access control block indicates to the Refresh control block that it may proceed with a Refresh operation by activating the Refresh Grant line. The access control block arbitrates between Memory Access requests and Refresh requests. In the case of simultaneous arrivals, Refresh requests are given priority to ensure that no stored information is lost.

As soon as the Refresh control block receives the Refresh Grant signal, it activates the Refresh line. This causes the address multiplexer to select the Refresh counter as the source for the row address, instead of the external address lines $ADRS_{15-8}$. Hence, the contents of the counter will be loaded into the row address latches of all memory chips when the RAS signal is activated. During this time, the $R/\overline{W}$ line of the memory bus may indicate a Write operation. It is important to ensure that this does not inadvertently cause new information to be loaded into some of the cells that are being refreshed. This needed protection can be provided in several ways. One way is to have the decoder block deactivate all CS lines to prevent the memory chips from responding to the $R/\overline{W}$ line. The remainder of the Refresh cycle is then the same as in a normal cycle. At the end, the Refresh control block increments the Refresh counter in preparation for the next Refresh cycle.

We should note that although it requires an 8-bit row address, the Refresh counter need only be 7 bits wide because of the cell organization inside its memory chips. The 256×256 array in Figure 8.8 in fact consists of two 128×256 arrays, each having its own set of Sense/Write circuits. One row in each of the two arrays is accessed during any memory cycle, depending upon the low-order 7 bits of the row address. The most significant bit of the row address is used only in a normal Read/Write cycle to select one of the two groups of 256 columns. Because of this organization, the frequency of Refresh operations can be reduced to half of what would be needed if the memory cells had been organized in a single 256×256 array.

The main purpose of the Refresh circuit is to maintain the integrity of the stored information. Ideally, its existence should be invisible to the remainder of the computer system. That is, other parts of the system, such as the CPU, should not be affected by the operation of the Refresh circuit. In effect, however, the CPU and the Refresh circuit compete for access to the memory. The Refresh circuit must be given priority over the CPU to ensure that no information is lost. Thus, the response of the memory to a request from the CPU, or from a DMA device, may be delayed if a Refresh operation is in progress. The amount of delay caused by Refresh cycles depends upon the mode of operation of the Refresh circuit. During a Refresh operation, all memory rows may be refreshed in succession before the memory is returned to normal use. A more common scheme, however, interleaves Refresh operations on successive rows with accesses from the memory bus. This results in shorter, but more frequent, Refresh periods. In either case, Refresh operations use less than 5 percent of the available memory cycles, so the time penalty caused by refreshing is small.

At this point, we should recall the discussion of synchronous and asynchronous buses in Chapter 6. There is an apparent increase in the access time of the memory when a request arrives while a Refresh operation is in progress. The resulting variability in access time is naturally accommodated on an asynchronous bus, provided that the maximum access time does not exceed the time-out period that usually exists in such systems. This constraint is easily met when the interleaved Refresh scheme is used. In the case of a synchronous bus, it may be possible to hide a Refresh cycle within the early part of a bus cycle if sufficient time remains after a Refresh cycle to carry out a Read or Write access. Alternatively, the Refresh circuit may request bus cycles in the same manner as any device with DMA capability.

8.4   SEMICONDUCTOR ROM MEMORIES

Chapter 5 discussed the use of read-only memory (ROM) units as the control store component in a microprogrammed CPU. Semiconductor ROMs are well suited for this application. They can also be used to implement parts of the main memory of a computer that contain fixed programs or data.

Figure 8.11 shows a possible configuration for a bipolar ROM cell. The word line is normally held at a low voltage. If a word is to be selected, the voltage of the corresponding word line is momentarily raised, which causes all transistors whose emitters are connected to their corresponding bit lines to be turned on. The current that flows from the voltage supply to the bit line can be detected by a sense circuit, as shown in Figure 8.3. The bit positions in which current is detected are read as 1s, and the remaining bits are read as 0s. Therefore, the contents of a given word are determined by the pattern of emitter to bit-line connections. Similar configurations are possible in MOS technology.

Data are written into a ROM at the time of manufacture. However, some ROM designs allow the data to be loaded by the user, thus providing a programmable ROM (PROM). Programmability is achieved by connecting a fuse between the emitter and the bit line in Figure 8.11. Prior to programming, then, the memory contains all 1s. The user can insert 0s at the required locations by burning out the fuses at these locations using high-current pulses. Of course, this process is irreversible.

PROMs provide flexibility and convenience not available with ROMs. The latter are economically attractive for storing fixed programs and data where high production volumes are involved. However, the cost of preparing the masks needed for storing a particular information pattern in ROMs makes them very expensive when only a small number is required. In this case, PROMs provide a faster and considerably less expensive approach, because they can be programmed directly by the user.

Another type of ROM chip allows the stored data to be erased and new data to be loaded. Such a chip is an erasable, reprogrammable ROM, usually called an

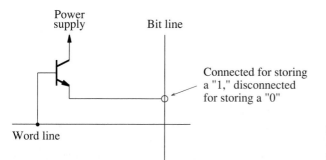

Power supply   Bit line

Connected for storing a "1," disconnected for storing a "0"

Word line

FIGURE 8.11
A storage cell for a bipolar read-only memory.

EPROM. It provides considerable flexibility during the development phase of digital systems. Since EPROMs are capable of retaining stored information for long periods, they can be used in place of ROMs while software is being developed. In this way, changes and updates can be easily implemented.

An EPROM cell bears considerable resemblance to the dynamic memory cell discussed in Section 8.2.3. As in the case of dynamic memory, information is stored in the form of a charge on a capacitor. The main difference is that the capacitor in an EPROM cell is very well insulated. Its rate of discharge is so low that it retains the stored information for over a year. However, the need for high insulation makes the process of writing new information into a cell more difficult than in other types of memories. A Write operation usually involves the application of a voltage higher than normal operating voltages in MOS circuitry. The high voltage is used to cause a temporary breakdown in insulation, and thus allow charge to be stored in the capacitor.

The contents of EPROM cells can be erased by increasing the discharge rate of the storage capacitors by several orders of magnitude. This can be accomplished by exposing the chip to ultraviolet light or by the application of a high voltage similar to that used in a Write operation. If ultraviolet light is used, all cells in the chip are erased at the same time. When electrical erasure is used, however, the process can be made selective. An electrically erasable EPROM, often referred to as an E^2PROM, offers another potential advantage. It need not be physically removed for reprogramming. This convenience is offset by the need to provide the high voltages required during the Write and Erase operations. For this reason, many manufacturers incorporate the circuitry for generating these voltages on the E^2PROM chip itself.

8.5 MULTIPLE-MODULE MEMORIES AND INTERLEAVING

If the main memory of a computer is structured as a collection of physically separate modules, each with its own address buffer register (ABR) and data buffer register (DBR), memory access operations may proceed in more than one module at the same time. Thus, the average rate of transmission of words to and from the total MM system can be increased. Extra controls will be required. However, because the MM speed is often the bottleneck in computation speeds, the expense involved is usually justified for large computers.

The way in which individual addresses are distributed over the modules is a critical factor in determining the average number of modules that can be kept busy as computations proceed. Two methods of address layout are indicated in Figure 8.12. In the first case, the MM address generated by the CPU is decoded as shown in Figure 8.12a. The high-order k bits name one of n modules, and the low-order m bits name a particular word in that module. If the CPU issues Read requests to consecutive locations, as it does when fetching instructions of a straight-line program, then only one module is kept busy by the CPU. However, devices with direct memory access (DMA) ability may be accessing information in other memory modules.

The second and more effective way to address the modules is shown in Figure 8.12b. It is called *memory interleaving*. The low-order k bits of the MM address

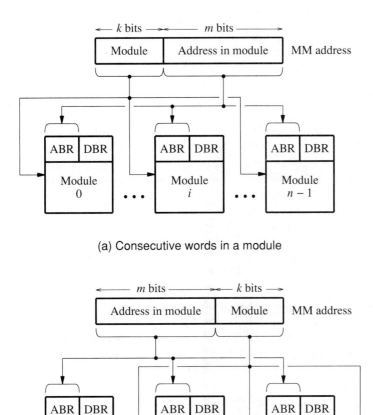

(a) Consecutive words in a module

(b) Consecutive words in consecutive modules

FIGURE 8.12
Addressing multiple-module memory systems.

select a module, and the high-order m bits name a location within that module. In this way, consecutive addresses are located in successive modules. Thus, any component of the system that generates requests for access to consecutive MM locations (such as the CPU or a DMA device) can keep a number of modules busy at any one time. This results in a higher average utilization of the memory system as a whole. To take advantage of memory interleaving, the CPU or the DMA device must be capable of initiating a memory access operation while waiting for a previous memory access to be completed.

In the system of Figure 8.12*b*, there must be 2^k modules; otherwise, there will be gaps of nonexistent locations in the MM address space. This raises a practical issue. The first system described, Figure 8.12*a*, is more flexible than the second in that any number of modules up to 2^k can be used. The modules are normally assigned consecutive MM addresses starting with 0. Hence, an existing system can be expanded simply by adding one or more modules as required. The second system must always have the full set of 2^k modules, and a failure in any module affects all areas of the address space. A failed module in the first system affects only a localized area of the address space.

To take advantage of an interleaved MM unit, the CPU should be able to issue the requests for memory words before these words are actually needed for execution. Obviously, this "lookahead" process is only useful for words in a straight-line program segment. Addressing of operands normally results in out-of-sequence requests to memory and therefore decreases the average rate of memory transfers. Furthermore, when a branch takes place, the words that have been prefetched from memory at the time of execution of the branch instruction have to be discarded. In summary, memory operands and program branching have a randomizing effect on the sequence of memory addresses generated by the CPU.

Consider a memory consisting of r modules. The effective cycle time of this memory is inversely proportional to the number of modules that can be kept busy at any given time. If all r modules are continuously busy, the effective memory cycle time is decreased by a factor of r relative to the cycle time of individual modules. In practical implementations of interleaved memories, the improvement factor depends upon the particular algorithm used to control access to individual memory modules. It is also affected by the randomizing effect of operand fetching. This factor is usually in the range of $\sqrt{r}$ to r. The number of modules in practical systems may be in the range of 16 to 32, which leads to a reduction in the effective memory cycle time by a factor of at least 4 to 6.

8.6   CACHE MEMORIES

Analysis of a large number of typical programs has shown that most of their execution time is spent on a few main routines in which a number of instructions are executed repeatedly. These instructions may constitute a simple loop, nested loops, or a few procedures that repeatedly call each other. The actual detailed pattern of instruction sequencing is not important. The main observation is that many instructions in a few localized areas of the program are repeatedly executed and that the remainder of the program is accessed relatively infrequently. This phenomenon is referred to as *locality of reference*.

If the active segments of a program can be placed in a fast memory, then the total execution time can be significantly reduced. Such a memory is referred to as a *cache* memory, which is inserted between the CPU and the main memory as shown in Figure 8.13. To make this arrangement effective, the cache must be considerably faster than the MM. This approach is more economical than the use of fast memory devices to implement the entire MM.

Conceptually, operation of a cache memory is very simple. The memory control circuitry is designed to take advantage of the property of locality of reference. When

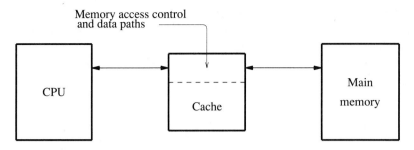

FIGURE 8.13
Use of a cache memory between the CPU and the main memory.

a Read request is received from the CPU, the contents of a block of memory words containing the location specified are transferred into the cache one word at a time. When any of the locations in this block is referenced by the program, its contents are read directly from the cache. Usually, the cache memory can store a number of such blocks at any given time. The correspondence between the MM blocks and those in the cache is specified by a *mapping function*. When the cache is full and a memory word (instruction or data) that is not in the cache is referenced, the cache control hardware must decide which block should be removed to create space for the new block that contains the referenced word. The collection of rules for making this decision constitutes the *replacement algorithm*.

The CPU does not need to know explicitly about the existence of the cache. It simply makes Read and Write requests using addresses that refer to locations in the MM. The memory-access control circuitry determines whether the requested word currently exists in the cache. If it does, the Read or Write operation is performed on the appropriate cache location. When the operation is a Read, the main memory is not involved. If the operation is a Write, however, the system can proceed in two ways. In the first technique, called *store-through*, the cache location and the MM location are updated simultaneously. The alternative is to update only the cache location and to mark it as updated with an associated flag bit, often called the *dirty* or *modified* bit. The permanent MM location of the word is updated later, when the block containing this marked word is to be removed from the cache to make way for a new block. The store-through method is clearly simpler, but it results in unnecessary Write operations in the MM when a given cache word is updated a number of times during its cache residency period.

When the addressed word in a Read operation is not in the cache, the block of words that contains the requested word is copied from the MM into the cache. Then, the particular word requested is forwarded to the CPU. The particular word that was requested may be forwarded to the CPU after the entire block is loaded into the cache. Alternatively, this word may be sent to the CPU as soon as it is read from the main memory. The latter approach, which is called *load-through*, reduces the CPU's waiting period somewhat. However, the resulting improvement in performance is often not worth the associated complexity, particularly in small to medium size computers.

During a Write operation, if the addressed word is not in the cache, then the information is written directly into the MM. In this case, there is little advantage in transferring the block containing the addressed word to the cache. A Write operation normally refers to a location in one of the data areas of a program rather than to the memory area containing program instructions. The property of locality of reference is not as pronounced in accessing data when Write operations are involved.

Finally, we should recall that in the case of an interleaved memory, contiguous block transfers are very efficient. Transferring data in blocks between the MM and the cache enables an interleaved MM unit to operate at its maximum possible speed. Similarly, block transfers to the cache can take advantage of the block or burst transfer mode available on most dynamic RAM chips.

8.6.1 Mapping Functions

In order to discuss possible methods for specifying where MM blocks are placed in the cache, we will use a specific example. Consider a cache consisting of 128 blocks of 16 words each, for a total of 2048 (2K) words, and assume that the main memory is addressable by a 16-bit address. For mapping purposes, the main memory will be viewed as composed of 4K blocks.

The simplest way to associate MM blocks with cache blocks is the *direct-mapping* technique. In this technique, block k of the MM maps onto block k modulo 128 of the cache, as depicted in Figure 8.14. Since more than one MM block is mapped onto a given cache block position, contention may arise for that position even when the cache is not full. For example, instructions of a program may start in block 128 and continue in block 256, possibly after a branch. As this program is executed, both of these blocks must be transferred to the block-0 position in the cache. Contention is resolved by allowing the new block to overwrite the currently resident block. In this case, the replacement algorithm is trivial.

An MM address can be divided into three fields, as shown in Figure 8.14. When a new block enters the cache, the 7-bit cache block field determines the cache position in which this block must be stored. The high-order five bits of the MM address of the block are stored in five tag bits associated with its location in the cache. As execution proceeds, the 7-bit cache block field of each address generated by the CPU points to a particular block location in the cache. The tag field of that block is compared to the tag field of the address. If they match, then the desired word is in that block of the cache. If there is no match, then the block containing the required word must first be read from the main memory and loaded into the cache. The direct-mapping technique is easy to implement, but it is not very flexible.

Figure 8.15 shows a much more flexible mapping method in which an MM block can potentially reside in any cache block position. In this case, 12 tag bits are required to identify an MM block when it is resident in the cache. The tag bits of an address received from the CPU are compared to the tag bits of each block of the cache to see if the desired block is present. This is called the *associative-mapping* technique. Because of the complete freedom this technique gives in block positioning, a wide range of replacement algorithms is possible. However, its cost of implementation is

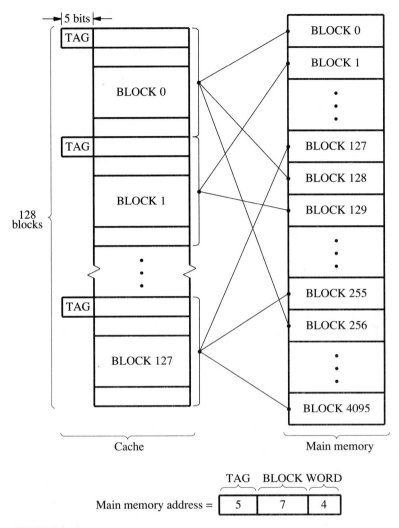

FIGURE 8.14
Direct-mapping cache.

somewhat higher than the cost of the direct-mapping scheme because of the need to search all 128 tag patterns to detemine whether a given block is in the cache. A search of this kind is called an *associative search*.

The final mapping method to be discussed is a combination of the two techniques mentioned above. Blocks of the cache are grouped into sets, and the mapping allows a block of the main memory to reside in any block of a specific set. Hence the contention problem of the direct method is eased by having a few choices for block placement. At the same time, the hardware cost is reduced by decreasing the size of the associative search. An example of this *block-set-associative-mapping* technique is

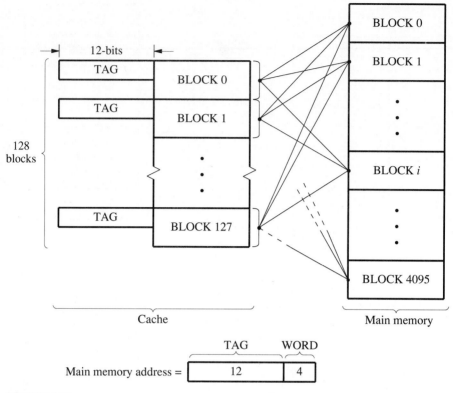

FIGURE 8.15
Associative-mapping cache.

given in Figure 8.16 for a cache with two blocks per set. The 6-bit set field of the address determines which set of the cache might contain the desired block. The tag field of the address must then be associatively compared to the tags of the two blocks of the set to check if the desired block is present. This two-way associative search is simple to implement.

We should note that the number of blocks per set is a parameter that can be selected to suit the requirements of a particular computer. Four blocks per set can be accommodated by a 5-bit set field, eight blocks per set by a 4-bit set field, and so on. The extreme condition of 128 blocks per set requires no set bits and corresponds to the fully associative technique, with 12 tag bits. The other extreme of one block per set is the direct-mapping method.

Another technical detail that should be mentioned, is the fact that a *valid bit* must usually be provided for each block. This bit indicates whether the block contains valid data. It should not be confused with the modified or dirty bit mentioned earlier. The dirty bit indicates whether the block has been modified during its cache residency and is needed only in systems that do not use the store-through method. The valid bits are all set to 0 when power is initially applied to the system or when the MM is

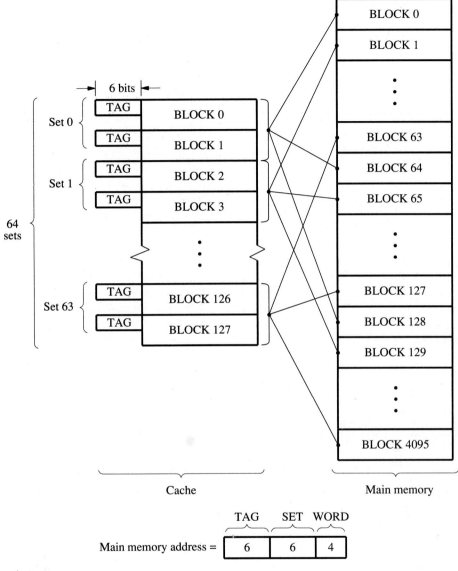

FIGURE 8.16
Block-set-associative-mapping cache with two blocks per set.

loaded with new programs and data from mass storage devices. Transfers from mass storage devices are carried out by a DMA mechanism, and normally bypass the cache. The valid bit of a particular cache block is set to 1 the first time this block is loaded from the MM, and it stays at 1 unless an MM block is updated by a source that bypasses the cache. In this case, a check is made to determine whether the block is currently in the cache. If it is, its valid bit is set to 0.

8.6.2 Replacement Algorithms

When a new block is to be brought into the cache and all the positions that it may occupy are full, the cache controller must decide which of the old blocks to overwrite. This problem has generated a great deal of interest among computer scientists, because the decision can potentially be a strong determining factor in system performance. In general, the objective is to keep blocks in the cache that are likely to be referenced in the near future. However, it is not easy to determine which blocks are about to be referenced. The property of locality of reference in programs gives a clue to a reasonable strategy. Because programs usually stay in localized areas for reasonable periods of time, there is a high probability that the blocks that have been referenced recently will be referenced again soon. Therefore, when a block is to be overwritten, it is sensible to overwrite the one that has gone the longest time without being referenced. This block is called the *least-recently-used (LRU)* block, and the technique is called the *LRU replacement algorithm*. In order to use the LRU algorithm, the cache controller must track the LRU block as computation proceeds. As a specific example, suppose it is required to track the LRU block of a four-block set. A 2-bit counter may be used for each block. When a *hit* occurs (when an access request is received for a word that is in the cache), the counter of the block that is referenced is set to 0. Counters with values originally lower than the referenced one are incremented by one, and all others remain unchanged. When a *miss* occurs and the set is not full, the counter associated with the new block loaded from the main memory is set to 0, and the values of all other counters are increased by one. When a miss occurs and the set is full, the block with the counter value 3 is removed, the new block is put in its place, and its counter is set to 0. The other three block counters are incremented by one. It can be easily verified that the counter values of occupied blocks are always distinct.

There are several replacement algorithms that require less overhead than the LRU approach. An intuitively reasonable rule would be to remove the "oldest" block from a full set when a new block must be brought in. Using this technique, no updating is needed when hits occur. However, because the algorithm does not take into account the recent pattern of access to blocks in the cache, it is generally not as effective as the LRU algorithm in choosing the best blocks to remove. The simplest algorithm is to choose the block to be overwritten at random. Interestingly enough, this simple algorithm has been found to be quite effective in practice.

8.6.3 Examples

Finally, let us discuss some typical cache parameter values that are found in commercially available computers. In general, cache memory access times of 50 ns or less are available in high-speed caches. This contrasts the 100- to 500-ns access times in MOS main memory modules. The percentage of memory accesses that result in finding the desired information in the cache ranges from 90 percent to over 99 percent. This parameter is usually called the *hit ratio* and depends mainly on the total size of the cache, as well as on the type of program being executed.

Caches are usually organized in the block-set-associative manner, with two to eight blocks per set. The number of bytes per block typically ranges from 4 to 64, and the total cache size ranges from 8K to 256K bytes. Naturally, the larger numbers apply to expensive, high-performance computers. For example, the IBM 3033 has a 64K-byte cache. It has 64 sets with 16 blocks per set, and there are 64 bytes per block. In the VAX 6200 multiprocessor system, each processor has a 256K-byte direct mapped cache with 64 bytes per block.

8.7 VIRTUAL MEMORIES

In any computer system in which the currently active programs and data do not fit into the physical MM space, secondary storage devices such as magnetic disks hold the overflow. The operating system automatically moves programs between the main memory and secondary storage. Thus, the application programmer does not need to be aware of the limitations imposed by the available main memory.

Techniques that automatically move program and data blocks into the physical MM when they are required for execution are called *virtual-memory* techniques. Programs, and hence the processor, reference an instruction and data space that is independent of the available physical MM space. The binary addresses that the processor issues for either instructions or data are called *virtual* or *logical addresses*. The mechanism that translates these into physical addresses is usually implemented by a combination of hardware and software components. If a virtual address refers to a part of the program or data space that is currently in the physical memory, then the contents of the appropriate location in the main memory are accessed immediately. On the other hand, if the referenced address is not in the MM, its contents must be brought into a suitable location in the MM before they can be used.

The simplest method of translation assumes that all programs and data are composed of fixed-length units called *pages*, each of which consists of a block of words that occupy contiguous locations in the MM or in secondary storage. Pages commonly range from 1K to 8K bytes in length. They constitute the basic unit of information that is moved back and forth between the MM and secondary storage whenever the translation mechanism determines that a move is required. This discussion clearly parallels many ideas that were introduced in the cache memory section. The cache is intended to bridge the speed gap between the processor and the MM and is implemented in hardware. The virtual-memory idea, on the other hand, is meant to bridge the size gap between the MM and secondary storage and is usually implemented in part by software techniques. Conceptually, cache techniques and virtual-memory techniques are very similar. They differ mainly in the details of their implementation.

A virtual memory address translation method based on the concept of fixed-length pages is shown schematically in Figure 8.17. Each virtual address generated by the processor, whether it is for an instruction fetch or an operand fetch/store operation, is interpreted as a page number (high-order bits) followed by a word number (low-order bits). Information about the disk or main memory location of each page is kept in a *page table* in the main memory. The starting address of this table is kept in a *page table base register*. By adding the page number to the contents of this register, the address of the corresponding entry in the page table is obtained. The contents of this location give the starting address of the page if that page currently resides in the MM; otherwise, they indicate where the page is to be found in secondary storage. In this

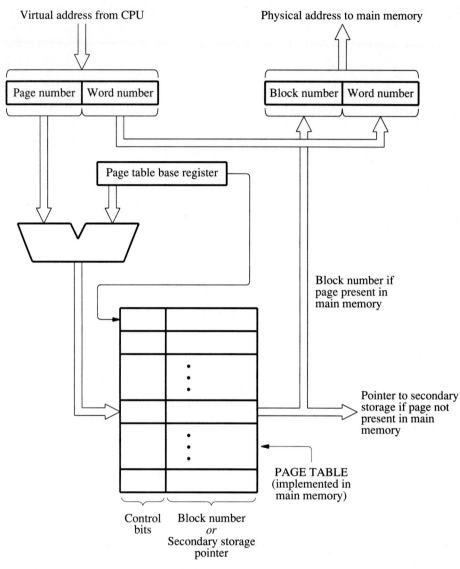

FIGURE 8.17
Virtual-memory address translation.

case, the entry in the table usually points to an area in the main memory where the secondary storage address of the page is held. Each entry also includes some control bits to describe the status of the page while it is in the MM. One control bit indicates whether the page has been modified during its residency in the MM. As with cache memories, this information is needed to determine whether to write the page back to secondary storage before removing it from the MM to make room for another page.

Other control information may also be recorded in the control bits, as we will describe in the VAX-11 example in Section 8.9.

If the page table is stored in the MM unit, as we assumed above, then two MM accesses must be made for every MM access requested by a program. This would result in a degradation of execution speed by a factor of two. However, a specialized cache memory is used in most systems to speed up the translation process by storing recently used virtual to physical address translations. Section 8.9 will describe how the VAX-11 does this.

When a program generates an access request to a page that is not in the MM, a *page fault* is said to have occurred. The whole page must be brought from secondary storage into the MM, usually via DMA, before access can proceed. Because a long delay is incurred while the page transfer takes place, the processor may execute another task whose pages are in the MM. It is the responsibility of the operating system to suspend execution of the program that caused the page fault and to start the execution of another program.

Once the MM is full, if a new page is brought from secondary storage, it must replace one of the resident pages. The problem of choosing the page to be removed is just as critical here as it is in a cache, and the notion that programs spend most of their time in a few localized areas is also applicable. Because main memories are considerably larger than cache memories, it should be possible to keep relatively larger portions of a program in the MM. This will reduce the frequency of transfers to and from secondary storage. Concepts similar to the LRU replacement algorithm can be applied to page replacement, and the required usage data can be kept in control bits in the page table entries.

8.8 MEMORY MANAGEMENT REQUIREMENTS

In our discussion of virtual-memory concepts, we have tacitly assumed that only one large program is being executed. If all of it does not fit into the available physical MM, parts of it (pages) are moved from secondary storage into the MM when they are to be executed and displace pages that have become idle. Although we have alluded to software routines that are needed to manage this movement of program segments, we have not been specific about the details. Of course, these management routines must also reside in the MM when they are executed.

The management routines are part of the operating system of the computer. It is convenient to assemble the operating system routines into a virtual address space, called the *system space*, that is separate from the virtual space in which user application programs reside. The latter space is called the *user space*. In fact, there may be a number of user spaces, one for each user. This can be arranged by providing a separate page table for each user. The particular table that is selected depends on the contents of the page table base register. By changing the contents of this register, the operating system can switch from one space to another. The physical MM is thus shared by the active pages of the system space and each of the user spaces. However, only the pages that belong to one of these spaces are accessible at any given time.

In any computer system in which independent user programs coexist in the MM, the notion of *protection* must be addressed. No program should be allowed to destroy either data or instructions of other programs in the MM. There is a number of ways in which such protection may be provided. Let us first consider the most basic form of protection. We have already introduced the notion of the state of the processor. In the simplest case there are two states, the *supervisor state* and the *user state*. As the names suggest, the processor is usually placed in the supervisor state when operating system routines are being executed, and in the user state to execute user programs. In the user state, some machine instructions cannot be executed. These *privileged instructions*, which include operations such as modification of the page table base register, can only be executed while the processor is in the supervisor state. Hence, a user program is prevented from accessing the page tables of other user spaces or of the system space.

It is often desirable for one application program to have access to pages belonging to another program. The operating system can arrange this by causing these pages to appear in both spaces. The shared pages will therefore have entries in two different page tables. The control bits in each table entry can be set to control the access privileges granted to each program. For example, one program may be allowed to read and write a given page, while the other program may be given only read access.

8.9 THE VAX-11 VIRTUAL-MEMORY SYSTEM

In order to appreciate the complexity of a virtual memory system, we will examine a commercial example. The VAX-11 system is described in this section.

The organization of the VAX-11 virtual-memory system follows the general scheme outlined in Figure 8.17. A virtual address in the VAX-11 is 32 bits long. It is interpreted as shown in Figure 8.18. The high-order bit, b_{31}, differentiates between user space and system space. User space is further divided into program and control

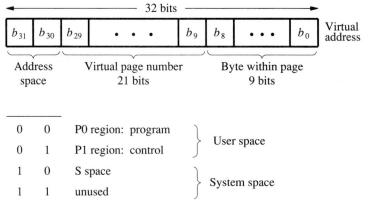

FIGURE 8.18
VAX-11 virtual-address format.

regions by bit b_{30}. The user program region contains programs and data, and the user control region contains the user stack and operating system data structures pertinent to a particular user. The system space contains operating system procedures (memory management software, user program scheduling, etc.) common to all users, and the page tables for all spaces. The remaining 30 bits of a virtual address specify a 21-bit virtual page number and a 9-bit address of a byte within that page. Thus, a page consists of 512 bytes. During the address translation process, the low-order 9 bits of a virtual address are taken directly as the low-order bits of the corresponding physical address.

The page is the basic unit that is transferred from secondary storage to the physical MM when successive parts of a program become active. The 21-bit virtual page number is used as an offset into a page table as shown in Figure 8.19. The address of the page table is held in a page table base register in the processor. Each page table entry is 32 bits long. Every entry contains a 21-bit physical page frame number that is used to construct a 30-bit physical address, as shown in the figure. The remaining 11 bits in the page table entry provide access control information for the referenced page.

The detailed format of a page table entry is shown in Figure 8.20. There are four fields in the access control section

Valid (1 bit) This bit is set to 1 if the page is currently resident in the MM. When a program generates an access request for a page whose valid bit is 1, translation continues. If this bit is 0, that is in the case of a page fault, the whole page must be brought into the MM before access can proceed.

Protection (4 bits) The protection field specifies the access privileges for programs that access the page.

Modified (1 bit) The value of this bit is 1 if there has been a Write operation to the page during its current MM residency period. This information is necessary when a page is to be removed from the MM. It determines whether the page must be written back into the secondary storage.

Own (5 bits) This field provides additional protection information that we will not discuss here.

8.9.1 The Translation Process

It is instructive to follow the details of translation from a virtual address to a physical address in the VAX-11 system. When the virtual address is in the system space, the translation steps are somewhat simpler than for a user space. We will consider both cases.

First, we should note a general aspect of the translation process shown in Figure 8.19. Two accesses to the MM are required for each virtual address access. First, a page table entry containing the physical page frame number is read from the MM, and then a second access to perform the requested Read or Write operation follows. This is a severe execution time penalty to pay for the flexibility of a virtual-memory system. Consecutive instruction fetches will usually reference the same physical page, so it would be helpful if a hardware mechanism were available to detect such occurrences.

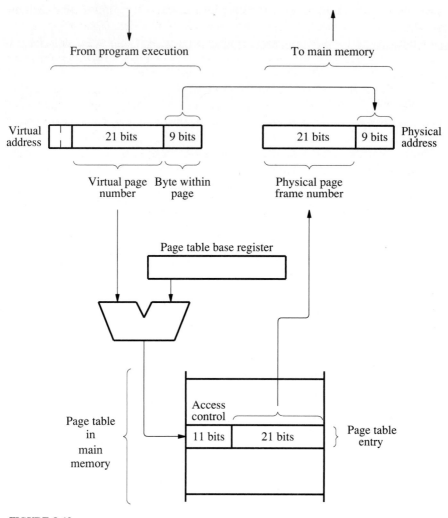

FIGURE 8.19
VAX-11 general address translation.

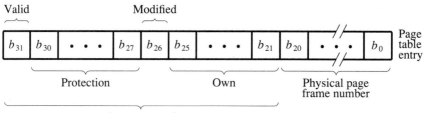

FIGURE 8.20
VAX-11 page table entry format.

The page table entry Read operation could then be avoided. The VAX-11 contains a small cache memory that holds the most recently used page table entries for this purpose. This address translation cache is distinct from the MM cache described in Section 8.6, which is also used in the VAX-11. We will give a discussion of the translation cache after describing the translation process itself.

SYSTEM SPACE TRANSLATION. A pictorial display of the required sequence of steps is given in Figure 8.21. There are two million possible virtual pages in each of the system and the user spaces. However, only a small fraction of these is in actual use in most applications. A register called the *system length register* (SLR) records the number of virtual pages in use in the system space. Programs prepared for execution on

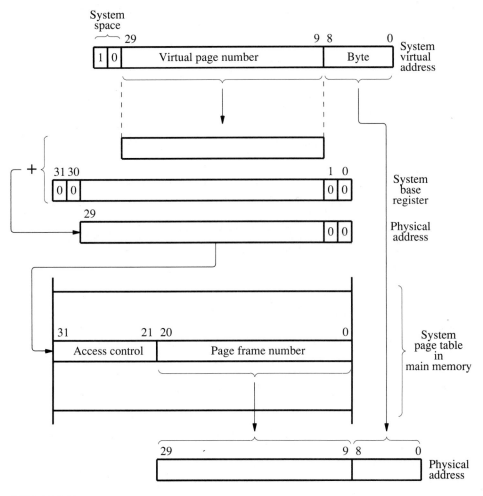

FIGURE 8.21
Translation of a system address.

a virtual-memory system always start at address 0 and occupy contiguous addresses. Therefore, the number in the SLR is one larger than the highest virtual page number in the system software. For each system virtual address generated by the processor the virtual page number is compared to the contents of the SLR. If it is smaller, the translation process continues. Otherwise, an interrupt is raised indicating an error.

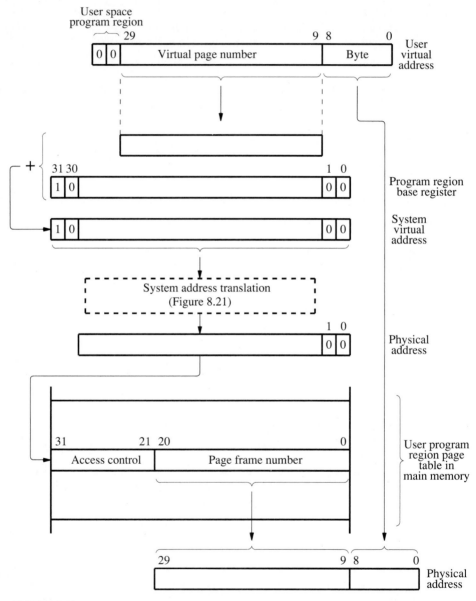

FIGURE 8.22
Translation of a user address in the program region.

A valid virtual page number is added to the contents of the *system base register* (SBR) to generate the physical address of the appropriate page table entry. This entry is then fetched from the main memory. First, the Valid bit in the access control field is checked. The protection bits are checked next to determine whether the program that generated the request has access rights. (Not all system software programs have the same access privileges.) Then a physical address is generated, and the requested Read or Write operation is performed. If the Valid bit is 0, a page fault has occurred, and a procedure must be invoked to load the requested page into the main memory. If the access protection check fails, that is, if the requested access is not authorized, an interrupt is raised.

USER SPACE TRANSLATION. The translation of user space virtual addresses is essentially the same as the translation of system space virtual addresses. The main difference is that user page tables are maintained at virtual addresses in the system space. Hence, they may not always be in the physical main memory. This contrasts with the system page table, which is always in the physical main memory.

Figure 8.22 shows a translation of an address in the program region of a user space. After a length check, the virtual page number is added to the base address of the corresponding page table. The result is a virtual address in the system space. This address is translated by the process shown in Figure 8.21 to yield the physical address of the page table entry, which is then fetched from the main memory. The remainder of the translation process is the same as we described for the system space. We should note that user space address translation requires two main memory accesses: first, to fetch the address of the page table entry, and then to fetch the entry itself. A third main memory access is finally needed to access the actual operand.

8.9.2   Translation Speedup Techniques

If every Read or Write operation in user space actually required three main memory accesses, as we described, the flexibility of the virtual-memory system would be overshadowed by the threefold increase in program execution time. Most commercial virtual-memory systems incorporate a mechanism that can avoid the bulk of the main memory accesses called for by the virtual-to-physical address translation process. This may be done with a cache memory called a *translation buffer*, which retains the results of recent translations.

In some VAX-11 computers, the translation buffer is a block-set-associative cache with 64 sets and 2 blocks per set, for a total of 128 address translation entries. It is divided into halves: one half is used for user space translations and the other half for system space translations. Figure 8.23 shows the organization of the translation buffer. This cache operates in the same way as the block-set-associative caches described in Section 8.6. A random replacement rule is used when an entry must be displaced from a set.

An additional address translation speedup technique is used during instruction fetches in the VAX-11. The number of the physical page frame that contains the current instruction stream is maintained in the processor. Consider the usual case in which instructions are being fetched from successive locations. When the page

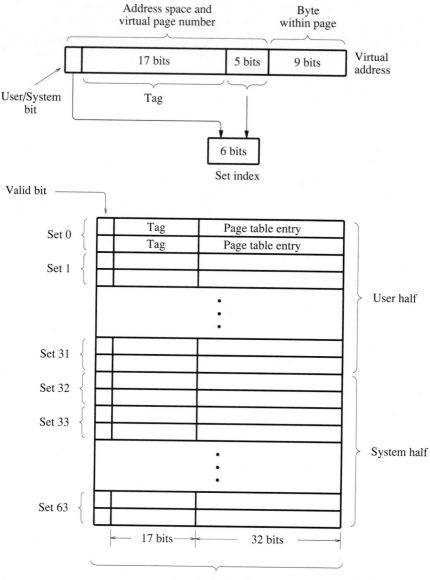

FIGURE 8.23
Address translation buffer in the VAX-11/780.

boundary is not crossed, the physical address of each instruction can be obtained simply by concatenating the current physical page frame number with the low-order 9 bits from the program counter. This technique is called *pretranslation* of instruction stream addresses because neither the translation buffer nor the main memory page tables are used in the process.

The combined use of pretranslation and the translation buffer has a significant impact on execution time. A simulation study[1] has shown that about two-thirds of all translation requests from the processor can be avoided by pretranslation. Furthermore, of all translation requests actually issued to the translation buffer, only about 1 percent result in misses. A miss indicates that the main memory page tables must be accessed to perform the translation.

8.9.3   Paging

The preceding discussion outlines the address translation mechanism and its associated hardware in the VAX-11 virtual memory system. However, we have only given details for the case in which the requested item, either an instruction or a data element, currently resides in the main memory. When it does not reside there, the page containing the item must be transferred into the main memory before execution of the program can continue. A great deal of the design effort in realizing virtual memory systems is concerned with determining how and when user program pages move between the main memory and secondary storage. Many issues are involved. A large computer system usually maintains sections of a number of different user programs in the main memory simultaneously, and the programs timeshare the processor. In such a setting, the overall strategy is to supply the processor with a steady work load and to minimize the shuffling of pages back and forth between the main memory and the secondary storage. A detailed study of these topics is beyond the scope of this book. Interested readers may consult reference 2 in Section 8.13 for a discussion of the techniques used in VAX-11 systems.

8.10   MEMORY MANAGEMENT HARDWARE

The implementation of memory management features requires considerable hardware support. This may include associative memories, address translation hardware, and high-speed memories for storing page tables. Such facilities are available for many computer systems.

Memory management hardware is typically provided in the form of a single chip that is compatible with the processor used. The memory management chip accepts a logical address from the processor and generates the corresponding physical address with its internal tables. Separate tables may be provided for user spaces and the system space. The processor loads the contents of these tables, which may contain protection and access restriction information. The processor also informs the memory management chip when it should switch from one user space to another or from a user space to the system space. We should note that most modern microprocessors are supported by memory management chips.

8.11   CONCLUDING REMARKS

The main memory is a major component in any computer. Its characteristics in terms of size and speed play an important role in determining the performance of a given computer. In this chapter, we have presented some of the technological and organizational details of the main memory.

Developments in technology have led to a considerable reduction in the cost of semiconductor memories. Bipolar memories are particularly useful in the implementation of cache memories because of their high-speed capabilities. MOS memories, on the other hand, are used in the main memory because of their relatively low cost.

Virtual-memory systems are rapidly increasing in number. Many new computer designs, including high-performance microcomputer systems, have virtual-memory capability as a part of their basic hardware and operating software. Others are designed to facilitate its implementation.

8.12 PROBLEMS

8.1. The address decoder in Figure 8.3 has 4 input lines and 16 output lines. Exactly one output line is selected (set to 1) for each possible 4-bit address. A decoder with the same general form as given in Figure A.32 can be used. It consists of 16 four-input AND gates and is called a *single-level decoder*.

For large numbers of inputs, a different form of decoder is more economical. Consider the three-input to eight-output configuration shown in Figure P8.1. It is called a *tree decoder*.

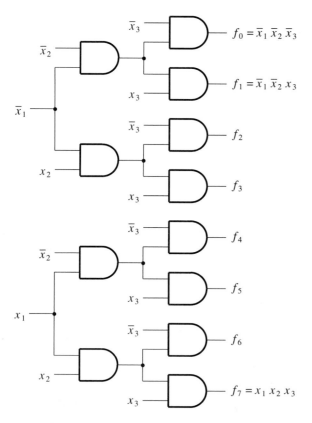

FIGURE P8.1
Three-variable tree decoder.

(*a*) Sketch the form of a 4-input to 16-output tree decoder.

(*b*) If decoder cost is determined by the total number of gates plus gate inputs, the cost of a three-input single-level decoder is 32, and the cost of a three-input tree decoder is 36. What are the corresponding costs for four-input and eight-input decoders?

8.2. It is possible to improve the tree-decoder scheme introduced in Problem 8.1. Consider the block diagram in Figure P8.2. The decoders shown are called *dual-tree* or *matrix decoders*. In Figure P8.2*a*, the four inputs are decoded in pairs in two-input decoders. The outputs of these decoders are combined in pairs in all possible ways by 16 AND gates in the final block to generate the required 16 outputs. The extension of this scheme

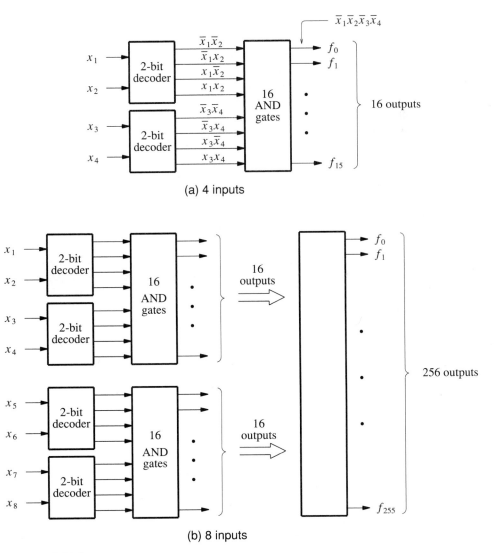

FIGURE P8.2
Dual-tree decoders.

to the eight-input case is shown in Figure P8.2*b*. Compute the cost (gates plus gate inputs) of four-input and eight-input dual-tree decoders and compare your results with the cost figures developed in Problem 8.1.

8.3. Show how to construct a 10-input decoder from resistors and diodes in a configuration similar to the AND array of the programmable logic array shown in Figure A.38. Which of the decoder forms from Problems 8.1 and 8.2 corresponds to this configuration?

8.4. Suppose an "Enable" input is added to an integrated circuit that performs the decoding function. When Enable $= 0$, all the outputs are held at 0; when Enable $= 1$, the circuit performs the decode function. This can be implemented internally by adding Enable as an input to each of the AND gates that generate the decoder outputs. Show how to use two-input decoders that have Enable inputs to implement a single four-input decoder.

8.5. Give a block diagram similar to the one in Figure 8.9 for a 4M $\times$ 16 memory using 256K $\times$ 1 memory chips.

8.6. Consider the dynamic memory cell of Figure 8.7. Assume that $C = 5$ picofarads and that leakage current through the transistor is about 2 nanoamperes. The voltage across the capacitor when it is fully charged is equal to 4.5 V. The cell must be refreshed before this voltage drops below 3 V. Estimate the minimum refresh rate.

8.7. A dynamic memory is connected to a synchronous bus, on which data transfers take place according to the timing diagram of Figure 6.15. The memory is controlled by a circuit similar to that in Figure 8.10. The processor asserts Memory-request at the beginning of a clock period in which it wishes to read data. If the memory control circuit accepts the request, it asserts MFC and the data transfer is completed in the normal manner. However, if a refresh request is generated during the same cycle, the refresh operation proceeds and MFC remains inactive. In this case, the processor waits for the next clock period, maintaining Memory-request in the active state. Give a suitable design for the Refresh Control and Access Control blocks.

8.8. It was pointed out in Section 8.3 that the cell array of the 64K dynamic IC shown in Figure 8.8 is usually implemented as two 128 $\times$ 256 arrays. Redraw Figure 8.8 to illustrate this. What would the refresh overhead be if the memory cells are organized as a single 256 $\times$ 256 array? Suggest a suitable organization for the cells of a 256K-bit memory IC assuming that they have the same refresh requirements as in the case of the 64K chip.

8.9. (*a*) Estimate the potential speedup in executing the program in Figure 2.5*c* if the MM is configured as shown in Figure 8.12*b* with $k = 2$.

(*b*) Repeat (*a*) for the PDP-11 program in Figure 2.21*b* or the 68000 program in Figure 2.32*b*.

8.10. In the bus transfers of Figures 6.15 and 6.16, the CPU requests a data transfer and maintains the address on the bus until the transfer is completed. This arrangement cannot realize the increase in speed made possible by the interleaved memory of Figure 8.12*b*. Suggest a modification for the way in which data transfers take place to enable simultaneous access to several memory modules.

8.11. A program consists of two nested loops, a small inner loop, and a much larger outer loop. The general structure of the program is given in Figure P8.3. The decimal memory addresses shown delineate the location of the two loops and the beginning and end of the total program. All memory locations in the various sections, 17–22, 23–164, 165–239, and so on, contain instructions to be executed in straight-line sequencing. The program is to be run on a computer that has an instruction cache organized in the direct-mapping manner (Figure 8.14) and that has the following parameters:

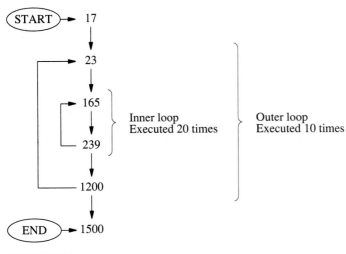

FIGURE P8.3
A program structure for Problem 8.11.

MM size	64K words
Cache size	1K words
Block size	128 words

The cycle time of the MM is 10τ s and the cycle time of the cache is 1τ s.

(a) Specify the number of bits in the TAG, BLOCK, and WORD fields in MM addresses.

(b) Compute the total time needed for instruction fetching during execution of the program in Figure P8.3.

8.12. A computer uses a small cache memory between the main memory and the CPU. The cache has four 16-bit words, and each word has an associated 13-bit tag, as shown in Figure P8.4a. Main memory locations are mapped on cache locations using the direct-

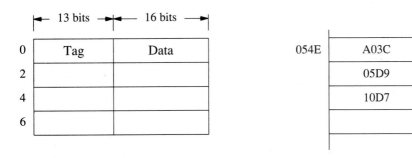

(a) Cache   (b) Main memory

FIGURE P8.4
Cache and main memory contents in Problem 8.12.

mapping technique. When a miss occurs on a read operation, the requested word is read from the main memory and sent to the CPU. At the same time, it is copied into the cache, and its block number is stored in the associated tag. Consider the following loop in a program

LOOP	Add	(R1)+,R0
	Decrement	R2
	BNE	LOOP

where all instructions and operands are 16 bits long. Assume that before this loop is entered, registers R0, R1, and R2 contain 0, 054E, and 3, respectively. Also assume that the main memory contains the data shown in Figure P8.4b, where all entries are given in hexadecimal notation. The loop starts at location LOOP = 02EC.

(a) Show the contents of the cache at the end of each pass through the loop.
(b) Assume that the access time of the main memory is 200 ns and that of the cache is 30 ns. Calculate the execution time for each pass. Ignore the time taken by the CPU between memory cycles.

8.13. Repeat Problem 8.12 for the case in which only instructions are stored in the cache. Data operands are fetched directly from the main memory and not copied into the cache. Why does this choice lead to faster execution than when both instructions and data are written into the cache? When might it be beneficial to use a cache that stores both instructions and data?

8.14. A block-set-associative cache consists of a total of 64 blocks divided into four-block sets. The MM contains 4096 blocks, each consisting of 128 words.
(a) How many bits are there in an MM address?
(b) How many bits are there in each of the TAG, SET, and WORD fields?

8.15. A computer system has an MM consisting of 1M 16-bit words. It also has a 4K-word cache organized in the block-set-associative manner, with four blocks per set and 64 words per block.
(a) Calculate the number of bits in each of the TAG, SET, and WORD fields of the MM address format.
(b) Assume that the cache is initially empty. Suppose that the CPU fetches 4352 words from locations 0, 1, 2, . . . 4351 (in that order). It then repeats this fetch sequence nine more times. If the cache is 10 times faster than the MM, estimate the improvement factor resulting from the use of the cache. Assume that the LRU algorithm is used for block replacement.

8.16. Repeat Problem 8.15, assuming that whenever a block is to be brought from the MM and the corresponding set in the cache is full, the new block replaces the most recently used block of this set.

8.17. When a DMA transfer is done between a disk and the main memory in a computer system that has a main memory cache, there are two ways to proceed. The transfer can go through the cache or it can bypass the cache. Discuss the advantages and disadvantages of each choice. (See Section 8.6.1.)

8.18. How might the value of k in the interleaved memory system of Figure 8.12b influence block size in the design of a cache memory to be used with the system?

8.19. In Section 8.9.1, it was pointed out that user page tables are located at virtual addresses in the system space. This means that the user page tables may not always be in the physical main memory. Is there any advantage to this arrangement?

8.20. Consider a computer system in which the available pages in the physical memory are divided among several application programs. When all pages allocated to a program are full and a new page is needed, it must replace one of the resident pages. The operating system monitors the page transfer activity and dynamically adjusts the page allocation to various programs. Suggest a suitable strategy that the operating system can use to minimize the overall rate of page transfers.

8.21. Suggest reasons why the page size in a virtual-memory system should be neither very small nor very large.

8.22. In a computer with a virtual-memory system, when a program generates a reference to a page that is not resident in the physical main memory, execution of the program is suspended until the requested page is loaded into the MM. What difficulties might arise when an instruction in one page has an operand in a different page? What capabilities must the CPU have to handle this situation?

8.23. Suppose that the program discussed in Problem 8.11 is to be run on a VAX-11 computer with a virtual-memory system (see Section 8.9). Assume that all addresses in this program are virtual byte addresses. Furthermore, assume that on average, an instruction occupies four bytes and that four bytes can be fetched from the memory in one memory access. A translation buffer and the pretranslation technique described in Section 8.9.2 are used. Estimate the total number of virtual-memory accesses (four bytes per access) requested by the CPU during execution of the program. If the complete program is resident in the main memory and the translation buffer is initially empty, what percentage of these accesses is handled by pretranslation and what percentage results in a hit in the translation buffer? What is the total number of translation buffer misses in this problem?

8.13 REFERENCES

1. Satyanarayanan, M., and D. Bhandarkov, "Design Tradeoffs in VAX-11 Translation Buffer Organization," *Computer*, 14, no. 12. December 1981, pp. 103–111.
2. Levy, H. M., and P. H. Lipman, "Virtual Memory Management in the VAX/VMS Operating System," *Computer*, 15, no. 3. March 1982, pp. 35–41.

CHAPTER
9

COMPUTER PERIPHERALS

In previous chapters we discussed hardware and software features of processors and main memories. We also discussed the means by which a computer communicates with external devices, including the hardware and software facilities that support program-controlled I/O, direct memory access, and interrupts. This chapter presents the characteristics of commonly used computer peripherals.

The word *peripheral* is used here to refer to any external device connected to a computer. In this context, the computer consists only of the processor and the main memory. Functionally, computer peripherals can be divided into two categories. The first category contains devices that perform input and output operations; this category includes keyboards, printers, and video display terminals. The second category contains devices that are intended primarily for secondary storage of data, with primary storage being provided by the main memory of the computer. These are mass storage devices, such as magnetic disk and tape units, which are capable of storing large amounts of data. Their main use is as an *on-line* extension to the main memory; however, another important use is for *off-line* storage of programs and data files, such as data stored on tape reels and disks that can be removed from the drive units when not in use.

9.1 I/O DEVICES

A wide range of devices may be used in conjunction with a computer for I/O purposes. Some of the commonly used devices are:

356

- Video terminals
- Graphic displays
- Printers
- Plotters

We will discuss the main features of these devices in the subsequent sections.

9.1.1   Video Terminals

Video terminals are the most commonly used I/O devices. They consist of a keyboard as the input device and a video display as the output device. They are used for direct human interaction with the computer, that is, for entering programs and data and receiving results of computations in an interactive environment. A video terminal may also be used by an operator for monitoring and controlling the overall operation of the computer system.

Early video terminals were functionally relatively simple, being able to perform only primitive I/O operations. Such terminals are sometimes called *dumb* terminals. The development of VLSI technology and the availability of microprocessors have had a great impact on the evolution of terminals. Inclusion of powerful microprocessors in terminals provides these devices with considerable processing capability, resulting in *smart* terminals. Such terminals often possess sophisticated graphics and text manipulation facilities.

We will discuss the display aspects of video terminals in subsequent sections. However, first we will consider how such terminals can be connected to a computer system. Since terminals are used for interaction with human operators, very high rates of data transmission are not necessary. Therefore, a simple, inexpensive, serial link, suitable for transmission of characters one bit at a time, is normally used to connect terminals. A standard format exists for transmitting such data, which we will describe next.

Serial transmission of data requires that both the transmitting and the receiving devices use the same timing information for interpretation of individual bits; thus, a clock signal must be used to indicate when each data bit occurs. There are two basic ways of realizing serial transmission. In a *synchronous* scheme, the receiver recovers the clock timing used by the transmitter by observing the positions of the transitions in the transmitted data signal. Alternatively, an *asynchronous* scheme may be used, where the sender and the receiver generate their clock signals independently. In this case, it is necessary to ensure that the two clocks have reasonably similar frequencies and that the start of a sampling period for each multibit unit of data can be identified.

The asynchronous serial transmission scheme that is commonly used for connection of terminals is known as the *start-stop* scheme. It is used for the transmission of alphanumeric characters, usually encoded in 8-bit data units, as shown in Figure 9.1. The line connecting the transmitter and the receiver is normally in the 1 state when idle. Transmission of a character is preceded by a 0 bit, referred to as the Start bit, followed by eight bits of data and one or two Stop bits (each with logic value 1). The Start bit alerts the receiver that data transmission is about to begin. Its leading edge is

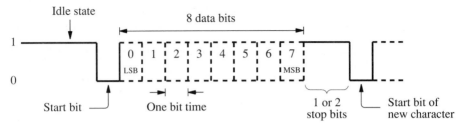

FIGURE 9.1
Asynchronous serial character transmission.

used to synchronize the receiver clock with that of the transmitter. The Stop bits at the end serve to delineate consecutive characters in the case of continuous transmission. If only one character is being transmitted, the line remains in the 1 state after the end of the Stop bits. During an input operation, it is the responsibility of the interface connecting the terminal to the I/O bus of the computer to remove the Start and Stop bits. The interface also assembles the eight serially transmitted data bits in its input data register in preparation for later parallel transfer to the computer when an input instruction is executed. The reverse sequence takes place for an output operation. An example of an interface of this type was given in Figure 6.19.

In order to ensure proper synchronization of the receiving end, the frequency of the local clock should be substantially higher than the transmission rate. Usually, the clock frequency is chosen to be 16 times the rate of transmission. This means that 16 clock pulses occur during each data bit interval. The receiver clock is used to increment a modulo-16 counter. This counter is reset to 0 when the leading edge of a Start bit is detected. Then, when the count reaches 8, in the middle of the Start bit, the value of the Start bit is sampled as a further check, and the counter is again reset to 0. From this point onward, the incoming data signal is sampled whenever the count reaches 16, which should be close to the middle of each bit transmitted. Therefore, as long as the relative positioning of bits within a transmitted character is not in error by more than eight clock cycles, the receiver will correctly interpret the bits of the encoded character.

A range of standard transmission rates is found in commercially available equipment. The most common rates are 300, 600, 1200, 2400, 4800, 9600, and 19,200 bits per second. A particular rate is chosen based on the characteristics of the transmission link, as well as on the nature of the application. The rate of transmission is often referred to somewhat incorrectly as the *baud* rate. A baud is actually a unit of signalling speed and refers to the number of times the state of a signal changes per second. For binary signals, the baud rate is the same as the bit rate. However, there exist more complicated signalling schemes where the baud rate is not the same as the bit rate. (See Problem 9.2 for an example.)

The transmitted characters are represented by the 7-bit ASCII code (see Appendix D) occupying bits 0 to 6 in Figure 9.1. The MSB, bit 7 of the transmitted byte, is usually set to 0. The ASCII character set consists of capital letters, numbers, and special symbols, such as $, +, and >. A number of nonprinting characters are also provided, for example EOT (end of transmission) and CR (carriage return). These characters may be used by the programmer to request specific actions, particularly when transmitting or receiving messages to or from a remote computer.

The start-stop scheme defines the format used for transmission of character data. There are several techniques for establishing the physical connection between the transmitter and the receiver. A popular standard that defines the electrical connections required is the RS-232-C, which will be discussed in Chapter 13.

9.1.2 Video displays

Video displays are used whenever visual representation of output information from a computer is needed, but where a hard copy of this information is not required. A video display is basically an output device. However, it can perform limited input functions when used in conjunction with a light pen, joystick, or mouse, as will be discussed later. In this section, we will present a brief description of the video display unit to give the reader an appreciation of the digital hardware involved. Detailed technological and engineering aspects of the design of the video display are beyond the scope of this book.

Let us start by describing how a picture is formed. A focused beam of electrons strikes a fluorescent screen, causing emission of light that can be seen as a bright spot against a dark background. The dot thus formed disappears when the beam is turned off or moved to another spot. Thus, in general, there are three independent variables that need to be specified at all times: the position of the beam, which can be specified in terms of its X and Y coordinates, and whether the beam is turned on, which is usually referred to as the Z-axis control. In color displays, additional information is needed to specify the color. The size of the spot formed on the screen by the electron beam determines the total number of distinct point positions that can be used on the screen. This is usually in the range of 300 to 1500 points along each of the X and Y coordinates. The amount of information required to define the status of all these points is very large. We will not quantify this parameter until we have defined the format in which the data are presented to the display. Usually, a considerable amount of hardware is provided in the display to convert data from the format generated by the computer to that required to drive the display screen.

There are basically two types of video displays: (1) alphanumeric and (2) graphic.

Alphanumeric displays. Alphanumeric displays are capable of displaying a character set such as that provided by the ASCII code. Because of the need to continuously refresh the display on the screen, the characters received from the computer should be stored in a local memory. An example of the organization of such a display terminal is shown in Figure 9.2. The four counters, Column counter, X counter, Row counter, and Y counter, in conjunction with the clock generate a *raster scan* of the screen. Each character is represented by a dot matrix. The Row and Column counters keep track of the row and column positions, respectively, within the dot matrix of any given character. Character positions on the screen are defined by the contents of the X

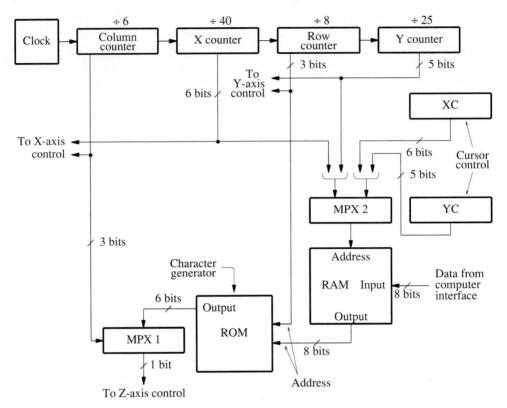

FIGURE 9.2
Control logic for an alphanumeric video display.

and Y counters. In the case of Figure 9.2, a 6×8 dot character pattern is assumed, and the screen has a capacity of 25 lines with 40 characters each.

A read-only memory (ROM) is used to store the dot pattern for each character and is thus called the *character generator*. The dot pattern for a given row of any character can be obtained by using the character code and the row number to address this memory. Multiplexer MPX 1 connects successive bits of this pattern to the Z-axis control as the beam scans across the screen. The character to be displayed at a given position on the screen is stored in the corresponding location of the random-access memory (RAM). Thus, as the values of the address counters change, the corresponding character codes are read from the RAM and sent to the character generator, which in turn provides the appropriate row pattern for Z-axis control.

Because of the need to refresh the display, the scanning process runs at a rate of about 60 full screen scans per second, providing a flicker-free display. In our example this requires a clock rate of approximately $60 \times (40 \times 6) \times (25 \times 8) \approx 3$ MHz. The RAM is addressed at one-sixth of this rate, or once every 2 μs.

To write new information on the screen, the contents of the RAM must be updated. The memory location where a new character can be written is defined by the two counters XC and YC. Multiplexer MPX 2 allows these two counters to replace the X counter and Y counter in providing the memory address during writing. The location thus defined is referred to as the *cursor* position. Counter XC is incremented by 1 every time a new character is entered. A carriage-return character causes XC to be reset to 0, and a line-feed character causes YC to be incremented by 1. Various controls may enable moving the cursor on the screen by changing the contents of the two counters XC and YC.

The example of Figure 9.2 illustrates the basic principles involved in most alphanumeric video displays. The total number of points and the order in which they are scanned vary from model to model.

Graphic displays. In many applications the output of a computer is best presented in graphical form. Computer-aided design applications provide one important example. The computer may be required to present to the designer a drawing representing the layout of an integrated circuit, a circuit diagram, or the outline of a structural member to be analyzed or modified. Real-time control applications provide another important example. From the viewpoint of a human operator, it is very convenient to represent the state of the switchgear in a power generating station or the valves in a chemical plant by familiar graphical symbols. In this way, operators can assess the overall state of the system much more quickly than if they have to interpret alphanumeric descriptions. Graphic displays are also used in applications such as video games, computer animation, and many others.

Graphical pictures can be constructed using a raster scan technique similar to that used in the alphanumeric display described above. A *bit map*, consisting of one bit for each dot position on the screen, represents the picture to be displayed. Hence, a screen with a 1000×1000 dot matrix requires a 1-Mbit memory. To refresh the display at the rate of 60 times per second, the data rate is 60 Mbps. Some high-quality terminals provide many intensity levels for each display point, thus requiring several bits to provide the *gray scale* information for each point. The display points are called *pixels*. Color displays also require several bits per pixel to provide color information.

The bit map approach is suitable for low- to medium-resolution displays. As the number of pixels increases, the necessary data rate becomes difficult to handle. An alternative approach is to specify a curvilinear path along which the electron beam can be moved to plot the required image directly. Such displays are known as *random scan displays*.

The random scan approach refreshes the display in much less time than the full screen approach. It also simplifies the job of defining the picture to be displayed. However, it requires a much more sophisticated design for the control circuitry of the display. This control circuitry is sometimes referred to as a *display processor*. The display processor accepts and executes commands of the type "Move the beam from its present position, point A, to point B," where point B is specified by absolute X and Y coordinates. Alternatively, point B can be specified relative to the current position of the beam. That is, only ΔX and ΔY, which are the X and Y coordinates of the vector AB, need be supplied. Each command should also indicate whether the beam should be turned on or off during its movement along the straight-line segment AB. In some displays, it is possible to specify the intensity of the beam and the type of line to be drawn, for example, solid or dashed. A sequence of such commands can be used to describe an arbitrary curve as a collection of straight-line segments.

Let us consider a very simple problem in which a rectangle is to be drawn on a graphic display. Suppose that the viewing area of the screen consists of 1024 addressable points along each of the X and Y axes, and assume that the display processor communicates with the remainder of the computer system using DMA. Figure 9.3 shows a block diagram of the overall system. The block of commands that instructs the display processor to draw the rectangle is assembled in an area of the main memory by a program. The program sends the starting address of this block of commands to the display processor, which then fetches the commands, one by one, from the main memory using cycle-stealing.

An outline of the block of commands that could be used to draw a rectangle of size 400×150 points is given in Figure 9.4. The long side of the rectangle is parallel to the X axis, and its lower left corner is at point (300, 400). The rectangle is drawn by proceeding clockwise from this corner. In this simple example, the display processor continually traces out the rectangle until it is halted by the CPU. Another possibility would be to replace command number 6 with a command to send an interrupt request to the CPU. The CPU could then update the commands, if desired, and restart execution. The ability to rapidly update the displayed picture is useful in producing such effects as "animation."

In the above discussion we introduced the basic ideas involved in raster scan and random scan displays. Both types of displays have found widespread use; both can be used as alphanumeric or graphic displays. Each has its own advantages and disadvantages, however. For example, the complexity of the picture has an effect on the displayed image when using the random scan technique. If a large number of line segments are involved in a given picture, the image will start to flicker if the display processor cannot keep up with the rate required for refreshing the screen. Raster scan displays have a

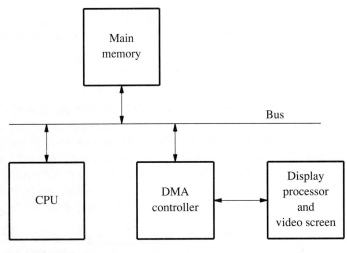

FIGURE 9.3
Graphic display in a computer system.

Command number	Block of commands in the main memory	Comments
1	Position beam to (300, 400), beam off	Get beam positioned at bottom left corner of rectangle.
2	Move incrementally (0, 150), beam on	Draw left side.
3	Move incrementally (400,0), beam on	Draw top side.
4	Move incrementally (0,–150), beam on	Draw right side.
5	Move incrementally (–400,0), beam on	Draw bottom side.
6	Branch to command number 1	Go back to beginning of block and begin refresh cycle.

FIGURE 9.4
Block of commands for drawing a rectangle on a graphic display.

fixed scanning rate, hence a fixed refresh rate. Their main drawback is that high resolution in the displayed image is not easy to achieve. On the positive side, raster scan displays are flicker-free, regardless of the complexity of the displayed picture. They also lend themselves to color applications.

9.1.3   Flat Panel Displays

Although cathode ray tube technology has dominated display applications, there has been considerable effort aimed at developing other display technologies. Flat panel displays are an interesting alternative. They are thinner, hence attractive for environments such as laptop computers. They provide better linearity and in some cases even higher resolution. However, high-quality flat panel displays are still relatively expensive.

Several types of flat panel displays have been developed, including

- Plasma panels
- Liquid crystal panels
- Electroluminescent panels

Plasma panels consist of two glass plates, separated by a thin gap filled with a gas such as neon. Each plate has a number of parallel electrodes running across it. The electrodes on the two plates run at right angles to each other. A voltage pulse applied between two electrodes, one on each plate, causes a small segment of gas at the intersection of the two electrodes to start glowing. The glow of gas segments turned on in this way is maintained by a lower voltage that is continuously applied to all electrodes. A similar pulsing arrangement can be used to selectively turn points off.

Liquid crystal panels may be constructed by sandwiching a thin layer of liquid crystal (that is, a liquid that exhibits crystalline properties) between two electrically conducting plates. The top plate has transparent electrodes deposited on it, and the back plate is a mirror. By applying proper electrical signals across the plates, various segments of the liquid crystal can be activated, causing changes in their light diffusing or polarizing properties. These segments will then either transmit or block the light. An image is produced by passing light through selected segments of the liquid crystal and then reflecting it back from the mirror to the viewer. Liquid crystal displays have found extensive use in calculators, watches, and other devices where small-size displays are needed.

Electroluminescent panels use a thin layer of phosphor between two electrically conducting panels. The image is created by applying electrical signals to the plates, making the phosphor glow.

The viability of flat panel displays is closely linked to developments in the competing cathode ray tube display technology, which continues to provide a good combination of price and performance and permits easy implementation of color displays.

9.1.4   Graphic Input Devices

It is important to have convenient and flexible means for creating and changing display images. In commonly used video terminals, a keyboard serves as the basic input device. It is used to enter both control commands and characters to be displayed. An operator can determine the position on the screen where the next input character will be displayed by controlling the position of the cursor. This may be done with key commands such as Space, Backspace, Carriage Return, Line Feed, and Tab.

In addition to basic cursor control from a keyboard, it is often desirable to have more powerful means of specifying locations on the screen. Simple input devices that can be used for this purpose include the light pen, the joystick, the trackball, and the mouse. The *light pen* consists of a pen with a light sensor mounted at its tip. When the tip is held near the screen, and when the electron beam illuminates a spot on the screen next to the sensor it produces an output pulse. This event can cause an interrupt request to be sent to the controlling processor. The X and Y coordinates of the beam at this moment are available for reference by the processor. This enables the programmer to use the light pen as an input device for defining points on the display screen.

The *joystick* is a short, pivoted stick that can be moved by hand to define a point in two dimensions. The position of the stick, hence the coordinates of that point, can be sensed by a suitable linear or angular position transducer, such as the potentiometer arrangement shown in Fig 9.5. The voltage outputs of the X and Y potentiometers are fed to two analog-to-digital (A/D) converters. The output of the A/D converters can be read by a computer, thus enabling the computer to sense the position of the joystick at any time.

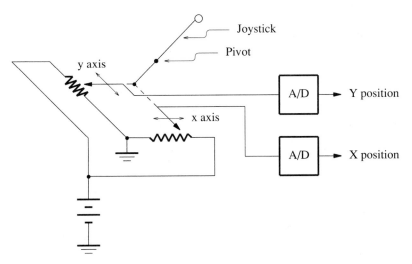

FIGURE 9.5
Joystick, using potentiometers as position transducers.

The *trackball* is fixed in a shallow well and can be rotated in any direction to move the cursor on the screen. The *mouse* is a small device that can be moved over a flat surface to cause the cursor to move in a corresponding way on the screen.

9.1.5 Printers

Printers are used to produce hard copy of output data or text. They are usually classified as either impact or nonimpact type, depending on the nature of the printing mechanism used. Impact printers use mechanical printing mechanisms, and nonimpact printers rely on electrostatic, thermal, or optical techniques. Mechanical printers can be only as fast as their mechanical parts allow. However, speeds upward of 1000 lines per minute are attainable. Considerably higher speeds can be achieved with nonimpact printers, where printing several thousand lines per minute is possible.

We will consider two representative examples of mechanical printers: drum and chain printers. Consider a drum line printer first. If a line contains *n* characters (132 characters is a popular choice), then the drum is divided into *n* tracks, each track consisting of a complete set of characters. A set of *n* print hammers (one per track) is used to press the printing paper and the ink ribbon against the characters on the drum. The line to be printed is held in a buffer, which is loaded by the output circuits of the computer. As the drum rotates, the characters on the drum are compared with those in the buffer. When a desired character passes in front of the hammer, the hammer is activated to print the character. Thus a complete line is printed within one revolution of the drum.

Chain printers employ a belt that contains a set of characters. As the belt rotates, the characters move along the line past the print hammers. Each hammer is activated when the character to be printed at that position passes in front of it. A complete line is printed within one revolution of the belt. Faster operation can be achieved if duplicate copies of the character set are used on the belt. For example, if five full sets of characters are used, a complete line can be printed in one-fifth of one revolution of the belt.

Nonimpact printers use fewer mechanical parts and can be operated at higher speeds. A number of different techniques are used in printers of this type. Photocopying technology has been used in laser printers. In this scheme, a drum coated with positively charged photoconductive material is scanned by a laser beam. The positive charges that are illuminated by the beam are dissipated. Then, a negatively charged toner powder is spread over the drum. It adheres to the positive charges, thus creating a page image that is then transferred to the paper. As the last step the drum is cleaned of any excess toner material to prepare it for printing the next page.

An electrostatic printing mechanism can be used in character and line printers. Characters are formed by charging the printing paper with character patterns under the control of electrodes. In this case, special paper containing electrically conductive material is used.

Other types of nonimpact printers include those using thermal and ink-jet principles. In a thermal printer, a heating element in the print head develops the character image on special heat-sensitive paper. In an ink-jet printer, electrically charged droplets of ink are fired from a nozzle. They are deflected by an electric field to trace out the desired character patterns on the paper they strike. Several nozzles with different color inks can be used to generate color output.

Printers are often referred to as either solid character or dot matrix printers. In the former, characters are formed as solid outlines. In dot matrix printers, characters are formed by printing dots in matrices that typically involve 5×7 or 7×9 dot positions. These printers are popular because they can easily accommodate a variety of fonts and can also be used for printing graphical images. A possible problem with dot matrix printers is poor definition of character outlines. This can be overcome by overlapping the dots and increasing their number.

Development of printers has been characterized by intense activity. A variety of different techniques have been developed and successfully applied in practice. Though this has resulted in lower costs, the cost of high-quality printers is still high.

9.2 ON-LINE STORAGE

Most computer systems require a storage space much larger than the available main memory. However, expansion of the main memory is limited by economic considerations. The required extra storage space can be provided by magnetic disks and tapes.

9.2.1 Magnetic-Disk Systems

As the name implies, the storage medium in a magnetic-disk system consists of one or more disks (platters) stacked one on another. A thin magnetic film is deposited on each disk, usually on both sides. The disks are mounted on a rotary drive such that the magnetized surfaces move in close proximity to Read/Write heads, as shown in Figure 9.6*a*. The disks rotate at a uniform speed. Each head consists of a magnetic yoke and a magnetizing coil, as in Figure 9.6*b*. Digital information can be stored on the magnetic film by applying current pulses of suitable polarity to the magnetizing coil. This causes the magnetization of the film in the area immediately underneath the head to be switched into a direction parallel to the applied field. The same head can be used for reading the stored information. In this case, changes in the magnetic field in the vicinity of the head caused by the movement of the film relative to the yoke induce a voltage in the coil, which now serves as a sense coil. The polarity of this voltage is monitored by the control circuitry to determine the state of magnetization of the film. It should be noted that only changes in the magnetic field under the head can be sensed during the Read operation. Therefore, if the binary states 0 and 1 are

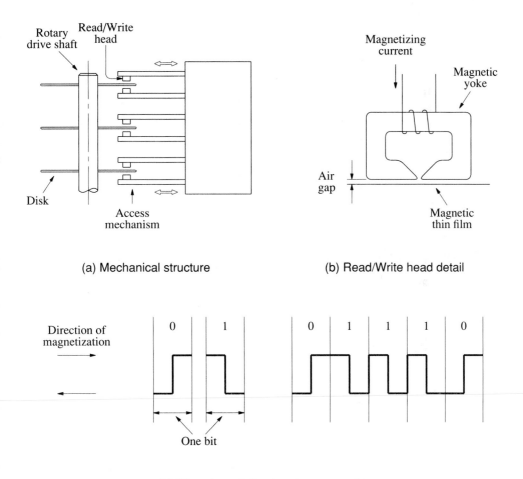

(a) Mechanical structure

(b) Read/Write head detail

(c) Bit representation by phase encoding

FIGURE 9.6
Magnetic disk principles.

represented by two opposite states of magnetization, a voltage is induced in the head only at 0 to 1 and 1 to 0 transitions in the bit stream. A long string of 0s or 1s will cause an induced voltage only at the beginning and end of the string. In order to determine the number of consecutive 0s or 1s stored, a clock must provide information for synchronization. The clock can be recorded on a separate track, where a change in magnetization is forced for each bit period. Then, a simple memory circuit that records the direction of the last change in magnetization on the data track, plus the clock signal, will allow correct reading of the stored data.

A number of different techniques for encoding data on magnetic disks have been developed. As an alternative to storing the clock on a separate track, the clocking information can be combined with the data. One popular scheme is depicted in Figure 9.6c. It is known as *phase encoding* or *Manchester encoding*. In this scheme, changes in magnetization occur for each data bit, as shown in the figure. Note that a change in magnetization is guaranteed at the midpoint of each bit period, thus providing the clocking information. With this type of encoding, it is not necessary to provide a separate track for clocking purposes, because the clock is easily extracted from the encoded data. The drawback of Manchester encoding is its poor bit-storage density. The space required to represent each bit must be large enough to accommodate two changes in magnetization. Other, more compact codes have been developed. They require more complex control circuitry but provide better storage density.

Read/Write heads must be maintained at a very small distance from the moving disk surfaces in order to achieve high bit densities and reliable Read/Write operations. When the disks are moving at their steady rate, air pressure develops between the disk surface and the head and forces the head away from the surface. This force can be counteracted by a spring-loaded mounting arrangement for the head that allows it to be pressed toward the surface. The flexible spring connection between the head and its arm mounting permits the head to "fly" at the desired distance away from the surface in spite of any small variations in the flatness of the surface.

Organization and accessing of data on a disk. The organization of data on a disk is illustrated in Figure 9.7a. Each surface is divided into concentric *tracks*, and each track is divided into *sectors*. The set of corresponding tracks on all surfaces of a stack of disks is said to form a *cylinder*. Data bits are stored serially on each track. Data on disks is addressed by specifying the surface number, the track number, and the sector number. In some cases, it is possible to specify an individual word within an addressed sector. However, in most disk systems, Read and Write operations always start at sector boundaries. If the number of words to be written is smaller than that required to fill a sector, the disk controller repeats the last bit of data for the remainder of the sector.

The Read/Write heads of a disk system are either fixed or movable. In the former case, a separate head is provided for each track of each surface. In the latter case, there is one head per surface; all heads are mounted on a comb-like arm that can move radially across the stack of disks to provide access to individual tracks, as shown in Figure 9.6a. In some moving-head disk systems, the stack of disks can be removed for off-line storage and is usually called a *disk pack*.

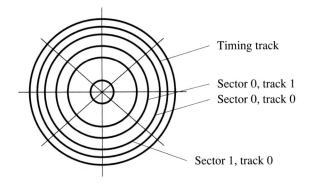

Timing track

Sector 0, track 1

Sector 0, track 0

Sector 1, track 0

(a) Organization of one surface of a disk

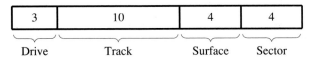

3	10	4	4
Drive	Track	Surface	Sector

(b) Format of a disk address word

FIGURE 9.7
Addressing of data on magnetic disks.

The fixed-head organization results in faster access to a sector location, because in the moving-head case the arm holding the Read/Write heads must first be positioned to the correct track. There are many other factors that should also be taken into account in comparing fixed-head systems with moving-head systems. For instance, there is more electronic circuitry involved in the one-head-per-track scheme than in the movable-head disk system. On the other hand, there is more mechanical complexity in the moving-arm organization.

It is common to have one or more permanently written tracks to provide timing pulses. The pulses, in conjunction with counters in the disk control circuits, can be used to determine sector and track origin positions on the data tracks. Figure 9.7a indicates a timing track at the outer edge of the surface. This is a feasible arrangement in fixed-head systems. The heads that operate on the timing tracks provide positional addressing information for the remainder of the tracks. In multiple-surface moving-head systems, one of the surfaces may be dedicated to providing timing-pulse information that can be used in addressing data on the remainder of the surfaces. In addition to these methods of deriving positional information from timing tracks, there are a number of ways in which additional timing information may be included in the data-encoding scheme, as we have described.

Let us consider an example of how a disk might be organized, using specific values for the various parameters. Suppose that the disk system has 16 data recording surfaces with 1024 tracks per surface. Tracks are divided into 16 sectors, and each sector of a track contains 1024 bytes (or characters) of data, recorded bit-serially. The total capacity of the disk is $16 \times 1024 \times 16 \times 1024 \approx 268$ million bytes. Assume that the diameter of the inner cylinder is 5 inches and that of the outer cylinder is 9 inches. Since the bit capacity of all tracks is the same, the maximum bit density occurs along the inner tracks, where it is $(16 \times 1024 \times 8)/5\pi \approx 8{,}400$ bits/in. Since there are 1024 tracks per surface, the track density is $1024/2 = 512$ tracks per inch.

The data transfer rate for this disk is calculated as follows. Assuming a rotational speed of 3600 revolutions per minute, a complete track can be read or written in $60/3600 \approx 0.017$ seconds. This corresponds to a byte transfer rate of $(16 \times 1024)/0.017 \approx 1{,}000{,}000$ bytes/s.

For a moving-head system, there are two components involved in the time delay between receiving an address and the beginning of the actual data transfer. The first, called the *seek time*, is the time required to move the Read/Write head to the proper track. This obviously depends on the initial position of the head relative to the track specified in the address. Average values in the 20-ms range are typical. The second component is the *rotational delay*, also called *latency time*. This is the amount of time that elapses after the head is positioned over the correct track until the starting position of the addressed sector comes under the Read/Write head. On average, this is the time for half a rotation of the disk, that is, $0.5(60/3600) = 8.3$ ms in the above example. The sum of these two delays is usually called the disk *access time*. We should note that if only a few sectors of data are moved in a single operation, the access time is about an order of magnitude longer than the actual data transfer period. Also, since the major component of the access time is the seek time, it is clear that fixed-head systems, which require no seek time, have a distinct time advantage over moving-head systems.

Disk operations. Communication between a disk and the main memory is done using DMA. The operation of this I/O access mechanism was described in Chapter 6. Here, we will concentrate on the logical requirements and will not be concerned with the method of implementation. The information that must be exchanged between the CPU and the disk controller in order to specify a transfer includes:

Main memory address—The address of the first main memory location of the block of words involved in the transfer.

Disk address—The location of the sector containing the beginning of the desired block of words.

Word count—The number of words in the block to be transferred.

We can assume, for convenience, that these three quantities are placed in registers in the disk controller.

The disk address format for our disk example is shown in Figure 9.7b. The lengths of the track, surface, and sector fields are consistent with the parameters we have used. The fourth field, named the drive field, specifies which of eight disk drives is involved. This applies to the case in which a number of disk drives are controlled by one controller.

The word count may correspond to fewer or more bytes than are contained in a sector. An interesting aspect of the disk-address word format of Figure 9.7*b* should be noted. Let us consider a data block that is longer than 16 sectors. The disk address register is incremented as successive sectors are read or written. When the sector count goes from 15 to 0, the surface count increases by 1. Thus, long data blocks are laid out on cylinder surfaces as opposed to being laid out on successive tracks of a single disk surface. This is efficient for the case of moving-head systems because successive 16-sector areas of data storage on the disk can be accessed by electrically switching from one Read/Write head to the next rather than by mechanically moving the arm from track to track. The track-to-track move will need to be made only at cylinder-to-cylinder boundaries.

The disk controller must be able to accept commands to initiate various functions in the disk drives, as well as handle the addressing and block-length information. The major functions are:

Seek—Selects the desired track. In the case of a moving-head system, the disk drive specified in the disk address register moves the Read/Write head arm from its current position to the track specified; in the case of a fixed-head system, the appropriate Read/Write head is selected electronically.

Read—Initiates a Read operation starting at the address specified in the disk address register. Data read serially from the disk are assembled into words and transferred to the main memory, starting at the location specified in the memory address register. The number of words transferred to memory is determined by the word count register. The word count is decremented after each word transfer, and the memory address is incremented. The disk address is incremented at the end of each sector.

Write—Transfers data from the main memory to the disk. Data transfers are controlled in a way similar to that given for the Read command.

Write Check—Can be used after a Write operation to ensure that no errors have been introduced during the transfer. The controller starts a Read operation on the disk and compares the contents of the addressed sector to the data read from the corresponding locations in the main memory. If a mismatch is detected, an error message is returned to the CPU via the interrupt system.

To synchronize the issuing of these commands from the CPU, the disk system may be arranged to raise an interrupt at the completion of a Seek operation in a moving-head disk. Interrupts will also normally be used to signal the completion of a Read, Write, or Write Check operation. In addition, many disk systems possess a lookahead register, which contains the address of the sector currently passing underneath the Read/Write head. This enables the operating system to check the disk position in order to efficiently schedule a series of input or output operations.

Winchester disks. Some advantages can be derived if the disk pack and the Read/Write heads are placed in a sealed, air-filtered enclosure. This approach is known as *Winchester technology*. In such units the Read/Write heads can operate closer to the magnetized track surfaces, because dust particles, which are a problem in unsealed assemblies, are absent. The closer the heads are to a track surface, the more densely the data can be packed along the track, and the closer the tracks can be to each other. Thus, Winchester disks have larger capacity for a given physical size, resulting in cheaper units. Another advantage of Winchester technology is that data integrity tends to be greater in sealed units where the storage medium is not exposed to contaminating elements.

Floppy disks. The devices discussed above are known as hard or rigid disk units. *Floppy disks* are smaller, simpler, and cheaper disk units that consist of a flexible plastic diskette coated with magnetic material. The diskette is enclosed in a cardboard or plastic jacket. The jacket has an opening where the Read/Write head comes in contact with the diskette. A hole in the center of the diskette allows a spindle mechanism in the disk drive to position and rotate the diskette.

Information is recorded on floppy disks by combining the clock and data information along each track. One of the simplest schemes used is essentially the same as phase or Manchester encoding, mentioned earlier. Disks encoded in this way are said to have *single density*. A more complicated variant of this scheme, called *double*

TABLE 9.1 Characteristics of some magnetic-disk systems.

Model	Type	Capacity per drive char. $\times 10^6$	Transfer rate, (char./s) $\times 10^6$	Average access time, ms	Speed of rotation, rpm
DEC:					
RA82	Winchester	855	2.4	32.3	3600
RA90	Winchester	1200	2.8	26.3	3600
RX50	Floppy	0.4	0.25	164.0	300
RX33	Floppy	1.2	0.5	92.0	360
IBM:					
3370	Winchester	730	1.9	30.1	2964
3380	Winchester	3780	3.0	24.3	3600
Control Data:					
9720	Winchester	1236	3.0	24.3	3600
97229	Winchester	1150	6.0	24.3	3600
Fujitsu:					
M2372	Winchester	824	2.5	24.3	3600
M2382	Winchester	1000	3.0	24.3	3620
Northern Telecom:					
8312	Winchester	592	1.9	29.3	3314

density, is frequently used. It increases the storage density by a factor of 2, but it also requires more complex circuits in the disk controller.

The main attraction of floppy disks is their low cost and shipping convenience. However, they have much smaller storage capacities and longer access times than hard disks. Floppy disks that can store 1 MByte of data are in common use, but units capable of storing up to 10 MBytes have been developed.

Disk technology has developed rapidly. We have discussed the main features of the commonly used disk types. In order to give the reader some feeling for the quantitative parameters of typical disk units, we have summarized these parameters for several disks in Table 9.1.

9.2.2 Magnetic-Drum Systems

Magnetic drums are similar to magnetic disks in their principle of operation. The main difference is that the magnetic film that serves as the storage medium is deposited on the surface of a drum instead of a disk. Tracks are organized around the surface of the drum as shown in Figure 9.8.

The storage capacity of a drum varies considerably from one system to another. It starts at around 2×10^6 characters and goes as high as 9×10^9 characters. Small drum systems are similar in performance to disk drives. Large drum systems, however, are capable of storing more information than currently available disk drives.

In many drum systems, a set of Read/Write heads is used to access the bits of a given character in parallel. With few exceptions, only one Read/Write head is enabled in a disk drive at any given time.

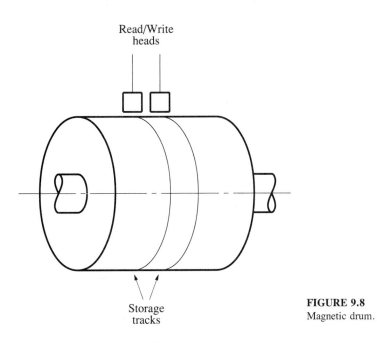

Read/Write
heads

Storage
tracks

FIGURE 9.8
Magnetic drum.

9.2.3 Magnetic-Tape Systems

Magnetic tapes are particularly suited for off-line storage of large amounts of data and are also used extensively for shipment of information when telecommunication facilities are either not available or not appropriate. Magnetic-tape recording uses the same principle as does recording data on disks. The main difference is that the magnetic film is deposited on a very thin 1/2-inch-wide plastic tape. Seven or nine bits (corresponding to one character) are recorded in parallel across the width of the tape, perpendicular to the direction of motion. A separate Read/Write head is provided for each bit position on the tape, so that all bits of a character can be read or written in parallel. One of the character bits is used as a parity bit.

Data on the tape are organized in the form of *records* separated by gaps, as shown in Figure 9.9. Tape motion is stopped only when a record gap is underneath the Read/Write heads. The record gaps are long enough to allow the tape to attain its normal speed before the beginning of the next record is reached. If a coding scheme such as that of Figure 9.6c is used for recording data on the tape, record gaps are identified as areas where there is no change in magnetization. This allows record gaps to be detected independently of the recorded data. To help in the organization of large amounts of data, a group of related records is called a *file*. The beginning of a file is identified by a *file mark*, as shown in Figure 9.9. The file mark is a special single- or multi-character record, usually preceded by a gap longer than the interrecord gap. The first record following a file mark may be used as a *header* or *identifier* for this file. This enables a tape containing a large number of files to be searched for a particular file.

The controller of a magnetic tape drive enables the execution of a number of control commands in addition to read and write commands. Control commands include the following operations:

- Rewind tape
- Rewind and unload tape
- Erase tape
- Write tape mark
- Forward space one record

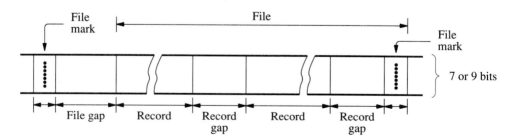

FIGURE 9.9
Organization of data on magnetic tape.

- Backspace one record
- Forward space one file
- Backspace one file

The tape mark referred to in the operation Write-tape-mark is similar to a file mark except that it is used for identifying the beginning of the tape. The end of the tape is sometimes identified by the EOT (end of tape) character (see Appendix D).

Two methods of formatting and using tapes are used. In one case, the records are variable in length. This allows efficient use of the tape, but it does not permit updating or overwriting of records in place. The second possibility is to use fixed-length records. In this case it is possible to update records in place. While this may seem to be a significant advantage, in practice it has turned out to be of little importance. The most common uses of tapes are for backing up information on magnetic disks and for archival storage of data. In these applications, a tape is written from the beginning to the end, so that the size of the records is immaterial.

The characteristics of some typical tape units are given in Table 9.2.

Cartridge tape system. A tape system that has been developed for backup of on-line disk storage uses an 8-mm tape housed in a cassette. These units are called cartridge tapes. They have capacities in the gigabyte range and handle data transfers at the rate of a few hundred kilobytes per second. Reading and writing is done by a helical scan system operating across the tape, similar to that used in video cassette tape drives. Bit densities of tens of millions of bits per square inch are achievable.

9.2.4   Other Mass Storage Technologies

Since the early days of computers, the majority of mass storage units have used magnetic disks, drums, and tapes. They offer high storage density combined with fast data

TABLE 9.2   Characteristics of some magnetic-tape systems.

Model	Channels	Tape speed, in/s	Density, bits/in	Transfer rate, (char./s) $\times$ 10^3
DEC:				
TU80	9	100	1600	160
TU79	9	125	1600/6250	781
Fujitsu:				
M2444	9	75	1600/6250	1000
Control Data Corp.:				
92185	9	75	1600/6250	770

transfer rates. However, because of the presence of moving parts, they are vulnerable to mechanical failures. Researchers continually seek alternative technologies that offer equivalent or better performance.

Several such alternative technologies have been developed. They include magnetic bubbles, charge-coupled devices, and optical storage. While these technologies have not replaced magnetic disks and tapes, they offer certain advantages that make them suitable for specialized applications. In what follows, we will briefly discuss some of these technologies.

Magnetic bubble devices. Crystals of certain magnetic materials strongly favor magnetization in a fixed direction relative to the crystalline axes. Bubble memories use thin slices of single crystals of such material, prepared so that the favored direction of magnetization is perpendicular to the surface of the slice. Vertical sections through the slice may be magnetized in opposite directions, as shown in Figure 9.10a.

Let us now assume that a uniform magnetic field H_b is applied to the slice of Fig 9.10a parallel to the Z-axis. The regions of the slice where magnetization is in the same direction as the H_b field will grow in size and those where magnetization is in the opposite direction will shrink. At a certain value of H_b, the regions with opposite magnetization collapse into very tiny cylinders, called *bubbles*, as shown in Figure 9.10b. They can be moved about in the slice by applying external magnetic fields. They maintain their size and shape as long as the H_b field remains constant.

The slice is divided into small areas, called cells, by a metallic pattern deposited on its surface. Binary information can be stored in the slice by stipulating that a cell stores a 1 if it contains a bubble and a 0 otherwise. It is possible to organize adjacent cells into loops. Bubbles can be introduced into loop cell positions at one point on the slice and then circulated around the loop. As loop information circulates past this point it can be read and/or modified. The introduction and removal of bubbles at such points is analogous to the writing action of heads in magnetic disk systems.

Commercially available bubble memories have a few hundred loops each, with a few thousand cells (bits) per loop, providing a total storage capacity on the order of a few megabits. The stored information can be accessed at a rate of about 100 Kbits/s. While bubble memories have not been able to compete with magnetic disks, the absence of moving parts makes them attractive in some mobile and airborne applications.

Charge-coupled devices. A charge-coupled device (CCD) is a high-density semiconductor storage device that can be accessed serially at high speed. A CCD consists of a silicon wafer on which tiny metal electrodes are deposited. When an electrical potential is applied to one of these electrodes, it forms a small pocket in the semiconductor material (the silicon wafer) in which an electric charge may be stored for a short time period. By applying an appropriate voltage waveform to the electrodes, the stored charge can be shifted between adjacent pockets. Hence, the structure functions as a shift register.

In order to use CCDs for storing information, the electrodes are organized in loops that incorporate refresh circuitry at regular intervals. The stored information,

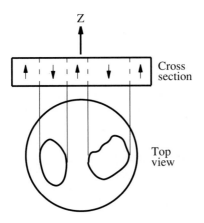

(a) Magnetization in a thin slice of magnetic bubble material

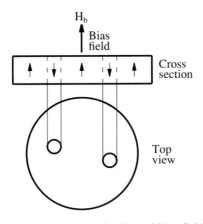

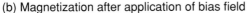

(b) Magnetization after application of bias field

FIGURE 9.10
Magnetic bubbles.

which is represented by the presence or absence of a charge, circulates continually around the storage loops. As in the case of bubble memories, appropriate structures are used for read and write operations.

CCDs are suitable for applications where a high-speed, serially accessed data buffer is needed. For example, they have been used as a cache memory between a magnetic disk and a computer. Because of their volatility, they are not suitable for long-term storage of information.

Optical storage devices. The spot of light produced by focusing a laser beam has a diameter of the order of 1 micron. A number of devices have been designed using such a spot in the process of storing and accessing information. Typically, the writing mechanism involves using a pulse of light to impart a well-controlled amount of heat to a tiny area of a suitable storage medium. This change in temperature causes a change in magnetization of a magnetic material or distorts a thin layer of metal. The stored information can be accessed by sensing the change in polarization or intensity of a light beam as it is transmitted through the storage medium or reflected from its surface. Elaborate mechanisms that may involve vibrating mirrors or rotating prisms move the light beam to different points of the storage medium. In some devices, the storage medium may also rotate in a manner similar to a magnetic disk. Optical storage devices are intended primarily for archival storage applications in which a very high storage density is needed.

9.3   FILE SERVERS

Widespread use of computer workstations has led to distributed computing systems. In a distributed system, most computational tasks are performed on local machines. These machines are connected to a network that includes a variety of computers and peripheral devices, enabling each machine to have access to other resources when needed.

One particular configuration of workstations connected to shared resources via a network has become very popular. Aside from printers and plotters, the major shared resource is a disk storage facility comprising at least one magnetic disk unit. Program and data files that may be accessed by any computer in the system are maintained in this facility. The workstations do not necessarily have local disks attached to them. A reasonably powerful processor is responsible for managing this fiie system and responding to the read and write requests that it receives over the network from the workstations. The combination of this processor and its disks is called a *file server*. Processing of application tasks is normally done on the workstations, not on the file server.

There are a number of economic and operational advantages to such a system. There is no disk unit noise at the workstation locations, which are usually individual offices or quiet office environments. Economy of scale favors the installation of a large disk storage facility, which can be built around large capacity disk units. Maintenance of the file system is more easily managed centrally.

A cost effective network for such a system consists of a single, bit-serial communication path over coaxial cable, fiber optic, or twisted-wire media. Such networks, called Local Area Networks (LANs), will be discussed in Chapter 13. For our purposes, it is useful to know that the bit rates on these networks range from about 5 Mbits/sec to 100 Mbits/sec. Such bit rates are adequate to support file transfer to and from the file server for a reasonable number of workstations. For example, suppose that 20 workstations are attached to a LAN and that each of them generates an average load of one or two 4KB file transfer operations per second. The aggregate data rate is thus at most $20 \times 2 \times 4 \times 10^3 \times 8 = 1.3$ Mbits/sec. This transfer rate represents reasonably intensive interaction between the file server and the workstations and is easily accommodated by current LANs.

9.4 CONCLUDING REMARKS

Input/output devices are a fundamental part of a computer system because they constitute the link for feeding information into a computer and for receiving the results. The choice of I/O device types and the way they are connected to the computer is an important design decision. The main concern in this decision is that no particular I/O device should create a "bottleneck" by forcing the rest of the computer system to idly wait for long periods of time until an input or output function is completed.

A slightly different situation is encountered in small computer systems. In this case, the cost of peripherals is often a major portion of the total system cost. Thus, utilization of the CPU is a less important consideration in the trade-offs of system design. An extreme example of this situation is encountered in microprocessor systems, where the cost of the CPU is very small.

9.5 PROBLEMS

9.1. The following components are provided.

- A 6-bit binary counter, with Clock and Clear inputs and six outputs
- A 3-bit serial-input–parallel-output shift register
- A clock running at eight times the input data rate
- Logic gates and JK flip-flops with Preset and Clear controls

Design a circuit using the above components to load 3 bits of serial data from an input data line into the shift register. Assume the data to have the format of Figure 9.1, but with only 3 bits of data instead of 8. The circuit you design should have two outputs, A and B. Output A should be set to 1 if a Stop bit is detected following the data bits. Otherwise, output B should be set to 1. Give an explanation of the operation of your design.

9.2. In Section 9.1.1 we defined the term "baud rate" and pointed out that in the case of binary signaling, the baud rate is the same as the bit rate. Consider now a communications channel in which 4-valued signals are used, as shown in Figure P9.1. If the channel is rated at 9600 baud, what is its capacity in bits per second?

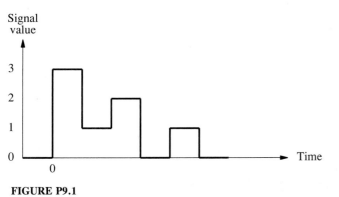

FIGURE P9.1
A 4-valued signal.

9.3. Show how Figure 9.2 can be modified so that all 6×8 points of a given character are displayed before moving to the next character.

9.4. Suggest suitable modifications to the video display controller of Figure 9.2 to implement a "roll page" feature. That is, upon receiving a special command from the computer, the displayed data moves upward slowly on the screen. Consider the following two cases.

(*a*) The entire picture on the screen moves upward in steps of one line at a time.

(*b*) The picture on the screen moves upward slowly, so that the characters on the top line progressively disappear and a new line gradually appears at the bottom of the screen. Once started, this process should proceed independently until all data has moved upward one line.

9.5. The display on a video screen must be refreshed at least 30 times per second to remain flicker-free. During each scan, the total time required to illuminate a point on the screen is 1 μs. The beam is then turned off and moved to the next point to be illuminated. On the average, this process takes 3 μs. Because of power-dissipation limitations, the beam cannot be turned on more than 10 percent of the time. Determine the maximum number of points that can be illuminated on the screen.

To illuminate more points than the above maximum, the display can be made to flash at the rate of once every 800 ms. In this case, the display is turned on for 500 ms and off for 300 ms. Determine the maximum number of points that can be illuminated under these conditions.

9.6. A disk unit has nine surfaces. The storage area on each surface has an inner diameter of 22 cm and an outer diameter of 33 cm. The maximum storage density along any track is 1600 bits/cm, and the minimum spacing between tracks is 0.25 mm.

(*a*) What is the maximum number of bits that can be stored in this unit?

(*b*) What is the data transfer rate in bytes per second at a rotational speed of 3600 rpm?

(*c*) Using a 32-bit word, suggest a suitable scheme for specifying the disk address.

(*d*) The main memory of a computer has a 32-bit word length and 0.3-μs cycle time. Assuming that the disk transfers data to or from the memory on a cycle-stealing basis, what percentage of the available memory cycles are stolen during the data transfer period?

9.7. The seek time plus rotational delay in accessing a particular data block on a disk is usually much longer than the data flow period for most disk transfers. Consider a long sequence of accesses to an IBM 3380 disk drive (see Table 9.1) for either Read or Write operations in which the average block being accessed is 4000 bytes long.

(*a*) Assuming that the blocks are randomly located on the disk, estimate the average percentage of the total time occupied by seek operations and rotational delays.

(*b*) Repeat part (*a*) for the situation in which the disk accesses have been arranged so that in 90 percent of the cases, the next access will be to a data block on the same cylinder.

9.8. The average seek time and rotational delay in a disk system are 20 ms and 8.3 ms, respectively. The rate of data transfer to or from the disk is 2 million bytes per second and all disk accesses are for 8 kilobytes of data. Disk DMA controllers, the CPU, and the main memory are all attached to a single bus. The bus data width is 32 bits, and a bus transfer to or from the main memory takes 300 nanoseconds.

(*a*) What is the maximum number of disk units that can be simultaneously transferring data to or from the main memory?

(*b*) What percentage of main memory cycles are stolen by a disk unit, on average, over a long period of time during which a sequence of independent 8-kilobyte transfers takes place?

9.9. Winchester magnetic disk technology has densities of 40×10^6 bits per square inch of surface.

(*a*) If the outer diameter of the recording area is 7 inches and the inner diameter is 4 inches, what is the average bit density along a track if radial track spacing density is 2000 tracks per inch?

(*b*) What is the transfer rate in bytes per second if the disk rotates at 3600 rpm?

(*c*) If such a disk is attached to a computer with a 32-bit word length, what memory cycle time (including bus delay) is needed if disk transfers are to steal no more than 50 percent of the bus cycles during the actual data flow time?

9.10. Given that magnetic disks are used as the secondary storage for program and data files in a virtual-memory system, suggest which disk parameter should influence the choice of page size.

9.11. A tape drive has the following parameters:

Bit density	1600 bits/in
Tape speed	200 in/s
Time to reverse direction of motion	225 ms
Minimum time spent at an interrecord gap	3 ms
Average record length	1000 characters

Estimate the percentage gain in time resulting from the ability to read records in both the forward and backward directions. Assume that records are accessed at random and that on average, the distance between two records accessed in sequence is four records.

9.12. Consider the operation of a line printer. The paper has to be stationary during the printing process. Assume that the total time required for printing a line is 10 ms. At the end of this period the paper is advanced to bring the next line to the printing position. This process takes T seconds. The speed v of the paper expressed as a function of time may be assumed to have the form

$$v = V_o\left(1 - \cos \frac{2\pi t}{T}\right)$$

where V_o is a constant. If the maximum acceleration that the paper can sustain without tearing is 65,000 cm/s^2, what is the maximum possible printing rate in lines per minute? Assume line spacing to be 4.2 mm.

9.13. Construct a flowchart for a main program and an interrupt-service routine to cause the rectangle drawn by the display program of Figure 9.4 to be increased in size from 150×400 to 190×440 in steps of 2 units. Assume that the computer has a clock that generates an interrupt every sixtieth of a second, at which time the rectangle size should be increased. When the rectangle size reaches its maximum (190×440), it is reset to the minimum size (150×400) at the next interrupt and then increased again.

9.14. A square of size 200×200 is to be drawn on a graphic display of size 1000×1000 that uses random scan. A block of commands similar to that shown in Figure 9.4 can be used. If the parameters 300 and 400 in command number 1 are replaced by references to variables XPOS and YPOS, then the square can be moved around on the screen. (XPOS and YPOS can have values in the 0 to 999 range.) As discussed in Section 9.1.2, if command number 6 is replaced by an interrupt command, the interrupt service routine can instruct the display processor to repeat the block of commands either with the same XPOS and YPOS values or with new values.

A clock interrupts the computer every sixtieth of a second. Assume that YPOS stays fixed at 400 but that after each interrupt, XPOS is incremented by 4. This should cause the square to move across the screen smoothly from left to right about once every 4 seconds. When the value of XPOS is between 0 and 799, the full square remains inside the screen boundaries. However, when XPOS is between 800 and 999, the right side of the square has moved off the screen.

Propose a way of sending appropriate blocks of commands to the display processor so that the part of the square that disappears off the right edge of the screen reappears at the left side of the screen.

CHAPTER
10

MICROPROCESSORS

One of the most significant technological advances of the past two decades has been the emergence of very large-scale integrated (VLSI) circuits. Improved technology and manufacturing methods have enabled production of very complex circuits on single chips. In the digital-logic domain, this evolution went through the stages of producing standard logic units in integrated circuit (IC) packages. The first stage yielded simple gates and flip-flops in small-scale integrated (SSI) chips and was followed by medium-scale integrated (MSI) chips that contained registers, counters, encoders, and decoders. In these forms, the required number of external connections to the package usually determines the number of distinct elements in any package. Thus it is typical to find an eight-input to one-output multiplexer or perhaps four flip-flops in a 16-pin package.

With the ability to place a large number of logic elements on a single chip, it became advantageous to consider circuits that require many logic elements but relatively few external connections. The result was the appearance of more complex packages, such as arithmetic and logic unit (ALU) chips, capable of performing the usual arithmetic and logic functions on 4-bit operands. The natural continuation of this trend brought the emergence of complete processors on a chip in the early 1970s. First, there were chips capable of operating on 4 bits in parallel. Because they had the processing capabilities but not the comparable size and speed of minicomputers, these new devices were named *microprocessors*. Soon thereafter, larger VLSI chips became available. At the present time a variety of microprocessor chips are manufactured that have word lengths in the range from 8 to 32 bits.

Increasing the processing capability of IC chips tends to increase the required number of external connections and results in larger packages. It is fairly standard to find 8-bit microprocessors in 40-pin packages. It is more difficult to fit a 16-bit microprocessor into a 40-pin package without time multiplexing the use of some pins. With time multiplexing, one set of pins is used for different functions at different times. Such time sharing is a viable possibility, but it is inevitably achieved at the cost of lower speed of operation and more complex external interfaces. The alternative is to use packages with more than 40 pins. The Motorola 68000 microprocessor, which was used as an example in Chapter 2, has 64 pins.

The term "microprocessor" was originally coined to refer to a processor characterized by very small physical size. In the early days (early 1970s), microprocessors were both physically small and computationally weak in comparison with commonly used computers. The phenomenal improvements in VLSI technology have changed this so that microprocessors are presently not only the processing elements in all modern workstations and personal computers, but they also serve as processing elements in very large multiprocessor machines, as will be discussed in Chapter 12.

Both of our major examples in Chapter 2, the 68000 and the PDP-11, have been realized in the form of microprocessors. In this chapter we will briefly consider some other popular microprocessors manufactured by Motorola and Intel. We will also discuss the support chips needed to build complete computers.

10.1 FAMILIES OF MICROPROCESSOR CHIPS

A computer is a complex machine. It is difficult to assemble all its components on a single chip. When it is subdivided into a few well-defined parts, however, the components may be implemented through a set of chips. It is quite feasible to fit the entire processor on one chip, but other chips are needed for the main memory. Yet more chips are needed to serve as interfaces to input and output devices. A number of chips are thus required for construction of a nontrivial machine.

Having established the need for various chips, we should consider the problem of interconnecting them. For economical reasons, it is important that interconnection requirements be simple and easy to meet. It is essential that signals generated by one VLSI chip can be used directly as inputs to other VLSI chips. Most manufacturers offer complete families of compatible chips. Furthermore, some of the more popular products have emerged as "standards," and their signal characteristics are used as desirable models for other products. Thus, it is not unusual to find compatibility among chips produced by different manufacturers.

As an example of a typical chip family, let us consider the Motorola 6809 microprocessor components.[1] Many basic parts are available, including:

1. 6809 (*microprocessor unit, MPU*) This is a 40-pin CPU chip that processes either 8 or 16 bits of data in parallel. It uses 16-bit addresses, allowing for memory sizes of up to 64K bytes. There are two 8-bit accumulators and five 16-bit registers that serve as a program counter, two index registers, and two stack pointers. Instructions are 1 to 5 bytes in length. The instruction set is fairly extensive, and a number of addressing modes can be used. Interrupt-handling capability is provided.

2. *PIA (peripheral interface adapter)* The PIA provides a simple means for interfacing peripheral devices to the 6809 bus. It has two I/O ports called A and B, each consisting of programmable control and data registers, as shown in Figure 10.1.

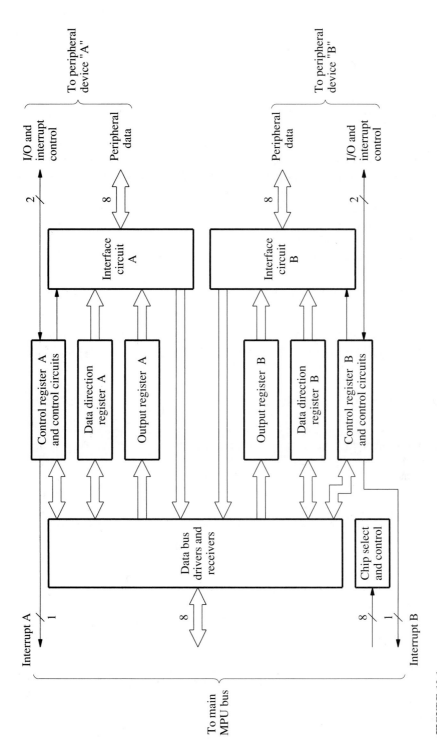

FIGURE 10.1
Peripheral interface adapter (PIA).

385

Each port provides a separate 8-bit bidirectional data interface and two control lines for connection to peripheral devices. Three internal 8-bit registers are associated with each port. An output register serves as a buffer in output transfers. A data-direction register governs the direction of I/O transfers on an individual line basis. For each bit in the register that is set to 1, the corresponding peripheral data line acts as an output and transfers the contents of the output register to the peripheral device. Similarly, for each bit set to 0, the corresponding peripheral data line acts as an input. There is no internal buffer for input transfers. Instead, input data is transferred directly to the main MPU bus. Use of the data-direction register in this fashion allows considerable flexibility in the deployment of the peripheral lines, because it is not necessary to use all of them as either inputs or outputs at any given time. A control register is provided to allow the MPU to control and monitor the status of the I/O and interrupt control lines. All three registers are accessible to the MPU as ordinary addressable locations.

3. *ACIA (asynchronous communications interface adapter)* The ACIA allows simple interfacing to devices that process data in bit-serial fashion. As Figure 10.2 indicates, the ACIA contains a transmitter circuit that accepts 8-bit parallel data from the main data bus and sends it to the peripheral device one bit at a time. This is accomplished by means of a "transmit" shift register which can be loaded in parallel. Similarly, a receiver circuit collects serial data from the device and assembles it into an 8-bit byte for transfer to the main data bus. The operation of the ACIA is controlled through two programmable control registers.

A number of other chips are also easily used with such a family of chips. In particular, memory chips (RAM, ROM, PROM, and EPROM) can be incorporated into a microprocessor system using the techniques discussed in Chapter 8.

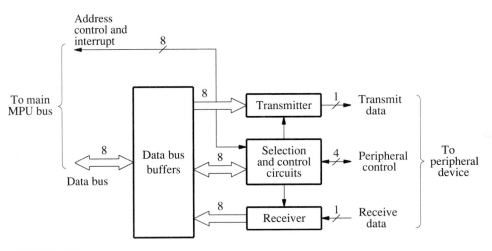

FIGURE 10.2
Asynchronous communications interface adapter (ACIA).

The key characteristic of the chips in a family is their total compatibility. They may be connected to form a simple, yet powerful, system as shown in Figure 10.3. The six chips in this configuration, together with a clock and a power supply, constitute a complete computer.

Complexity of support chips tends to increase as microprocessors themselves become more complex. This may be illustrated with the example of support chips for the Motorola 68000 class of microprocessors. There are two chips that serve as parallel and serial interfaces, which correspond functionally to the PIA and ACIA chips discussed above. The first, called PI/T (*parallel interface/timer*), provides three parallel I/O ports. Two of these ports, A and B, are similar to the equivalent ports in the PIA. However, these ports have more versatile modes of operation. Each can be used as a unidirectional 8-bit port, where the direction of each line is controlled by a bit in a data-direction register, as in the PIA. The additional modes allow these ports to function as a single 16-bit port or as bidirectional ports where the direction of the lines is controlled dynamically by the state of four *handshake* control lines. Port C is an extra 8-bit port, which makes multiplexed use of 8 pins that may also be used for control purposes.

The timer is based on a 24-bit counter. It provides such capabilities as producing a square wave output signal, generating periodic interrupts, and raising a single interrupt request after a programmed time period.

The second chip is a serial interface known as DUART (*dual asynchronous receiver/transmitter*), which is a much enhanced device of the ACIA class. It contains two independent full-duplex receiver/transmitter channels, each of which allows simultaneous transmission and reception of bit-serial data. In order to increase its versatility, the DUART also contains one parallel input port and one parallel output port.

The PI/T and DUART chips differ from the PIA and ACIA chips in one other significant way. They are intended for connection to an asynchronous bus of the type used in a 68000 system. In contrast, the PIA and ACIA chips are intended for connection to a synchronous bus, as used in 6809 systems.

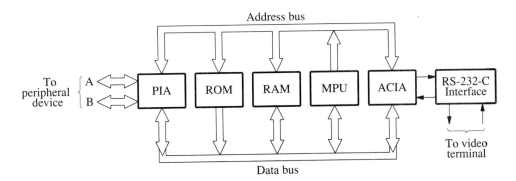

FIGURE 10.3
A simple microprocessor system.

10.2 6809 MICROPROCESSOR

The 6809 is one of the most advanced 8-bit microprocessors. It was developed as a successor to the highly popular 6800 microprocessor, with the goal of overcoming some shortcomings of the earlier model. The 6809 uses 16-bit addresses, providing for an address space of 64K bytes. It physically manipulates data in 8-bit quantities, although many operations use 16-bit words at the programming level.

10.2.1 Register Structure

Figure 10.4 shows the internal registers in the 6809. There are two 8-bit accumulators, A and B, which may be used separately or may be manipulated as a single 16-bit accumulator D. There are two index registers, named X and Y, and two stack pointers, S and U. Stack pointer S is used to maintain the system stack used in

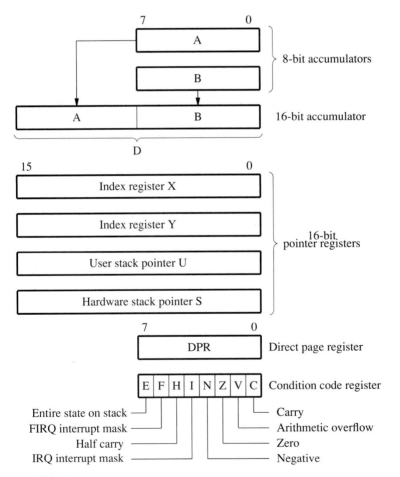

FIGURE 10.4
Register structure in the 6809 microprocessor.

subroutine linkage and interrupt servicing. The second stack pointer, U, enables the programmer to implement a second stack, called the user stack. This stack provides increased flexibility to the programmer, who may use the stack for passing subroutine parameters or for organizing temporary storage. Both stack pointers can also be used as extra index registers.

The direct page register (DPR) supports a short form of absolute addressing, as we will explain in the next section. The condition code register (CCR) has eight flags, as indicated in Figure 10.4. The C, V, Z, and N flags have the same meaning as those covered in our introductory discussion in Section 2.7.5. The H flag, known as half carry, is set if there is a carry from the fourth bit position. It is useful for processing binary-coded-decimal (BCD) data in which two BCD digits are stored in one byte. We will illustrate this in a subsequent example. Flags I, F, and E, which are used for interrupt purposes, will be discussed in Section 10.3.1.

10.2.2 Addressing Modes

The 6809 has eight basic addressing modes, plus an indirect version of five of these modes. The basic modes are:

Implied register mode. The operand location is one of the registers in the microprocessor.

Absolute mode. (called *extended* mode by Motorola) An absolute address is specified by the two bytes that follow the OP code.

Absolute short mode. (called *direct* mode by Motorola) This is a short version of the absolute mode, where the 8 low-order bits of a 16-bit address are given in the byte that follows the OP code, and the 8 high-order bits are the contents of the Direct Page Register.

Immediate mode. The operand is contained in one or two bytes that follow the OP code.

Indexed mode. The effective address is the contents of register R (R = X, Y, U or S) plus either one or two bytes that follow the OP code, or the contents of one of the accumulators.

Autoincrement mode. The effective address is the contents of register R (R = X, Y, U, or S). Having accessed the operand, the contents of R are incremented automatically by 1 or 2 as specified in the instruction.

Autodecrement mode. The contents of register R (R = X, Y, U, or S) are decremented by 1 or 2 as specified in the instruction. Then, the updated contents of R are used as the effective address.

Relative mode. The effective address is the contents of the program counter plus either an 8-bit or a 16-bit signed offset specified in one or two bytes that follow the OP code.

In addition to these basic modes, an *indirect mode* is also available. It can be used in conjunction with extended, indexed, autoincrement, autodecrement, and relative modes. In each case, the address generated by the basic mode indicates the memory location that holds the address of the desired operand. A summary of address-ing modes and their syntax is given in Table 10.1.

The 6809 addressing modes follow the general types described in Chapter 2. The only significant difference is in the two forms of the absolute mode. The extended version is the standard form of absolute addressing. The direct version allows implementation of more compact object code, because only one byte of an address needs to be included in an instruction. In this mode the addressable space is effectively partitioned into 256 pages, pointed to by the 8 bits of the DPR register. Each page is 256 bytes long. The DPR is set under programmer control. Although there is no single instruction provided for this purpose, the desired page address may be placed into the DPR by first loading it into one of the accumulators and then transferring it into the DPR. At start-up time, when a Reset signal is applied to the microprocessor, the DPR register is cleared to zero so that it points to page zero.

When writing a source program, the programmer may specify whether the extended or the direct mode is to be used, as indicated in Table 10.1. For example, the instruction

$$\text{CLR} \quad > \text{LOC}$$

uses the extended mode even if the address LOC is in the page pointed to by the DPR. If neither mode is explicitly specified, then the assembler chooses the direct mode if possible. Thus, in the instruction

$$\text{CLR} \quad \text{LOC}$$

the direct mode will be used if LOC is in the page pointed to by the DPR; otherwise the extended mode will be used. It is important to note that during the assembly process the assembler must know what the contents of the DPR will be at run-time. There exists an assembler command for this purpose that has to be included in the source code.

The first byte of any instruction is the OP code. It specifies the operation to be performed and the addressing mode to be used. However, a single byte does not have sufficient bit space to provide all of the necessary information. Some instructions need two-byte OP codes. In addition to the OP code byte(s), yet another byte may be used to define the nature of the operation. This byte, called the *post-byte* by Motorola, is appended to the OP code in the case of indexed, autoincrement, autodecrement, relative, and extended indirect modes. The format for the post-byte is shown in Table 10.2. The table is largely self-explanatory. Note that three different sizes of offsets can be specified in the indexed mode. The shortest is a 5-bit offset that is given within the post-byte. Other possibilities are 8- and 16-bit offsets that are specified in 1 or 2 bytes that follow the post-byte. In all cases the offsets are interpreted as signed 2's-complement numbers. Thus, offsets as large as $\pm 2^{15}$ may be used.

The relative mode is indicated as

$$\text{Value,PCR}$$

where Value is the desired effective address of the operand, usually expressed as a label. At execution time, the processor generates this address by adding a signed offset to the current value of the PC. The required offset is computed by the assembler and inserted in the instruction. It occupies 1 or 2 bytes following the post-byte, depending

TABLE 10.1   Syntax for 6809 Addressing Modes.

Mode	Syntax	Addressing function
Implied	Included in the OP code	Operand = [Implied register]
Absolute (extended)	>Value or Value	EA = Value
Absolute short (direct)	<Value or Value	EA = [DPR] ‖ SValue
Immediate	#Value	Operand = Value
Indexed	Value,R SValue,R Q,R or ACCUM,R	EA = Value + [R] EA = SValue + [R] EA = Q + [R] EA = [ACCUM] +[R]
Autoincrement	,R + or ,R + +	EA = [R] R ← [R] + 1 EA = [R] R← [R] + 2
Autodecrement	,−R or , − −R	R← [R] − 1 EA = [R] R← [R]−2 EA = [R]
Relative	Value,PCR	EA = Value encoded as: Offset + [PC]
Indexed indirect	[Value,R] [Svalue,R] or [ACCUM,R]	EA = [indexed EA]
Autoincrement indirect	[,R + +]	EA = [autoincrement EA]
Autodecrement indirect	[,− −R]	EA = [autodecrement EA]
Relative indirect	[Value,PCR]	EA = [relative EA]
Extended indirect	[Value]	EA = [Value]

Notes:		
R	=	X, Y, U, or S register
ACCUM	=	A, B, or D register
EA	=	effective address
a‖b	=	16-bit number where *a* is the most significant byte and *b* is the least significant byte
Value	=	16-bit signed number
SValue	=	8-bit signed number
Q	=	5-bit signed number
PC	=	Program Counter
DPR	=	Direct Page Register

TABLE 10.2 Post-byte format in 6809.

Post-byte bits								Assembler syntax	Addressing mode
7	6	5	4	3	2	1	0		
0	r	r	q	q	q	q	q	Q,R	Indexed with 5-bit signed offset
1	r	r	0	0	0	0	0	,R +	Autoincrement
1	r	r	i	0	0	0	1	,R + +	
1	r	r	0	0	0	1	0	,−R	Autodecrement
1	r	r	i	0	0	1	1	,− −R	
1	r	r	i	0	1	0	0	,R	Indexed with zero offset
1	r	r	i	0	1	0	1	B,R	Indexed with accumulator offset
1	r	r	i	0	1	1	0	A,R	
1	r	r	i	1	0	0	0	SValue, R	Indexed with 8-bit signed offset
1	r	r	i	1	0	0	1	Value,R	Indexed with 16-bit signed offset
1	r	r	i	1	0	1	1	D,R	Indexed with register D offset
1	r	r	i	1	1	0	0	Value, PCR	Relative with 8-bit signed offset
1	r	r	i	1	1	0	1	Value, PCR	Relative with 16-bit signed offset
1	r	r	1	1	1	1	1	[Value]	Extended indirect

Notes: r r specifies register R where $0\,0 \Rightarrow R = X$
$\qquad\qquad\qquad\qquad\qquad 0\,1 \Rightarrow R = Y$
$\qquad\qquad\qquad\qquad\qquad 1\,0 \Rightarrow R = U$
$\qquad\qquad\qquad\qquad\qquad 1\,1 \Rightarrow R = S$
$\qquad$ Q = (q q q q q) is a 5-bit signed number
$\qquad$ i = 1 specifies indirect address mode

on its size. Note that the assembler recognizes the relative mode by the presence of the symbol PCR (program counter relative). The execution of an instruction that uses the relative mode is handled in the same way as for the indexed mode, with the PC serving as the index register.

10.2.3 Instruction Set

The instruction set of the 6809 is summarized in Table 10.3. For each instruction, the table shows all allowable addressing modes, the OP codes, the number of bytes, the function performed, and the effect on the flags in the CCR register. In order to save space in the table, some instructions are combined. For example, the Add instruction that uses accumulator A has the mnemonic ADDA, and its OP code for the immediate address mode is 8B. The same instruction using accumulator B has the mnemonic ADDB, and its OP code for the immediate mode is CB. The two instructions are combined in the table as ADDA/B, and the immediate mode OP codes are shown as 8B/CB. The number of bytes required for each addressing mode is also given. Note that the entries for the indexed mode are stated as $n +$. This indicates that at least n bytes are needed, but additional bytes may be involved if 8- or 16-bit offsets are used. In the column that indicates the function performed, the symbol "M" represents the effective address of the operand.

The autoincrement, autodecrement, relative, and indirect addressing modes are not shown explicitly in Table 10.3. They are all implemented by means of the post-byte, as was indicated in Table 10.2. The OP-code byte of any instruction using these modes is the same as that for the indexed mode.

The number of cycles needed to execute an instruction is not shown in Table 10.3 because it would take too much space. A single memory access, which involves 8 bits of data, can be completed within one clock cycle. Thus, the execution time of various instructions is largely determined by the number of bytes that need to be fetched from or written into the memory. However, additional time is needed to perform arithmetic and logic operations within the microprocessor. Typically, for an arithmetic operation such as addition or subtraction, the execution time is increased by one cycle for each required 8-bit operation. For example, consider the ADDD instruction in the indexed mode in which a 16-bit offset is used. This instruction is four bytes long, consisting of the OP-code byte, the post-byte, and two bytes for the offset. Its execution requires the following cycles. Two cycles are needed to fetch the OP code and the post-byte. During the next two cycles the 16-bit offset value is read from the memory. Then two cycles are used to add the offset and the contents of the index register, to generate the effective address of the source operand. Now, another two cycles are needed to read the source operand from the memory. Finally, the 16-bit source operand is added to the contents of accumulator D, which requires two more cycles. Hence, a total of ten cycles are used to execute the instruction. Similar situations exist with other instructions, although most of them require fewer cycles because they are less complex.

Table 10.3 indicates which flags are affected by a given instruction. An "x" indicates that a particular flag is set to 1 if the condition it represents is true; otherwise, it is cleared to 0. A 1 or 0 indicates that the flag is unconditionally set or cleared, respectively. A blank entry denotes that the flag is not affected by the instruction. For branch instructions, the table shows how the flags are used to form the test conditions.

The 6809 has some instructions whose usefulness is not obvious at first glance. When parameters have to be passed to subroutines, it is often convenient to deal with the addresses of operands rather than with the operands themselves. Thus, a machine instruction that can determine the address of an operand in a simple way is likely to be valuable. The LEA instructions provide a facility of this type. These instructions load the effective address derived in the indexed addressing mode into a designated 16-bit pointer register. For example, suppose that the address of the sixth entry in a

TABLE 10.3 6809 microprocessor instruction set.

Operation	Mnemonic	IMMED OP code	#	DIRECT OP code	#	EXTEND OP code	#
Add	ADDA/B	8B/CB	2	9B/DB	2	BB/FB	3
	ADDD	C3	3	D3	2	F3	3
Add with carry	ADCA/B	89/C9	2	99/D9	2	B9/F9	3
Add accum. B to index register X unsigned	ABX						
AND	ANDA/B	84/C4	2	94/D4	2	B4/F4	3
	ANDCC	1C	2				
	CWAI	3C	2				
Bit test	BITA/B	85/C5	2	95/D5	2	B5/F5	3
Clear	CLR			0F	2	7F	3
	CLRA/B						
Compare	CMPA/B	81/C1	2	91/D1	2	B1/F1	3
	CMPD	1083	4	1093	3	10B3	4
	CMPS	118C	4	119C	3	11BC	4
	CMPU	1183	4	1193	3	11B3	4
	CMPX	8C	3	9C	2	BC	3
	CMPY	108C	4	109C	3	10BC	3
Complement (1's)	COM			03	2	73	3
	COMA/B						
Decimal adjust A	DAA						
Decrement	DEC			0A	2	7A	3
	DECA/B						
Exclusive-OR	EORA/B	88/C8	2	98/D8	2	B8/F8	3
Exchange register contents	EXG (R_1,R_2)						
Increment	INC			0C	2	7C	3
	INCA/B						
Load	LDA/B	86/C6	2	96/D6	2	B6/F6	3
	LDD/U	CC/CE	3	DC/DE	2	FC/FE	3
	LDS	10CE	4	10DE	3	10FE	4
	LDX	8E	3	9E	2	BE	3
	LDY	108E	4	109E	3	10BE	4
Load effective address	LEAS/U						
	LEAX/Y						
Multiply	MUL						

| Address modes | | | | Performed function | Condition code flags affected | | | | |
| INDEX | | IMPLIED | | | H | N | Z | V | C |
OP code	#	OP code	#						
AB/EB	2+			A ← [A] + [M]	x	x	x	x	x
E3	2+			D ← [D] + [M]	x	x	x	x	x
A9/E9	2+			A ← [A] + [M] + [C]	x	x	x	x	x
		3A	1	X ← [X] + [B] (unsigned)					
A4/E4	2+			A ← [A] ∧ [M]		x	x	0	
				CCR ← [CCR] ∧ [M]	x	x	x	x	x
				CCR ← [CCR] ∧ [M] store registers on S stack; wait for interrupt	x	x	x	x	x
A5/E5	2+			[A] ∧ [M]		x	x	0	
6F	2+			M ← 0		0	1	0	0
		4F/5F	1	A ← 0		0	1	0	0
A1/E1	2+			[A] − [M]		x	x	x	x
10A3	3+			[D] − [M]		x	x	x	x
11AC	3+			[S] − [M]		x	x	x	x
11A3	3+			[U] − [M]		x	x	x	x
AC	2+			[X] − [M]		x	x	x	x
10AC	3+			[Y] − [M]		x	x	x	x
63	2+			M ← [M̄]		x	x	0	1
		43/53	1	A ← [Ā]		x	x	0	1
		19	1	Converts binary sum of BCD characters into BCD format		x	x	0	x
6A	2+			M ← [M] − 1		x	x	x	
		4A/5A	1	A ← [A] − 1		x	x	x	
A8/E8	2+			A ← [A] ⊕ [M]		x	x	0	
		1E	2	R$_1$ ↔ R$_2$					
6C	2+			M ← [M] + 1		x	x	x	
		4C/5C	1	A ← [A] + 1		x	x	x	
A6/E6	2+			A ← [M]		x	x	0	
EC/EE	2+			D ← [M]		x	x	0	
10EE	3+			S ← [M]		x	x	0	
AE	2+			X ← [M]		x	x	0	
10AE	3+			Y ← [M]		x	x	0	
32/33	2+			S ← EA					
30/31	2+			X ← EA	x				
		3D	1	D ← [A] × [B] (unsigned)		x			x

TABLE 10.3 (Continued)

Operation	Mnemonic	IMMED OP code	#	DIRECT OP code	#	EXTEND OP code	#
Negate (2's complement)	NEG NEGA/B			00	2	70	3
No operation	NOP						
OR (inclusive)	ORA/B ORCC	8A/CA 1A	2 2	9A/DA	2	BA/FA	3
Push	PSHS/U (reg. list)						
Pull	PULS/U (reg. list)						
Rotate left	ROL ROLA/B			09	2	79	3
Rotate right	ROR RORA/B			06	2	76	3
Shift left (arithmetic)	ASL ASLA/B			08	2	78	3
Shift right (arithmetic)	ASR ASRA/B			07	2	77	3
Shift left (logical)	LSL LSLA/B			08	2	78	3
Shift right (logical)	LSR LSRA/B			04	2	74	3
Sign extend B into A	SEX						
Store	STA/B STD STS STU/X STY			97/D7 DD 10DF DF/9F 109F	2 2 3 2 3	B7/F7 FD 10FF FF/BF 10BF	3 3 4 3 4
Subtract	SUBA/B SUBD	80/C0 83	2 3	90/D0 93	2 2	B0/F0 B3	3 3
Subtract with carry	SBCA/B	82/C2	2	92/D2	2	B2/F2	3
Transfer register to register	TFR (R_1,R_2)						
Test	TST TSTA/B			0D	2	7D	3

Address modes				Performed function	Condition code flags affected				
INDEX		IMPLIED							
OP code	#	OP code	#		H	N	Z	V	C
60	2+			$M \leftarrow 0 - [M]$		x	x	x	x
		40/50	1	$A \leftarrow 0 - [A]$		x	x	x	x
		12	1	No operation					
AA/EA	2+			$A \leftarrow [A] \vee [M]$		x	x	0	
				$CCR \leftarrow [CCR] \vee [M]$	x	x	x	x	x
		34/36	2	Push registers on S/U stack					
		35/37	2	Pull registers from S/U stack					
69	2+			M, A rotate left through carry (C, b_7 ... b_0)		x	x	x	x
		49/59	1			x	x	x	x
66	2+			M, A rotate right through carry (C, b_7 ... b_0)		x	x		x
		46/56	1			x	x		x
68	2+			M, A shift left (C, b_7 ... b_0 ← 0)		x	x	x	x
		48/58	1			x	x	x	x
67	2+			M, A shift right (b_7 ... b_0, C)		x	x		x
		47/57	1			x	x		x
68	2+			M, A shift left (C, b_7 ... b_0 ← 0)		x	x	x	x
		48/58	1			x	x	x	x
64	2+			M, A logical shift right (0 → b_7 ... b_0, C)	0	x			x
		44/54	1		0	x			x
		1D	1	Set all bits in A to equal the sign bit in B		x	x	0	
A7/E7	2+			$M \leftarrow [A]$		x	x	0	
ED	2+			$M \leftarrow [D]$		x	x	0	
10EF	3+			$M \leftarrow [S]$		x	x	0	
EF/AF	2+			$M \leftarrow [U]$		x	x	0	
10AF	3+			$M \leftarrow [Y]$		x	x	0	
A0/E0	2+			$A \leftarrow [A] - [M]$		x	x	x	x
A3	2+			$D \leftarrow [D] - [M]$		x	x	x	x
A2/E2	2+			$A \leftarrow [A] - [M] - [C]$		x	x	x	x
		1F	2	$R_2 \leftarrow [R_1]$		x	x	0	
						x	x	0	
6D	2+			$[M] - 0$					
		4D/5D	1	$[A] - 0$					

TABLE 10.3 (Continued)

Operation	Mnemonic	Address modes											Branch test
		RELATIVE		DIRECT		EXTEND		INDEX		IMPLIED			
		OP code	#	OP code	#	OP code	#	OP code	#	OP code	#		
Branch always	BRA	20	2										None
	LBRA	16	3										
Branch if carry clear	BCC	24	2										$[C] = 0$
	LBCC	1024	4										
Branch if carry set	BCS	25	2										$[C] = 1$
	LBCS	1025	4										
Branch if $= 0$	BEQ	27	2										$[Z] = 1$
	LBEQ	1027	4										
Branch if ≥ 0	BGE	2C	2										$[N] \oplus [V] = 0$
	LBGE	102C	4										
Branch if > 0	BGT	2E	2										$[Z] \vee ([N] \oplus [V]) = 0$
	LBGT	102E	4										
Branch if higher	BHI	22	2										$[C] \vee [Z] = 0$
	LBHI	1022	4										
Branch if higher or same	BHS	24	2										$[C] = 0$
	LBHS	1024	4										
Branch if ≤ 0	BLE	2F	2										$[Z] \vee ([N] \oplus [V]) = 1$
	LBLE	102F	4										
Branch if lower	BLO	25	2										$[C] = 1$
	LBLO	1025	4										
Branch if lower or same	BLS	23	2										$[C] \vee [Z] = 1$
	LBLS	1023	4										

Operation	Mnemonic		#		#		#		#	Condition
Branch if < 0	BLT		2							$[N] \veebar [V] = 1$
	LBLT	102D	4							
Branch if minus	BMI	2B	2							$[N] = 1$
	LBMI	102B	4							
Branch if ≠ 0	BNE	26	2							$[Z] = 0$
	LBNE	1026	4							
Branch if plus	BPL	2A	2							$[N] = 0$
	LBPL	102A	4							
Branch never	BRN	21	2							None
	LBRN	1021	4							
Branch if overflow clear	BVC	28	2							$[V] = 0$
	LBVC	1028	4							
Branch if overflow set	BVS	29	2							$[V] = 1$
	LBVS	1029	4							
Branch to subroutine	BSR	8D	2							
	LBSR	17	3							
Jump	JMP	0E	2	7E	3	6E	2+			
Jump to subroutine	JSR	9D	2	BD	3	AD	2+			
Return from interrupt	RTI							3B	1	
Return from subroutine	RTS							39	1	
Software interrupt	SWI							3F	1	
	SWI2							103F	2	
	SWI3							113F	2	
Wait for interrupt	SYNC							13	1	

Notes: # = number of bytes in the instruction; EA = effective address;

For two-byte operands: $R \leftarrow [M]$ implies $R_H \leftarrow [M]$ and $R_L \leftarrow [M + 1]$

character list pointed to by register Y is to be placed in register X. If Y contains the address of the first entry in the list and each entry occupies 1 byte, then the desired operation can be performed with the instruction

$$\text{LEAX} \qquad 5,\text{Y}$$

The effective address is computed as $5 + [\text{Y}]$ and is loaded into register X.

The LEA instructions are useful for writing position-independent code in which data is addressed relative to the current contents of the program counter. For example, register Y can be loaded with the starting address of a list with the instruction

$$\text{LEAY} \qquad \text{LIST,PCR}$$

The fact that a signed number (offset) is added to the register contents in the LEA instructions makes these instructions suitable for doing addition and subtraction on the pointer registers. A register, say X, may be decremented with the instruction

$$\text{LEAX} \qquad -1,\text{X}$$

Most instructions that use the implied addressing mode are only 1 byte long. However, there are four exceptions in which a second byte is needed to indicate the registers involved. In EXG and TFR instructions, registers R_1 and R_2 may be any pair of 8-bit registers or any pair of 16-bit registers. The assembler syntax in this case is

$$\text{EXG} \qquad \text{R1,R2}$$

In the PSH and PUL instructions, the second byte indicates which of the eight processor registers are to be pushed on the stack or pulled from the stack. Bits b_7 to b_0 are used to specify PC, U or S, Y, X, DP, B, A, and CCR, in that order. This is the order in which the registers are transferred, regardless of the order in which they are listed in the assembly language instruction. For example, the instruction

$$\text{PSHS} \qquad \text{PC,U,B,A}$$

pushes the four indicated registers onto the stack. When assembled, the second byte of this instruction will have bits b_7, b_6, b_2 and b_1 set to 1, and the remaining bits equal to 0.

10.2.4   Example

To illustrate the use of the 6809 instruction set, let us consider a small program for subtraction of two numbers represented in BCD form. Numbers P and Q are 16 digits long and are stored in locations NUMP and NUMQ. Each number spans 8 bytes, and the two most significant digits occupy the lowest-address byte. We would like to subtract the number at NUMQ from that at NUMP and to store the result at NUMP.

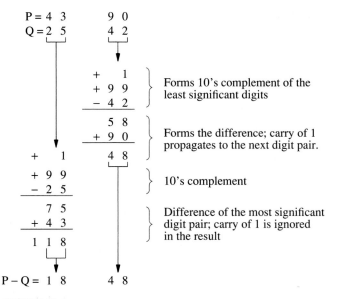

FIGURE 10.5
An example of BCD subtraction for 4-digit operands.

The main difficulty in performing this subtraction is the fact that a BCD operation is to be carried out using simple binary arithmetic. When 2 bytes containing two BCD digits each are added in an 8-bit binary adder, the result is not necessarily in the correct BCD format. A special instruction, called Decimal Adjust (DAA), can be used to make the required transformation. An algorithm that performs the desired subtraction forms the 10's complement of the subtrahend Q and adds it to the minuend P to obtain the difference. The formation of the complement and the addition step can be combined into a single iterative cycle as indicated in the four-digit example of Figure 10.5. The two numbers are scanned from right to left.

Figure 10.6 shows how this task can be implemented using the 6809. The program uses index registers X and Y as pointers to the BCD operands involved in the process. The BCD numbers and the program itself are placed in specific memory locations by the three assembler commands at the beginning of the program. This was done to enable the reader to see what the actual assembled object code looks like when loaded in the memory. The memory addresses and their contents are also shown in the figure.

10.3 INPUT/OUTPUT IN MICROPROCESSOR SYSTEMS

Perhaps the most important hardware aspect of a microprocessor system, from a user standpoint, is the I/O structure. A thorough appreciation of the I/O details from both the software and hardware points of view is likely to prove beneficial in many ways. This section will deal with I/O in microprocessor systems in some detail and will

Location (hex)	Contents (hex)	Assembler format for instructions			Comments
		NUMP	EQU	$2000	
		NUMQ	EQU	$3000	
			ORG	$100	
100	8E		LDX	#NUMP	Register X points to NUMP.
101	20				
102	00				
103	10		LDY	#NUMQ	Register Y points to NUMQ.
104	8E				
105	30				
106	00				
107	C6		LDB	#7	Set B as a byte counter.
108	07				
109	1A		ORCC	#1	Set carry for 10's complement.
10A	01				
10B	86	SLOOP	LDA	#$99	Form 10's complement of Q
10C	99				for one digit pair.
10D	89		ADCA	#0	
10E	00				
10F	A0		SUBA	B,Y	
110	A5				
111	AB		ADDA	B,X	Form P − Q in binary.
112	85				
113	19		DAA		Decimal Adjust.
114	A7				
115	85		STA	B,X	Store the digit pair of the difference
116	5A		DECB		into NUMP.
117	2C				
118	F2		BGE	SLOOP	Loop until last byte is processed.

FIGURE 10.6
Program for subtraction of 16-digit BCD operands for 6809.

discuss applicable techniques and typical interfaces. In order to give the reader a feeling for the complexity of I/O structures, we will give some detailed examples using the 6809 microprocessor.

10.3.1 Control of I/O Activity

Chapter 6 discussed two basic schemes for controlling I/O activity. The first scheme involved continuous checking of the status of an I/O device by the processor. The second used interrupts raised by a device to indicate changes in its status. These schemes are applicable to all computers, regardless of size, and are commonly used in microprocessor systems.

Continuous status checking is the simplest to implement. It requires the I/O device status information to be available in the I/O interface in a form suitable for reading by the processor. A practical way to realize this scheme is to include one or more status registers that can be accessed as addressable locations in the I/O interface. The actual arrangement is influenced mostly by the nature of the I/O devices and the structure of the interface chips used. It is essentially independent of the choice of the microprocessor (that is, the CPU) because most microprocessors are capable of executing simple instructions to poll these addressable locations.

Interrupt-driven I/O is more complex. Since the interrupt mechanism that can be implemented depends mainly upon the corresponding capability of the microprocessor, varying degrees of interrupt-handling capability exist in commercially available microprocessors. Although the fundamental principles are the same as we outlined in Chapter 6, the scope of interrupt structure and capability may differ considerably for different microprocessors.

Let us consider the interrupt characteristics of the 6809 microprocessor. The 6809 chip has four input connections, or pins, that are dedicated to interrupts. An active signal on one of these inputs indicates an interrupt request. The four interrupt inputs are Reset, Interrupt request (IRQ), Fast interrupt request (FIRQ), and Nonmaskable interrupt (NMI). The signals on these inputs are active when low. It is customary in the technical literature to indicate this fact by writing a bar (as in complementation) over the names of such inputs. Thus, the 6809 interrupt inputs are denoted as $\overline{\text{Reset}}$, $\overline{\text{IRQ}}$, $\overline{\text{FIRQ}}$, and $\overline{\text{NMI}}$.

The IRQ is enabled or disabled by setting the I flag (bit 4) in the CCR register to 0 or 1. When the I flag equals 1, the 6809 ignores interrupt requests on the IRQ line. If an IRQ request arrives when I equals 0, the processor stores its entire state on the S stack and sets the I flag to 1 (disabling further IRQ requests). It then enters the interrupt-service routine.

The entire state consists of all registers in the processor. It takes considerable time to store these registers. In some real-time applications it is impractical to spend this time saving the registers, particularly if the interrupt-service routine will not affect the contents of most registers. A faster response can be obtained with the FIRQ request. In this case, only the contents of the program counter and the CCR register are stored on the stack. The FIRQ interrupt is masked with the F flag (bit 6) in the CCR in the same way as the IRQ interrupt is masked by the I flag. The FIRQ request has higher priority than the IRQ request; hence, its occurrence sets the I flag as well as the F flag to 1.

The difference between IRQ and FIRQ is the number of registers saved. Both interrupts are handled by interrupt-service routines that end with an RTI (Return-from-Interrupt) instruction. Since this instruction restores the saved registers, it is essential to have some mechanism for remembering the type of interrupt that occurred. This is done by including the E flag (bit 7) in the CCR. In response to an IRQ request, this flag is set to 1 before the contents of the CCR are saved on the stack as part of the entire state. It is cleared to 0 if FIRQ occurs. Then, when a Return-from-Interrupt is performed, after the completion of the interrupt-service routine, the state of bit 7 in the status word that is reloaded into the CCR indicates whether or not all processor registers were saved and hence must be restored.

The 6809 also provides a nonmaskable interrupt NMI. This interrupt request cannot be ignored. The interrupt sequence starts when the 6809 detects a negative-going transition on its NMI input. The NMI is therefore an edge-triggered interrupt. This means that the user should not connect more than one device to the NMI input, because if two or more devices activate the NMI line at the same time, only one interrupt request will be recognized and the rest will be lost. The NMI interrupt has higher priority than either IRQ or FIRQ. Hence, it sets both I and F flags to 1.

The highest priority interrupt is Reset, whose activation resets the 6809 to the initial state. Reset is used to start the operation of a microprocessor system at power-up time or to recoup when computation has gone hopelessly astray and system software cannot be used to recover from the inadvertently reached, undesired state. Activation of the Reset input disables IRQ and FIRQ interrupts by setting I and F flags to 1, clears the contents of the DPR register, and then starts the execution of the Reset routine. The reader should note that although we have referred to Reset as an interrupt, its function is somewhat different. When Reset is activated, the current state of the processor is abandoned. Therefore, when the Reset routine is completed, no RTI instruction can be meaningfully executed.

In addition to the hardware interrupts, the 6809 has three software interrupts generated by the execution of machine instructions SWI, SWI2, and SWI3. The entire processor state is saved on the stack for these interrupts. The SWI interrupt has higher priority than IRQ or FIRQ, but SWI2 and SWI3 have lower priority.

An interrupt-service routine is associated with each interrupt. The starting addresses of these routines are stored in fixed locations in the memory, as shown in Figure 10.7. Two bytes are needed to store each 16-bit address.

The 6809 has no hardware means for distinguishing interrupt requests that come from two or more devices connected to the same interrupt input. Software polling may be used to identify the interrupting devices.

10.3.2 I/O Interface Circuits

Chapter 6 dealt with the general problem of interfacing I/O devices to a computer bus. In the microprocessor environment it is common to use interface chips such as the PIA and the ACIA described in Section 10.1. In this section we will consider a

Interrupt	Memory location of interrupt vector
Reset	FFFE, FFFF
NMI	FFFC, FFFD
SWI	FFFA, FFFB
IRQ	FFF8, FFF9
FIRQ	FFF6, FFF7
SWI2	FFF4, FFF5
SWI3	FFF2, FFF3

FIGURE 10.7
Memory locations where addresses of interrupt-service routines are stored in 6809.

parallel interface circuit similar to the PIA to illustrate the nature and complexity of interfacing techniques in more detail.

The diagram in Figure 10.1 shows a parallel interface that has two ports that handle 8 bits of data each. A port includes input and output data paths and control information, all of which are accessible as addressable memory locations. Instead of pursuing the PIA example in this section, we will define a simplified version of a typical interface that will allow us to discuss the relevant issues without worrying about unnecessary details of a specific product.

Figure 10.8 shows the block diagram of a parallel interface circuit (PIC). The PIC has two 8-bit I/O ports labelled A and B, each of which has three registers directly associated with it. The input (IR) and output (OR) registers hold 8 bits of data during input and output transfers. A data direction register (DDR) determines the direction of the I/O transfer for each data line in a port. If bit k ($k = 0, 1, \ldots, 7$) in the DDRA (DDRB) is 0, then line k in port A(B) acts as an input line. If this bit is 1, then the corresponding line acts as an output line.

Two control lines are used with each port. CA1(CB1) is an input line that may, for example, be used by an I/O device to indicate its busy/idle status. CA2(CB2) is a bidirectional line for exchange of control signals between the PIC and a connected device. The nature of signals on these control lines is determined by the content of the control signal register (CSR), as will be explained later.

The I/O devices can use control lines to raise interrupt requests. The status of

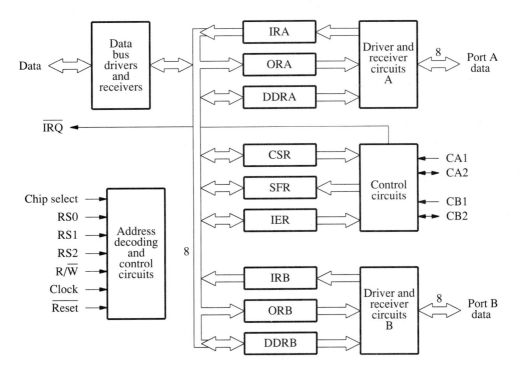

FIGURE 10.8
A parallel interface circuit (PIC).

these lines is recorded in the status flag register (SFR), and this information is used to activate the $\overline{\text{IRQ}}$ (interrupt-request) line of the microprocessor bus. The activation of the $\overline{\text{IRQ}}$ line depends upon the setting of bits in the interrupt-enable register (IER).

On the processor side, the PIC has eight data bus drivers and receivers, as well as address decoding and control circuits. The addressing information consists of a chip select input, register select (RS) inputs that identify specific registers, and the R/$\overline{\text{W}}$ input that indicates whether a read or a write operation is required. The clock input allows synchronization of operations in the PIC with the rest of the system. The Reset input is used to clear all registers in the PIC and is usually connected to the reset inputs of all other units in the system, including the one in the processor.

The PIC registers are addressable as memory locations. Figure 10.9 shows a map of the registers and the addressing codes that distinguish them. Because there are nine registers, four input signals are needed to specify any given register. Register select signals RS0, RS1, and RS2 and the R/$\overline{\text{W}}$ control input are used for this purpose. Note that the same value of RS inputs refers to both the input and the output registers in each port. The two are distinguished by the value of the R/$\overline{\text{W}}$ input.

In order to access the PIC from the microprocessor bus, the chip select input must be activated. An address decoder circuit may be used for this purpose, to de-

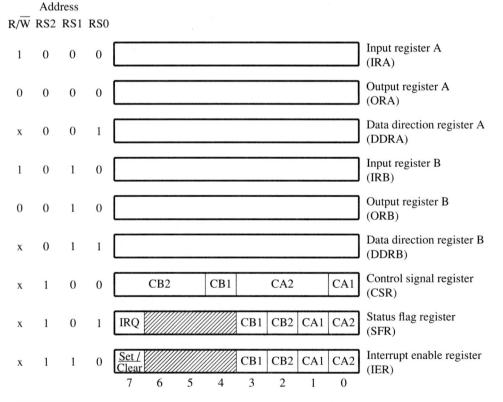

FIGURE 10.9
Addressable registers in the PIC.

code the high-order 13 bits of a 16-bit address. When an address assigned to a PIC register appears on the bus, the decoder's output activates the chip select input. The three low-order address lines are connected directly to the RS0, RS1, and RS2 inputs.

A set of distinct input, output, and data-direction registers is provided in each port. Additional control and status information is incorporated into the CSR, SFR, and IER registers, which serve both ports as indicated in the figure.

The exact meaning of the bits in the PIC registers is described in Figure 10.10. The figure deals only with the bits pertaining to port A, but the same meaning applies to

Bit position	Bit state	Function
$DDRA_k$ ($k = 0, \ldots, 7$)	0	Line k in port A acts as an input line.
	1	Line k in port A acts as an output line.
CSR_0	0	Negative (high to low) is the active transition on the CA1 line.
	1	Positive (low to high) is the active transition on the CA1 line.
SFR_0	0	Indicates that no active transition has been received on the CA2 line.
	1	Indicates that an active transition has been received on the CA2 line. This flag is cleared by reading from IRA, writing into ORA, or writing a 0 into SFR_0.
SFR_1	0	Indicates that no active transition has been received on the CA1 line.
	1	Indicates that an active transition has been received on the CA1 line. This flag is cleared by reading from IRA, writing into ORA, or writing a 0 into SFR_1.
SFR_7	IRQ	$IRQ = SFR_3 \cdot IER_3 + SFR_2 \cdot IER_2 + SFR_1 \cdot IER_1 + SFR_0 \cdot IER_0$
$IER_{0,1}$	0	Disable the corresponding interrupt.
	1	Enable the corresponding interrupt.
IER_7	0,1	Used to control the setting of bits in IER. See the explanation in the text.

FIGURE 10.10
Meaning of bits in PIC, for port A.

the corresponding bits in port B. Most entries in this figure are self-explanatory. Note that interrupt requests can be generated through the CA1(CB1) and CA2(CB2) control lines. Thus, there are four possible sources of interrupt requests, each of which can be enabled by setting the corresponding bit in the IER register to 1. An IRQ request to the processor is made if an active signal appears on a control line while interrupts for that line are enabled. It is useful to be able to easily set or clear individual bits in the IER without disturbing the rest of the bits, which can be done with the aid of bit 7 in the IER. When this Set/Clear bit is a 1 in an 8-bit word that the CPU writes into the IER, then for each 1 in bit positions 0 through 3 of the word, the corresponding IER bit is set to 1. When bit 7 is a 0, then each 1 in bit positions 0 to 3 clears the corresponding bit in IER.

Control lines CA2 and CB2 can be used in a very flexible fashion. Figure 10.11 describes the possible modes for CA2. The mode information for CA2 is specified in bits 1 through 3 of the CSR register. The CB2 line has the same modes of operation, specified by CSR bits 5 through 7. The description of the modes in the figure should

CSR_3	CSR_2	CSR_1	Mode
0	0	0	Automatic flag clear – SFR_0 is set by a negative transition on the CA2 line; it is cleared by reading from IRA or writing into ORA.
0	0	1	Independent flag clear – SFR_0 is set by a negative transition on the CA2 line; it is cleared by writing into SFR_0.
0	1	0	Automatic flag clear – SFR_0 is set by a positive transition on the CA2 line; it is cleared by reading from IRA or writing into ORA.
0	1	1	Independent flag clear – SFR_0 is set by a positive transition on the CA2 line; it is cleared by writing into SFR_0.
1	0	0	Handshake mode – CA2 goes low upon reading from IRA or writing into ORA; it is restored high by an active transition on the CA1 line.
1	0	1	Pulse acknowledgement mode – CA2 goes low for one clock cycle after reading from IRA or writing into ORA.
1	1	0	Direct CA2 control mode – CA2 is held low.
1	1	1	Direct CA2 control mode – CA2 is held high.

FIGURE 10.11
Modes of operation for the CA2 line in PIC.

be self-explanatory. Note that the corresponding status flag in SFR can be set by either a positive or a negative transition on the CA2 line. The status flag can be cleared either by performing a data transfer to or from the port, or by writing new control information into the SFR. Other modes allow for implementation of handshake control and an acknowledgment scheme in which a pulse that is one clock cycle in duration is sent to the connected device. The state of the CA2 line may also be set directly from the processor.

In order to show how a chip with the structure of the PIC may be used in a microprocessor system, we will give two simple examples.

10.3.3 Example 1

Let us assume that a keyboard and a printer are to be connected to a microcomputer so that 8-bit encoded characters typed at the keyboard can be sent to the printer. The keyboard has eight data pins that indicate the encoded character corresponding to a pressed key. It also has one control line to indicate that valid data is available on the data pins. The printer has eight input connections and two control lines. One control line informs the printer that data is available, and the other indicates the busy/idle status of the printer. The desired connections may be achieved with the aid of a PIC, as shown in Figure 10.12. The keyboard is connected to port A, with the CA1 line indicating the availability of the data. The printer is connected to port B, with control lines CB2 and CB1 indicating the availability of data and the status of the printer. A 6809 microprocessor is the CPU used to execute the required transfers. The task to be implemented is:

- The keyboard indicates that valid data is ready on its data pins by a positive-going signal on the Data Ready line.
- The CPU polls the status of the keyboard to determine when the data is available.

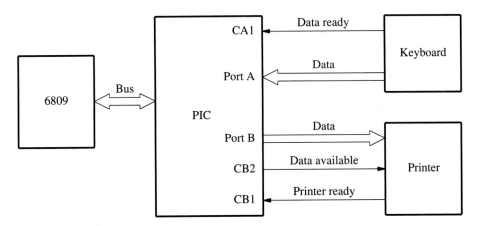

FIGURE 10.12
A parallel interface circuit for connection to a keyboard and a printer.

- The CPU transfers the 8-bit character to the printer and informs it that data is available for printing. Note that the action of reading this character from Port A clears the keyboard status flag SFR_1.
- The printer indicates its availability to receive another character by a negative-going signal on the Printer Ready line.

In order to meet these requirements, the PIC must be initialized as follows

Port A
- The data lines of port A must be configured as inputs; therefore, all bits in DDRA must be cleared to 0.
- CA1 is used as the Data Ready line and must be conditioned to respond to positive transitions from the keyboard. Thus, the control bit CSR_0 must be set to 1, as shown in Figure 10.10.

Port B
- The data lines of port B must be configured as outputs, so all bits in DDRB must be set to 1.
- CB2 is used as the Data Available line. A handshake between the PIC and the printer is required. Thus, the handshake mode in Figure 10.11 is chosen by setting $CSR_{7-5} = 100$.
- CB1 is used as the Printer Ready line. It must be conditioned to recognize negative transitions, by setting $CSR_4 = 0$.

This means that the desired CSR bit setting is

$$10000001 = 81_{16}$$

Since CA2 is not used, it can be specified in any mode (0 in our example).

A 6809 program capable of performing the required task is given in Figure 10.13. It includes an initializing sequence that configures the PIC according to the preceding requirements. It also disables interrupts because CPU polling of the device status is the I/O mode of operation used.

This example is merely intended to illustrate how a typical commercially available parallel interface integrated circuit may be used to connect to input and output devices. The actual arrangement of transferring characters directly from a keyboard to a printer is unlikely to be of significant value. In practical applications, the processor would perform some manipulation on the input characters before sending the results to a printer.

10.3.4 Example 2

In the previous example, we considered a simple connection to a keyboard and a printer, in which the processor controlled the I/O activity by polling the status of

*Initializing sequence for the PIC

```
        LDA     #$0F        Disable interrupts.
        STA     IER
        CLR     DDRA        Set port A lines as inputs.
        LDA     #$FF
        STA     DDRB        Set port B lines as outputs.
        LDA     #$81        Load the required pattern into CSR.
        STA     CSR
                  :
                  :
```

*Transfer one character from keyboard to printer

```
WAITR   LDA     SFR         Test keyboard status, on line CA1.
        ANDA    #$02
        BEQ     WAITR       Wait if character not ready.
        LDB     IRA         Read character from keyboard.
WAITW   LDA     SFR         Test printer status, on line CB1.
        ANDA    #$08
        BEQ     WAITW       Wait if printer not ready.
        STB     ORB         Send character to printer.
                  :
                  :
```

FIGURE 10.13
A program for Example 1.

both devices. We will now modify that arrangement by using interrupts in dealing with the keyboard. Let the required operation be as follows.

A line of alphanumeric characters is to be read from the keyboard and stored in the main memory. The availability of a new character is indicated to the processor by an IRQ interrupt. When a carriage return is encountered, the stored line of text is processed by calling a subroutine LINE. Processed results are then printed. This is similar to the example in Figure 6.11.

The physical connection can be made as shown in Figure 10.12. The control signalling between the PIC and the I/O devices will be the same as in Example 1, but in the present case, an active transition on the CA1 line will be used to raise an IRQ interrupt request.

The required initialization sequence is shown in Figure 10.14. This sequence configures port A as input and port B as output and sets up the control lines as described in Example 1. Assuming that the first line is to be stored in a main memory buffer starting at location LOC, this address is placed in a pointer location MEMADR that will subsequently be updated to contain the address where the next character is to be stored. Next, interrupts generated by active transitions on the CA1

*Initialization sequence for the PIC

```
            LDA      #$0F            Disable interrupts.
            STA      IER
            LDX      #KBDINT         Initialize interrupt vector.
            STX      $FFF8
            CLR      DDRA            Set port A lines as inputs.
            LDA      #$FF
            STA      DDRB            Set port B lines as outputs.
            LDA      #$81            Load the required pattern
            STA      CSR               into the CSR.
            LDX      #LOC            Place the starting address of
            STX      MEMADR            the memory buffer in MEMADR.
            LDA      #$82            Enable interrupt requests
            STA      IER               on the CA1 line.
            ANDCC    #%11101111      Clear IRQ mask in CCR.
                       ⋮
```

*Interrupt-service routine for reading one character

```
KBDINT      LDA      SFR             Check if the interrupt was
            ANDA     #$02              originated by the CA1 line.
            BEQ      OTHER           Some other interrupt occurred.
            LDX      MEMADR          Use register X as a buffer pointer.
            LDA      IRA             Transfer a character into the
            STA      ,X+               memory buffer.
            STX      MEMADR          Store the updated pointer value.
            CMPA     #$0D            Check if carriage return.
            BNE      DONE
            BSR      LINE            Process input line.
DONE        RTI
OTHER       Check for other sources of interrupts.
```

FIGURE 10.14
Initialization sequence and interrupt-service routine for Example 2.

line are enabled. This is done by writing a word with bits 7 and 1 equal to 1 ($= 82_{16}$), into the IER. Finally, the IRQ interrupt mask bit in the CCR register is cleared.

An interrupt-service routine is also shown in the figure. It first checks to see if the CA1 line caused the IRQ request. Should the request be from some other source, either from the same PIC or from another device that may be connected to the $\overline{\text{IRQ}}$ input of the 6809, a branch is made to the routine OTHER. Index register X is used in the autoincrement mode to access successive memory locations in transferring characters from the IRA into the memory buffer. Upon encountering a carriage return ($0D_{16}$), a call to the line processing subroutine LINE is made.

10.3.5   Commercial Interface Chips

We defined the PIC to simplify the discussion and focus on the most basic aspects of I/O interfacing. Although the PIC is not a commercial product, it has a structure that corresponds closely to Motorola's PIA. It also resembles the main part of the VIA (Versatile Interface Adapter) produced by Synertek.[2] In addition to two parallel ports, the VIA contains a serial port and two timers. The serial port allows connection to devices that handle data in a bit-serial manner. The timers consist of counters that can be used to count externally produced pulses and to generate programmable-frequency square wave signals.

Numerous other interface chips are available that support various forms of serial and parallel data transfer schemes. Many of these chips incorporate useful timing capabilities. These I/O interface chips can often be used with a number of different microprocessors. Their versatility is an important characteristic.

10.4   MOTOROLA 32-BIT MICROPROCESSORS

We have considered Motorola's 6809 as an example of an 8-bit microprocessor. In Chapter 2 we introduced the 68000, which is a good example of 16-bit microprocessors. In this section we will discuss the key features of Motorola's next level of microprocessors, which use full 32-bit address and data buses. These are the 68020, 68030, and 68040 microprocessors.

The 68020 is much more powerful than the 68000, due in large measure to some significant architectural enhancements. These advances were made possible by improved VLSI technology and larger packages that removed many pin-limitation constraints. Although the 68030 is superior to the 68020, the difference between them is less significant. In fact, as far as the programming model is concerned, they are essentially identical. Both have some instructions that are not available in the 68000 instruction set. The 68000 is upward compatible with the 68020, 68030, and 68040, which means that the 68000 code can be executed on the other microprocessors without modification, but not vice-versa. The 6809 is not compatible at all with the 68000 series of microprocessors.

In the following discussion, we will deal first with the common features of the 68020, 68030, and 68040 microprocessors. We will refer to the 68020 by name most of the time, assuming that the reader is aware that the same comments apply to the 68030 and 68040. Later, we will describe the enhancements found in the 68030 and 68040.

10.4.1   68020 Microprocessor

This section highlights the main differences between the 68020 and the 68000 microprocessors.

ADDRESS AND DATA BUSES. The 68020 has external connections for 32-bit addresses and 32-bit data. Its address space is 4 gigabytes ($=2^{32}=4,294,967,296$

bytes). Although its data bus is 32 bits wide, the 68020 can deal efficiently with devices that transfer 8, 16, or 32 bits at a time. The microprocessor can adjust dynamically to the data bus width requirements of a particular device in a manner that is transparent to the programmer. The 68020 bus includes control lines that are activated by the devices connected to the bus to indicate the required size of their data transfers. Thus, the microprocessor can deal with devices of different data transfer sizes without knowing the actual size prior to the initiation of a data transfer.

The 68000 restriction that word operands must be aligned on even address boundaries has been eliminated in the 68020. Operands of any size may start at any address. This means that 16- and 32-bit operands can occupy parts of two 32-bit locations in the main memory. Two access cycles are therefore needed to reach such an operand. The two accesses are performed automatically by the microprocessor, which knows from the address which 32-bit locations must be accessed and the pattern in which the individual bytes from these locations should be assembled to obtain the desired operand. For details of these mechanisms and other aspects of the 68020 bus, the reader may consult more specialized literature.[3,4]

REGISTER SET AND DATA TYPES. Like the 68000, the 68020 has user and supervisor modes of operation. In the user mode, the registers available are essentially the same as those given in Figure 2.23 for the 68000. In the supervisor mode, however, the 68020 has several additional control registers, which are intended to simplify implementation of operating system software.

The 68000 data types are bit, byte, word, long word, and packed BCD. In addition to these, the 68020 allows quad word, unpacked BCD, and bit-field data types. A quad word consists of 64 bits. Unpacked BCD has one BCD digit per byte. A bit-field consists of a variable number of bits in a 32-bit long word and is specified by the location of its leftmost bit and the number of bits in the field.

ADDRESSING MODES. All 68000 addressing modes, shown in Table 2.3, are available in the 68020. Several extra versions of the indexed mode have been added to provide better support for running programs written in high-level languages.

The full indexed mode has been made more powerful by allowing a range of displacements (offsets) and providing for a scaling factor. Recall that the 68000 syntax for the full indexed mode is

$$disp(An,Rk.size)$$

where the displacement is a signed 8-bit number and the size designation indicates whether 32 or 16 bits of the Rk register are to be used in computing the effective address. The 68020 version of this mode allows the displacement to be an 8-, 16-, or 32-bit value. It also introduces a scale factor by which the contents of Rk are multiplied. The value of the scale factor may be 1, 2, 4, or 8. The syntax for the mode is

$$(disp,An,Rk.size*scale)$$

Note that the displacement is indicated within the parentheses in this case. The effective address is computed as

$$EA = disp + [An] + [Rk] \times scale$$

This mode is useful when dealing with lists of items that are 1, 2, 4, or 8 bytes long. If the scale factor is chosen equal to the size of the items, then successive items in the list can be accessed by incrementing the contents of Rk by 1.

Another powerful extension of indexed addressing is "memory indirect indexed modes," in which an address operand is obtained indirectly from the main memory. There are two such modes. In *memory indirect post-indexed* mode an address is fetched from the memory before the normal indexing process takes place. Its syntax is

([basedisp,An],Rk.size*scale,outdisp)

and the effective address is computed as

$$EA = [basedisp + [An]] + [Rk] \times scale + outdisp$$

Note that two displacements are used. A "base displacement" (16 or 32 bits) is used to modify the address in An, which is then used to fetch the address operand from the memory. The second displacement is the normal displacement used in indexed addressing. It is called "outer displacement" to distinguish it from the base displacement. This mode is similar to the method of indexing used in VAX-11 computers that was described in Section 3.4.2.

The second version is the *memory indirect pre-indexed* mode, in which most of the indexing modification is done before the address operand is fetched. The syntax for it is

([basedisp,An,Rk.size*scale],outdisp)

and the effective address is determined as

$$EA = [basedisp + [An] + [Rk] \times scale] + outdisp$$

In both of these modes, the user specified values An, Rk, basedisp, and outdisp are optional. They are not included in the computation of the effective address unless specified. These addressing modes are useful for dealing with lists in which contiguous memory locations are used to store addresses of data items, rather than data items themselves which can be anywhere in memory.

A relative version of all indexed modes is available in which the program counter is used in place of the address register, An.

INSTRUCTION SET. All 68000 instructions are available in the 68020. Some have extra flexibility. For example, branch instructions can have 32-bit displacements, and several instructions have the option of using longer operands. A number of new instructions have been provided. There is a set of instructions that deals with bit-field type of operands and also a set that allows interaction with coprocessors (see Section 10.4.4).

ON-CHIP CACHE. The 68020 chip includes a small instruction cache that has 256 bytes organized as 64 long-word blocks. A direct-mapping scheme is used when loading new words into the cache.

10.4.2   Enhancements in 68030

The 68030 differs from the 68020 in two significant ways. In addition to the instruction cache, the 68030 has another cache of the same size for data. The data cache organization has 16 blocks of 4 long words each. The 68030 also contains a memory management unit, MMU.

The execution unit in the 68030 generates virtual addresses. The cache access circuitry determines if the desired operand is in the cache, based on virtual addresses. The MMU translates the virtual address into a physical address in parallel with the cache access, so that in the case of a cache access miss, the physical address needed to access the operand in the main memory is immediately available.

The MMU function need not be used unless it is desired. It can be disabled either by software or external hardware. This allows even the possibility of using a different external MMU with a 68030 microprocessor.

10.4.3   68040 Microprocessor

VLSI technology has been advancing at a very rapid pace. Each year it becomes possible to substantially increase the number of transistors on a microprocessor chip. Technology has reached the stage where several large circuits that previously had to be implemented as separate chips can now be incorporated into a single chip. In the previous subsection we saw that the 68030 microprocessor includes an instruction cache, a data cache, and a memory management unit in addition to the integer processing unit. When it becomes feasible to manufacture a larger chip (in terms of the number of transistors), the designers of microprocessors must decide what additional capability should be provided. The possible choices include expanded caches, inclusion of I/O controllers, and provision of specialized functions.

The 68040 is a high-performance microprocessor that makes good use of the advances in technology. Its main part is an integer processing unit that is object-code compatible with other microprocessors in the 68000 family. It has instruction and data caches, which we have already encountered in the case of the 68030 microprocessor. Its memory management unit is improved over that in the 68030, to provide better performance. This unit has two independent address translation caches that permit simultaneous translation of addresses for both instructions and data. The 68040 has a "pipelined" structure that permits fetching of instructions while previous instructions are still being processed. The concept of pipelining will be discussed in Chapter 11.

The internal structure of the 68040 features multiple buses. Two of these are used to transfer instructions and data from the respective caches. These buses, in conjunction with the two address translation circuits, allow simultaneous accessing of instruction and data caches.

The 68040 also includes a floating-point unit, which implements the IEEE floating-point standard described in Chapter 7. This unit has the same functionality as the MC68881 coprocessor chip (see the next section), which has been used to provide floating-point capability in machines based on microprocessors of the 68000 family.

Finally, the 68040 includes circuits that monitor the activity on the external bus. This feature is intended to make the 68040 suitable for use in multiprocessor systems. In such systems, which will be discussed in Chapter 12, one of the key requirements is to maintain consistency of the common data that may temporarily reside in several caches associated with different processors. Bus monitoring circuits are helpful in observing changes in cache information, as such changes take place by means of bus transfers.

10.4.4 Support Chips

There is a variety of support chips available for use with 68020 and 68030 microprocessors. Here, we will mention only two of the more important ones.

Neither microprocessor has the ability to perform floating-point operations in hardware. This capability is provided through a special floating-point coprocessor chip, MC68881,[5] which handles operands represented in the IEEE Standard format discussed in Section 7.10.4. A *coprocessor* is a processing unit that performs a specialized function in support of another processor. Usually, it has the ability to execute special instructions, which expands the capability of the main processor. The MC68881 provides an extra set of registers and instructions used solely for floating-point operations.

The 68020 chip does not include memory management circuitry. Instead, the memory management capability can be achieved with an MMU chip known as MC68851.[6] This chip includes a 64-entry associative address translation cache. It allows separate address translation tables to be used at different protection levels. Accessing these tables requires interaction with the main memory, which is done by means of specialized instructions. Hence, the MC68851 can be thought of as a coprocessor for the 68020 microprocessor.

10.5 INTEL MICROPROCESSORS

In the preceding sections, we have used Motorola chips as examples of microprocessor elements. An understanding of one microprocessor family and the support chips that it includes provides a good foundation for dealing with other microprocessor products. Like all computers, microprocessors of different families are based on the same principles. However, their architectures sometimes exhibit striking differences. As an example of such differences, we will consider the 8086 architecture in the Intel family of microprocessors.

Intel microprocessors have attained enormous popularity, helped greatly by the fact that they have been used in IBM personal computers (PCs). The Intel company became a major force in the microprocessor market in the 1970s with its 8080 and 8085 chips. These were 8-bit chips comparable to Motorola's 6800 and 6809 microprocessors. Then, in the 1980s, Intel produced a series of microprocessors based on a new architecture. The cornerstone of this architecture is the 8086 microprocessor, which deals externally with 20-bit addresses and 16-bit data. Because it comes in a 40-pin package, the address and data values are time-multiplexed on the same set of pins. Progressively more powerful microprocessors using the same basic architecture have since been introduced. These are the 80186, 80286, 80386, and 80486. The first two are 16-bit chips, and the other two are 32-bit chips whose external addresses and data are handled in 32-bit quantities. The 32-bit chips come in large packages that obviate the need for multiplexing. Although they retain the fundamentals of the 8086 architecture, they have features that enhance their computing power. There is also a simpler version than the 8086. A chip known as 8088 has the same logical and programming structure as the 8086, but it handles external data in 8-bit quantities only. Thus, it is really an 8-bit microprocessor.

We will not discuss the Intel microprocessors in detail. However, we will consider some of their features that notably differ from their counterparts in either the Motorola microprocessors or the PDP-11 machines that have served as our main examples. We will concentrate in particular on the way they access main memory and I/O devices. Since the 8086 is the basic component of the Intel family and has a relatively simple structure, we will use it as a representative example in the discussion that follows.

10.5.1   Memory Segmentation

The 8086 microprocessor views the memory as being organized in sets of segments, each 64K bytes in size. The microprocessor has four registers that serve as pointers to the segments. Instructions and data are addressed relative to these pointers. One of these registers, called the Code Segment register (CS), is used to access instructions only. Another, called the Data Segment register (DS), is used when accessing data. This means that the most natural way to write programs for the 8086 is to fully separate the instruction space from the data space. This separation of program and data spaces is sometimes referred to as *Harvard architecture*, as contrasted with the more familiar *von Neumann architecture* in which instructions and data share the same space as in our previous examples. Note that the segments may overlap, which happens if the segment registers are loaded with values that are within 64K of each other. In addition to the DS register, there is an Extra Segment register (ES) that is also used for accessing data. The fourth register of this type is the Stack Segment register (SS), which defines the 64K-byte area where a stack is located. It points to the base address of the stack segment. Since the contents of the SS register can be changed by the program, a number of different stacks can be created.

The concept of memory segmentation as implemented in the 8086 is conducive to modular software development. Individual modules can be independent, but can also share some common data. Using the CS register to point to the segment that is currently being executed provides an efficient mechanism for relocatability. A program module can be accessed in different locations in the memory by changing the code segment value associated with it. Data is normally placed in the DS segment. By default, most instructions use the DS register when accessing data. If an instruction is to access data in the ES segment, a prefix byte is added to the instruction. The ES segment is convenient for storing data common to two or more program modules.

10.5.2   Register Structure in the 8086 Microprocessor

Figure 10.15 shows the register structure of the 8086 microprocessor. In addition to the segment registers, it has a set of data, pointer, and index registers.

The four data registers are general purpose registers that can be used for temporary storage of data. However, some instructions implicitly assign a more specific

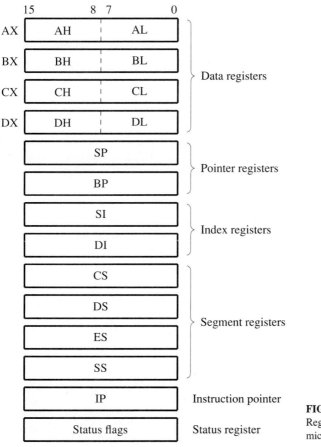

FIGURE 10.15
Register structure in the 8086 microprocessor.

function to these registers. The AX register is normally used as the accumulator. The BX register is used to hold a base address, typically the starting address of a list or an array of data in the main memory. The CX register contains the count for shift and rotate instructions, which indicates the number of bit positions that the operand is to be shifted or rotated. The DX register holds the address of an I/O device during some I/O operations. All four data registers can be accessed either as 16-bit words or as individual bytes. When a byte is to be accessed, the register name specifies the desired byte. For example, AH and AL refer to the high- and low-order bytes of accumulator AX.

Register SP is the usual stack pointer. Its contents are added to the contents of the SS register to obtain the address that defines the top of the stack. Note that the bottom of the stack is not necessarily defined by the value in SS alone. It is defined by the value in SS plus the initial contents of SP.

The base pointer register, BP, provides another option in based addressing. It is often used to hold the base address of a list or an array. Recall that this addressing function can also be achieved with the BX register.

Index registers SI and DI are used in various versions of the index addressing mode in conjunction with the BP and BX registers. When strings are used as operands, these registers provide source index and destination index.

Although the pointer and index registers have specific functions as we explained in the preceding paragraphs, they can also be used to hold general operands. These operands can only be accessed as 16-bit words.

The instruction pointer, IP, has the function of a program counter, but it does not normally contain the actual address of the current instruction. This address is the sum of the contents of IP and the code segment register, CS. The status register contains condition code flags and status flags.

By now, the reader has probably reached a conclusion that the 8086 does not have a very general register structure like the 68000 or PDP-11 processors. Although most registers can be used as general purpose data registers, their roles are often constrained to specific functions as we have discussed. In this respect, the 8086 is similar to the 6809 microprocessor, which uses specialized assignment of registers. Perhaps the main reason for selecting this approach was Intel designers' desire to make the 8086 compatible with its 8-bit predecessor, the 8085. The 8086 has an operation mode in which it can execute programs written for the 8085. In order to achieve this, the AL, BH, BL, CH, CL, DH, DL, SP and IP serve the same function as the corresponding registers in the 8085. Note that only the low byte of the AX register is used, because the 8085 has only an 8-bit accumulator. Such upward compatibility of a new product allows customers to use their existing application software without significant modifications, but it also constrains freedom of design.

10.5.3 Generation of Memory and I/O Addresses

The registers in the 8086 are 16 bits long. In order to generate a 20-bit memory address, the contents of a segment register used in the computation of the address are

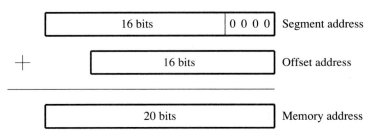

FIGURE 10.16
Generation of a memory address.

multiplied by 16 and then added to a 16-bit offset address, as shown is Figure 10.16. The offset address is the 16-bit value determined from the addressing mode involved. Intel literature calls this offset the "effective address." Note that if the offset address is continuously incremented it will go from FFFF to 0000, which means that addresses wrap around at the end of a segment.

Although I/O devices can be mapped into memory address space, the 8086 also has special I/O instructions that use a separate I/O address space. I/O addresses consist of 16 bits, which allows access to as many as 64K byte-sized I/O locations. If 16-bit I/O registers are used, they should be located at even addresses so that a single operation can transfer a 16-bit quantity between the I/O device and the microprocessor.

Two special instructions, IN and OUT, transfer data between an I/O device and the 8086. These instructions may include an 8-bit address as an immediate value, which can be used to directly access the first 256 I/O locations. The remaining I/O locations are accessed indirectly, using the address in the DX register. The IN and OUT instructions are more compact and faster to execute than the memory reference instructions that are used if I/O devices are memory mapped.

10.5.4   Intel 80186 Microprocessor

Considerable hardware improvements, in the form of new features, are found in the 80186 microprocessor. In addition to the circuitry needed to implement the 8086 architecture, this chip includes

- A two-channel DMA controller
- A programmable interrupt controller
- Three programmable timers
- 13 chip-select signals for memory devices and peripheral controllers

These circuits reduce the amount of external hardware needed to build a complete system.

For example, the chip-select signals reduce the amount of address decoding in the device interfaces. A given chip select line is activated when the 80186 generates an address within a specific range. The boundaries of the range are under program control.

From the application programmer's point of view, the 80186 has essentially the same structure as the 8086 microprocessor plus a few additional instructions.

10.5.5 Intel 80286 and 80386 Microprocessors

The 80286 is a 16-bit microprocessor that enhances the 8086 architecture by including on-chip memory management circuitry. Its overall capabilities, including the memory management facility, are not as extensive as those found in the 80386 microprocessor. Hence, we will discuss this facility in conjunction with the 80386.

The 80386 is a 32-bit microprocessor. Its register structure, as seen by the programmer, is basically that shown in Figure 10.15. The significant difference is the fact that all registers are 32 bits long except for the segment registers, which are 16 bits long. Also, the 80386 has six segment registers rather than four. The two extra registers are used to point to data segments.

In addition to memory segmentation, the 80386 provides a virtual memory paging capability. The segmentation and paging features are not necessarily used at the same time. In fact, the memory can be organized in the following ways

- As a flat 32-bit address space in which the effective address is used as the physical address
- As one or more variable-length segments (without paging)
- As a 32-bit space divided into one or more 4K-byte pages
- As a structure that combines segmentation and paging

Figure 10.17 shows the most general way to generate a physical address. A 32-bit *effective address* may be determined in normal indexed mode in which the contents of the index register may be multiplied by a scale factor of 1, 2, 4, or 8. One of the six segment registers is used to specify the required segment. Only the most-significant 14 bits of the register are used. These bits, called a *selector*, are used as an index into a segment descriptor table from which a 32-bit *linear base address* is obtained. This address is added to the effective address to produce a 32-bit *linear address*. The paging unit translates the linear address into a 32-bit *physical address* using a page table. Note that together, the 14-bit selector and the 32-bit effective address can be thought of as a 46-bit virtual address as indicated in Figure 10.17. Therefore, the total address space of the 80386 is 64 terabytes (2^{46}).

The segment descriptor and page tables are large, and are therefore kept in the main memory. In order to ensure fast address translation, on-chip caches are included in the 80386 to hold the active parts of these tables. An address translation cache holds the physical addresses of the 32 most recently used pages. A set of *descriptor registers* is provided for the linear base addresses. One such register is associated with each segment register. It contains three entries: a linear base address, a limit value that defines the maximum size of the segment, and an access rights field. Whenever a new value is loaded into one of the segment registers, the corresponding descriptor register is updated automatically.

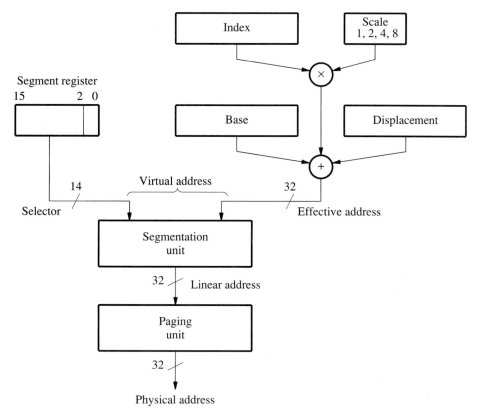

FIGURE 10.17
Address generation in 80386.

The address translation mechanism described above takes place in a so-called *protected mode* of operation. The 80386 can also operate in another mode, called the *real mode*. In this mode it behaves as an 8086 processor, except that it can use 32-bit registers. Memory addressing and segmentation are done as explained in Section 10.5.3.

Segmentation and paging are two key features of the 80386 microprocessor. Segmentation allows the application programmer to organize the main memory in logical modules. Paging provides a convenient mechanism for the system programmer to manage the physical memory.

The 80386 is a powerful and complex processor. We have considered in detail only its addressing mechanism, which differs from those we examined in earlier chapters. Interested readers can find other details about the 80386 in the manufacturer's literature.

10.5.6   Intel 80486 Microprocessor

The Intel 80486 microprocessor was one of the first chips to contain 1 million transistors. This processor provides significantly improved performance over the

80386 class of chips, an advance made possible by the expanded circuitry. It includes both integer and floating-point processing units, an 8K-byte cache, and support for multiprocessor applications.

The integer unit is fully compatible with the 80386 microprocessor. The floating-point unit implements the IEEE floating-point standard presented in Chapter 7. In 80386-based computers, the same capability may be achieved using a coprocessor chip called 387DX. Paging and memory management support in the 80486 is the same as in the 80386.

A four-way set-associative cache is included for instructions and data. The loading of new information into the cache is enhanced by a burst data transfer mechanism, which enables four 32-bit words to be read as a block and loaded into the cache. The cache has a write-through feature, whereby any data written into the cache is also automatically written into the main memory.

The 80486 is suitable for use in multiprocessor systems, which will be presented in Chapter 12. One feature that facilitates such applications is the *snoopy cache*. When several processors that contain a cache are connected to a common bus, the control circuits associated with each cache monitor the bus to detect data transfers to the main memory. When a processor writes data into a memory location that has an image in other caches, the control circuits associated with these caches invalidate their copy. This ensures that stale data in a cache will not be used. A similar feature is found in the Motorola 68040 microprocessor, which was discussed in Section 10.4.3.

In order to achieve high performance, the 80486 exploits parallelism and pipelining to a great extent. Both the integer unit and the floating-point unit can execute instructions in parallel. When one instruction is being executed, the subsequent instructions are fetched from the memory. Execution of frequently used instructions requires fewer clock cycles than in the 80386, with those that load and store data or perform register to register operations requiring only one cycle. The design of the 80486 was influenced by the RISC approach, which will be explained in Chapter 11, to achieve high performance. However, instead of using a RISC-like instruction set that consists of relatively simple instructions, the well-established 80386 instructions were retained. This maintains compatibility with the previous microprocessors in the 8086 family and allows the use of existing software.

10.6   CONCLUDING REMARKS

Progress in VLSI technology has been rapid and its impact upon microprocessors has been very pronounced. New chips are developed and marketed every year. Chips tend to be increasingly more versatile and powerful. This has led to a situation in which any given microprocessor is likely to have a relatively short lifetime because newer products inevitably make it obsolete.

Because of this fast pace, it is perhaps dangerous to refer to any particular microprocessor in a discussion of the topic. We used a few specific examples in this chapter to help illustrate the concepts involved in microprocessors in general. Thus, although they may become obsolete soon, the basic principles will remain useful and will continue to be found in other products.

10.7 PROBLEMS

10.1. Figure 2.32 shows a byte-sorting program. Write a program to perform the same task using the 6809 microprocessor. How many bytes of storage are needed for your program?

10.2. Comment on the relative merits of the 6809 and 68000 microprocessors with respect to the preceding byte-sorting task.

10.3. Write a 6809 program to multiply two 16-bit signed numbers using the Booth algorithm from Section 7.7. Assume that the multiplicand, multiplier, and the resultant 32-bit product occupy 8 consecutive bytes of RAM.

10.4. Write a 6809 program to convert a two-digit BCD number stored in 1 byte into an 8-bit binary number.

10.5. Consider a 6809 system that has four peripheral devices connected to two PICs (described in Section 10.3.2), with one device per port. All four devices can raise interrupts. Each interrupt request is wire-ORed and appears as an IRQ signal on the corresponding pin of the microprocessor.

   An interrupt cannot be accepted until the execution of the current instruction is completed. Estimate the maximum delay that the lowest-priority device will experience before its request is serviced, given that it is the only interrupting device and that the interrupt mask (bit I in the condition code register) is not set. Assume that the number of cycles needed to execute an instruction is the same as the number of memory accesses needed. Note that prior to servicing any interrupt request, the 6809 will automatically store the contents of its internal registers on the stack. This process takes 12 cycles.

10.6. Two 7-segment displays are connected to a 6809 system, one to each port of a PIC. The displays have the organization indicated at the top of Figure A.33, and each segment is connected directly to one port data line (i.e., a BCD-to-7-segment decoder circuit is not used). Write a program capable of displaying 10 two-digit BCD numbers stored in a list in RAM, with two digits per byte. Each number should be displayed for approximately two seconds. Assume that the number of cycles needed to execute an instruction is the same as the number of memory accesses needed, and that the clock speed is 2 MHz.

10.7. Write a 6809 program that reverses the order of bits in accumulator A. For example, if the starting pattern in the accumulator is 10110100, the result left in the accumulator should be 00101101.

10.8. Assume that a string of ASCII characters is stored in the main memory starting at location 1000_{16}. Each character occupies 1 byte, consisting of the 7-bit ASCII code (see Appendix D) and a 0 in the most significant bit position. The character string is terminated by the null character, which is encoded as 00_{16}. Write a 6809 program to count the number of occurrences of the definite article "the" in the string.

10.9. Generalize the part that searches for the definite article in the program of Problem 10.8 and make it capable of finding an arbitrary string of characters in a given text. Write the program as a subroutine in which the starting address of the text and the starting address of the buffer that holds the string that is to be searched for are passed as parameters.

10.10. A commonly used input device is a hexadecimal keypad, which has 16 keys corresponding to the 16 hex digits. Internally, the hex keypad consists of four row wires (R0,R1,R2,R3) and four column wires (C0,C1,C2,C3) in a matrix arrangement. The wires are normally isolated from each other. When a key is pressed, the corresponding row and column wires are connected. Assume that the keys corresponding to the hex digits 0, 1, . . . , 9, A, . . . , E, F establish connections between the row/column pairs R0/C0, R0/C1, . . . , R2/C1, R2/C2, . . . , R3/C2, R3/C3, respectively.

Let the hex keypad be connected to one of the ports of a PIC. The closure of any switch can then be detected by writing a 0 to all row wires and by reading the column wires, and vice versa. Write a 6809 program to read the keys pressed on the keypad and store the values read in successive memory locations.

10.11. One of the problems with mechanical switches is that their contacts often bounce (open and close several times) before making a firm electrical connection. Modify your program for Problem 10.10 to "debounce" the switches on the keypad (that is, to ensure that an input pattern will be read only after it has settled to a correct value). Assume that bouncing lasts about 2 ms.

10.12. Design a 6809 system in conjunction with a PIC for the following application. Two devices are to be connected to the system. One device, D_1, is a timer circuit that generates a 100-μs-long negative-going pulse once every second. The second device, D_2, is a part of a controller that needs the exact time of day. Whenever it requires the time of day, D_2 raises an interrupt request to the microcomputer by means of a positive-going signal. This signal remains high until the end of the transfer of data that represents the time of day. The required data consists of 6 bytes in ASCII code, in which 2 bytes are used to denote each of the number of hours, minutes, and seconds. Each byte transmitted to D_2 is to be accompanied by a pulse on a control wire indicating that valid data is available on the 8 data lines.

Note that the 6809 must maintain the necessary information about the time of day. This feature in a computer system is often referred to as a *real-time clock*.

10.13. Write a 6809 program to multiply two matrices using the approach explained in Section 3.3.

10.14. Discuss the similarities and differences between Motorola and Intel microprocessors.

10.15. The 68030 microprocessor has a 256-byte instruction cache and a 256-byte data cache. Is this better than having a 512-byte instruction cache and no data cache? What are the advantages and disadvantages of these two alternatives?

10.16. What are the advantages and disadvantages of memory-mapped I/O in comparison with schemes in which a separate I/O space is defined? What I/O arrangements can be used with Motorola and Intel microprocessors?

10.17. In Section 10.5.5 it was explained that the 80386 microprocessor can view the memory as being organized in four different ways, depending on how the segmentation and paging are used. Give some examples of applications in which each of the four possibilities is beneficial.

10.8   REFERENCES

1. *MC6809 Microprocessor Manual,* Motorola Inc., 1979.
2. *Versatile Interface Adapter (VIA),* Synertek Inc., 1979.
3. *MC68020 32-bit Microprocessor User's Manual,* Motorola Inc., 1986.
4. Vranesic, Z. G., and S. G. Zaky, *Microcomputer Structures.* Holt, Rinehart and Winston, New York, NY, 1989.
5. *MC68881 User's Manual,* Motorola Inc., 1986.
6. *MC68851 Paged Memory Management Unit User's Manual,* Motorola Inc., 1986.

CHAPTER
11

RISC
PROCESSORS

The basic ideas of computer instructions and machine-level programming were described in Chapter 2. It was pointed out in Chapter 3 that modern computers evolved in one of two ways. In one approach, a computer has a large number of instructions, many of which are capable of performing complex tasks. The instruction sets of Motorola 68000, DEC VAX, and IBM 370 computers were described as examples. A computer that follows this approach is referred to as a *complex-instruction-set computer* (CISC). The idea behind the CISC design philosophy is to minimize the number of instructions needed to perform a given task. Thus, the machine becomes easier to program in assembly language. Support for high-level languages is provided in the form of instructions that closely match typical constructs found in high-level language programs. The proponents of the CISC approach believe that the availability of such instructions simplifies the task of designing compilers and leads to an overall improvement in performance.

The second approach follows a diametrically opposite philosophy. It has evolved following a number of studies of the way high-level language compilers use the instructions of a given machine. The results of these studies showed that complex instructions that perform specialized tasks tend to appear infrequently, if at all, in the code generated by a compiler. Although such instructions are useful when programming in assembly language directly, they are much more difficult to generate automatically by a compiler. A *reduced-instruction-set computer* (RISC) is one in which the design of the instruction set is heavily guided by compiler considerations. Only those instructions that are easily used by compilers and that can be efficiently implemented in hardware are included in the instruction set. More complex tasks are left to the compiler to construct from simpler operations. Thus, the design of the instruction set of a RISC machine is streamlined for efficient use by the compiler to maximize performance for programs written in high-level languages.

In many computers, a hardware organization called pipelining is used to increase the effective speed of execution of instructions. The instruction sets of RISC machines are often designed to take maximum advantage of the opportunities for performance improvement through pipelined execution. Although the number of single instructions needed to perform a given task may be large, their pipelined execution can be shorter than the time needed to perform the same task using more complex instructions. RISC machines require a somewhat larger memory to accommodate the larger programs. Also, to achieve high performance, more involved compilation techniques are needed to make effective use of this organization. Because RISC machines place heavy demands on compilers, achieving high performance is often contingent on the use of the so-called "optimizing compilers." Such compilers use sophisticated techniques to minimize the movement of data between the main memory and CPU registers. They may also rearrange the sequence in which some operations are performed to eliminate any redundant steps. The RISC approach can be viewed as a trade-off in which hardware complexity is reduced at the expense of increased compiler complexity, compilation time, and the size of object code.

The IBM 801 was the first commercial processor to use the RISC approach in the design of its instruction set.[1] Since then, this approach has gained prominence in the marketplace, resulting in high-performance computers and workstations that include products from IBM, SUN, Hewlett-Packard, and MIPS.[2] RISC microprocessor chips are manufactured by a wide range of suppliers. In this chapter, the Motorola 88000 microprocessor family of chips will be used to illustrate RISC machines and the trade-offs involved in their design.

11.1 INTRODUCTION

Although no single feature characterizes the instruction set of a RISC computer, certain properties are found in most designs. We will introduce some of them in this section and others later in the chapter.

It was pointed out in Chapter 4 that a processor executes instructions by performing a sequence of steps. Hence, the time required to perform a given task may be expressed in the form:

$$\text{Execution time } = N \times S \times T \tag{11.1}$$

where N is the number of instructions
S is the average number of steps per instruction
T is the time needed to perform one step

A higher speed of execution can be achieved by reducing the value of any or all of these three parameters. In general, it can be said that CISC machines attempt to decrease the value of N and that the goal in the design of a RISC machine is to have small values for S and T. As will be explained in the next section, pipelining can be used to make the effective value of S very close to 1, which means that most of the time, the computer can complete the execution of one instruction in every CPU clock cycle. To reduce the value of T, the clock period, the number of logic levels in the hardware that decodes the instructions and generates various control signals must be kept to a minimum. This means that instructions should be simple and their number small.

When considering an instruction for inclusion in a RISC processor, the instruction's effect on the execution time of an average task (as given by Equation 11.1) should be kept clearly in mind. For example, if a particular instruction causes the value of S or T to increase by 5 percent, it should be included only if it is likely to be used sufficiently frequently that it would reduce the average value of N by at least that much.

Let us examine some common features of RISC machines and their instruction sets. The instruction

$$\text{MOVE} \qquad 50(A2),(A5)+$$

in the 68000 microprocessor copies the source operand, whose address is obtained by adding the number 50 to the contents of register A_2, into the destination location, which is pointed to by register A_5. Register A_5 is then incremented. On another computer that does not allow memory-to-memory operations and does not provide an autoincrement addressing mode, the same task requires a sequence of instructions such as the following:

$$
\begin{array}{ll}
\text{MOVE} & 50(A2),D3 \\
\text{MOVE} & D3,(A5) \\
\text{ADD} & \#2,A5
\end{array}
$$

where D_3 is a register being used as a temporary location. As we will show in Section 11.2, instruction fetch operations in a pipelined CPU are carried out in parallel with internal operations and do not contribute to the execution time of a program. However, read and write operations on data operands do. Let us assume that the source operand of the preceding ADD instruction is a short immediate operand that is included in the OP-code word. After excluding instruction fetch operations, the three instructions given above involve the same number of memory transfers as an equivalent single instruction. The time required to perform these memory transfers represents the shortest possible time in which the task can be performed, no matter how fast the CPU is. The premise on which a RISC machine is designed is that the use of simple instructions makes it possible to approach this ideal situation.[3] A key point in this argument is that a high degree of pipelining can be achieved.

Most RISC machines have a *load-store* architecture. That is, load and store instructions are provided to transfer data between the CPU registers and the main memory. All data manipulation instructions are limited to operands that are either in CPU registers or are contained within the instruction word. The addressing modes used in load and store instructions are limited to those that require only a single access to the main memory. Addressing modes requiring several internal operations in the CPU are also avoided. For example, most RISC computers do not provide an autoincrement addressing mode because it usually requires an additional clock cycle to increment the contents of the register. More importantly, the autoincrement mode is rarely used by compilers.

Only a few bits are needed to name a register that contains a data operand. Many machines take advantage of that fact by using three-operand instructions, making it possible for tasks such as

$$R_i \leftarrow [R_j] + [R_k]$$

to be implemented in a single instruction. Such instructions are particularly suitable for use by optimizing compilers. They are more powerful than their two-operand counterparts, yet they do not require more clock cycles to execute.

In general, it is beneficial for a computer to have a large number of CPU registers to reduce the need for frequent transfers of data between the CPU and the main memory. Modern compilers use a variety of sophisticated algorithms to take maximum advantage of the registers available in a given computer, because operations on variables assigned to registers require less time to perform. A data operand that is used several times needs to be loaded into a register only once, provided that the register can be dedicated to that operand for the duration of the task. However, if the number of registers is small, the operand may have to be loaded from the main memory every time it is needed. In other words, a small number of registers leads to an increase in the number of load and store instructions needed to implement a given task. We will see in the next section that load and store instructions often can slow down the operation of a pipelined CPU. Hence, it is particularly advantageous to reduce the number of load and store operations by providing more registers. On the other hand, a large number of registers may waste space unnecessarily if the compiler cannot use them effectively. Most RISC computers have at least 32 registers, and some have as many as 128. Because of the importance of reducing the number of data transfers to or from the main memory, hardware features have been devised to enable compilers to make better use of the CPU registers. These will be discussed in Section 11.7.

An important concern in the design of single-chip RISC processors is the area of the integrated circuit chip occupied by the hardware components that implement various features. It was pointed out in Chapter 4 that the CPU contains an ALU, registers, and interconnections, controlled by signals generated by a control unit. The size of the chip area occupied by the control unit is a function of the number and complexity of the machine instructions. Complex, multistep instructions require a large number of words in the microprogram memory. In a hardwired control unit, complex logic circuitry is needed. A machine that has a small number of simple instructions requires a small area for its control unit. The area saved can be used to provide other facilities, such as a larger number of registers or a cache memory.

FLOATING-POINT INSTRUCTIONS. Floating-point computation is used extensively in many computer applications, including scientific computations, digital signal processing, and graphics. Many computers have special provisions to speed up floating-point computations, and RISC machines are no exception. Most RISC machines have special instructions for floating-point operations and hardware that performs these operations at high speed.

Floating-point instructions involve a complex, multistep sequence of operations to handle the mantissa and the exponent and to carry out such tasks as operand alignment and normalization. The incorporation of such instructions in the instruction set of a computer may appear inconsistent with the RISC design philosophy, but this is not the case. In fact, floating-point instructions are a good example of the trade-offs that define the RISC approach. A given instruction is included in the instruction set if it leads to better overall performance. In this respect, a key consideration is the frequency of use of that instruction in a typical application. Because floating-point computations are used extensively, the incorporation of floating-point instructions that speed up these computations is justified.

An important consideration in the instruction set of a pipelined CPU is that most instructions should take about the same time to execute. Because of the number of steps involved, it is difficult to arrange for floating-point instructions to be completed in the same time as their integer counterparts. Hence, the two types of instructions cannot be integrated into a single pipelined structure. Instead, floating-point hardware usually constitutes an independent processor that has its own internal pipelining arrangement. It is often referred to as a floating-point *coprocessor*. The floating-point coprocessor may be housed on the same chip as the CPU, or it may be implemented as a separate chip connected to the CPU via an appropriate bus. It is particularly useful if the hardware allows both the integer and the floating-point processors to operate in parallel, under control of the software. In such a case, sufficient information must be kept by hardware about the progress of computation in each unit to ensure correct operation when interrupts and other types of exceptions occur.

CACHE MEMORY. Another prominent functional block found in all RISC computers is a cache memory. Although a cache memory is useful in any type of computer, it plays a particularly important role in a RISC machine. The reason for this is that the memory access time directly affects the values of S and T in Equation 11.1. A long access time requires either using a long CPU clock cycle or using more than one clock cycle for each memory access. The effect of memory access time on pipelined operation will be discussed in the next section.

11.2 PIPELINING

An important feature that is common to most RISC designs is pipelined instruction execution. The idea of pipelining was encountered in earlier chapters. Pipelining is used in many high-performance computers, but it is a key element in the implementation of the RISC architecture. In this section we will examine the idea of pipelining, paying special attention to its influence on the design of the instruction set of a computer.

The CPU executes a program by fetching and executing instructions one after the other. Assume that F_i and E_i refer to the fetch and execute steps for instruction I_i. The execution of a sequence of instructions I_1, I_2, and so on consists of a sequence

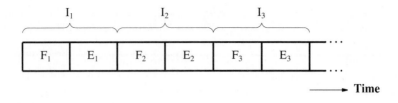

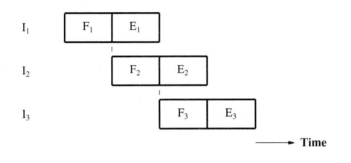

FIGURE 11.1
Basic idea of instruction pipelining.

of fetch and execute stages, as is represented diagramatically in Figure 11.1a. Let us assume that for all instructions of some computer, the fetch and execute stages require roughly the same amount of time. Let us further assume that the computer has two hardware units, one for fetching instructions and the other for executing them. Instruction execution may now be organized as in part (b) of the figure, in which the clock speed is chosen such that the fetch and the execute operations can each be completed in one clock cycle. After fetching instruction I_1 (step F_1), the instruction fetch unit begins fetching instruction I_2 (step F_2). Meanwhile, the execution unit performs the operation specified by instruction I_1 (step E_1). By the time the execution of instruction I_1 is completed, instruction I_2 is available. Hence, step E_2 may proceed immediately. In this manner, both the fetch and execute units are kept busy all the time. Clearly, if the pattern of Figure 11.1b can be sustained for a long period, the speed of instruction execution is twice that of sequential operation depicted in part (a) of the figure.

The processing of an instruction need not be divided into only two stages. For example, a pipelined CPU may process each instruction in four stages, as follows:

F	Fetch the instruction
S	Decode the instruction and fetch the source operand(s)
O	Perform the operation
D	Store the result in the destination location

The sequence of events for this case is shown in Figure 11.2. Four instructions are in progress at any given time, each at a different stage. The rate at which instructions are executed is four times that of sequential operation.

Pipelining refers to the type of computation parallelism that is illustrated in Figure 11.2, in which several instructions are being executed simultaneously, each at a different stage of its processing sequence. Clearly, some constraints must be imposed to guarantee correct results. The most important of these is that no two operations performed in parallel can depend on each other. This rather obvious condition has far-reaching consequences. An understanding of its implications is the key to understanding the variety of design alternatives and trade-offs encountered in pipelined computers.

Let us consider first the two-stage pipeline of Figure 11.1b. Stage F_2 must not depend on E_1, F_3 must not depend on E_2, and so forth. In other words, the operation of fetching an instruction must be independent of the execution phase of the previous instruction. There are two immediate consequences of this condition:

1. Pipelined operation cannot be maintained in the presence of branch or jump instructions because the address of the instruction to be fetched next is not known until execution of the branch instruction is completed.
2. The data paths for fetching instructions must be separate from those involved in the execution of an instruction.

Instruction

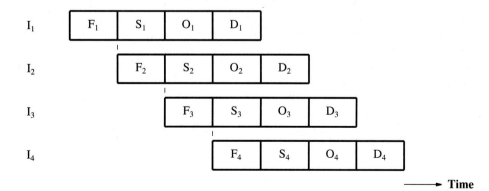

FIGURE 11.2
A 4-stage pipeline.

For longer pipelines, in which the execution phases of two successive instructions overlap, we must introduce a third condition:

3. If one instruction requires data generated by a previous instruction, it is essential to ensure that the correct values are used.

We will examine each of these aspects in the next section.

11.2.1 Instruction and Data Paths

The hardware of a pipelined machine should be organized to minimize interruptions in the flow of work through the stages of the pipeline. Pipelined operation is interrupted whenever two operations being attempted in parallel need the same hardware component. Clearly, such a conflict can occur if the execution phase of an instruction requires access to the main memory, which also contains the next instruction that should be fetched at the same time. The two operations can proceed in parallel only if they involve different memory units and if two separate buses are provided between the CPU and the main memory. Many high-performance computers, including most RISC machines, have two memory buses, one for instructions and one for data. The extra cost of providing duplicate buses is justified by the gain in performance.

A related question is that of the memory access time. Pipelining provides maximum benefit if the operations performed in different pipeline stages require the same amount of time to complete. If one stage takes a long time, the operations that are being performed in parallel have to be extended in time to maintain the proper logical relationship among pipeline stages. This is important when selecting the operations that should take place in each stage of the pipeline. Memory access, whether to fetch an instruction or to read or write data, is almost always much slower than internal CPU operations. Hence, in a pipelined machine, it is important to decrease the memory access time.

It was pointed out in Chapter 8 that a cache memory reduces the memory access time as seen by the CPU. For this reason, two cache memories are often used, one for instructions and one for data. Motorola's 88000 microprocessor system, which is introduced next, exemplifies this approach.

MOTOROLA 88000. The Motorola 88000 chip family is an example of a high-performance set of components designed according to the RISC philosophy. Its main component is the CPU chip, 88100,[4] which comprises the functional blocks shown in Figure 11.3. The instruction and data units are responsible for fetching instructions and data from the main memory. There are two execution units: an integer unit for handling most integer computations and a floating-point unit for executing floating-point arithmetic and integer division. The instruction, data, and execution units communicate via the register file, which consists of 32 registers. All internal and external data paths are 32 bits wide.

Figure 11.4 shows a typical organization of an 88000 system. The CPU chip has two buses, one for instructions and one for data. In the manufacturer's nomenclature, each bus is called a P bus. The buses are connected to their respective caches, which

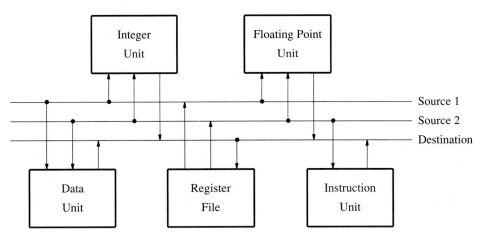

FIGURE 11.3
Internal organization of the 88100 processor.

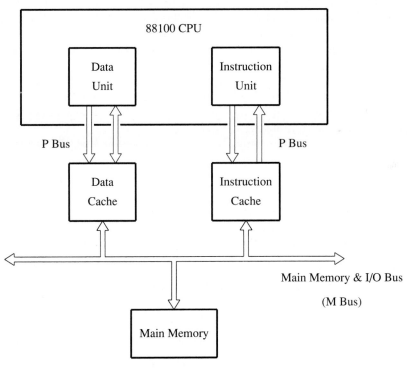

FIGURE 11.4
A typical arrangement for an 88000 system.

in turn are connected to the main memory bus, called the M bus. One of the support chips in the 88000 family is the cache, 88200, which provides the cache memory and performs the memory management operations needed to implement a virtual memory system.

The organization shown in Figure 11.4 allows several operations to proceed in parallel. The instruction unit in the microprocessor contains the logic circuitry needed to fetch instructions, to decode branch instructions, and to compute branch addresses. Most of the time, the instructions and data are available in the cache memories. Hence, instruction and data transfers can be carried out simultaneously and in parallel with the computations in the execution units. The floating-point unit is capable of performing two internal operations simultaneously. In total, the microprocessor may have up to five operations in progress at the same time, comprising an instruction fetch from the instruction cache, a data transfer to or from the data cache, and three internal data manipulation operations.

11.2.2 Branching

A pipelined machine must provide some mechanism for dealing with branch instructions. Consider the sequence of instructions shown in Figure 11.5, in which instructions I_j and I_{j+1} are stored at successive locations in the main memory, and I_j is a branch instruction. Let the branch target be instruction I_k. By the time the branch address is computed, instruction I_{j+1} will have been fetched. At this point, the machine must discard I_{j+1} and begin fetching instruction I_k, as shown. The hardware unit that was to perform step E_{j+1} must be told to do nothing. Thus, in effect, instruction I_{j+1} is replaced by a NOP (no operation) instruction. The time lost as a result of a branch instruction is often referred to as the branch penalty. In the case of Figure 11.5, it is equal to one clock cycle.

Branch instructions occur frequently. In fact, they represent about 20 percent of the dynamic instruction count of most programs. (The dynamic count means the

Instruction

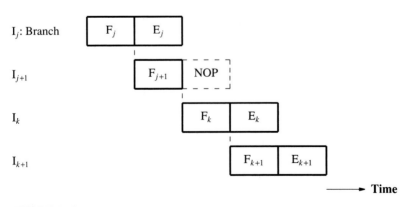

FIGURE 11.5
NOP cycles caused by branch instruction.

number of instructions actually executed, taking into account the fact that some program instructions are executed many times because of loops.) This is a large percentage that, because of the branch penalty mentioned above, would limit the utility of pipelined machines to specialized applications where branches occur only infrequently. Fortunately, there are several ways to handle branch instructions to reduce their negative impact on the rate of execution of instructions.

DELAYED BRANCH. The CPU will begin fetching instruction I_{j+1} in Figure 11.5 before it determines whether the current instruction, I_j, is a branch instruction. When execution of I_j is completed and a branch needs to be made, the CPU must discard the instruction that was fetched and fetch instead the instruction at the branch target. The location containing an instruction that may be fetched and then discarded because of the branch is called a *branch delay slot*. In general, if there are more than two pipeline stages, there will be several delay slots following a branch instruction. For example, the pipeline in Figure 11.2 has three delay slots. If instruction I_1 is a branch instruction, instructions I_2 to I_4 will be fetched but may all have to be discarded. A technique called *delayed branching* can be used to minimize the penalty incurred in such cases. The idea is very simple. Because the instructions in the delay slots will always be fetched and at least partially executed, we should attempt to ensure that these instructions need to be executed whether or not the branch is taken.

Consider, for example, the instruction sequence given in Figure 11.6a. Register R2, which is assumed to contain a value greater than zero, is used as a counter to determine the number of times the contents of register R1 are shifted left. For a CPU with a two-stage pipeline and delayed branch instructions, the instructions may be reordered as shown in part (b) of the figure. In this case, the shift instruction will be fetched while the branch instruction is being executed. After evaluating the branch condition, the CPU will fetch the instruction at LOOP or at NEXT, depending

LOOP	Shift_left	R1
	Decrement	R2
	Branch_if=0	LOOP
NEXT	. . .	

(a) Program loop

LOOP	Decrement	R2
	Branch_if=0	LOOP
	Shift_left	R1
NEXT	. . .	

(b) Organization for a delayed branch

FIGURE 11.6
Reordering of instructions for a delayed branch.

Instruction

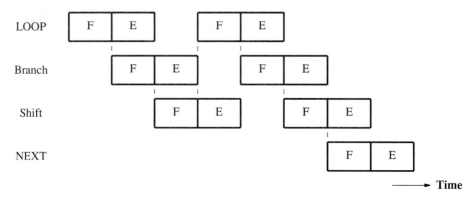

FIGURE 11.7
Execution timing for the loop in Figure 11.6*b*.

on whether the branch condition is true or false, respectively. In either case, it will complete execution of the shift instruction. The sequence of events during the last two passes in the loop is illustrated in Figure 11.7. Pipelined operation will not be interrupted at any time, and there is no need for NOP instructions. Logically, the program is executed as if the branch instruction were placed after the shift instruction. That is, branching takes place one instruction later than where the branch instruction appears in the instruction sequence, which explains the name "delayed branch." The instruction that appears sequentially after the branch instruction will always be executed.

For a machine that uses the delayed branch approach, it is the responsibility of the compiler to place appropriate instructions in the branch delay slots. If there is nothing useful to be done in these slots, NOP instructions must be used. Hence, the effectiveness of the delayed branch approach depends on how often it is possible to reorder instructions (as was done in the program of Figure 11.6). Experimental data collected from a large number of programs indicate that sophisticated compilation techniques can make use of a branch delay slot in as many as 85 percent of the cases.[5] For a machine with two branch delay slots, such as MIPS-X,[6] the compiler attempts to find two instructions preceding the branch instruction that it can move to the delay slots without introducing a logical error. The chances of finding two such instructions are considerably less than in the case of one delay slot. Thus, part of the speed advantage gained from increasing the number of pipeline stages may be lost because of the branch penalty.

11.3 DATA DEPENDENCY

A pipeline in which instruction fetch and execution are overlapped requires special handling for branch instructions, because the address of the next instruction is dependent on the result of execution of the current instruction. If the pipeline allows two or more data fetch or manipulation operations to be carried out in parallel, similar dependencies arise. In this case, a particular operation may not proceed until another operation is completed. Such dependencies cause pipelined operation to stall. They limit the potential performance advantage of a pipelined structure. As with branch instructions, data dependencies require special handling to reduce their impact on performance. We will first discuss this problem in general; then we will return to the 88100 microprocessor for examples.

Consider a CPU that uses the 4-stage pipeline in Figure 11.2. During the first stage, an instruction is fetched from the program memory. The instruction is decoded and the source operands are read from the register file in the second stage. During the third stage, an ALU operation is performed, and the result is stored in the destination register in the fourth stage. Assume that the CPU has 3-operand instructions that can have two source operands and one destination operand. A hardware organization that supports these features is shown in Figure 11.8. The register file allows three different locations to be accessed simultaneously. Two locations provide the two source operands, which can be transferred in parallel to the input registers of the ALU. Meanwhile, the data at the output of the ALU are stored in a third location in the register file.

Consider the following two instructions:

$$I_1: \quad \text{Add} \quad\quad R_1, R_2, R_3$$
$$I_2: \quad \text{Shift\_left} \quad R_3$$

The execution of these two instructions is depicted in Figure 11.9. The Add instruction performs the operation $R_3 \leftarrow [R_1] + [R_2]$. The contents of the two source registers, R_1 and R_2, are read during the second pipeline stage and are clocked into registers SRC1 and SRC2 at time t_2. Their sum is generated by the ALU and loaded into the ALU output register, RSLT, during the third stage, and then is stored in register R_3 in the register file between t_3 and t_4. The question now arises as to what happens to the source operand of instruction I_2. The CPU hardware must detect the fact that this operand is the same as the destination operand of the previous instruction and ensure

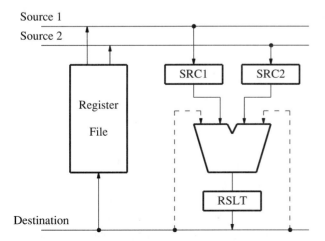

Source 1

Source 2

SRC1   SRC2

Register

File

RSLT

Destination

FIGURE 11.8
Part of the data paths of a CPU.

Instruction

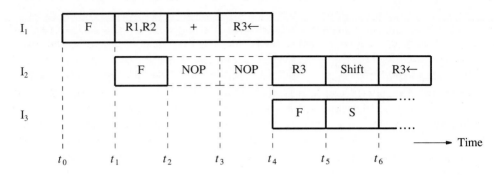

FIGURE 11.9
Interruption of pipelined operation because of data dependency.

that the updated value is used. Without some special provision, the read operation for the source operand of instruction I_2 must be postponed until after t_4, causing the pipeline to be stalled for two cycles, as shown.

To avoid the NOP cycles, the hardware can be organized to enable the data at the output of the ALU to be available for another ALU operation in the immediately following cycle. This technique is called *operand forwarding*. The dashed-line connections in Figure 11.8 may be added for this purpose. After detecting that the source operand of I_2 is the same as the destination operand of I_1, the control hardware chooses register RSLT instead of SRC1 or SRC2 as one of the inputs to the ALU. Execution of I_2 may now proceed without interruption, as shown in Figure 11.10. During the second clock cycle of this instruction, the ALU determines that operand forwarding should be used and enables the appropriate path from RSLT to one of the two inputs of the ALU during the following clock cycle.

A similar data dependency arises when reading data from the main memory. Consider, for example, these two instructions:

Instruction

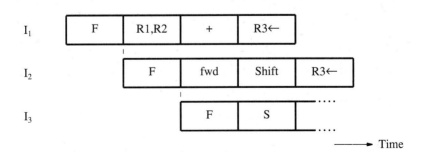

FIGURE 11.10
Instruction execution using operand forwarding.

$$I_1: \quad \text{Load} \quad M,R_1$$
$$I_2: \quad \text{Add} \quad R_1,R_2,R_3$$

A possible sequence of events while executing these instructions is shown in Figure 11.11. We have assumed that the CPU uses one clock cycle to obtain the address of the memory operand, M, perhaps from a register. Two cycles are then used to read it from the main memory. Because the destination register, R_1, appears as a source register in I_2, the memory data are forwarded to the ALU during the same cycle in which they are stored in R_1. In this case, even when forwarding is used, a NOP cycle is still needed because of the memory access time. The NOP cycle may be inserted automatically by the hardware after detecting the data dependency. However, in some machines this task is left to the compiler, which must now generate the following sequence:

$$\text{Load} \quad M,R_1$$
$$\text{NOP}$$
$$\text{Add} \quad R_1,R_2,R_3$$

The compiler may attempt to place useful instructions in the NOP slots, as in the case of delayed branching.

11.3.1 Side Effects

The data dependency encountered above is explicit and easily detected because the register involved is named as the destination in instruction I_1, and as a source in I_2. Sometimes an instruction may change the contents of a register other than the one named as the destination. A simple example is an instruction that uses an autoincrement or autodecrement addressing mode. In addition to storing new data in its destination location, such an instruction will also change the contents of a source register used to access one of its operands. All the precautions needed to handle data dependencies involving the destination location must also be used for the registers affected by an autoincrement or autodecrement operation. Stack instructions, such as push and pop, produce similar side effects because they implicitly use the autoincrement and autodecrement addressing modes.

Another side effect encountered in machines such as the PDP-11 and 68000 involves the condition codes. The condition code bits are changed by most instructions.

Instruction

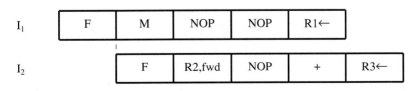

FIGURE 11.11
Data dependency involving a load instruction.

They are later used by other instructions such as conditional branches and add-with-carry. Hence, condition codes must also be regarded as giving rise to data dependencies and be handled accordingly.

From this discussion, it is clear that instructions that have side effects introduce data dependencies that are not easily detected and that lead to a substantial increase in the complexity of the hardware or software needed to resolve them. The complexity becomes even greater when interrupts and exceptions are considered. For this reason, the instruction set of a RISC machine is carefully designed to reduce side effects or possibly to eliminate them. This means that only the contents of the register or memory location named as the destination may be affected by any given instruction.

The requirement that instructions have no side effects may appear to be too restrictive. Chapters 2 and 3 showed that autoincrement and autodecrement addressing modes are potentially useful. Condition codes are also needed for recording such information as the generation of a carry or the occurrence of overflow in an arithmetic operation. We will show in the following sections that the functionality provided by these features can be provided by other means that are consistent with a pipelined organization and with the needs of optimizing compilers.

11.4 ADDRESSING MODES

The discussion in previous sections outlined the objectives of a RISC architecture and some of the features and constraints associated with pipelined hardware. We will now begin the discussion of the way the RISC philosophy influences instruction set design by considering its effect on the choice of addressing modes.

It was pointed out in Chapter 2 that addressing modes should provide the means for accessing a variety of data structures simply and efficiently. Useful addressing modes include index, indirect, autoincrement, and autodecrement. Chapter 3 described several machines that provide various combinations of these modes to increase the flexibility of their instruction sets. Complex addressing modes, such as those involving double indexing, are commonly found in many computers.

In choosing the addressing modes to be implemented on a RISC machine, the effect of the addressing modes on aspects such as the clock period, chip area, and the instruction execution pipeline should be considered. But most importantly, the extent to which these modes are likely to be used by compilers should be studied. To compare various approaches, we will assume a simple model for accessing operands in the main memory. The instruction

$$\text{Move} \quad (R_1), R_2$$

reads the contents of the memory location pointed to by R_1 and stores the result in R_2. The execution of this instruction can be organized to fit the four-stage pipeline of Figure 11.2 by using the source cycle, S, to read the contents of R_1 from the register file and to send them to the data unit responsible for reading data from the memory. Access to the main memory takes place during the third stage of the pipeline. We will assume that memory can make the requested data available in time to be stored in R_2 during the fourth stage of the pipeline.

Many of the complex addressing modes require several accesses to the main memory to reach the named operand. For example, consider the following instruction:

$$\text{Move} \qquad (X(R_1)),R_2$$

Assume that the index offset, X, is a short value given as a part of the instruction word. While executing this instruction, the CPU needs to access the main memory twice to read $[X + [R_1]]$ and then $[[X + [R_1]]]$. To accommodate this instruction in the pipeline, the execution phase will occupy five clock cycles, as shown in Figure 11.12a, allowing one cycle for computing $X + [R_1]$. The same move operation requires several instructions when it is implemented using only simple addressing modes. For example, on a computer that allows three operand addresses we may write

$$\text{Add} \qquad \#X,R_1,R_2$$
$$\text{Move} \qquad (R_2),R_2$$
$$\text{Move} \qquad (R_2),R_2$$

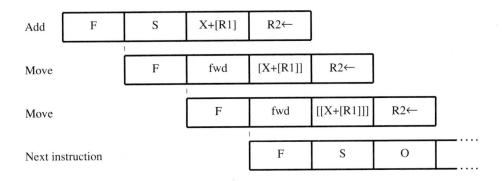

(a) Complex addressing mode

(b) Simple addressing modes

FIGURE 11.12
Equivalent operations using complex and simple addressing modes.

The Add instruction performs the operation $R_2 \leftarrow X + [R_1]$. The two Move instructions fetch the address and then the operand from the main memory. Because of pipelining, this sequence of instructions takes exactly the same number of clock cycles as the original single Move instruction. This is shown in part (b) of Figure 11.12. We have assumed that the machine has the operand forwarding capability described earlier. Hence, while executing the first Move instruction, the CPU sends the value $X + [R_1]$ directly to the memory to read $[X + [R_1]]$. Operand forwarding also takes place in the second Move instruction to read the final value to be deposited in R_2.

The above example indicates that in a pipelined machine capable of starting a new instruction in every clock cycle, complex addressing modes that involve several accesses to the main memory do not necessarily lead to faster execution. The main advantage of such modes is that they reduce the number of instructions needed to perform a given task and thereby reduce the space needed in the main memory. Their main disadvantage is that considerably more complicated hardware is needed to decode and execute them.

Complex control hardware uses more chip area and often requires a longer clock cycle. Also, many studies of compilation techniques and compiler-generated code have shown that complex addressing modes are not convenient to work with and, hence, are not frequently used. In other words, the inclusion of complex addressing modes in the instruction set of a machine tends to increase the value of T, but it does not lead to an offsetting reduction in the value of N in Equation 11.1. For these reasons, almost all RISC designs avoid complex addressing modes.

As a result of these considerations, the addressing modes found in RISC machines often have the following features:

1. Access to an operand does not require more than one access to the main memory.
2. Access to the main memory is restricted to load and store instructions.
3. The addressing modes used do not have side effects.

Three basic addressing modes that have these features are register, register indirect, and indexed. With indexed addressing, the operand address is the sum of the contents of a CPU register and an offset value. The offset may be given in a second register. Alternatively, if the range of values of the offset is limited so that it can be represented by a small number of bits, then it can be given as a part of the instruction word. In either case, only one access to the main memory will be needed to get the operand. Relative addressing is also used in RISC machines because it is a special case of indexed addressing in which the program counter is used as the index register.

11.5 INSTRUCTION SET OF THE 88100 MICROPROCESSOR

The design of the 88100 instruction set and addressing modes is a good example of the RISC approach because it follows very closely the criteria presented above. Access to operands in the main memory is restricted to three load and store instructions: Load, Store, and Exchange Memory (XMEM). The first two require a single data access to the main memory, except in the case of double word operands in which two transfers are needed. The third instruction, XMEM, requires a read operation followed by a write operation. This is a special instruction needed to support software synchronization operations, which we will discuss in Section 12.3.7. All other instructions manipulate data operands that are either stored in CPU registers or given as part of the OP-code word of the instruction. We will next give a brief description of the 88100 instruction set to illustrate the influence of the RISC philosophy on various aspects of instruction set design. For further details, the reader should consult the manufacturer's literature.[4]

Most 88100 instructions use the three-operand format. The operands are usually in CPU registers, but they can also be given as immediate operands that are a part of the OP-code word of the instruction. We will use the case of register operands to illustrate the operations performed by various instructions. Other addressing modes will be discussed in the next subsection.

In assembler notation, instructions are written in the form

OP-code   RD,RS1,RS2

The source operands are the contents of registers RS1 and RS2. These two registers are not affected by the instructions. The result of the operation specified by the OP code is deposited in the register named in the RD field.

The instruction set of the 88100 is summarized in Table 11.1, which gives a brief description of the function performed by each instruction. Although most instructions will be familiar to the reader, we will highlight a few features.

INTEGER ARITHMETIC AND LOGIC INSTRUCTIONS. All instructions use the three-operand format and operate on 32-bit quantities, which are regarded as either signed or unsigned values in 2's-complement representation. The operation specified is performed, and the result is stored in a CPU register. The Add and Subtract instructions may specify that a carry-out be produced or that a carry-in be included in the operation. Handling of the carry will be discussed in Section 11.6.

Unlike other machines encountered earlier in this book, the 88100 stores the Compare instruction's result in the destination register because it does not have the conventional condition code bits. The reason for this will also be discussed in Section 11.6.

FLOATING-POINT ARITHMETIC INSTRUCTIONS. Several instructions are available for floating-point operations and for conversion between integer and floating-point representations. Either single- or double-precision arithmetic may be specified according to IEEE Standard 754, which was presented in Chapter 7. A single-precision operand is 32 bits long and fits in a single CPU register. A double-precision operand is stored in two adjacent registers.

The mode of operation of the floating-point unit is controlled by several control registers. A control register may be read from or written into by transferring data between it and one of the 32 general-purpose registers of the CPU.

TABLE 11.1 88100 instruction set.

Mnemonic	Name	Description
		Integer Arithmetic Instructions
ADD	Add	RD ← [RS1] + [RS2]
ADDU	Add Unsigned	RD ← [RS1] + [RS2]
CMP	Compare	Compare [RS1] with [RS1] and record result in RD (see Sec. 11.6).
DIV	Divide signed	RD ← [RS1]/[RS2]
DIVU	Divide Unsigned	RD ← [RS1]/[RS2]
MUL	Multiply	RD ← [RS1] × [RS2]
SUB	Subtract	RD ← [RS1] − [RS2]
SUBU	Subtract Unsigned	RD ← [RS1] − [RS2]
		Floating-Point Instructions
FADD	FP Add	RD ← [RS1] + [RS2]
FCMP	FP Compare	Compare the two FP numbers in RS2 and RS1 and record results in RD.
FDIV	FP Divide	RD ← [RS1]/[RS2]
FLDCR	FP Load from CR	Load RD from one of the control registers of the floating-point unit.
FLT	Convert	Convert integer in RS1 to FP representation and store in RD.
FMUL	FP Multiply	RD ← [RS1] × [RS2]
FSTCR	FP Store into CR	Store [RS1] into one of the control registers of the floating-point unit.
FSUB	FP Subtract	RD ← [RS1] − [RS2]
FXCR	FP Exchange CR	Copy [RS1] into one of the FP control registers and store the original contents of that register into RD.
INT	Round to Integer	Round the FP number in RS2 to an integer and store into RD. The rounding method is specified in a control register.
NINT	Round to Nearest Integer	Round the FP number in RS2 using IEEE 754 round-to-nearest method and store into RD.
TRNC	Truncate to Integer	Truncate the FP number in RS1 to an integer and store in RD.
		Logical Instructions
AND	Logical And	RD ← [RS1] ∧ [RS2]
MASK	Mask	RD ← low- or high-order 16 bits of RS1 ANDed with an immediate operand.
OR	Logical Or	RD ← [RS1] ∨ [RS2]
XOR	Xor	RD ← [RS1] ⊕ [RS2]

TABLE 11.1 88100 instruction set. *Cont'd.*

Mnemonic	Name	Description
Bit-Field Instructions		
CLR	Clear bit field	RD ← [RS1], with the bit field specified in RS2 cleared to 0.
EXT	Extract	Bit field specified in RS2 is extracted from RS1, sign-extended and stored in RD.
EXTU	Extract unsigned	Same as EXT, but field is zero-extended.
FF0	Find First 0	RD ← number of most-significant 0 in RS2.
FF1	Find First 1	RD ← number of most-significant 1 in RS2.
MAK	Make Bit Field	A bit field extracted from the low end of RS1 and padded with 0s is deposited in RD with the offset specified in RS2.
ROT	Rotate	RD ← [RS1] rotated right by the number of bits specified in RS2.
SET	Set bit field	RD ← [RS1], with the bit field specified in RS2 to set to 1.
Load/Store/Exchange Instructions		
LD	Load	RD is loaded from memory.
LDA	Load Address	The effective address is loaded into RD.
LDCR	Load Control Register	RD is loaded from a control register.
ST	Store	[RD] is stored in memory.
STCR	Store Control Register	[RS1] is stored in a control register.
XCR	Exchange Control Register	Control register ← [RS1] , and RD ← [control register]
XMEM	Exchange With Memory	Exchange RD and a memory location.
Flow Control Instructions		
BB0	Branch on Bit Clear	Branch if a specified bit in RS1 is 0.
BB1	Branch on Bit Set	Branch if a specified bit in RS1 is 1.
BCND	Branch on Condition	Inspect RS1 and branch if the specified condition is true.
BR	Branch	Unconditional branch.
BSR	Branch to Subroutine	
JMP	Jump	Jump to the absolute address given in RS2.
JSR	Jump to Subroutine	Jump to the subroutine whose absolute address is given in RS2.
RTE	Trap On Bit Clear	A software interrupt occurs if the specified bit in RS1 is 0.
TB1	Trap on Bit Set	A software interrupt occurs if the specified bit in RS1 is 1.
TBND	Trap on Bounds Check	A software interrupt occurs if [RS1] > [RS2].
TCND	Conditional Trap	A software interrupt occurs if [RX1] indicates that the specified conditon is true.

BIT-FIELD INSTRUCTIONS. These instructions operate on a bit field, which consists of a number of contiguous bits within a register. A bit field is specified by its width, or the number of bits it contains, and its offset, which is the number of its least-significant bit. For example, a field consisting of bits b_8 to b_{24} has a width of 17 and an offset of 8. The two 5-bit numbers needed to specify the width and offset are given in register RS2, as shown in Figure 11.13.

Bit field instructions implement a variety of bit manipulation operations. For example, the CLR and SET instructions copy the contents of source register RS1 into the destination register RD, with the bits in the field specified by RS2 either cleared to 0 or set to 1, respectively. The FF0 and FF1 instructions scan register RS2, starting from the most-significant bit, to find the first 0 or 1. If a bit with the required value is found, its number is stored in RD. Otherwise, RD is set to the value 32.

The EXT and MAK instructions can be regarded as generalized shift instructions. They differ from the familiar arithmetic and logical shift instructions in that the shift operation is restricted to the specified bit field. The bits not involved in the shift are either filled with zeros or are filled by sign-extending the value in the bit field. For example, consider the Extract instruction

$$\text{EXT} \qquad \text{R3,R14,R15}$$

where registers R_{14} and R_{15} contain the bit patterns shown in Figure 11.14. Register R_{15} specifies a 10-bit field starting at bit b_{18}, which the EXT instruction treats as a signed quantity. Hence, it copies bits b_{18} to b_{27} from register R_{14} into bits b_0 to b_9 of R_3. The most-significant bit is replicated to fill the remaining bits of R_3.

The result of the preceding EXT instruction is an arithmetic shift right by 18 bit positions. If a logical shift is desired, the Extract Unsigned (EXTU) instruction should be used instead. The reader may verify that the Make Bit Field instruction (MAK) can be used to perform a shift-left operation.

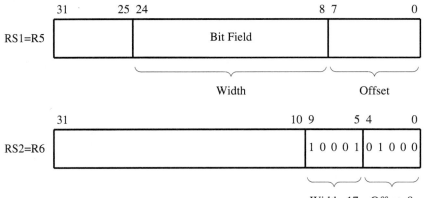

FIGURE 11.13
Example of a bit-field specification.

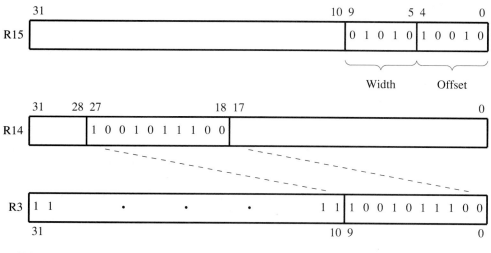

FIGURE 11.14
An example of an arithmetic shift right operation.

LOAD/STORE/EXCHANGE INSTRUCTIONS. The 88100 microprocessor deals with three distinct types of storage: the main memory, the register file, and a number of control registers that define the mode of operation of various units within the CPU. The load/store/exchange instructions move data between the register file and either a control register or a main memory location.

FLOW CONTROL INSTRUCTIONS. This group includes branch, jump, call subroutine, and software interrupt instructions. A single conditional branch instruction is available, in which the branch condition is specified as an operand. This instruction will be discussed further in Section 11.6.

The 88100 microprocessor has a total of 51 instructions, 12 of which are dedicated to floating-point operations. Most of the basic functions normally found in the instruction set of a computer are provided. However, an important feature of the 88100 is that most of its instructions operate only on the contents of CPU registers. The three instructions that refer to memory operands have three addressing modes.

Some necessary operations appear to be missing from Table 11.1. Although it is not obvious, most of these operations can be performed with the instructions provided. For example, there is no instruction to copy the contents of one register into another. To facilitate this and other tasks, register R_0 is implemented as a special register that always contains the value 0. Thus, register R_5 may be copied into register R_6 by adding it to R_0 and specifying R_6 as the destination. Writing the result of an operation into R_0 amounts to discarding that result. This feature can be useful in a variety of situations. For example, if we wish to set the carry condition code bit without affecting anything else, we may execute any instruction that produces a carry and writes the result into R_0.

11.5.1 Addressing Modes

All data manipulation instructions use the three-operand format. The operands may be in three registers, RD, RS1, and RS2, as discussed in the preceding sections. Alternatively, the third operand may be an immediate 10-bit or 16-bit constant included in the OP-code word of the instruction. We will refer to this constant as Imm10 or Imm16, depending on its length. Hence, there are three basic instruction forms:

Triadic:	OP-Code	RD,RS1,RS2
Immediate-16:	OP-Code	RD,RS1,Imm16
Immediate-10:	OP-Code	RD,RS1,Imm10

The result of the operation specified by the OP code is deposited into the register named in the RD field. The other two fields specify the source operand(s) of the instruction.

For arithmetic and logic instructions, either the triadic or the immediate-16 format is used. The two source operands are the contents of RS1 and RS2 or RS1 and Imm16. In the latter case, the immediate constant is interpreted as an unsigned value, and the constant is zero-extended to obtain a 32-bit value. The immediate-10 format is used for instructions that operate on a bit field within a register. In this case the operand is in register RS1, and the bit field is specified as a 10-bit immediate constant.

Memory reference instructions use either the triadic or immediate-16 formats. The two values given in the source fields are combined to compute a memory address according to one of the three modes given in Table 11.2. For a Load instruction, a word is fetched from this address and deposited into register RD. In the case of a Store instruction, the contents of RD are written into the memory. For each entry in the table, the first line of the description is the name given in the manufacturer's literature. This is followed by an expression for the effective address used to access memory.

All three entries in Table 11.2 represent different forms of indexed addressing. In the first entry, index offset Imm16 is given as a 16-bit constant in the OP-code word. The second entry represents indexed addressing with the index offset given in the second source register, RS2. Finally, in the case of the third entry, the contents

TABLE 11.2 88100 addressing modes for accessing the data memory.

Syntax	Description
RD,RS1,Imm16	Register indirect with unsigned immediate A_{eff} = [RS1] + Imm16
RD,RS1,RS2	Register indirect with index A_{eff} = [RS1] + [RS2]
RD,RS1,[RS2]	Register indirect with scaled index A_{eff} = [RS1] + scale factor×[RS2]

of RS2 are multiplied by a scale factor before being added to the contents of RS1. The scale factor is 1, 2, 4, or 8, depending on the length of the operand specified in the OP-code of the instruction. This mode facilitates access to items in a list, irrespective of the length of each item. The value of the address offset used will be adjusted automatically for byte, half-word, word, or double-word items. The multiplication operation needed to adjust the value of the offset is easily implemented by shifting the contents of RS2.

We should emphasize that the choice of addressing modes in the 88100 is consistent with the discussion in Section 11.4. None of the addressing modes in Table 11.2 require access to the main memory to compute the effective address of the operand. All the information needed is either contained in a register or in the OP-code word of the instruction. Also, the addressing modes do not produce any side effects because address computations do not cause a change in the contents of any register.

11.5.2 Instruction Encoding

It is important that the OP-code word be easy to decode. A decoder that must examine a large number of OP-code bits simultaneously requires a correspondingly large number of levels of logic gates and introduces a large delay. On the other hand, if the OP-code is divided into small fields and a separate decoder is used for each field, the decoding delay will be much smaller. For the clock cycle in a RISC machine to be as short as possible, the OP-code word is usually divided into fields that can be decoded independently.

Figure 11.15 gives the formats used in the 88100 instructions. The first three formats are used for data manipulation instructions and the fourth is used in flow-control instructions such as Branch and Branch-to-subroutine. The branch offset is given as a 26-bit signed immediate value. In all cases, there is a 6-bit OPCODE field. In data manipulation instructions, this is followed by two 5-bit fields for specifying registers RD and RS1. The remaining 16 bits either are used to specify a 16-bit immediate operand or are split between an operand specification and a field called SUBOPCODE. This latter field completes the specification of the operation to be performed.

The OPCODE field also determines which of the units in Figure 11.3 will be responsible for completing the execution of the instruction and so should read the information on the source buses. The selected execution unit decodes the SUBOPCODE field to determine what action to take. Interpreting the bit patterns in this field depends upon the result of decoding the OPCODE field. However, since the SUBOPCODE information is not needed until a later stage in the execution pipeline, the clock period need only be long enough for one field to be decoded. Note also that the bit fields containing the OPCODE and the register specifiers are always at the same place within the instruction word. Decoding of these fields can therefore proceed in parallel, immediately after the instruction is fetched.

11.5.3 Comparison with the 68000

It is instructive to compare the instruction set of the 88100 with that of a CISC machine such as the 68000, which is summarized in Appendix C. A quick comparison might

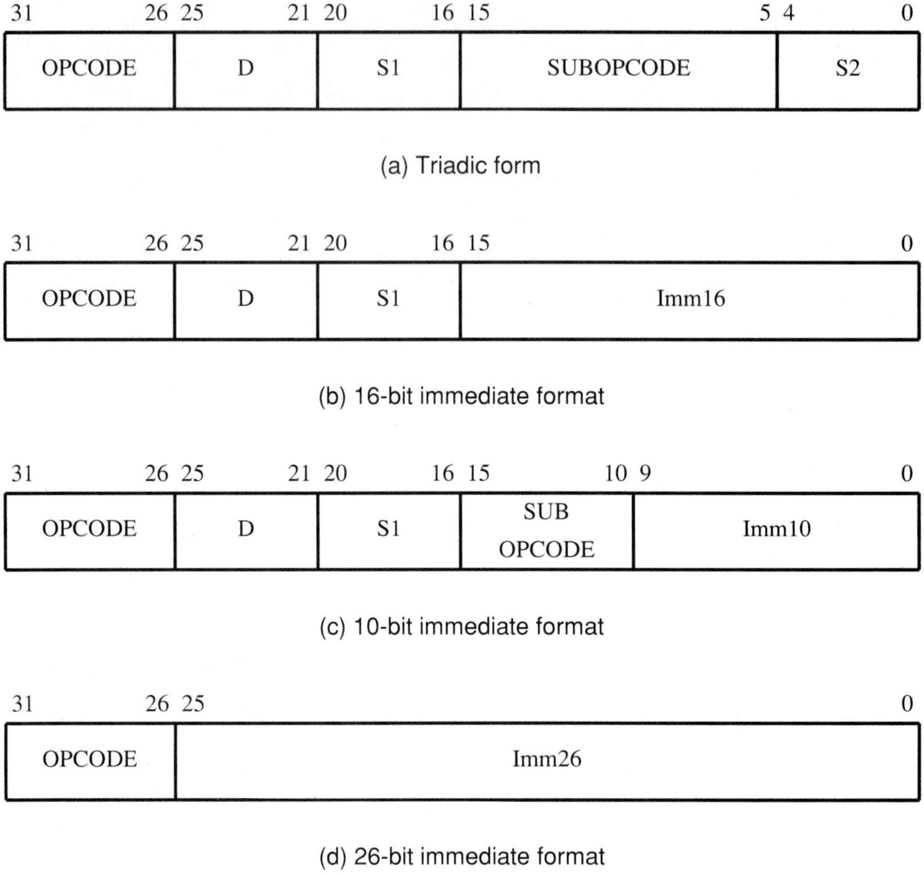

31	26 25	21 20	16 15	5 4	0
OPCODE	D	S1	SUBOPCODE	S2	

(a) Triadic form

31	26 25	21 20	16 15	0
OPCODE	D	S1	Imm16	

(b) 16-bit immediate format

31	26 25	21 20	16 15	10 9	0
OPCODE	D	S1	SUB OPCODE	Imm10	

(c) 10-bit immediate format

31	26 25	0
OPCODE	Imm26	

(d) 26-bit immediate format

FIGURE 11.15
Instruction formats of the 88100 microprocessor.

suggest that the 88100 has fewer instructions. However, closer inspection reveals that almost all the operations that can be performed by the 68000 instructions are available in the 88100. As we pointed out earlier, some of the operations that do not appear explicitly in Table 11.1 are available through the use of register R_0 or through special cases of the bit manipulation instructions. Also, as we will show in the next section, the conditional branch instruction of the 88100 can be used to specify any of the conditions available in the 68000 instruction set. Hence, the number of distinct operations that can be performed by the 88100 instructions is comparable to the number available in the 68000. The main difference between the two instruction sets lies in the fact that the 88100 instructions have been chosen as an efficient target for high-level language compilers. Only those operations that need to be implemented in hardware to achieve a high speed of execution are included in the instruction set. More complex operations, such as complex addressing modes, are left to the compiler to construct using a sequence of machine instructions.

11.6 CONDITION CODES

In machines such as the PDP-11 and the 68000, the condition code bits, which are a part of the processor status register, are set or cleared based on the result of instructions. They may be tested by subsequent conditional branch instructions to change the flow of program execution. It was pointed out in Section 11.2.2 that the compiler for a RISC microprocessor attempts to reorder instructions to eliminate NOP cycles caused by branches or by data dependency between two successive instructions. The condition-code bits themselves cause data dependencies and complicate the task of the compiler, which must ensure that reordering will not cause a change in the outcome of a computation.

Consider the following sequence of instructions in some computer:

Increment	R_5
Add	R_1, R_2
Add-with-carry	R_3, R_4

The carry that results from the second instruction is used in the third instruction. This introduces a data dependency that must be recognized by both the compiler and the hardware. The compiler needs to know about it because it must not reverse the order of the two instructions while attempting to fill NOP slots. Also, it must not put the Increment instruction between the two Add instructions, because the Increment instruction may change the value of the carry. The hardware must know about the data dependency because it may have to delay the second Add instruction until the first one is completed. Although detecting and dealing with such data dependencies is a relatively straightforward task for the compiler, it is a difficult task for the hardware.

Hence, the condition code bits should not be updated automatically after every instruction. They should be changed only when explicitly requested in the instruction OP-code. This makes the task of detecting and dealing with the resulting data dependency much easier.

Let us again return to the 88100 microprocessor for examples of the ways in which these constraints might influence the design of the instruction set. Of the four condition code flags that are normally found in most machines, N, Z, V, and C, only the carry flag is provided in the 88100. The carry-out resulting from an arithmetic operation is stored in the C flag only when this action is explicitly requested in the instruction. An arithmetic instruction such as ADD does not affect the carry flag. To affect the carry flag, the suffix CO is added in the assembler notation, resulting in the instruction ADD.CO. If an add-with-carry operation is desired, the carry-in option is specified by using ADD.CI. The instruction ADD.CIO uses a carry-in and produces a carry-out that is stored in the C flag.

In machines such as the PDP-11 or 68000, the V flag is used to record the occurrence of arithmetic overflow. The programmer may inspect it by using appropriate conditional branch instructions to determine whether overflow has occurred. In the 88100, arithmetic overflow will always lead to an exception, so there is no need for a flag to record the occurrence of overflow.

Let us now consider the N and Z flags. These are normally used to record the fact that a given operand or the result of an arithmetic operation is positive, negative, or zero. The determination of branch conditions such as "greater than" or "lower or same" also requires inspection of the C and V flags. In the 88100, only one instruction can be used to evaluate such conditions. This is the Compare instruction, CMP. The result of the comparison is recorded in the destination register named in the instruction. The same register can then be named in a conditional branch instruction. For example, the instruction

$$\text{CMP} \qquad \text{R3,R5,R6}$$

subtracts the contents of R_6 from R_5 and stores a 9-bit pattern in register R_3, indicating the result of the comparison. Each of the 9 bits corresponds to one of the conditions: equal, greater than, higher, etc. Because the contents of R_0 are always equal to 0, the CMP instruction may be used to test the contents of a single register by comparing them to R_0.

The CMP instruction may be followed by a conditional branch instruction such as

$$\text{BCND} \qquad \text{GT0,R3,500}$$

This instruction is always given in the immediate-16 format. It specifies R_3 as its source register and uses the field normally reserved for the destination register to specify the branch condition. The contents of the immediate field are interpreted as a signed 16-bit branch offset. This instruction inspects the 9-bit pattern stored in R_3 and branches if the bit corresponding to the condition specified is equal to 1.

The branch instruction need not come directly after the compare instruction, provided that the intervening instructions do not change the contents of R_3. The intervening instructions may even contain another compare instruction that uses a different destination register. For example, if we wish to implement a 3-way branch depending on the contents of R_{14}, we may write the following:

```
CMP     R7,R14,R20
CMP     R8,R14,R21
BCND    EQ,R7,120
BCND    EQ,R8,−50
```

A branch with an offset of +120 will take place if $[R_{14}] = [R_{20}]$, and with an offset of −50 if $[R_{14}] = [R_{21}]$. If neither condition is true, the next sequential instruction will be executed.

31		26	25		21	20		16	15		0
1 1 0 0 1	N		M5			S1			Imm16		

FIGURE 11.16
Instruction format for a conditional branch instruction.

Conditional branch instructions are encoded as shown in Figure 11.16. A 5-bit field called M5, which specifies the branch condition, occupies the field that normally contains the number of the destination register, RD. Bit b_{26}, called N for next, allows the compiler to select delayed branching. The assembler command BCND.N causes N to be set to 1, in which case the instruction sequentially following the branch will be executed whether or not the branch is taken. All flow control instructions in Table 11.1 provide a delayed branch option in a similar manner, except for the trap instructions which cause a software interrupt.

11.7 REGISTER SETS

Most computers provide a number of registers in the CPU. Data stored in these registers can be accessed faster than data stored in the main memory. Moreover, since the number of registers is much smaller than the number of main memory locations, fewer bits are needed to specify the location of an operand when that operand is in a CPU register.

High-level language programs do not refer to CPU registers. During the compilation of a program, the compiler uses the registers to store intermediate results during the evaluation of arithmetic expressions or to hold the values of some frequently referenced variables. In doing so, it is common to divide the available registers between global variables and variables that are local to given procedures. When one procedure calls another, the registers common to both procedures must be saved in the memory and be restored upon return to the calling procedure. An important goal for the register allocation strategy used by the compiler is to make maximum use of the available registers, while minimizing the need to save and restore registers during execution of a program.[7]

Increasing the number of registers will improve the computer's performance only to the extent that the compiler can make effective use of the enlarged register set. A discussion of register allocation strategies is outside the scope of this book, but we will describe one hardware feature called *register windows*, which is intended to simplify the problem of register allocation when a large number of registers are available. Register windows have been implemented on some RISC machines. However, the idea is equally applicable to CISC computers.

11.7.1 Register Windows

In most computers, all CPU registers are available for use at any time. The decision as to which registers are used in a given procedure is left entirely to the software. The idea of register windows is to divide the available registers into groups called *windows*, as shown in Figure 11.17. When a procedure is called, a new register window is assigned to it. Thus, register R_0 of the called procedure will be physically different from register R_0 of the calling procedure. A procedure can access only the registers in its window.

Register windows are assigned to procedures as if they were entries on a stack. Referring to Figure 11.17, let window 0 be assigned to some procedure A. When another procedure, B, is called by A, window 1 is assigned to it. If B calls a third

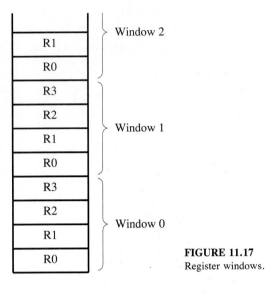

FIGURE 11.17
Register windows.

procedure C, then window 2 is assigned to C, and so on. As each procedure returns, the window stack is popped, so that the registers that are accessible at any given time are those in the window assigned to the currently active procedure.

A typical high-level language program has a large number of nested procedure calls. Hence, the available windows are likely to be used up quickly. When this happens, some of the windows assigned to procedures that are higher up in the call chain should be freed so that they may be reassigned to new procedures. Of course, the contents of the registers in a window that will be reassigned must first be saved in the main memory and may be pushed onto the system stack.

Figure 11.18 shows the case of a CPU with a total of four register windows. The letter inside each box representing a window is the name of the procedure to which that window has been assigned. Part (*a*) of the figure depicts the situation at the end of a call chain involving procedures A, B, and C. Window 3 is still unassigned. Suppose that procedure C calls procedure D, which in turn calls another procedure E. Before procedure E can be executed, the contents of window 0 are saved on the stack. That window is then assigned to E. Thus as the window stack grows past the top window, it wraps around to location 0. A storage buffer managed in this way is called a *circular buffer*. The situation after E calls F is illustrated in part (*b*) of the figure. Register contents for procedure B are now at the top of the stack in the memory.

The CPU registers may be regarded as an extension of the memory stack. Thus the effective top of the stack, which contains the variables of the currently active procedure, F, is window 1. If F calls another procedure, window 2 must be freed by having its contents copied into the memory part of the stack. Window 2 then becomes the new top of the stack. These actions are reversed when procedures return. Because

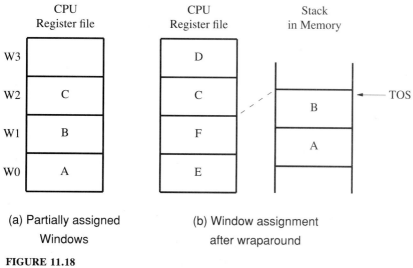

(a) Partially assigned
Windows

(b) Window assignment
after wraparound

FIGURE 11.18
Saving windows on the stack.

register windows can be viewed in this way, the scheme bears some resemblance to the way stack frames are handled in a stack machine, as discussed in Chapter 3.

In general, the register window scheme is most effective when there are long periods of time during the execution of a program in which the top of the window stack moves up and down within a small range. During such periods there will be little need for moving register window contents back and forth between the CPU registers and the main memory.

11.7.2   Overlapping Windows

The window scheme described above gives each procedure exclusive access to the registers in the window assigned to it. The compiler allocates these registers to local variables of the procedure. Because other procedures cannot access these registers, the procedure cannot use them to pass parameters. There are also many situations in which procedures require access to global variables or to some of the variables of procedures that are higher up in the call chain. The extent to which such accesses are allowed depends on the scope rules of the language used. When such variables are accessed often, it is desirable to place them into CPU registers. This is not possible in the window scheme as described, because no register can be accessed by more than one procedure.

The window scheme can be modified to accommodate global variables and to provide an easy mechanism for passing parameters. To support global variables, a few registers can be made accessible to all procedures. These registers may also be used to pass parameters. However, an even more convenient arrangement for passing

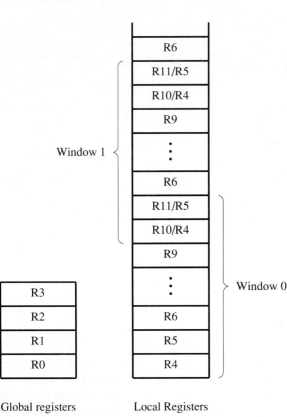

Window 1

Window 0

Global registers   Local Registers

FIGURE 11.19
Overlapping windows and global registers.

parameters between two procedures is to arrange for their windows to overlap. This makes the top few registers of the calling procedure the bottom registers of the called procedure, as illustrated in Figure 11.19. In this figure, four global registers are referenced by all procedures as registers R_0 to R_3. Each procedure is also assigned one of the local register windows, which contain eight registers each. The registers in the window are seen by the procedures as registers R_4 to R_{11}. Of these, R_{10} and R_{11} of window 0 are the same registers as R_4 and R_5 of window 1. Hence, they can be used to pass parameters between their respective procedures. For example, if procedures A and B are assigned windows 0 and 1, respectively, any information written by procedure A in register R_{10} will be available to procedure B in register R_4.

The window scheme has some advantages and some drawbacks. It simplifies the problem of register allocation and reduces the need for saving and restoring registers, but the number of registers allocated to a procedure is fixed. In principle, the window size can be made variable. However, this would lead to considerable increase in the complexity of the hardware that controls access to the registers.

Register windows represent one way of storing frequently accessed data on the CPU chip. An alternative is to provide fewer registers combined with an on-chip data cache. Such a cache is a fast memory to which data items that are being used frequently will migrate. Hence, it serves a similar purpose to that of a large register file.

11.8 CONCLUDING REMARKS

This chapter described the main features of a reduced instruction set computer, a computer intended to efficiently execute programs written in high-level languages. The term RISC was first used by researchers at Berkeley who developed a processor with the same name.[8] Its instruction set consists of instructions that are easily used by compilers and that can be executed at a high rate using techniques such as pipelining. RISC instructions perform simple, basic operations and use a small number of addressing modes. Access to memory is usually limited to load and store instructions. Floating-point operations are also typically provided as an integral part of the instruction set.

The execution speed of a RISC machine comes at the expense of increased compiler complexity and compilation time. Also, the size of the machine code needed to perform a given task may be much larger than the code for a CISC machine.

11.9 PROBLEMS

11.1. A program loop ends with a conditional branch to the beginning of the loop. How would you implement this loop on a pipelined computer that uses delayed branching with one delay slot? Under what conditions would you be able to put a useful instruction in the delay slot?

11.2. Consider a pipelined computer in which the instruction in the branch delay slot is always executed. If a branch is to take place, the results of that instruction are discarded, and the instruction at the branch target is fetched and executed instead. Suggest a way to implement program loops efficiently on this computer.

11.3. Assume that 20 percent of the instructions executed on a computer are branch instructions. Delayed branching is used, with one delay slot. Estimate the gain in performance if the compiler is able to utilize 85 percent of the delay slots.

11.4. Write the sort routine shown in Figure 2.21 or 2.32 for the 88100 microprocessor. Assume that one delay slot follows a load or a branch instruction and attempt to fill the slots where possible.

11.5. The instruction

$$\text{Add} \quad X(R_1, R_2), R_3$$

adds the contents of location $X + [R_1] + [R_2]$ in the memory to register R_3. The index value X is stored in the memory word following the instruction OP code. Show how to perform this operation using the 88100 instructions and addressing modes. Show the execution stages for both the above single instruction and the 88100 equivalent sequence of instructions, assuming an instruction execution pipeline similar to that shown in Figure 11.12.

11.10 REFERENCES

1. Radin, G., "The 801 minicomputer," *Proc. Symposium on Architectural Support for Programming Languages and Operating Systems*, Palo Alto, CA, March 1982, pp. 39–47.
2. Gimarc, C. E., and V. M. Milutinovic, "A Survey of RISC Processors and Computers of the Mid-1980s," *Computer*, September 1987, vol. 20, pp. 59–69.
3. Chow, P., and J. Hennessy, "Reduced Instruction Set Computer Architectures," *Computer Architectures: Concepts and Systems*. V. Milutinovic, ed., North Holland Publications, New York, NY, 1988.

4. *MCX88100 Reduced Instruction Set Computer (RISC) User's Manual*, Motorola Inc., 1988.
5. McFarling, S., and J. Hennessy, "Reducing the Cost of Branching," *Proc. 13th Annual International Symposium on Computer Architecture*, Tokyo, June 2–5, 1986, pp. 396–403.
6. Chow, P., and M. Horowitz, "Architectural Tradeoffs in the Design of MIPS-X," *Proc. 14th Annual International Symposium, Computer Architecture,* June 1987, pp. 300–308.
7. Flynn, M. J., C. L. Mitchell, and J. M. Mulder, "And Now a Case for More Complex Instruction Sets," *Computer*, September 1987, vol. 20, pp. 71–83.
8. Patterson, D. A., "Reduced Instruction Set Computers," *Communications of the ACM*, vol. 28, No. 1, Jan. 1985, pp. 8–21.

CHAPTER
12

MULTIPROCESSORS

When a computer application requires a very large amount of computation that must be completed in a reasonable amount of time, it becomes necessary to use machines with correspondingly large computing capacity. Such machines are called *supercomputers*. Typical applications that require supercomputers include weather forecasting; simulation of large, complex, physical systems; and computer-aided design (CAD) using high-resolution graphics.

None of the machines discussed in previous chapters are in the supercomputer class. As a general quantitative measure, a supercomputer should have the capability to execute at least 100 million instructions per second. This is approximately an order of magnitude better than any of the machines discussed earlier.

In the development of powerful computers, two basic approaches can be followed. The first possibility is to build the system around a high-performance single processor, and to use the fastest circuit technology available. Architectural features such as multiple functional units for arithmetic operations, pipelining, large caches, and separate buses for instructions and data can be used to achieve very high throughput. The price paid in using this approach is hardware that is difficult to design and expensive to maintain. However, because the design is based on a single processor, the system is relatively easy to use from a software standpoint because conventional software techniques can be applied.

The second approach is to configure a system that contains a large number of conventional processors. The attractive feature of this approach is that the individual processors do not have to be complex, high-performance units. They can be standard microprocessors. The system derives its high performance from the fact that many computations can proceed in parallel. The difficulty in using such a system efficiently is that it may not be easy to break an application down into small tasks that can be assigned to the individual processors for simultaneous execution. Determining these tasks and then scheduling and coordinating their execution on multiple processors requires sophisticated software techniques.

Multiprocessor systems are economically very attractive and are beginning to rival conventional, uniprocessor supercomputers in some applications. This chapter deals mainly with multiprocessor systems, examining a number of issues involved in their design.

12.1 FORMS OF PARALLEL PROCESSING

There are many opportunities for parts of a given computational task to be executed in parallel in a computer system. We have already seen a number of them in earlier chapters. For example, in dealing with I/O operations, most computer systems have hardware to perform direct memory access (DMA) between an I/O device and main memory. The transfer of data in either direction between the main memory and a magnetic disk can be accomplished under the direction of a DMA controller that operates in parallel with the CPU.

When a block of data is to be transferred from disk to main memory, the CPU initiates the transfer by sending instructions to the DMA controller. While the controller transfers the required data using cycle stealing, the CPU continues to perform some computation that is unrelated to the data transfer. When the controller completes the transfer, it sends an interrupt request to the CPU to signal that the requested data is available in the main memory. In response, the CPU switches to a computation that uses the data. This simple example illustrates two fundamental aspects of parallel processing. First, the overall task has the property that some of its subtasks (a CPU computation and an I/O transfer) can be done in parallel by different hardware components—the CPU and the DMA controller. Second, some means must exist for initiating and coordinating the parallel activity. Initiation is done when the CPU sets up the DMA transfer and then continues with another computation. The coordination needed when the transfer is completed is triggered by the interrupt signal from the DMA controller to the CPU. This allows the CPU to move to the computation that operates on the transferred data.

The preceding example illustrates a trivial case of parallelism, one involving only two tasks. In general, large computations can be divided into many parts that can be performed in parallel. Several hardware structures can be used to support such parallel computations.

12.1.1 Classification of Parallel Structures

A general classification of forms of parallel processing has been proposed by Flynn.[1] In this classification, a single-processor computer system is called a *Single Instruction stream, Single Data stream* (SISD) system. A program executed by the processor constitutes the single instruction stream, and the sequence of data items that it operates on constitutes the single data stream. In the second scheme, a single stream of instructions is broadcast to a number of processors. Each processor operates on its own data. This scheme, in which all processors execute the same program, is called a *Single Instruction stream, Multiple Data stream* (SIMD) system. The multiple data streams are the sequences of data items accessed by the individual processors in their own memories. The third scheme involves a number of independent processors, each executing a different program and accessing its own sequence of data items. Such machines are called *Multiple Instruction stream, Multiple Data stream* (MIMD) systems. The fourth possibility is a *Multiple Instruction stream, Single Data stream* (MISD) system. In such a system, a common data structure is manipulated by separate processors, and each executes a different program. This form of computation does not arise often in practice, so it will not be pursued here.

This chapter will concentrate on MIMD structures. However, we will first briefly consider the SIMD structure to illustrate the kind of applications for which it is well suited.

12.2   ARRAY PROCESSORS

The SIMD form of parallel processing, also called *array processing*, was historically the first form to be studied and implemented. In the 1960s, a system named ILLIAC-IV[2] was designed at the University of Illinois and later built by Burroughs Corporation. We will use the structure shown in Figure 12.1, which is similar to ILLIAC-IV, to illustrate array processors. A two-dimensional grid of processing elements executes an instruction stream *broadcast* from a central control processor. As each instruction

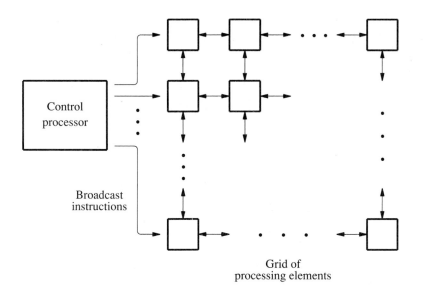

FIGURE 12.1
Array processor.

is broadcast, all elements execute it simultaneously. Each processing element is connected to its four nearest neighbors for purposes of exchanging data. Endaround connections may be provided on both rows and columns, but they are not shown in the figure.

It is instructive to consider a specific computation in order to understand the capabilities of the SIMD architecture. The grid of processing elements can be used to generate solutions to two-dimensional problems. For example, if each element of the grid represents a point in space, the array can be used to compute the temperature at points in the interior of a conducting plane. Assume that the edges of the plane are held at some fixed temperatures. An approximate solution at the discrete points represented by the processing elements is derived as follows. The outer edges are initialized to the specified temperatures. All interior points are initialized to some arbitrary values, not necessarily the same. Iterations are then executed in parallel at each element. Each iteration consists of calculating an improved estimate of the temperature at a point by averaging the current values of its four nearest neighbors. The process stops when successive estimates are closer than some predefined small difference.

The capability needed in the array processor to perform such calculations is quite simple. Each element must be able to exchange values with each of its neighbors over the paths shown in the figure. Each processing element has a few registers and some local memory to store data. It also has a register, which we will call the network register, that is used to facilitate movement of values to and from its neighbors. The central processor can broadcast an instruction to shift the values in the network registers one step up, down, left, or right. Each processing element also contains an ALU to execute arithmetic instructions broadcast by the control processor. Using these basic facilities, a sequence of instructions can be broadcast repeatedly to implement the iterative loop. The control processor must be able to determine when each of the processing elements has developed its component of the temperature to the required accuracy. To do this, each element sets an internal status bit to 1 to indicate this condition. The grid interconnections include a facility that allows the controller to detect when all status bits are set at the end of an iteration.

Array processors are highly specialized machines. They are well suited to numerical problems that can be expressed in matrix or vector format. However, they are not very useful in speeding up general computations.

12.3 GENERAL PURPOSE MULTIPROCESSORS

The array processor architecture described in the preceding section is a design for a computer system that corresponds directly to a class of computational problems that exhibits an obvious form of data parallelism. In more general cases in which the parallelism is not so obvious, it is useful to have an MIMD architecture, which involves a number of processors capable of independently executing different routines in parallel.

A general MIMD configuration, usually called a *multiprocessor*, is shown in Figure 12.2. An *interconnection network* permits n processors to access k memories

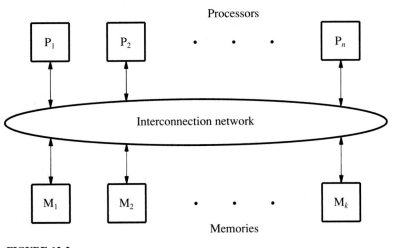

FIGURE 12.2
A general multiprocessor.

so that any of the processors can access any of the memories. The interconnection network introduces considerable delay between a processor and a memory. Because of the extremely short instruction execution times achievable by processors, the network delay in fetching individual instruction and data words from the memories is likely to be unacceptable. An attractive alternative, which allows a high computation rate to be sustained in all processors, is to attach some local memory directly to each processor. This organization is shown in Figure 12.3. The way in which the local memory is used varies from one system to another.

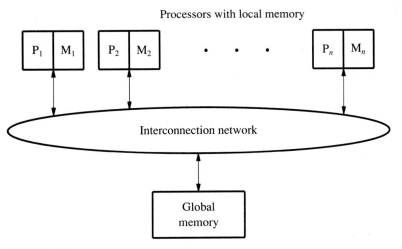

FIGURE 12.3
A global memory multiprocessor.

Normally, each processor accesses instructions and data from its own local memory. The interconnection network provides access from any processor to a *global memory*. This memory holds programs and data that can be shared among the processors, providing a means for interaction among the tasks performed by the processors. These tasks may be components of a single large application that has been divided into subtasks. They may also be independent tasks that require the use of some shared resources such as printers or magnetic disks.

The relationship between the information stored in the local memories and that stored in the global memory of Figure 12.3 will be explored next. One of the key issues is how to interpret the addresses issued by each processor.

12.3.1 Single Global Address Space

A simple organization is to have all processors reference a single global address space. All addresses refer to locations in the global memory. Each of the local memories acts as a cache containing the segments of program and data that are currently being accessed by its associated processor. This interpretation is illustrated in Figure 12.4. From the software standpoint, this is the simplest assumption about the address space. However, the use of multiple caches creates a problem. The problem arises when multiple copies of some items from the global memory exist in various caches. If these *shared variables* are updated, then different values of the same variable might be created in different caches and lead to incorrect results. Some control must be exerted to prevent this problem. We will examine solutions later in Section 12.3.8.

12.3.2 Global and Private Address Spaces

It is also possible that some part of the address range issued by an individual processor references a *private address space*, which is mapped onto a local memory associated with the processor. The remainder of the address range references a global address

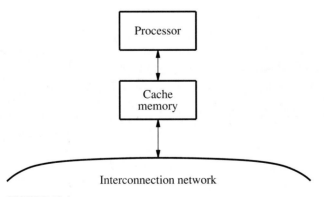

FIGURE 12.4
Processor with cache.

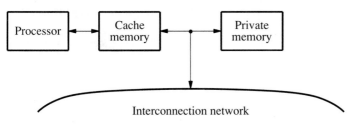

FIGURE 12.5
Processor with cache and private memory.

space as was previously described. This possibility is indicated in Figure 12.5. A cache memory that can contain items from either address space is included for execution efficiency. An advantage of this configuration of the address space is that there are more memory locations overall in the system. However, the management of the private address spaces and the global address space is more complex from a software standpoint.

12.3.3 Exclusively Private Address Spaces

The extreme in which all addresses issued by a processor reference only a private memory is not usually called a multiprocessor. The term *multicomputer* is more widely used for this configuration. Any interaction among programs running on the individual processors must be implemented by sending *messages* from one computer to another. In this form of communication, the interconnection network is seen by each processor as an I/O device. This is the easiest way to connect a number of computers into a large system. However, communication between tasks running on different computers will be relatively slower because messages are exchanged through I/O transfers. We will consider this type of system in Section 12.5.

12.3.4 Centralized and Distributed Global Memory

Memory access time is a key factor in the performance of any computer system. For multiprocessors, access to the global memory is of concern. Several schemes may be used alone or in combination to reduce this access time. The first possibility is to provide cache memories as we already described. Another possibility is to implement global memory in the form of a number of separate memory modules. The modules can be accessed independently and in parallel. Maximum performance will be achieved if access requests from the processors are evenly spread across all modules. One way to achieve this is to interleave addresses across the modules, as was described in Chapter 8. With interleaved addressing, access requests to successive words in the address space are directed to different memory modules. This address assignment is particularly effective when a miss occurs at one of the processor caches and a block must be transferred from the global memory to the cache. Because a block consists of words at successive addresses, several modules will be accessed to satisfy the transfer request. Thus the time required to transfer the block will be much less than the time required in the case in which all requests are directed to a single module. Of course, this gain in performance is possible only if the interconnection network allows access to the memory modules to proceed in parallel.

This discussion has implicitly assumed that the global memory is implemented centrally as shown in Figure 12.3 and is accessed uniformly through the interconnection network by all processors. An alternative that has potential performance benefits is to distribute the global memory modules, locating them close to the processors, at the same point as the private memory in Figure 12.5. The interconnection network is still needed when a processor accesses a global memory location that is not in the module at its location. However, the network is not involved when a processor accesses a global memory module at its location. Obviously, address interleaving across memory modules at different locations should not be used. With distributed global memory, it is important to attempt to place the instructions and data at the processor location at which they are used. It is the responsibility of the system software to arrange for this to happen as much as possible.

12.3.5 Virtual Memory

For the same reasons that it is valuable in uniprocessors, virtual memory capability is useful in multiprocessors and can be implemented in the same way. The virtual memory mapping operation must be done at each processor. When the distributed version of global memory implementation is used, the placement of page tables and the pages themselves into physical page frames in which they are most likely to be accessed is an important consideration.

12.3.6 Program Parallelism and Shared Variables

In the preamble to this chapter, we mentioned that it is difficult to break large tasks down into subtasks that can be executed in parallel on a multiprocessor. There are some special cases, however, in which the division is easy. A trivial observation is that if the large task originates as a set of independent programs, then these programs can simply be executed on different processors. Unless these programs block each other in competing for shared I/O devices, the multiprocessor is fully utilized by such a workload.

The next easy case occurs when the high-level source programming language has constructs that allow an application programmer to explicitly declare that certain subtasks of a program can be executed in parallel. Figure 12.6 shows such a construct, often called a PAR segment. The PARBEGIN and PAREND control instructions bracket a list of procedures, named Proc1 to ProcK, that can be executed in parallel. The order of execution of this program is as follows. When segment i of the program is completed, any or all of the K parallel procedures may be started immediately, depending upon the number of idle processors available. They may be started in any

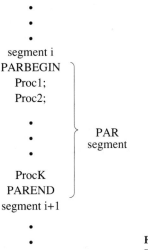

```
    •
    •
    •
segment i
PARBEGIN  ⎫
  Proc1;   ⎪
  Proc2;   ⎪
          ⎪
    •      ⎬  PAR
    •         segment
    •      ⎪
          ⎪
  ProcK    ⎪
PAREND    ⎭
segment i+1
    •
    •
    •
```

FIGURE 12.6
Parallel programming construct.

order. Execution of the part of the program labeled segment $i + 1$ is allowed to begin only after all of the K procedures have completed execution. In summary, segment i, followed by the PAR segment and then by segment $i + 1$, must be executed in sequential order with the internal procedures of the PAR segment being executed in any order.

If this program is the only one being executed on the multiprocessor, then the burden of efficient utilization of the processors is placed on the application programmer. The number and size of the PAR segments relative to the sequential segments and their degree of parallelism, K, will determine the level of utilization achievable by the multiprocessor.

The most challenging case to handle in developing high utilization of the multiprocessor is that in which the language compiler is required to automatically detect parallelism in a user program. The potential usefulness of automatic detection of parallelism is based on the following reasoning. An application programmer tends to think most naturally about programming a task as a set of serially performed basic operations. However, even though the programmer specifies the operations as a serial list of instructions in some high-level language, there may be many opportunities for executing various groups of instructions in parallel. A simple case is that of successive passes through a loop. If no *data dependency* is involved, then successive passes may be executed in parallel. On the other hand, if the first pass through the loop generates data that is needed in the second pass, and so on, then parallel execution is not possible. In general, data dependencies need to be detected by the compiler to determine which operations can be done in parallel and which cannot. The design of compilers that can detect parallelism for exploitation in multiprocessors is complicated. Even after the parallel parts of a program are identified, their subsequent scheduling for execution on a multiprocessor with a limited number of processors is a nontrivial task. It must be done at runtime by the operating system.

We will not pursue this topic of determining and scheduling tasks that can be executed in parallel. Instead, we will turn to the issue of accessing shared variables that are modified by programs running in parallel on different processors of a multi-processor system.

12.3.7 Accessing Shared Variables

Assume that two tasks that can run in parallel on a multiprocessor have been identified. The tasks are largely independent, but from time to time they access and modify some common, shared variable in the global memory. For example, let a shared variable SUM represent the balance in an account. Moreover, assume that several tasks running on different processors need to update the account. Each task manipulates SUM in the following way. The task reads the current value from SUM, performs an operation that depends on this value, and writes the result back into SUM. It is easy to see how errors can occur if such *read-modify-write* accesses to SUM are performed by tasks T1 and T2 running in parallel on processors P1 and P2, respectively. Suppose that both T1 and T2 read the current value from SUM, say 17, and then proceed to modify it locally. T1 adds 5 for a result of 22, and T2 subtracts 7 for a result of 10. They then proceed to write their individual results back into SUM with T2 writing first, followed by T1. SUM then contains the value 22, which is wrong. SUM should contain the value 15 (= 17 + 5 − 7), which is the intended result after applying the modifications strictly one after the other, in either order.

In order to guarantee correct manipulation of the shared variable SUM, each task must have exclusive access to it during the complete read-modify-write sequence. This can be provided by using a global *lock* variable, LOCK, and a machine instruction called Test-and-Set. The variable LOCK will contain one of two possible values, 0 or 1. It will be used as a guard to ensure that only one task at a time is allowed access to SUM during the time needed to execute the instructions that update the value of this shared variable. Such a sequence of instructions is called a *critical section*. LOCK is manipulated as follows. It is equal to 0 when neither task is in its critical section that operates on SUM. When either task wishes to modify SUM, it first checks the value of LOCK and then sets it to 1, regardless of its original value. If the original value was 0, then the task can safely proceed to work on SUM because no other task is currently doing so. On the other hand, if the original value of LOCK was 1, then the task knows that some other task is operating on SUM and must wait until that task resets LOCK to 0 before it can proceed. This desired mode of operation on LOCK is made foolproof by the Test-and-Set instruction. As its name implies, this instruction performs the critical steps of testing and setting LOCK in an indivisible sequence of operations executed as a single machine instruction. While this instruction is executing, the memory module involved must not respond to access requests from any other processor.

As a specific example, let us consider the Test-and-Set instruction denoted as TAS in the Motorola 68000 microprocessor. This instruction has one operand that is always a byte. Assume that it is stored in the memory at location LOCKBYTE. Bit b_7, the most significant bit of this operand, serves as the variable LOCK discussed above. The TAS instruction does the uninterruptible test and set operations on bit b_7. Condition code flag N (Negative) is set to the original value of b_7. Thus after completion of execution of TAS, the program can continue into its critical section if N equals 0, but it must wait if N equals 1. The easiest way to implement this decision is to follow TAS with a conditional branch instruction. This instruction should cause a branch back to TAS if $N = 1$, resulting in a wait loop that continues to execute TAS on the operand in location LOCKBYTE until it finds b_7 equal to 0. The branch instruction fails if TAS is executed when b_7 is 0, allowing the program to continue into its critical section. When the program is finished with its critical section, it should clear LOCKBYTE, thus resetting b_7 to 0 and allowing any waiting program to proceed into its critical section. Figure 12.7 shows the way in which tasks T1 and T2 manipulate LOCKBYTE to gain access to critical sections of code in which they update the shared variable SUM.

The TAS instruction is an example of a simple machine instruction that can be used to implement the concept of a lock. Most computers include an instruction of this type. These instructions may provide additional capabilities, such as the incorporation of a conditional branch based on the result of the test.

12.3.8 Cache Coherency

Shared variables give rise to another problem in a multiprocessor machine that has multiple caches. Copies of a shared variable may reside in a number of caches. When any processor writes to such a variable in its own cache, all other caches that

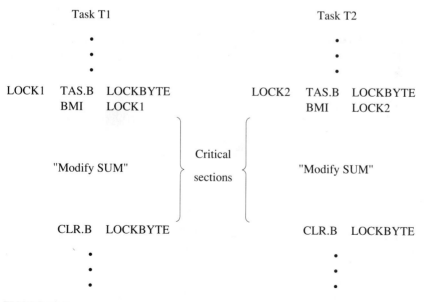

FIGURE 12.7
Mutually exclusive access to critical sections.

contain a copy of that variable will now have the old incorrect value. They must be informed of the change so that they can either update their copy to the new value or invalidate it. *Cache coherency* is defined as the situation in which all cache copies of a shared variable have the same value at all times.

Assume that the interconnection network broadcasts all writes from processors. When a write occurs to a particular variable, the global memory and all caches containing a copy of the variable can update their values. The advantage of this write-through policy is that unnecessary cache invalidations are avoided. This should lead to better hit ratios than those achieved when cache copies are invalidated when a write is observed from another processor. The disadvantage of this policy is the high level of network traffic and cache and global memory updating. However, the global memory always contains the correct value of all variables. When a read miss occurs in any cache, the global memory always supplies the requested value, which simplifies operations.

If the preceding write-through policy based on cache updating instead of invalidation is judged to be inappropriate, then the following policy can be used. Whenever a processor writes to a cache-resident variable for the first time, the cache entry is marked as dirty, and the write is broadcast into the network. The global memory updates its value, and all other caches invalidate their copy. The processor that did the write is now considered to be the owner of the variable. It can do further writes on the same variable without broadcasting them. If it does do more writes, then the global memory will not contain the correct value of the variable. Therefore, if the owner observes a read access to this variable on the network, it must supply the correct value to the requesting processor. The global memory is informed that an owner is supplying the correct value by a broadcast signal from the owner, and the global memory updates its value. Finally, the owner marks its copy as clean. Operation now proceeds with multiple cache copies of the variable and the global memory all having tne consistent correct value. In the case in which a dirty value must be replaced to make room for a new variable, a write-back operation to the global memory must be done. A similar technique is used for cache coherency control in the Sequent Symmetry multiprocessor.[3]

In order to implement the cache coherency operations, special hardware features are needed in the interconnection network. The most important of these is the need to broadcast a processor write operation to all other processor caches attached to the network. All caches must monitor the network for broadcast writes, and they must either update or invalidate their own cache copies when a match is detected. The monitoring actions are sometimes referred to as *snoopy cache* controls.

We should note that the requirement for lock guard controls on access to shared variables is independent of the need for cache coherency controls. Both types of controls are needed. To see this, consider the case in which cache coherency is maintained by using the write-through policy accompanied by cache updating of writes to shared variables. Suppose that the contents of SUM in the example in the previous section have been read into the caches of the two processors that execute the tasks T1 and T2. If the read operations are part of an update sequence and are not made mutually exclusive by the use of a lock guard control, then it is easy to see that the original error can still occur. If task T1 writes its new value last, as before, then SUM will contain the value 22, which is wrong. Cache coherency is maintained throughout this sequence of events. However, incorrect results were obtained because lock guard controls were not used. Lock variables themselves need to be handled in a special way. Instruction execution must be arranged in such a way that Test-and-Set instructions can only be applied to lock variables in a global memory module. The module is then responsible for keeping the operations of the Test-and-Set instruction indivisible.

12.3.9 Performance Considerations

Section 12.3.4 claimed that maximum performance in terms of bandwidth between processors and global memory modules is achieved if access requests are evenly spread across all modules. This assumes that the modules can be accessed independently and in parallel. Address interleaving will certainly help in spreading access requests evenly. Before describing specific interconnection networks that can be used to carry this traffic, it is instructive to see the average number of modules that can be kept busy at a time processing access requests. We will make the ideal assumption that the interconnection network has zero delay and can simultaneously provide as many independent paths to modules as are needed. Therefore, the performance measure derived is an upper limit on the average bandwidth that can be provided by any network. The only way a processor request can be blocked is if another processor is using the memory module that it wishes to access. This is referred to as a *memory conflict*.

Consider the following model of processor accesses to global memory modules. Time is divided into discrete intervals called cycles, each of which has a length equal to the memory module read or write access time. Suppose there are n processors and k memories, as shown in Figure 12.2. At the beginning of each cycle, each processor independently generates a request. A request from a particular processor is directed to a particular memory with probability $1/k$. The probability that a particular memory is not selected by a particular processor is $1 - 1/k$, and the probability that a particular memory is not selected by any processor is $(1 - 1/k)^n$. Therefore, the probability that a memory is selected by at least one processor is $p = 1 - (1 - 1/k)^n$. Assume that when multiple requests are directed to a memory, one gains access and the others are blocked. Then p represents the fraction of memories that are busy processing requests in any cycle, on average.

A few numerical examples illustrate the effect of memory conflicts in the preceding model. Suppose that the number of processors and memories is the same and is very large. Then p approaches

$$\lim_{n \to \infty} 1 - \left(1 - \frac{1}{n}\right)^n$$

This is $(1 - 1/e) = 0.63$. That is, under the independent and uniform request pattern model, an average of 63 percent of memory modules are busy in large systems. If $n = k = 8$, then p is 0.66, which is not much different from the value for large systems. These results should be kept in mind as we study specific interconnection networks.

12.4   INTERCONNECTION NETWORKS

In this section we will examine some of the possibilities for implementing the interconnection network that provides the path between the processors and the global memory. To be more specific, the interconnection network provides for transfers between the caches or private memories shown in Figures 12.4 and 12.5 and the memory modules that implement the global memory. As was discussed earlier, the global memory can be centralized or distributed. If it is centralized, then all transfers to and from the global memory go through the network. On the other hand, if the decentralized implementation is used, the network is involved in the transfer only if the required information is not in a local module of the global memory. Our discussion on interconnection network design will not need to distinguish between these two cases.

The network provides for two-way transfer of data between multiple sources of requests and multiple destinations that will respond to these requests. The sources are the processors, caches, or local memories; the destinations are the global memory modules. Note that we associate the terms source and destination with the request, not with the actual transfer of data. Thus, a read request results in a data transfer from the destination to the source, and a write request leads to a data transfer from the source to the destination.

12.4.1   Single Bus

The simplest and most economical means for interconnecting the multiple sources with the multiple destinations is to use a single bus. All requests must be processed sequentially over the bus. The detailed aspects of bus design, as discussed earlier in Chapter 6, apply here as well. Since there are multiple sources, it is necessary to determine the order of access when a number of requests are outstanding. An arrangement similar to that shown in Figure 6.7 for handling device interrupts can be used. Each source has a bus request line to an arbitration circuit that is activated to indicate that the source wishes to use the bus for transferring data. Each source also has a bus grant input activated by the arbitration circuit, which indicates to the source that it can use the bus. For fair sharing of the bus, the arbitration circuit can be arranged to honor requests on a round-robin basis.

In normal operation, the bus is dedicated to a particular source-destination pair for the full duration of the requested transfer. Hence, only one global memory module (destination) will be actively processing a request at any time. We would like to arrange for a number of destinations to be simultaneously active in processing requests. In order to see how this can be done, we will examine the detailed steps involved in handling an individual request. Let us assume that the request is for a read operation. First, the address of the location to be read is transferred over the bus from the source to the destination. The memory module then begins an access cycle to retrieve the requested word. The bus is idle during this access cycle. When the word becomes available, the bus is used to transfer it to the source to complete the request. The bus can now be assigned to handle the next request.

Suppose that a bus transfer takes T time units and that memory access time is $4T$ units. It then takes $6T$ units to complete a read request. This results in the bus being idle for two-thirds of the time. A scheme known as *split-cycle operation* makes it possible to use the bus during the idle period to serve another request. Consider the following way of handling a series of read requests. After transferring the address involved in the first request, the bus may be assigned to transfer the address for the second request. Assuming that this request is to a different memory module, we now have the situation in which two modules are proceeding with read access cycles in parallel. If neither module has finished with its access, the bus may be assigned to a third request, and so on. Eventually, the first memory module will finish its access cycle and the bus will be needed to transfer the word to the source that requested it. As other modules complete their cycles, the bus will be used to transfer their words to the corresponding sources. Note that the actual length of time between address transfer and word return is not critical. Address and data transfers for different requests represent independent uses of the bus that can be interleaved in any order.

Split-cycle operation results in a more fully utilized bus and in increased total bandwidth between sources and destinations. The improved performance is achieved at a cost of increased bus complexity. The main problem is that a memory module needs to know which source initiated a given read request. This may be done by including a source identification tag with each request. This tag is later used to send the requested data to the source. Complexity is also increased because a destination must be able to request use of the bus to transfer the requested data to the source. The bus arbiter becomes considerably more complicated.

The performance improvement associated with split-cycle operation depends upon the relationship between the bus transfer time and the memory access time.

Examples. A number of split-cycle bus systems are commercially available. The size of these systems is from 4 processors to 30 processors, each with a cache memory. All systems have multiple-module global memories.

Digital Equipment Corporation markets the VAX 6200 system[4] with up to 4 processors. Bus transfer time is 64 nanoseconds. The bus has 64 data lines, and block access requests for 32 bytes are provided. Such requests require five bus transfers— one for the starting address (multiplexed over the data lines) and four for the data transfer. Thus, 320 nanoseconds of bus time is needed to transfer 32 bytes of data. If all bus cycles are utilized to handle requests from the multiple processors, then the maximum achievable bandwidth is 100 megabytes per second if all requests are for 32-byte block transfers. Such a block is the unit requested by a processor cache on a cache miss.

Encore Computer Corporation manufactures a 20-processor system called the Multimax[5] that also has a split-cycle bus. A bus transfer takes 80 nanoseconds. It has separate address and data lines, and the data bus has 64 lines. If requests are interleaved so that the data bus transfers 8 bytes every 80 nanoseconds, then the maximum bandwidth supportable is 100 megabytes per second, the same as in the VAX 6200 system.

Our final example is the Symmetry multiprocessor,[3] which is manufactured by Sequent Computer Systems. Up to 30 processors are included, and the split-cycle bus has a 100 nanosecond transfer time. Addresses are multiplexed over the 64-bit data bus, and block requests for 16 bytes are provided. The maximum data transfer rate across the bus is 53.3 megabytes per second.

If split-cycle operation of a single bus cannot meet the memory bandwidth demands, then multiple paths are needed in the interconnection network. The first step in this direction is to provide multiple buses. If this trend is extended until the number of buses equals the number of destinations, then the resulting network is called a crossbar.

12.4.2 Multiple Buses and Crossbars

Consider the *two-bus system* shown in Figure 12.8. Half of the destinations are connected to one bus, and the other half are connected to the other bus. Assuming that requests are uniformly spread across all destinations, this configuration will increase the performance over that of the single bus system. Connection cost is obviously higher, however, because each source must be connected to both buses to enable it to access any of the destinations.

Although it is not essential for connectivity reasons, each destination could be connected to both buses. Then when a request originates from a source, it can be assigned to the first free bus. This has certain performance advantages, especially if the requests are unevenly distributed across the destinations. In addition, there is a definite reliability advantage, because if either of the buses becomes faulty, the other still maintains full connectivity between sources and destinations. These advantages are offset by the added cost of the extra connections between buses and destinations.

Extending the preceding pattern of adding more buses to improve performance reaches a limit when there are as many buses as there are destinations. The resulting configuration indicated in Figure 12.9 is called a *crossbar switch*. If requests from the sources are directed to distinct destinations, then they all proceed simultaneously. Hence, the crossbar is called a *non-blocking switch*. Other networks with fewer buses

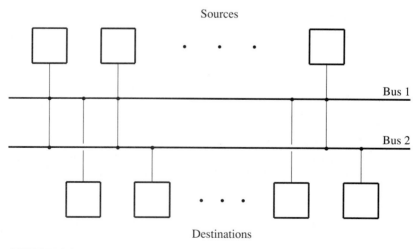

FIGURE 12.8
Two-bus interconnection network.

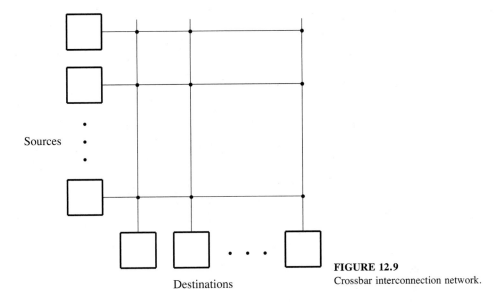

FIGURE 12.9
Crossbar interconnection network.

will block some requests, even if they are to distinct destinations, if a bus is not available to make the connection.

Control of access to the multiple-bus system, including the crossbar case, can be done as an extension of the single-bus case; that is, an arbiter is used for each bus. The address issued from a source determines which bus is involved.

Because the crossbar is a non-blocking switch, the bandwidth it supports between processors and memory modules in a multiprocessor is limited only by memory conflicts. It was shown in Section 12.3.9 that an average of 63 percent of the modules can be kept busy in large systems in which access requests from the processors are uniformly distributed across the modules. If a fixed number of buses are used, the maximum bandwidth provided is fixed and independent of the number of memory modules.

12.4.3 Multistage Networks

The bus systems described above use a single stage of switching to gain access to a particular bus. It is also possible to implement interconnection networks that use multiple stages of switches to set up paths between sources and destinations. Such networks are less costly than the crossbar structure, yet they provide a reasonably large number of parallel paths between sources and destinations. The idea of multistage switching is best illustrated by an example. Figure 12.10 shows a three-stage network connecting eight sources to eight destinations. It is called a *shuffle network*. The term shuffle is used to describe the pattern of connections from the outputs of one stage to the inputs of the next stage. The pattern is identical to the repositioning of playing cards in a deck that is shuffled by splitting the deck into two halves and interleaving the halves.

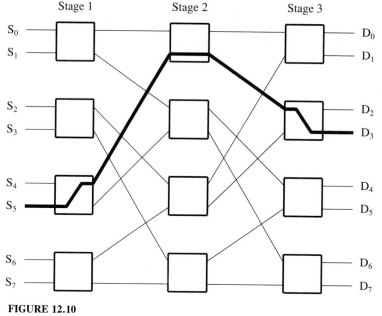

FIGURE 12.10
Multistage shuffle network.

Each box in the figure is a 2×2 switch that can route either input to either output. If the inputs request distinct outputs, then they can both be routed simultaneously in the straight-through or crossed pattern. If both inputs request the same output, only one request can be satisfied. The other one is blocked until the first request finishes using the switch. It is easy to show that there is exactly one path from each input to any particular output. Therefore, this network provides full connectivity between sources and destinations. Many request patterns, however, cannot be satisfied simultaneously: For example, sources S_0 and S_1 cannot be connected simultaneously to destinations D_0 and D_1.

A particular request can be routed through the network using the following scheme. The source sends a binary pattern representing the destination number into the network. As the pattern moves through the network, each stage examines a different bit to determine switch settings. Stage 1 uses the most significant bit, stage 2 the middle bit, and stage 3 the least significant bit. When a request arrives on either input of a switch, it is routed to the upper output if the controlling bit is a 0 and to the lower output if the bit is a 1. For example, a request from source S_5 for destination D_3 moves through the network as shown in the figure by the bold lines. Its route is controlled by the bit pattern 011, which is the destination address. In a multiprocessor in which the destinations are memory modules, this first pass through the network sets up the path. Succeeding passes can be used to transfer the address in the module and then to transfer data in either direction, depending upon whether the request is a read or a write access.

Networks such as this were first developed to provide for flexible interconnections in certain SIMD architectures between the processors and an equal number of shared memory modules. A number of different interstage connection patterns are possible. Particular patterns are chosen to correspond to memory access patterns that arise naturally in certain numerical SIMD applications. Multistage interconnection networks can also be used for the more general class of MIMD architectures that are the focus in this chapter.

Example. The BBN Butterfly[6] is a multiprocessor manufactured by BBN Advanced Computers. A 64-processor model of this system contains a three-stage network built with 4×4 switches. The routing through each stage of these switches is determined by successive 2-bit fields of the destination address.

It is interesting to compare the bandwidth provided by multistage networks with that provided by crossbars, assuming the uniform access probability model discussed in Section 12.3.9. Assume that the number of memory modules is the same as the number of processors in a multiprocessor system. From our earlier discussion, we know that systems with eight or more processors can keep about 65 percent of the memory modules busy if a crossbar interconnection network is used. Although we will not give the calculations here, it can be shown that the comparable figures for a multistage network of 2×2 switches are 52 percent for 8 processors, 35 percent for 64 processors, and successively smaller values as the number of processors increases.[7] Note that at 64 processors, blocking in the multistage network cuts the bandwidth to about half of what it is when limited only by memory conflicts.

12.5 MULTICOMPUTERS AND MESSAGE PASSING

In our earlier discussion of address spaces in Section 12.3, we briefly discussed the case in which there is no shared, global memory in the system. All processors directly reference only their own private, local memory. We will refer to the combination of a processor and its private memory as a computer module, or simply a computer. The interconnection network is seen by each computer as an I/O device and is used to pass messages between them.

Systems organized along these lines are usually called message-passing multicomputers. They are not referred to as multiprocessors, because that term is normally used for systems in which there is shared global memory. The terms *loosely-coupled* and *tightly-coupled* have also been associated with multicomputer and multiprocessor structures, respectively.

Physical implementations of interconnection networks for multicomputers usually involve bit-serial lines driven by I/O device interfaces. An interface circuit reads a message from the memory of the source computer using the DMA technique, converts it into bit-serial format, and transmits it over the network to the destination computer. Source and destination addresses are included in a header of the message for routing purposes. The message is routed to the destination computer, where it is written into a memory buffer by the I/O interface of that computer. The network may be a simple broadcast facility such as a bus, or it may consist of multiple paths.

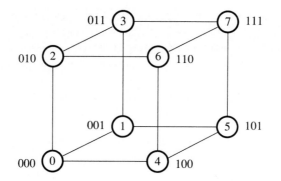

(a) 3-dimensional hypercube

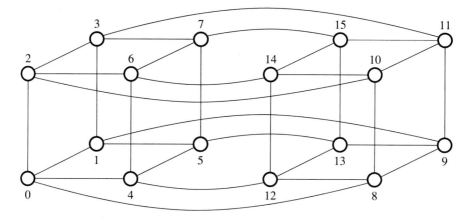

(b) 4-dimensional hypercube

FIGURE 12.11
Hypercube interconnection structure.

We will discuss one example of a multiple-path interconnection structure called the *hypercube*. Its 3- and 4-dimensional forms are shown in Figure 12.11. Each small circle represents a node in the network to which a computer is attached, and the lines represent bidirectional communication links between neighboring nodes. In an n-dimensional hypercube, each node is directly connnected to n neighbors. A useful way to label the nodes is to assign binary addresses to them in such a way that the addresses of any two neighbors differ in exactly one bit position. Such an assignment for the 3-dimensional hypercube is shown in Figure 12.11a. Part (b) of the figure shows an extension of this labeling pattern for the 4-dimensional hypercube, using decimal equivalents.

Routing messages through the hypercube is particularly easy. If the computer at node C_i wishes to send a message to the computer at node C_j, it proceeds as follows. The binary addresses of the source, i, and the destination, j, are compared from least to most significant bits. Suppose that they differ first in position p. Node C_i then sends the message to its neighbor, whose address, k, differs from i in bit position p. Node C_k forwards the message to the appropriate neighbor using the same address comparison scheme as used by node C_i. The message gets closer to destination node C_j with each of these hops. For example, a message from node C_2 to node C_5 in the 3-dimensional hypercube requires 3 hops, passing through nodes C_3 and C_1. The maximum distance that any message needs to travel in an n-dimensional hypercube is n hops.

Scanning address patterns from right to left is only one of the methods that can be used to determine message routing. Any other scheme that moves a message closer to its destination on each hop is equally acceptable, as long as the routing decision can be made locally at each node on the path. This feature of the hypercube is attractive from the reliability viewpoint. The existence of multiple paths between two computers means that when faulty links are encountered, they can usually be avoided by simple, local routing decisions. If one of the shortest routes is not available, it may be feasible to send a message over a longer path. However, if this is done, care must be taken to avoid looping, the situation in which the message circulates in a closed loop and never reaches its destination.

Hypercube multicomputers can be operated in MIMD or SIMD modes. In MIMD mode, messages are passed among computers that cooperate in the solution of some task. Thus message traffic will vary in intensity and occur in a variety of patterns, depending upon the particular application. On the other hand, if a hypercube machine is used in SIMD mode, then regular patterns of synchronized message passing will occur. For example, we will show how to apply a 4-dimensional hypercube machine consisting of 16 computers to the array update problem that we discussed in Section 12.2. First, we redraw Figure 12.11b in the grid form shown in Figure 12.12.

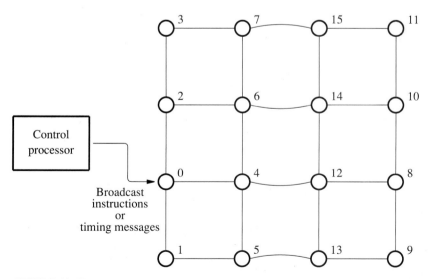

FIGURE 12.12
SIMD operation in a hypercube.

The row and column endaround connections that exist in the hypercube network are not shown explicitly. The control processor shown in the figure is needed to broadcast instruction or synchronization timing messages to the node computers. In the simplest form of hypercube machines, the processors at the nodes are simply ALUs that execute instructions that are broadcast throughout the hypercube network by the control processor. This is a generalization of the array processor structure discussed previously. If each node consists of a complete computer, then copies of the nearest neighbor update routine can be kept in each node computer. In this case, the control processor only needs to broadcast synchronization timing messages to keep the computers in lock step as they execute successive iterations of the update algorithm. In either case, the network is also used to exchange grid values among neighboring nodes in performing an update step.

In order to broadcast a message throughout a hypercube network, it is desirable to use an algorithm that will cause each node to receive the message exactly once and that will flood the message to all nodes as quickly as possible. A scheme that does this in n steps for an n-dimensional hypercube is as follows. Assume that node C_0 initiates the broadcast by sending the message to node C_1 at time 0. Then at time 1, C_0 sends the message to C_2; it then sends the message at succeeding times to nodes C_4, C_8, and so on up to node $C_{2**(n-1)}$. When a node receives the message at time t, it sends the message out at successive times $t + 1$, $t + 2$, and so on to each of its neighbors along the dimensions corresponding to the high order zeroes in its own address. Thus, for example, in a 4-dimensional hypercube, node C_3 receives the message at time 1 from node C_1, and then proceeds to send it on to nodes C_7 and C_{11} at times 2 and 3, respectively. The reader should verify that all 15 nodes, other than C_0, receive the message exactly once and that broadcasting is completed at the end of time 3.

This discussion has shown that the hypercube structure is potentially quite versatile. Under the direction of a synchronizing controller, a hypercube multicomputer can be applied fairly directly to SIMD applications. Although we have only shown how a square grid of 16 nodes can be mapped onto a 4-dimensional hypercube, embedding other regular structures into hypercubes is not difficult. A hypercube machine can also perform MIMD computations if its node computers have general-purpose processing capabilities. Whether or not a message-passing multicomputer such as a hypercube machine is a more useful architecture than a shared-memory multiprocessor is an open question. Both structures are certainly very effective in providing large amounts of computing power. The hardware and software overhead involved in message-passing on multicomputers is larger than the overhead involved in controlling access to shared data in the global memory of multiprocessors. However, if the application does not require very frequent interchange of messages among processors, then this overhead may not be critical. These types of applications have been called *coarse-grained*. If message-passing needs to be very intensive, which is the characteristic of *fine-grained* applications, then multiprocessors or array processors may be more effective. Because of the high costs involved in the implementation of parallel buses or multistage interconnection networks, large multiprocessors tend to be more expensive than multicomputers with a comparable number of processors. This offsets their potential performance advantage.

EXAMPLES. A large SIMD multicomputer with hypercube interconnections is manufactured by the Thinking Machines Corporation. It is named the Connection Machine,[8] and its CM-2 version has up to 64K processing element nodes. Each of the elements is based on an 8-bit ALU. All 64K elements simultaneously execute an instruction stream that is broadcast through the hypercube network from a control sequencer.

Intel Corporation produces a hypercube machine with MIMD capabilities called the iPSC,[9] which can have up to 128 computer nodes. Each node contains a 32-bit microprocessor and has general computation capability.

12.6 CONCLUDING REMARKS

Multiprocessors have been commercially available for several years. A number of different interconnection network architectures have been developed with varying degrees of parallelism to meet shared memory bandwidth needs. Multiple buses[10] and multistage networks[11] are relatively complex hardware structures. Their use in SIMD and MIMD multiprocessors is cost-justified only for large numerical applications that have obvious and significant levels of parallelism. However, multiprocessors with moderate interconnection network complexity seem certain to increase in popularity as more suitable system and application software is developed for them.

Multicomputers[12] are also evolving rapidly. Both SIMD and MIMD hypercube machines are commercially available. Assuming that software overhead can be suitably controlled in these message-passing systems, multicomputers can compete favorably with multiprocessors over a range of applications.

An interesting and cost-effective possibility is to implement a multicomputer system using personal workstations interconnected by a local area network. Traditionally, workstations are used to execute programs for a single user. However, as local area network speeds increase, it is quite feasible for a number of workstations to cooperatively execute single, large programs in MIMD style,[13] at performance levels comparable to other multicomputer structures. This possibility is attractive because it can be implemented with currently available hardware technology. The development of suitable operating system and communication software would make this structure a viable multicomputer architecture.

12.7 PROBLEMS

12.1. Write a program loop whose instructions can be broadcast from the control processor in Figure 12.1 that will enable an array processor to iteratively compute temperatures in a plane, as discussed in Section 12.2. In addition to instructions that shift the network register contents between adjacent processing elements (PEs), assume that there are two-operand instructions for moves between PE registers and local memory and for arithmetic operations. Assume that each PE stores the current estimate of its grid point temperature in a local memory location named CURRENT and that a few registers, R_0, R_1, and so on, are available for processing. Each boundary PE maintains a fixed boundary temperature value in its network register and does not execute the broadcast program. A small value stored in location EPSILON in each PE is used to determine when the local temperature has reached the required level of accuracy. At the end of each iteration of the loop, each PE must set its status bit, STATUS, to 1 if its new temperature satisfies the following condition:

$$| \text{New-temperature} - [\text{CURRENT}] | < [\text{EPSILON}]$$

Otherwise, STATUS is set to 0.

12.2. Let processing elements in an $n \times n$ array processor be labeled as PE(i,j), $0 \leq i$, $j \leq n - 1$, with i naming rows and j naming columns. If element (i,j) of a matrix is stored in PE(i,j), it is easy to see that addition of matrices can be done in a small, fixed number of steps independent of n. Matrix multiplication is not as easy. The Pascal program for matrix multiplication shown in Figure 3.3 requires a number of steps proportional to n^3 on a uniprocessor. Since there are n^2 PEs in an $n \times n$ array processor, it may be possible to do matrix multiplication in a number of steps proportional to n. All PEs will need to execute in parallel when doing the "multiply/add" operation in the inner loop of the Pascal program. Devise a suitable program for matrix multiplication on an array processor. *Hint:* Accumulate element (i,j) of the product matrix in PE(i,j) by shifting the relevant (i,k), (k,j) pairs through it. To facilitate doing this in parallel for all (i,j) positions, you will need to develop an initial layout of the two operand matrices that is a skewed version of the natural layout used above for matrix addition. The wraparound feature of nearest neighbor routing will also be needed.

12.3. What are the data transfer rates in the DEC VAX 6200, Encore Multimax, and Sequent Symmetry systems if all transfers involve only eight bytes of data? (See Section 12.4.1.)

12.4. Assume that a bus transfer takes T seconds and memory access time is $6T$ seconds. A read request over a conventional bus then requires $8T$ seconds to complete. How many conventional buses are needed to equal or exceed the bandwidth of a split-cycle bus that operates with the same time delays? Consider only read requests, ignore memory conflicts, and assume that all memory modules are connected to all buses in the multiple bus case. Does your answer increase or decrease if memory access time increases?

12.5. Assume that the cost of a 2×2 switch in a shuffle network is twice the cost of a crosspoint in a crossbar switch. There are n^2 crosspoints in an $n \times n$ crossbar switch. As n increases, the crossbar becomes more costly than the shuffle network. What is the smallest value of n for which crossbar cost is five times more costly than the shuffle network?

12.6. Shuffle networks can be built from 4×4 and 8×8 switches, for example, instead of from 2×2 switches. Draw a 16×16 ($n = 16$) shuffle network built from 4×4 switches. If the cost of a 4×4 switch is four times the cost of a 2×2 switch, compare the cost of shuffle networks built from 4×4 switches with those built from 2×2 switches for n values in the sequence $4, 4^2, 4^3$, and so on. Qualitatively compare the blocking probability of these two different ways of building shuffle networks.

12.7. Suppose that each procedure of a PAR segment (see Figure 12.6) requires 1 unit of time to execute. A program consists of three sequential segments. Each segment requires k time units, and must be executed on a single processor. The three sequential segments are separated by two PAR segments, each of which consists of k procedures that can be executed on independent processors.

Derive an expression for speedup for this program when run on a multiprocessor with n processors, where Speedup $= T_1/T_n$, with T_i defined as execution time on a multiprocessor system with i processors. Assume $n \leq k$. What is the limiting value of Speedup when k is large and $n = k$? What does this result tell you about the effect of sequential segments in programs that have some segments with substantial parallelism?

12.8. The analysis given in Section 12.3.9 for p, the fraction of memories kept busy in a multiprocessor system, applies to any system with a non-blocking interconnection network such as a crossbar. Under the same assumptions as we used there, develop a method for computing p where the network is a shuffle network built from 2×2 switches, with $k = n$. Check your method against the numerical values claimed in Section 12.4.3.

12.9. The shortest distance a message travels in an n-dimensional hypercube is 1 hop, and the longest distance a message needs to travel is n hops. Assuming that all possible source/destination pairs are equally likely, is the average distance a message needs to travel larger or smaller than $(1 + n)/2$? Justify your answer.

12.10. A task that "busy-waits" on a lock variable by using a Test-and-Set instruction in a two-instruction loop, as in Figure 12.7, wastes bus cycles that could otherwise be used for computation. Suggest a way around this problem that involves a centralized queue of waiting tasks that is maintained by the operating system. Assume that the operating system can be called by a user task and that the operating system determines which task is to be executed on a processor from among those ready for execution.

12.11. What are the arguments for and against invalidation and updating as strategies for maintaining cache coherency?

12.12. It was argued in Section 12.3.8 that cache coherency controls cannot replace the need for lock variables. Can the use of lock variables replace the need for explicit cache coherency controls?

12.13. Shared-memory multiprocessors and message-passing multicomputers are architectures that support simultaneous execution of tasks that need to interact with each other. Which of these two architectures can emulate the action of the other one more easily? Briefly justify your answer.

12.14. A *mailbox memory* is a RAM memory with the following feature. A full/empty bit, F/E, is associated with each memory word location. The instruction

PUT R0,BOXLOC,WAITSEND

is executed indivisibly as follows. The F/E bit associated with mailbox memory location BOXLOC is tested. If it is 0 (denoting "empty"), then the contents of register R0 are written into BOXLOC, F/E is set to 1 (denoting "full"), and execution continues with the next sequential instruction. Otherwise (i.e., for F/E = 1), no operations are performed and execution control is passed to the instruction at location WAITSEND in program memory.

(*a*) Give an appropriate definition for the instruction

GET R0,BOXLOC,WAITREC

that is complementary to the PUT instruction.

(*b*) Suppose two tasks, T_1 and T_2, running on different processors in a multiprocessor system, pass a stream of one-word messages from T_1 to T_2 using PUT and GET instructions on a shared mailbox memory unit. Write program segments for T_1 and T_2 in assembly language style that accomplishes the same thing on a shared-memory multiprocessor system that does not have a mailbox memory unit but does have a TAS instruction as described in Section 12.3.7.

12.8 REFERENCES

1. Flynn, M. J., "Very High-Speed Computing Systems," *Proceedings of the IEEE*, vol. 54, December 1966, pp. 1901–1909.
2. Slotnick, D. L., "The Fastest Computer," *Scientific American*, vol. 224, February 1971, pp. 76–88.
3. Lovett, T., and S. Thakkar, "The Symmetry Multiprocessor System," *Proceedings of the International Conference on Parallel Processing*, vol. 1, The Pennsylvania State University Press, August 1988, pp. 303–310.
4. Allison, B. R. "An Overview of the VAX 6200 Family of Systems," *Digital Technical Journal*, no. 7, August 1988.
5. Billig, R. R., S. S. Corbin, and R. L. Moore, "A Fast Backplane Cluster Heralds a 1000-MIPS Computer," *Electronic Design*, July 9, 1987.
6. BBN Advanced Computers Inc., "Inside the GP1000," October 1988.
7. Patel, J., "Performance of Processor-Memory Interconnections for Multiprocessors," *IEEE Transactions on Computers*, vol. C-30, October 1981, pp. 771–780.
8. Hillis, W. D., "The Connection Machine," MIT Press, 1985.
9. Intel Corporation, "A New Direction in Scientific Computing," 1985.
10. Mudge, T. N., J. P. Hayes, and D. C. Winsor, "Multiple Bus Architectures," *IEEE Computer*, vol. 20, no. 6, June 1987, pp. 42–48
11. Siegel, H. J., "Interconnection Networks for Large-Scale Parallel Processing," Lexington Books, 1985.
12. Athas, W., and C. L. Seitz, "Multicomputers: Message-Passing Concurrent Computers," *IEEE Computer*, vol. 21, no. 8, August 1988, pp. 9–24.
13. Cheriton, D. R., "The V Distributed System," *Communications of the ACM*, vol. 31, no. 3, March 1988, pp. 314–333.

CHAPTER

13

COMPUTER COMMUNICATIONS

In our discussion of interface design in Chapter 6, we implicitly assumed that input and output devices are close to the processor and that they are connected to it and the main memory by a bus. From the implementation point of view, the main constraint on the location of I/O devices relates to the distance over which the bus signals need to travel. Longer distances mean longer propagation delays, and hence slower speed. The total length of the bus is typically limited to a few meters, which is the length required to connect all the I/O interfaces. The interfaces are connected to their I/O devices via cables that may be somewhat longer (3 to 10 m). The format of data transfer along these cables depends upon the nature of the devices. In the case of high-speed devices, the information is usually transferred in parallel, thus requiring multiconductor cables. Slow devices may use a serial link with an asynchronous start-stop transmission format similar to that discussed in Section 9.1.1.

In many computer applications, the usefulness of a computer system can be enhanced considerably if some of the I/O devices can be situated at remote locations. This, in fact, generates a whole set of applications that would not otherwise be possible. Consider, for example, the following situations.

1. *Remote terminals.* A computer system is typically accessed from terminals placed in user-convenient locations. These terminals are likely to be scattered throughout a building or a plant site. Sometimes access to a computer is required from different

points in a city or even from different cities. In all of these cases, a communication facility is needed to transfer data between the computer and the terminals.

2. *Computer-to-computer communication.* It is often necessary to transfer data from one computer to another. For example, Chapter 9 pointed out that workstations are often connected to other computers that provide file storage facilities, additional computing power, and access to specialized resources. The required connections are achieved through a communications network. Networks that span a small geographic area with distances not exceeding a few kilometers are called *local area networks*. Networks that cover larger areas that involve distances up to thousands of kilometers are referred to as *long-haul networks*, or *wide area networks*. Such networks provide service nationally or internationally.

Terminal-to-computer and computer-to-computer data transfers impose different requirements on a communication network. The former are characterized by transmission of small amounts of data per transfer. Moreover, their interactive nature requires short delays. On the other hand, communication between two computers often involves transferring large record blocks or complete files at high speed. A computer communication network should enable both types of traffic to be handled efficiently and economically.

Terminal networks, local area networks, and long-haul networks represent three distinct types of data communication networks, each characterized by its own speed of transmission, type of transmission lines, and organization. We shall start this chapter by considering the means available for communicating with a single remote terminal. This will be followed by a discussion of multiplexing a number of remote terminals onto a single communication facility and descriptions of local and long-haul networks for computer-to-computer communication.

13.1 COMMUNICATION WITH A REMOTE TERMINAL

When a computer and an I/O terminal are situated a considerable distance apart, a multiconductor cable connection between them for parallel data transfer may become impractical. The cost of such cables may be excessive. Moreover, as the length of the cable increases, so does the data skew (see Section 6.5.1). This places an upper limit on the data rate, thus eliminating the main advantage of parallel transmission. A more reasonable approach is to convert the parallel data to a serial format at the transmitting end and then convert it back to the parallel format at the receiving end. This approach is normally used with remote terminals, irrespective of the nature of the I/O device.

Two important aspects of serial transmission of digital data need to be considered:

- The nature of the transmitted signal
- The format of transmission

13.1.1 Transmission of Digital Data

The simplest transmission line arrangement suitable for digital data is a *current loop*. As shown in Figure 13.1*a*, the transmitter is a simple ON/OFF switch. The receiver is arranged such that when the transmitter switch is closed, a current *I* flows in the circuit. The terms *mark* and *space* are used to describe the situations when the transmitter switch is closed or open, corresponding to logic values 1 and 0, respectively. The receiver senses the state of the line and generates an output logic signal. The scheme of Figure 13.1 enables installation of terminals either locally or hundreds of meters away. Four wires are used to enable transmission in both directions. Data transmission is in the asynchronous start-stop format described in Section 9.1.1.

Some precautions are often necessary when transmitting signals over long distances. Long cables are likely to pick up electrical noise from the environment, so the receiver at the end of a long cable may detect signals on the line even when nothing is being transmitted at the sending end. These signals may be picked up from nearby communication or power cables. If the noise signal level at the receiver is comparable to that of the transmitted signals, the receiver cannot separate them and errors will occur. An effective and economical way to separate the two components of the received signal is to take advantage of some of the differences in the characteristics of the noise current and the transmitted signal current. The most important difference

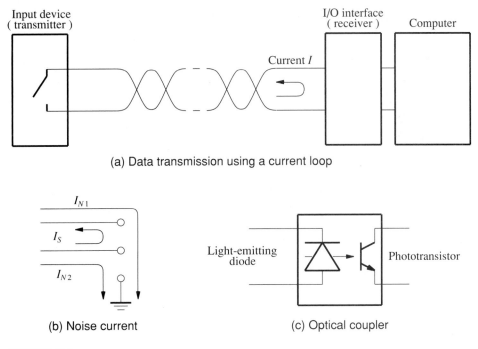

(a) Data transmission using a current loop

(b) Noise current

(c) Optical coupler

FIGURE 13.1
Connection of a remote device using a current loop.

is illustrated in Figure 13.1*b*. Signal current flows around the loop, but noise currents flow from either side of the loop to ground. Hence, the receiver should be designed to detect only the component of the current that flows around the loop, which has the magnitude $I_S + I_{N2} - I_{N1}$. Moreover, the transmission line should be designed such that the two currents I_{N1} and I_{N2} are as close to each other as possible. When this situation holds, the transmission line is said to be *balanced*. Balancing can be achieved through the use of a twisted pair of wires to form the transmission line. The average value of I_{N1} and I_{N2} is usually referred to as the *common-mode* signal, and the loop current constitutes the *differential-mode* signal. A receiver amplifier that is sensitive only to the differential component is referred to as a differential amplifier. Such amplifiers are capable of detecting differential-mode signals that are thousands of times smaller than the common-mode component.

Another important precaution relates to the protection of semiconductor circuits whenever such circuits are used as a part of the receiver or the transmitter. Semiconductor circuits can be designed to withstand a few tens of volts or even a few hundreds of volts before they break down. However, equipment connected to a long cable is subject to large voltage surges that may result, for example, from lightning strikes. Voltages of 1000 V or higher may be encountered in such situations. It is thus necessary to isolate the sensitive circuitry from the lines that may carry such high voltages. A device that is highly suitable for this purpose is the *optical isolator*, represented schematically in Figure 13.1*c*. An optical source (light-emitting diode) and an optical sensor (phototransistor) are contained in a small sealed package. When the loop current flows through the diode, the emitted light causes the transistor to become conducting; otherwise, it is nonconducting. Thus the receiver circuitry can sense the presence or absence of loop current without direct electric connection to the transmission line. It should also be noted that the diode carries only the loop current and is not affected by the common-mode component. Therefore, in addition to providing the required protection, the optical isolator enables rejection of the common-mode noise currents on the line.

Figure 13.1*a* requires the link to allow transmission of DC (direct current) signals. If the transmission link is a part of the public telephone network, however, this is usually not possible to achieve. A *voice-grade* link will only allow signals with frequencies in the range of 300 to 3600 Hz to be transmitted without excessive attenuation. Unless special arrangements are made with the telephone company, no DC path exists between the two ends of a telephone connection (because of the intervening central office equipment). This means that to transmit data on such links, an encoding scheme has to be used to represent the 0 and 1 logic values by signals whose frequencies lie within the transmission band of the line. This function is performed by *modems* (MOdulator-DEModulators), which are installed at each end of the line.

Two transmission channels can be established on a single line by an appropriate choice of the transmission frequencies for each direction. A commonly used scheme, referred to as frequency-shift keying (FSK), is shown in Figure 13.2. One of the channels is used for transmission in one direction, and the other is used for the opposite direction.

	Frequency, Hz	
Logic state	0 (space)	1 (mark)
Channel 1	1075	1275
Channel 2	2025	2225

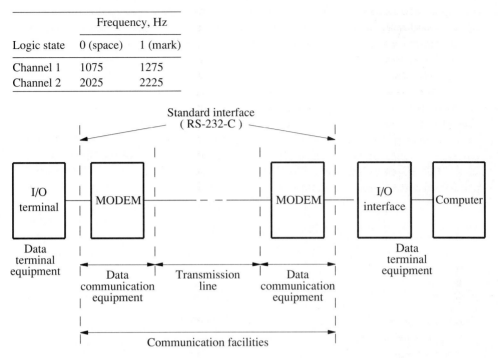

FIGURE 13.2
Remote connection of an I/O terminal over a dedicated telephone line using frequency-shift keying.

13.1.2 Synchronous and Asynchronous Transmission

The asynchronous start-stop format mentioned earlier is most commonly used for communication with remote terminals, particularly over the dialed public network. However, for higher-speed devices the start and stop bits of this transmission format are wasteful of the line *bandwidth*. Line bandwidth roughly corresponds to the transmission capacity of the line in bits per second. Better utilization of the transmission link can be attained through the use of synchronous transmission. In this case, data is transmitted in blocks consisting of several hundreds or thousands of bits each. The beginning and end of each block is marked by an appropriate coding technique, and data within a block is organized according to a known set of rules. These rules constitute an important part of the *data link protocol* used by the transmitter and the receiver. Synchronous data link protocols will be discussed in Section 13.3.

When transmitting long blocks of data bits, there must be some means provided for the receiver to synchronize with the successive bit positions in the incoming data stream. This is necessary because the receiver does not have direct access to the clock timing signal used by the transmitter in sending the data bits. Several clock recovery methods can be used to synchronize the receiver with the transmitter. One such method, called phase encoding, was described in Chapter 9 in connection with magnetic recording techniques. A guaranteed change in the signal during each bit period is used to recover the clock. However, simple phase encoding requires significant extra bandwidth, which defeats the potential advantage of synchronous transmission. Other encoding techniques require less additional bandwidth. We will examine one of them in Section 13.3. Modems using such encoding techniques present the receiving data terminal with the data bit stream and the recovered clock on separate lines. Many modems require a significant "start-up" time. This time is needed to complete such operations as transmitting and detecting carrier frequencies and establishing synchronization. In some modems, the start-up time is also used to adapt the modem circuits to the current transmission properties of the link.

Modems with data rates up to 9,600 bits per second can be used on specially conditioned telephone system lines.

13.1.3 Full-Duplex and Half-Duplex Links

In general, a communication link may be one of the following three types:

1. *Simplex* allows transmission in one direction only.
2. *Half duplex (HDX)* allows transmission in either direction, but not at the same time.
3. *Full duplex (FDX)* allows simultaneous transmission in both directions.

The simplex configuration is useful only if the remote location contains an input or an output device, but not both. Hence, it is seldom used. The choice between half and full duplex is basically a trade-off between economy and speed of operation.

With a transmission scheme such as the current loop, a pair of wires enables transmission in one direction only, that is, simplex operation. To obtain a half-duplex link, it is necessary to use switches at both ends to connect either the transmitter or the receiver, but not both, to the line. When transmission in one direction is completed, the switches are reversed to enable transmission in the reverse direction. Control of the position of the switches is a part of the function of the devices at each end of the line.

Full-duplex operation can be achieved on a four-wire link that has two wires dedicated to each direction of transmission. Alternatively, a two-wire link with two nonoverlapping frequency bands can be used to create two independent transmission channels, one for each direction. Figure 13.2 gave an example of such a full-duplex link in which the two channels have the signaling frequencies 1275/1075 and 2225/2025 Hz.

In the case of synchronous half-duplex operation, a time delay is encountered whenever the direction of transmission is reversed, because the transmitting modem may have to transmit an initializing sequence of signals to allow the receiving end to adapt to the conditions of the channel. The amount of delay encountered depends upon the modem and the transmission facilities and may be anywhere from a few milliseconds to several hundred milliseconds.

The above discussion relates directly to the characteristics of the transmission link and the modems. Other important factors that influence the choice between half- and full-duplex operation are the nature of the data traffic and the means by which the system reacts to the occurrence of errors during transmission. The former is discussed below; the latter will be dealt with in Section 13.2.

Many computer applications require the computer to receive input data, perform some processing, and then return output data. Basically, this is half-duplex operation. A half-duplex link will not only satisfy the requirements for such an application, but it will also enable data transmission to take place at the maximum possible speed. If the messages exchanged between the two ends are short and frequent, however, the delay encountered in reversing the direction of transmission becomes significant. For that reason alone, many such applications utilize full-duplex transmission facilities, although actual data transmission never takes place in both directions at the same time.

There are situations in which simultaneous transmission in both directions can be used to considerable advantage. Let us again consider the system of Figure 13.2, with the remote terminal being a simple video terminal. Each character entered at the keyboard should be echoed back to be displayed on the screen. This may be done locally, by the control circuitry of the terminal, for example, or remotely by the computer or its peripherals. The latter provides an automatic checking capability to ensure that no errors have been introduced during transmission. If a half-duplex link is used in such a case, transmission of the next character must be delayed until the first character has been echoed back. No such restriction is necessary with full-duplex operation. Another example can be found in high-speed computer communication networks. Messages traveling in opposite directions on any given link often bear no relation to each other; hence, they can be transmitted simultaneously.

13.1.4 Standard Communications Interface

To allow interconnection of equipment made by different manufacturers, it is useful to develop standards that define how these devices may be interconnected. Such standards should define both the physical and functional characteristics of the interface. As pointed out in Section 6.6, a standard interface refers to the dividing line, or the collection of points at which two instruments are connected together. One such standard that has gained acceptance is the EIA (Electronics Industry Association) Standard RS-232-C. Outside North America, it is known as the CCITT (Comité Consultatif International Télégraphique et Téléphonique) Recommendation V24. It completely specifies the interface between data communication devices (for example, modems) and data terminal equipment (for example, the computer and the I/O terminal in Figure 13.2). The RS-232-C interface consists of 25 connection points, which are described in Table 13.1.

For illustration purposes, let us discuss a simple but frequently encountered example. Consider the link of Figure 13.2, assuming the remote terminal to be a video terminal and the connection to be over the dialed telephone network. The modem on the computer side, which we will refer to as modem A, is capable of going on-

TABLE 13.1 Summary of the EIA Standard RS-232-C Signals
(CCITT Recommendation V24)

	Name		
EIA	CCITT	Pin* no.	Function
AA	101	1	Protective ground
AB	102	7	Signal ground-common return
BA	103	2	Transmitted data
BB	104	3	Received data
CA	105	4	Request to send
CB	106	5	Clear to send
CC	107	6	Data set ready
CD	108.2	20	Data terminal ready
CE	125	22	Ring indicator
CF	109	8	Received line signal detector
CG	110	21	Signal quality detector
CH	111	23§	Data signal rate selector (from DTE† to DCE‡)
CI	112	23§	Data signal rate selector (from DCE‡ to DTE†)
DA	113	24	Transmitter signal element timing (DTE†)
DB	114	15	Transmitter signal element timing (DCE‡)
DD	115	17	Receiver signal element timing (DCE‡)
SBA	118	14	Secondary transmitted data
SBB	119	16	Secondary received data
SCA	120	19	Secondary request to send
SCB	121	13	Secondary clear to send
SCF	122	12	Secondary received line signal detector

*Pins 9 and 10 are used for testing purposes and pins 11, 18, and 25 are spare.
†Data terminal equipment.
‡Data communication equipment.
§The signal on this pin is given a different name, depending upon its direction.

and off-hook under computer control as well as detecting the ringing signal on the telephone line. A similar modem, called B, is used on the I/O terminal side. Figure 13.3 gives the sequence of logic signals needed to establish a connection, transmit data, and terminate the connection. The steps involved in this process are described briefly below.

1. When the computer is ready to accept a call, it sets the data terminal ready signal (CD) to 1.

2. Modem A monitors the telephone line, and when it detects the ringing current that indicates an incoming call, it signals the computer by setting the ring indicator (CE) to 1. If CD = 1 at the time the ringing current is detected, the modem automatically answers the call by going off-hook. It then sets the modem ready signal (CC) to 1.

Step no.	Terminal	Interface signals	Modem B	Modem A	Interface signals	Computer
1				Enable automatic answering	CD	←1
2	Dialed digits →			1 → Goes off hook 1 →	CE CC	
3		CF	←1	←2225 Hz 1 →	CA CB	←1
4	1 →	CA CB CC	1275 Hz → ←1 ←1	1 →	CF	
5	Output data ← Input data →	BB BA	← Data 1275—1075 Hz →	←2225—2025 Hz Data →	BA BB	← Output data → Input data
6		CF	←0	Drop 2225 Hz and disconnect 0 → 0 → 0 →	CA CD CF CC CB	←0 ←0
7	(0 →)	CA CB CC	Drop 1275 ←0 ←0			
8	Terminate connection				CD	←1

FIGURE 13.3
RS-232-C standard signalling sequence.

3. The computer instructs modem A to start transmitting the frequency representing a mark condition (2225 Hz) by setting request to send (CA) to 1. When this is accomplished, modem A responds by setting clear to send (CB) to 1. The detection of the mark frequency at modem B causes it to set the received line signal detector (CF) to 1.

4. The terminal sets CA to 1, causing transmission of the 1275-Hz signal. Modem B then sets CB and CC to 1. When modem A detects the 1275-Hz frequency, it sets CF to 1.

5. A full-duplex link is now established between the computer and the remote terminal. The computer can transfer data to and from the remote terminal in the same way as in the case of local terminals. Interface pins BA (transmitted data) and BB (received data) are used for this purpose; all other signals in the interface remain unchanged.

6. When the user signs off, the computer sets the request to send and data terminal ready signals (CA and CD) to 0, causing modem A to drop the mark condition and disconnect from the line. Signals CB, CF, and CC are set to 0 by modem A. When modem B senses the disappearance of the mark condition on the line, it sets the received line signal detector (CF) to 0.

7. Modem B responds by removing its mark frequency from the line and setting CB and CC to 0. The user terminates the connection by going on-hook.

8. The computer sets data terminal ready (CD) to 1 in preparation for a new call.

We should point out that the above description pertains specifically to the case of a transmission link involving a modem. The RS-232-C interface is much more general because it can be used to provide a serial connection between any two digital devices. Of course, the interpretation of individual signals such as CA and CD depends on the functional capabilities of the devices involved. When these signals are not needed, they are simply ignored by both devices. In some situations, a device such as a computer requires an active signal on certain lines (for example, on the data terminal ready (CD) line). If the terminal connected to the computer does not generate an active signal on this line, the interface wiring should provide the required active level.

13.2 ERROR CONTROL

In the previous section, some elementary concepts related to communication between a computer and a remote terminal were introduced. Such communication takes place in much the same way as local communications. So far, only one substantial difference between the two cases has been encountered: The remote terminal, unlike a local terminal, requires some means for establishing and breaking the connection with the computer. With local terminals the link exists, in effect, as long as power is supplied to the equipment. The next and even more fundamental difference between local and remote peripherals is that errors are much more likely to occur during communication with a remote peripheral. The detection of these errors and the provision of some means for recovery are important functions of the communications hardware and software.

13.2.1 Detection of Transmission Errors

The simplest method for error detection is the use of *parity* bits, which may be inserted in the data stream in a variety of ways. For example, a parity bit may be added to each character to form either odd or even parity. For a 7-bit character $b_6 b_5 \ldots b_0$, an even-parity bit P may be transmitted as an eighth bit, where

$$P = b_6 \oplus b_5 \oplus \cdots \oplus b_0$$

The symbol $\oplus$ denotes the *Exclusive-OR*, or *modulo 2 sum*, function. If odd parity is used, P is replaced by $\overline{P}$ ($= 1 \oplus P$). The receiving end can easily check whether each of the received characters has the appropriate parity. If a character with the wrong parity is received, a transmission error has occurred. This form of error checking is usually referred to as *vertical redundancy checking* (VRC). Another parity scheme, referred to as *longitudinal redundancy checking* (LRC), introduces a single checking character at the end of a group of characters that constitute a message. For example, a message consisting of a group of 7-bit characters is followed by a 7-bit *check sum* $P_6 P_5 \ldots P_0$. Each of the parity bits P_6 to P_0 is equal to the modulo 2 sum of all the corresponding bit positions in the characters of the message. The VRC and LRC schemes may be combined as shown in Figure 13.4 to enhance the error-detection capability.

The preceding error-detection schemes are very useful when bit errors occur as isolated events. Unfortunately, errors on telephone channels usually occur in bursts, particularly at higher transmission speeds. As an example, switching transients on nearby power lines may cause errors in a number of consecutive bits. The bursty nature of errors on telephone lines limits the usefulness of the VRC and LRC schemes. A number of other error-detection schemes have been developed for use in such environments. A powerful and commonly used scheme is the *cyclic-redundancy-checking* (CRC) technique. Similar to LRC, the CRC scheme uses a check sum at the end of the message. The check sum is generated by computing the modulo-2 sum of the message bits after grouping them in a special way. The number of bits in the check sum is usually 16 or 32, depending upon the length of the message and the desired error-detection capability. A thorough treatment of this subject may be found in *Coding and Information Theory*, by R. W. Hamming.[1]

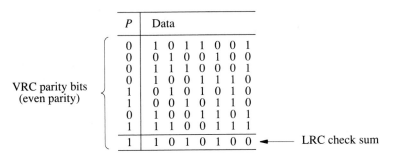

FIGURE 13.4
Use of VRC and LRC parity checking.

13.2.2   Procedures for Recovery
from Transmission Errors

In general, recovery from transmission errors may be achieved in one of two ways:

1. *Forward error correction* (FEC)—This approach works by including enough redundancy to enable the receiver to reconstruct the transmitted message even when some of the received bits are in error.
2. *Automatic repeat request* (ARQ)—This approach uses an error-detection scheme and requests retransmission when an error is detected.

FEC PROTOCOLS. A well-known example of FEC codes can be found in the Hamming codes, which are a special case of the CRC techniques. One problem with error-correcting codes is that they require a large number of additional check bits. For example, a 7-bit message containing 4 bits of information and 3 check bits enables the receiver to reconstruct the original message after the occurrence of an error in 1 bit at most. In general, n check bits enable correction of a 1-bit error in a message that is $2^n - 1$ bits long (including the check bits). More check bits are necessary if the capability for correcting errors in more than 1 bit is required. For this reason, such codes are only suitable for use when channels have very low error rates or when a reverse channel is not available to request retransmission. Examples of the use of forward error correction can be found in radio and satellite communications.

ARQ PROTOCOLS. The most commonly used approach for error control on telephone channels is ARQ. The simplest of these protocols is referred to as *stop-and-wait* ARQ. After the sending end completes transmission of a message, it stops and waits until either a positive or a negative acknowledgment is received from the remote end. An acknowledgment is a coded message that the receiving end sends to the sending end when the reception of a message is completed. A positive acknowledgment indicates that no errors have been detected; that is, the check sum computed by the receiver matches that at the end of the message. A negative acknowledgment indicates an error condition, and it is interpreted by the sending end as a request for retransmission of the same message. A system using this protocol should also allow for the possibility that the acknowledgment message might not reach the sending end. In order to save the transmitter from waiting indefinitely for a reply, a watchdog timer is used. After a time-out period, the sender assumes that its message has been lost and starts retransmission. This may be attempted a few times, after which the sender assumes that the transmission link is broken.

The stop-and-wait protocol is very simple to implement and can be used with either full- or half-duplex lines. Its main disadvantage, however, is that line utilization is low because considerable time is spent waiting for acknowledgments. The situation is depicted in Figure 13.5, where T is the message transmission time and W is the waiting time before the next message can be transmitted. Thus message transmission takes place only $T/(T + W)$ of the available time. Furthermore, if we assume that P is the probability of an erroneous message, only $1 - P$ of the transmitted messages are received correctly. The remaining messages are discarded by the receiving end

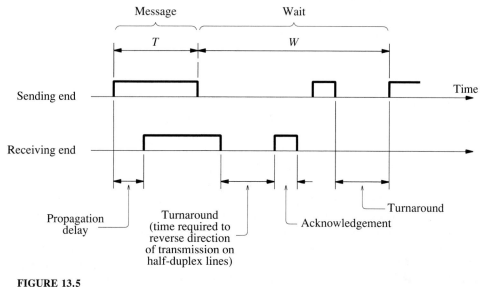

FIGURE 13.5
Stop-and-wait ARQ scheme.

because of the presence of errors. Thus we can define a transmission efficiency factor η as

$$\eta = \frac{T}{T + W}(1 - P)$$

Let the speed of transmission be ν bits/s and the message length be n bits; then,

$$\eta = \frac{n/\nu}{n/\nu + W}(1 - P)$$

$$= \frac{n}{n + W\nu}(1 - P)$$

It can be easily seen from Figure 13.5 that the waiting time W consists of three components: the round-trip propagation delay, the time required to reverse the direction of transmission twice, and the transmission time of the acknowledgment message. As an example, let us consider a 4800-bit/s communication link over the public telephone network. The propagation delay may be estimated at 4 ms/100 mi. The turnaround time varies considerably and will be assumed to be 150 ms. The transmission time for the acknowledgment message is a function of the number of characters it contains. Because this involves the transmission of only a few characters, the transmission time is short and may be neglected. Assuming a 300-mi link, we obtain

$$W = 2(4 \times 3 + 150) = 324 \text{ ms}$$

Next, let us consider the probability of error P. Obviously, this is a function of the message length n. For n in the range of 10 to 10^4 bits, a rough estimate for P for a

4800-bit/s link may be obtained from the equation

$$P = 0.15 \times 10^{-4}n$$

Then, for a message length of 1000 bits, we obtain

$$\eta = \frac{1000(1 - 0.015)}{1000 + 0.324 \times 4800} = 0.39$$

The effective rate of transmission under these conditions is $0.39 \times 4800 = 1870$ bits/s. For message lengths such that $P \ll 1$, the transmission efficiency improves as the message length increases. For $n = 200$, η drops to 0.11, while for $n = 5000$, $\eta = 0.71$.

Let us now consider the effect of increasing the modem speed to 9600 bits/s. The new value for η for a 1000-bit message becomes 0.24, and the effective rate of transmission is $0.24 \times 9600 = 2300$ bits/s. It is interesting to observe that doubling the transmission speed results in increasing the effective rate of transmission by only 23 percent (from 1870 to 2300 bits/s) because transmission takes place only 24 percent of the time at the higher speed.

We can see from the above discussion that the stop-and-wait ARQ scheme is inherently inefficient. However, because of its simplicity it is widely used. Note that if the transmission facilities are full duplex, the turnaround time is reduced to zero. Because this is the dominant parameter in the above example, a significant increase in the transmission efficiency can be expected. In fact, for a 4800-bit/s link and for $n = 200$, 1000, and 5000 bits, η is equal to 0.63, 0.90, and 0.97, respectively.

For long-distance transmission, the efficiency of the stop-and-wait scheme is low even with full-duplex transmission. Significant improvement can be achieved if the wait period is eliminated, which is the case with the continuous-ARQ scheme described briefly below.

Continuous ARQ. With full-duplex facilities, the transmitting end may continue sending messages without waiting for the arrival of acknowledgments. When a negative acknowledgment is received, the sending end starts retransmitting the messages that were received in error. This implies several details:

1. Messages are kept in memory buffers until the corresponding acknowledgments are received.
2. Messages and their acknowledgments should be numbered so that the transmitting end can retransmit the correct messages.

The continuous-ARQ method is considerably more involved than the stop-and-wait scheme. It is used in situations in which line utilization and overall throughput are important factors.

13.3 MULTITERMINAL CONFIGURATIONS

We now consider the problem of connecting a number of remote terminals to a computer. Three possible configurations suitable for this purpose are given in

Figure 13.6. These are the following:

- Star configuration
- Multipoint line
- Loop configuration

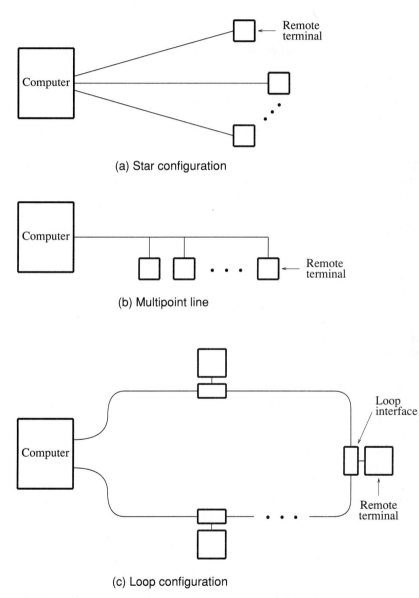

(a) Star configuration

(b) Multipoint line

(c) Loop configuration

FIGURE 13.6
Connection of remote terminals.

13.3.1 Star Configuration

This is the simplest configuration. A separate transmission link is used between each terminal and the computer, as shown in Figure 13.6a. The links in such a network may be either dedicated transmission lines or a part of the dialed telephone network. Each link has a configuration similar to that of Figure 13.2 and may be connected to the computer by means of a separate I/O interface. When the number of remote terminals is large, it becomes advantageous to connect the lines to the main computer by using a *multiplexer*. The multiplexer collects data characters from individual lines and presents them to the computer with an address identifying the source terminal. A reverse process takes place during output: The computer sends a data character and a line address to the multiplexer, which in turn transmits the character to the appropriate terminal. Multiplexing is usually one of the functions performed by a communications controller, if one exists.

13.3.2 Multipoint Line

The second configuration (Figure 13.6b) is the *multipoint*, or *multidrop*, line. In this case, a single transmission line is used for connecting a number of terminals. This can lead to a substantial saving in cabling costs, but, it introduces some new problems related to the way in which a communication path is established between the computer and one of the terminals. In the following discussion we will assume that full-duplex operation is possible, which is usually the case with multipoint lines. This means that at any given time, the computer can be transmitting to one or more terminals and receiving from one terminal. A control scheme (protocol) has to be established to deal with two activities:

1. Addressing of individual terminals
2. Scheduling the use of the transmission line

ADDRESSING OF INDIVIDUAL TERMINALS. When the computer transmits a message, it should be able to select only one of the terminals to receive this message. It accomplishes this by transmitting the message preceded by the terminal address. Thus a protocol is required to allow all devices connected to the line to identify the address and data components of a message unambiguously. Two such protocols are described below.

ASCII data link control. This protocol is used on synchronous transmission links for both point-to-point and multipoint connections. It is based on transmitting the address, control, and data bits in 7- or 8-bit characters. The standard ASCII 7-bit character set is given in Appendix D. The 8-bit code usually consists of the standard 7-bit code plus one parity bit. A few characters are reserved for establishing character synchronization and identifying various sections of a transmitted message.

Let us consider first the problem of character synchronization. Because transmission on a communication link is in the bit-serial mode, the receiver needs to identify the beginning and end of each character. The character SYN is used for this purpose. The binary code for this character is 0010110, which has the property that upon circular shifting, the code repeats itself only after a full 7-bit cycle. This means that if a sequence of SYN characters is transmitted, the receiver can unambiguously identify their boundaries, thus establishing character synchronization for subsequent characters.

Having established the character boundaries, the receiver must separate the address, control, and data components of a message. The message can be divided into two parts: the *message header* consisting of the address and control information and the *message text*, which is the actual data transmitted. Special characters are used to identify each part. The exact format of the message and the particular characters used as "delimiters" vary from one application to another. An example of a full ASCII message is given in Figure 13.7. In this case, the characters SOH (start of header), STX (start of text), and ETX (end of text) are used to identify the beginning and end of the header and text.

This simple ASCII scheme can be used for addressing terminals on a multipoint line. However, it has a few limitations, as follows:

1. The user is restricted to transmitting 8-bit entities.
2. The user is prohibited from using the codes corresponding to the reserved control characters. In the case of traffic consisting of printing characters this limitation is not important because the control characters are always chosen from the 32 nonprinting characters of the ASCII code (see Appendix D). If the user wishes to transmit all possible codes, then a slight modification of the ASCII protocol is needed, based on the use of the character DLE (data link escape). Control characters can be uniquely identified if they are always preceded by DLE. In the text portion of the message, any occurrence of the DLE character is duplicated by the transmitting end. At the receiving end, the first DLE character is always dropped. If the next character is another DLE, it is regarded as part of the text; otherwise, it is treated as a control character.
3. The protocol does not guarantee the occurrence of 0 to 1 transitions in the user's text. Thus a transmission scheme has to be used that does not depend on these transitions for recovering the clock at the receiving end.

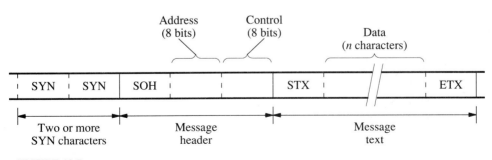

FIGURE 13.7
A typical ASCII message.

High-level data link control (HDLC). This control protocol overcomes the difficulties encountered in the ASCII scheme. With minor variations, it is also known as SDLC (synchronous data link control), ADCCP (advanced data communication control procedure), and LAP (link-access protocol). This scheme has two basic characteristics:

1. The notion that a fixed-size character is a fundamental transmission unit is discarded.
2. A unique 8-bit combination, referred to as a flag, is introduced to serve as the only delimiter in the system. The uniqueness of this flag is guaranteed in a way that is transparent to the user.

   The format of a message using this protocol is given in Figure 13.8. The flag has the code 01111110. The same flag is used to indicate the beginning and the end of a message. Any number of flags may be transmitted between messages for synchronization purposes. Whenever five consecutive 1s appear in the user's message, the transmitting end automatically inserts a 0. Similarly, the receiving end automatically discards a 0 following five 1s. Therefore, six consecutive 1s is a unique code encountered only in the flag. Recovery of the transmission clock at the receiving end is also facilitated by the encoding scheme used. A 0 is encoded as a state change on the line (that is, by either a high to low or a low to high transition), and a 1 is transmitted by maintaining the same state as in the preceding bit period. Hence, because the maximum length of a string of 1s is 6 bits, it is relatively easy to reconstruct the transmission clock from the received signal. The user need not be aware of the insertion and deletion of 0s. This function is automatically performed by the transmitting and receiving hardware.
   The address and control fields have fixed lengths of 8 bits each. These are followed by the message text, which may consist of any number of bits. The last 16 bits in the message consist of a CRC check sum for error-detection purposes.

SCHEDULING THE USE OF THE TRANSMISSION LINE. Let us consider the situation in which some of the terminals of Figure 13.6*b* are ready to transmit data to the

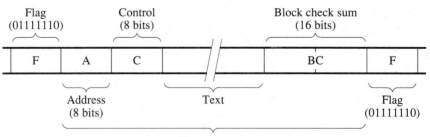

FIGURE 13.8
High-level data link protocol.

computer. Obviously, only one terminal can be allowed to transmit at any given time. Coordination of this process has to be under control of the computer. Three commonly used schemes for this purpose are *roll polling*, *hub polling*, and *contention*.

Roll polling. This is the simplest of the control procedures for a multipoint line. The computer starts by transmitting a short poll message to one of the terminals. If the terminal is ready for transmission, it responds by transmitting its data. Otherwise, it transmits a "not ready" message. The computer then polls the next terminal, and so on. In this scheme, the computer transmits and all terminals receive on the outbound channel of the full-duplex link. The selected terminal transmits and the computer receives on the inbound channel. Thus, outbound messages, other than poll messages, may be overlapped with terminal-to-computer transmission.

Hub polling. This is a modification of the roll-polling scheme aimed at reducing the polling overhead. The computer starts by sending a poll message on the outbound channel to terminal 1. If this terminal is ready for transmission, it responds as before by transmitting its message. If it is not ready, however, it transmits the poll message to terminal 2 on the inbound channel. This can be accomplished simply by inserting the address of terminal 2 into the address space of the poll message. Thus, terminal 2 must be able to receive messages on the inbound channel. Of course, all terminals must also be able to receive messages from the computer on the outbound channel. When any terminal finishes transmitting a message, it should send the poll message to the next terminal on the inbound channel.

The hub-polling scheme results in a significant reduction in the polling overhead. The computer only initiates the polling process by sending a poll message on the outbound channel to terminal 1. While polling proceeds on the inbound channel, the computer is free to use the outbound channel for sending output messages. Moreover, if propagation delay is taken into consideration, it can be shown that the delay involved in polling all the terminals on the line is substantially decreased in comparison with the roll-polling scheme.

Contention. When terminal traffic is light, the probability of more than one terminal becoming ready for transmission at the same time is fairly low. This is sometimes exploited by allowing terminals to start transmitting as soon as they have a message ready, preceding their messages with an identifying address. Whenever the computer receives garbled data resulting from more than one terminal starting transmission at the same time, it issues a command causing all terminals to stop transmission. It then starts polling terminals in order. This method is obviously inefficient at times of high terminal activity, so the messages "enable transmission" and "disable transmission" are usually provided to allow the computer to switch between the polling and contention modes of operation.

13.3.3   Loop Organization

The main difference between the loop configuration of Figure 13.6c and the multipoint line is the fact that the loop consists of separate point-to-point links interconnecting the loop interfaces. Transmission around the loop always takes place in the same direction: either clockwise or counterclockwise. Thus, all line segments operate in the simplex mode. Data received at the input side of a loop interface are either sent to the attached terminal or transmitted, after some delay, on the next segment of the loop. The loop interface may also transmit data received from its associated terminal. Obviously, a loop protocol is required to determine the time at which an interface can place this data on the loop and the format in which this transmission can take place.

13.3.4 Multiplexing

The role of a multiplexer was explained in the discussion of the star configuration in Section 13.3.1. If a cluster of terminals is remote from a computer, the multiplexer can be conveniently located at the cluster site. A high-speed line can be used to transmit multiplexed terminal data between the computer and the multiplexer. This section describes some techniques for transmission of multiplexed data.

Let us consider the case in which the cluster consists of n terminals. The multiplexer, in effect, uses the high-speed line to establish the equivalent of n independent links to the computer, one for each terminal. Each of these links has a capacity equal to one of the low-speed lines connecting the terminals to the multiplexer. Two general multiplexing techniques are commonly used: *frequency-division multiplexing* (FDM) and *time-division multiplexing* (TDM).

Frequency-division multiplexing (FDM). The transmission frequency band of the high-speed line is divided into n frequency slots or channels. Individual terminal line signals are then shifted in frequency to fit into these slots. This process is called *modulation*. The reverse process, *demodulation*, takes place at the receiving end. Note that no further addressing information is required during transmission because individual terminals are identified by the frequency slot they occupy. The FDM technique has long been used in voice communications on the telephone network, in which individual voice signals are combined for transmission on high-speed lines between central offices.

Synchronous time-division multiplexing (STDM). This scheme requires the time for transmitting one character on the high-speed line to be less than $1/n$th of the corresponding transmission time on the low-speed lines. The multiplexer consists of a switch that continuously scans the low-speed lines in such a way that one character is transmitted from line 1, followed by one character from line 2, and so on. When line n is reached the scanning process is repeated. A special framing character is usually transmitted at the beginning of each scan to enable the receiving end to identify the data from individual lines. The first character following the framing character belongs to line 1, the second character belongs to line 2, and so on. The resulting transmission format is shown in Figure 13.9. The time period corresponding to one transmission frame is divided into $n + 1$ time slots. The first of these slots is always occupied by the framing character. The next n slots provide n independent channels, which

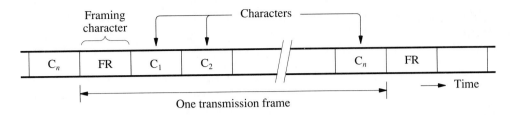

FIGURE 13.9
Transmission format in synchronous time-division multiplexing.

are assigned to the n low-speed lines. As in the case of FDM, no further addressing information is needed, because individual lines are identified by their relative positions within the transmission frame.

We should note that when the scanner switch is connected to any line i, it is possible that there is no character to be sent on that particular line. In this case, the multiplexer transmits a "null" character. The receiving end automatically discards null characters. Thus, proper operation of the system requires two characters to be reserved for the framing and null functions, so these characters must not be included in the character set that the terminals use.

It is interesting to investigate the operation of the character buffers needed to couple two transmission lines operating at different speeds. The double-buffer arrangement of Figure 13.10 is needed for this purpose. Bits from the low-speed line are serially shifted into an input buffer. When a complete character has been received, it is transferred to the output buffer, where it is stored until it can be transmitted in the appropriate time slot. Meanwhile, the next character is assembled in the input buffer. The figure shows the buffers needed for transmission from the terminal to the computer. For full-duplex operation, a similar arrangement is required for transmission in the opposite direction.

Remote terminals are seldom all busy at the same time, and terminal operation involves long periods of inactivity. Therefore, a significant proportion of the time slots of STDM and the capacity of the channels of FDM will be wasted. The next

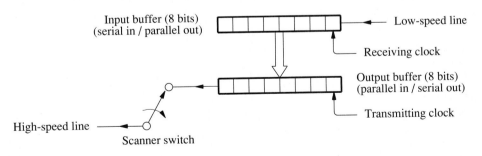

FIGURE 13.10
Double-buffer arrangement for an STDM source line.

scheme to be discussed allows the capacity of the high-speed line to be reduced to less than the sum of the capacities of the low-speed lines by taking advantage of the idle-time property of the terminals.

Asynchronous time-division multiplexing (ATDM). The basic idea of this scheme is to discard the fixed n-slot assignment of STDM and to let time slots be assigned only to terminals that have data ready for transmission. In such a case, the use of a fixed transmission frame and addressing by position within it are no longer possible. A part of each time slot must be used as an address field to identify the terminal. A framing character is also required to establish the beginning of each time slot. The length of the time slot, and hence the number of characters per slot, must be increased considerably if the framing and addressing overhead is to be kept to a minimum. The resulting transmission format is given in Figure 13.11.

The organization of the STDM multiplexer can be used for ATDM purposes with minor modifications. First, the scanner switch should be controlled so that it can skip positions whose output buffers are empty. Second, the size of the character buffers must be increased to correspond to at least the number of characters to be transmitted in one time slot. An organization that is well suited to this application is the queue, or first-in first-out (FIFO) buffer. A hardwired FIFO buffer may have the structure shown in Figure 13.12. After a character is assembled in the input buffer, it is entered into the top position of the FIFO buffer. The control hardware automatically shifts the character downward through successive character positions in the buffer until it reaches the lowest unoccupied position. When the output buffer is emptied, the character occupying the lowest location is shifted out, causing all characters in the FIFO buffer to move downward one position. Thus the FIFO buffer of a given line is filled at the low input rate until a time slot is assigned to this line. At this time a number of characters corresponding to the contents of one time slot are transmitted at the high output rate.

The maximum length of the queue in any line buffer is a function of the input traffic on this line and of the output rate, which is also affected by traffic on other lines. The size of the FIFO buffer should be chosen to accommodate the expected maximum length. If under extreme conditions this length is exceeded, some characters will be lost. The system design should provide some means for rectifying these situations or preventing them from happening.

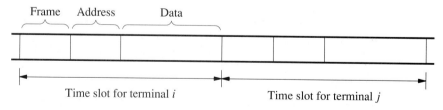

Frame   Address   Data

Time slot for terminal i Time slot for terminal j

FIGURE 13.11
Asynchronous time-division multiplexing.

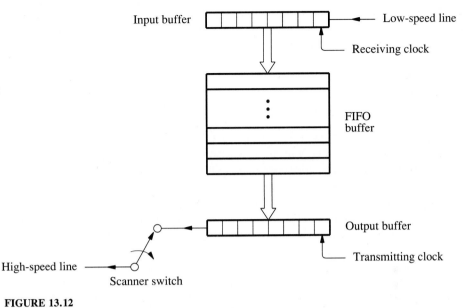

FIGURE 13.12
Use of a FIFO buffer in an ATDM system.

13.3.5 Hierarchy of Control

Before proceeding to more complex networks, we will pause briefly to examine an aspect of the information we have encountered so far regarding the control of data transfers between a computer and a collection of terminals. In using the ATDM technique to multiplex terminal data onto a high-speed line, addressing is required to identify the individual terminals, in addition to any protocols that are needed to control data flow over the high-speed link. These protocols may still use any of the data link control procedures discussed in Section 13.3.2. In fact, the multiple-message format of Figure 13.11 is a substructure for the message text portion of Figures 13.7 or 13.8.

We have identified two levels of control. One level deals with data transfer between the multiplexer and the central computer, and a higher level handles the routing of data to and from individual terminals. A still higher level is needed for handling the text received by the central computer from an individual user. For example, consider a user who is communicating with an interactive operating system. All commands, data, or control characters that are needed for this communication are simply treated as text by the other two levels. The user need not be aware of any of the details of the first two levels except for the possible restriction on the transmission of some reserved characters. This hierarchy of control and the requirement that lower levels of protocol be transparent to higher levels are important features of a properly designed computer communications network. The requirement for independence between various levels becomes more important as the size and complexity of the network increases. Independence allows each level to be developed or updated from time to time without affecting other levels in the network. The term *hierarchical networks* is used to describe computer networks in which a hierarchy of levels can be clearly identified in the control structure of the network. Individual levels are often referred to as *protocol layers*.

13.4 CIRCUIT AND MESSAGE SWITCHING

The previous discussion dealt with networks that connect a number of terminals to a single central computer. We will now consider a more general class of networks that interconnect an arbitrary collection of terminals and computers. Data transfer may take place between a terminal and a computer or between two computers. The service provided by such a network is akin to the service provided by the public telephone network. Indeed, the latter can be used for this purpose, and sometimes is. The dialed connection discussed in Section 13.1 is an example of such a use. There are several advantages in using networks designed specifically for computer communications because of the special nature of this type of communication. In this case, the dialed network can still be useful for back-up purposes.

Two fundamental differences can be readily identified between voice communications for which the telephone network is designed and computer communications:

- Computer traffic is bursty in nature.
- Computers are far less tolerant of transmission errors.

In the traditional telephone network, a transmission path is established between the calling and the called parties soon after dialing. The facilities involved are dedicated to this call throughout its duration. That is, they cannot be shared with other users, even during long periods of silence. Such schemes for connecting two points are referred to as *circuit* or *line switching*. In computer communications, the majority of the network traffic consists of short bursts of data separated by relatively long periods of inactivity. When this type of traffic is carried on a circuit-switched network, the utilization of the transmission facilities is very low. A possible alternative is to place a separate call for each burst of data, but this is likely to be inefficient because the setup time (that is, the time required to establish a call) is often long in comparison with the transmission time of a burst of data. A better alternative is a network that operates on the basis of dynamic allocation of resources. That is, a number of users should be able to share the use of the transmission facilities on a demand basis.

A scheme that satisfies this requirement is known as *message switching*. A source of data presents its message, preceded by the address of its intended destination, to the communications network. The network temporarily stores the message at the node where the message is received. It then selects an appropriate route for the message depending upon the destination address and the current traffic in the network. As the message is transferred along this route, it is stored at each node until a transmission link to the next node is available. This mode of operation is called *store-and-forward*. It represents an extension of the ideas presented in Section 13.3.4 regarding the use of ATDM in the multiplexer application.

The other important difference between the telephone network and a computer network relates to their error performance. As we mentioned in Section 13.2, fairly complex procedures are required to enable error-free transfer of data. In a network designed specifically for computer communications, such procedures can be incorporated as an integral part of the network protocols.

13.4.1 Network Design Considerations

Let us consider a network, such as the one shown in Figure 13.13, that is used to interconnect a number of terminals and computers. The network is capable of providing communication paths between any pair of users. For example, terminal A may want to communicate with computer B while data transfer is taking place between computers C and D. The store-and-forward mode of operation requires the controller at each node of the network to perform the following functions:

- Store a message.
- Select an appropriate outgoing link, based on the destination address.
- Transmit the message when this link is free.

These tasks are required in addition to error control and other data link control

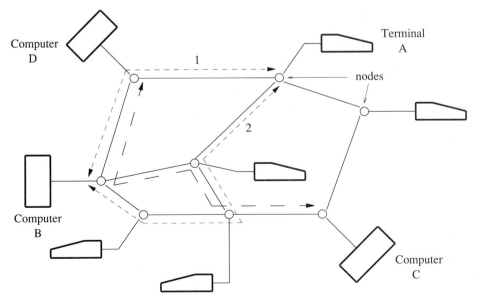

FIGURE 13.13
An example of an 8-node store-and-forward network.

functions required to transfer a message between any two nodes. Because of the complexity of these tasks, a small computer is normally used as the node controller. We will briefly present several important issues related to the operation of a message-switching network.

TYPE OF SERVICE. In a telephone network, the connection between the calling and the called parties is maintained until the call is terminated. A number of network resources are dedicated to this connection to provide a transmission path between the two ends. In the case of message switching, two types of networks can be identified. In the first, the network service appears to the user very much like that provided by a telephone network. After establishing a connection, two users can exchange messages for any period of time, then close down the connection. The network nodes keep track of the connection by means of table entries at various nodes. Thus, user messages need not carry the address of their destination. Such a logical connection between two users is called a *virtual circuit*. Note that actual physical transmission links are allocated to the connection only while a message is being transmitted.

The concept of a connection is discarded in the second type of network, at least as far as the network is concerned. Each message must carry an address, which is used by the network to deliver the message to the intended destination. Since individual messages are handled independently, the network does not guarantee that they will be delivered in the same order in which they were presented to the network by the source. In fact, the network does not guarantee that they will be delivered at all. Because of transmission errors and subsequent retransmissions, several copies of a given message may be delivered to the destination. It is up to the network users to detect lost or duplicate messages and to take appropriate corrective action. Because the service provided by such a network bears some resemblance to that of the post office, it is referred to as *datagram* service.

MESSAGE ROUTING. When a message is received by any node in the network, the node processor inspects the destination address field in order to select an appropriate outgoing transmission link. This selection is usually based on routing tables stored in the computer memory. In a network such as that of Figure 13.13, a number of alternative routes exist between any two points. For example, paths 1 and 2 are possible choices for a message from terminal A to computer B. It is advantageous to have as much flexibility as possible in choosing a suitable path, taking into account such considerations as broken links and heavily loaded links or nodes.

CONTROL OF DATA FLOW. Congestion in the network (the situation in which a large percentage of the buffer space is occupied) can lead to undesirable results. Consider two node computers, X and Y, exchanging messages. Messages arriving at each computer destined for the other are buffered in an output queue. As the traffic increases, the lengths of both output queues increase until they occupy all the buffer space available. At this point no further message transfers can take place between the two computers. Computer X cannot accept any message from Y or from any other computer because it has no buffer space available to store the message. Similarly, computer Y cannot accept any messages from X. A *deadlock* is said to have occurred, and message traffic stops. To avoid the occurrence of such deadlocks, the buffer allocation scheme in computer Y should ensure that at least one message buffer space is always available for receiving messages from computer X, and vice versa.

In general, network protocols must be provided to control the flow of messages into the network. In addition to preventing the occurrence of deadlocks, these protocols protect against the occurrence of excessive delays.

CHOICE OF MESSAGE LENGTH. Message length is an important parameter that has a significant effect on network performance. The statistical distribution of message length depends upon the application. In interactive traffic, for example, messages are relatively short and are limited to a maximum, such as the length of a line of text on a terminal. On the other hand, when transferring data files from one computer to another, messages can be very long. In a store-and-forward network, long messages require a large amount of buffer storage and may adversely affect the network throughput. They also require long transmission time, thus leading to slower response time for other users. This is highly undesirable if the network also services interactive terminals. Very short messages lead to inefficient operation because network overhead (for example, addressing, routing, and acknowledgments) is independent of the message length. Thus there is an optimal message length that provides an acceptable compromise between efficiency and response time.

It is not convenient to force the network user to limit all messages to the optimal length required by the network. This suggests the following mode of operation. Variable-length messages may be accepted by the network, which then breaks each message down into smaller messages that correspond to the optimal message length in the network. These shorter messages can now be transmitted through the network. When they reach the destination point, they are reassembled into the original format and delivered to the receiver. Such short messages that travel through the network are referred to as *packets*, and the technique is known as *packet switching*. Networks using this approach can transfer long messages without a significant degradation in service to users with short messages. A maximum message length, which can be several times the packet length, is usually imposed because of buffer storage limitations.

13.5 LOCAL AREA NETWORKS

As we discussed in the introduction to this chapter, a local area network (LAN)[2] is a computer network that is limited to a geographically small area. It interconnects computers, terminals, and other digital devices within a plant site, a university campus, an office building, and so forth.

The most popular local area networks use either the ring or the bus topology. A ring LAN has the general topology of Figure 13.6c, without the controlling computer. In the loop of that figure all messages flow either to or from the controlling computer.

In a ring LAN, all message flow is in one direction, and any device can communicate directly with any other device. For bus LANs, all devices are connected to the bus through an appropriate interface.

The transmission media for either ring or bus LANs can be twisted wire pair, coaxial cable, or optical fiber. Bit-serial transmission is used, and rates in the 1 to 20 megabits per second (Mbps) range are common. Only one message packet at a time can be successfully transmitted onto the single shared path. Source and destination device addresses precede the data field of a packet, and appropriate delimiters indicate the start and end of the packet. Some form of error control is used, and the error control bits are usually placed immediately before the end delimiter. In general, packets have variable length ranging from tens of bytes to over 1000 bytes.

A protocol that implements distributed access control is needed to determine orderly transfer of packets between arbitrary pairs of communicating devices. We will sketch the basic ideas involved in three widely used protocols: the token ring, the token bus, and the Ethernet bus. All three of these protocols are specified in detail in an IEEE Standard.[3]

13.5.1 Token Ring

A single, appropriately encoded flag, called a *token*, circulates continuously around the ring. The arrival of the token at a ring station represents permission to transmit. If the station has nothing to transmit, it forwards the token to the next station downstream with as little delay as possible. If the station has data ready for transmission, however, it inhibits the propagation of the token and instead transmits a packet of information preceded by an appropriately encoded header flag. As the packet is transmitted around the ring, its contents are read and copied as it travels past the destination station. The packet continues to travel around the ring until it reaches the source station, where it is discarded. When the source station completes transmitting a packet, it releases the permission token, which again starts to circulate around the ring. The packet size on a token ring is variable and is limited only by the amount of buffer memory available in each station.

13.5.2 Token Bus

A short token packet is used to pass transmission permission among the devices attached to a bus LAN. A designated station initiates operation by addressing a token packet to a particular device. As the packet is transmitted onto the bus, it propagates toward both ends of the bus and is absorbed in electrical terminations at the ends of the bus. Therefore, every device attached to the bus observes the packet. The addressed device acquires permission to transmit a message packet when it observes the token packet. After transmitting a message packet, this device then addresses a token packet to the next device. If the first device has no message packet to transmit, it immediately addresses a token packet to the next device. All devices are polled in this manner, and then the cycle repeats.

13.5.3 Ethernet (CSMA/CD) Bus

The Ethernet bus access protocol, also called the Carrier Sense Multiple Access with Collision Detection (CSMA/CD) protocol, is conceptually simpler than the token bus protocol. Whenever an attached device has a message to transmit, it waits until it senses that the bus is idle and then begins transmission. The device then monitors the bus for 2τ seconds as it transmits its message, where τ is the end-to-end bus propagation delay. If the device does not observe any distortion of its transmitted signal during the 2τ interval, then it can assume that no other station has started transmission and can continue to complete its own transmission. On the other hand, if distortion is observed, caused by the beginning of a transmission from some other device, then both devices must stop transmitting. The mutually destructive distortion of the two transmitted signals is called a *collision*, and the time interval 2τ is called the *collision window*.

Messages that have been destroyed by collision must be retransmitted. If the devices involved in the collision attempt to retry immediately, their packets will almost certainly collide again. A basic strategy used to prevent collision of the retries is as follows. Each device independently waits for a random amount of time, then waits until the bus is idle, and then begins retransmission. If the random waits are a few multiples of 2τ, the probability of repeated collisions is reduced.

13.6 CONCLUDING REMARKS

This chapter has presented an overview of the concepts involved in computer communication networks. Applications of such networks are virtually limitless. They cover widely differing areas such as scientific research, banking, library services, medical services, and weather forecasting. Many networks have been implemented and many others are in the planning stages. Interconnection of these networks is an important topic that has not been dealt with in this chapter; ground, underwater, and satellite communication links are being used for this purpose. Other important issues include economic, regulatory, and reliability considerations.

13.7 PROBLEMS

13.1. Consider a modem connection to a computer through an RS-232-C interface. Assume that the control signals associated with this interface can be accessed by the computer by means of an I/O register, as shown in Figure P13.1. The status change bit, b_{15}, is set to 1 whenever there is a change in the state of bits b_{12} or b_{13} or when b_{14} is set to 1. It is cleared when this register is accessed by the CPU. Write a computer program for either the PDP-11 or the 68000 to implement the control sequence required to establish a telephone connection according to steps 1 to 4 of Figure 13.3.

13.2. Ten terminals are connected to a computer via a single, full-duplex, multipoint line. The computer periodically polls each terminal for input data. Estimate the time required for a complete polling cycle, not including data transmission, for both the roll-polling and hub-polling schemes described in Section 13.3.2. Assume the following parameters:

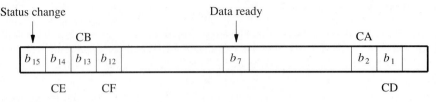

FIGURE P13.1
Organization of an I/O register for a modem interface.

Distance between two terminals	5 km
Distance between computer and first terminal	10 km
Propagation delay	3 ms/100 km
Transmission speed	2400 bits/s
Length of poll message	40 bits
Length of reply message	40 bits

13.3. Ten terminals are connected to a computer in a multipoint line configuration. Transmission of data from the terminals to the computer is on a contention basis. On average, each terminal transmits data for 100 ms in every 10-s period. The time required for any terminal to recognize that another terminal is transmitting is 5 ms. Estimate the probability of two terminals starting transmission at the same time. When a terminal tries to use the line and finds the line busy, it will retry later. How does the retry strategy affect the above probability?

13.4. Consider a half-duplex communication link between two computers that are 400 km apart. The parameters for this link are as follows:

Propagation delay	3 ms/100 km
Turnaround time	50 ms
Transmission speed	4800 bits/s
Length of Acknowledge message	40 bits
Probability of error in a transmission block	$2 \times 10^{-5}n$

where n is the number of bits in a transmission block. Assume that the stop-and-wait ARQ protocol is used. Plot a curve of the effective transmission rate over this link versus the block size n for n in the range 100 to 30,000 bits. Estimate the block size that results in a maximum effective transmission rate.

13.5. Repeat Problem 13.4, assuming that the transmission speed is doubled but that all other parameters remain the same.

13.6. The communication link of Problem 13.4 is operated in a full-duplex mode. Calculate the resulting percentage increase in the effective transmission rate over this link for $n = 1000$.

13.7. Consider a continuous-ARQ transmission scheme. Assume that when an error is detected all messages are retransmitted, starting with the message in which the error was detected.
   (*a*) Give a diagram similar to that of Figure 13.5 that shows a transmission sequence in which an error is detected.
   (*b*) Derive an expression for the transmission efficiency factor η in this case.

13.8. Consider a synchronous time-division multiplexing scheme similar to that of Figure 13.9. Assume that each transmission frame contains character data from 15 different devices and that each character is 8 bits long. The framing character is also 8 bits long.

  (*a*) What is the effective data rate for each of the 15 devices if the transmission speed on the high-speed line is 4800 bits/s?

  (*b*) If only 3 of the 15 devices are transmitting data at any given time, what data rate can each of them have?

13.9. The transmission scheme of Problem 13.8 is replaced by an asynchronous time-division multiplexing scheme.

  (*a*) Suggest a suitable format for transmission.

  (*b*) What is the average data rate for each device when only 3 of the 15 devices are transmitting? Assume that on the average, five data characters are transmitted in each time slot.

13.10. Give a block diagram showing how to implement the FIFO buffer of Figure 13.12 using random-access memory and control logic.

13.11. Consider the following scheme for routing messages in a multiconnected network. When a message is received at any node, its address field is inspected. If the message is addressed to that node, it is accepted; otherwise, copies of the message are transmitted to all neighboring nodes. This scheme is called "flooding." It will obviously cause multiple copies of a given message to arrive at the destination. Assume that this scheme is used in the network of Figure P13.2 and that a message originates at node A addressed for node G. What sequence of transmissions will result in the first arrival of that message at node G? Suggest how the flooding scheme may be used for establishing the shortest route between any two points in a network using distributed control.

13.12. The relative efficiency of Local Area Network (LAN) access protocols depends on two major factors—the total utilization of the LAN; and the ratio, A, of LAN propagation delay to message transmission time. LAN utilization, U, is usually expressed as the fraction of time the LAN is successfully transferring message packets as opposed to being idle, carrying control overhead such as tokens or token packets, or being in a collision state. Assume that a large number of stations are attached to the LAN and that the total length of a bus or ring needed to connect them is the same. Message packets arrive at the LAN from the stations in some random fashion. For purposes

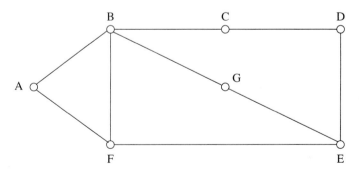

FIGURE P13.2
Connections in a store-and-forward message network.

of this question, we will assume that efficiency is determined by the average delay experienced by a message between the time it is generated at a station and the beginning of its successful transmission onto the LAN.

For both the light utilization (U < 0.1) and heavy utilization (U > 0.5) cases, qualitatively compare the efficiency of all three LAN types discussed in Section 13.5 for both A << 1 and for A ≈ 1.

13.13. In the discussion of the LAN token ring access protocol in Section 13.5.1, it was implicitly assumed that the time to transmit a message onto the ring is longer than propagation delay around the ring. Therefore, a station is still transmitting when its message header arrives back at the input side of the station after propagating around the ring. The header flag (and thus the message) is deleted from the ring by being discarded while the station is still transmitting. Now consider the case in which transmission time is much shorter than ring propagation delay. When a station finishes transmitting a packet, it appends the token immediately, as before. It is then possible for a "train" of short messages to develop on the ring. The single token trails the train, and messages are separated by header flags.

How does a source station recognize the header of its own message so that it can remove the message from the ring by transforming the header pattern into idle bits?

13.14. Why is the collision window of length 2τ and not τ in the Ethernet bus LAN protocol?

13.15. The Ethernet bus LAN protocol is really only suitable when message transmission time is significantly larger than 2τ, where τ is the end-to-end bus propagation delay. Consider the case where transmission time is less than τ. Is it possible for a destination station to correctly receive an undistorted message, even though the source station observes a collision inside the 2τ collision window period? If not, justify your answer. If you think it is possible, give the relative locations of the source, destination, and interfering stations on the bus and describe the relevant event times.

13.16. Justify or refute the following claim: "As bit rates increase into the 100s of megabits per second range, the token ring LAN access protocol becomes superior to both the token bus and Ethernet bus protocols."

13.8 REFERENCES

1. Hamming, R. W., *Coding and Information Theory*, 2d ed., Prentice-Hall, Englewood Cliffs, NJ, 1986.
2. Stallings, W., *Local Networks, An Introduction*, 2d ed., Macmillan, New York, NY, 1987.
3. *IEEE Local Area Network Standard 802*, 1985.

APPENDIX
A

LOGIC CIRCUITS

Information in digital computers is represented and processed by electronic networks called *logic circuits*. These circuits operate on *binary variables* that assume one of two distinct values, usually called 0 and 1. In this appendix we will give a concise presentation of logic functions and circuits for their implementation, including a brief review of integrated circuit technology.

A.1 BASIC LOGIC FUNCTIONS

It is helpful to introduce the topic of binary logic by examining a practical problem that arises in all homes. Consider a light bulb whose on-off status is controlled by two switches, x_1 and x_2. Each switch can be in one of two possible positions, 0 or 1, as shown in Figure A.1a. It can thus be represented by a binary variable. We will let the switch names serve as the names of the associated binary variables. The figure also shows an electrical power supply and a light bulb. The way the switch terminals are interconnected determines how the switches control the light. The light will be on only if a closed path exists from the power supply through the switch network to the light bulb. Let a binary variable f represent the condition of the light. If the light is on, $f = 1$, and if the light is off, $f = 0$. Thus $f = 1$ means that there is at least one closed path through the network, and $f = 0$ means that there is no closed path. Clearly, f is a function of the two variables x_1 and x_2.

519

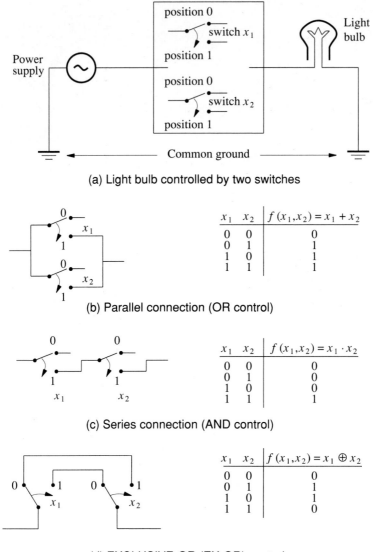

(a) Light bulb controlled by two switches

x_1	x_2	$f(x_1,x_2) = x_1 + x_2$
0	0	0
0	1	1
1	0	1
1	1	1

(b) Parallel connection (OR control)

x_1	x_2	$f(x_1,x_2) = x_1 \cdot x_2$
0	0	0
0	1	0
1	0	0
1	1	1

(c) Series connection (AND control)

x_1	x_2	$f(x_1,x_2) = x_1 \oplus x_2$
0	0	0
0	1	1
1	0	1
1	1	0

(d) EXCLUSIVE-OR (EX-OR) control

FIGURE A.1
Light switch example.

Let us consider some possibilities for controlling the light. First, suppose that the light is to be on if either switch is in the 1 position; that is, $f = 1$ if

$$x_1 = 1 \qquad \text{and} \qquad x_2 = 0$$

or

$$x_1 = 0 \qquad \text{and} \qquad x_2 = 1$$

or

$$x_1 = 1 \quad \text{and} \quad x_2 = 1$$

The connections that implement this type of control are shown in Figure A.1b. A logic *truth table* that represents this situation is shown beside the wiring diagram. The table lists all possible switch settings, along with the value of f for each setting. In logic terms, this table represents the OR function of the two variables, x_1 and x_2. The operation is represented algebraically by a "$+$" sign or a "$\bigvee$" sign, so that

$$f = x_1 + x_2 = x_1 \bigvee x_2$$

We say that x_1 and x_2 are the *input* variables and f is the *output* function.

We should point out some basic properties of the OR operation. It is commutative; that is,

$$x_1 + x_2 = x_2 + x_1$$

It can be extended to n variables, so that

$$f = x_1 + x_2 + \cdots + x_n$$

has the value 1 if any of the x_i variables has the value 1. This represents the effect of connecting more switches in parallel with the two switches in Figure A.1b. Also, inspection of the truth table shows that

$$1 + x = 1$$

and

$$0 + x = x$$

Now, suppose that the light is to be on only when both switches are in the 1 position. The connections for this, along with the corresponding truth-table representation, are shown in Figure A.1c. This is the AND function, which uses the symbols "$\cdot$" and "$\bigwedge$" and is denoted as

$$f = x_1 \cdot x_2 = x_1 \bigwedge x_2$$

Some basic properties of the AND operation are

$$x_1 \cdot x_2 = x_2 \cdot x_1$$

$$1 \cdot x = x$$

and

$$0 \cdot x = 0$$

The AND function also extends to n variables, with

$$f = x_1 \cdot x_2 \cdots x_n$$

having the value 1 only if all the x_i variables have the value 1. This represents the case in which more switches are connected in series with the two switches in Figure A.1c.

The final possibility that we will discuss for the way the switches determine the light status is another common situation. If we assume that the switches are at either end of a stairway, it should be possible to turn the light on or off from either switch position. That is, if the light is on, changing either switch position should turn it off; correspondingly, if it is off, changing either switch position should turn it on. Assume that the light is off when both switches are in the 0 position. Then, changing either switch to the 1 position should turn the light on. Now suppose that the light is on with $x_1 = 1$ and $x_2 = 0$. Switching x_1 back to 0 will obviously turn the light off. Furthermore, it must be possible to turn the light off by changing x_2 to 1; that is, $f = 0$ if $x_1 = x_2 = 1$. The connections to implement this type of control are shown in Figure A.1d. The corresponding logic operation is called the EXCLUSIVE-OR (EX-OR) function, which is represented by the symbol "$\oplus$". Some of its properties are

$$x_1 \oplus x_2 = x_2 \oplus x_1$$
$$1 \oplus x = \overline{x}$$

and

$$0 \oplus x = x$$

where $\overline{x}$ denotes the NOT function of the variable x. This single-variable function, $f = \overline{x}$, has the value 1 if $x = 0$ and the value 0 if $x = 1$. We say that the input x is being *inverted* or *complemented*.

A.1.1 Electronic Logic Gates

The use of switches, closed or open electrical paths, and light bulbs to illustrate the idea of logic variables and functions is convenient because of their familiarity and simplicity. The logic concepts that have been introduced are equally applicable to the electronic circuits that are used to process information in digital computers. The physical variables are electrical voltages and currents instead of switch positions and closed or open paths. For example, consider a circuit that is designed to operate on inputs that are at either +5 or 0 V. The circuit outputs are also at either +5 or 0 V. Now, if we say that +5 V represents logic 1 and that 0 V represents logic 0, then we can describe what the circuit does by specifying the truth table for the logic operation that it performs.

With the help of transistors, it is possible to design simple electronic circuits that perform logic operations such as AND, OR, EX-OR, and NOT. It is customary to use the name *gates* for these basic logic circuits. Standard symbols for these gates are shown in Figure A.2. A somewhat more compact graphical notation for the NOT operation is used when inversion is applied to a logic-gate input or output. In such cases, the inversion is denoted by a small circle.

The electronic implementation of logic gates will be discussed in Section A.5. We will now proceed to discuss how basic gates can be used to construct logic networks that implement more complex logic functions.

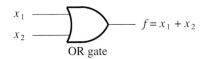

OR gate

$f = x_1 + x_2$

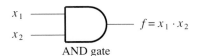

AND gate

$f = x_1 \cdot x_2$

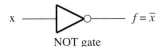

NOT gate

$f = \overline{x}$

EX-OR gate

$f = x_1 \oplus x_2$

FIGURE A.2
Standard logic gate symbols.

A.2 SYNTHESIS OF LOGIC FUNCTIONS USING AND, OR, AND NOT GATES

Consider the network composed of two AND gates and an OR gate that is shown in Figure A.3a. It can be represented by the expression

$$f = \overline{x}_1 \cdot x_2 + x_1 \cdot \overline{x}_2$$

The construction of the truth table for this expression is shown in Figure A.3b. First, the values of the AND terms are determined for each input valuation. Then the values of the function f are determined using the OR operation. The truth table for f is identical to the truth table for the EX-OR function, so the three-gate network in Figure A.3a is an implementation of the EX-OR function using AND, OR, and NOT gates. The logic expression $\overline{x}_1 \cdot x_2 + x_1 \cdot \overline{x}_2$ is called a *sum-of-products* form because the OR operation is sometimes called the "sum" function and the AND operation the "product" function.

We should note that it would be more proper to write

$$f = ((\overline{x}_1) \cdot x_2) + (x_1 \cdot (\overline{x}_2))$$

to indicate the order of applying the operations in the expression. To simplify the appearance of such expressions, we define a hierarchy among the three operations AND, OR, and NOT. In the absence of parentheses, operations in a logic expression should be performed in the following order: NOT, AND, then OR. Furthermore, it is customary to omit the "·" operator whenever there is no ambiguity.

Returning to the sum-of-products form, we will now explain how any logic function can be synthesized in this form directly from its truth table. Consider the

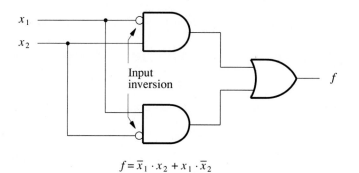

$$f = \overline{x}_1 \cdot x_2 + x_1 \cdot \overline{x}_2$$

(a) Network for the EX-OR function

$x_1\ x_2$	$\overline{x}_1 \cdot x_2$	$x_1 \cdot \overline{x}_2$	$f = \overline{x}_1 \cdot x_2 + x_1 \cdot \overline{x}_2$ $= x_1 \oplus x_2$
0 0	0	0	0
0 1	1	0	1
1 0	0	1	1
1 1	0	0	0

(b) Truth table construction for $\overline{x}_1 \cdot x_2 + x_1 \cdot \overline{x}_2$

FIGURE A.3
Implementation of the EX-OR function using AND, OR, and NOT gates.

truth table of Table A.1 and suppose we wish to synthesize the function f_1 using AND, OR, and NOT gates. For each row of the table in which $f_1 = 1$, we include a product (AND) term in the sum-of-products form. The product term includes all three input variables. The NOT operator is applied to these variables individually so that the term is 1 only when the variables have the particular valuation that corresponds to

TABLE A.1 Two 3-variable functions

x_1	x_2	x_3	f_1	f_2
0	0	0	1	1
0	0	1	1	1
0	1	0	0	1
0	1	1	1	0
1	0	0	0	1
1	0	1	0	1
1	1	0	0	0
1	1	1	1	0

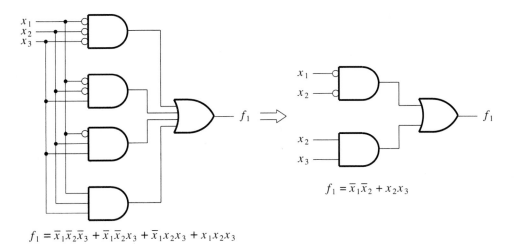

$$f_1 = \overline{x}_1\overline{x}_2\overline{x}_3 + \overline{x}_1\overline{x}_2x_3 + \overline{x}_1x_2x_3 + x_1x_2x_3$$

$$f_1 = \overline{x}_1\overline{x}_2 + x_2x_3$$

FIGURE A.4
A logic network for f_1 of Table A.1 and an equivalent minimal network.

that row of the truth table. This means that if $x_i = 0$, then $\overline{x}_i$ is entered in the product term, and if $x_i = 1$, then x_i is entered. For example, the fourth row of the table has the function entry 1 for the input valuation

$$(x_1, x_2, x_3) = (0, 1, 1)$$

The product term corresponding to this is $\overline{x}_1x_2x_3$. Doing this for all rows in which the function f_1 has the value 1 leads to

$$f_1 = \overline{x}_1\overline{x}_2\overline{x}_3 + \overline{x}_1\overline{x}_2 x_3 + \overline{x}_1 x_2x_3 + x_1x_2x_3$$

The logic network corresponding to this expression is shown on the left side in Figure A.4. As another example, the sum-of-products expression for the EX-OR function can be derived from its truth table by this technique. This approach can be used to derive sum-of-products expressions and the corresponding logic networks for truth tables of any size.

A.3 MINIMIZATION OF LOGIC EXPRESSIONS

We have shown how to derive one sum-of-products expression for each truth table. In fact, there are many equivalent expressions and logic networks for any particular truth table. Two logic expressions or logic-gate networks are equivalent if they have identical truth tables. An expression that is equivalent to the sum-of-products expression that we derived for f_1 in the previous section is

$$\overline{x}_1\overline{x}_2 + x_2x_3$$

To prove this, we construct the truth table for the simpler expression and show that

TABLE A.2 Evaluation of the expression $\bar{x}_1\bar{x}_2 + x_2x_3$

x_1	x_2	x_3	$\bar{x}_1\bar{x}_2$	x_2x_3	$\bar{x}_1\bar{x}_2 + x_2x_3 = f_1$
0	0	0	1	0	1
0	0	1	1	0	1
0	1	0	0	0	0
0	1	1	0	1	1
1	0	0	0	0	0
1	0	1	0	0	0
1	1	0	0	0	0
1	1	1	0	1	1

it is identical to the truth table for f_1 in Table A.1. This is done in Table A.2. The construction of the table for $\bar{x}_1\bar{x}_2 + x_2x_3$ is done in three steps. First, the value of the product term $\bar{x}_1\bar{x}_2$ is computed for each valuation of the inputs. Then x_2x_3 is evaluated. Finally, these two columns are ORed together to obtain the truth table for the expression. This truth table is identical to the truth table for f_1 given in Table A.1.

To simplify logic expressions we will perform a series of algebraic manipulations. The new logic rules that we will use in these manipulations are the distributive rule

$$w(y + z) = wy + wz$$

and the identity

$$w + \bar{w} = 1$$

Table A.3 shows the truth-table proof of the distributive rule. It should now be clear

TABLE A.3 Truth-table technique for proving equivalence of expressions

w	y	z	$y + z$	Left-hand side $w(y + z)$	wy	wz	Right-hand side $wy + wz$
0	0	0	0	0	0	0	0
0	0	1	1	0	0	0	0
0	1	0	1	0	0	0	0
0	1	1	1	0	0	0	0
1	0	0	0	0	0	0	0
1	0	1	1	1	0	1	1
1	1	0	1	1	1	0	1
1	1	1	1	1	1	1	1

that rules such as this can always be proved by constructing the truth tables for the left-hand side and the right-hand side to show that they are identical. Logic rules, such as the distributive rule, are sometimes called *identities*. Although we will not need to use it here, another form of distributive rule that we should include for completeness is

$$w + yz = (w + y)(w + z)$$

The objective in logic minimization is to reduce the cost of implementation of a given logic function according to some criterion. More particularly, we wish to start with a sum-of-products expression derived from a truth table and simplify it to an equivalent *minimal sum-of-products* expression. To define the criterion for minimization, it is necessary to introduce a size or cost measure for a sum-of-products expression. The usual cost measure is a count of the total number of gates and gate inputs required in implementing the expression in the form shown in Figure A.4. For example, the larger expression in this figure has a cost of 21, composed of a total of 5 gates and 16 gate inputs. Input inversions are ignored in this counting process. The cost of the simpler expression is 9, composed of 3 gates and 6 inputs. We are now in a position to state that a sum-of-products expression is minimal if there is no other equivalent sum-of-products expression with a lower cost. In the simple examples that we will introduce, it is usually reasonably clear when we have arrived at a minimal expression. Thus we will not give rigorous proofs of minimality.

The general strategy in performing algebraic manipulations on a given expression in order to simplify it is as follows. First, group product terms in pairs that differ only in that some variable appears complemented ($\bar{x}$) in one term and true (x) in the other. When the common subproduct consisting of the other variables is factored out of the pair by the distributive rule, we are left with the term $x + \bar{x}$ that has the value 1. Applying this procedure to the first expression for f_1, we obtain

$$\begin{aligned}
f_1 &= \bar{x}_1\bar{x}_2\bar{x}_3 + \bar{x}_1\bar{x}_2x_3 + \bar{x}_1x_2x_3 + x_1x_2x_3 \\
&= \bar{x}_1\bar{x}_2(\bar{x}_3 + x_3) + (\bar{x}_1 + x_1)x_2x_3 \\
&= \bar{x}_1\bar{x}_2{\cdot}1 + 1{\cdot}x_2x_3 \\
&= \bar{x}_1\bar{x}_2 + x_2x_3
\end{aligned}$$

This expression is minimal. The network corresponding to it is shown in Figure A.4.

The grouping of terms in pairs so that minimization can lead to the simplest expression is not always as obvious as it is in the above example. A rule that is often helpful is

$$w + w = w$$

This allows us to repeat product terms so that a particular term can be combined with more than one other term in the factoring process. As an example of this, consider the function f_2 in Table A.1. The sum-of-products expression that can be derived for it directly from the truth table is

$$f_2 = \bar{x}_1\bar{x}_2\bar{x}_3 + \bar{x}_1\bar{x}_2x_3 + \bar{x}_1x_2\bar{x}_3 + x_1\bar{x}_2\bar{x}_3 + x_1\bar{x}_2x_3$$

TABLE A.4 Rules of binary logic

Name	Algebraic identity	
Commutative	$w + y = y + w$	$wy = yw$
Associative	$(w + y) + z = w + (y + z)$	$(wy)z = w(yz)$
Distributive	$w + yz = (w + y)(w + z)$	$w(y + z) = wy + wz$
Idempotent	$w + w = w$	$ww = w$
Involution	$\overline{\overline{w}} = w$	
Complement	$w + \overline{w} = 1$	$w\overline{w} = 0$
de Morgan	$\overline{w + y} = \overline{w}\ \overline{y}$	$\overline{wy} = \overline{w} + \overline{y}$
	$1 + w = 1$	$0 \cdot w = 0$
	$0 + w = w$	$1 \cdot w = w$

By repeating the first product term $\overline{x}_1\overline{x}_2\overline{x}_3$ and interchanging the order of terms (by the commutative rule), we obtain

$$f_2 = \overline{x}_1\overline{x}_2\overline{x}_3 + \overline{x}_1\overline{x}_2x_3 + x_1\overline{x}_2\overline{x}_3 + x_1\overline{x}_2x_3 + \overline{x}_1\overline{x}_2\overline{x}_3 + \overline{x}_1x_2\overline{x}_3$$

Grouping the terms in pairs and factoring yields

$$f_2 = \overline{x}_1\overline{x}_2(\overline{x}_3 + x_3) + x_1\overline{x}_2(\overline{x}_3 + x_3) + \overline{x}_1(\overline{x}_2 + x_2)\overline{x}_3$$

$$= \overline{x}_1\overline{x}_2 + x_1\overline{x}_2 + \overline{x}_1\overline{x}_3$$

The first pair of terms is again reduced by factoring, and we obtain the minimal expression

$$f_2 = \overline{x}_2 + \overline{x}_1\overline{x}_3$$

This completes our discussion of algebraic simplification of logic expressions. The obvious practical application of this mathematical exercise stems from the fact that networks with fewer gates and inputs are cheaper and easier to implement. Therefore, it is of economic interest to be able to determine the minimal expression that is equivalent to a given expression. The rules that we have used in manipulating logic expressions are summarized in Table A.4. They are arranged in pairs to show their symmetry as they apply to both the AND and OR functions. So far, we have not had occasion to use either involution or de Morgan's rules, but they will be found useful in the next section.

A.3.1 Minimization Using Karnaugh Maps

In our algebraic minimization of the functions f_1 and f_2 of Table A.1, it was necessary to guess the best way to proceed at certain points. For instance, deciding to repeat the term $\overline{x}_1\overline{x}_2\overline{x}_3$ as the first step in minimizing f_2 is not obvious. There is a geometric technique that can be used to quickly derive minimal expressions for logic functions of a few variables. The technique depends on a different form for presentation of the truth table, a form called the *Karnaugh map*. For three-variable functions, the map is a rectangle composed of eight squares arranged in two rows of four squares each, as shown in Figure A.5a. Each square of the map corresponds to a particular valuation of the input variables. For example, the third square of the top row represents the valuation $(x_1, x_2, x_3) = (1, 1, 0)$. Because there are eight rows in a three-variable truth table, the map obviously requires eight squares. The entries in the squares are the function values for the corresponding input valuations.

The key idea in the formation of the map is that horizontally and vertically adjacent squares correspond to input valuations that differ in only one variable. When two adjacent squares contain 1s, they indicate the possibility of an algebraic simplification. In the map for f_2 in Figure A.5a, the two 1 values in the left two squares of the top row correspond to the product terms $\overline{x}_1 \overline{x}_2 \overline{x}_3$ and $\overline{x}_1 x_2 \overline{x}_3$. As we have already seen, the simplification

$$\overline{x}_1 \overline{x}_2 \overline{x}_3 + \overline{x}_1 x_2 \overline{x}_3 = \overline{x}_1 \overline{x}_3$$

was performed in minimizing the algebraic expression for f_2. This simplification can be obtained directly from the map by grouping the two 1s as shown. The product term that corresponds to a group of squares is the product of the input variables whose values are constant on these squares. If the value of input variable x_i is 0 for all 1s of a group, then $\overline{x}_i$ is entered in the product, but if x_i has the value 1 for all 1s of the group, then x_i is entered in the product. Adjacency of two squares includes the fact that the left-end squares are adjacent to the right-end squares. Continuing with our discussion of f_2, the group of four 1s consisting of the left-end column and the right-end column simplifies to the single-variable term $\overline{x}_2$ because x_2 is the only variable whose value remains constant over the group. All four possible combinations of values of the other two variables occur in the group.

Karnaugh maps can be used for more than three variables. A Karnaugh map for four variables can be obtained from 2 three-variable maps. Examples of four-variable maps are shown in Figure A.5b, along with minimal expressions for the functions represented by the maps. In addition to two- and four-square groupings, it is now possible to form eight-square groupings. Such a grouping is illustrated in the map for g_3. Note that the four corner squares constitute a valid group of four and are represented by the product term $\overline{x}_2 \overline{x}_4$ in g_2. As in the case of three-variable maps, the term that corresponds to a group of squares is the product of the variables whose values do not change over the group. For example, the grouping of four 1s in the upper right-hand corner of the map for g_2 is represented by the product term $x_1 \overline{x}_3$ because $x_1 = 1$ and $x_3 = 0$ over the group. The variables x_2 and x_4 have all the possible combinations of values over this group. It is also possible to use Karnaugh maps for five-variable functions. In this case, 2 four-variable maps are used, one of them corresponding to the 0 value for the fifth variable and the other corresponding to the 1 value.

The general procedure for forming groups of two, four, eight, and so on in Karnaugh maps is readily derived. Two adjacent pairs of 1s can be combined to form a group of four. Similarly, two adjacent groups of four can be combined to form a

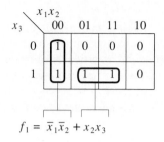

$$f_1 = \overline{x}_1\overline{x}_2 + x_2x_3$$

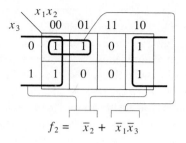

$$f_2 = \overline{x}_2 + \overline{x}_1\overline{x}_3$$

(a) 3-variable maps

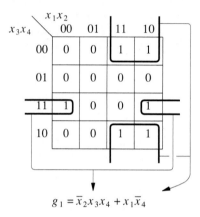

$$g_1 = \overline{x}_2x_3x_4 + x_1\overline{x}_4$$

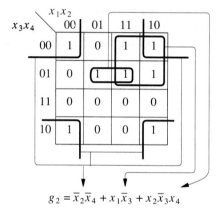

$$g_2 = \overline{x}_2\overline{x}_4 + x_1\overline{x}_3 + x_2\overline{x}_3x_4$$

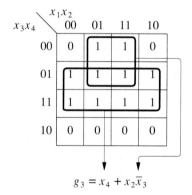

$$g_3 = x_4 + x_2\overline{x}_3$$

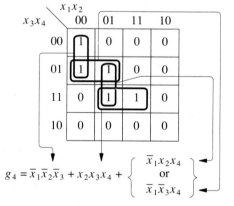

$$g_4 = \overline{x}_1\overline{x}_2\overline{x}_3 + x_2x_3x_4 + \begin{cases} \overline{x}_1x_2x_4 \\ \text{or} \\ \overline{x}_1\overline{x}_3x_4 \end{cases}$$

(b) 4-variable maps

FIGURE A.5
Minimization using Karnaugh maps.

group of eight. In general, the number of squares in any valid group must be equal to 2^k, where k is an integer.

We will now consider a procedure for using Karnaugh maps to obtain minimal sum-of-products expressions. As can be seen in the maps of Figure A.5, a large group of 1s corresponds to a small product term. Thus, a simple gate implementation results from covering all the 1s in the map with as few groups as possible. In general, we should choose the smallest set of groups, picking large ones wherever possible, that cover all the 1s in the map. Consider, for example, the function g_2 in Figure A.5b. As we have already seen, the 1s in the four corners constitute a group of four that is represented by the product term $\bar{x}_2\bar{x}_4$. Another group of four exists in the upper right-hand corner and is represented by the term $x_1\bar{x}_3$. This covers all the 1s in the map except for the 1 in the square where $(x_1, x_2, x_3, x_4) = (0, 1, 0, 1)$. The largest group of 1s that includes this square is the two-square group represented by the term $x_2\bar{x}_3x_4$. Therefore the minimal expression for g_2 is

$$g_2 = \bar{x}_2\bar{x}_4 + x_1\bar{x}_3 + x_2\bar{x}_3x_4$$

Minimal expressions for the other functions shown in the figure can be derived in a similar manner. Note that in the case of g_4 there are two possible minimal expressions, one including the term $\bar{x}_1x_2x_4$ and the other including the term $\bar{x}_1\bar{x}_3x_4$. It is often the case that a given function has more than one minimal expression.

In all our examples, it is relatively easy to derive minimal expressions. In general, there are formal algorithms for this process (see references 1 through 7 in section A.16) but we will not consider them here.

A.3.2 Don't-Care Conditions

In many situations, some valuations of the inputs to a digital circuit never occur. For example, consider the binary-coded decimal (BCD) number representation. Four binary variables b_3, b_2, b_1, and b_0 represent the decimal digits 0 through 9, as shown in Figure A.6. These four variables have a total of 16 distinct valuations, only 10 of which are used for representing the decimal digits. The remaining valuations are not used. Therefore, any logic circuit that processes BCD data will never encounter any of these six valuations at its inputs.

Figure A.6 gives the truth table for a particular function that may be performed on a BCD digit. We do not care what the function values are for the unused input valuations: Hence, they are called *don't-cares* and are denoted as such by the letter "d" in the truth table. To obtain a circuit implementation, the function values corresponding to don't-care conditions can be arbitrarily assigned to be either 0 or 1. The best way to assign them is in such a manner as to lead toward a minimal logic-gate implementation. We should interpret don't-cares as 1s whenever they can be used to enlarge a group of 1s. Because larger groups correspond to smaller product terms, minimization is enhanced by the judicious inclusion of don't-care entries.

The function in Figure A.6 represents the following processing on a decimal digit input: The output f is to have the value 1 whenever the inputs represent a nonzero digit that is evenly divisible by 3. Three groups are necessary to cover the three 1s of the map, and don't-cares have been used to enlarge these groups as much as possible.

Decimal digit represented	Binary coding b_3 b_2 b_1 b_0	f
0	0 0 0 0	0
1	0 0 0 1	0
2	0 0 1 0	0
3	0 0 1 1	1
4	0 1 0 0	0
5	0 1 0 1	0
6	0 1 1 0	1
7	0 1 1 1	0
8	1 0 0 0	0
9	1 0 0 1	1
	1 0 1 0	d
	1 0 1 1	d
unused	1 1 0 0	d
	1 1 0 1	d
	1 1 1 0	d
	1 1 1 1	d

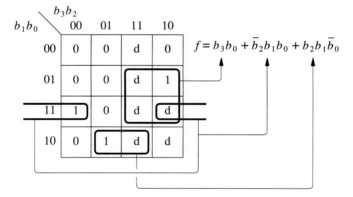

FIGURE A.6
Four-variable Karnaugh map illustrating don't-cares.

A.4 SYNTHESIS WITH NAND AND NOR GATES

We will now consider two other basic logic gates called NAND and NOR, which are extensively used in practice because of their simple electronic realizations. The truth table for these gates is shown in Figure A.7. They implement the equivalent of the AND and OR functions followed by the NOT function, which is the motivation for the names and standard logic symbols for these gates. Letting the arrows " ↑ " and " ↓ " denote the NAND and NOR operators, respectively, and using de Morgan's rule in Table A.4, we have

x_1	x_2	f
0	0	1
0	1	1
1	0	1
1	1	0

x_1	x_2	f
0	0	1
0	1	0
1	0	0
1	1	0

$$f = x_1 \uparrow x_2 = \overline{x_1 x_2} = \overline{x}_1 + \overline{x}_2$$

$$f = x_1 \downarrow x_2 = \overline{x_1 + x_2} = \overline{x}_1\, \overline{x}_2$$

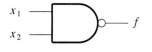

(a) NAND

(b) NOR

FIGURE A.7
NAND and NOR gates.

$$x_1 \uparrow x_2 = \overline{x_1 x_2} = \overline{x}_1 + \overline{x}_2$$

and

$$x_1 \downarrow x_2 = \overline{x_1 + x_2} = \overline{x}_1 \overline{x}_2$$

NAND and NOR gates with more than two input variables are available, and they operate according to the obvious generalization of de Morgan's law as

$$x_1 \uparrow x_2 \uparrow \cdots \uparrow x_n = \overline{x_1 x_2 \cdots x_n} = \overline{x}_1 + \overline{x}_2 + \cdots + \overline{x}_n$$

and

$$x_1 \downarrow x_2 \downarrow \cdots \downarrow x_n = \overline{x_1 + x_2 + \cdots + x_n} = \overline{x}_1 \overline{x}_2 \cdots \overline{x}_n$$

Logic design with NAND and NOR gates is not as straightforward as with AND, OR, and NOT gates. One of the main difficulties in the design process is that the associative rule is not valid for NAND and NOR operations. We will expand on this problem later. First, however, let us describe a simple, general procedure for synthesizing any logic function using only NAND gates. There is a direct way to translate a logic network expressed in sum-of-products form into an equivalent network composed only of NAND gates. The procedure is easily illustrated with the aid of an example. Consider the following algebraic manipulation of a logic expression corresponding to a four-input network composed of 3 two-input NAND gates:

$$(x_1 \uparrow x_2) \uparrow (x_3 \uparrow x_4) = \overline{(\overline{x_1 x_2})(\overline{x_3 x_4})}$$

$$= \overline{\overline{x_1 x_2} + \overline{x_3 x_4}}$$

$$= x_1 x_2 + x_3 x_4$$

We have used de Morgan's rule and the involution rule in this derivation. Figure A.8 shows the logic network equivalent of this derivation. Since any logic function can be synthesized in a sum-of-products (AND-OR) form and because the preceding derivation is obviously reversible, we have the result that any logic function can be synthesized in the NAND-NAND form. It is easily seen that this result is true for functions of any number of variables. The required number of inputs to the NAND gates is obviously the same as the number of inputs to the corresponding AND and OR gates.

Let us return to the comment that the nonassociativity of the NAND operator can be an annoyance. In designing logic networks with NAND gates using the procedure illustrated in Figure A.8, a requirement for a NAND gate with more inputs than can be found on standard commercially available gates may arise. If this happens when one is using AND and OR gates, there is no problem because the AND or OR operators are associative and a straightforward cascade of limited fan-in gates can be used. The case of implementing three-input AND and OR functions with two-input gates is shown in Figure A.9a. The solution is not as simple in the case of NAND gates. For example, a three-input NAND function cannot be implemented by a cascade of 2 two-input NAND gates. Three gates are needed, as shown in Figure A.9b.

A discussion of the implementation of logic functions using only NOR gates proceeds in a similar manner. Any logic function can be synthesized in a product-of-sums (OR-AND) form. Such networks can be implemented by equivalent NOR-NOR networks.

The above discussion introduced some basic concepts in logic design. Detailed discussion of the subject can be found in any of a number of textbooks (see references 1 through 6 in Section A.16).

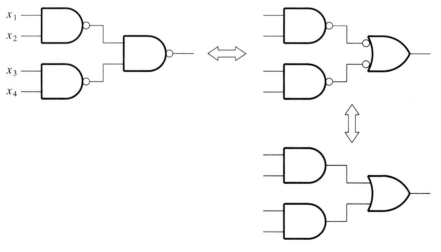

FIGURE A.8
Equivalence of NAND-NAND and AND-OR networks.

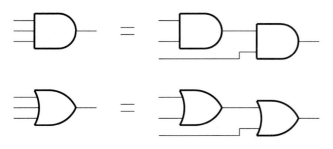

(a) Implementing 3-input AND and OR functions with 2-input gates

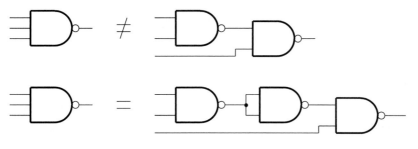

(b) Implementing a 3-input NAND function with 2-input gates

FIGURE A.9
Cascading of gates.

A.5   PRACTICAL IMPLEMENTATION OF LOGIC GATES

Let us now turn our attention to the means by which logic variables can be represented and logic functions can be implemented in practice. The choice of a physical parameter to represent logic variables is obviously technology-dependent. In electronic circuits, either voltage or current levels can be used for this purpose.

To establish a correspondence between voltage levels and logic values or states, the concept of a *threshold* may be used. Voltages above a given threshold may be taken to represent one logic value, and voltages below that threshold represent the other. In practical situations, the voltage at any point in an electronic circuit undergoes small random variations owing to a variety of reasons. Because of this "noise," the logic state corresponding to a voltage level near the threshold cannot be reliably determined. To avoid such ambiguity, a "forbidden range" should be established, as shown in Figure A.10. In this case, voltages below $V_{0,max}$ represent the 0 value, and voltages above $V_{1,min}$ represent the 1 value. In subsequent discussion, we will often use the terms "low" and "high" to represent the voltage levels corresponding to logic values 0 and 1, respectively.

Consider the circuits in Figure A.11. When switch S in Figure A.11a is closed, the output voltage V_{out} is equal to 0 (ground). On the other hand, when S is open, the

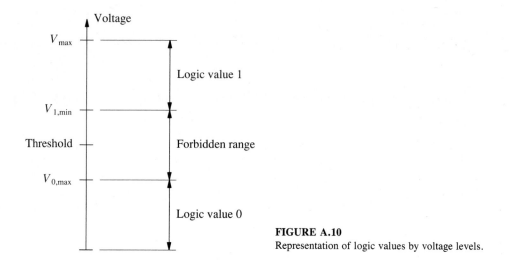

FIGURE A.10
Representation of logic values by voltage levels.

output voltage V_{out} is equal to the supply voltage. The same effect can be obtained in Figure A.11b, in which a transistor Q is used to replace the switch S. When no current is supplied to the base of the transistor (that is, when the input voltage $V_{in} = 0$), the transistor is equivalent to an open switch, and $V_{out} = V_{supply}$. As V_{in} increases, V_{out} starts to drop until V_{out} is very close to 0. The rate at which this happens is a function of the values of resistors R_1 and R_2 and the characteristics of the transistor. Through proper choice of these components, it is possible to establish the two levels $V_{1,min}$ and $V_{0,max}$ so that

$$\text{if} \qquad V_{in} \leq V_{0,max}, \qquad \text{then} \qquad V_{out} > V_{1,min}$$

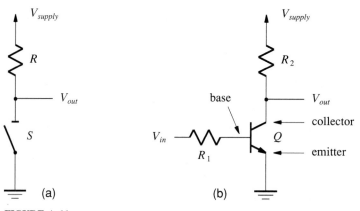

FIGURE A.11
An inverter circuit.

and

$$\text{if} \quad V_{in} \geq V_{1,min}, \qquad \text{then} \qquad V_{out} < V_{0,max}$$

Under these conditions, the circuit performs the function of a logic NOT gate.

We can now discuss the implementation of more complex logic functions. Figure A.12 shows a circuit realization for a NOR gate. In this case, V_{out} in Figure A.12a is high only when both switches S_a and S_b are open. Similarly, V_{out} in Figure A.12b is high only when both inputs V_a and V_b are low. Thus the circuit is equivalent to a NOR gate in which V_a and V_b correspond to two logic variables x_1 and x_2. It is easily verified that a NAND gate can be obtained by connecting the transistors as shown in Figure A.13. The logic functions AND and OR can be implemented by using NAND and NOR gates, respectively, followed by the inverter of Figure A.11. The circuits of Figures A.11 to A.13 form a "logic family" that is generally referred to as *resistor-transistor logic* (RTL).

It is interesting to note that in the RTL family, NAND and NOR gates are simpler in their circuit implementation than AND and OR gates. It will be seen shortly that the same applies to most other logic families, with the notable exception of emitter-coupled logic. Hence, it is not surprising to find that practical realizations of logic functions use NAND and NOR gates extensively. Many of the examples given in this book show circuits consisting of AND, OR, and NOT gates for ease of understanding. In practice, logic circuits contain all five types of gates.

A.5.1 Logic Families

The RTL circuits of Figures A.11 to A.13 are very simple. Their use, however, is subject to limitations arising from their electrical characteristics. A number of other logic families have been developed to overcome these limitations. Of course, all

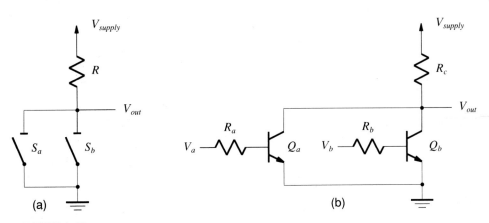

FIGURE A.12
A transistor circuit implementation for a NOR gate.

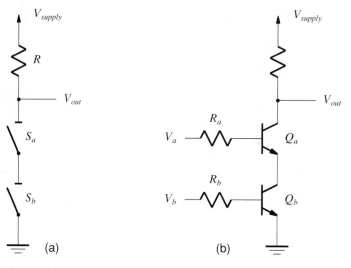

FIGURE A.13
A transistor circuit implementation of a NAND gate.

logic families perform the same logic functions: They differ only in their electrical and physical characteristics. Although we do not intend to study these characteristics in detail, we will present a summary of those parameters that affect the choice of the logic family to be used in a given application.

Circuits belonging to different logic families exhibit a number of trade-offs among three basic properties: speed, power, and packaging density. Speed is measured by the rate at which state changes can take place at the output of any logic gate. A related parameter is the *propagation delay*, which is defined in Figure A.14. When a state change takes place at a gate input, a delay is encountered before the corresponding change at the gate output is observed. This propagation delay is usually measured between the 50 percent points of the transitions, as defined in the figure. Another important parameter is the *transition time*, which is normally measured between the 10 and 90 percent points on the waveform, as shown. The maximum speed at which a logic circuit can be operated decreases as the propagation delay through different paths within that circuit increases. The delay along any path is the sum of individual gate delays along this path.

Power consumption is the next parameter in the characterization of logic families. High power consumption requires complex and costly packaging to enable dissipation of the heat produced. The cost of the power supply is also increased. Power consumption is particularly significant in the case of *very large-scale integration* (VLSI). This is the case when a logic subsystem consisting of a large number of gates is fabricated on a single integrated circuit chip.

For a general circuit configuration such as the one in Figure A.11, it is possible to obtain a number of designs that differ in their speed and power characteristics. However, as the speed capability increases, so will the power consumption. Roughly,

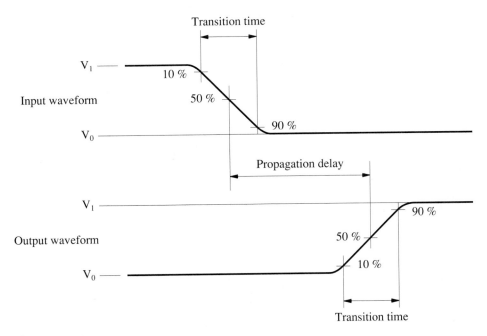

FIGURE A.14
Definition of propagation delay and transition time.

the product of power dissipation per gate and propagation delay remains constant for a given logic family technology. This power-delay product is often used as a figure of merit that describes the capabilities of a given technology.

In addition to the basic characteristics presented above, other important properties should be taken into consideration when comparing logic families. These include the following:

Noise immunity, which refers to the ability to reject interference from neighboring circuits

Drive requirement, which is the electrical load presented by a gate input to the circuit preceding it (for example, the input current in the circuit of Figure A.11)

Drive capability, which is the maximum amount of current that can be drawn from a gate output without serious degradation of its performance

The combination of drive requirement and drive capability determines two important parameters:

Fan-in, which is the maximum number of inputs that a logic gate can have

Fan-out, which is the maximum number of gates that can be driven from the output of a single gate

With the preceding considerations in mind, we shall now present a review of some of the commonly used logic families.

TRANSISTOR-TRANSISTOR LOGIC (TTL). A TTL configuration for a NAND gate is shown in Figure A.15a. To understand the operation of this gate, let us consider the circuit of Figure A.15b. This circuit belongs to an earlier logic family known as *diode-transistor logic* (DTL). First consider the case when the two inputs V_a and V_b are high. Because a diode conducts current only in the forward direction, no appreciable

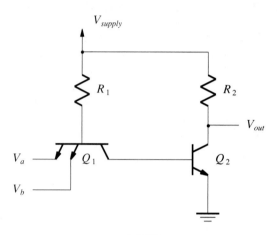

(a) TTL

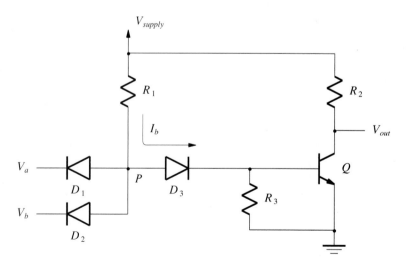

(b) DTL

FIGURE A.15
TTL and DTL NAND gates.

current flows through D_1 or D_2. Diode D_3, however, is forward-biased and allows a current I_b to flow to the base of transistor Q. Thus Q is turned on, and V_{out} is close to ground, indicating a logic value of 0. If either V_a or V_b drops to the 0 state, the corresponding diode starts to conduct. This causes the voltage at point P to drop to a value below that required to maintain the flow of I_b. Thus transistor Q turns off, and V_{out} rises to the supply voltage. In other words, this circuit performs the NAND function.

When the above DTL circuit is implemented in an integrated circuit form, the three diodes D_1, D_2, and D_3 can be combined to form transistor Q_1 of Figure A.15a, reducing the chip area required for the gate. This also leads to an improvement in performance because of the higher speed with which transistor Q_2 can be changed from the on to the off state. Detailed discussion of these properties can be found in texts on electronics, such as references 8 and 9 in section A.16. The logic family based on the circuit configuration of Figure A.15a is referred to as *transistor-transistor logic*.

To enhance the output drive capability of the circuit of Figure A.15a and hence to improve the fan-out, a driver stage is usually added. This yields the standard TTL circuit configuration given in Figure A.16. The output stage contains two transistors, Q_3 and Q_4. When the output is in the 0 state, transistor Q_3 is off, and transistor Q_4 is

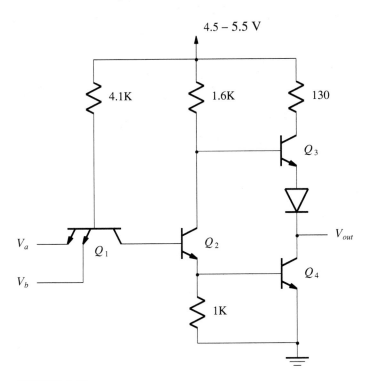

FIGURE A.16
A standard TTL NAND gate.

on. Conversely, when the output is in the 1 state, Q_3 is on, and Q_4 is off. This allows higher load currents to be handled without excessive power dissipation or reduction in speed.

The 0 and 1 voltage levels for the TTL logic family are defined in Figure A.17. It is important to note that the values of $V_{0,max}$ and $V_{1,min}$ defined earlier are different for the input and output sides of the gate. This is necessary to guarantee that the output of a gate will not lie within the forbidden range of the input to the next gate, even in the presence of a small amount of noise. The difference between the corresponding levels for the input and output defines the *noise margins* for the logic family. In the case of TTL, the noise margin for both the 0 and 1 states is 0.4 V.

The TTL logic family has been the workhorse in computer and logic applications for a long time. Many variations of the circuit in Figure A.16 have evolved for low-power or high-speed applications. One important variation is known as low-power Schottky TTL. It uses Schottky transistors, which are characterized by very short turn-off time (transistor turn-off time is the limiting factor for the speed of standard TTL). This circuit combines low power and high speed and is particularly suited for VLSI applications. It has a typical propagation delay of 8 ns and power dissipation of 4 mW (milliwatts) per gate. The corresponding values for standard TTL are 10 ns and 10 mW.

COMPLEMENTARY METAL-OXIDE SEMICONDUCTOR (CMOS) LOGIC. Numerous logic families have been developed using metal-oxide semiconductor (MOS) transistors instead of the bipolar transistors used in TTL. For the purposes of this review, the reader need not be concerned with the differences between various types of transistors. Interested readers may consult references 8 and 9 in section A.16. Depending on the manufacturing process, MOS transistors are known as either p- or n-channel transistors. In general, MOS circuits operate at lower speeds in comparison with bipolar circuits. Their major advantage, however, is that they are well-

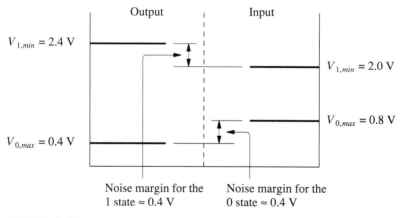

FIGURE A.17
TTL logic levels.

suited to VLSI. Logic families based on either p- or n-channel transistors are extensively used in VLSI applications. Important examples of this are the memory and microprocessor chips discussed in Chapters 8 and 10.

A logic family that combines p- and n-channel MOS transistors on the same chip is known as the *complementary MOS* or CMOS family. The circuit configuration for a CMOS inverter is given in Figure A.18b. Operation of this inverter circuit is similar to operation of the circuit in Figure A.18a, in which the two switches S_1 and S_2 are linked so that switch S_2 is open when switch S_1 is closed, and vice versa. In the CMOS circuit, when V_{in} is high, the n-channel transistor is on and the p-channel transistor is off. Thus the output terminal is at 0 V. As the input voltage changes from high to low, the p-channel transistor starts to conduct and the n-channel transistor turns off, causing V_{out} to rise to the supply voltage. Extension of this circuit to obtain NAND and NOR functions is straightforward. A NOR gate is illustrated in Figure A.19.

Advantages of CMOS logic circuits include high noise immunity and low power consumption. The noise immunity occurs because the noise margin for the basic inverter circuit of Figure A.18 is roughly equal to a third of the supply voltage. With V_{supply} in the range of 3.5 to 15 V, the noise margin is in the range of 1 to 5 V. The low power of CMOS circuits can be appreciated by inspection of Figure A.18. Consider first the case in which V_{in} is held near either 0 or V_{supply}. In either case one of the two transistors is in the nonconducting mode, so no significant flow of current takes place from the power supply to ground. Only a very small amount of "leakage" current exists, thus leading to very low power dissipation. While switching between the two logic states, however, there is a short period of time when both transistors are in the conducting mode. This causes a short current pulse to be observed at the power supply, associated with every change of state. Therefore, power dissipation in CMOS circuits is dependent on the rate at which state changes take place. In fact,

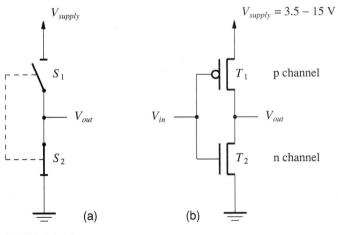

FIGURE A.18
A CMOS inverter.

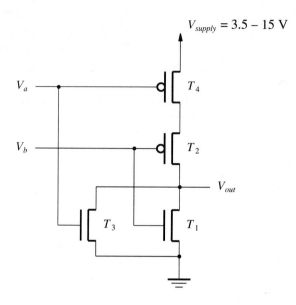

FIGURE A.19
A two-input CMOS NOR gate.

it increases linearly with the frequency of operation. At 1 MHz, power dissipation is about 1 mW per gate. In comparison with TTL, a considerable saving in power is achieved up to frequencies of a few megahertz. Propagation delay for CMOS gates is in the range of 25 to 100 ns.

In addition to regular CMOS circuits, a high-performance class of such circuits exists, known as *high-speed CMOS*. These circuits have a gate propagation delay of 8ns. Their power dissipation is about 1mW per gate at a frequency of 20 MHz.

EMITTER-COUPLED LOGIC (ECL). This logic family provides the highest-speed logic devices that are presently commercially available. ECL gates have propagation delays of the order of 1 or 2 ns. The basic configuration of an ECL NOT gate is illustrated in Figure A.20. In this figure, current flows from the ground terminal to a negative power supply. Operation of the circuit can be described as follows. When the input voltage V_{in} is below the fixed reference voltage V_{ref}, transistor Q_2 is in the conducting mode and transistor Q_1 is turned off. Thus a current I flows through resistor R_2. When V_{in} rises above V_{ref}, the situation is reversed, causing the same current I to flow through R_1. Only a small change in V_{in}, of the order of a few tenths of a volt, is required for this change of state to take place. As V_{in} rises from its low state (V_L) to its high state (V_H), the voltage at point P drops from 0 to $-IR_1$. A simple voltage-level-shifting network produces output voltages of V_H and V_L when point P is at 0 and $-IR_1$, respectively.

In summary, state changes in the circuit of Figure A.20 take place by "steering" the current I from one branch of the circuit to the other. This is in contrast to switching the supply current on and off in the RTL and TTL families. The use of current steering and the attendant low-voltage changes are the main reasons for the high speed of ECL

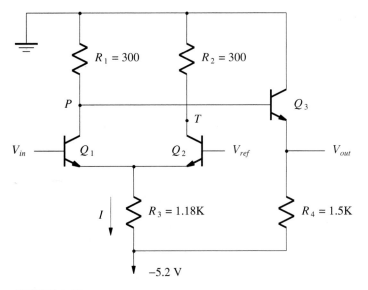

FIGURE A.20
An ECL logic inverter.

logic. We should note, however, that this is accomplished at the expense of increased power consumption. For a 2-ns gate, power dissipation is about 25 mW.

The logic levels for the ECL family are as follows.

Output: $V_{1,min} = -0.850$ V
$V_{0,max} = -1.500$ V

Input: $V_{1,min} = -1.025$ V
$V_{0,max} = -1.325$ V

Therefore the noise margin for both the 0 and 1 states is 0.175 V.

It is interesting to note that the state of point T in the circuit of Figure A.20 is always the complement of the state of point P. Thus, at the small expense of an extra level-shifting network, both the output and its complement can be made available. This is illustrated in Figure A.21, which gives the organization of an ECL OR-NOR circuit. The two outputs are represented symbolically as shown in the figure.

A comparison of the three logic families presented in this brief review is given in Table A.5.

A.5.2 Integrated Circuit Packages

Individual logic gates are commercially available in integrated circuit (IC) form. An IC chip is mounted inside a sealed protective package, which has a number

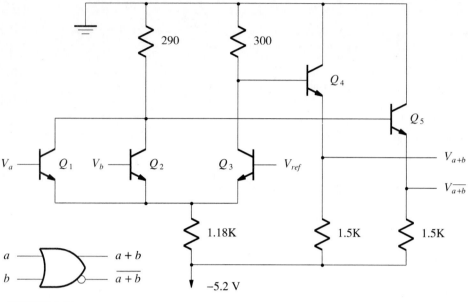

FIGURE A.21
An ECL OR-NOR gate.

of metallic pins for external connections. Standard IC packages are available with different numbers of pins. A typical package containing four NAND gates is shown in Figure A.22. The four gates utilize common power supply and ground pins. Such ICs comprising only a few logic gates are referred to as *small-scale integrated* (SSI) circuits.

We should note that the speed and power dissipation figures given in this section apply to gates in SSI form. In any VLSI implementation, these figures can be considerably smaller. Moreover, they may vary from gate to gate depending upon size and geometry.

TABLE A.5 Comparison of logic families

Logic family	Typical gate delay, ns	Power dissipation, mw	Propagation delay-power product, pJ
RTL	12	12	144
Standard TTL	10	10	100
Low-power TTL	33	1	33
Schottky TTL	4	35	140
Low-power Schottky TTL	8	4	32
CMOS (regular)	70	1 (at 1 MHz)	70
CMOS (high speed)	8	1 (at 20 MHz)	8
ECL	2	25	50

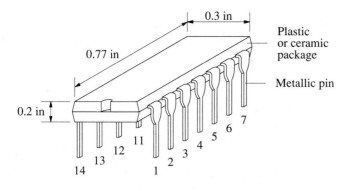

(a) Physical appearance

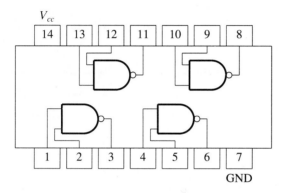

(b) Schematic of an integrated circuit providing four 2-input NAND gates

FIGURE A.22
A 14-pin dual in-line integrated circuit package (DIP).

A.6 FLIP-FLOPS

In the majority of applications of digital logic, there is a need for storing information. For example, in the familiar problem of a combination lock, it is necessary to remember the sequence in which the digits are dialed in order to decide whether to open the lock. Another important example is the storage of programs and data in the memory of a digital computer.

The basic electronic element for storing binary information is termed a *flip-flop*. Consider the two cross-coupled NOR gates in Figure A.23*a*. Let us examine this circuit, starting with the situation in which R $= 1$ and S $= 0$. Simple analysis shows that $Q_a = 0$ and $Q_b = 1$. Under this condition, both inputs to gate G_a are equal to 1. Thus if R is changed to 0, no change will take place at the outputs Q_a and Q_b. If S is set to 1 with R equal to 0, Q_a and Q_b will become 1 and 0, respectively, and will remain in this state after S is returned to 0. Hence this logic circuit constitutes a memory element, or a flip-flop, that remembers which of the two inputs S and R

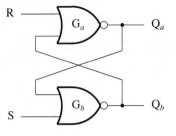

S	R	Q_a	Q_b
0	0	0/1	1/0
0	1	0	1
1	0	1	0
1	1	0	0

(a) Network   (b) Truth table

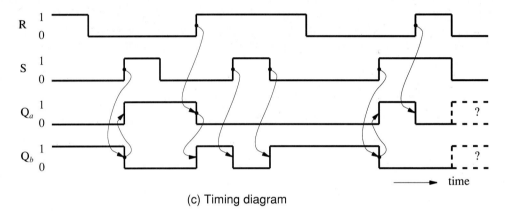

(c) Timing diagram

FIGURE A.23
An RS flip-flop.

was most recently equal to 1. A truth table for this flip-flop is given in Figure A.23*b*. Some typical waveforms that characterize the flip-flop are shown in Figure A.23*c*. The arrows in Figure A.23*c* indicate the cause-effect relationships among the signals. Note that when both the R and S inputs change from 1 to 0 at the same time, the resulting state is undefined. In practice, the flip-flop will assume one of its two stable states at random. The input valuation $R = S = 1$ is not used in most applications of RS flip-flops.

Because of the nature of operation of the above circuit, the S and R lines are referred to as the *set* and *reset* inputs, and Q_a and Q_b are usually represented by Q and $\overline{Q}$, respectively. Furthermore, the circuit is called an *RS flip-flop*. We should note that in this context, $\overline{Q}$ should be regarded merely as a symbol representing the second output of the flip-flop rather than as the complement of Q, because the input valuation $R = S = 1$ yields $Q = \overline{Q} = 0$.

A.6.1 Clocked Flip-Flops

Many applications require that the time at which a flip-flop is set or reset be controlled from an input other than R and S, termed a *clock* input. The resulting configuration is called a *clocked RS flip-flop*. A logic circuit and characteristic waveforms for such a flip-flop are given in Figure A.24. When the clock Cl is equal to 1, points S' and R' follow the inputs S and R, respectively. On the other hand, when $Cl = 0$, the S' and R' points are equal to 0, and no change in the state of the flip-flop can take place.

In technical literature, the basic storage element consisting of two cross-coupled NOR gates, such as the one in Figure A.23a, is often called a *latch*. The term flip-flop is then used to denote a circuit in which a clock input is included, such as the one in Figure A.24a.

So far we have used truth tables to describe the behavior of logic circuits. A truth table gives the output of a network for various input valuations. Logic circuits whose outputs are uniquely defined for each input valuation are referred to as *combinational circuits*. This is the class of circuits discussed in Sections A.1 to A.4. When memory elements are present, a different class of circuits is obtained. The output of such circuits is a function not only of the present valuation of the input variables but also

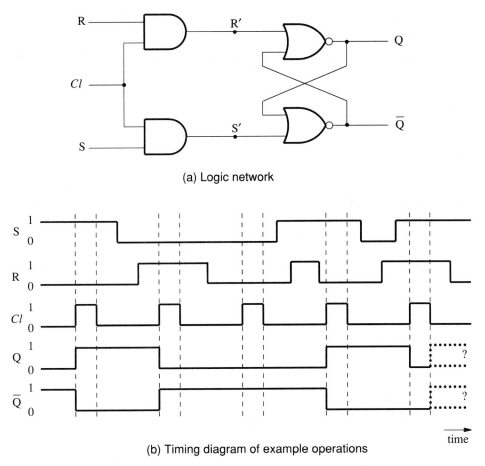

(a) Logic network

(b) Timing diagram of example operations

FIGURE A.24
Clocked RS flip-flop.

TABLE A.6 Truth table for a clocked RS flip-flop

S	R	Q_{n+1}
0	0	Q_n (no change in state)
0	1	0
1	0	1
1	1	X (undefined)

of their previous behavior. An example of this is shown in Figure A.23. These types of circuits are called *sequential circuits*.

Because of the memory property of a flip-flop, a flip-flop's truth table should be modified to show the effect of its present state. Table A.6 describes the behavior of the clocked RS flip-flop, where Q_n denotes its present state. The transition to the next state, Q_{n+1}, occurs at a clock pulse time. Note that the state following a clock pulse with the input valuation $S = R = 1$ is shown as undefined for reasons discussed earlier.

A second type of flip-flop, called the *D flip-flop*, is given in Figure A.25. In this case, the two signals S and R are derived from a single input D. At a clock pulse, the Q output is set to 1 if $D = 1$ or is reset to 0 if $D = 0$. This means that the D flip-flop samples the D input at the time the clock is high and stores that information until a subsequent clock pulse arrives.

A.6.2 Master-Slave and Edge-Triggered Flip-Flops

In the circuit of Figure A.24 we assumed that while $Cl = 1$, the inputs S and R do not change. Inspection of the circuit reveals that the outputs will respond immediately to any change in the S or R inputs during this time. Similarly, for the circuit of Figure A.25, $Q = D$ while $Cl = 1$. This is undesirable in many cases, particularly in circuits involving counters and shift registers, which will be discussed later. In

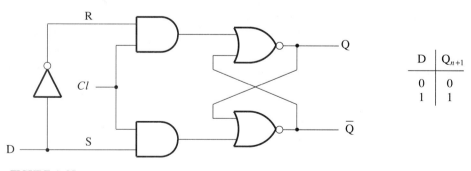

FIGURE A.25
D flip-flop.

such circuits, immediate propagation of logic conditions from the data inputs (R, S, or D) to the flip-flop outputs may lead to incorrect operation. The concept of a *master-slave* organization eliminates this problem. Two flip-flops can be connected to form a master-slave RS flip-flop, as shown in Figure A.26a. The first, referred to as the master, is connected to the input lines when $Cl = 1$. A 1 to 0 transition of the clock isolates the master from the input and transfers the contents of the master stage to the slave stage. The thresholds at which logic transitions occur in particular gates are arranged as shown in Figure A.26b. It is easily seen that no direct path ever exists from the inputs to the outputs.

It should be noted that while $Cl = 1$, the state of the master stage is immediately affected by changes in the inputs S and R. The function of the slave stage is to hold the output of the flip-flop while the master stage is being set up to the next-state value determined by the S and R inputs. In most applications, this means that the S and R inputs should have reached the correct levels for determining the next state before the 0 to 1 transition on Cl and should hold these levels while $Cl = 1$. The new state is then transferred from the master to the slave after the 1 to 0 transition on Cl. At this point, the master stage has been isolated from the inputs so that further changes in the S and R inputs will not affect this transfer. The master-stage outputs Q' and $\overline{Q}'$ are the slave-stage inputs S' and R', respectively, as shown in the figure. Examples of state transitions for various S and R input combinations are shown in Figure A.26c.

Another very useful type of flip-flop is the *JK flip-flop*. A truth table defining its operation is given in Table A.7. The first three entries in this table exhibit the same behavior as those in Table A.6, so that J and K correspond to S and R. For the input valuation $J = K = 1$, the next state is defined as the complement of the present state of the flip-flop. That is, when $J = K = 1$, the flip-flop functions as a *toggle*, or a modulo-2 counter. A JK flip-flop can be implemented using an RS flip-flop connected such that

$$S = J\overline{Q} \quad \text{and} \quad R = KQ$$

This means that feedback connections are required from the outputs Q and $\overline{Q}$ to the inputs R and S. It is important, therefore, that the flip-flop does not allow input changes to be propagated immediately to the output. Otherwise, a steady state can never be reached when $J = K = 1$, because a change in the output causes a change in the input. This leads to a further change in the output, and so on. In other words, the circuit will oscillate. A master-slave organization can be used to guarantee proper operation. Figure A.27a gives an implementation of a master-slave JK flip-flop derived

TABLE A.7 Truth table for a JK flip-flop

J	K	Q_{n+1}
0	0	Q_n
0	1	0
1	0	1
1	1	$\overline{Q}_n$

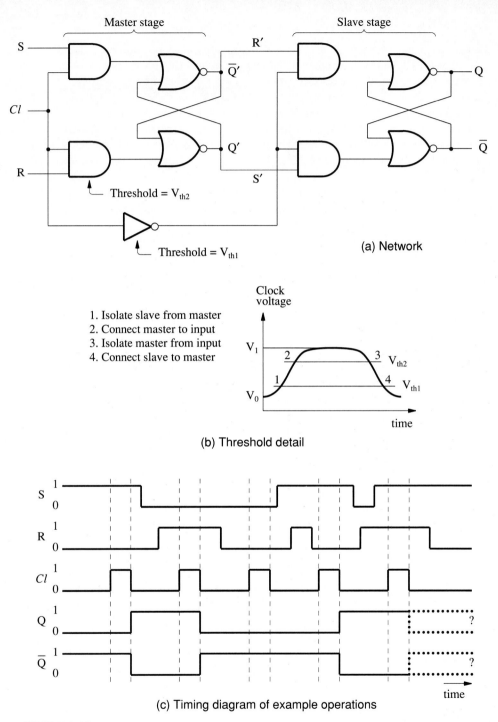

(a) Network

1. Isolate slave from master
2. Connect master to input
3. Isolate master from input
4. Connect slave to master

(b) Threshold detail

(c) Timing diagram of example operations

FIGURE A.26
Master-slave RS flip-flop.

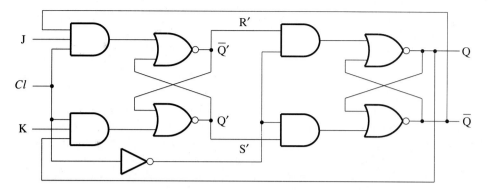

(a) Implementation of a JK flip-flop from a master-slave RS flip-flop

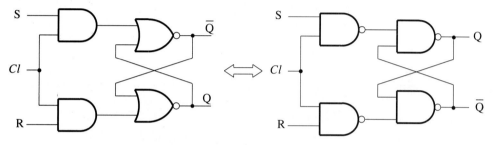

(b) NAND gate implementation of a clocked RS flip-flop

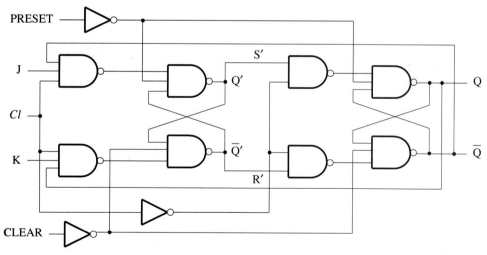

(c) NAND gate implementation of a JK flip-flop

FIGURE A.27
Master-slave JK flip-flops.

by adding the appropriate feedback connections to the master-slave RS flip-flop shown in Figure A.26. The remainder of Figure A.27 shows how a JK flip-flop can be constructed using NAND gates only. Figure A.27b illustrates the implementation of a clocked RS flip-flop using NAND gates. The reader should verify that the NAND network operates as desired. Figure A.27c shows how two NAND gate flip-flops can be used to implement the JK flip-flop. Two additional control inputs are shown in this implementation. These are PRESET and CLEAR, which force the flip-flop into the 1 or 0 state, respectively, independent of the J, K, and Cl inputs. When both PRESET and CLEAR inputs are equal to 0, the flip-flop is controlled by the other inputs in the normal way. When PRESET = 1, the flip-flop is forced to the 1 state; and when CLEAR = 1, the flip-flop is forced to the 0 state. These additional controls are also often incorporated in the other flip-flop types.

A slightly different approach to the control of data transfer from the input to the output of a flip-flop is known as *edge-triggering*. In this case, data present at the input are transferred to the output only at a transition in the clock signal. The input and output are isolated from each other at all other times. The terms "leading (positive) edge-triggered" and "trailing (negative) edge-triggered" describe flip-flops in which data transfer takes place at the 0 to 1 and 1 to 0 clock transitions. For proper operation, edge-triggered flip-flops require the triggering edge of the clock pulse to be well-defined and to have a very short transition time. An example of a *negative edge-triggered D flip-flop* is given in Figure A.28a.

Let us consider the operation of this flip-flop. If $Cl = 1$, the outputs of gates 2 and 3 are both 0. Therefore the flip-flop outputs Q and $\overline{Q}$ maintain the current state of the flip-flop. It is easy to verify that during this period, points P3 and P4 immediately respond to changes at D. P3 is kept equal to $\overline{D}$, and P4 is maintained at D. When Cl drops to 0, these values are transmitted to P1 and P2 by gates 2 and 3, respectively. Thus the output latch, consisting of gates 5 and 6, acquires the new state to be stored.

We now verify that while $Cl = 0$, further changes at D do not change points P1 and P2. Consider two cases. First, suppose D $= 0$ at the trailing edge of Cl. The 1 at P2 maintains an input of 1 at each of the gates 2 and 4, holding P1 and P2 at 0 and 1, independent of further changes in D. Second, suppose D $= 1$ at the trailing edge of Cl. The 1 at P1 means that further changes at D cannot affect the output of gate 1, which is maintained at 0.

When Cl goes to 1 at the start of the next clock pulse, points P1 and P2 are again forced to 0, isolating the output from the remainder of the circuit. Points P3 and P4 then follow changes at D, as we have previously described.

An example of the operation of this type of D flip-flop is shown in Figure A.28b. The state acquired by the flip-flop upon the 1 to 0 transition of Cl is equal to the value on the D input immediately preceding this transition. However, there is a critical time period T_{CR} around the trailing edge of Cl during which the value on D should not change. This region is split into two parts, the *setup time* before the clock edge and the *hold time* after the clock edge as shown in the figure.

Other flip-flop types are available in the edge-triggered configuration, but we will not discuss any of their details.

We have introduced a number of flip-flop configurations that differ in their data input and clock requirements. The data input can take the form of RS, D, and JK

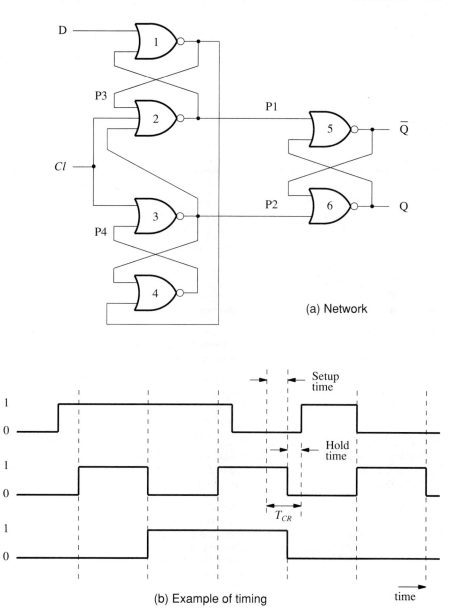

(a) Network

(b) Example of timing

FIGURE A.28
A negative edge-triggered D flip-flop.

inputs. Clocking may consist of simple input gating, edge-triggering, or a master-slave arrangement. This gives considerable flexibility in the choice of a particular type of flip-flop for a given application. In general, the input configuration is chosen to simplify any external logic circuitry that may be required. Choice of the clocking arrangement is dependent upon the timing constraints.

Flip-flops are available in IC form with two or four flip-flops to a package. The number of flip-flops in a package is limited by the number of pins available, which is either 14 or 16 for SSI circuits. A variety of ICs are also available that contain a number of gates and flip-flops connected to implement small logic subsystems. Such ICs represent *medium-scale integration* (MSI). Some examples of MSI circuits will be given in the following sections.

A.7   REGISTERS

Individual flip-flops can be used to store a few bits. However, in machines in which data are handled in words consisting of many bits (perhaps as many as 64), it is more convenient to have larger devices capable of holding several bits of data. Such devices are usually called *registers*. The simplest form of a register in a single IC package consists of a few flip-flops whose operations are synchronized by a common clock signal. A 24-pin MSI package may have as many as 10 D-type flip-flops.

The number of pins in an IC package is often the factor that determines the number of circuits that can be usefully included on an IC chip. If a register consists of individual flip-flops and if each flip-flop needs a certain number of input and output connections, then it is apparent that pin limitation constrains the size of the register. An interesting and useful alternative is to put more than one register on a single chip, sharing some of the external connections. Thus a "register file" is obtained that contains an array of flip-flops organized into several register sections. A typical configuration may involve four 4-bit sections, or perhaps eight 2-bit sections. The chip must obviously have some inputs that can select the desired section. Such register files provide economical means for the implementation of general-purpose registers in computers. We should note that the concept of register files is readily extendable to larger-scale circuits, where they in effect become full-fledged memory chips that may store thousands of bits of data. Of course, the access circuitry in memory chips is considerably more complex. See Chapter 8 for details.

A.8   SHIFT REGISTERS

Processing of digital data often requires the capability to shift and rotate the data, so it is necessary to provide the hardware with this facility. A simple mechanism for realizing both operations is to devise a register whose contents may be shifted to the

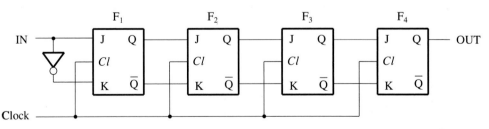

FIGURE A.29
A simple shift register.

right or left one bit position at a time. As an example, consider the 4-bit shift register in Figure A.29. It consists of JK flip-flops connected so that each clock pulse will cause transfer of the contents (state) of F_i to F_{i+1}, thus effecting a "right shift." Data is shifted serially into and out of the register.

Proper operation of a shift register requires that its contents be shifted exactly one position for each clock pulse. This places a constraint on the type of flip-flops that can be used. Flip-flops that have simple input gating, as in Figures A.24 or A.25, are not suitable for this purpose. While the clock is high, the data applied to the input of these flip-flops quickly propagate to its output. From there, the data propagate through the next flip-flop in the same manner. Hence there is no control over the number of shifts that will take place during a single clock pulse. This number depends on the propagation delays of the flip-flops and the duration of the clock pulse. The solution to the problem is the use of either the master-slave or the edge-triggered flip-flops described in Section A.6.2. In the remainder of this appendix we will assume that one of these two types is used.

A particularly useful form of a shift register is one that can be loaded and read in parallel. This can be accomplished with some additional gating as illustrated in Figure A.30, which shows a 4-bit register constructed with RS flip-flops. The register can be

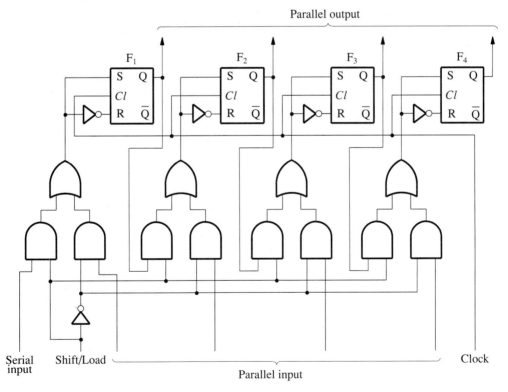

FIGURE A.30
Parallel-access shift register.

loaded either serially or in parallel. When the register is clocked, a shift takes place if Shift/Load $= 1$; otherwise, a parallel load is performed.

Shift registers of this type are commercially available in many different configurations. In addition to providing the shifting in one direction, some extra logic can be added to provide the ability to shift in the opposite direction as well. One readily finds shift-register chips that allow parallel data access and shifting in either direction.

A.9 COUNTERS

In the preceding section we discussed the applicability of flip-flops in the construction of shift registers. They are equally useful in the implementation of *counter* circuits. It is hardly necessary to justify the need for counters in digital machines. In addition to being hardware mechanisms for realizing ordinary counting functions, counters are also used to generate control and timing signals. A counter driven by a high-frequency clock can be used to produce signals whose frequencies are submultiples of the original clock frequency. In such applications a counter is said to be functioning as a *scaler*.

A simple four-stage (or 4-bit) counter constructed with JK flip-flops is given in Figure A.31. Recall that when the J and K inputs are both equal to 1, the flip-flop acts as a toggle; that is, its state changes with each successive clock pulse. Thus two

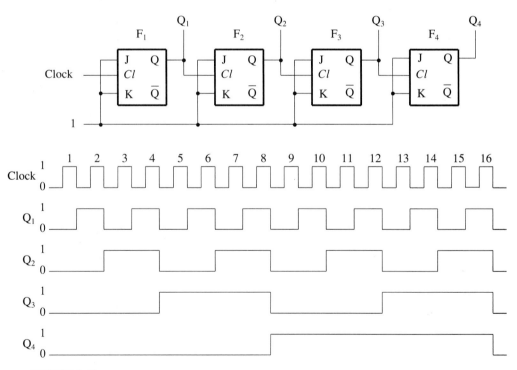

FIGURE A.31
A four-stage counter and associated signal waveforms.

clock pulses will cause F_1 to change from the 1 state into the 0 state and back into the 1 state or from 0 to 1 to 0. This means that the output waveform of F_1, denoted in the figure as Q_1, has half the frequency of the clock. Similarly, because F_2 is driven by the output of F_1, the waveform at Q_2 has half the frequency of Q_1, or one-fourth the frequency of the clock. Note that we have assumed that the trailing edge of the clock input to each flip-flop triggers the change of its state.

The above counter is often called a "ripple" counter because the effect of an input clock pulse ripples through the counter. For example, the trailing edge of pulse 8 will change the state of F_1 from 1 to 0. This change in Q_1 will then force Q_2 from 1 to 0. Next, Q_3 is changed from 1 to 0, which in turn forces Q_4 from 0 to 1. If each flip-flop introduces some delay Δ, then the delay in setting Q_4 is 4Δ. Such delays can be a problem when very fast operation of counter circuits is required. In many applications, however, they are small in comparison with the length of the clock pulses and can be neglected.

With the addition of some extra logic gates, it is possible to construct a "synchronous" counter in which each stage is under the control of the common clock so that all flip-flops can change their states simultaneously. Such counters are capable of operation at higher speed because the total propagation delay is reduced considerably.

A.10   DECODERS

Much of the information in computers is handled in a highly encoded form. In an instruction, an n-bit field may be used to denote 1 out of 2^n possible choices for the action to be taken. To perform the desired action, the encoded instruction must first be decoded. A circuit capable of accepting an n-variable input and generating the corresponding output signal on one out of 2^n output lines is called a *decoder*. A simple example of a two-input to four-output decoder is given in Figure A.32. One

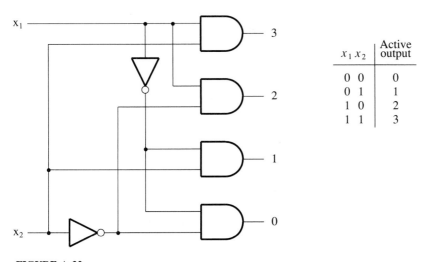

$x_1 \, x_2$	Active output
0 0	0
0 1	1
1 0	2
1 1	3

FIGURE A.32
A two-input to four-output decoder.

No.	x_1	x_2	x_3	x_4	a	b	c	d	e	f	g
0	0	0	0	0	1	1	1	1	1	1	0
1	0	0	0	1	0	1	1	0	0	0	0
2	0	0	1	0	1	1	0	1	1	0	1
3	0	0	1	1	1	1	1	1	0	0	1
4	0	1	0	0	0	1	1	0	0	1	1
5	0	1	0	1	1	0	1	1	0	1	1
6	0	1	1	0	1	0	1	1	1	1	1
7	0	1	1	1	1	1	1	0	0	0	0
8	1	0	0	0	1	1	1	1	1	1	1
9	1	0	0	1	1	1	1	1	0	1	1

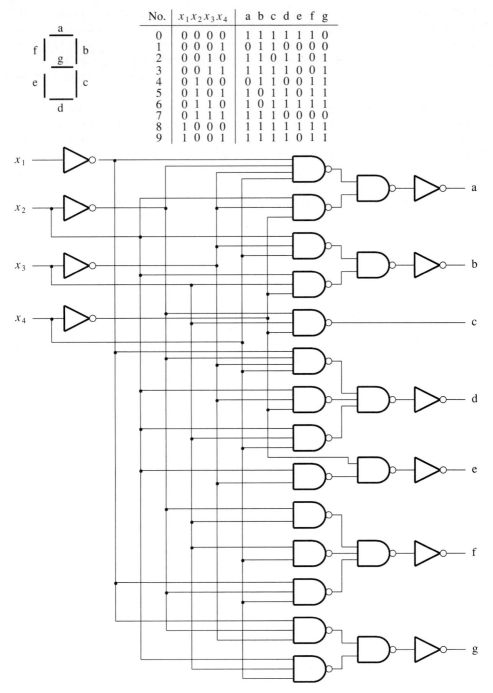

FIGURE A.33
A BCD to seven-segment display decoder.

of the four output lines is selected by the inputs x_1 and x_2, as indicated in the figure. The selected output has the logic value 1, and the remaining outputs have the value 0.

So far, we have considered only the simplest kind of decoders, but many others exist. For example, using information in BCD form often requires decoding circuits in which a four-variable BCD input is used to select 1 out of 10 possible outputs. As another specific example let us consider a decoder suitable for driving a seven-segment display. Figure A.33 shows the structure of a seven-segment element used for display purposes. It is easily seen that any decimal number from zero to nine can be displayed with this element simply by turning some segments on (light), while leaving others off (dark). The necessary functions are indicated in the table. They can be realized using the decoding circuit shown in the figure. Note that the circuit is constructed with NAND gates. We encourage the reader to verify that the circuit indeed implements the required functions.

A.11 MULTIPLEXERS

In the preceding section we saw that decoders select one output line on the basis of input signals. The selected output line has a logic value 1, while the other outputs have the value 0. Another class of very useful selector circuits exists, in which any one of n inputs can be selected to appear as the output. The choice is governed by a set of "select" inputs. Such circuits are called *multiplexers*. An example of a multiplexer circuit is shown in Figure A.34. It has two select inputs, w_1 and w_2. Their four possible valuations are used to select one of four inputs, x_1, x_2, x_3, or x_4, so that the selected input appears as the output z. A simple logic circuit that can implement the required operation is also given. Obviously, the same structure can be used to realize larger multiplexers, in which k select inputs are used to connect one of the 2^k data inputs to the output.

The obvious application of multiplexers is in the gating of data that may come from a number of different sources. For example, loading a 16-bit data register loaded from one of four distinct sources can be accomplished with 16 four-input multiplexers that come in eight IC packages.

Multiplexers are also very useful as basic elements for implementing logic functions. Consider a function f defined by the truth table of Figure A.35. It can be represented as shown in the figure by factoring out the variables x_1 and x_2. Note that for each valuation of x_1 and x_2, the function f corresponds to one of four terms: 0, 1, x_3, or $\overline{x}_3$. This suggests the possibility of using a four-input multiplexer circuit, in which x_1 and x_2 are the two select inputs that choose one of the four data inputs. Then, if the data inputs are connected to 0, 1, x_3, or $\overline{x}_3$ as required by the truth table, the output of the multiplexer will correspond to the function f. The approach is completely general. Any function of three variables can be realized with a single four-input multiplexer. Similarly, any function of four variables can be implemented with an eight-input multiplexer, and so on.

Using multiplexers in this fashion is a straightforward approach that often reduces the total number of ICs needed to realize a given function. If the function of Figure A.35 is constructed with AND, OR, and NOT gates, its minimal form is

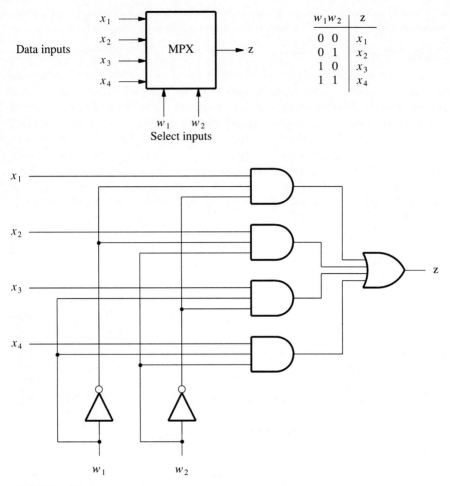

FIGURE A.34
A four-input multiplexer.

$$f = x_1\overline{x}_2 + x_1\overline{x}_3 + \overline{x}_1x_2x_3$$

This implies a network of three AND gates and one OR gate, and thus parts of more than one IC are needed for this implementation. In general, the multiplexer approach is more attractive for functions that do not yield simple sum-of-products expressions. Of course, the relative merits of the two approaches should be judged by the number of ICs needed to implement a given function.

A.12 PROGRAMMABLE LOGIC ARRAYS (PLAs)

Sections A.2 and A.3 showed how a given switching function can be represented in terms of sum-of-products expressions and implemented in terms of the corresponding

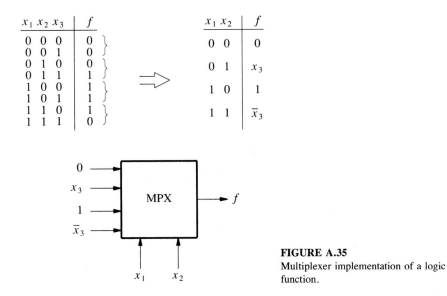

x_1	x_2	x_3	f
0	0	0	0
0	0	1	0
0	1	0	0
0	1	1	1
1	0	0	1
1	0	1	1
1	1	0	1
1	1	1	0

$\Rightarrow$

x_1	x_2	f
0	0	0
0	1	x_3
1	0	1
1	1	$\overline{x}_3$

FIGURE A.35
Multiplexer implementation of a logic function.

AND-OR gate networks. Section A.11 showed how multiplexers can be used to realize switching functions. In this section we will consider another class of circuits that can be used for the same purpose. These circuits consist of arrays of switching elements that can be programmed to allow implementation of sum-of-products expressions. They are called *programmable logic arrays*.

Figure A.36 shows the block diagram of a PLA. It has n input variables $(x_1, \ldots, x_n)$ and m outputs $(f_1, \ldots, f_m)$. Each function f_i is realized as a sum of product terms that involve the input variables. The variables $x_1, \ldots, x_n$ are

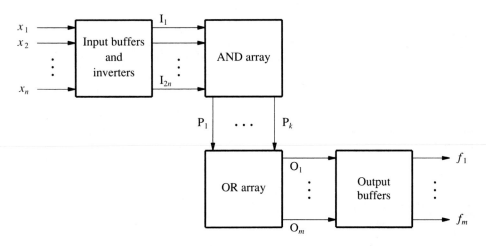

FIGURE A.36
A block diagram for a PLA.

presented in true and complemented form to the AND array, where up to k product terms are formed. These are then gated into the OR array, where the output functions are formed. Some of the product terms may be used in the synthesis of more than one of the output functions.

Let us consider a specific example of a three-input two-output PLA in which the output functions are

$$f_1 = x_1 x_2 + x_1 \bar{x}_3 + \bar{x}_1 \bar{x}_2 x_3$$

and

$$f_2 = x_1 x_2 + x_1 x_3 + \bar{x}_1 \bar{x}_2 x_3$$

Its structure can be modeled by an equivalent logic-gate network as shown in Figure A.37. Note that only four product terms are needed, because two terms can be shared by both functions. A simplified circuit for a PLA programmed to implement these functions is given in Figure A.38. Diodes are used to implement the product terms in

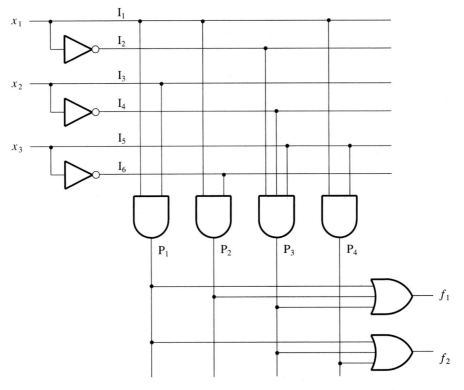

$$f_1 = x_1 x_2 + x_1 \bar{x}_3 + \bar{x}_1 \bar{x}_2 x_3$$
$$f_2 = x_1 x_2 + x_1 x_3 + \bar{x}_1 \bar{x}_2 x_3$$

FIGURE A.37
Logic gate equivalent of an example PLA.

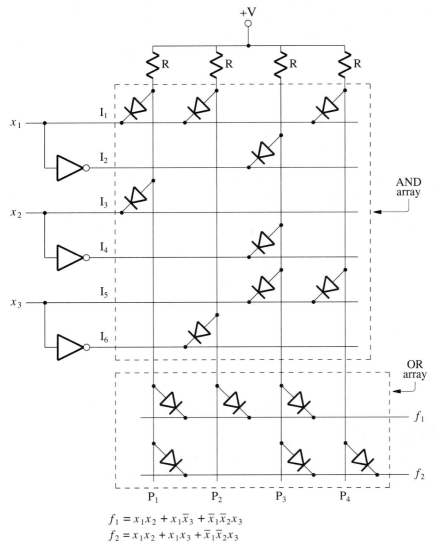

$$f_1 = x_1x_2 + x_1\overline{x}_3 + \overline{x}_1\overline{x}_2x_3$$
$$f_2 = x_1x_2 + x_1x_3 + \overline{x}_1\overline{x}_2x_3$$

FIGURE A.38
An example of a PLA.

the AND array and to realize the desired sums in the OR array. The operation of this circuit follows the principles described in Section A.5.1. Note that the absence of a diode at any given crosspoint merely indicates that the corresponding variable does not appear in the particular product term.

A PLA has switching elements available at each crosspoint of both AND and OR arrays. However, they do not provide an actual conducting path until they are programmed. Programming is typically the last step in the manufacturing process.

PLAs provide a simple way of implementing logic functions. The number of functions that can be implemented depends upon the size of the PLA. For example, one can obtain a PLA that has 14 input variables, 8 output functions, and up to 48 internal product terms in the AND array. Clearly, such a device can be used to realize a fairly complex logic network.

A.13 PAL DEVICES

In a PLA, the inputs to both the AND array and the OR array are programmable. A similar device, in which the inputs to the AND array are programmable but the connections to the OR gates are fixed, has found great popularity in practical applications. Such devices are known as *programmable array logic* (PAL) chips. In order to make PALs easily programmable by the user, their AND array inputs incorporate fuses that may be blown by applying a higher than normal current to them.

Figure A.39 shows a simple example of a PAL. It illustrates how two specific functions may be implemented by blowing certain fuses. Note that the number of

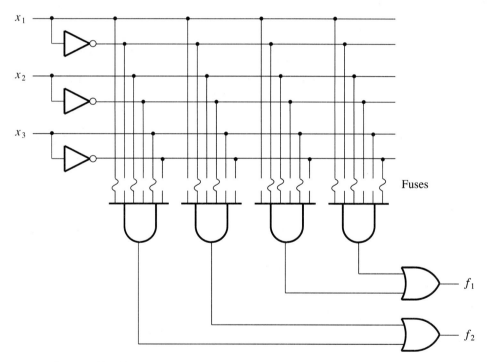

$$f_1 = x_1 x_2 \overline{x}_3 + \overline{x}_1 x_2 x_3$$
$$f_2 = \overline{x}_1 \overline{x}_2 + x_1 x_2 x_3$$

FIGURE A.39
An example of a PAL.

AND gates connected to each OR gate determines the maximum number of product terms that can be realized in a sum-of-products representation of a given function.

PAL chips are available in various configurations. A substantial number of inputs and outputs can be provided, allowing complex functions to be realized. The versatility of a PAL may be enhanced further by including flip-flops in the outputs from some of the OR gates. Such PALs can enable the designer of a digital system to implement a relatively complex logic network using a single chip.

A.14 CONCLUDING REMARKS

IC technology has revolutionized the art of logic design. A variety of IC components are commercially available at ever decreasing costs, and new developments and technological improvements are constantly adding to this collection. In this appendix we introduced some of the basic components that are useful in the design of digital systems. Several others are discussed in the main body of the book: For example, ICs that implement arithmetic functions are dealt with in Chapter 7. Very large-scale integrated (VLSI) circuits as used in the microprocessor environment are treated in Chapter 10. In these cases, it is more natural to talk about particular components within the framework of their typical applications.

From the designer's point of view, the obvious parameter to keep in mind is the cost of the resultant circuits. This implies that the number of IC packages used should be as low as possible.

Although the component cost in a digital system is a significant factor, two other design objectives are becoming increasingly important. The ability to easily test the resultant circuits simplifies the task of proving that newly produced equipment works correctly as well as the task of repairing it in the case of failure. Furthermore, it is often desirable to increase the reliability of a system with the help of additional redundant logic circuits (for example, by duplicating some parts). Both these objectives are likely to lead to increased component cost. It is the designer's job to arrive at a satisfactory trade-off between these considerations.

A.15 PROBLEMS

A.1. Implement the COINCIDENCE function in sum-of-products form in which COINCIDENCE $= \overline{\text{EX-OR}}$.

A.2. Prove the following identities by using algebraic manipulation and also by using truth tables.

(a) $\overline{a \oplus b} \oplus c = \overline{a}\overline{b}\overline{c} + a\overline{b}c + \overline{a}bc + a\overline{b}\overline{c}$

(b) $x + w\overline{x} = x + w$

(c) $x_1\overline{x}_2 + \overline{x}_2x_3 + x_3\overline{x}_1 = x_1\overline{x}_2 + x_3\overline{x}_1$

A.3. Derive minimal sum-of-products forms for the 4 three-variable functions f_1, f_2, f_3, and f_4 given in Figure PA.1. Is there more than one minimal form for any of these functions? If so, derive all of them.

A.4. Two 2-bit numbers $A = a_1a_0$ and $B = b_1b_0$ are to be compared by a four-variable function $f(a_1, a_0, b_1, b_0)$. The function f is to have the value 1 whenever

$$v(A) \le v(B)$$

x_1	x_2	x_3	f_1	f_2	f_3	f_4
0	0	0	1	1	d	0
0	0	1	1	1	1	1
0	1	0	0	1	0	1
0	1	1	0	1	1	d
1	0	0	1	0	d	d
1	0	1	0	0	0	d
1	1	0	1	0	1	1
1	1	1	1	1	1	0

FIGURE PA.1
Logic functions for Problem A.3.

where $v(X) = x_1 \times 2^1 + x_0 \times 2^0$ for any 2-bit number. Assume that the variables A and B are such that $|v(A) - v(B)| \leq 2$. Synthesize f using as few gates as possible.

A.5. A number code in which consecutive numbers are represented by binary patterns that differ in one bit position only is called a Gray code. A truth table for a 3-bit Gray-code to binary-code converter is shown in Figure PA.2a.

(a) Implement the three functions f_1, f_2, f_3 using only NAND gates.

(b) A lower-cost network for performing this code conversion can be derived by noting the following relationships between the input and output variables.

3-bit Gray code inputs			Binary code outputs		
a	b	c	f_1	f_2	f_3
0	0	0	0	0	0
0	0	1	0	0	1
0	1	1	0	1	0
0	1	0	0	1	1
1	1	0	1	0	0
1	1	1	1	0	1
1	0	1	1	1	0
1	0	0	1	1	1

(a) Three-bit Gray code

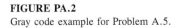

(b) Code conversion network

FIGURE PA.2
Gray code example for Problem A.5.

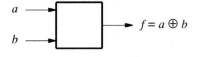

FIGURE PA.3
Combinational network for the EX-OR function.

$$f_1 = a$$

$$f_2 = f_1 \oplus b$$

$$f_3 = f_2 \oplus c$$

Using these relationships, specify the contents of a combinational network N that can be repeated, as shown in Figure PA.2b, to implement the conversion. Compare the total number of NAND gates required to implement the conversion in this form to the number required in part (a).

A.6. In the production of ICs it is desirable to have circuits with as few wire crossovers as possible. Implement the EX-OR function using only NAND gates, so that there are no wire crossovers inside the box shown in Figure PA.3.

A.7. Figure A.33 defines a BCD to seven-segment display decoder. Give an implementation for this truth table using AND, OR, and NOT gates. Verify that the same functions are correctly implemented by the NAND-gate circuits shown in the figure.

A.8. In the logic network shown in Figure PA.4, gate 3 fails and produces the logic value 1 at its output F1 regardless of the inputs. Redraw the network, making simplifications wherever possible, to obtain a new network that is equivalent to the given faulty network and that contains as few gates as possible. Repeat this problem, assuming that the fault is at position F2 and that it is stuck at a logic value 0.

A.9. The circuit configuration for a CMOS two-input NOR gate is given in Figure A.19. Show how the four MOS transistors can be connected to obtain a two-input NAND gate.

A.10. Consider the DTL circuit in Figure A.15. Assume that the voltage drop across each diode is 0.7 V when the diode is conducting and that the transistor is turned off when the base-emitter voltage V_{BE} is less than 0.4 V. When the transistor is fully on, the collector-emitter voltage is 0.2 V and $V_{BE} = 0.7$ V. For V_{BE} between 0.4 and 0.7 V,

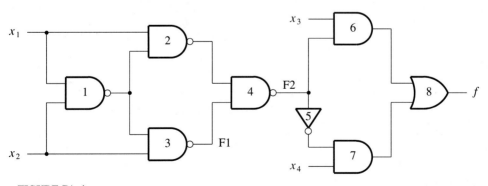

FIGURE PA.4
A faulty network.

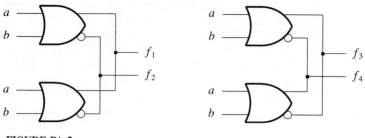

FIGURE PA.5
Wired output configurations.

the transistor is partially conducting. Plot the I/O characteristics for this circuit with the two inputs tied together. Suggest suitable values for $V_{1,min}$ and $V_{0,max}$ at the input for proper operation as a logic inverter.

A.11. The ECL logic family provides considerable flexibility in implementing logic functions by allowing gate outputs to be tied together. By inspection of the circuit configuration for an ECL NOR gate, derive the logic expressions for the functions f_1 to f_4 in Figure PA.5.

A.12. Logic circuits for JK master-slave flip-flops are given in Figure A.27. Draw the waveforms at S', R', Q, and $\overline{Q}$ for the input waveforms shown in Figure PA.6, assuming that the flip-flop is initially in the 0 state.

A.13. Derive the truth table for the NAND-gate circuit in Figure PA.7. Compare it to the truth table in Figure A.23b and then verify that the equivalence shown in Figure A.27b is correct.

A.14. Compute both the setup time and the hold time in terms of NOR-gate delays for the negative edge-triggered D flip-flop shown in Figure A.28.

A.15. Figure A.29 shows a shift-register network that shifts the data to the right one place at a time under the control of a clock signal. Modify this shift register to make it capable of shifting data either one or two places at a time under the control of the clock and an additional control input ONE/TWO.

A.16. A 4-bit shift register that has three inputs—INITIALIZE, RIGHT/LEFT, and CLOCK— is required. When INITIALIZE is set to 1, the binary number 1000 should be loaded

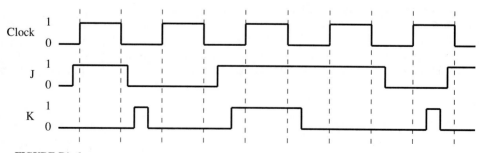

FIGURE PA.6
Input waveforms for a JK flip-flop.

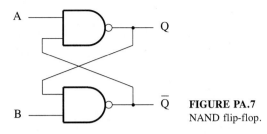

A

B

Q

$\overline{Q}$

FIGURE PA.7
NAND flip-flop.

into the register independently of the clock input. When INITIALIZE = 0, pulses at the CLOCK input should rotate this pattern. The pattern moves right or left when the RIGHT/LEFT input is equal to 1 or 0, respectively. Give a suitable design for this register using JK flip-flops that have PRESET and CLEAR inputs as shown in Figure A.27.

A.17. Derive a three-input to eight-output decoder network, with the restriction that the gates to be used cannot have more than two inputs.

A.18. JK flip-flops are useful in constructing counters because of their toggle effect when J = K = 1. Isolating this feature in a separate storage circuit leads to a "T" flip-flop, shown in Figure PA.8.

(a) Derive a T flip-flop using a D flip-flop and any additional logic gates that may be required.

(b) Construct a modulo 8 counter using the T flip-flops.

A.19. Figure A.31 shows a four-stage "up counter." A counter that counts in the opposite direction (that is, 15, 14, . . . , 1, 0, 15, . . . ,) is called a "down counter." A counter capable of counting in both directions under the control of an UP/DOWN signal is called an "up-down counter." Show a logic diagram for a four-stage up-down counter that can also be preset to any state through parallel loading of its flip-flops from an external source. A LOAD/COUNT control is used to determine whether the counter is being loaded or is operating as a counter.

A.20. In digital systems it is often necessary to be able to load a register from a number of different sources. Section A.11 suggested that multiplexer circuits can be used for this purpose very conveniently. However, suppose that the required gating is to be accomplished using AND, OR, and NOT gates in separate IC packages. Let these gates have fan-out of 10. How many such gates are needed in a circuit that would permit loading a 16-bit register from one of four distinct sources?

A.21. A switching function to be implemented is described by the expression

$$f(x_1, x_2, x_3, x_4) = x_1 x_3 \overline{x}_4 + \overline{x}_1 \overline{x}_3 x_4 + \overline{x}_2 \overline{x}_3 \overline{x}_4$$

(a) Show an implementation of f in terms of an eight-input multiplexer circuit.

(b) Can f be realized with a four-input multiplexer circuit? If so, show how.

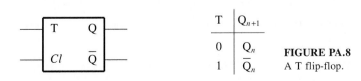

T	Q_{n+1}
0	Q_n
1	$\overline{Q}_n$

FIGURE PA.8
A T flip-flop.

A.22. Repeat Problem A.21 for

$$f(x_1, x_2, x_3, x_4) = x_1\overline{x}_2x_3 + x_2x_3x_4 + \overline{x}_1\overline{x}_4$$

A.23. Find the simplest sum-of-products form for the function f using the don't-care condition d, where

$$f = x_1(x_2\overline{x}_3 + x_2x_3 + \overline{x}_2\overline{x}_3x_4) + x_2\overline{x}_4(\overline{x}_3 + x_1)$$

and

$$d = x_1\overline{x}_2(x_3x_4 + \overline{x}_3\overline{x}_4) + \overline{x}_1\overline{x}_3x_4$$

A.24. Implement the following function with no more than six NAND gates, each having three inputs.

$$f = x_1x_2 + x_1x_2x_3 + \overline{x}_1\overline{x}_2\overline{x}_3x_4 + \overline{x}_1\overline{x}_2x_3\overline{x}_4$$

Assume that both true and complemented inputs are available.

A.25. Show how to implement the following function using six or fewer two-input NAND gates. Complemented input variables are not available.

$$f = x_1x_2 + \overline{x}_3 + \overline{x}_1x_4$$

A.26. Implement the following function as economically as possible using only NAND gates. Assume that complemented input variables are not available.

$$f = (x_1 + x_3)(\overline{x}_2 + \overline{x}_4)$$

A.27. Repeat Problem A.4 for $f = 1$ whenever

$$v(A) > v(B)$$

subject to the input constraint

$$v(A) + v(B) \leq 4$$

A.28. (a) What is the total number of distinct functions, $f(x_1, x_2, x_3)$, of three binary variables?

(b) How many of these functions are implementable with one PAL circuit of the type shown in Figure A.39?

(c) What is the smallest change in the circuit in Figure A.39 that should be made to allow any 3-variable function to be implemented with a single PAL circuit?

A.29. Consider the PAL circuit in Figure A.39. Suppose that the circuit is modified by adding a fourth input variable, x_4, which is connected in its uncomplemented and complemented forms to all four AND gates in the same way as the variables x_1, x_2, and x_3.

(a) Can this modified PAL be used to implement the function

$$f = x_1\overline{x}_2\overline{x}_3 + \overline{x}_1x_2\overline{x}_3 + \overline{x}_1\overline{x}_2x_3$$

If so, show how.

(b) How many functions of three variables cannot be implemented with this PAL?

A.16 REFERENCES

1. Kohavi, Z. *Switching and Finite Automata Theory,* 2d ed., McGraw-Hill, New York, NY, 1978.
2. Dietmeyer, D. L., *Logical Design of Digital Systems,* 2d ed., Allyn and Bacon, Boston, MA, 1978.

3. Hill, F. H., and G. R. Peterson, *Introduction to Switching Theory and Logical Design,* 3d ed., Wiley, New York, NY, 1981.

4. McCluskey, E. J., *Logic Design Principles,* Prentice-Hall, Englewood Cliffs, NJ, 1986.

5. Mano, M. M., *Digital Design,* Prentice-Hall, Englewood Cliffs, NJ, 1984.

6. Breeding, K. J., *Digital Design Fundamentals,* Prentice-Hall, Englewood Cliffs, NJ, 1989.

7. Fletcher, W. I., *An Engineering Approach to Digital Design,* Prentice-Hall, Englewood Cliffs, NJ, 1980.

8. Taub, H., and D. Schilling, *Digital Integrated Electronics,* McGraw-Hill, New York, NY, 1977.

9. Sedra, A. S., and K. C. Smith, *Microelectronic Circuits,* 2d ed., Holt, Rinehart and Winston, New York, NY, 1987.

APPENDIX

B

INSTRUCTION SET
FOR PDP-11
MINICOMPUTERS

This appendix contains a list of instructions used in PDP-11 minicomputers. There are a number of different models of these computers involving differing instruction sets. In general, larger models have all the instructions found in the smaller ones, plus some additional instructions that are either standard or a part of an optional feature. For illustrative purposes in this book, it is adequate to consider a relatively basic set. The instruction set given in this appendix can be found in most models of the PDP-11 computer.

The addressing scheme for the PDP-11 was fully described in Chapter 2 and will not be repeated here. The instructions are listed below in tabular form, with most entries being self-explanatory. However, some notational abbreviations are used to keep the table as compact as possible. Instructions that have both word and byte formats are combined as single entries; for example, MOV and MOVB are shown as MOV {B}. Such instructions are distinguished by the most significant bit of the OP code, which is 0 in the case of a word instruction and 1 for a byte instruction. This fact is denoted by the character "β." Manipulation of the condition codes is indicated for each instruction, where they are affected. In a typical statement it may be indicated that a flag corresponding to a particular condition code is set to 1 if a given condition is met. It is implicitly assumed that the flag is reset or cleared to 0 if this condition is not met. Thus, instead of writing in full "Condition Code Z: set if result = 0; cleared otherwise," we will show simply "Z: set if result = 0."

Following is a summary of the symbols and abbreviations used:

β   0 for word and 1 for byte instructions
MSB   Most significant bit
PC   Program counter
SP   Stack pointer (that is, register 6)
PSW   Processor status word
temp Internal temporary storage register in the CPU
∧   Logical AND operation
∨   Logical OR operation
⊕   Logical EXCLUSIVE-OR operation
[ ]   Denotes the contents of the register or memory location specified

TWO-OPERAND INSTRUCTIONS

There are two formats for two-operand instructions. The first one allows complete freedom in specifying the source and destination operands, using any of the addressing modes. The format is

OP code	src	dst
15 12	11 6	5 0

It is used in the following instructions:

Mnemonic (name)	OP code (octal)	Operation performed	Condition codes
MOV{B} (Move)	β1	dst ← [src] In MOVB, if dst is a register, then MSB of the low-order byte is extended into the high-order byte	N set if [src] < 0 Z set if [src] = 0 V reset C not affected
ADD (Add)	06	dst ← [src] + [dst]	N set if result < 0 Z set if result = 0 V set if arithmetic overflow occurs C set if carry from MSB of result occurs
SUB (Subtract)	16	dst ← [dst] − [src]	N, Z, V same as in ADD C set if no carry from MSB of result occurs
CMP{B} (Compare)	β2	[src] − [dst] Neither of the operands is affected	Same as in SUB

Mnemonic (name)	OP code (octal)	Operation performed	Condition codes
BIT{B} (Bit test)	β3	$[src] \land [dst]$ Neither of the operands is affected	N set if MSB of result = 1 Z set if result = 0 V reset C not affected
BIC{B} (Bit clear)	β4	$dst \leftarrow \overline{[src]} \land [dst]$	Same as in BIT
BIS{B} (Bit set)	β5	$dst \leftarrow [src] \lor [dst]$	Same as in BIT

The second format for two-operand instructions allows full flexibility in specifying only one operand, either the source or the destination. The second operand is restricted to be in one of the registers, thus requiring only a 3-bit field to specify it. The format is

OP code	reg	src/dst
15	9 8 6 5	0

It is used in the following instructions:

Mnemonic (name)	Op code (octal)	Operation performed	Condition codes
XOR (Exclusive-OR)	074	$dst \leftarrow [reg] \oplus [dst]$	Same as in BIT
MUL (Multiply)	070	$reg, reg \lor 1 \leftarrow [reg] \times [src]$ The double-length product is stored in reg and the next higher-numbered register if reg is even. If reg is odd, then only the low-order word is stored in reg.	N set if product < 0 Z set if product = 0 V reset C set if result is not within the range -2^{15} to $2^{15}-1$.
DIV (Divide)	071	$reg, reg \lor 1 \leftarrow [reg, reg \lor 1] \div [src]$ reg must be even, quotient goes to reg and remainder to the next higher-numbered register (that is, reg $\lor$ 1)	N set if quotient < 0 Z set if quotient = 0 V set if $[src] = 0$ or if $|[reg]| > |[src]|$ C set if divide by 0 is attempted
ASH (Arithmetic shift)	072	Contents of reg are shifted right or left according to the count in the low-order 6 bits of src. Negative	N set if result < 0 Z set if result = 0 V set if MSB of reg changed during shifting

Mnemonic (name)	OP code (octal)	Operation performed	Condition codes
		count results in right shift and positive in left shift	C loaded by the last bit shifted out of reg

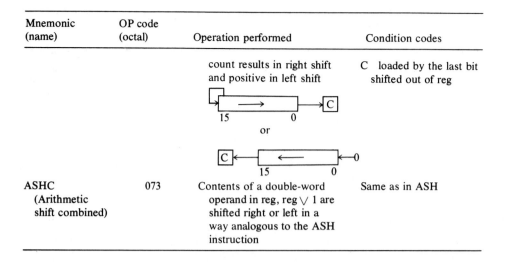

Mnemonic (name)	OP code (octal)	Operation performed	Condition codes
ASHC (Arithmetic shift combined)	073	Contents of a double-word operand in reg, reg $\vee$ 1 are shifted right or left in a way analogous to the ASH instruction	Same as in ASH

ONE-OPERAND INSTRUCTIONS

The format for one-operand instructions is

OP code		dst
15	6 5	0

The operand can be specified using any of the addressing modes. Instructions in this group are:

Mnemonic (Name)	OP code (octal)	Operation performed	Condition codes
CLR{B} (clear)	β050	dst ← 0	N, V, C reset Z set
COM{B} [Complement (1's)]	β051	dst ← $\overline{[dst]}$	N set if MSB of result is 1 Z set if result = 0 V reset C set
INC{B} (Increment)	β052	dst ← [dst] + 1	N set if result < 0 Z set if result = 0 V set if [dst] was 077777 C not affected
DEC{B} (Decrement)	β053	dst ← [dst] − 1	N, Z, C same as in INC V set if [dst] was 100000

Mnemonic (name)	OP code (octal)	Operation performed	Condition codes
NEG{B} [Negate (2's compl.)]	$\beta054$	dst ← − [dst]	N, Z same as in INC V set if result = 100000 C reset if result = 0, set otherwise
ADC{B} (Add carry)	$\beta055$	dst ← [dst] + [C]	N, Z, V, C same as in ADD
SBC{B} (Subtract carry)	$\beta056$	dst ← [dst] − [C]	N, Z, V, C same as in SUB
TST{B} (Test)	$\beta057$	dst ← [dst]	N, Z same as in INC V, C reset
ROR{B} (Rotate right one place)	$\beta060$	C → [15 → 0] (rotate right); C → [7 → 0] (15) (8)	N, Z same as in ASH V set to $N \oplus C$
ROL{B} (Rotate left one place)	$\beta061$	C ← [15 ← 0] (rotate left); C ← [7 ← 0] (15) (8)	N, Z, V same as in ROR
ASR{B} (Arithmetic shift right one place)	$\beta062$	[15 → 0] → C; [7 → 0] → C (15) (8)	N, Z, V same as in ROR
ASL{B} (Arithmetic shift left one place)	$\beta063$	C ← [15 ← 0] ← 0; C ← [7 ← 0] ← 0 (15) (8)	N, Z, V same as in ROR
SWAB (Swap bytes)	0003	$dst_{15-8} \leftarrow [dst_{7-0}]$ $dst_{7-0} \leftarrow [dst_{15-8}]$	N set if b_7 of result set Z set if low-order byte of result = 0 V, C reset
SXT (Sign extended)	0067	dst ← 0 if [N] = 0 dst ← −1 if [N] = 1	N, C not affected Z set if [N] = 0 V reset

BRANCH INSTRUCTIONS

Branch instructions use the format

OP code	Offset
15 8 7	0

If the branch condition is satisfied, the new value of the program counter is
PC $\leftarrow$ [updated PC] + 2 $\times$ Offset, where the updated PC is equal to the address
of the branch instruction plus 2, and the Offset is interpreted as a signed 8-bit
number. Condition codes are not affected by the branch instructions.

Mnemonic	Name	OP code (binary)	Branch condition
BR	Branch unconditionally	00000001	None
BNE	Branch if $\neq$ 0	00000010	$Z = 0$
BEQ	Branch if = 0	00000011	$Z = 1$
BPL	Branch if plus	10000000	$N = 0$
BMI	Branch if minus	10000001	$N = 1$
BVC	Branch if overflow clear	10000100	$V = 0$
BVS	Branch if overflow set	10000101	$V = 1$
BCC	Branch if carry clear	10000110	$C = 0$
BCS	Branch if carry set	10000111	$C = 1$
BGE	Branch if $\geq$ 0	00000100	$N \oplus V = 0$
BLT	Branch if < 0	00000101	$N \oplus V = 1$
BGT	Branch if > 0	00000110	$Z \vee (N \oplus V) = 0$
BLE	Branch if $\leq$ 0	00000111	$Z \vee (N \oplus V) = 1$
BHI	Branch if higher	10000010	$C \vee Z = 0$
BLOS	Branch if lower or same	10000011	$C \vee Z = 1$
BHIS*	Branch if higher or same	10000110	$C = 0$
BLO*	Branch if lower	10000111	$C = 1$

*Instructions BHIS and BLO are the same as BCC and BCS.
These mnemonics are included for convenience purposes only.

The instructions BHI, BLOS, BHIS, and BLO are normally used after a
Compare instruction. They are based on interpreting the data which caused the
setting of the condition codes as positive 16-bit integers. This is in contrast to
the instructions BGE, BLT, BGT, and BLE, which are based on interpreting the
data as 16-bit signed integers in 2's-complement representation.

JUMP AND SUBROUTINE INSTRUCTIONS

In the description of bit patterns for this group of instructions the following
notation is used:

DD Represents a 6-bit destination (dst) in any of the standard addressing modes

R Represents a general-purpose register (reg)

QQ Represents a 6-bit positive number

The condition codes are not affected by these instructions.

Mnemonic	Name	Code (octal)	Operation performed
JMP	Jump	0001DD	PC ← dst
JSR	Jump to subroutine	004RDD	temp ← dst SP ← [SP] − 2 [SP] ← [reg] reg ← [PC] PC ← [temp]
RTS	Return from subroutine	00020R	PC ← [reg] reg ← [[SP]] SP ← [SP] + 2
MARK	Mark	0064QQ	SP ← [SP] + 2 × QQ PC ← [reg 5] reg 5 ← [[SP]] SP ← [SP] + 2
SOB	Subtract one and branch	077RQQ	reg ← [reg] − 1 If result ≠ 0, then PC ← [PC] − 2 × QQ

The MARK instruction is used to facilitate return from subroutines when subroutine parameters are to be removed from the processor stack. The SOB instruction provides a convenient means for controlling program loops.

TRAP AND INTERRUPT INSTRUCTIONS

Mnemonic	Name	Code (octal)	Operation performed	Condition codes
RTI	Return from interrupt	000002	PC ← [[SP]] SP ← [SP] + 2 PSW ← [[SP]] SP ← [SP] + 2	N, Z, V, C loaded from the processor stack
TRAP	Trap	104400–104477	SP ← [SP] − 2 [SP] ← [PSW] SP ← [SP] − 2 [SP] ← [PC] PC ← [loc. 34] PSW ← [loc. 36]	N, Z, V, C loaded from the trap vector

There are four other trap and return from interrupt instructions, for which the reader may consult the manufacturer's manuals. Note that trap instructions are, in effect, software-generated interrupts. The new values for the PC and PSW are obtained from a two-word trap vector at a fixed memory location. The above trap instruction is defined by the high-order byte only, while the low-order byte may be used to transmit data to the trap routine.

CONDITION CODE INSTRUCTIONS

A set of 10 instructions is provided to enable setting and resetting of condition codes. Their format is

0	0	0	0	0	0	0	0	1	0	1	0/1	N	Z	V	C
15															0

Condition codes N, Z, V, and C are manipulated if the corresponding bits in positions b_3 to b_0 are set. The selected condition codes are set if $b_4 = 1$ and reset if $b_4 = 0$. Note that all 16 bits of these instructions, in effect, constitute an OP code.

Mnemonic	Name	OP code (octal)
CLC	Clear C	000241
CLV	Clear V	000242
CLZ	Clear Z	000244
CLN	Clear N	000250
SEC	Set C	000261
SEV	Set V	000262
SEZ	Set Z	000264
SEN	Set N	000270
SCC	Set all condition codes	000277
CCC	Clear all condition codes	000257

MISCELLANEOUS INSTRUCTIONS

These instructions are used for control purposes and do not affect the condition codes:

Mnemonic	Name	OP code (octal)	Function
HALT	Halt	000000	Stops the processor
WAIT	Wait for interrupt	000001	Causes the processor to wait for an external interrupt
RESET	Reset external bus	000005	All devices on the Unibus are reset
NOP	No operation	000240	No operation is performed

APPENDIX

C

INSTRUCTION SET FOR MOTOROLA 68000 MICROPROCESSOR

This appendix contains a summary of the instructions for the 68000 microprocessor. An introductory discussion of the main characteristics of this microprocessor was given in Chapter 2. It included a description of the register structure and the addressing modes, summarized in Figure 2.23 and Table 2.3, respectively. Note that Table 2.3 includes the assembler syntax for the addressing modes.

The general format for encoding the address field for an operand is shown in Table C.1. A 6-bit field is used to specify the addressing mode and the register involved. In the modes in which it is not necessary to specify a particular register, the register field is used as an extension of the mode field having the bit patterns shown in the table.

The names of addressing modes in Table C.1 are consistent with those used in this book. We should caution the reader that some of these names are different from those used in Motorola literature. Because the reader will undoubtedly find it useful to consult the manufacturer's data sheets and user manuals, we have summarized the differences in the terminology in Table C.2. It is apparent that the Motorola terminology is highly descriptive, but somewhat awkward to use for discussion purposes.

TABLE C.1
Address field encoding for 68000

Addressing mode	Mode field	Register field
Data register direct	000	Register number
Address register direct	001	Register number
Address register indirect	010	Register number
Autoincrement	011	Register number
Autodecrement	100	Register number
Indexed basic	101	Register number
Indexed full	110	Register number
Absolute short	111	000
Absolute long	111	001
Relative basic	111	010
Relative full	111	011
Immediate or status register	111	100

The 68000 instructions are presented in this appendix in the form of a table. In order to keep the table reasonably small, extensive notational abbreviations are used.

Table C.3 gives the notational symbols and their meanings. Note that symbols that correspond to bit patterns in the OP-code field have one letter for each bit position involved.

Table C.4 provides a complete listing of the available instructions. The addressing modes allowed for each instruction are indicated in a matrix format. For each source (destination) addressing mode provided, all destination (source) addressing modes permitted are denoted with an x. For example, for the AND instruction, if the source is a data register, the destination mode may be (An), (An) + , − (An), d(An),

TABLE C.2
Differences from Motorola terminology

Terminology used in this text	Motorola terminology
Autoincrement	Address register indirect with postincrement
Autodecrement	Address register indirect with predecrement
Indexed basic	Address register indirect with displacement
Indexed full	Address register indirect with index
Relative basic	Program counter with displacement
Relative full	Program counter with index

TABLE C.3
Notation for Table C.4

Symbol	Meaning
s	Source operand
d	Destination operand
An	Address register n
Dn	Data register n
Xn	An address or data register, used as an index register
PC	Program counter
SP	Stack pointer
SR	Status register
CCR	Condition code flags in SR
AAA	Address register number
DDD	Data register number
rrr	Source register number
RRR	Destination register number
eeeee	Effective address of the source operand
EEEEE	Effective address of the destination operand
MMM	Effective address mode of destination
CCCC	Specification for a condition code test
P. . .P	Displacement
Q. . .Q	Quick immediate data
SS	Size: 00≡byte, 01≡word, 10≡long word (for most instructions)
	01≡byte, 11≡word, 10≡long word (for MOVE and MOVEA instructions)
VVVV	Trap vector number
u	Condition code flag state is undefined (meaningless)
d(An)	Indexed basic addressing mode
d(An,Xi)	Indexed full addressing mode
d(PC)	Relative basic addressing mode
d(PC,Xi)	Relative full addressing mode

d(An,Xi), Abs.W, or Abs.L. Moreover, if the destination is a data register, the source can be specified in any of the 11 modes shown in the table.

The OP-code column shows the actual bit pattern of the first 16-bit word of an instruction. Instructions that have immediate source data use a second word for 8- and 16-bit operands, and a second and third word for 32-bit operands. For the indexed and relative addressing modes, the required index value (displacement) is given in the word that follows the OP code.

Shift and rotate instructions can specify a count of the number of bit positions by which the operand is to be shifted or rotated. The count can be given as the contents of a data register or as an immediate 3-bit value within the OP code. If a memory operand is involved, however, then the count is always equal to 1.

Branch instructions are listed in Table C.5. The branch offset (displacement) is a signed 2's-complement number that specifies the relative distance in bytes. For conditional branch instructions, as well as for Scc (set on condition) instructions, the condition code suffix possibilities (cc) are shown in Table C.6. The table also indicates the condition that is tested to determine if a branch is to be taken.

The operation performed for a given instruction is indicated in Tables C.4 and C.5. For most instructions the action taken is obvious. However, for a few instructions, additional comments are in order. The instructions labeled with an asterisk in the mnemonic column are discussed further in the following paragraphs.

BCHG, BCLR, BSET, and BTST. All of these instructions test a specified bit of the destination operand. The number of the bit position to be tested (bit#) is indicated either as the contents of a data register or as an immediate value within the instruction. The test is made by loading the complement of the tested bit into the condition flag Z.

MOVEM. This instruction moves the contents of one or more registers to or from consecutive memory locations. The registers involved in the transfer are specified in the second word of the instruction. Bits 0 to 7 correspond to D0 to D7, and bits 8 to 15 correspond to A0 to A7. This arrangement is valid for all addressing modes except the autodecrement mode, in which case the order of registers is reversed.

MOVEP. This instruction is useful for data transfers between the 68000 and 8-bit peripheral devices. The data is transferred in bytes, with the memory address incremented by 2 after each byte. Thus, if the starting address is even, all bytes are transferred to or from even numbered address locations by means of the high-order eight lines of the data bus. Similarly, if the starting address is odd, then all transfers are done via the low-order eight lines of the data bus. The high-order byte of a data register is transferred first and the low-order byte last.

As pointed out in Chapter 2, the 68000 has two basic modes of operation. In the supervisor mode all instructions can be used. In the user mode, some instructions cannot be executed. Instructions that can be used in the supervisor mode only are called *privileged* instructions. These are

- ANDI, EORI, ORI, and MOVE instructions when the destination is the status register SR
- MOVE instruction which moves the contents of the user stack pointer to or from an address register
- RESET, RTE, and STOP instructions

The information presented in this appendix should enable the reader to write and debug assembly language programs for the 68000. The size and structure of assembled instructions can be determined on the basis of the OP codes given and the addressing modes employed. Lack of space has prevented inclusion of timing information such as the number of machine cycles needed to execute a given instruction. This information, as well as further details about the instruction set, can be found in the manufacturer's literature.

TABLE C.4
68000 instruction set

Mnemonic (Name)	Size	Addressing mode	Dn	An	(An)	(An)+	-(An)	d(An)	d(An,Xi)	Abs.W	Abs.L	d(PC)	d(PC,Xi)	Immed	SR or CCR
ABCD (Add BCD)	B	s = Dn d =	x												
		s = -(An) d =					x								
ADD (Add)	B,W,L	s = Dn d =	x		x	x	x	x	x	x	x				
		d = Dn s =	x	x	x	x	x	x	x	x	x	x	x	x	
ADDA (Add address)	W	d = An s =	x	x	x	x	x	x	x	x	x	x	x	x	
	L	d = An s =	x	x	x	x	x	x	x	x	x	x	x	x	
ADDI (Add immediate)	B,W,L	s = Immed d =	x		x	x	x	x	x	x	x				
ADDQ (Add quick)	B,W,L	s = Immed3 d =	x	x	x	x	x	x	x	x	x				
ADDX (Add extended)	B,W,L	s = Dn d =	x												
		s = -(An) d =					x								
AND (Logical AND)	B,W,L	s = Dn d =			x	x	x	x	x	x	x				
		d = Dn s =	x		x	x	x	x	x	x	x	x	x	x	
ANDI (AND immediate)	B,W,L	s = Immed d =	x		x	x	x	x	x	x	x				x
ASL (Arithmetic shift left)	B,W,L	count = [Dn] d =	x												
		count = QQQ d =	x												
		count = 1 d =			x	x	x	x	x	x					
ASR (Arithmetic shift right)	B,W,L	count = [Dn] d =	x												
		count = QQQ d =	x												
		count = 1 d =			x	x	x	x	x	x					
BCHG* (Test a bit and change it)	B	bit# = [Dn] d =			x	x	x	x	x	x	x				
		bit# = Immed d =			x	x	x	x	x	x	x				
	L	bit# = [Dn] d =	x												
		bit# = Immed d =	x												
BCLR* (Test a bit and clear it)	B	bit# = [Dn] d =			x	x	x	x	x	x	x				
		bit# = Immed d =			x	x	x	x	x	x	x				
	L	bit# = [Dn] d =	x												
		bit# = Immed d =	x												

| | | Condition flags | | | | |
OP code $b_{15} \ldots b_0$	Operation performed	X	N	Z	V	C
1100 RRR1 0000 0rrr 1100 RRR1 0000 1rrr	d ← [s] + [d] + [X] Binary-coded decimal addition	x	u	x	u	x
1101 DDD1 SSEE EEEE 1101 DDD0 SSee eeee	d ← [Dn] + [d] Dn ← [s] + [Dn]	x x	x x	x x	x ·x	x x
1101 AAA0 11ee eeee 1101 AAA1 11ee eeee	An ← [s] + [An]					
0000 0110 SSEE EEEE	d ← s + [d]	x	x	x	x	x
0101 QQQ0 SSEE EEEE	d ← QQQ + [d]	x	x	x	x	x
1101 RRR1 SS00 0rrr 1101 RRR1 SS00 1rrr	d ← [s] + [d] + [X] Multiprecision addition	x	x	x	x	x
1100 DDD1 SSEE EEEE 1100 DDD0 SSee eeee	d ← [Dn] ∧ [d]		x	x	0	0
0000 0010 SSEE EEEE	d ← s ∧ [d]		x	x	0	0
1110 rrr1 SS10 0DDD 1110 QQQ1 SS00 0DDD 1110 0001 11EE EEEE		x	x	x	x	x
1110 rrr0 SS10 0DDD 1110 QQQ0 SS00 0DDD 1110 0000 11EE EEEE		x	x	x	x	x
0000 rrr1 01EE EEEE 0000 1000 01EE EEEE 0000 rrr1 01EE EEEE 0000 1000 01EE EEEE	Z ← (bit# of d); then complement the tested bit in d.				x	
0000 rrr1 10EE EEEE 0000 1000 10EE EEEE 0000 rrr1 10EE EEEE 0000 1000 10EE EEEE	Z ← (bit# of d); then clear the tested bit in d.				x	

TABLE C.4
(*continued*)

Mnemonic (Name)	Size	Addressing mode		Dn	An	(An)	(An)+	-(An)	d(An)	d(An,Xi)	Abs.W	Abs.L	d(PC)	d(PC,Xi)	Immed	SR or CCR
BSET* (Test a bit and set it)	B	bit# = [Dn]	d =			x	x	x	x	x	x	x				
		bit# = Immed	d =			x	x	x	x	x	x	x				
	L	bit# = [Dn]	d =	x												
		bit# = Immed	d =	x												
BTST* (Test a bit)	B	bit# = [Dn]	d =			x	x	x	x	x	x	x				
		bit# = Immed	d =			x	x	x	x	x	x	x				
	L	bit# = [Dn]	d =	x												
		bit# = Immed	d =	x												
CHK (Check register against bounds)	W	d = Dn	s =	x		x	x	x	x	x	x	x	x	x	x	
CLR (Clear)	B,W,L		d =	x		x	x	x	x	x	x	x				
CMP (Compare)	B,W,L	d = Dn	s =	x	x	x	x	x	x	x	x	x	x	x	x	
CMPA (Compare address)	W	d = An	s =	x	x	x	x	x	x	x	x	x	x	x	x	
	L	d = An	s =	x	x	x	x	x	x	x	x	x	x	x	x	
CMPI (Compare immediate)	B,W,L	s = Immed	d =	x		x	x	x	x	x	x	x				
CMPM (Compare memory)	B,W,L	s = (An)+	d =				x									
DIVS (Divide signed)	W	d = Dn	s =	x		x	x	x	x	x	x	x	x	x	x	
DIVU (Divide unsigned)	W	d = Dn	s =	x		x	x	x	x	x	x	x	x	x	x	
EOR (Exclusive OR)	B,W,L	s = Dn	d =	x		x	x	x	x	x	x	x				
EORI (Exclusive OR immediate)	B,W,L	s = Immed	d =	x		x	x	x	x	x	x	x				x
EXG (Exchange)	L	s = Dn	d =	x	x											
		s = An	d =	x	x											
EXT (Sign extend)	W		d =	x												
	L		d =	x												

OP code $b_{15} \ldots b_0$	Operation performed	X	N	Z	V	C
0000 rrr1 11EE EEEE 0000 1000 11EE EEEE 0000 rrr1 11EE EEEE 0000 1000 11EE EEEE	$Z \leftarrow \overline{(\text{bit\# of d})}$; then set to 1 the tested bit in d.			x		
0000 rrr1 00EE EEEE 0000 1000 00EE EEEE 0000 rrr1 00EE EEEE 0000 1000 00EE EEEE	$Z \leftarrow \overline{(\text{bit\# of d})}$			x		
0100 DDD1 10ee eeee	If $[Dn] < 0$ or $[Dn] > [s]$, then raise an interrupt.		x	u	u	u
0100 0010 SSEE EEEE	$d \leftarrow 0$		0	1	0	0
1011 DDD0 SSee eeee	$[d] - [s]$		x	x	x	x
1011 AAA0 11ee eeee 1011 AAA1 11ee eeee	$[An] - [s]$		x	x	x	x
0000 1100 SSEE EEEE	$[d] - [s]$		x	x	x	x
1011 RRR1 SS00 1rrr	$[d] - [s]$		x	x	x	x
1000 DDD1 11ee eeee	$d \leftarrow [d] \div [s]$, using 32 bits of d and 16 bits of s.		x	x	x	0
1000 DDD0 11ee eeee	$d \leftarrow [d] \div [s]$, using 32 bits of d and 16 bits of s.		x	x	x	0
1011 rrr1 SSEE EEEE	$d \leftarrow [Dn] \oplus [d]$		x	x	0	0
0000 1010 SSEE EEEE	$d \leftarrow s \oplus [d]$		x	x	0	0
1100 DDD1 0100 0DDD 1100 AAA1 0100 1AAA 1100 DDD1 1000 1AAA	$[s] \leftrightarrow [d]$					
0100 1000 1000 0DDD 0100 1000 1100 0DDD	(bits 8–15 of d) ← (bit 7 of d) (bits 16–31 of d) ← (bit 15 of d)		x x	x x	0 0	0 0

TABLE C.4
(continued)

Mnemonic (Name)	Size	Addressing mode		Dn	An	(An)	(An)+	-(An)	d(An)	d(An,Xi)	Abs.W	Abs.L	d(PC)	d(PC,Xi)	Immed	SR or CCR
JMP (Jump)		d =				x			x	x	x	x	x	x		
JSR (Jump to subroutine)		d =				x			x	x	x	x	x	x		
LEA (Load effective address)	L	d = An	s =			x			x	x	x	x	x	x		
LINK (Link and allocate)		disp = Immed	s =		x											
LSL (Logical shift left)	B,W,L	count = [Dn]	d =	x												
		count = QQQ	d =	x												
	W	count = 1	d =			x	x	x	x	x	x	x				
LSR (Logical shift right)	B,W,L	count = [Dn]	d =	x												
		count = QQQ	d =	x												
	W	count = 1	d =			x	x	x	x	x	x	x				
MOVE (Move)	B,W,L	s = Dn	d =	x	x	x	x	x	x	x	x	x				
		s = An	d =	x	x	x	x	x	x	x	x	x				
		s = (An)	d =	x	x	x	x	x	x	x	x	x				
		s = (An)+	d =	x	x	x	x	x	x	x	x	x				
		s = -(An)	d =	x	x	x	x	x	x	x	x	x				
		s = d(An)	d =	x	x	x	x	x	x	x	x	x				
		s = d(An,Xi)	d =	x	x	x	x	x	x	x	x	x				
		s = Abs.W	d =	x	x	x	x	x	x	x	x	x				
		s = Abs.L	d =	x	x	x	x	x	x	x	x	x				
		s = d(PC)	d =	x	x	x	x	x	x	x	x	x				
		s = d(PC,Xi)	d =	x	x	x	x	x	x	x	x	x				
		s = Immed	d =	x	x	x	x	x	x	x	x	x				
	W	d = CCR	s =	x	x	x	x	x	x	x	x	x	x	x	x	
		d = SR	s =	x	x	x	x	x	x	x	x	x	x	x	x	
		s = SR	d =	x	x	x	x	x	x	x	x	x				
	L	s = SP	d =		x											
		d = SP	s =		x											
MOVEA (Move address)	W,L	d = An	s =	x	x	x	x	x	x	x	x	x	x	x	x	

OP code b_{15} ... b_0	Operation performed	X	N	Z	V	C
0100 1110 11EE EEEE	PC ← effective address of d					
0100 1110 10EE EEEE	SP ← [SP] − 4; [SP] ← [PC]; PC ← effective address of d					
0100 AAA1 11ee eeee	An ← effective address of s					
0100 1110 0101 0AAA	SP ← [SP] − 4; [SP] ← [An]; An ← [SP]; SP ← [SP] + disp					
1110 rrr1 SS10 1DDD 1110 QQQ1 SS00 1DDD 1110 0011 11EE EEEE	$\boxed{C} \leftarrow \boxed{\text{operand}} \leftarrow 0$, $\boxed{X} \leftarrow$	x	x	x	0	x
1110 rrr0 SS10 1DDD 1110 QQQ0 SS00 1DDD 1110 0010 11EE EEEE	$0 \rightarrow \boxed{\text{operand}} \rightarrow \boxed{C}$, $\rightarrow \boxed{X}$	x	x	x	0	x
00SS RRRM MMee eeee	d ← [s]		x	x	0	0
0100 0100 11ee eeee	CCR ← [s]	x	x	x	x	x
0100 0110 11ee eeee	SR ← [s]	x	x	x	x	x
0100 0000 11EE EEEE	d ← [SR]					
0100 1110 0110 1AAA	d ← [SP]					
0100 1110 0110 0AAA	SP ← [d]					
00SS AAA0 01ee eeee	An ← [s]					

TABLE C.4
(continued)

Mnemonic (Name)	Size	Addressing mode	Dn	An	(An)	(An)+	-(An)	d(An)	d(An,Xi)	Abs.W	Abs.L	d(PC)	d(PC,Xi)	Immed	SR or CCR
MOVEM* (Move multiple registers)	W	s = Xn d =			x		x	x	x	x	x				
		d = Xn s =			x	x		x	x	x	x	x	x		
	L	s = Xn d =			x			x	x	x	x				
		d = Xn s =			x	x		x	x	x	x	x	x		
MOVEP* (Move peripheral data)	W	s = Dn d =						x							
	L	s = Dn d =						x							
	W	s = d(An) d =	x												
	L	s = d(An) d =	x												
MOVEQ (Move quick)	L	s = Immed8 d =	x												
MULS (Multiply signed)	W	d = Dn s =	x		x	x	x	x	x	x	x	x	x	x	
MULU (Multiply unsigned)	W	d = Dn s =	x		x	x	x	x	x	x	x	x	x	x	
NBCD (Negate BCD)	B	d =	x		x	x	x	x	x	x	x				
NEG (Negate)	B,W,L	d =	x		x	x	x	x	x	x	x				
NEGX (Negate extended)	B,W,L	d =	x		x	x	x	x	x	x	x				
NOP (No operation)															
NOT (Complement)	B,W,L	d =	x		x	x	x	x	x	x	x				
OR (Logical OR)	B,W,L	s = Dn d =			x	x	x	x	x	x	x				
		d = Dn s =	x		x	x	x	x	x	x	x	x	x	x	
ORI (OR immediate)	B,W,L	s = Immed d =	x		x	x	x	x	x	x	x				x
PEA (Push effective address)	L	s =			x			x	x	x	x	x	x		

OP code $b_{15} \ldots b_0$	Operation performed		X	N	Z	V	C
		Condition flags					
0100 1000 10EE EEEE	d← [Xn]	A second word is					
0100 1100 10ee eeee	Xn ← [s]	used to specify					
0100 1000 11EE EEEE	d ← [Xn]	the registers					
0100 1100 11ee eeee	Xn ← [s]	involved.					
0000 DDD1 1000 1AAA	Alternate bytes of d ← [Dn]						
0000 DDD1 1100 1AAA							
0000 DDD1 0000 1AAA	Dn ← alternate bytes of d						
0000 DDD1 0100 1AAA							
0111 DDD0 QQQQ QQQQ	Dn ← QQQQQQQQ			x	x	0	0
1100 DDD1 11ee eeee	Dn ← [s] × [Dn]			x	x	0	0
1100 DDD0 11ee eeee	Dn ← [s] × [Dn]			x	x	0	0
0100 1000 00EE EEEE	d ← 0 − [d] − [X] using BCD arithmetic		x	u	x	u	x
0100 0100 SSEE EEEE	d ← 0 − [d]		x	x	x	x	x
0100 0000 SSEE EEEE	d ← 0 − [d] − [X]		x	x	x	x	x
0100 1110 0111 0001	none						
0100 0110 SSEE EEEE	d ← $\overline{[d]}$			x	x	0	0
1000 DDD1 SSEE EEEE	d ← [s] ∨ [d]			x	x	0	0
1000 DDD0 SSee eeee							
0000 0000 SSEE EEEE	d ← s ∨ [d]			x	x	0	0
0100 1000 01ee eeee	SP ← [SP] − 4 [SP] ← effective address of s						

TABLE C.4
(continued)

Mnemonic (Name)	Size	Addressing mode	Dn	An	(An)	(An)+	-(An)	d(An)	d(An,Xi)	Abs.W	Abs.L	d(PC)	d(PC,Xi)	Immed	SR or CCR
RESET															
ROL (Rotate left without X)	B,W,L W	count = [Dn] d = count = QQQ d = count = 1 d =	x x		x	x	x	x	x	x	x				
ROR (Rotate right without X)	B,W,L W	count = [Dn] d = count = QQQ d = count = 1	x x		x	x	x	x	x	x	x				
ROXL (Rotate left with X)	B,W,L W	count = [Dn] d = count = QQQ d = count = 1 d =	x x		x	x	x	x	x	x	x				
ROXR (Rotate right with X)	B,W,L W	count = [Dn] d = count = QQQ d = count = 1 d =	x x		x	x	x	x	x	x	x				
RTE (Return from exception)															
RTR (Return and restore CCR)															
RTS (Return from subroutine)															
SBCD (Subtract BCD)	B	s = Dn d = s = -(An) d =	x				x								
Scc (Set on condition)	B	d =	x		x	x	x	x	x	x	x				

OP code $b_{15} \ldots b_0$	Operation performed	Condition flags				
		X	N	Z	V	C
0100 1110 0111 0000	Assert RESET output line.					
1110 rrr1 SS11 1DDD 1110 QQQ1 SS01 1DDD 1110 0111 11EE EEEE	C ← operand ← (rotate left through C)		x	x	0	x
1100 rrr1 SS11 1DDD 1110 QQQ0 SS01 1DDD 1110 0111 11EE EEEE	operand → C (rotate right through C)		x	x	0	x
1110 rrr1 SS11 0DDD 1110 QQQ1 SS01 0DDD 1110 0101 11EE EEEE	C ← operand ← X (rotate left through X)	x	x	x	0	x
1110 rrr0 SS11 0DDD 1110 QQQ0 SS01 0DDD 1110 0100 11EE EEEE	X → operand → C (rotate right through X)	x	x	x	0	x
0100 1110 0111 0011	SR ← [[SP]]; SP ← [SP] + 2; PC ← [[SP]]; SP ← [SP] + 4	x	x	x	x	x
0100 1110 0111 0111	CCR ← [[SP]]; SP ← [SP] + 2; PC ← [[SP]]; SP ← [SP] + 4	x	x	x	x	x
0100 1110 0111 0101	PC ← [[SP]]; SP ← [SP] + 4					
1000 RRR1 0000 0rrr 1000 RRR1 0000 1rrr	d ← [d] − [s] − [X] Binary-coded decimal subtraction	x	u	x	u	x
0101 CCCC 11EE EEEE	Set all 8 bits of d to 1 if cc is true, otherwise clear them to 0.					

TABLE C.4
(*continued*)

Mnemonic (Name)	Size	Addressing mode		Dn	An	(An)	(An)+	−(An)	d(An)	d(An,Xi)	Abs.W	Abs.L	d(PC)	d(PC,Xi)	Immed	SR or CCR
STOP (Load SR and stop)			s =												x	
SUB (Subtract)	B,W,L	s = Dn	d =			x	x	x	x	x	x	x				
		d = Dn	s =	x	x	x	x	x	x	x	x	x	x	x	x	
SUBA (Subtract address)	W	d = An	s =	x	x	x	x	x	x	x	x	x	x	x	x	
	L	d = An	s =	x	x	x	x	x	x	x	x	x	x	x	x	
SUBI (Subtract immediate)	B,W,L	s = Immed	d =	x		x	x	x	x	x	x	x				
SUBQ (Subtract quick)	B,W,L	s = Immed3	d =	x	x	x	x	x	x	x	x	x				
SUBX (Subtract extended)	B,W,L	s = Dn	d =	x												
		s = −(An)	d =					x								
SWAP (Swap register halves)	W		d =	x												
TAS (Test and set)	B		d =	x		x	x	x	x	x	x	x				
TRAP (Trap)																
TRAPV (Trap on overflow)																
TST (Test)	B,W,L		d =	x		x	x	x	x	x	x	x				
UNLK (Unlink)					x											

		Condition flags				
OP code $b_{15} \ldots b_0$	Operation performed	X	N	Z	V	C
0100 1110 0111 0010	SR ← s; Wait for interrupt.	x	x	x	x	x
1001 DDD1 SSEE EEEE 1001 DDD0 SSee eeee	d ← [d] – [s]	x	x	x	x	x
1001 AAA0 11ee eeee 1001 AAA1 11ee eeee	An ← [An] – [s]					
0000 0100 SSEE EEEE	d ← [d] – s	x	x	x	x	x
0101 QQQ1 SSEE EEEE	d ← [d] – QQQ	x	x	x	x	x
1001 RRR1 SS00 0rrr 1001 RRR1 SS00 1rrr	d ← [d] – [s] – [X]	x	x	x	x	x
0100 1000 0100 0DDD	$[Dn]_{31-16} \leftrightarrow [Dn]_{15-0}$		x	x	0	0
0100 1010 11EE EEEE	Test d and set N and Z flags: set bit 7 of d to 1.		x	x	0	0
0100 1110 0100 VVVV	SP ← [SP] – 4; [SP] ← [PC]; SP ← [SP] – 2; [SP] ← [SR]; PC ← vector					

0100 1110 0111 0110	If V = 1, then
	  SP ← [SP] – 4;
	  [SP] ← [PC];
	  SP ← [SP] – 2;
	  [SP] ← [SR];
	  PC ← TRAPV vector					

0100 1010 SSEE EEEE	Test d and set N and Z flags.		x	x	0	0
0100 1110 0101 1AAA	SP ← [An]; An ← [[SP]]; SP ← [SP] + 4					

TABLE C.5
68000 branch instructions

Mnemonic (Name)	Displacement size	OP code	Operation performed
BRA (Branch always)	8	0110 0000 PPPP PPPP	PC ← [PC] + disp
	16	0110 0000 0000 0000 PPPP PPPP PPPP PPPP	
Bcc (Branch conditionally)	8	0110 CCCC PPPP PPPP	If cc is true, then
	16	0110 CCCC 0000 0000 PPPP PPPP PPPP PPPP	PC ← [PC] + disp
BSR (Branch to subroutine)	8	0110 0001 PPPP PPPP	SP ← [SP] − 4; [SP] ← [PC];
	16	0110 0001 0000 0000 PPPP PPPP PPPP PPPP	PC ← [PC] + disp
DBcc (Decrement and branch conditionally)	16	0101 CCCC 1100 1DDD PPPP PPPP PPPP PPPP	If cc is false, then Dn ← [Dn] − 1; If [Dn] ≠ − 1, then PC ← [PC] + disp
DBRA (Decrement and branch)	The assembler interprets this instruction as DBF (see the DBcc entry).		

TABLE C.6
Condition codes for Bcc, DBcc, and Scc instructions

Machine code CCCC	Condition suffix cc	Name	Test condition
0000	T	True	Always true
0001	F	False	Always false
0010	HI	High	$C \lor Z = 0$
0011	LS	Low or same	$C \lor Z = 1$
0100	CC	Carry clear	$C = 0$
0101	CS	Carry set	$C = 1$
0110	NE	Not equal	$Z = 0$
0111	EQ	Equal	$Z = 1$
1000	VC	Overflow clear	$V = 0$
1001	VS	Overflow set	$V = 1$
1010	PL	Plus	$N = 0$
1011	MI	Minus	$N = 1$
1100	GE	Greater or equal	$N \oplus V = 0$
1101	LT	Less than	$N \oplus V = 1$
1110	GT	Greater than	$Z \lor (N \oplus V) = 0$
1111	LE	Less or equal	$Z \lor (N \oplus V) = 1$

T and F suffixes cannot be used in the Bcc instruction.

APPENDIX
D

CHARACTER
CODES
AND NUMBER
CONVERSION

D.1 CHARACTER CODES

Information storage and processing in digital computers involves coding the individual items of information by using a number of binary variables. In most scientific computers, positive and negative numbers are represented in some variation of the binary number system. The most usual formats are presented in Chapter 7, where both integer and floating-point numbers are discussed.

In computers that are used mainly for business data processing, it is useful to represent and process numbers in the base-10 (decimal) format. Table D.1 gives the most usual coding for individual digits, called the binary-coded decimal (BCD) code. This code is simply the first 10 values (0–9) of the 4-bit binary number system. Strings of these 4-bit code values can be used to represent any desired range of positive and negative integers, with an appropriate code being used for the sign position.

Alphabetic characters (A–Z), operators, punctuation symbols, and control characters (+ − / , : ; LF CR EOT), as well as numbers, need to be represented for text storage and editing and high-level language input, processing, and output operations. Two standard codes for this purpose are the American Standards Committee on Information Interchange (ASCII) code and the Extended Binary Coded Decimal Interchange Code (EBCDIC). The standard ASCII code is a 7-bit code, and the EBCDIC code is an 8-bit code. Tables D.2 and D.3 show the standard ASCII and EBCDIC codes, respectively.

Table D.1 BCD encoding of decimal digits

Decimal digit	BCD code
0	0000
1	0001
2	0010
3	0011
4	0100
5	0101
6	0110
7	0111
8	1000
9	1001

Table D.2 The 7-bit ASCII code

Bit positions 3210	Bit positions 654							
	000	001	010	011	100	101	110	111
0000	NUL	DLE	SPACE	0	@	P	'	p
0001	SOH	DC1	!	1	A	Q	a	q
0010	STX	DC2	"	2	B	R	b	r
0011	ETX	DC3	#	3	C	S	c	s
0100	EOT	DC4	$	4	D	T	d	t
0101	ENQ	NAK	%	5	E	U	e	u
0110	ACK	SYN	&	6	F	V	f	v
0111	BEL	ETB	'	7	G	W	g	w
1000	BS	CAN	(	8	H	X	h	x
1001	HT	EM	)	9	I	Y	i	y
1010	LF	SUB	*	:	J	Z	j	z
1011	VT	ESC	+	;	K	[	k	{
1100	FF	FS	,	<	L	\	l	l
1101	CR	GS	−	=	M	]	m	}
1110	SO	RS	.	>	N	^	n	~
1111	SI	US	/	?	O	—	o	DEL

NUL	Null/Idle		SI	Shift in
SOH	Start of header		DLE	Data link escape
STX	Start of text		DC1-DC4	Device control
ETX	End of text		NAK	Negative acknowledgement
EOT	End of transmission		SYN	Synchronous idle
ENQ	Enquiry		ETB	End of transmitted block
ACK	Acknowledgement		CAN	Cancel (error in data)
BEL	Audible signal		EM	End of medium
BS	Back space		SUB	Special sequence
HT	Horizontal tab		ESC	Escape
LF	Line feed		FS	File separator
VT	Vertical tab		GS	Group separator
FF	Form feed		RS	Record separator
CR	Carriage return		US	Unit separator
SO	Shift out		DEL	Delete/Idle

Bit positions of code format = | 6 | 5 | 4 | 3 | 2 | 1 | 0 |

Table D.3 The 8-bit EBCDIC code

Bit positions 3210	Bit positions 7654															
	0000	0001	0010	0011	0100	0101	0110	0111	1000	1001	1010	1011	1100	1101	1110	1111
0000	NULL				SP	&	–									0
0001							/		a	j			A	J		1
0010									b	k	s		B	K	S	2
0011									c	l	t		C	L	T	3
0100	PF	RES	BYP	PN					d	m	u		D	M	U	4
0101	HT	NL	LF	RS					e	n	v		E	N	V	5
0110	LC	BS	EOB	UC					f	o	w		F	O	W	6
0111	DEL	IL	PRE	EOT					g	p	x		G	P	X	7
1000									h	q	y		H	Q	Y	8
1001									i	r	z		I	R	Z	9
1010			SM		¢	!		:								
1011					.	$	,	#								
1100					<	*	%	@								
1101					(	)	_	'								
1110					+	;	>	=								
1111					|	¬	?	"								

NULL	Null/Idle	NL	New line	PRE	Prefix	
PF	Punch off	BS	Backspace	SM	Set mode	
HT	Horizontal tab	IL	Idle	PN	Punch on	
LC	Lower case	BYP	Bypass	RS	Reader stop	
DEL	Delete	LF	Line feed	UC	Upper case	
RES	Restore	EOB	End of block	EOT	End of transmission	
				SP	Space	

Bit positions of code format = | 7 | 6 | 5 | 4 | 3 | 2 | 1 | 0 |

In many applications it is preferable to use 8-bit quantities, thus the basic ASCII code is often extended to 8-bits. A common way of doing this is to set the high-order bit position (bit 7) to zero. Another popular possibility is to use bit 7 as a parity bit for the encoded character.

Some comments about the structure of the ASCII and EBCDIC codes are helpful. Note that in both codes the low-order 4 bits of the decimal character codes (0–9) are the BCD codes of Table D.1. This facilitates two operations. First, the comparison of two characters that represent decimal digits to determine which is larger can be done with the same type of logic circuits that are used to perform the standard arithmetic operations on binary numbers. This is helpful when strings of decimal numbers need to be sorted into numerical order. Second, when it is determined by context that consecutive 7- or 8-bit codes in some input string represent a decimal number that is to be stored and processed as a single entity, then it is sometimes practical to remove the leftmost 3 or 4 bits of each digit code and compress the number being represented into a string of 4-bit BCD digits. Of course, this compression or packing of data requires starting and ending delimiters, but it is justified in many situations where storage space requirements are a concern. Similar comments apply to the codes for the alphabetic characters. The fact that their binary bit patterns are in numerical sequence facilitates alphabetic sorting.

D.2 DECIMAL TO BINARY CONVERSION

This section will show how to convert a fixed-point decimal number to its binary equivalent. The value represented by the binary number

$$B = b_n b_{n-1} \cdots b_0 . b_{-1} b_{-2} \cdots b_{-m}$$

is given by

$$V(B) = b_n \times 2^n + b_{n-1} \times 2^{n-1} + \cdots + b_0 \times 2^0$$
$$+ b_{-1} \times 2^{-1} + b_{-2} \times 2^{-2} + \cdots + b_{-m} \times 2^{-m}$$

To convert a fixed-point decimal number into binary, the integer and fraction parts are handled separately. First, the integer part is converted as follows. It is divided by 2. The remainder is the least significant bit of the integer part of the binary representation. The quotient is again divided by 2, and the remainder is the next bit of the binary representation. The process is repeated up to and including the step in which the quotient becomes 0.

Second, the fraction part is converted by multiplying it by 2. The part of the product to the left of the decimal point (which is either 0 or 1) is a bit in the binary representation. The fractional part of the product is again multiplied by 2, generating the next bit of the binary representation. The first bit generated is the bit immediately to the right of the binary point. The next bit generated is the

Convert $(927.45)_{10}$

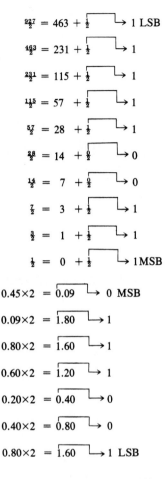

$$0.45 \times 2 = 0.09 \rightarrow 0 \text{ MSB}$$

$$0.09 \times 2 = 1.80 \rightarrow 1$$

$$0.80 \times 2 = 1.60 \rightarrow 1$$

$$0.60 \times 2 = 1.20 \rightarrow 1$$

$$0.20 \times 2 = 0.40 \rightarrow 0$$

$$0.40 \times 2 = 0.80 \rightarrow 0$$

$$0.80 \times 2 = 1.60 \rightarrow 1 \text{ LSB}$$

$(927.45)_{10} = (1110011111.0111001\cdots)_2$ **Figure D.1** Conversion from decimal to binary.

second bit to the right, and so on. The process is repeated until the required accuracy is attained.

Figure D.1 shows an example of conversion from $(927.45)_{10}$ to binary. Note that conversion of the integer part is always exact, but the binary fraction for an exact decimal fraction may not be exact. For example, the fraction $(0.45)_{10}$ used in Figure D.1 does not have an exact binary equivalent. This is obvious from the pattern developing in the figure. In such cases, the binary fraction is generated to some desired level of accuracy. In general, the maximum absolute error e in generating a k-bit fractional representation is bounded as $e \leq 2^{-k}$. Of course, some decimal fractions have an exact binary representation. For example, $(0.25)_{10} = (0.01)_2$.

BIBLIOGRAPHY

Abd-alla, A. M., and A. C. Meltzer: *Principles of Digital Computer Design*, Prentice Hall, Englewood Cliffs, NJ, 1976.

Abrams, M. D., and P. G. Stein: *Computer Hardware and Software: An Interdisciplinary Introduction*, Addison-Wesley, Reading, MA, 1973.

Baer, J.-L.: *Computer Systems Architecture*, Computer Science Press, Potomac, MD, 1980.

Bartee, T. C.: *Digital Computer Fundamentals*, 4th ed., McGraw-Hill, New York, 1977.

Bell, C. G., J. C. Mudge, and J. E. McNamara: *Computer Engineering*, Digital Press, Bedford, MA, 1978.

Bell, C. G., and A. Newell: *Computer Structures: Reading and Examples*, McGraw-Hill, New York, 1971.

Bowen, B. A., and R. J. A. Buhr: *The Logical Design of Multiple-Microprocessor Systems*, Prentice Hall, Englewood Cliffs, NJ, 1980.

Chirlian, P. M.: *Analysis and Design of Digital Circuits and Computer Systems*, Matrix, Champaign, IL, 1976.

Chu, Y.: *Computer Organization and Microprogramming*, Prentice Hall, Englewood Cliffs, NJ, 1972.

Eckhouse, R. H.: *Minicomputer Systems: Organization and Programming*, Prentice Hall, Englewood Cliffs, NJ, 1975.

Flores, I.: *Computer Organization*, Prentice Hall, Englewood Cliffs, NJ, 1969.

Foster, C. C.: *Computer Architecture*, Van Nostrand Reinhold, New York, 1970.

Gear, C. W.: *Computer Organization and Programming*, 4th ed., McGraw-Hill, New York, 1985.

Gschwind, H. W., and E. J. McCluskey: *Design of Digital Computers*, Springer-Verlag, New York, 1975.

Hayes, J. P.: *Computer Architecture and Organization*, 2d ed., McGraw-Hill, New York, 1988.

Hayes, J. P.: *Digital System Design and Microprocessors*, McGraw-Hill, New York, 1988.

Hellerman, H.: *Digital Computer System Principles*, 2d ed., McGraw-Hill, New York, 1973.

Hennessy, J., and D. Patterson: *Computer Architecture: A Quantitative Approach*, Morgan Kaufman, San Mateo, CA, 1990.

605

Hilburn, J. L., and P. N. Julich: *Microcomputers/Microprocessors: Hardware, Software, and Applications*, Prentice Hall, Englewood Cliffs, NJ, 1976.

Hill, F. H., and G. R. Peterson: *Digital Systems: Hardware Organization and Design*, 2d ed., Wiley, New York, 1978.

Husson, S.: *Microprogramming: Principles and Practices*, Prentice Hall, Englewood Cliffs, NJ, 1970.

Hwang, K., and F. A. Briggs: *Parallel Computer Architecture*, McGraw-Hill, New York, 1984.

Kain, R. Y.: *Computer Architecture—Software and Hardware*, 2 volumes, Prentice Hall, Englewood Cliffs, NJ, 1989.

Katzan, H., Jr.: *Computer Systems Organization and Programming*, Science Research, Chicago, 1976.

Kogge, P. M.: *The Architecture of Pipelined Computers*, McGraw-Hill, New York, 1981.

Langdon, G. G., Jr.: *Computer Design*, Computeach Press, Inc., San Jose, CA, 1982.

Langholz, G., J. Francioni, and A. Kandel: *Elements of Computer Organization*, Prentice Hall, Englewood Cliffs, NJ, 1989.

Lewin, D.: *Theory and Design of Digital Computers*, Nelson, London, 1972.

Mano, M. M.: *Computer System Architecture*, 2d ed., Prentice Hall, Englewood Cliffs, NJ, 1982.

Murray, W. D.: *Computer and Digital System Architecture*, Prentice Hall, Englewood Cliffs, NJ, 1990.

Nashelsky, L.: *Introduction to Digital Computer Technology*, 2d ed., Wiley, New York, 1977.

O'Malley, J.: *Introduction to the Digital Computer*, Holt, New York, 1972.

Osborne, A.: *An Introduction to Microcomputers, Vol. 2: Some Real Products*, Adam Osborne and Associates, Berkeley, CA, 1976.

Pfleeger, C. P.: *Machine Organization*, Wiley, New York, 1982.

Poppelbaum, W. J.: *Computer Hardware Theory*, McGraw-Hill, New York, 1972.

Rafiquzzaman, M., and R. Chandra: *Modern Computer Architecture*, West, St. Paul, MN, 1988.

Siewiorek, D. P., C. G. Gell, and A. Newell: *Computer Structures: Principles and Examples*, McGraw-Hill, New York, 1982.

Sloan, M. E.: *Computer Hardware and Organization*, Science Research, Chicago, 1976.

Sobel, H. S.: *Introduction to Digital Computer Design*, Addison-Wesley, Reading, MA, 1970.

Stallings, W.: *Computer Organization and Architecture—Principles of Structure and Function*, Macmillan, New York, 1987.

Stone, H. S.: *High-Performance Computer Architecture*, Addison-Wesley, Reading, MA, 1987.

Stone, H. S. (ed.): *Introduction to Computer Architecture*, 2d ed., Science Research, Chicago, 1980.

Stone, H. S.: *Microcomputer Interfacing*, Addison-Wesley, Reading, MA, 1982.

Stone, H. S., and D. P. Siewiorek: *Introduction to Computer Organization and Data Structures: PDP-11 Edition*, McGraw-Hill, New York, 1975.

Tanenbaum, A. S.: *Structured Computer Organization*, 3rd ed., Prentice Hall, Englewood Cliffs, NJ, 1990.

Vranesic, Z. G., and S. G. Zaky: *Microcomputer Structures*, Holt, Rinehart and Winston, New York, 1989.

Wakerly, J.: *Microcomputer Architecture and Programming*, Wiley, New York, 1981.

Wakerly, John F.: *Microcomputer Architecture and Programming—The 68000 Family*, Wiley, New York, 1989.

Weitzman, C.: *Distributed Micro/Minicomputer Systems*, Prentice Hall, Englewood Cliffs, NJ, 1980.

INDEX